T0375142

THE LAND OF THE ELEPHANT KINGS

The Land of the Elephant Kings

Space, Territory, and Ideology in the Seleucid Empire

PAUL J. KOSMIN

 Harvard University Press

Cambridge, Massachusetts
London, England

First Harvard University Press paperback edition, 2018
Second printing

Library of Congress Cataloging-in-Publication Data

Kosmin, Paul J., 1984–
    The land of the elephant kings : space, territory, and ideology in the Seleucid
Empire / Paul J. Kosmin.
        pages cm
    Includes bibliographical references and index.
    ISBN 978-0-674-72882-0 (hardcover : alk. paper)
    ISBN 978-0-674-98688-6 (pbk.)
    1. Seleucids.   2. Syria—History—333 B.C.–634 A.D.   I. Title.
    DS96.2.K67 2014
    935'.062—dc23   2013042033

To my parents

Contents

Maps

Illustrations

Abbreviations

Classical authors according to the *Oxford Classical Dictionary* (3rd edition); in addition:

AD	Sachs, Abraham and Hermann Hunger. 1988–1996. *Astronomical Diaries and Related Texts from Babylonia.* Vienna.
AIIS	*Annali dell'Istituto italiano per gli studi storici*
AJA	*American Journal of Archaeology*
AJAH	*American Journal of Ancient History*
ANS MN	*American Numismatic Society: Museum Notes*
ArchPF	*Archiv für Papyrusforschung und verwandte Gebiete*
ASNP	*Annali della Scuola Normale di Pisa*
BASOR	*Bulletin of the American Society of Oriental Research*
BCH	*Bulletin de correspondance hellénique*
BCHP	Finkel, Irving and Robert van der Spek. 2012. *Babylonian Chronicles of the Hellenistic Period,* published online at www.livius.org/cg-cm/chronicles/chron00.html
BICS	*Bulletin of the Institute of Classical Studies*
BMCR	*Bryn Mawr Classical Review*
BNJ	Worthington, Ian. 2012–. *Brill's New Jacoby,* published online at http://referenceworks.brillonline.com
BSA	*Annual of the British School at Athens*
BSOAS	*Bulletin of the School of Oriental and African Studies*
CA	*Classical Antiquity*
CM	*Classica et Mediaevalia*
CP	*Classical Philology*
CQ	*Classical Quarterly*

CR	*Classical Review*
CRAI	*Comptes rendus de l'Académie des Inscriptions et Belles-Lettres*
EMC	*Échos du monde classique*
FGrHist	Jacoby, Felix. 1923–. *Die Fragmente der griechischen Historiker.* Berlin.
G&R	*Greece & Rome*
GRBS	*Greek, Roman and Byzantine Studies*
HSCP	*Harvard Studies in Classical Philology*
ICS	*Illinois Classical Studies*
IEJ	*Israel Exploration Journal*
IEOG	Rossi, Canali de. 2004. *Iscrizioni dello estremo oriente greco.* Bonn.
IGIAC	Rougemont, Georges. 2012. *Inscriptions grecques d'Iran et d'Asie centrale.* London.
IGLS	Jalabert, L., R. Mouterede, and J.-P. Rey-Coquais (eds.). 1929–. *Inscriptions grecques et latines de la Syrie.* Paris.
IstMitt	*Istanbuler Mitteilungen*
JANES	*Journal of the Ancient Near Eastern Society*
JAOS	*Journal of the American Oriental Society*
JCS	*Journal of Cuneiform Studies*
JDAI	*Jahrbuch des deutschen archäologischen Instituts*
JEA	*Journal of Egyptian Archaeology*
JHS	*Journal of Hellenic Studies*
JJS	*Journal of Jewish Studies*
JNES	*Journal of Near Eastern Studies*
JRA	*Journal of Roman Archaeology*
JRAS	*Journal of the Royal Asiatic Society of Great Britain and Ireland*
JRS	*Journal of Roman Studies*
JS	*Journal des Savants*
MDAI (A)	*Mitteilungen des deutschen archäologischen Instituts. Abteilung Athen.*
MDAI (I)	*Mitteilungen des deutschen archäologischen Instituts. Abteilung Istanbul.*
NC	*Numismatic Chronicle*
NNM	*Numismatic Notes and Monographs*
OGIS	Dittenberger, W. 1903. *Orientis graeci inscriptiones selectae.* Leipzig.
PP	*La Parola del passato*
RA	*Revue archéologique*

RC	Welles, C. 1934. *Royal Correspondence in the Hellenistic Period.* London.
RE	*Real-Encyclopädie der classischen Altertumswissenschaft*
REA	*Revue des études anciennes*
REG	*Revue des études grecques*
RN	*Revue numismatique*
SCO	*Studi classici e orientali*
SEG	*Supplementum Epigraphicum Graecum*
SNR	*Schweizerische numismatische Rundschau*
TAPA	*Transactions of the American Philological Association*
VDI	*Vestnik drevnej istorii*
ZATW	*Zeitschrift für die alttestamentliche Wissenschaft*
ZDPV	*Zeitschrift des Deutschen Pälastina-Vereins*
ZPE	*Zeitschrift für Papyrologie und Epigraphik*

Introduction

Three elephants.

The road to Mount Karasis peters out in a lemon orchard. It is Ramadan and July, so we do not disturb the farmers snoozing through the heat and hunger of the early afternoon for a guide. A brutal climb up goat trails and dry streambeds—an unsigned path long since mislaid—abruptly comes to a wall of vast Hellenistic masonry that hugs the mountain ridge. One last clamber and we are within a citadel of the late third or early second century BCE, spotted for the first time by helicopter in 1994 and still to be excavated.[1] To the north the Taurus piedmont crumples into the high chain that dominates central Turkey. To the south, beyond the city of Kozan, the wet plains of Cilicia spread to the Mediterranean, invisible in the heavy haze, and on to distant Syria. The fort's walls are a somber grey, without inscription or life, except for a single image: we see carved in relief on the doorway of a tower, stomping across the lintel with trunk raised in eternal salute, an Indian elephant (Figure 1).

A fragmentary clay tablet, now in the British Museum, closely impressed with the cuneiform wedges of Akkadian and Sumerian: the diary entry of an anonymous priest of Bel-Marduk, from the Esagil temple of Babylon.

24th Adarru (274 BCE). The satrap of Babylonia brought out much silver, cloth, goods, and utensils from Babylon and Seleucia, the city of kingship, and twenty elephants, which the satrap of Bactria had sent to the king, to Ebir-nari into the presence of the king.[2]

1

Figure 1 An elephant! Mount Karasis fort, Cilicia.

The dynastic chronicle of the Hasmonaean kings of Judea, known to us in its Greek translation as 1 Maccabees, celebrates the Jewish struggle for independence from the Seleucid empire. The battle of Beth-Zechariah, in 162 BCE, pitted the exhausted and outnumbered Jewish fighters against the massed ranks of the professional Seleucid army under the command of Lysias, guardian of the child-king Antiochus V. The chronicle exaggerates an imperial army of 100,000 infantrymen, 20,000 cavalry, and, most terrifying of all, thirty-two war elephants. To each beast were assigned 1,000 infantry and 500 picked cavalry. Strong wooden howdahs, strapped to the elephants' backs, held four men, and Indian mahouts steered from the necks. Against such odds the Jewish resistance stood no chance, and Beth-Zechariah was a total Seleucid victory. But the rebels had their glory. For our chronicler records that Eleazar Avaran, brother of Judas Maccabaeus, seeing one elephant towering over the others in royal armor and mistakenly identifying its mahout as the Seleucid king Antiochus V himself, carved his way through the phalanx, got beneath the beast, buried his spear in its exposed belly, and killed the elephant, which crushed the Samson-like hero in its fall.[3]

*   *   *

Eleazar's error—confusing the mahout guiding his war elephant for the monarch ruling his kingdom—has a symbolic logic. For the great Seleucid empire, founded at the end of the fourth century by Seleucus I Nicator, a king titled "elephant-commander" (ἐλεφαντάρχης) by his enemies,[4] took as its dynastic blazon the Indian elephant. Marching elephants and elephant-chariots and elephant-scalps adorned official coins and seals.[5] Elephants lined up at the foundation of Antioch-by-Daphne, the empire's most famous colony, to mark out the city wall.[6] Elephant-trophies commemorated Seleucid military victories.[7] An epic poem sung of the elephants' triumph over barbarian Galatians.[8] Elephants, chosen as emblems of empire, were speared or hamstrung by Seleucid enemies.[9] To think Seleucid is to see elephants, and, like the beasts, the Seleucid empire, enormous and vulnerable, brutally powerful and self-defeating, was as much a work of the imagination as a creature of war.

The Seleucid empire was a sprawling offcut from the carcass of Alexander the Great's conquests. It extended geographically from the oasis cities of Central Asia to the riding plains of Bulgaria, from the uplands of Armenia to the Bahrain archipelago, and chronologically from Seleucus I Nicator's conquest of Babylonia in 311 down to Pompey's provincialization of Syria in 64.[10] Four decades after Alexander the Great's death in 323 his unitary world-empire had fragmented and multiplied into a peer-kingdom international system, dominated by three "Great Powers": the Antigonid kingdom in the Macedonian and Greek homeland, the Ptolemaic kingdom in Egypt, and the Seleucid kingdom across the Near East. Whereas their peers in Macedonia and Egypt governed monocultural and bicultural states respectively, the Seleucid kings, as our three opening elephant episodes demonstrate, headed an expansive, continent-wide empire of astonishing linguistic, religious, and social diversity. Their multicultural territory encompassed, to name only the major players, Greek and Phoenician city-states, Anatolian and Jewish theocracies, vast Babylonian conurbations, Iranian dynasts, Central Asian nomads, and Macedonian adventurers. Furthermore, in contrast to every previous Near Eastern empire, the Seleucid monarchs were sundered from their ancestral homeland: Greece and Macedonia, the origins of the dynasty and much of its ruling class, lay beyond the kingdom's western horizon. The Seleucids did not rule this complex space on the basis of appointment or inheritance or any kind of natural geographical unity; rather, the empire consisted of the lands that Seleucus

I, Alexander's general and the kingdom's founder, had managed to conquer, hold, and pass on.

So how could the Seleucid kings hope to govern such an arbitrary and complicated space and to legitimize their rule over it? Scholars have offered three kinds of answer. They did not, according to the once dominant interpretation. The empire was seen as little more than a ramshackle, overstretched march-state in perpetual decline, characterized by inadequate provincial administration and peripheral collapse.[11] William Tarn, the Scottish classicist and Alexander hagiographer, notoriously compared the empire to a crustacean, invertebrate and without core strength.[12] In comparison to the apparently well-ordered Ptolemaic domains or mighty Rome, the Seleucid territorial imprint was regarded as shallow and insignificant—the Sick Man of the Hellenistic world.[13] Over the last couple of decades the rhetoric has mostly shifted, and a new approach has brought salutary recognition to the duration, sophistication, and local adaptability of the Seleucid state;[14] here the kingdom's success is attributed above all to its adoption of tried and tested Near Eastern, specifically Achaemenid, systems of imperial rule, an approach that emphasizes structural and ideological continuities between the Persian and Seleucid periods.[15] But most influential of all has been a systematic devaluing of the importance of territory for the Hellenistic kingdoms. Numerous historians have asserted that the Seleucid empire was not in fact territorial but a "personal monarchy," according to which the state, unnamed, was made up of a set of institutions—king, court, and army—without a strong spatial attachment and in which royal legitimacy was based in certain unmoored kingly practices, primarily warfare and benefaction. The Seleucid kings, the argument continues, retained ambitions to universal rule and so refused to admit territorial borders.[16]

There is much to commend each of the approaches, but in their arguments the full richness of Seleucid territory—as landscape, experience, spectacle, aspiration—falls from view. Seleucid state control did indeed fluctuate and ultimately collapse, but not their claims or legacy. The Seleucids did owe much to their Persian predecessors, but their imperial space was not a given. Indeed, as we will see, early Seleucid imperial ideology explicitly, and at some cost to its legitimacy, denied any connection to the preceding regimes. And arguments of personal kingship underplay the basic physicality of Seleucid power and the territorial commitment of its rulers: monarchic action becomes as abstracted and placeless as walking on a treadmill instead of in the world.

This book examines how the Seleucid kings—outsiders ruling over a heterogeneous land—worked hard to make the imperial space their own, how they tried to transform the landscape over which they ruled into a meaningful and legitimate territory. The land had to *become* Seleucid, and king and court put extraordinary effort into getting to know, sanctifying, and articulating their imperial space. We will see that the Seleucids responded to the enormous opportunities and challenges of their empire's political landscape with a range of ideological constructions and practical interventions, ranging from border diplomacy to colonial foundations, geographic exploration to royal parade, territorial baptisms to acts of war. These had major historical significance: the imperial space was invested with symbols of power and memories of kingly heroism, and so became both a source of royal legitimacy and a proving ground for its rulers; its landscape was bounded, measured, and segmented, and thereby made administratively legible at the same time as it was cut with the fault lines along which later it would tear.

My approach in this book is built on two relatively recent developments in scholarship, one historical and one theoretical. The first is the recent boom of Seleucid studies, as much a response to our more sophisticated understanding of the preceding Achaemenid empire as to new archaeological or epigraphic discoveries and the better availability of Near Eastern sources. Several game-changing monographs have been published over the last couple of decades. Amélie Kuhrt and Susan Sherwin-White's stimulating *From Samarkhand to Sardis* drew overdue, if overplayed, attention to the significance of Near Eastern prototypes and the Babylonian and Upper Satrapies.[17] John Ma's *Antiochos III and the Cities of Western Asia Minor* set a new bar in understanding the sophistication of imperial rhetoric at the western frontier.[18] Laurent Capdetrey's *Le pouvoir séleucide* offered a subtle reexamination of Seleucid institutions and imperial practices, fully informed by developments in Achaemenid studies.[19] Andrea Primo's *La storiografia sui Seleucidi* for the first time considered the Seleucid court as a cultural producer of literary texts.[20] These and many more have laid down roadways through the tangle of source criticism and institutional history and so provided much of the historical undergirding for my project. Even if, in the course of this book, I disagree with some of their conclusions, I remain profoundly in their debt.

The second, much broader development is the migration of investigations of space and spatiality from cultural geography, urban studies, and anthropology into the humanities and social sciences, a phenomenon commonly known to the beneficiaries as the "spatial turn." This movement is based on a fundamental reconceptualization of the ontology of space. In brief, to the Cartesian *res extensa*—a geometric, isotropic, unproblematic container within which humans think and act—has been added an understanding of space as relational and relative, historically contingent and culturally constructed, with the capacity both to discipline social behaviors and to be molded, manipulated, and resisted by historical agents.[21] While the origins of this new thinking lie in Leibniz' anti-Newtonian metaphysics and, more recently, a *soixante-huitard* spatialization of Marxist dialectic, in which the Cartesian model is revealed as the supposed buttress of capitalism and imperialism, the implications and applications for historians are much wider and more profound. The spatial turn is being felt throughout ancient studies, allowing novel interpretations of topics such as state formation,[22] Mediterranean historical dynamics,[23] Hellenistic poetry,[24] and imperial ideology.[25] The most successful of this bountiful crop have been able meaningfully to link thoughts about space (e.g., maps, literary descriptions, imagery, phenomenology) with things in space (e.g., historical geography, material conditions, political processes, physical movement).

Building on these two developments, this book aims as much as possible to connect the production of Seleucid territory at the level of words and imagination to the space-making practices, experiences, and strategies that ordered the imperial terrain. The work has its particular focus—the land of the elephant kings—and makes no claim to being a total history of the Seleucid empire. But nor is our hermeneutic like George Eliot's candle on the pier-glass, which lights up only those scratches pointing toward it. For, as we shall see, the basic characteristics of the Hellenistic world and the Seleucid empire gave the spatial concerns of the ruling dynasty—the desire for geographical coherence and connectedness, the making of home and taking of ownership, and the forms of statecraft that developed these—an orchestrating role in the unfurling history of the kingdom, the region, and the period.

The launderings of time have been unkind to the Seleucid empire. The Seleucids are not a name to conjure with: no nation proclaims their descent, no politician invokes their example, no landscape admits their presence. And without heirs, Seleucid traditions have not been passed down to us for their own sake. Indeed, the one breathing response to the Seleucid empire, the Jewish winter festival, Chanukah, shunts aside the persecutor kingdom in favor of long-burning oil. If all ancient history is a form of necromancy, the Seleucid ghost is fainter than most. So to orient the reader in the upcoming chapters, the following sections of this introduction briefly run through our surviving source material, the physical geography of Seleucid territory, and a basic outline of the empire's political history. Those in the know can leapfrog to the naming of parts.

Scene Setting

Sources

To study the Seleucids we are obliged to gather the empire's history from its material detritus, woken from the sleep of centuries by excavation or chance discovery, and the narrative accounts of its hostile neighbors and subject communities, often fragmentary, always telling their own story. Seleucid studies is bricolage: we can but hope for a kind of epistemological teepee, with different struts giving mutual support as they converge. Our three opening elephant episodes—fort, tablet, chronicle—demonstrate the typological diversity of the kingdom's surviving evidence—archaeology, epigraphy, and textual traditions.

Archaeology offers our most unmediated access to the basic physicality of the Seleucid empire: its construction of urban and military spaces, its architectural and sculptural styles, its landscape interventions. Currently available data represent a mere fraction of what must survive from a kingdom of such size and duration, to be explained at least in part by the political turmoil that has truncated or damaged excavation in Afghanistan, Iraq, Iran, and now Syria as well as by expeditionary preferences for pre- or post-Hellenistic strata. Even so, I refer throughout this book to a number of Seleucid foundations that have been explored through excavation, survey, subsurface prospection, or aerial photography. Four sites are exclusively Seleucid, founded by the dynasty and abandoned at its fall: the fortress on Mount Karasis, with the Indian elephant relief; the settlement of Apamea-on-the-Euphrates, on the left bank opposite the more famous Seleucia-Zeugma; the military colony of Jebel Khalid, on the right bank of the upper-middle Euphrates; and the temple-fort of Icarus, on Failaka island in the Persian Gulf. But most Seleucid colonies were so successfully situated that they continued to be inhabited for centuries after the empire's demise. These include the great city of Aï Khanoum in eastern Afghanistan, turned into a royal center of the independent Graeco-Bactrian dynasty; Seleucia-on-the-Tigris, south of Baghdad, and Dura-Europus, on the middle Euphrates, both of which continued to prosper after the Parthian conquest; and the colonies of Asia Minor and northern Syria, which blossomed under the Caesars and, in some cases, to this day.[26] The Seleucid phase of these settlements is known only partially or indirectly, but the promise of future excavation holds out hope for further, perhaps paradigm-changing, discoveries.

Inscriptions, text-bearing durable artifacts exposed in excavation or identified from later reuse, have contributed in a different way to our understanding of the Seleucid empire. As contemporary records or public documents they manifest, in some cases, the instructions of the Seleucid state and its agents and, in others, indigenous responses to empire. There are two concentrations of Seleucid epigraphy—Akkadian clay tablets from Babylonia and Greek stone inscriptions, mostly from the kingdom's Aegean fringe but also a smattering from its more central and eastern provinces.

Cuneiform tablets, Loeb-sized blocks of clay impressed with a reed stylus by *ṭupšarrū* scribes, were already a millennia-old technology by the time Babylonia fell under Seleucid control. They were typically composed in a combination of Akkadian syllabograms and Sumerian logograms, ancient languages no longer spoken in the later first millennium but retained by the literate temple elite, much as Latin in the monasteries of mediaeval Europe. During the Seleucid and early Parthian periods these cuneiform tablets were slowly being replaced by parchment and papyrus documents written in the simpler alphabetic Greek or Aramaic scripts, but these "paper" texts have entirely vanished into the alluvium's underground moistness, leaving behind, like a glass slipper, only the clay rings that once bound the rolls.[27] Even though this systematic climatic privileging of the more conservative and archaizing elements of the Babylonian textual world has no doubt distorted our understanding of the region's development, the use of imperishable clay tablets by Seleucid-period Babylonian scribes has preserved for the modern scholar an unparalleled wealth of information on temple rituals, judicial and economic proceedings, literary composition, and scribal training. In this book I mostly make use of two cuneiform genres, the Astronomical Diaries and the Babylonian Chronicles, written in Babylon's main temple, Esagil. The Diaries, from which I culled the elephant fragment at the opening, were records that correlated in six-month units the movements of heavenly bodies and meteorological phenomena with earthly events of political or economic importance.[28] The Chronicles, compiled from these Diaries' historical notices and other sources, were dated lists of political or religious events in Babylonia and occasionally the wider Near East, narrated in a sober third-person voice.[29]

These two quasi-historiographical genres are a font of antiquarian information on Seleucid-period *Realien* and state events, ranging from the elephant march to the market price of mustard, from notices of royal death to the outbreak of plague.

In contrast to these privately composed and temple-archived Babylonian tablets, Greek stone inscriptions gained their social meaning from being official documents publicly erected in the most conspicuous places within sanctuaries, cities, and forts. Two major Greek epigraphic modes are examined in this book. Honorific inscriptions, issued by both cities and high-ranking Seleucid courtiers, formally expressed gratitude to a king or an individual for services to the state; somewhat related inscriptions granted citizenship to individuals or entire communities or recognized the promotion of a settlement's political or religious status. The motivation clauses of these inscriptions, detailing the reasons for which the honorand had earned such rewards, give self-contained historical narratives of great significance. Inscribed royal letters, issued in a recognizable chancery style by the Seleucid court or its agents, delivered instructions, appointed officials, established cults, and bestowed benefactions. These letters, sometimes inscribed alongside the forwarding notes of subordinates, provide crucial information for the titles, terminology, and hierarchical organization of the imperial administration. Other royal inscriptions include boundary markers, religious dedications, and milestones, some with Aramaic précis.[30]

A final epigraphic-type source used in this book are the coins, in precious metals and bronze, struck by the Seleucid state and semiautonomous cities within the empire, stamped with royal or civic iconography, and inscribed with Greek or indigenous legends.[31] Like Greek inscriptions, coins were formal productions of the state, displaying officially approved words and images, but their circulatory nature means they would have reached a far wider audience.

Most important for reconstructing Seleucid history are the written sources of the Jewish and Graeco-Roman traditions that over generations unbroken have been read, copied, recopied, printed, and now digitized. As literary works, they offer our most detailed and sophisticated characterizations of the empire and its impact, along with evident authorial biases that are of historical interest in their own right.

The desecration of the Jerusalem temple and the persecution of Judaism by Antiochus IV prompted the composition of Jewish resistance literature, apocalyptic and historiographical texts that delegitimized the Seleucid empire and heroized martyrdom and the Maccabaean revolt. The Hebrew Bible's book of Daniel, composed in its final form in 165 BCE in a combination of Aramaic and Hebrew, encodes in typological antecedents, eschatological visions, and *vaticinia ex eventu* the horrors of the Antiochid persecution. Its rich symbolic imagery and long-view historical sensibility reveal a particular and influential mode of conceptualizing Seleucid imperial dominance. By contrast, 1 Maccabees and 2 Maccabees narrate without disguise the events and aftermath of the Jewish revolt. Originally written in Hebrew in the style of the Bible's historical books and now surviving only in a Greek translation, 1 Maccabees focuses on the emergence of the Hasmonaean dynasty as divinely approved leaders and defenders of the faith; the Eleazar elephant attack episode, described earlier, is typical of the work's focus on national liberation through battle. The author's use of Jerusalem archives, diplomatic correspondence, and Seleucid royal edicts is invaluable. 2 Maccabees, an epitome of a five-book history written by the otherwise unknown Jason of Cyrene, narrates the Jewish-Seleucid encounter in a Greek historiographical style but with a distinctly Jewish Deuteronomistic theological vision that reduces the cause and meaning of all events to the (im)piety of the Jewish people and the appropriate divine response. Here the Antiochid persecution is brought to an end by the suffering of martyrs: "*Not* by power, *not* by might, but by My spirit, says the Lord of Hosts."[32] These works, under-utilized by Hellenistic historians,[33] provide our most detailed provincial perspective on the Seleucid state.

Royal-sponsored literary production in Greek, the prestige language for the whole Hellenistic world, occupied as central a place at the Seleucid court as at its Ptolemaic, Antigonid, and Attalid peers; indeed, Part I of this book, "Border," is intended to bring overdue attention to fragmentary Seleucid ethnographers and geographers. But almost all Seleucid historiography has disappeared. Accordingly, for our basic historical narratives we rely on a set of external and mostly hostile Greek authors. The works of Hieronymus of Cardia, Phylarchus, and Nymphis of Heraclea Pontica, though lost, have been paraphrased or quoted by several later historians and give us the basic political and chronological framework for the empire's foundation and consolidation.[34] We are in a more fortunate position for the high empire of the later third and first half of the second centuries since Polybius, a leading politician of the Achaean League and then an exile in Rome, in his forty-book account of Rome's rise to Mediterranean dominance between 220 and 146, treats in some detail the reigns of Antiochus III, Antiochus

IV, and Demetrius I, a fellow hostage at Rome whom he befriended and helped escape to Syria. Despite his Roman focus, Polybius tells us much concerning the Seleucid empire's geography, warfare, court politics, diplomacy, and benefactions and betrays in several places the influence of official Seleucid discourses. Our only complete account of the slow agony of Seleucid dissolution is Appian's *Syriaca,* a short monograph on the Seleucid dynasty composed by the second-century CE Alexandrian lawyer and historian as part of his region-by-region account of Rome's rise. Other fragments for (early and) late Seleucid history are found in the encyclopaedic *Deipnosophistai,* "Wise Banqueters," of Athenaeus of Naucratis, himself responsible for a now lost work on the Seleucid kings. Both Appian and Athenaeus made use of, among many other authors, the Apamean polymath Posidonius, who continued Polybius' *Histories* down to the year 88. Finally, we have access to the civic histories of Antioch-by-Daphne in Libanius' "Encomium to Antioch" and Malalas' *Chronographia,* the former a fourth-century CE pagan rhetorician and friend of emperors, the latter a sixth-century Christian chronicler, both proud Antiochians. The Seleucids have a limited presence in Latin accounts: the great Roman historian Livy paraphrases certain lost sections of Polybius, and Justin's epitome of the Augustan-period Pompeius Trogus' history of the Hellenistic kingdoms contains some important material not found elsewhere.

From this brief survey it should be clear that the different regions of empire had their own mnemonic traditions as well as their distinct patterns of evidentiary survival; it is to be regretted above all that so little remains from the Seleucids' vast Iranian provinces. Combining such multilingual, fragmentary, and scattered evidence can be hard work for reader and author alike, but there is an intellectual thrill and profit to bringing into contact worlds isolated by the academy's disciplinary geography. Such an inclusive and comparative approach to the evidence makes clear that the Seleucid state could prompt the various discourses that described it, expressing in local idiom the empire's unitary ideas, structures, and symbols, as plants from different gardens grow toward the same sun. One need only recall the Indian war elephants carved onto an Anatolian lintel, marched through a Babylonian diary, and killed in a Hasmonaean royal chronicle. Furthermore, regional approaches to the empire, examining a single type or language of evidence, run the risk of confusing imperial strategy for character, obscuring the pan-imperial, boundary-crossing, fundamentally foreign nature of the Seleucid monarchy beneath its localized performances of long-established pre-Hellenistic identities. Like the proverb of the blind men and the elephant, Seleucid regional studies have felt the tail and pulled a rope, embraced the trunk and hugged a tree, touched the flank and hit a wall. While the Seleucid elephant will always remain obscured and historians forever blinded by the overwhelming losses of antiquity, we can at least hope for a fuller sense of the beast by uniting its parts. Accordingly, all textual sources used in this book have been studied in their original languages and within their respective genres; this has required a certain amount of exposition of sources unfamiliar to the various academic fields intruded upon. A glossary, at the end of the book, identifies the more significant terms, names, and places.

Geography

The Greeks conventionally divided the "inhabited world" (Gr. *oikoumené*) into three continents—Europe, lying to the north of the Mediterranean; Libya (our Africa), to its south; and Asia, to its east. This "Asia," approximate to the bloc of lands over which the Seleucid dynasty ruled in the first half of the third and early second centuries and after which the kingdom was named, was an oblong-shaped landmass, extending about 4,000 kilometers east-west and 1,500 kilometers north-south in the area of today's Middle East (excluding north Africa), Pakistan, and the southern parts of Central Asia.

The basic skeletal anatomy of this "Asia" are the high mountain chains that dominate its northern and eastern parts, the bones showing through the skin—the Taurus range in Turkey, the Zagros between Iraq and Iran, the Elburz below the Caspian Sea, and the knotted massif of the Hindu Kush, Pamir, and Karakoram. All are crunched upward by the slow northward subduction of the Arabian and Indian tectonic plates beneath the Eurasian. To the Hellenistic geographers Dicaearchus and Eratosthenes, these ranges formed a continuous horizontal spine across "Asia" and the central dividing line of the *oikoumené*.[35] They functioned as internal peripheries between relatively discrete lowland regions, canalizing travel along their most accessible passes, fructifying the most important riverine systems with their snow melt, and parching much of the remaining piedmont in their rain shadow. They break down the enormously varied landscape of Seleucid "Asia" into four regional zones, each of which is represented by our opening elephants—Asia Minor, on the southern edge of which the Mount Karasis fort was constructed; the Levant, where Eleazar speared the elephant and to where, under the ancient Babylonian name Ebir-nari, "Across the River (Euphrates)," the twenty elephants were being delivered; Mesopotamia, home of our Babylonian scribe; and the Upper Satrapies, from which the twenty elephants were dispatched. Detailed discussion of each area's topography, climate, natural resources, and agricultural productivity can be found in the more specialized geographies referenced in the endnotes;[36] here I want merely to identify the features and administrative names most germane to the book's arguments. I recommend consulting Map 1 with the following descriptions.

Asia Minor, the sea-washed Turkish peninsula, was formed of a central steppe tableland, walled off to the east by the Taurus range and descending along the valleys of westward-running rivers to the Greek-colonized Aegean coastline. Three of these rivers are particularly important: the Caïcus, flowing through Mysia and beneath Pergamum, the royal seat of the Attalid house; the Hermus, running by Sardis, the ancient capital of Lydia and most significant Seleucid center in the west; and the Maeander, debouching near the great port of Ephesus and guiding the main eastward trunk road up to Apamea-Celaenae in inland Phrygia. The southern coast of Asia Minor, disputed between the Ptolemies and Seleucids, alternated topographically from west to east between the upland regions of Caria and Lycia, the low fertile plain of Pamphylia, the steep bluffs of the Taurus in Rough *(Tracheia)* Cilicia, and the Taurus-ringed riviera of Smooth *(Pedias)* Cilicia. The northern half of Asia Minor remained in the hands of the non-Macedonian dynasties of Bithynia and Cappadocia, with whom the Seleucids enjoyed occasional kinship, alliance, and contest.

The Levant, made up of today's Hatay province of Turkey, Syria, Lebanon, Israel, the Palestinian territories, and Jordan, is a dry-agriculture Mediterranean region sundered from Asia Minor by the Taurus range and from Mesopotamia and Egypt by desert. The most stable core of the Seleucid empire, termed the "Seleucis" after the dynasty, was located at the top of the Levant along the Orontes river and the coastline of Hatay and northern Syria. This heavily colonized region offered the shortest route to the Euphrates and inner Asia. The central and southern portion of the Levant, called in Greek sources Coele ("Hollow") Syria and Phoenicia and disputed with the Ptolemies throughout the third century, was made up of three bands separated from one another by two high mountain ranges: a thin coastal strip occupied by ancient Phoenician cities; the inland rift valley of

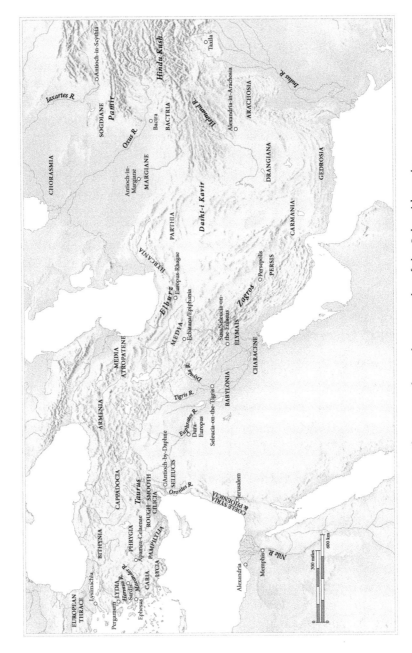

Map 1 The geography and topography of the Seleucid empire.

the Beqa' and Jordan river, with the hill country of Judea and its capital, Jerusalem, on its western bank; and on the eastern, far side the oasis cities of the Decapolis, including Damascus.

Mesopotamia, roughly equivalent to modern-day Iraq, was separated from the Levant by a great sand desert. The region lay between and around the Euphrates and Tigris rivers, which flow southeast into the Persian Gulf (the Greeks' Erythraean Sea). While northern Mesopotamia, today's Jazirah and once heartland of the Assyrian kingdom, allowed limited dry farming, central and southern Mesopotamia (satrapal name "Babylonia") were entirely dependent on elaborately engineered irrigation systems that would lapse into saltbrush desert without periodic dredging. Under the Seleucid monarchs, the storied capital Babylon, located on the Euphrates, was overshadowed by Seleucus I's eponymous foundation, Seleucia-on-the-Tigris, a deeper-running and more navigable river. The southern reaches of the Euphrates and the Tigris formed a gateway region for Gulf trade, known in ancient sources as Characene, Mesene, or the Satrapy of the Erythraean Sea. In modern Khuzistan to its east, bridging the Mesopotamian and Iranian worlds, lay Susiane/Elymaïs with its capital, Susa, refounded as Seleucia-on-the-Eulaeus.[37]

The eastern hemisphere of "Asia" was known to the Seleucids, with their Mediterranean inland gaze, as the Upper Satrapies. This was a cavalry land of rugged mountains and oasis-dotted salt deserts. At its western edge the Zagros range, a 200-kilometer-wide barrier between the worlds of Mesopotamia and Iran, massed in a southeasterly direction from semiautonomous Armenia and independent Media Atropatene, approximately modern Azerbaijan, through the satrapy of Media to Persis, the old heartland of the Achaemenid empire. The key route from Mesopotamia passed up the Diyala valley behind Seleucia-on-the-Tigris to the Median capital, Ecbatana, modern Hamadan. To the east of the Zagros glacis Iran extends as a high plateau, fenced to the north by the Elburz mountains and rising to the peak country of Afghanistan. The most important trans-Iranian route for the Seleucids, known as the Khorasan highway, filed its way between the Elburz and the Dasht-i Kavir wasteland through Hyrcania and Parthia to the oasis city of Antioch-in-Margiane, modern Merv in Turkmenistan, and into Bactria. Sogdiana and Bactria, in Uzbekistan-Tajikistan and Afghanistan respectively, lie to the north and south of the river Oxus, modern Amu Darya, which coils from the roof of the world, the Pamir mountains, through the Scythian steppes to the oasis of Chorasmia, modern Khwarezm, by the Aral Sea. The satrapies of Gandhara, Aria, and Arachosia, in part or whole, were early on ceded to the Mauryan kingdom of India. The unrelieved desert of Gedrosia, today's Baluchistan on the shores of the Indian Ocean, was left an unclaimed wilderness.

History

The Seleucids ruled over a great part of this landscape of "Asia," depositing their evidentiary trace, for almost two and a half centuries. The diversity and size of the empire and its neighbors and the patchiness of source survival have rendered its political history both byzantine and dispiritingly lacunose. So here I will merely sketch the chronological outline of the empire's development, interstate and internecine conflicts, and territorial losses in order to clarify the historical framework within which the book's chapters operate.[38] The narrative is accompanied by a simplified family tree of the Seleucid dynasty (see Figure 2).

The empire's political history falls into four periods, beginning with the rise and reign of its eponymous founder, Seleucus I Nicator. Seleucus was born to non-royal Macedonian nobility in the early 350s, making him an exact peer of Alexander. He played a significant but not leading role during Alexander's decade-long conquest of the Persian empire (334–323), appearing in the Alexander Historians as the commander of the Macedonian elite infantry, the *hypaspistai* or "shield-bearers," during the Indian campaign and as the husband of Apame, daughter of the Sogdian chieftain Spitamanes, at the mass marriage of Macedonian generals to Iranian noblewomen at Susa in 324. After Alexander's death in 323, Seleucus remained of second-rank importance until he was rewarded at the conference of Triparadisus in 320 with the satrapy of Babylonia for his part in the assassination of Perdiccas, regent of the conqueror's incapacitated heirs. Seleucus governed Babylonia as satrap, cultivating indigenous support, until he was chased from the city by Antigonus Monophthalmus in 315. For the next three years, he found refuge in the entourage of Ptolemy, satrap of Egypt, serving as his naval commander in the eastern Mediterranean. But following Ptolemy's victory over Antigonid forces at Gaza in 312, Seleucus hurried through the Arabian desert with a tiny band of followers to reclaim his satrapal command; this triumphal return to Babylon marked the birth of the Seleucid empire. Over the next thirty years Seleucus absorbed most of Alexander's Asian conquests. Between 311 and 304 he extended his

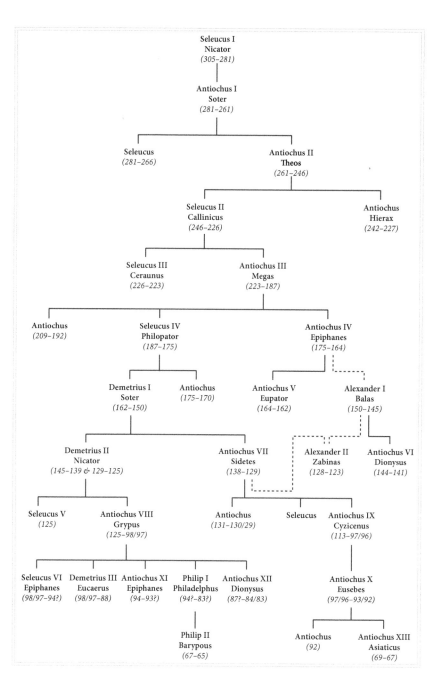

Figure 2 The house of Seleucus (simplified).

control over the Zagros mountains, the Iranian plateau, and Central Asia, taking the royal diadem and so formally becoming a king in 305/4. Turning to the west, he joined a coalition with the successors Cassander, Lysimachus, and Ptolemy I against his *bête noire,* the one-eyed Antigonus, who was defeated and killed at the battle of Ipsus in Phrygia in 301. In consequence, Seleucus absorbed the north Syrian and southeastern Anatolian parts of Antigonus' kingdom, for the first time giving him access to the Mediterranean; against Seleucus' protestations, Ptolemy took over Coele Syria and Phoenicia and so stored up a generations' conflict between their descendants. Marching westward once again, in 281, at the battle of Corupedium in Lydia, an elderly Seleucus defeated and killed Lysimachus, ruler of western Asia Minor, Thrace, and Macedonia. In September of the same year he crossed to Europe with plans for further conquest but was soon struck down by his ward, Ptolemy Ceraunus. "Conqueror of conquerors,"[39] last of Alexander's peers to die, in half a century Seleucus had forged a kingdom that stretched from Afghanistan to the Aegean.

The second coherent period of Seleucid history covers the vertical inheritance of this territory during the reigns of Antiochus I Soter (281–261), Antiochus II Theos (261–246), Seleucus II Callinicus (246–225), and Seleucus III Ceraunus (225–223); it is characterized by conflict with the Ptolemies (the First, Second, and Third Syrian Wars), dynastic struggle, and the consequent loss of the kingdom's eastern and western peripheries. Antiochus I Soter (281–261), son of Seleucus I Nicator and Apame, had already been appointed crown prince and ruler of the Upper (i.e., Iranian and Central Asian) Satrapies by Seleucus I in 294. The challenges faced by Antiochus I at the death of his father, discussed in some detail in Chapter 3, included Ptolemaic conquests in northern Syria and Asia Minor (the War of Syrian Succession and the First Syrian War), the migration into Asia Minor of the Galatians, whose defeat by his elephant force in the Elephant Battle of the mid-270s did not remove their threat, and, at the end of his reign, the emancipation of Pergamum under Eumenes I. His second son, Antiochus II Theos, powerfully answered these threats. In the Second Syrian War (260–253), details mostly unknown, Seleucid forces won back from Ptolemy II most of his conquests along the Aegean and southeastern coastline of Asia Minor, including the important cities of Miletus and Ephesus. Antiochus II also personally campaigned to reassert Seleucid control in European Thrace.

The Second Syrian War was closed by a dynastic marriage of devastating consequence, precipitating a triple collapse of Seleucid authority. Antiochus II divorced his wife, Laodice, dispatching her to western Asia Minor with vast estates as alimony, in order to marry Ptolemy II's daughter Berenice. But a couple of years later, perhaps pining for Laodice, Antiochus established his court at Ephesus with his first wife and their sons, Seleucus (II) and Antiochus Hierax, abandoning Berenice and their baby boy in Antioch-by-Daphne. At Antiochus II's suspicious death in 246, two rival courts in Ephesus and Antioch, headed by the young sons and their mothers, claimed the throne and territory. In the Third Syrian War (246–241), sometimes called the Laodicean War after Antiochus II's first wife, the recently enthroned Ptolemy III invaded on behalf of his sister Berenice, arriving in Antioch too late to save her life but nonetheless conquering the Syrian Seleucis, capturing the Seleucids' Indian elephants, retaking many of the western provinces lost to Antiochus II in the Second Syrian War, and marching as far as Babylon. When an indigenous revolt obliged Ptolemy III to return to Egypt in 241, Seleucus II Callinicus, Antiochus II's eldest son by Laodice, regained most of the Syrian Seleucis. The second disaster, known as the War of the Brothers, followed immediately, when Seleucus II was challenged by his younger sibling, Antiochus Hierax, "the Hawk," who eventually inflicted a severe defeat on his older brother's forces at Ancyra and established himself as an independent king over Seleucid Asia Minor. During the 230s and early 220s Attalus I of Pergamum gained control of Antiochus Hierax' kingdom, returning royal monopoly to the Seleucid house at the cost of its territories in Asia Minor. Our third catastrophe, evidently a response to this crisis at center, were the breakaways of the great eastern satrapies of Parthia, initially under its satrap, Andragoras, and then under the nomadic Parni (who quickly became known as the Parthians), and of Bactria, under the satrap Diodotus. Seleucus II's eastward expedition of reconquest, to be dated sometime between 230 and 227, achieved nothing, and the king died shortly thereafter. The nadir was reached when the new king, Seleucus II's son Seleucus III Ceraunus, having crossed into Asia Minor to regain the territories lost to Antiochus Hierax and Attalus I, was killed by an army conspiracy in the second year of his reign.

The third period, that of the mature kingdom during the reigns of Antiochus III Megas (223–187), Seleucus IV Philopator (187–175), and Antiochus IV Epiphanes (175–164), is dominated by the empire's encounter with Rome. Antiochus III, younger brother of Seleucus III, spent three decades restoring Seleucid authority across "Asia." From the moment of his accession he prioritized the conquest of Coele Syria, claimed by the Seleucids but occupied by the Ptolemies since the battle of Ipsus in 301: a first invasion, the Fourth Syrian War (219–217), recaptured Seleucia-in-Pieria at the mouth of the Orontes but was defeated by Ptolemy IV at Raphia on the Egyptian border; a second, the Fifth Syrian War (202–200), managed to overcome Ptolemaic forces at Panium, in the Golan, and so to incorporate Judea and the major Phoenician cities into the empire for the first time. Antiochus campaigned three times in Asia Minor: between 216 and 213 he took action against the pretender Achaeus, a relative who had taken over Seleucus III's army and title, besieging and then torturing him to death at Sardis; an expedition in 204 and 203 conquered parts of Caria; and the campaign of 198–193 swept up most of the remaining Ptolemaic and Attalid possessions and independent *poleis* of the coastline and interior of Asia Minor and European Thrace, symbolically concluding with the refoundation of Lysimachia in the Thracian Chersonese, eponymous capital of the successor Lysimachus. Antiochus III also reasserted Seleucid dominance in the Upper Satrapies. In 220 he defeated Molon, the rebellious satrap of Media, and imposed suzerainty on Artabazanes, the ruler of Media Atropatene. Antiochus' second inland expedition, or *anabasis*, fired the imagination of the world and established his reputation as the greatest of the Hellenistic monarchs: following his dismemberment of the pretender Achaeus in Asia Minor, Antiochus III committed seven years, 212–205, to campaigning in the Iranian and Central Asian provinces—forcing the submission of Armenia and its dynast Xerxes; campaigning in Media; imposing vassalage on Arsaces II of Parthia; besieging Euthydemus of Bactria for two years and then recognizing him as an independent ally; descending into northwestern India, where he received elephants from the local king, Sophagasenus; sailing the Persian Gulf to the Arabian oasis of Gerrha and the island of Bahrain; and returning to northern Syria via Seleucia-on-the-Tigris and Babylon.

By 193 Antiochus III Megas had established his authority over most of the lands ruled or claimed by his ancestors. But his good fortune was brought to an abrupt end by his overambitious and ill-prepared invasion of Greece, a Roman protectorate since the Republic's defeat of Philip V, Antigonid king of Macedonia, in 197. A first Roman success at Thermopylae—a moral location that has ever since characterized the Seleucid empire as the Achaemenid *redivivus*—was followed up by the triumph of Scipio Asiaticus at the battle of Magnesia in 189. Victor imposed on vanquished the Peace of Apamea (188), according to which Antiochus III formally and forever ceded all Seleucid lands in cis-Tauric Asia Minor, reduced his military forces, including elephants, paid an enormous war indemnity, and surrendered twenty senior Seleucid hostages to Rome. The once great Antiochus III spent his final years in a third *anabasis,* killed in 187 in an attempt to reassert Seleucid authority over Elymaïs. His successor, Seleucus IV Philopator, focused on paying off the indemnity and rebuilding diplomatic alliances, achieved little of prominence; he was murdered in 175 by his chief minister, Heliodorus.

Seleucus IV was succeeded by his younger brother, Antiochus IV Epiphanes, since his eldest son, Demetrius (I), remained a hostage at Rome. Antiochus IV, an energetic ruler and reformer, embarked on the Sixth—and, fortunately, final—Syrian War (170–168), twice invading Egypt and besieging Alexandria until, on the "Day of Eleusis," he was humiliated into retreat by the ultimatum of the Roman legate, Popilius Laenas. His subsequent desecration of the Jerusalem Temple and persecution of Judaism in 167 provoked the Maccabaean revolt, which would eventually result in Judea's independence under the Hasmonaean dynasty. In 165, as the Jewish revolt strengthened, Antiochus IV embarked on an eastern *anabasis,* reconquering Armenia and reasserting the Seleucid presence in the Gulf, but died of disease or divine punishment in Iran in 164 before more could be achieved.

The fourth phase of Seleucid history, from Antiochus IV's death in 164 to the final dissolution of the kingdom in 64/3, is a bewildering chaos of dynastic conflict, Parthian conquest, and indigenous insurrection. The historical processes are explored thematically in Chapter 8, so the outline here will be narrowly dynastic and chronological; regnal successions do not of course make adequate history, but they are the only landmarks for navigating the unforgiving complexity and onomastic repetition of what follows.

The premature death of Antiochus IV Epiphanes exploded into rivalry between his descendants and those of Seleucus IV Philopator, his older brother and predecessor. The throne was immediately occupied by Antiochus IV's young son, Antiochus V Eupator (164–162), represented by his guardian, Lysias. The Roman determination to weaken the empire still further was quickly made evident when a visiting delegation, headed by Cn. Octavius, hamstrung the entire Seleucid elephant herd, an act of symbolic violence to "cripple the royal power."[40] In 162, Seleucus IV's son, Demetrius I Soter (162–150), having failed to persuade the Senate to release him, fled Rome to retake his ancestral kingdom; Antiochus V and Lysias were soon disappeared. Despite Demetrius I's efforts to win the support of his former detainers, within a year he was doubly undermined by the Senate's alliance with the insurgent Hasmonaean Jews and recognition of Timarchus, rebellious satrap of Media, as an independent king. Although Demetrius I managed to defeat Timarchus in 160, seven years later Timarchus' brother Heraclides won his revenge by persuading the Senate to recognize a certain Alexander, supposed son of Antiochus IV, as legitimate Seleucid king. Demetrius I Soter fell in 150, fighting his rival's invasion of Syria, and Alexander I Balas (150–145) was secured in his position by marriage to the daughter of Ptolemy VI, Cleopatra Thea. Alexander I, in his turn, was challenged by Demetrius I's son, Demetrius II Nicator, who landed with Cretan mercenaries in Phoenicia in 147. By 145 Demetrius II had won control of most of Syria; Ptolemy VI, once more determining the victor, transferred his daughter, Cleopatra Thea, from Alexander I to Demetrius II. Demetrius II Nicator (first reign, 145–138) faced immediate opposition from the military commander Diodotus Tryphon, who raised a revolt in the name of Alexander Balas' son, Antiochus VI Dionysus (144–141), and then, after murdering the child, proclaimed himself king (141–138); the Seleucid heartland was fragmented once again into warring factions. In an attempt to break the stalemate, gain resources, and win legitimacy, in 139 Demetrius II crossed the Euphrates for the empire's eastern provinces.

Dynastic strife and Timarchus' revolt had fatally eroded Seleucid authority in the Upper Satrapies: under Mithridates I, the Parthian kingdom had expanded from the Caspian region to occupy Media in 148/7, Babylonia in 141, and Elymaïs in 140. Demetrius II's *anabasis* to recover these lands was terminated by his capture and imprisonment at the Parthian court, where he was given away to Mithridates I's daughter Rhodogune. Demetrius II's younger brother, Antiochus VII Sidetes (138–129), now sailed to Syria to fill his captive brother's empty throne and bed, marrying Cleopatra Thea at Seleucia-in-Pieria. Antiochus VII finally defeated Diodotus Tryphon in 138, bringing some measure of stability to Syria, and reasserted Seleucid authority in Judea, razing the walls of Jerusalem in 133. In 131 the king led out an 80,000-strong army from Antioch-by-Daphne for the east, intending to win back from the Parthians both the Upper Satrapies and his brother, Demetrius II. The reigning Parthian, Phraates II, hoping to stir dynastic conflict between the two brothers—a fair assumption—returned Demetrius II to Syria. The siblings switched places: Antiochus VII Sidetes, after some early and significant successes against Parthian forces, fell somewhere in western Iran in 129; Demetrius II Nicator, back in Syria, enjoyed a second reign (129–125), once again with Cleopatra Thea as his queen. The Seleucid empire, its Upper Satrapies now irrecoverable, was reduced to its north Syrian and Cilician rump. And the nine offspring of Cleopatra Thea, by Alexander I Balas, Demetrius II, Antiochus VII, and Demetrius II for a second time, would between themselves tear apart this small territory.

Demetrius II's marriage to Cleopatra Thea had involved him in the dynastic disputes of the Ptolemaic house, in which he supported his mother-in-law, Cleopatra II, against her brother Ptolemy VIII Physcon. In response, Ptolemy VIII sponsored a challenger to the Seleucid throne, Alexander II Zabinas (128–123), supposed son of Alexander I Balas or adopted son of Antiochus VII Sidetes. Syria split once more, and Egyptian forces drove Demetrius II to flight; he was killed in 125 by the commander of Tyre. Alexander II Zabinas, soon abandoned by Ptolemy VIII, was killed for his sacrilegious exactions from Antioch-by-Daphne; Demetrius II's son, Seleucus V Philometor (125), took the diadem without his mother's permission and so was shortly disposed of in favor of another son by Demetrius II, Antiochus VIII Grypus (125–98/7), to whom Ptolemy VIII married his daughter Cleopatra Tryphaena. Antiochus VIII anticipated his mother with poison in 121, and under his rule Syria enjoyed almost a decade of calm before Antiochus IX Cyzicenus (113–96), Cleopatra Thea's son by Antiochus VII Sidetes and an obsessive puppeteer, invaded in 113 to challenge his half-brother and cousin; the war dragged on for fifteen years, further benefiting the Parthians, who captured the Euphratene colony of Dura-Europus, the Hasmonaeans, who consolidated their independence and sacked Samaria, the cities of the Syro-Phoenician littoral, which exacted economic and political privileges from the kings, and the pirates of the Cilician coastline, who could swashbuckle at will.

Following the assassination of Antiochus VIII Grypus by his general, Heracleon, in 98/7, his sons Seleucus VI Epiphanes (98–94?) and Demetrius III Eucaerus (98–88) declared themselves kings in Cilicia and Syria, respectively; it seems that Demetrius III refounded Damascus as his eponymous capital. In 97/6 Seleucus VI defeated Antiochus IX Cyzicenus and occupied Antioch-by-Daphne but was immediately challenged by Antiochus IX's son, Antiochus X Eusebes (97/6–93/2), who pursued his father's vanquisher to Mopsuestia in Cilicia, where, an unwilling Sardanapalus, he was burned to death with his *philoi* in the royal palace. Seleucus VI's twin brothers, Antiochus XI Epiphanes (94/3) and Philip I Philadelphus (94–83?), avenged his death. At some point, Philip I, now based out of Beroea

(Aleppo), turned on his brother Demetrius III Eucaerus, who was captured and dethroned by the Parthians; Damascus was then occupied by another brother, the fifth and youngest son of Cleopatra Tryphaena and Antiochus VIII Grypus, Antiochus XII Dionysus (87/6–84/3), who was defeated and killed by the Nabataeans.

In 83 Syria and Cilicia were absorbed into the Armenian kingdom of Tigranes II, and many of its inhabitants resettled in the king's eponymous new city, Tigranocerta. When Tigranes and his army were forced by the Roman general L. Lucullus to evacuate Syria in 69, the land was handed over to Antiochus XIII Asiaticus (69–64), son of Antiochus X Eusebes. The rot had reached so deep that even this Roman creature was challenged, by Philip II Barypous (67–65), son of Philip I, with the support of the Arab chieftain Aziz. In the winter of 64/3 Pompey the Great declared Syria a possession of the Roman people. Antiochus XIII Asiaticus was put to death by Sampsigeramus, ruler of Emesa and deep ancestor of the Severan emperors; the Seleucid empire had died long before.

The Naming of Parts

The Land of the Elephant Kings is organized into four parts, of two chapters each, that take us thematically and chronologically from the kingdom's establishment to its final dissolution.

Part I, "Border," examines the demarcation of the Seleucid empire's eastern boundary during the reigns of Seleucus I and Antiochus I. Chapter 1, "India—Diplomacy and Ethnography at the Mauryan Frontier," demonstrates the importance for the empire's spatial identity of Seleucus I's military encounter at the end of the fourth century with Chandragupta Maurya, founder of the Mauryan empire of northern India, and the subsequent Treaty of the Indus, which established peace between the two powers for generations. A close reading of the major ethnographic composition of the early Seleucid court, the *Indica* of Megasthenes, Seleucus I's ambassador to the Mauryan kingdom, shows that the work responded to the new political geography by recentering India on the Ganges valley and refashioning the kingdom as a non-utopian peer. By comparing Megasthenes' ethnography with the Greek and Prakrit inscriptions of the Mauryan king Ashoka, Chandragupta's grandson, we see that both empires presented their bilateral border in the Hindu Kush as the shared periphery of two natural and self-contained geographical units.

Chapter 2, "Central Asia—Nomads, Ocean, and the Desire for Line," explores how the Seleucids, lacking a powerful, external state to their north against which they could delineate themselves, worked hard to impose an ideological *limes* on the problematically porous landscape of Central Asia. We see that religious dedications, preserved on stone or in the fragmentary autobiography of the Seleucid general Demodamas, attempted to sanctify the northern frontier of imperial space as the boundary of the civilized world. More bizarre was the unified aquatic edge at the kingdom's north, fabricated by the Seleucid admiral and Caspian explorer Patrocles.

Together, the two chapters demonstrate the significant contribution of Seleucid geographers and ethnographers—active soldiers and diplomats not, like their Ptolemaic and Antigonid peers, "armchair" scholars—to the reshaping of the Graeco-Macedonian (and therefore Roman and mediaeval) understanding of the farther east.

Part II, "Homeland," investigates the closing of the empire's territory in the west, addressing the tension between the natal origins of the Seleucid dynasty, in Macedonia, and the place of its kingship, in Asia. I concentrate on two moments. Chapter 3, "Macedonia—From Center to Periphery," investigates Seleucus I's failed attempt to conquer his Macedonian homeland in 281, half a century after he had left it with Alexander. It combines Babylonian sources and Greek historiography to argue that the imperial court depicted the founder-king's invasion of Europe as a *nostos*, the homeward journey of a homesick king. We see that, when Seleucus I was assassinated and the expedition aborted, European Thrace was established as the kingdom's loosely administered and ideologically demoted western periphery.

Chapter 4, "Syria—Diasporic Imperialism," examines how Antiochus I and his successors made sense of Seleucus I's tragic fate and the consequent externality of Macedonia. Oracles and dream omens, preserved in an official biographical tradition of Seleucus I, presented Macedonia as a forbidden land. In its place, northern Syria was constructed as the empire's new heartland. This *translatio patriae*, the relocation of the ruling dynasty's affective home associations from one place to another, was achieved by the burial of Seleucus I in the Syrian Seleucis, by the invention of a continuous year-count, the Seleucid Era, and by the formal relabeling of the urban and natural landscape of northern Syria with names borrowed from Macedonia and the ruling family.

A brief Interlude shows that this Seleucid territory, bounded at east and west, was assimilated to the Greek geographical concept of "Asia" and the empire consequently named the "kingdom of Asia." The second half of the book explores how this closed space was articulated and practiced.

Part III, "Movement," looks at the role of the itinerant court in the construction of Seleucid territorial identity. A short Chapter 5, "Arrivals and Departures," uses royal entrances into and departures from the imperial territory, in peace and war, to explore the ways in which the Seleucid landscape could bestow legitimacy on kings. It is shown that Seleucid expansions beyond the territory framed or claimed by Seleucus I and Antiochus I—the island of Euboea by Antiochus III in the Roman War, most of lower Egypt by Antiochus IV in the Sixth Syrian War—required rituals of integration that marked these new conquests as external to Seleucid space.

Chapter 6, "The Circulatory System," explores how the Seleucid kings took possession of their empire by progressing through it. Greek, Jewish, and Babylonian texts are paralleled to show that the traveling kings used the same limited repertoire of ceremonial interactions throughout their diverse territory. Arrival and departure ceremonies performed at urban settlements asserted Seleucid sovereign claims in a quasi-religious mode and temporarily co-opted indigenous elites into the royal court. The itinerant king hosted regular in-the-field banquets, pulling inward and then redistributing local food resources, to pose as agricultural patron and greatest giver. "Traffic-flow" maps of all known royal journeys identify the directionality and frequency of the kings' movement and the practical and ideological significance of Royal Roads. It is shown that royal mobility was the major mechanism of provincial integration and an index for evaluating individual monarchs.

The book's final section, Part IV, "Colony," examines how the Seleucids' astonishingly ambitious program of colonization transformed the landscape of Asia and manifested or undercut Seleucid sovereignty. Chapter 7, "King Makes City," explores the spatial pattern of Seleucid colonization at three scales: at the continental level, we see that the new colonies shifted the gravitational centers of the political landscape to the previously underdeveloped regions of the middle Tigris valley and northern Syria; at the regional, they reconfigured population groups and economic production; at the city level, their cookie-cutter grid plans represented an entirely new kind of urbanism that characterized the empire as modern, scientific, and rational. We see that Seleucid colonial onomastics and official foundation narratives represented a coherent imperial ideology of urbanism and space.

Chapter 8, "City Makes King," investigates how, under the afflictions of dynastic strife, these colonies grew to replace the king's mobile court as the main center of legitimate authority. I trace the emergence of an emphatically non-Seleucid civic identity for the urban foundations, through the gradual demarcation of royal palaces in these colonies as "forbidden cities" separate from civic areas and through the colonies' invention of mythological archaic origins to displace their actual Seleucid founders. I show that colonial populations came to form a discrete public sphere with which kings negotiated, by which they were monitored, and from which they deduced at least part of their legitimacy.

In the Conclusion we see that the ways in which the Seleucid landscape was articulated and made administratively legible also generated the fault lines along which it fell apart.

PART I

Border

CHAPTER 1

India—Diplomacy and Ethnography at the Mauryan Frontier

From Alexander the Great's death at Babylon in 323 until the first decades of the third century the lands over which he had ruled were convulsed by the ambitions, assassinations, and alliances of his greatest generals. With almost forty years of warfare and betrayal, vertiginous collapse and unexpected rise, it is no surprise that *Tychē*, capricious Fate, achieves new causal prominence in the historiography of this period.[1] But if we stand at a distance from what Braudel called history's "crests of foam," we can understand the playing out of the succession crisis as the birth pangs of a new, but not unfamiliar, world order: the peer-kingdom international system.

Alexander's kingdom, like the Achaemenid imperial structure he conquered and reelaborated, was a hegemonic world empire characterized by an emphasis on totality and exclusivity.[2] The Persian Great King and Alexander monopolized legitimate sovereignty and recognized no entity as external and equivalent. The fragmentation of this all-embracing imperial formation after Alexander's death and the stabilization of independent kingdoms multiplied the royal persona and state. A diachronic succession of world-empires (Achaemenids to Alexander) was replaced with the synchronic coexistence of bounded kingdoms. The emergence of a few "Great Powers" (Antigonid Macedonia, Ptolemaic Egypt, Seleucid Asia, as well as Attalid Pergamum, Mauryan India, the Anatolian kingdoms, and Rome) gradually developed into a system of peer states with semiformalized procedures of interaction. In other words, the east Mediterranean–west Asian region settled back into the multipolarity that had characterized it in the Neo-Babylonian period, immediately before Cyrus' conquests and the foundation of the Persian empire, and in the famous Late Bronze Age of Amarna.[3]

This historical process of division and multiplication can be traced throughout the Wars of Succession that followed Alexander's death.[4] By the third century, a developed and unquestioned international order was operating within the broader Hellenistic world; multipolarity was the assumed framework for everything from *asylia* (recognition of a city's inviolability)[5] and festival requests[6] to benefactions following natural disasters.[7] Of paramount importance to such a system was the "border," both in its technical definition and its ideological implications. Kingdoms had to be recognized as spatially limited units, as bounded territories with shared frontiers. In this first part of *The Land of the Elephant Kings* I investigate the construction of the Seleucid empire's political boundary in the east.

In 305 or 304, Macedonian forces once again issued out of the Hindu Kush, more than two decades after they had first entered the Indus valley behind Alexander the Great:[8] for Seleucus I Nicator, who over the previous half decade had extended his authority from Babylonia to Bactria, now led his army in a second Indian invasion. This campaign and the diplomatic agreement that concluded it formed the foundational moment of Seleucid imperial space. For the first time, Seleucus I's rule was formally bounded and thereby territorialized, fixing the empire's southeastern border for at least a century. Furthermore, the encoding of this new political situation in Seleucid court ethnography—specifically, the *Indica* of Megasthenes, Seleucus' ambassador to the Indian court—demonstrates the profound impact of this historical moment on traditional geographical and ethnological ideas.

The Treaty of the Indus

In contrast to the untidy patchwork of rival principalities and *gana-sangha* oligarchies encountered by Alexander, the land Seleucus entered had recently been annexed and united by Chandragupta Maurya, the new ruler of the first pan-north Indian imperial entity.[9] Chandragupta, appearing in classical sources as (S)androcottus,[10] was a peer of the Macedonian Successors and integrated into their world and its struggles.[11] Like them, the new Indian potentate is shown emphasizing his links to Alexander: Plutarch records that king Sandrocottus claimed to have met Alexander as a youth,[12] compared himself to the great Macedonian,[13] and sacrificed on the altars erected by Alexander on the bank of the Hyphasis (mod. Beas) whenever he crossed the river.[14] The course of Seleucus' campaign against this Indian emperor is not known in detail—an obscurity that has tempted modern historians to political allegory and forgery.[15] Certainly, Seleucus crossed his forces over the river Indus, so invading India proper,[16] but whether Seleucid and Mauryan armies fought a pitched battle is still debated. Whatever happened, at some point, in a momentous and foundational act of the new world order, Seleucus and Chandragupta decided to make peace. The ancient historians Justin, Appian, and Strabo preserve the three main terms of what I will call the Treaty of the Indus:[17]

(i) Seleucus transferred to Chandragupta's kingdom the easternmost satrapies of his empire, certainly Gandhara, Parapamisadae, and the eastern parts of Gedrosia,[18] and possibly also Arachosia and Aria as far as Herat.[19]

(ii) Chandragupta gave Seleucus 500 Indian war elephants.[20]

(iii) The two kings were joined by some kind of marriage alliance (ἐπιγαμία or κῆδος); most likely Chandragupta wed a female relative of Seleucus.[21]

The terms are interrelated: Seleucus' receipt of elephants is framed as an exchange (Strabo's verb is ἀντιλαμβάνω, "I take in return") for the territory or the marriage, and the marriage itself may have functioned as the security and guarantee of the treaty, with the ceded land considered a dowry.[22]

This territory-for-elephants exchange was mutually beneficial. Geopolitically, Seleucus abandoned territories he could never securely hold in favor of peace and security in the east: the treaty and elephants allowed him to turn his attention to his rival, Antigonus Monophthalmus, Syria, and the Mediterranean.[23] Chandragupta gained unchallenged expansion into India's northwest corridor.[24] His gift of elephants may have alleviated the burden of fodder and the return march. Ambassadors and caravans, not conquering armies, would now pass through the intermediate zone. Moreover, the fact and terms of the treaty were a recognition of equal, royal status for kings who lacked the legitimacy of appointment or inheritance. It is even possible that Seleucus used the occasion of this treaty—a wedding on the Indus?—for formally completing his long march from satrap to king.[25]

The Treaty of the Indus was a constitutive act of the Hellenistic state system, creating the Seleucid empire's eastern frontier by transferring land out of Seleucus' control. This act of delimitation marked the boundary of Seleucid power and sovereign claims. As such, it was a radical departure

from two centuries of Achaemenid and Alexandrian universalist pretensions. Persian kings had recognized no independent, equal monarchy to its
east, and in Achaemenid geography, as far as it can be grasped through its
Herodotean and Ctesian refractions, the world simply faded into nothing-
ness beyond Persia's imperial possessions in India. The eastern boundary
of Alexander's conquests was more problematic. From its outset, his *anabasis* had been a relentless march toward the eastern edge of the world; he was
halted only at the Hyphasis river by an army mutiny, a form of internal
historical agent entirely consistent with his empire's effacement of external
powers. By contrast, the termination of Seleucus' eastern conquest was ex-
ternally motivated. Seleucus, like Alexander, crossed the river Indus (a me-
tonymy for royal invasion),[26] but he met his equal, Chandragupta. In other
words, diplomacy is to bounded political space what mutiny is to universal
political space. The new world order's multicentrism results in a historical
narrative of multiple agency.

The terms of the treaty, no doubt much negotiated, indicate an economy
of exchange. Space is convertible. Seleucid power was not yet embedded in
a defined territory: its eastern lands function, like Chandragupta's elephants,
as one resource of the kingdom. The very fact of the treaty's territorial clause
indicates that land was still a possession to be negotiated over and divided up
unproblematically. Moreover, the treaty created new spatial units, ignoring
the boundaries of ethnic communities and the historical precedents of Achaemenid and Alexandrian imperialism.

The Treaty of the Indus satisfactorily secured the eastern periphery of
the Seleucid empire and the western periphery of the Mauryan empire. The
Seleucid frontier with the Indian kingdom, settled once and for all, never
became an important location for the legitimating of monarchic identity
through territorial claims or military aggression; there was no attempt to
reconquer the ceded territories or to redraw the border, a clear contrast to the
ping-pong regions of Coele Syria and Asia Minor. Likewise, the Mauryan
kingdom, satisfied with its territorial gains in the northwest, appears to
have turned its attentions eastward and southward.[27] Friendly contacts
were maintained by Seleucid diplomats resident in the Mauryan capital,
Pataliputra (Gr. Palimbothra, mod. Patna), including, as we will see, Seleucus I's envoy Megasthenes, and it is very probable that Chandragupta's
representatives were attached to the Seleucid court; his grandson Ashoka
certainly sent them.[28] Relations continued into the kingdoms' second generation: Strabo reports that Megasthenes was replaced by Deimachus, am-

bassador of Seleucus' successor, Antiochus I, to Chandragupta's successor, Amitrochates (Bindusara).[29]

In the new context of permanent, amicable diplomacy opened by the Treaty of the Indus, the land-for-elephants agreement was reperformed as regular, ceremonial gift-giving, exchanges that generated solidarity and renewed equality of rank, as in the Bronze Age "Great Powers" system of Amarna diplomacy,[30] rather than functioning as unidirectional signs of subservience, as in Persepolitan imperialism.[31] The Hellenistic historian Phylarchus, in a passage preserved by Athenaeus, indicates that Chandragupta sent Seleucus a gift package, including Indian aphrodisiacs.[32] The incense trees that Seleucus attempted to import by sea from India[33] and the tigers he sent to the Athenians (see Chapter 4) may well have originated as Chandragupta's diplomatic gifts. Athenaeus repeats Hegesander's report that Chandragupta's son, Amitrochates (Bindusara), requested from Antiochus I wine, figs, and a sophist. Antiochus responded, ἰσχάδας μὲν καὶ γλυκὺν ἀποστελοῦμέν σοι, σοφιστὴν δ' ἐν Ἕλλησιν οὐ νόμιμον πωλεῖσθαι, "The figs and sweet wine we will send you, but it is not lawful among the Greeks for a sophist to be sold."[34] This delightful passage demonstrates not only that the diplomatic gift exchange between the Seleucid and Mauryan kings was well known and recorded by contemporary authors but also that it was imagined to be open to curiosity, request, negotiation, and refusal: giving is complemented by keeping.[35] The frequency with which the exchanged gifts appear to be of an ethnographic character may be a consequence of our sources' parodoxographical preferences, but the sending of figs eastward or tigers westward could only reinforce the new world order's assertion of independent, essentially external territories.

Almost a century after Seleucus I had given land for peace, the greatest of his successors, Antiochus III, led a new imperial army into India. No Seleucid ruler had penetrated to the distant eastern borders of the kingdom since Seleucus Nicator had delineated them at the Treaty of the Indus. Polybius describes this second encounter of Seleucid and Indian monarchs:

[Antiochus III] crossed the Caucasus and descended into India, renewed his friendship (τήν τε φιλίαν ἀνενεώσατο) with Sophagasenus, king of the Indians (τὸν βασιλέα τῶν Ἰνδῶν), and received more elephants, raising their number to a total of one hundred and fifty, and provisioned his army once more on the spot. He himself broke camp with his troops, leaving behind Androsthenes of Cyzicus to bring back the treasure which the king (Sophagasenus) had agreed to give him.[36]

King Sophagasenus, a name probably derived from Subhagasena,[37] is here identified as ὁ βασιλεὺς τῶν Ἰνδῶν, "the king of the Indians." This title falsely suggests a unified Indian kingdom such as Chandragupta's: a projection of imperial stability in line with Antiochus III's own internally rejuvenating objectives. In fact, the Mauryan state entity had disintegrated, for various reasons, following the death of Ashoka in 232; Sophagasenus was ruler of a northwestern splinter kingdom. Without doubt, the "renewal of friendship" was imposed from a position of strength on the Indian king by the sudden arrival of a large, well-tested, recently reinforced and rested army. In practical terms, it was not an alliance between equals: Androsthenes of Cyzicus was left behind to transport Sophagasenus' own treasure, while king Antiochus simply took the elephants (compare his λαβὼν ἐλέφαντας "taking the elephants" with Seleucus I's ἀντιλαβὼν ἐλέφαντας "taking in return the elephants"; that is, seizure versus reciprocal exchange[38]). Given his immediate, on-the-ground advantages, it is striking that Antiochus III neither claimed superiority of status nor attempted to integrate these trans-Caucasian territories into his imperial structure, a clear contrast with his actions earlier in his eastern expedition, where he had framed a similar payment from Xerxes, the local ruler of Armenia, as the legitimate extraction of long-overdue tribute[39] and had made an extraordinary, but ultimately unsuccessful, effort to avoid recognizing the royal status and independence of Euthydemus of Bactria.[40] Antiochus' activities in India are explicitly considered an act of renewal. The encounter of Antiochus and Sophagasenus is very clearly framed as a historical reenactment of the Seleucus-Chandragupta Treaty of the Indus (τήν τε φιλίαν ἀνενεώσατο, "he renewed the friendship"), guaranteeing amicable relations and uncontested boundaries between the Seleucid and Indian kingdoms by means of, as before, mutual recognition of equivalent status and the gift of elephants. The continuity is, as we have seen, an engineered ideological fiction. Antiochus' actions in northwestern India, a curious combination of compulsion and renunciation, demonstrate his unproblematic acceptance of the Treaty of the Indus and its century-old territorial transfer. Despite marching his army over the Hindu Kush, Antiochus made no attempt to "conquer" India. Rather, he acknowledged the spatial limitation of his own sovereignty, which is to say, the boundedness of Seleucid imperial territory. As we will see in Chapter 5, Antiochus' changed behavior on crossing the border constitutes a kind of threshold ritual: the king distinguished, in his own person, interior from exterior, Seleucid from non-Seleucid territory.

Demonstrably, the Treaty of the Indus retained its salience within the kingdom's official dynastic memory, both as a magnificent episode of grand royal encounter and as a first act of territorial delimitation.[41] In addition to its continued geopolitical importance, the peace treaty also provided the ideological motivation and diplomatic conditions for perhaps the greatest and most influential literary work of the Seleucid court—the *Indica* of Megasthenes, Seleucus' envoy to the Mauryan court—to which we now turn.

Megasthenes' *Indica*

Seleucus I's relationship with India was complex. On the one hand, his kingdom's security and ultimate success were founded on his relationship with the Mauryan empire: the 500 war elephants received from Chandragupta defeated Antigonus Monophthalmus at Ipsus in 301.[42] Seleucus' coinage and the kingdom's official historiography depicted the Treaty of the Indus as a success and celebrated it accordingly.[43] On the other hand, Seleucus had abandoned the very territories in which he had first achieved prominence; he had diminished, not extended, Macedonian rule; Alexander's Graeco-Macedonian settlers in the Hindu Kush would now be Yona minorities on the periphery of the Indian kingdom. So when Seleucus was toasted as ἐλεφαντάρχης, "elephant-commander," at the banquets of his rival, Demetrius Poliorcetes, the son of Antigonus Monophthalmus, it is likely that he was being mocked for his withdrawal from India, much as Agathocles of Syracuse, whose dream to expand from Sicily to Africa had recently collapsed, was hailed as νησιάρχης, "island-commander," at the same feast.[44]

I will argue here that Megasthenes' ethnography of India, as a sensitive engagement with the new, multipolar world order, attempted to neutralize this embarrassing, ideologically confusing contradiction. We will see that the ethnography legitimized Seleucus' formal renunciation of the Macedonian conquests in India, reformulated Indian geography to naturalize the post-treaty Mauryan-Seleucid border, and established India as an analogous kingdom for thinking through Seleucid state formation. More generally, an examination of Megasthenes' *Indica*, the best known and preserved of a host of ethnographies written for the Seleucid kingdom in its pioneering phase, will uncover the considerable energies devoted to generating, order-ing, and deploying a governmentally useful spatial knowledge.

Even though historical narrative and monarchic ideology inevitably emplot the Treaty of the Indus as the meeting of two great rulers, it cannot be doubted that the negotiations were parleyed by Indian and Graeco-Macedonian regional experts. It is possible that Megasthenes was Seleucus' main negotiator in 305/4,[45] probable that he was the main literary source for the diplomatic terms,[46] and certain that he was the Seleucid ambassador to the court of Chandragupta Maurya, at Pataliputra on the Ganges; the Appendix discusses the *testimonia* for Megasthenes' career. At some point during or after his tenure as ambassador, Megasthenes published an ethno-graphic treatise, titled *Indica*. The work, like so much of Hellenistic literature, has not survived from antiquity in its own right[47] and so must be recon-structed from the quotations, paraphrases, and allusions of later, extant authors. But we are unusually lucky: the rise of Parthia, the emancipation of Graeco-Bactria, and the collapse of the Mauryan empire after Ashoka's death restricted land access to the Ganges; the discovery of the Gulf trade winds (and the consequent commerce in Indian luxuries) in the first cen-tury exploited the west Indian littoral rather than the country's interior. As a result, Megasthenes' *Indica* was established as the most authoritative ethnography of the Gangetic basin, quickly becoming the standard descrip-tion of the Indian interior.[48] Extensive and overlapping portions of the *In-dica* have been preserved in Diodorus Siculus, Strabo, and Arrian, as well as brief but eye-catching passages in the Jewish/Christian and paradoxo-graphical literary traditions.[49] Broad similarities of content as well as spe-cific equivalences of vocabulary and phrase permit a relatively unproblem-atic identification of Megasthenes' material even when he is not explicitly named.[50] The reconstruction of the work's structure and internal logic is greatly aided both by the unity of Diodorus' epitome and by a basic similar-ity to Hecataeus of Abdera's *Aigyptiaca*.[51] It is likely that Megasthenes wrote the *Indica* in three books:[52] the first discussed India's geography, natural his-tory, and climate; the second, the country's primitive life, early civilization, and historical developments; the third, the customs and administration of the contemporary Mauryan state.

The *Indica*'s historical account narrated a culture myth, explicitly repre-sented as indigenous Indian tradition, of the transformation of Indian soci-ety by a conquering Dionysus and an autochthonous Heracles.[53] Such "as-cent of man" narratives were regularly treated in universal histories and ethnographic treatises.[54] The *Indica*'s *Kulturgeschichte* establish the important ethnographic principles and patterns of historical causation that the work will systematically deploy. Accordingly, they play a central role in the logic of Megasthenes' Seleucid apology: as the modalities of cultural formation play out over the course of Indian history, Seleucus' territorial abandonment is made inevitable.

Prehistoric India, that is, India before the arrival of Dionysus and the beginnings of cultural memory, is a world without cities. In the characterization of primitive India's state of nature, this absence is mentioned first and functions as the primary and determinant condition for all other barbarous behaviors:

> Long ago the Indians were nomads, just like the nonagricultural Scythians, who, wandering in their wagons, exchange one part of Scythia for another at one time or another (ἄλλοτε ἄλλην), neither inhabiting cities nor honoring shrines of the gods (οὔτε πόληας οἰκέοντες οὔτε ἱερὰ θεῶν σέβοντες).[55]

In Megasthenes' stagist model, the earliest condition of Indian man was indicated not only by a lack of urbanism or religious piety but also by an absence of territoriality. Indian space was unmarked and expansive and, like the Scythian steppe, uninvested with meaning; it could be abandoned willy-nilly (effectively underlined by the juxtaposition ἄλλοτε ἄλλην). The *Indica*'s language here is strikingly Herodotean, and the comparison clearly points toward Herodotus' Scythian ethnography.[56] Megasthenes' account moves on emphatically to associate the absence of cities and religion with the stock elements of a generic barbarity: wearing skins, not clothes; eating bark, not grain; devouring meat raw, not cooked.[57] This absence of cities is, for Megasthenes, the very condition of Dionysus' conquest. India is an open, accessible space: "[Dionysus] overran all of India, since there was no important city (μηδεμιᾶς οὔσης ἀξιολόγου πόλεως) powerful enough to oppose him."[58] India could be conquered because the Indians were nomads. Megasthenes establishes a connection between urban power and resistance to conquest that resonates throughout his treatise.

Dionysus' invasion puts an end to this timeless, primitive India. Arrian paraphrases:

> When Dionysus came and became master of the Indians he founded cities and established laws in the cities (πόληάς τε οἰκίσαι καὶ νόμους θέσθαι τῇσι πόλεσιν), he dispensed wine to the Indians, just as to the Greeks, he taught

them to sow the land, giving them seeds . . . Dionysus was the first to yoke
the oxen to the plough, and made the majority of Indians agriculturalists
instead of nomads; he also armed them with weapons of war. Dionysus
also taught them to worship other gods, but himself most of all, clashing
cymbals and playing drums.[59]

Megasthenes has avoided the naturalistic, impersonal, random, and gradualist historical anthropology associated with Democritus, Protagoras, and
Dicaearchus[60] in favor of Dionysus' momentous role as benefactor, teacher,
and inventor. Culture arrives with monarchy: Megasthenes' *Kulturgeschichte*
construct, with other early Hellenistic texts, an image of the monarchic
monopoly of historical agency, the royal profile of master-builder, and the
cocreation of a political and spatial centrality.[61] And, as in much of Hellenistic literature, Dionysus' violence is suppressed; though bearing the cult-
title ὠμάδιος or ὠμηστής ("devourer of raw flesh") in the Greek world, he
leads Megasthenes' Indians from the raw to the cooked.[62] Alongside the
standardly Bacchic satyric dance, long hair, perfumery, invention of wine,
and visibility of women, the continued performances of which were witnessed in India at the time of Alexander's invasion, it is Dionysus' role as
city founder that is most unusual and striking. Just as the lack of cities was
primitive life's first mentioned and fundamental absence, so the creation of
cities is the first mentioned act of civilization and the requirement for associated cultural processes. In Diodorus' parallel account, Dionysus' urban
foundations invest the landscape with difference: the unstriated space of
prehistoric India is now marked with value (τοὺς εὐθέτους τόπους, "well-
placed sites") where the cities are located.[63] Moreover, Diodorus' Dionysus is
an oecist of πόλεων ἀξιολόγων, "important cities": the diction here responds
directly to primitive India's absence of a single *important* city, which was, as
we have seen, the precondition of Dionysus' very conquest.

  Dionysus' city-founding activities abolish the very circumstance that permitted the success of his own invasion, making it a unique episode in Indian history. Dionysus is also the inventor of Indian warfare, arming the
population with weapons of war and influencing their battle order, which
obviously goes hand in hand with the land's new urban defensibility.
Alongside its generic civilizing function, therefore, the invasion of Dionysus
operates as a guarantee of India's future isolation and impregnability, characteristics which Megasthenes' ethnographic descriptions and continued
historical narrative repeatedly emphasize. As demonstrated by the failure of

all subsequent invasions (see later), this foundational act transforms a penetrable, open space into a closed, fortified, and unconquerable territory.

The *Indica* introduces a second civilizing superman, Heracles, fifteen generations after Dionysus' invasion; as before, the account is attributed to Indian authority.[64] In accordance with the now established ethnographic principle, Heracles is no invader. Despite the similarity of his clothing and weapon to those of the Theban hero,[65] the new impregnability and inaccessibility of the land require that he be an autochthonous son of India. In addition to purging land and sea of wild beasts,[66] we are told that Heracles "was the founder of not a few cities (κτίστην τε πόλεων οὐκ ὀλίγων), the most distinguished and largest of which he called Palimbothra. In it he built an expensive palace and established a great number of settlers; he fortified the city with worthy ditches filled with river water (τήν τε πόλιν ὀχυρῶσαι τάφροις ἀξιολόγοις ποταμίοις ὕδασι πληρουμέναις)."[67] Heracles continues the urbanization, and thus fortification, of India on a grand scale (πόλεων οὐκ ὀλίγων). Palimbothra, the Mauryan capital, Pataliputra, stands out as the only named city. That it is founded by Heracles, not Dionysus (i.e., its emergence in the second, not the first, stage of cultural development), may encode the city's late rise to primacy under the last Nandas and Chandragupta.[68] The adjective ἀξιόλογος appears again, here qualifying the city's defensive works (τάφροις ἀξιολόγοις)—precisely the feature of urbanism that Megasthenes' ethnographic principle should underline.

The ethnographic logic outlined in Indian prehistory—the correlation of urbanism and unconquerability—plays out in Megasthenes' discussion of contemporary India. By the time of Megasthenes' sojourn there, he reports that progressive urbanization has transformed India from an empty expanse of aimless nomadic wanderings into a land garrisoned by countless cities: "One cannot enumerate accurately the cities in India because of their number."[69] The *Indica*'s description of Palimbothra should be understood as the culminating instantiation of this development. Having established the city as the index of indigenous power, Megasthenes deploys this principle in the synchronous ethnography of his third book to demonstrate the might of the new Mauryan kingdom:

At the junction of this (the Ganges) and the other river (the Erranoboas, mod. Son), Palimbothra was established, eighty stades in length, fifteen in width, in the shape of a parallelogram, surrounded by a perforated wooden construction, such that arrows can be shot through the holes. A

ditch lies in front, as a defense and as a reservoir for the sewerage from the
city. The *ethnos* in which the city is located is called the Prasii, and is the
most distinguished of all. The ruler must be named after the city (τὸν δὲ
βασιλεύοντα ἐπώνυμον δεῖν τῆς πόλεως εἶναι), called "Palimbothros" in addition to his family name, such as Sandrocottus to whom Megasthenes
was sent.[70]

The capital city of the Mauryan kingdom is the largest of all Indian urban
foundations, populated by the most distinguished of all Indian tribes. We
can note Megasthenes' careful enumeration of Palimbothra's unimaginably
large size.[71] As in the account of its foundation by Heracles (given earlier),
the city's defenses receive the most attention. The large wooden palisade,
uncovered by the late nineteenth-century excavations,[72] the 570 towers,[73]
the network of arrow slits, and the encircling ditch φυλακῆς . . . χάριν, "for
defense," make this city a bastion against foreign conquest. Importantly, a
direct identification is made between city and king: the Mauryan emperor
takes the city's name as a royal title, eliding the city's impregnability with
his own invincibility. Moreover, the *Indica*, describing the contemporary
Mauryan administration, delineated six groups of city administrators, assigned to various tasks of urban construction and upkeep[74] and so underscores the importance of a *city* bureaucracy. The city/Palimbothra is the
fixed and unmoving point that makes it possible for Indian space to constitute itself as a territory ruled by a power.

In the context of earlier Greek Indography, Megasthenes' urbanism is
doubly radical. First, city foundation gives a temporal structure to Indian
history. Herodotus' India is populated by nomadic and settled peoples concurrently: ἔστι δὲ πολλὰ ἔθνεα Ἰνδῶν καὶ οὐκ ὁμόφωνα σφίσι, καὶ οἳ μὲν αὐτῶν
νομάδες εἰσὶ οἳ δὲ οὔ, "There are many tribes of Indians, and they do not all
speak the same language; some are nomads, others not."[75] Megasthenes
transforms this uncomplicated and synchronic μὲν . . . δέ opposition into a
diachronic stagism. Indian history can now be periodized into preurban
and urban eras. In doing so, he gives India the chronological depth it was
denied in earlier paradoxographical, edge-of-the-earth ethnographies. It is
important to note that the cultural heroism of Dionysus and Heracles and
the urban trajectory of Indian history do not eradicate nomadism in its
entirety. Megasthenes, describing contemporary Mauryan society in the
Indica's third book, observes that nomadism has been shifted to the mountainous margins of the Mauryan kingdom and incorporated as a specific

economic occupation within the monarch-centered "caste system": the shepherds and hunters, the third μέρος or "class," "live a wandering tent-living existence";[76] "they do not live in cities or villages, but are nomads and live up in the mountains."[77] They receive a regular food allowance from the king in return for freeing the land from wild beasts. That is to say, the single civilizing act of Heracles has become the socially embedded caste identity of a particular group, whose marginal, nomadic existence guarantees the settled, urban life for the rest of the kingdom. The Mauryan kingdom accomplishes its own ever-renewing cultural heroism through occupational differentiation. Similarly, Megasthenes tells of ascetic Garmanes, who enact a conscious primitivism, living in the wild, gathering fruit, refraining from wine, clothed in the bark of trees.[78] The primitive lifestyle functions here, just as for the Cynics in Greece, as an entirely modern rejection of the urban; its cultural forms depend on the *Kulturgeschichte* outlined earlier.

Second, Megasthenes has inverted a key and ubiquitous principle of Greek ethnography. As we have seen, his description of primitive India makes clear reference to Herodotus' Scythian *logoi*, paralleling early Indian and contemporary Scythian nonagricultural nomads. One of the most famous passages in all of Herodotus' histories is his statement that Scythian nomadism was the greatest of all human discoveries because it was the key to unconquerability:

> But the Scythian people has made the cleverest discovery that we know in what is the most important of all human affairs; I do not praise the Scythians in all respects, but in this, the most important: that they have contrived that no one who attacks them can escape, and no one can catch them if they do not want to be found. For when men have no established cities or forts (τοῖσι γὰρ μήτε ἄστεα μήτε τείχεα ἦ ἐκτισμένα), but are all nomads and mounted archers, not living by tilling the soil but by raising cattle and carrying their dwellings on wagons, how can they not be invincible and unapproachable (ἄμαχοί τε καὶ ἄποροι προσμίσγειν)?[79]

The causation could not be clearer. Herodotus' Scythians are ἄμαχοί τε καὶ ἄποροι, "invincible and unapproachable," because they are nomads. Scythian nomadism is a cultural discovery, a strategy of space, and a deliberate choice. It is not associated, as in Megasthenes, with primitivism: the Scythians sacrifice, cook, and wear clothes. Rather, in Hartog's felicitous formulation, nomadism is a strategy which is in addition a way of life.[80] And it works: Herodotus is emphatic that Darius I's great invasion of Scythia failed because of the absence of cities. Comparable assertions of nomadic unconquerability recur throughout post-Herodotean ethnography and historiography. In Arrian's *Bithynica*, for example, contemporary Scythian nomadism is represented as a historically situated rejection of an earlier farming and urban phase, when the settled Scythians had been overrun by the Thracians.[81] Similarly, for Hieronymus of Cardia, a peer of Megasthenes, the Nabataeans of Arabia secured their independence from Antigonid aggression by means of their dogmatic opposition to settled habitation and agriculture;[82] for Agatharchides, nomadism had allowed the Nabataeans to successfully resist Assyrian, Persian, and Macedonian imperial ambitions.[83] A passage in Quintus Curtius Rufus, most likely deriving from Cleitarchus[84] (another contemporary), depicts a Sacan embassy's use of this trope in an attempt to deter Alexander from crossing the Iaxartes river in Central Asia.[85] Greek ethnographic literature in general characterized the nomadic life as permanently hostile and aggressive.[86] In striking contrast, nomadism in Megasthenes' *Indica* functions as a vulnerability. It is an aberrant way of life, defined only by its deficiencies. Megasthenes represents Indian nomadism as anterior, primitive, and unmarked. It is the baseline of existence, superseded by cultural discovery. Nomadism, that is to say, the absence of cities, allows Dionysus' invasion to succeed.

Can we trace the genealogy of Megasthenes' inversion? I would suggest that the *Indica*'s principle of urban defensibility is a sensitive response to two, perhaps three, traditions. In the historiographical tradition's accounts of prehistory, the civilizing quality of city foundation appears in several instances of comprehensive cultural heroism but does not have a defensive function.[87] We must look, instead, to strands of fifth- and fourth-century Greek *Kulturgeschichte*. Here the independent city-state naturally manifested the *telos* of the civilizing process, and nomadism the primordial state of nature out of which humanity laboriously dragged itself. The primitive nomad was an exposed, vulnerable being, culturally naked, and defenseless against beast and nature.[88] For certain naturalistic models, perhaps deriving from Democritean anthropology,[89] city foundation was motivated by communal defensive requirements, albeit of a limited and local nature.[90] Aristotle's model of heroic kingship's benefactions focuses, like that of Megasthenes, on synoecism and defensibility.[91]

Political and military activities of the fourth century manifest a growing awareness of the transformative potential of urban foundations. The first major demonstrations of a deliberate urbanistic strategy within Greece

were the Theban general Epaminondas' synoecisms of Messene and Megalopolis in the 360s as bastions against Sparta: Megalopolis is considered
explicitly a defensive foundation to strengthen Arcadian resistance.[92] However, this is not quite the urbanism of Megasthenes' ethnography. Peloponnesian synoecism was more a matter of politics than space, associated
with people power and an anti-Spartan foreign policy, which threatened the
alliance of oligarchic interests on which Lacedaemon's soft imperialism in
the Peloponnese depended.[93] Moreover, there is an important distinction
between city foundation as the generating act of a single, independent political community, such as Megalopolis or Messene, and urbanization as a form
of nodal, defensible power in the creation of an expansive, territorial, monarchic state. This second type, separating a city's military function from
any autonomous political pretensions, developed as a spatial strategy of the
Macedonian kingdom.[94] Philip II's numerous fortified settlements, concentrated in Thrace and Upper Macedonia, were primary foundations of previously nonurbanized peoples, designed to bring security to rugged areas.[95]

It seems that Megasthenes combined the practical motivation behind
Macedonian kings' urbanization and the theoretical musings of prehistoric anthropology into an ethnographic causal principle. Moreover, the
possibility of Mesopotamian influence should not be ignored. The primacy of city foundation, the single moment of cultural heroism, the divine identity of the founder figure, the cocreation of urbanism and religion, the polarity of nomad and city, and the coexistence of multiple urban
foundations within a single kingdom are all elements, albeit not explicitly
theorized, of Babylonian genesis accounts.[96] It is not impossible, given
Megasthenes' praise of Nebuchadnezzar II (see later) and his attachment to
the Seleucid court, as well as Seleucus' own participation in Babylonian
religious culture, that these Near Eastern myths helped to shape the *Indica*'s prehistory.

The *Indica*'s emphatic urbanism, a historical trajectory culminating in the
contemporary Mauryan empire and its megalopolis of Palimbothra, has an
apologetic function. The founding of cities means the closing of India. By
the time of Megasthenes, the country is, quite simply, unconquerable and
Seleucus' treaty with "Sandrocottus-Palimbothros" is a recognition of this
basic power reality.[97] Moreover, the ethnographic principle encoded in the
Indica's *Kulturgeschichte*, historical narrative, and contemporary ethnography
is an eminently suitable representation of Seleucus' own city-founding activities. That is to say, Megasthenes does not merely legitimate a territorial

retreat but also, perhaps more importantly, transforms this limiting of Seleucid imperial space into an act of cultural self-identification. The *Indica*'s
urbanism is a valorizing affirmation of one of the central acts of early Seleucid monarchy—city foundation. The identity of city and king is a reflection of early Hellenistic practice: the Indian monarch was named after his
capital, the Seleucid cities were named after their monarchs. As we will
see in Chapter 7, Megasthenes' transformative, civilizing, territorializing,
defensive, royal, administrative city is the Seleucid colony in its essence.

In addition to rewriting Indian history, Megasthenes reformulated Indian
geography. His ethnography created the spatial field in which his account
of India's historical, cultural, and political dynamics play out,[98] and this
cartography differed strikingly from both classical-period Indographers
and the Alexander Historians. Pre-Megasthenic Indian geography displays
a broadly stable structure: the most civilized core of "India" is the Indus
river basin, paradoxically frontier, center, and main artery of travel;[99] to the
river's east and south one meets a progressively increasing strangeness, uto-
pianism, or barbarism, as is to be expected from the edge of the world. For
Herodotus, presumably using the report of Scylax of Caryanda, who had
been commissioned by the Achaemenid king Darius I to explore the region,[100] the land beyond the Indus just fades away:[101] black-skinned vege-
tarians to the south, nomads to the east, and eventually an impenetrable,
waterless desert.[102] For Ctesias of Cnidus, writing a generation later, India
was still the territory watered by the river Indus[103] and enclosed by the great
sand desert in the east[104] but was now a unified vassal kingdom of Persia.[105]
Ctesias, in an important precedent for Megasthenes, linked the freakish
margins to the ruler: the Pygmies, found deep in the heart of India, serve in
the royal army,[106] and the Dogheads, who live between the Indus and the
mountains, receive gifts from the royal court every five years.[107] Alexander's
campaigning in India (326–325) had permitted, for the first time since
Scylax' expedition, autopsy and firsthand investigation,[108] and therefore in
the Alexander Historians the land's geography has a finer grain and wider
horizons;[109] however, the Macedonian army's restriction to the Punjab maintained the primacy of the Indus valley in narrative and geography. In sum,
then, Indian geography before Megasthenes reproduced the Indus-centered
Achaemenid *dahạyāuš*, or provincial district, of *Hi^nduš*:[110] Herodotus and
Ctesias respond to Persian imperial structures, the Alexander Historians
to the revitalization of Achaemenid territory and Herodotus' relevance in

the new world.[111] As we will see elsewhere, the seismic rupture in the classical worldview occurs not with Alexander but after his death.[112]

Megasthenes changed the shape of India, rotating it ninety degrees and reducing its size.[113] The country no longer fades off toward an impenetrable desert or an undetermined margin. India now has a terminal, Oceanic boundary to the south and east as well as the long-recognized one to the west:[114] where Alexander's unrelenting quest for the eastern edge of the world had failed, Megasthenes' diplomatic mission succeeds. That one can now circumnavigate India and sail from the ocean up the Ganges to the Mauryan capital, Palimbothra,[115] will prove important for the imaginary voyage of the Seleucid geographer Patrocles, discussed in Chapter 2. Most important of all, India is now centered on the Ganges, not Indus, valley: the first and third books in particular privilege the *ethnos* of the Prasii, the city of Palimbothra, and the royal administration located there. This is the inevitable geographical consequence of Chandragupta's unification of northern India around the Gangetic core of Maghada and Megasthenes' diplomatic residence in Pataliputra, the imperial capital: Megasthenes' eye gazes out from the Mauryan heartland. We have seen that in earlier Indography, the river Indus was made to function, oddly, as both center and border. Megasthenes resolves this awkwardness. Whereas the Indus flowed at the edge of the country, the Ganges meandered through its core, with India on both sides.[116] Palimbothra, stretching along the northern bank of India's main river, functions as the point from which geographical distance is now measured.[117] Indeed, the notion of a capital city abutting a central river is familiar from the new urban foundations of the Seleucid empire: Seleucia-on-the-Tigris, with which Palimbothra suggestively shares some basic characteristics,[118] and Antioch-by-Daphne.

The spatializing operation of the *Indica* not only focalizes a new center but also delineates a periphery. No *Indica* would be complete, or believable, without its wonders. Just as the Gangetic core of the Mauryan state is associated with normative humanity in its recognizable form, so the kingdom's boundaries are the site of various freakish phenomena. This is achieved, in part, through a Herodotean zoning of information by autopsy or report. For example, the gold-digging ants, whose skins had been observed by Alexander's general Nearchus in the Macedonian camp on the Indus are known to Megasthenes through ἀκοή, "oral report," alone.[119] The gynocracy of Pandaea, where nature is accelerated, is found to the south of the Mauryan kingdom: women give birth at age six or seven, men die before their fortieth year, fruits mature and decay more quickly.[120] The gold and pearls of Taprobane (Sri Lanka) are larger and more abundant than elsewhere in India.[121] Megasthenes populates the mountains of India's northwestern frontier with peoples freakish in *nomos* (human custom), such as having sex in public or eating their dead relatives, and bizarre in *physis* (nature), such as having no mouths or noses, sleeping in their giant ears, or walking on inverted feet.[122]

Megasthenes links the core and peripheries of his Indian kingdom through a deliberate centripetal policy. The spatial dynamics of Sandrocottus' court reverse the more standard royal procession from center to edge (see Chapter 6); in India, the borders are transported to the king. For example, the Astomoi, the mouthless people who live at the source of the Ganges in the northwest[123] and nourish themselves with smells, "were brought" (ἀχθῆναι) to the royal camp, where they could barely survive the bad odors of military life;[124] the Wild Men, with their feet back to front, "could not be conveyed" (μὴ κομισθῆναι) to the king because they would starve themselves to death.[125] Similarly, Aelian reports that beasts and birds of all kinds were gathered and presented to the Indian monarch.[126] We may even see an echo of the Mauryan king's magnetic pull, as well as Megasthenes' career at court, in a fragment of the almost entirely lost utopian novel of Iambulus:[127] the Odyssean hero, shipwrecked upon a sandy and marshy coast of India, "was brought by the natives into the presence of the king at Palimbothra, many days' journey from the sea" (ὑπὸ τῶν ἐγχωρίων ἀναχθῆναι πρὸς τὸν βασιλέα εἰς πόλιν Παλίβοθρα, πολλῶν ἡμερῶν ὁδὸν ἀπέχουσαν τῆς θαλάττης), from where he was granted safe conduct back to Greece.[128] If this is a parody of the *Indica*, Iambulus, the normative Greek man, functions as one of the marginal oddities to be brought to court from the kingdom's far periphery.[129]

Megasthenes' restructuring of Indian space transforms the nature of the land. It is no longer the eastern margin of an imperial structure whose capital district lies far to the west or the bizarre, hypertrophic fringe of a Greece-centered *oikoumenē*. Rather, India is now an organized space, a territorialized kingdom with its own center and its own peripheries. The classical and Alexandrian ethnographers and historians had located India within a geographical model of the world, which, in its fundamental Oceanic structure, was organized as a smoothly graded circle around a single center, from which increasing distance correlated with increasing weirdness: the farther from Greece, the more peripheral the region.[130] In this light, Alexander's expedition was a journey outward, into margin and myth, and India's strangeness merely affirmed his achievement. Megasthenes has fragmented this model and reproduced it in miniature. India has its center at Palimbothra and its peripheral circumference. The key point is that one of India's peripheries now lies *between* its center and the Greek world. The Seleucid and Mauryan empires have different centers but a shared periphery in the mountains of northwestern India. In short, Megasthenes has made India its own continent. In part, as we will see, this must represent a shift from the imperial discourse of the Achaemenids and Alexander to that of the Mauryas.[131] But more importantly, it is a sensitive geographical response to the fragmentation of the Achaemenid-Alexandrian empire in the Successor period and the consequent multiplication of king, state, and capital.

The apologetic function we have observed in the *Indica*'s prehistory can be detected here as well. The spatial operation performed by the *Indica* encodes in ethnographic discourse the terms of the Seleucus-Chandragupta peace. Just as Indian territory is unconquerable, so Indian space is self-contained and relatively isolated. This plays itself out in the *Indica*'s insistence on economic autarky and the absence of adventures into the outside world.[132] Megasthenes draws India more fully into the *oikoumenē* in order to exclude it from Seleucid space. The sovereign, mutually recognized Mauryan and Seleucid political landscapes that followed the Treaty of the Indus, with their shared mountainous border, are refashioned by Megasthenes into natural geographical units. Moreover, the new geography reinterprets Alexander's Indian conquests: like Seleucus, he crossed the Indus but never conquered the heartland; like Seleucus, he turned back in the face of the Gangetic kingdom, a state which subsequently had expanded westward.[133] India is as much a separate spatial entity as Ptolemaic Egypt or mainland Greece. In between them all lies the Seleucid empire.

This new geography changed the function of Indian ethnography. Megasthenes transformed India from a site of freakish difference and symmetrical opposition, to be wondered at or assimilated by imperial expansion, into a space of similarity and submerged cultural identity. India is now good to think with. The land has become an analogue of the Seleucid state and the *Indica* a text for working through issues of Seleucid state formation.

While Chandragupta Maurya's multiethnic, polyglot, expansionist kingdom certainly resembled the Seleucid state in outline[134] and probably generated parallel mechanisms of territorial control, Megasthenes' ethnography went beyond this to emphasize consonance with the Seleucid world:[135]

certain of India's characteristics, appearing for the first time in ethnography, resemble Seleucid state structures too closely to be anything but observations or fabrications of similarity. The strongest case is the existence of autonomous, democratically governed cities within Megasthenes' Indian kingdom.[136] The coexistence of independent and dependent cities within the same realm is one of the most striking characteristics of the Seleucid empire; it is unattested for the Mauryan kingdom.[137] Megasthenes seems to have deliberately constructed a parallel system of irregular political sovereignty to better support the analogy between the two states. Other parallels include royal land ownership, the capital-on-the-river, the construction of roads and milestones, and various duties of the monarch.

More fundamentally, a new and central characteristic of the Megasthenic India, consequent on the spatializing operation described earlier, is the normalization of the land. In contrast to the timeless, idealized, edge-of-the-earth qualities that had characterized India in earlier ethnographies, the key to the land's new analogous function is that it is *not* utopian.[138] The idealized utopias of the Greek imagination were a function of distance, temporal or geographical, and thereby inaccessibility.[139] The tendency to correlate peripheral geography with a flattening of historical time fashioned the most distant, enormous kingdoms of ethnography—including India—into static and unchanging moral *paradeigmata*.[140] For example, Ctesias contrasts a visitable, historical Persia, where Achaemenid monarchs suffer treason and defections, with an eternal India of perfect justice, devoted subjects, and natural abundance.[141] Megasthenes' ethnography contains certain well-paralleled utopian tropes: India's gentle climate and fertile superabundance guarantees a double harvest, removing all danger of famine;[142] the earth is well veined with precious metals;[143] the land's inhabitants are beautiful, skilled, and autochthonous;[144] none is a slave;[145] a seven-tiered "caste system" institutionalizes hierarchy, endogamy, occupational fixity and exclusivity, with philosophers on top;[146] the Indians honor truth and virtue and so trust to leave their houses unguarded, rely on unwritten law, and avoid unnecessary litigation.[147] However, the new Indian geography prevents a mere flight into fantasy. India is now an accessible land[148] with chronological depth, historical development,[149] and some negative social forms. The land's great productivity is the result of, not spontaneous or toilless production of food, but the developed state structure of the Mauryan kingdom, in which irrigation is widespread, agriculture is an exclusive and unavoidable social function for part of the population, and, in times of war, farmers are inviolate and agricultural lands unravaged.[150] Crime and misdemeanor exist and are kept in check by a harsh sanctioning system of somatic punishments.[151] More strikingly, the monarch's lot is not a happy one: a spying network of overseers and courtesans informs in secret from the capital and the military camp;[152] the king is forced to change beds at night because of plots.[153] The sense of reality and recognizability in Megasthenes' India is achieved—what an indictment!—through war, violence, corruption, and law. The land resembles Ctesias' Persia much more closely than his India. Simply put, India is no longer too good to be true.[154]

The Indian analogy is about recognition, not aspiration. In this light, recalling that the text was written soon after Seleucus' adoption of the royal diadem and self-transformation from satrap to king, the *Indica*'s unproblematic and casually assumed monarchism is noteworthy. The monarchic thread runs right through the ethnography: in the *Kulturgeschichte,* culture arrives with kingship; in the description of contemporary India, every aspect of Indian society is structured for and by Sandrocottus: he is the source of all administrative and military employment, the node around which society articulates itself, and the purpose for which all activity is undertaken. In classical-period Greek ethnography, kingship was a fundamental element in the construction of ethnic alterity: "all barbarian power, without further specification of its exact nature or the manner in which it is exercised, simply because it *is* power, tends to appear as royalty."[155] Kingship is otherness. The basic political development of the early Hellenistic period was the creation of large territorial states under Graeco-Macedonian kings. To most Near Eastern populations this could be seen as an exchange of one foreign dynasty for another, but to the Greek world it was revolutionary. Monarchy, formerly of ethnographic interest as foreign and exotic, is now the court author's own environment and must be naturalized. A key element of the Megasthenic analogy is that monarchy is described in a rhetoric of likeness, not difference. This is, of course, most apparent in Megasthenes' description of Sandrocottus and the world he visits.[156] But it is also found in India's earlier history and in nature. One of the most important of Megasthenes' fragments, preserved by Strabo and Arrian in parallel passages, lists a catalogue of unsuccessful royal expeditions against India:

Megasthenes, moreover, agrees with this point of view when he urges disbelief in the ancient accounts of India, for no army was ever sent outside by the Indians, nor did any from outside invade and conquer them, except that with Heracles and Dionysus and now with the Macedonians. But Sesostris the Egyptian, and Tearcon the Ethiopian advanced as far as Europe, and Nebuchadnezzar, esteemed more among the Chaldaeans than Heracles, went as far as the Pillars and Tearcon also went that far and led an army from Iberia into Thrace and to Pontus. Idanthyrsus the Scythian overran Asia as far as Egypt, but none of these touched India, and Semiramis died before her attempt. The Persians sent for the Hydracae from India as mercenaries, but did not take an expedition there, only coming near it when Cyrus attacked the Massagetae.[157]

The chronicle of never undertaken or failed invasions, even effacing Darius I's actual conquest, repeatedly confirms the *Indica*'s ethnographic principle of post-Dionysus unconquerability. The apologetic force is evident: by inventing precedents for Seleucus' territorial withdrawal, Megasthenes normalizes and vindicates the Treaty of the Indus.[158] The new careers of Semiramis, Sesostris, and Idanthyrsus demonstrate the *Indica*'s creative engagement with its literary environment;[159] Tearcon and Nebuchadnezzar are Megasthenes' own discovery, perhaps from Babylonian or Jewish sources.[160] Megasthenes' chronicle of invasions generates a historical rhythm of power and its limits in Asia, in which monarchy is figured as the entirely standard, unquestionable form of government. Seleucus can be slipped unproblematically into the catalogue.

Kingship, existing throughout the world and in the past, is also found below the waves. A passage in Arrian's *Indica*, directly attributed to Megasthenes, gives the natural history of the Indian pearl:

> There is also a king or queen among the pearls, just like bees. Should anyone happen to catch him, a net can easily be thrown over the rest of the pearls, but if the king escapes, the others can no longer be caught.[161]

This account appears in the context of early Indian monarchy. Having discovered pearls in the sea, the autochthonous culture-hero Heracles considers them a suitable adornment for Pandaea, his daughter-wife and queen of the south.[162] The single attestation of pearls in all extant earlier Greek literature, a short description in the *de lapidibus* of Theophrastus,[163] merely locates their point of origin in India and the islands of the Persian Gulf. So, the *Indica*'s natural history of the pearl is most likely Megasthenes' own creation. Megasthenes' pearls inhabit a social structure of absolute, total monarchy: the fate of the swarm depends in its entirety on the independence of the king or queen. As Megasthenes observed, the pearls behave like bees,[164] which have a well-established function as a metaphor for good kingship.[165] Such natural monarchy is transferred in the *Indica* to a geographically appropriate species. It is difficult to imagine a stronger idealization of early Hellenism's philosophy of monarchy;[166] the pearl king could justly boast, "L'état, c'est moi."

Kings in Egypt, Ethiopia, Assyria, Scythia, and Babylonia; king Seleucus and king Chandragupta; kings under the sea. By asserting the geographical and historical ubiquity of monarchy, the *Indica* denies its ethnic salience; by finding kingship in the animal world, the *Indica* naturalizes it. Megasthenes conventionalizes royal power.

To assert that ethnography speaks to ourselves while describing The Other has become a banality. Nonetheless, the relationship between the Seleucid and Mauryan kingdoms, as between historical reality and ethnographic textuality, works here in a specific and novel way. Megasthenes enacts analogy, not allegory, tempering the utopian fables of his generic inheritance with the realistic tones of the Hellenistic world. The early Seleucid ethnography of India is in many ways similar to classical Athenian writings on Sparta: both describe a legitimate, parallel, and equivalent state, capable of peer relations, whose territorial independence is beyond question, and whose externality turns it into a site of political theorizing. Such treatment of India as an analogous kingdom is not merely a narrative device for thinking through Seleucid state formation. In very real terms, this was the inescapable implication of the transformed political spaces brought about by the Treaty of the Indus. The meeting of kings, acts of exchange, and marriage alliance in themselves established India as an equivalent state and separate territory. So, India's ethnographic function as an analogue is, in an important sense, an epiphenomenon of the high-level diplomacy that brought about Megasthenes' mission. The *Indica* is a textual reproduction of the very condition of its own creation.

The Reproduction of the Boundary

To an *engagé* and influential hermeneutic, the (European) investigation and categorization of foreign peoples is implicated in the broader project of western colonial oppression, in which space is to be possessed and consumed by an imperial cartography of illegitimate seizure.[167] But Megasthenes could not be further from this profile. The historical context and biographical condition of the *Indica*'s very creation is Seleucid withdrawal, not expansion. Megasthenes is an envoy of renunciation, and this is both a historical fact and a rhetorical choice. The fragments give no hint of Megasthenes' renaming the landscape, populations, or cities of India; they entirely lack the linguistic baptisms found in, say, Seleucid Syria, where Macedonian or dynastic names were superimposed on indigenous ones (see Chapter 4). Megasthenes never registers the problem of cross-cultural communication.[168] Nor was the *Indica*'s spatializing operation unidirectional, for the new southeastern border of the Seleucid kingdom was recognized, acknowledged, and reperformed by the Mauryan state.

The evidence for this is in fact rather exciting. Following the death in 273/2 of Chandragupta's successor, Bindusara (Greek Amitrochates), and a subsequent struggle for succession among his sons,[169] king Ashoka acceded to his father's throne in 269/8 as the third king of the Mauryan dynasty. Ashoka is one of the more outstanding figures of the ancient world. In brief, his conquest of the east Indian state of Kalinga in his eighth regnal year so horrified the king that henceforth he forsook all wars of aggression, converted to a pacifist form of Buddhism, and pursued, with obsessive and missionary zeal, *dhamma*—a broad social ethic and practice including abstinence from killing, considerate family relations, and welfare programs.[170] Importantly, the king's devotion to the propagation of *dhamma* generated an unprecedented epigraphic habit—fourteen Major Rock Edicts, numerous Minor Rock Edicts, and seven Pillar Edicts survive from his reign—that demonstrates, among other things, the Mauryan empire's own spatial ideology.[171] We see this in two ways: the findspots of the inscriptions and their content.

The locations of Ashoka's Major Rock Edicts (see Map 2) beat the boundaries of Mauryan imperial territory: the eastern seaboard of conquered Kalinga, the southern Deccan, the western coast, and the northwestern periphery of the Mauryan state, where it bordered the Seleucid empire. At Alexandria-in-Arachosia (mod. Kandahar) a bilingual Greek-Aramaic text, urging vegetarianism and filial piety, was cut into the cliff face by the side of the main trade road. The inscription demonstrates a keen awareness of the culturally specific traditions and languages of the region's "Yona and Kamboja" (Greek and Persian) populations: the Greek version combines vocabulary appropriate to oracular pronouncement and contemporary philosophy,[172] while the Aramaic version, heavily influenced by Old Persian, assimilates *dhamma* to Zoroastrian truth.[173] Another inscription, found on a stone block at Kandahar, freely translates into Greek parts of Ashoka's

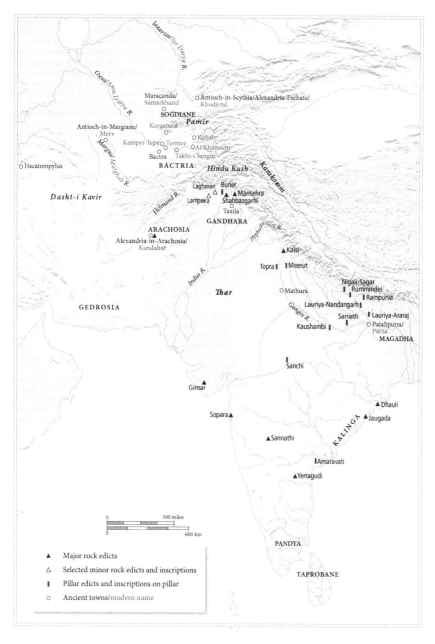

Map 2 Central Asia and India, with Ashoka's inscriptions.

Twelfth and Thirteenth Rock Edicts: it is probable that all fourteen Major Rock Edicts of the Indian king were recorded on some kind of stone construction, perhaps with a full Aramaic version.[174] Aramaic inscriptions of Ashoka's edicts have been found at Taxila (in Pakistan), Lampaka, and Laghman (both in Afghanistan). Two more inscriptions, in Karoshti (a script derived from Imperial Aramaic), have been found in the North West Frontier Province of Pakistan (at Shahbazgarhi and Mansehra). These inscriptions, while constituting direct evidence for Mauryan control of this region by the reign of Ashoka, indicate through their use of local languages its frontier status within the Mauryan polity, as Megasthenes' ethnography had implied: all other Ashokan inscriptions from the subcontinent, including those of the southern Deccan, are in the Prakrit language and the Brahmi script.[175]

The region's marginality within Mauryan political geography is confirmed by the content of several of Ashoka's edicts. In the king's own speech-act, the Gandharas, Kambojas, and Yonas are explicitly identified as his empire's "borderers." The Thirteenth Edict, in a quasi-ethnographic observation, states: "Except among the Yonas, there is no land where the religious orders of *brahmans* and *śramaṇas* are not to be found, and there is no land anywhere where men do not support one sect or another."[176] Similarly, the *Majjhima Nikaya*, a composition most likely of the Mauryan period, has the Buddha expound in ethnographic mode on the strangely fluid and simple social order of the Greek and Iranian world: "In Yona-Kamboja and adjacent regions (*jānapada*) there are only two *varṇas*: masters and slaves. One who has been a master may become a slave, and one who has been a slave may become a master."[177] The Thirteenth Edict continues, in a passage of exceptional historical importance:

> The Beloved of the Gods considered victory by *dhamma* to be the foremost victory. And moreover the Beloved of the Gods has gained this victory on all his frontiers to a distance of six hundred *yojanas,* where reigns the Yona king named Antiyoko, and beyond the realm of that Antiyoko in the lands of the four kings (*a ṣaṣu pi yojanaśateṣu yatra Aṁtiyoko nama Yonaraja paraṁ ca tena Atiyokena chature 4 rajani*) named Turumaye, Antikini, Maka, and Alikasudaro; and in the south over the Cholas and Pandyas as far as Tamraparni. Likewise here in the imperial territories among the Yonas and the Kambojas, Nabhakas and Nabhapanktis, Bhojas and Pitinikas, Andhras and Parindas, everywhere the people follow the Beloved of the Gods' instructions in *dhamma*.[178]

The king of India lists five peers in the Hellenistic west: Antiochus II Theos of the Seleucid empire, Ptolemy II Philadelphus of Egypt, Antigonus II Gonatas of Macedon, Magas of Cyrene, and Alexander of Epirus (or Corinth). The overlap of kings determines the chronology for this inscription and so for Ashoka's entire reign: the only possible dates are between 260 and 258. The universalist notion of *dhammavijaya, dhamma*-conquest, contrasting with simple *vijaya,* (territorial) conquest, generated this description of the western and southern worlds beyond the horizon of Mauryan political sovereignty. The passage pivots on the opposition of exterior and interior: Ashoka expounds on the total victory of *dhamma* first outside his kingdom ("on all his frontiers to a distance of six hundred *yojanas*") and then within his kingdom ("here in the imperial territories"). The Mauryan empire, like the Seleucid, was bounded to the west by peer kingdoms. The Seleucid kingdom performs an important spatial function here. It is the point to which distance is measured: 600 *yojanas* translate to between 4,800 and 6,000 miles.[179] Accordingly, Antiochus II is held to rule an astonishingly large kingdom, several thousand miles from the Mauryan frontier in the Hindu Kush to his distant residence. It is significant that, paralleling the spatializing operation of Megasthenes' *Indica,* the Seleucid empire holds a position of centrality, situated between Mauryan India to the east and the four other Hellenistic states to the west. The Ptolemaic, Antigonid, Cyrenean, and Epirote kingdoms are located by reference to the Seleucid monarch ("to a distance of six hundred *yojanas,* where reigns the Yona king named Antiyoko, and beyond the realm of that Antiyoko in the lands of the four kings"). The Seleucid kingdom, bounded to the east and west, occupies the same place in the Second Major Rock Edict, which describes Ashoka's welfare programs throughout the world. Here, too, Antiochus appears both in his own right and as place marker for the more distant Hellenistic powers:

Everywhere in the dominions of king Priyadarshin, Beloved of the Gods, and likewise in the bordering territories *(aṁtā)* of the Cholas, Pandyas, the Satika-putra, Tamraparni, the Yona king named Antiyoka and also the kings who are the neighbors of the said Antiyoka *(Aṁtiyoge nāma Yonalājā ye cā aṁne tasā Aṁtiyogasā sāmaṁtā lājāno)*—everywhere king Priyadarshin, Beloved of the Gods, has arranged for two kinds of medical treatment, medical treatment for men and medical treatment for animals.[180]

In both the Second and Thirteenth Edicts, Antiochus, alone of the Hellenistic kings, is termed the *Yonaraja*, the "Greek king."[181] The inscriptions, therefore, present Greek populations living both within and outside the Mauryan kingdom: the political frontier between the Mauryan and Seleucid sovereignties divides an ethnic community, a result of the Treaty of the Indus and the westward retreat of Macedonian sovereignty. Finally, by recognizing the distant Antiochus II as his direct neighbor Ashoka acknowledges the legitimacy of Seleucid sovereignty in the Upper Satrapies. The powerful, nearby satraps—soon to revolt from the kingdom—are not even mentioned.

The Indian evidence, supporting the Greek, points to a cooperative and mutual process of delineation. Each kingdom recognized the territorial independence and legitimate sovereignty of the other. In the spatial ideology of Ashoka, as in that of Antiochus III, the Treaty of the Indus retained practical effect and ideological salience. Seleucid diplomacy and Megasthenes' ethnography had closed an imperial boundary at the kingdom's southeast and opened a dialogue with Mauryan India of profound historical significance.

CHAPTER 2

Central Asia—Nomads, Ocean, and the Desire for Line

We have seen in Chapter 1 that Seleucid territory in India was closed off by diplomacy. Structural similarities and equality of status between the Seleucid and Mauryan empires allowed the formation of a bilateral border. But Seleucid Central Asia—the provinces of Bactria, Sogdiana, Aria, Margiane, and Parthia in the approximate area of modern Afghanistan, Tajikistan, Uzbekistan, Turkmenistan, and northeastern Iran (see Map 2)—presented Seleucus I with a very different place: no large, territorial, centralized state was recognized beyond Seleucus' kingdom.[1] Whereas in India (as well as Asia Minor, Egypt, and Europe) the Seleucid kings had partners with whom they could negotiate treaties and exchange gifts, ambassadors, and women, in Central Asia they had no one. Accordingly, how was Seleucid territory to be bounded? How could the edge of sovereignty be marked? The Seleucid solution, as far as it can be reconstructed from the scanty and shattered evidence, was an intriguing combination of religious ritual, geographic invention, anthropological theory, and historical precedent. The spatial problem that was (and remains) Central Asia resulted in a multi- and overdetermined border, which attempted to impose an ideological *limes* on a complex and porous zone of frontier interaction.

There were two periods of early Seleucid royal involvement in Central Asia: the first, between Seleucus' resecuring of Babylonia and the Treaty of the Indus (307–304), and the second, during Antiochus I's coregentship (294–281).

Of the first almost nothing is known.[2] In 308/7, Antigonus Monophthalmus and Seleucus Nicator, who had been battling for control of Babylonia, turned their backs on one another to pursue their respective western and eastern interests: while Antigonus was extending his influence into Greece and the Aegean, Seleucus was adding the Central Asian provincial ensemble to his Babylonian and west Iranian territories. Seleucus encountered a landscape that had tumbled into chaos following Alexander's death. The Graeco-Macedonian military veterans, who had been forcibly settled in the region by Alexander, had revolted and been massacred.[3] There is some evidence for a great nomadic incursion from the north.[4] The weakening of both the colonial presence in these provinces and the imperial mechanisms that subordinated them to the central authority[5] is witnessed in the issuing of coins by two non-Greek or -Macedonian indigenous dynasts, Sophytos[6] and Wakhshuvar.[7] Wakhshuvar's coins are particularly interesting. They are gold staters of Macedonian style and fabric that depict, on the obverse, a satrap's head with Persian (satrapal) tiara and the name *Vḥšvr* in Aramaic, and, on the reverse, a four-horse chariot. *Vḥšvr* has been identified as Oxyartes, father of Alexander's wife, Rhoxane. The coins' use of Achaemenid-era iconography and script for, of all people, Alexander's father-in-law indicates a reassertion of a pre-Macedonian language of legitimacy; it implies, if not sovereign independence, at least practical autonomy. Unfortunately, we do not know how Seleucus, confronted with such a situation, transformed the region's quasi-independent satraps and local dynasts into subordinate officials of his kingdom. The ease of the process is often assumed, but the campaign may have taken several years and faced tough resistance.[8]

Seleucus had sufficiently consolidated his control of Central Asia to descend into India in 305 or 304, as we saw in Chapter 1. His success may be explained by a policy of light-footed tolerance (retaining personnel; limiting tribute demands; not interfering with administrative structures) that asserted only formal authority;[9] or his forces may have been considered a bulwark against the threats of Mauryan expansion[10] or nomadic razzia.[11] We should not underestimate the exploitable ideological capital of Seleucus' first queen, Apame, the daughter of the Sogdian dynast Spitamenes. In any case, for the purpose of this chapter, it must be emphasized that Seleucus' incorporation of the Central Asian provinces does not appear to have been accompanied with significant spatializing gestures. His activities were military, not discursive and symbolic. As far as we can tell, no boundaries were demarcated, no space was privileged. It seems that Seleucus absorbed the scaffolding of Alexander's territorial arrangements in Central Asia without major effort at changing, problematizing, or privileging them.

By contrast, the second period, from 294 to 281, is far more historically significant and ideologically creative. In response to the extraordinary size of his kingdom—stretching from Syria to Central Asia—and in an effort to avoid dynastic strife following his second marriage to Stratonice, daughter of Demetrius Poliorcetes,[12] in 294 Seleucus transferred to his eldest son, Antiochus, the kingship of the Upper Satrapies and with it, notoriously, his own second wife, Stratonice. The impact of Antiochus I's kingship in Central Asia is immediately apparent on the ground. The Macedonian colonies, abandoned since Alexander's death by their restless settlers or destroyed by barbarian incursions, were refounded and renamed. Classical geographers mention Artacabene in Aria,[13] Antioch (formerly Alexandria)[14] and Achaïs (formerly Heraclea)[15] in Margiane, Soteira, Calliope, and Charis in Parthia, Hecatompylus in Hyrcania, and Antioch-in-Scythia (formerly Alexandria-Eschate) on the edge of Sogdiana.[16] Excavation supports this literary evidence[17] and also demonstrates an otherwise unattested panregional (re)construction of fortified settlements,[18] increase of colonial population, expansion of irrigation,[19] and part monetization of the economy.[20] These Seleucid city-founding practices will be examined in Chapter 7, but here we should note that Antiochus' role as builder-king in the Upper Satrapies is of great importance as a territorializing strategy.

Two Seleucid generals joined Antiochus in his Central Asian endeavors— Demodamas and Patrocles. Their actions and writings, now fragmentary, participated in the demarcation of the kingdom's *limes* in this region. They responded to the Seleucid desire for line in very different ways—Demodamas sanctified the land and divided its peoples, Patrocles opened the sea and sailed its width. I will deal with each in turn.

Demodamas

Only the bare outlines of Demodamas' career can be reconstructed. He was already associated with the Seleucid dynasty at the very beginning of the third century, sponsoring two decrees (dated to 300/299 or 299/298) in his Ionian hometown of Miletus in honor of Seleucus' Sogdian wife, Apame, and their son, Antiochus.[21] The Roman encyclopaedist Pliny the Elder records that he served in Central Asia as *Seleuci et Antiochi regum dux,* "general of kings Seleucus and Antiochus."[22] The mention of both kings indicates that his military command in the Upper Satrapies belongs in the second period under discussion, during the dual monarchy and Antiochus' vice-royship in this region.[23] Pliny tells:

> Beyond [the Bactrians] are the Sogdians and the town of Panda, and, on the farthest confines of their territory, Alexandria, founded by Alexander the Great. At this place there are altars set up by Hercules and Father Liber, and also by Cyrus and Semiramis and by Alexander, all of whom found their limit in this region of the world, where they were shut in by the river Iaxartes, which the Scythians call the Silis and which Alexander and his soldiers thought to be the Tanaïs. Demodamas, the general of king Seleucus and king Antiochus, whom we are chiefly following in this part *(quem maxime sequimur in his)*, crossed this river and set up altars to Apollo of Didyma *(transcendit eum amnem . . . arasque Apolloni Didymaeo statuit)*.[24]

Pliny identifies the source he follows here as Demodamas himself:[25] the Milesian general wrote an autobiographical account of his military activities in Central Asia. The erection of altars at a watery edge (fluvial or oceanic) was a thank-offering to the gods, a memorial to achievements, and, above all, a bounding of territory. We have seen, for instance, that Alexander erected twelve altars on the banks of the Hyphasis river in the Punjab, at the eastern limit of his imperial territory;[26] two further altars at the mouth of the Indus and twelve on the Hellespont demarcated his Asian conquests.[27] In the second century CE, the explorer Demetrius of Tarsus commemorated the northern edge of his travels by founding altars at York.[28] The Carthaginians marked the edge of their African territory in the same way.[29] Accordingly, Demodamas' altars should be understood as a spatializing gesture: they indicate the edge of Seleucid sovereignty in this region and identify the Iaxartes (mod. Syr Darya) river as the kingdom's north-eastern boundary. The act clearly echoes Alexander's; indeed, the *Tabula Peutingeriana*, the best-preserved example of antique cartography, expressly indicates the edge of Sogdiana with a square altar labeled *Ara Alexandri*, "Altar of Alexander"[30] (see later). As a spatial mechanism, the altar's location on the water's bank used the river-run to unfurl this single point into a linear edge, thereby circumscribing the kingdom.

If Pliny's passage, as he suggests, derives from Demodamas' own writings, then the Milesian general not only founded altars on the Iaxartes river but also invented a series of historical precedents for this spatial act: the god Dionysus, the hero Heracles, the Assyrian queen Semiramis, the Persian king Cyrus, and the Macedonian Alexander. It is noteworthy that, as we saw in Chapter 1, each of these great Asian conquerors had already functioned in some sense as Seleucid prototypes in Megasthenes' *Indica*. Just as Megasthenes had created precedents for Seleucus' withdrawal from India, so Demodamas naturalized Antiochus' bounding of sovereignty in Central Asia. Such repetitive patterning of symbolic limits by successive kingdoms may have been a trope of the Seleucid kingdom's emerging spatial ideology: Demodamas inscribed himself and his king in the history of imperial dominance in the region.

According to Demodamas' narrative, then, he and his king, Antiochus, replayed in this region the great feats of previous conquerors. Demodamas' expedition to the Iaxartes and planting of altars there may also have been the occasion for the reconstruction and repopulation of Alexander's colony, Alexandria-Eschate ("Alexandria the Farthest"), as a new Seleucid city, Antioch-in-Scythia.[31] Alexandria-Eschate/Antioch-in-Scythia—modern Khodjend (or, to use its more recent imperial name, Leninabad)—stood, like Demodamas' altars, on the Iaxartes river. As its name ("the Farthest") suggests, Alexander's city functioned to demarcate the northern edge of his empire, an ideological significance evident in its inclusion in the *Marmor Parium*, a third-century chronicle of Greek history inscribed on the Aegean island of Paros.[32] The colony replaced Cyropolis, believed by the Greeks to have been founded during Cyrus the Great's last campaign on the Iaxartes.[33] This Persian city, too, had marked the limit of empire. Strabo described it as ὅριον τῆς Περσῶν ἀρχῆς, "the boundary of Persian rule";[34] it was also known as Cyreschata ("Cyr-the-Farthest").[35] Like the altars, Antiochus' foundation of Antioch-in-Scythia reperformed Cyrus' Cyropolis and Alexander's Alexandria-Eschate. Three successive kingdoms rhythmically marked their imperial boundary on the Iaxartes.

Demodamas' spatializing operation not only distinguished Seleucid from non-Seleucid territory. By honoring Apollo of Didyma (also known as Branchidae), the main god of Miletus, Demodamas bracketed this far-flung corner of the Seleucid kingdom with Miletus, the Aegean, Old World Greece, and everything they stood for.[36] That Miletus was within Lysimachus' kingdom at this time was unproblematic, for Milesian mercenaries had fought for Seleucus,[37] Seleucus had sent precious gifts to Didyma and restored Apollo's cult statue from its exile in Media,[38] and Antiochus had paid for the construction of a *stoa* in the Milesian agora.[39] Worship of Apollo of Didyma is directly attested in Bactria, where amphorae of uncertain date, found at Dilberjin in northern Afghanistan, bear the inscriptions Βρο|αγχιδ and

Βρο|αγχ, a dialect form of "Branchidae."[40] And it was, of course, natural for Demodamas of Miletus to honor his home city's deity. Similarly, Milesians in Egypt consecrated a statue of Didymaean Apollo at Medinet-Habu, the west bank of Luxor.[41] Nonetheless, the embracing of Old World Greece and Central Asia by religious homage is a recurring spatial gesture in this region. We will see in Chapter 8 that the philosopher Clearchus of Soli set up maxims of the Seven Sages of archaic Greece, inscribed at Delphi, at the Seleucid colony of Aï Khanoum in eastern Bactria, thereby locating the colony in geographical and religious relation to Delphi.[42] Both Demodamas and Clearchus sanctified the Central Asian boundary of the Seleucid kingdom by honoring there two of the most ancient and holy shrines of the Greek motherland far to the west, Delphi and Didyma. Another example: an Iranian or Bactrian named Atrosoces dedicated a small bronze figurine of Marsyas with double-flute to the deified river Oxus at the Takht-i Sangin sanctuary[43] (see Figure 3). Among the many things this dedication is doing, it brackets Marsyas, the Phrygian deity of his eponymous river, a tributary of the Maeander in Asia Minor, with the mighty Oxus.[44] No doubt such an identification would have derived from Asia Minor colonists. Each of these gestures of religious bracketing is strongly associated with the kingdom: a general on campaign, a philosopher in a Seleucid settlement, a Hellenized local in a Seleucid-sponsored temple.

It is probable that Demodamas included in his memoirs of the Central Asian expedition an account of Antiochus' colonizing activities. This work lies behind the brief statements of Pliny and Strabo[45] that a number of Graeco-Macedonian settlements were destroyed by "barbarians" after Alexander's death and then refounded, expanded, fortified, and renamed by Antiochus I.[46] In order to explain the post-Alexander destruction scholars have conjured from the steppes a mass nomadic invasion, razing cities as far apart and as far south as Merv and Termez; the viceroyship of Antiochus and the expedition of Demodamas are interpreted as the appropriate Seleucid response.[47] While this great razzia thesis can be neither confirmed nor dismissed on the basis of current archaeological evidence,[48] we are able to recognize the repeated instances of barbarian destruction between Alexander and Antiochus as a narrative pattern. Demodamas again and again emplotted Antiochus' settling of the Upper Satrapies as a three-stage narrative—the foundation of a colony by Alexander, its destruction by nomads, and its refoundation by Antiochus I—that casts the new ruler of the east in the ideologically potent role of builder-king, restorer, and, above all, defender of civilization.

In Chapter 1 I argued that the key principle of Megasthenes' *Kulturge-schichte* is the distinction between nomadism and urbanism. This fundamental opposition of Greek anthropology reemerges in Central Asia. In India, nomad and city dweller were divided temporally; in Central Asia, nomad and city dweller were divided spatially. In part, this was an understandable, if schematic, depiction of the ethnocultural landscape of Central Asia. In part, it was the inevitable response to the lack of an external,

Figure 3 Atrosoces' dedication to river Oxus, from the Takht-i Sangin temple, southern Tajikistan.

bounding peer state. Accordingly, Antiochus' colonization narrative constructed Central Asia as a contested space. In contrast to the diplomatically established and unchanging Indian border, the northeastern edge of
the Seleucid kingdom had to be periodically and energetically fixed by
royal military expeditions and colonial settlements. Whereas Indian
nomadism had been abolished by Dionysus or otherwise co-opted into
the urban social order, Demodamas' narrative pattern (royal foundation—
barbaric destruction—royal foundation) characterized Central Asian nomadism as an ever-present danger, threatening to reassert itself at any opportunity, and kept at bay only by the urbanizing activities of the watchful
and protective monarch; somewhat like Aristeas of Proconessus' unending
battle of Arimaspians against the Gryphons. All this means that the delimitation of Seleucid sovereignty in the Upper Satrapies could be considered a function of anthropology—the Seleucid kingdom and civilization
were coterminous.

  We see this principle at play almost a century after Demodamas. The
spotlight of our Greek narrative sources falls on the kingdom's provincial
landscape almost solely during episodes of royal presence (see Chapter 6).
As before, the second *anabasis,* or inland expedition, of Antiochus III permits a rare illumination of the Seleucid empire's northeastern boundary.
Polybius reports how, several decades after Bactria had emancipated itself
from the Seleucid kingdom, the Bactrian king Euthydemus I successfully
resisted Antiochus' siege of his capital, Bactra, for two years (208–206) and
then defended by argument the legitimacy of his independent kingship.
According to what may be an official Seleucid record of the meeting,[49] the
rebel prince foregrounded the nomadic danger:

> [N]either of them would be safe if [Antiochus] did not yield to the demands.
> For not a small number of nomads were close by, who were a danger to
> both; the land would, they could agree (ὁμολογουμένως), be utterly barba-
> rized (ἐκβαρβαρωθήσεσθαι δὲ τὴν χώραν) if they admitted them.[50]

The barbaric menace is total and apocalyptic: the nomadic population is
not named, counted, or located. The lack of particularity here draws attention to the instrumental and rhetorical nature of Euthydemus' use of the
nomad-civilization binary.[51] As ὁμολογουμένως ("they could agree") indicates, the Bactrian king is justifying his rule on the basis of the already
existing Seleucid anthropological-spatial discourse about this region. In
his opposition to nomadism, just as in various other cultural performances,

the legitimacy of Euthydemus' kingship rests on his correct performance of the categories and responsibilities of Seleucid monarchy.[52] Euthydemus was a participant in the defense of civilization; he and Antiochus were two kings in alliance against barbarism.[53]

This Seleucid situation is new. Unlike the fundamental nomad fear typical of urbanized Greece and Babylonia,[54] as far as we can tell the Persian kings saw no essential division between their sedentary and pastoral subjects.[55] The "double morphology" (Mauss' formulation) of the Central Asian environment—fertile oases or floodplains separated by long tracts of desert and steppe—required the structural interpenetration of nomadic and settled populations.[56] Interactions between the Achaemenid state and the nomadic groups must have been complex and variable but, outside the hostile and limited campaigns of the Great Kings, mostly regulated by gift-giving and exchange services.[57] Moreover, the region's Achaemenid-era urban settlements had been destroyed not by nomads but by Alexander's armies. Accordingly, the anthropological basis of the Seleucid frontier in Central Asia, as revealed by general Demodamas' and king Euthydemus' similar depictions of the barbarian threat and royal duty, reinterpreted the basic nomad-sedentary polarity as a nomad-monarchy one; the opposition is found elsewhere at the Seleucid court.[58] If the Indian border established Seleucid territory as central, the Central Asian *limes* marked that space as civilized.

Patrocles

We now turn to Patrocles, our second author-general of Antiochus' coregency in the Upper Satrapies. We actually know quite a lot about him. He was an imperial official of the top rung, and his career in the royal service spanned chronologically from Seleucus' coronation to, at least, Antiochus' accession and geographically from Sogdiana to Asia Minor. As a "trusted Friend" of Seleucus Nicator, Patrocles accompanied the founder-king back to Babylon in 312,[59] where he was immediately appointed the region's governor.[60] During the joint monarchy of Seleucus I and Antiochus I—the period we are looking at—he was assigned an unspecified command over Bactria and Sogdiana.[61] He is later found by Seleucus I's side in Syria[62] and then, following Seleucus' murder and Antiochus I's difficult accession in 281, campaigning to restore Seleucid authority in Asia Minor.[63] At some point during his Central Asian appointment, Patrocles was commissioned by his royal masters to lead a voyage of exploration, called a *periplus*, along the coastline of the Caspian Sea;[64] subsequently, he published an account of this *periplus'* geographical and ethnological discoveries. The work proved extraordinarily influential, owing both to his trustworthy reputation[65] and to the simple fact that he was the only Greek explorer to describe the Caspian firsthand.[66] As we will see, Patrocles determined the Hellenistic and Roman understanding of this region's geography for centuries.

In itself, Seleucus' and Antiochus' commissioning of a Caspian *periplus* was a gesture of demarcation. Before we even examine Patrocles' account it is possible to identify some of his *periplus'* significance, both as a royal-sponsored act of empire formation and as a literary work operating within a specific horizon of expectations.

Peripli are, in essence, acts of delegation, directed from the court center toward the extreme peripheries of royal space. The exploratory voyages establish the field in which royal power plays out its strategies of possession. We can see this most clearly in Herodotus, who records in succession three separate exploratory voyages: pharaoh Neco's and king Xerxes' commissioning the circumnavigation of Africa and Darius I's tasking Scylax of Caryanda, as we have seen in Chapter 1, to sail along the Indus river and the Persian Gulf.[67] These missions, combining the unsurpassed resources of imperial power with individual kings' *vouloir-savoir*, constitute a significant intersection of imperial ideologies and geographic imagination. The Indian *periplus* of Scylax, for example, was preceded by Darius' wish to know (βουλόμενος . . . εἰδέναι) where the river Indus entered the sea; then, "after these had sailed round (μετὰ δὲ τούτους περιπλώσαντας), Darius subdued the Indians and made use of this sea."[68] It is crucial to recognize that this Herodotean representation reflects an actual Achaemenid practice and discourse. An Old Persian inscription from Suez (known by the abbreviation DZc) commemorates in Darius I's own voice such an imperial voyage:

> Darius the king says: I am a Persian. From Persia I seized Egypt. I ordered this canal to be dug *(adam ni[ya]štāyam imām [yauviyā]m ka^ntanaiy)*, from the river called Pirāva (Nile), which flows in Egypt, to the ocean, which goes from Persia *(hacā Pārsā)*. Afterward, this canal was dug, just as I ordered, and ships came from Egypt through this canal to Persia *(abiy Pārsam)*, just as I desired *(yaθā mā[m kāma āha])*.

Darius' inscription, like Herodotus' account, underscores the driving effectiveness of royal will, the interaction of conquest and *periplus*, the imperial objective of maritime connectivity, and the geographic centrality of the Persian homeland (note *hacā Pārsā* and *abiy Pārsam*).[69] Alexander the Great, uniting the Achaemenid precedent with Aristotelian natural historical inquiry, commissioned *peripli* of the Indus river and Persian Gulf[70] and of Arabia.[71] Most relevantly, just before his death Alexander sent a certain Heraclides to explore the Caspian Sea, "for a desire seized him" (πόθος γὰρ εἶχεν αὐτόν) to find out whether it connected to the Black Sea or Indian Ocean.[72] The project died with Alexander.[73] So, by assigning a Caspian *periplus* to Patrocles, Seleucus I and Antiochus I were both fulfilling an interrupted last plan of Alexander and locating themselves within an established royal and Persian tradition of maritime exploration.

As a literary genre, *peripli* generate a particular kind of space.[74] The texts standardly list various points on a line (places, towns, peoples) from the perspective of a ship coasting along the shore and relate these points to one another by abstract measurements of distance or sailing time. The *periplus* genre is thus concerned with marking out an edge, not with what lies between or beyond,[75] and thereby generates coherent and roundable land units.

Accordingly, in precedent and genre alone, Patrocles' *periplus* was an eminently suitable method of fixing the kingdom's territory. By the naval gaze—the possessive glance from ship to shore—Patrocles' voyage would delimit Seleucid sovereign claims in the kingdom's northeast. Although it is impossible to reconstruct with any certainty the duration, direction, and starting or ending points of Patrocles' actual voyage,[76] his literary account made three key, and utterly revolutionary, geographical claims:

The Northeast Passage

Greek geography since Homer had assumed that a single, unitary Ocean flowed around the continental landmass and into the Mediterranean (and so the Black Sea), the Red Sea, and the Persian Gulf. Patrocles reported that the Caspian Sea, which is of course a large saltwater lake, also opened to this encircling Ocean through a narrow mouth, στόμα, at its northernmost point.[77] Consequently, in passages dependent on his account, the Caspian is consistently referred to as "the gulf," ὁ κόλπος. The claim is preserved and accepted by all major classical geographers up to Ptolemy. Even the *Tabula Peutingeriana*, the famous reproduction of a late antique Roman map, makes the Caspian Sea a gulf of Ocean[78] (see Figure 4). The belief

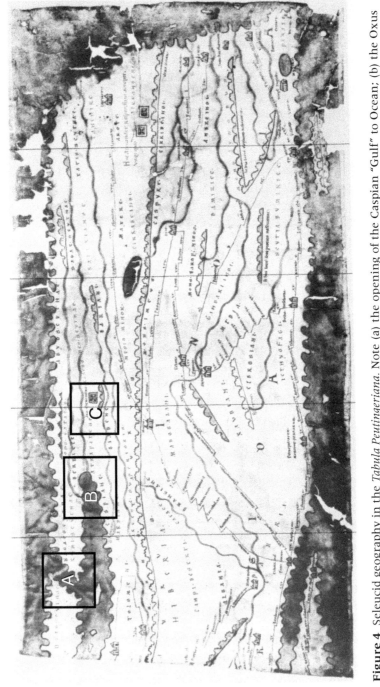

Figure 4 Seleucid geography in the *Tabula Peutingeriana*. Note (a) the opening of the Caspian "Gulf" to Ocean; (b) the Oxus and Iaxartes rivers debouching into the Caspian; and (c) the *Ara Alexandri*, "Altar of Alexander."

persisted into the early modern period.[79] Patrocles' report is not only complete fabrication; it also overturned the standard geographical understanding of this region. While it is uncertain whether Hecataeus of Miletus considered the Caspian to be a lake or gulf,[80] Herodotus could not be clearer that the Caspian was an isolated sea, surrounded by land and unconnected to Ocean: "the Caspian Sea is by itself, not joined to the other Sea (i.e., Ocean)" (ἡ δὲ Κασπίη θάλασσά ἐστι ἐπ' ἑωυτῆς, οὐ συμμίσγουσα τῇ ἑτέρῃ θαλάσσῃ);[81] Aristotle[82] and the Alexander Historians[83] followed this lake model. The so-called Gazetteer of Satrapies, a geographical description of the Macedonian empire confidently dated to the period immediately following Alexander's death and preserved in Diodorus Siculus,[84] also treated the Caspian as a self-enclosed lake.[85] Patrocles redrew the map. Perhaps responding to the symmetrical impulse of ancient cartography, whereby the Red Sea was made to mirror the Black and the Danube river the Nile, so the Caspian Gulf (κόλπος) came to resemble the Persian Gulf.[86] No longer an isolated and static phenomenon of limited regional importance, the Oceanic Caspian could now participate in global geography and big-picture imperialism.

The Caspian's transformation from a closed lake into a waterway meant that one could sail into and out of it. Patrocles suggested that a voyage from India into the Caspian was now possible[87] and, according to Pliny, had even completed this impossible journey with his royal sponsors: "Seleucus, Antiochus, and Patrocles, the commander of their fleet, actually sailed around into the Hyrcanian and Caspian Sea" (circumvectis etiam in Hyrcanium mare et Caspium).[88] While such a journey is geographically and historically absurd,[89] Pliny's version may be explained by Patrocles' narration of his geographical account from the perspective of a ship entering the Caspian Gulf through its supposed northern opening (στόμα) and then sailing counterclockwise along the coast to the mouth of the Iaxartes.[90] Even if Pliny read Patrocles' words incorrectly, he sensitively interpreted the political force of the Seleucid admiral's geographic invention:

> Similarly in the east the whole region under the same star from the Indian Ocean to the Caspian Sea was navigated by Macedonian forces in the (joint-)reign of Seleucus and Antiochus (pernavigata est Macedonum armis Seleuco atque Antiocho regnantibus), who desired that it be called "Seleucis" and "Antiochis" after themselves (qui et Seleucida et Antiochida ab ipsis appellari voluere). And around the Caspian many coasts of Ocean have been explored,

and very nearly the whole of the north has been sailed from one side or the other.[91]

The association of royal-sponsored naval exploration with territorial renaming highlights the possessive, imperial implications of the Caspian periplus.[92] In other words, Patrocles' northeast passage gave to the *oikoumenē* a hitherto unrecorded oceanic boundary to the north and to Seleucid territory a natural roundability and territorial unity.[93]

Oxus and Iaxartes Debouch into the Caspian

The two great rivers of Central Asia, the Oxus and the Iaxartes, today debouch into the much-reduced and oversalinated Aral Sea.[94] This was almost certainly the case in the Hellenistic period as well.[95] Yet Patrocles, in a second fabrication, asserted that both rivers flowed into the Caspian Gulf[96] and that their mouths were separated by eighty *parasangs* (a Persian measurement).[97]

While the course of these rivers may not at first appear of great significance, the invention served a wider geographical purpose. Patrocles claimed that the Oxus river, flowing into the Caspian Sea from its source in the Hindu Kush,[98] was navigable (εὔπλουν)[99] and that trade goods could be carried easily from India into the Caspian Sea, and then portered across the Caucasian isthmus into the Black Sea.[100] Such an east-west Caspian trade route never existed. No cities or ports were established on the Caspian Sea, and no regular Seleucid fleet succeeded Patrocles' exploratory *periplus*. Rather, the geographical invention should be understood as an ideological operation, providing the Seleucid kingdom with a second northern route to India by boat. Patrocles' Oxus river journey, like the Oceanic voyage, emphasized the ease of communications, travel, and trade between the worlds of Mauryan India and Seleucid Central Asia. It belongs in the diplomatic context of the Indus Treaty and Megasthenes' tenure at Pataliputra.

Excepting the short-lived colonial outposts in Sogdiana, the Oxus basin marked the northern edge of achievable sovereignty in the kingdom's opening decades. Patrocles was not alone in privileging this Central Asian river. It was also the recipient of official and unparalleled Seleucid cultic veneration. A unique royal bronze coin issue from Bactria, dating to Antiochus' viceroyship in the region, depicts the Oxus in the standard Greek iconography of a river-god—a human-headed humped bull.[101] The same deity was worshipped at the enormous royal-sponsored temple complex at Takht-i Sangin on the river's northern bank,[102] where, as we have seen (Figure 3), Atrosoces dedicated a Marsyas statue "to Oxus."

The full importance of an Oceanic Caspian and a navigable Oxus, however, can be understood only in the light of Patrocles' final and most outrageous suggestion.

Canalization of the Caucasian Isthmus

The separation of the Eurasian landmass into the continents "Europe" and "Asia" has always been artificial, for, in contrast to the clear maritime break of the Bosporus and the Hellespont, the dry land to the north of the Black Sea runs without break from Portugal to Kamchatka. Greek geography had long considered the Tanaïs river, flowing into Lake Maeotis at the northeastern corner of the Black Sea, the dividing line between Europe and Asia. Aristotle and the Alexander Historians had identified the Tanaïs with the Iaxartes, stating that a branch of the Central Asian river meandered through the steppes north of the Caspian and debouched into the Maeotis and the Black Sea, at some point having changed its name to Tanaïs.[103] In other words, the continents of Europe and Asia were separated, to north and south, by a river flowing continuously east to west. Patrocles' model of a Caspian Gulf made this impossible. On the one hand, the Caspian's Oceanic inlet meant that there was now no contiguous landmass north of the Caspian through which the Iaxartes-Tanaïs could flow. Patrocles' new geography, in which the Iaxartes debouched into the Caspian alone and did not enter the Black Sea, did away with the simple, continuous, and linear boundary between Europe and Asia. On the other hand, Patrocles' *periplus* demonstrated that the Caspian's western coastline continued without break from Oceanic inlet to southern shore; he discarded the possibility, held by Alexander among others,[104] that the Caspian itself flowed into the Black Sea. Ultimately, Patrocles' cartographic inventions had joined the Caspian Sea to Ocean in the north (via the inlet) and to India in the east (via the Oxus) at the expense of any connection to the Black Sea in the west.

An obscure project of Seleucus I belongs within the logical framework of this geography. Pliny reports, "Claudius Caesar has informed us that the distance from the Cimmerian Bosporus (in the Black Sea) to the Caspian Sea is 150 miles, and that Seleucus Nicator contemplated cutting through this isthmus at the time when he was killed by Ptolemy Ceraunus."[105] This proposal is entirely dependent on Patrocles' bizarre geographic inventions.[106] By artificially connecting the Black and Caspian Seas, the Seleucid monarch would accomplish for the new geography of Patrocles the form that nature had given to the old. As we have seen, the difficulty of northern Seleucid space was the absence of an external bounding mechanism to delimit royal sovereignty. The proposed canalization of the Caucasus, together with the already discussed notions of an Oceanic Caspian Gulf and a navigable Oxus river, works toward some kind of answer: river, Gulf, and canal gave the Seleucid kingdom a northern edge. Significantly, Claudius located this proposal at the Hellespont, for Seleucus I was assassinated while sacrificing near Lysimachia just after he had crossed out of Asia (see Chapter 3). Accordingly, the canalization project was directly tied to the kingdom's full east-west geographic expanse. A continuous watery line would run along the northern edge of the kingdom from the Hellespont to India.

The Seleucid proposal has a spatial configuration similar to the Egyptian canal of Darius I.[107] The Persian king's excavation, as we have seen, linked the otherwise unconnected Mediterranean and Red Seas as the Caucasian canal would join the Caspian and Black Seas. Both projects generate a linear maritime route out of a river-canal-Ocean unit.[108] It is interesting to note that one of the ways in which Seleucus I's great-great-great-grandson Antiochus IV was denounced in 2 Maccabees, the epitome of Jason of Cyrene's history of the Jewish revolt against the Seleucid kingdom, was as a new Xerxes, arrogantly inverting natural geography by canalizing the land: "Antiochus, thinking in his arrogance to make the earth sailable."[109] Perhaps this was not simply a generic accusation; does Seleucus' proposition lie in the background?

Patrocles' cartography and Seleucus' canal—natural geography and royal will—gave the northern Seleucid empire, from India to the Hellespont, the conceptual coherence and roundability of peripleutic space. We will see in Chapter 3 that this "littoral" reading of Seleucid territory shares much with older Oceanic models of world geography.[110]

For Aelius Aristides, the power of Rome was unlimited by man or nature. "The course of the sun and your possessions are equal and the sun's course is always in your land. No marine rocks and no Chelidonean and Cyanean islands define your empire, nor the day's ride of a horse to the sea, nor do you rule within fixed boundaries, nor does another prescribe the limit of your power":[111] οὐδέ γε δεῖ νῦν περιήγησιν γῆς γράφειν, "We don't need geographers any more."[112]

The early third century, when Alexander's unitary empire had fragmented into a multicentric new world order, was the precise inverse of this. Geographers and ethnographers were at the vanguard of the kingdoms' territorialization, working alongside kings, diplomats, and armies to imagine and make natural the new sovereign territories. The Treaty of the Indus between Seleucus and Chandragupta had programmatically demarcated historically unprecedented spatial units. Seleucus' assertion of a territorially limited sovereignty was a double gesture, directed both inward and outward. By contrast, the Central Asian place constructed by the coregent Antiochus I and his author-generals Demodamas and Patrocles was only inward facing and demonstrated far greater continuity with its Alexandrian and Achaemenid predecessors. The absence of an external power in the northeast meant that the universalism of world empire was retained for this area alone. In a sense, circumscribing power here was natural. The *oikoumenē* simply faded away, as it always had. The multiple and various attempts to demarcate the "natural" edge of Seleucid territory indicate both the continuing need for a clearly identifiable *limes* and its practical impossibility. The ingenious operations of Demodamas and Patrocles were discursive formulations, attempting to translate a network of isolated settlements and structurally interdependent subject and nonsubject, settled and nomadic populations into a graspable notion of imperial territory. It was a desire for line. Later centuries would respond with the construction of the enormous walls at Gongar, the Sadd-i Iskandar.[113] As inventive as Patrocles, Nizami, the late twelfth-century Persian poet, extended this "Rampart of Alexander," identified with the Quran's Wall of Gog and Magog,[114] into the world's northern boundary:

> Who thus established a barrier on the mountain?
> - Sikandar, who effected the prosperousness of 'Ajam
> The Iskandrian wall of shelter is from where to where?
> - From the circle of Chin in the east to the boundary of the west.[115]

By the end of Seleucus I's reign an enormous, contiguous, coherent, and politically unified block of land had been bounded by nature and treaty, territorialized, invested with dynastic identity, subordinated to court and king, and incorporated as a unit into the international system. This had been achieved thanks, above all, to certain high officials of Seleucus I's court, Megasthenes, Demodamas, and Patrocles. In salutary contrast to the armchair scholars of Ptolemaic Alexandria, the Seleucid court author actively participated in the physical formation of the empire he described. The early Seleucid kingdom and its privileged interest in ethnography and geography, far more than Alexander and his Historians, settled into place a new conception of the world and its shape.

PART II

Homeland

CHAPTER 3

Macedonia—From Center
to Periphery

The bounding of Seleucid territory was, in process if not result, agglomerative. Its genesis was coterminous with the founder-king's step-by-step victories and personal decisions: satrapal rule in Babylonia, conquest in Central Asia, peace in India. Even if Seleucus I's successors, their subjects, and their peers inherited and reenunciated a notion of legitimate bounded space, for Seleucus himself the land over which he extended his rule was arbitrary: aside from his marriage to the Central Asian princess Apame, Seleucus had no inherent, deeply rooted, ancestral connection to the regions over which he ruled. The historical accidents of Alexander's campaigns and the various power-sharing agreements after his death had, almost whimsically, placed Seleucus on this stage.

Victory over Antigonus Monophthalmus at the battle of Ipsus in 301 inaugurated a new westward phase of Seleucid territorial expansion. The dismemberment of Antigonus' kingdom by peer agreement gave Seleucus Syria and Lysimachus western Asia Minor;[1] Ptolemy, who had played no part in the battle and in consequence had been accorded no territory, nonetheless occupied Coele Syria and Phoenicia (mod. Lebanon, Israel, Palestinian territories, and Jordan).[2] Seleucus' expansion into regions long in contact with the Hellenic world, offering access to the Mediterranean Sea and proximity to the Old World of the Graeco-Macedonian mainland, brought to the surface the underlying tension between the identity of the king and the space of his kingdom. In this second part of the book I investigate the establishment of the Seleucid kingdom's far western boundary in European Thrace and the consequent externality of the Macedonian homeland.

Murder, not Macedonia

Seleucus I Nicator had shown an interest in western Asia Minor from the opening years of the third century, showering benefactions on the cult of Didymaean Apollo.[3] But in the division of spoils following the battle of Ipsus in 301 the region, along with Thrace and Macedonia, had fallen to king Lysimachus, a former comrade in Alexander's army and now a rival for his inheritance. Strife between the two neighbors was inevitable. In an already familiar pattern of the geographically separated powers uniting, like the wings of a triptych, against the central power, Ptolemy in Egypt and Lysimachus in Asia Minor made an alliance against Seleucus, directly threatening his new possessions in Syria and Cilicia.[4] Relations soured further over Seleucus' refusal to murder Antigonus' son, Demetrius Poliorcetes.[5] In 282 the tensions resolved into a showdown, the last of Alexander's funeral games. Our sources, no doubt inflected with Seleucus' legitimizing propaganda, depict Lysimachus at this time as a senile ruler, manipulated into murdering his eldest son, Agathocles, his realm disintegrating of its own accord, and allegiances transferred to Seleucus.[6] Welcoming this opportune turn of events, Seleucus invaded.[7] In early 281 he defeated and killed Lysimachus at the battle of Corupedium[8] and absorbed into his kingdom Lysimachus' territories in Asia Minor. Seleucus' kingdom now extended to the shores of the Aegean (see Map 3).

The aftermath of Seleucus' Corupedium campaign is associated with an ideological enunciation of exceptional importance. Following the battlefield death of Lysimachus, Seleucus could have claimed his enemy's entire kingdom in Asia Minor, Thrace, and Macedonia by right of conquest.[9] Instead, he characterized his incorporation of Lysimachus' trans-Aegean realm as a *nostos,* the homeward journey of a homesick king. Like a lumbering elephant, the elderly Macedonian was going home to die. This homecoming narrative appears in two contemporary but strikingly different historiographical traditions—the local history written by Nymphis, from the *polis* of Heraclea Pontica on the Black Sea coast of Anatolia, and the priestly cuneiform record known as the Babylonian Chronicle.[10] Individually and together, these two sources underscore the wide dissemination and courtly genesis of Seleucus' proclaimed homesickness.

Nymphis was a leading figure at Heraclea Pontica, returning from exile after Lysimachus' death in 281 and negotiating on the city's behalf with the Galatians in 250. He composed a history of his home city from its mythical foundation down to the accession of Ptolemy III Euergetes in 246 and a narrative account of Alexander, the Successors, and the Epigoni (the successors of the Successors).[11] Nymphis' writings reach us thirdhand: they were excerpted by the Heracleote historian Memnon in the late Hellenistic or early imperial period,[12] whose own history in turn was comprehensively

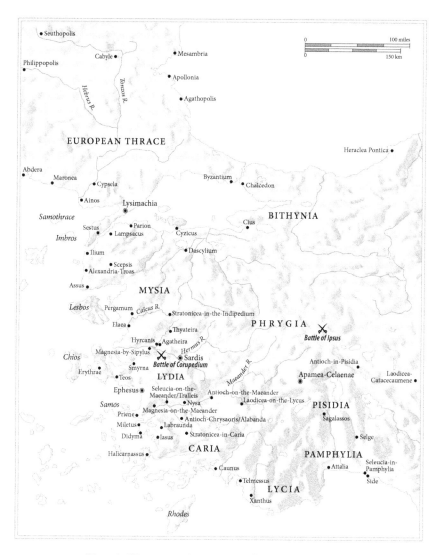

Map 3 Western Asia Minor and European Thrace.

epitomized by the Byzantine patriarch Photius in the ninth century CE.[13] It is nonetheless clear that Nymphis narrates the history of Heraclea as the typical Hellenistic tale of the gradual interweaving of *polis* and world affairs, moving from a dynastically structured series of tyrant biographies and a focus on the city's internal battle for its democratic institutions to the wider canvas of conflict between Alexander's Successors and the city's desperate attempts to preserve its autonomy from the Seleucid empire. On the whole, Nymphis' treatment of Seleucus I seems to have been laudatory and influenced by official Seleucid pronouncements.[14] Describing the aftermath of Seleucus' victory at Corupedium, Photius, in his epitome of Memnon's quotation of Nymphis, writes:

> Seleucus, buoyed by his successes over Lysimachus, set out to cross over to Macedonia, having a longing for his homeland (πόθον ἔχων τῆς πατρίδος), out of which he had marched with Alexander; he intended to live out what was left of his life there, since he was already an old man, and to assign Asia to his son Antiochus.[15]

Seleucus' homesickness is expressed by a marked term, *pothos*. Generally, the word indicates a personal desire for someone or something that is absent or lost or out of reach, a sorrowful yearning, a crying out for.[16] A new and unusual sense of *pothos* had been developed in the course of Alexander's campaign. This was an existential *pothos* that combined geographical exploration and conquering zeal—Alexander's bursting need to press forward, to penetrate unknown regions, to cross the next ridge.[17] Seleucus' *pothos* inherits from Alexander's the identification of imperial conquest with the personal fulfillment of the king's deep-seated desire, but its direction has been reversed: where Alexander's *pothos* had driven him ever farther from Macedonia, Seleucus' brings him home.[18] Such yearnings for home had been expressed during Alexander's reign by mutinying soldiers in India[19] and by settlers in Bactria;[20] certainly this was a traditional meaning.[21] But these instances were exclusively in subversion of monarchic authority—rebellions against empire and crushed accordingly. For Seleucus after the battle of Corupedium, in a profound rejection of Alexander's legacy, *pothos* for Macedonia became authorized policy. Nymphis' account is echoed by the second-century CE travel writer Pausanias, who reports that Seleucus, having defeated Lysimachus and entrusted Asia to his son Antiochus I, "pressed on for Macedonia" (αὐτὸς δὲ ἐς Μακεδονίαν ἠπείγετο).[22] The verb ἐπείγω, used in the passive voice, indicates haste and eagerness.

The influence of official Seleucid ideology on the Nymphis passage is confirmed by our second source, a Babylonian Chronicle narrating the final two years of Seleucus' reign (282–281). The Chronicles were Babylonia's dominant historiographical genre in the second half of the first millennium BCE. They are sober, terse prose lists of dated events in the third person, compiled from various sources by the priestly scribal elite of the Esagil, the main temple of the god Marduk in the heart of Babylon.[23] Accordingly, much like Nymphis' local history, they constitute an unofficial, indigenous, and contemporary response to current events. The Chronicle for Seleucus' final years is fragmentary, and the nature of the cuneiform writing system—no word breaks, variable signs with multiple phonetic values, and a combination of Akkadian syllabograms and Sumerian logograms—adds further uncertainty. Even so, repetitive patterning and regular formulae allow fairly certain reconstruction of the following passage:

> Year 30, month Siwan. That month king Seleucus mustered his troops [in Babylonia] and marched to the land of S[ardis]. . . .
> Year 31, month [. . . That month king Seleucus mustered] his [troops] from the land of Sard[is]. He and his army crossed the sea to Macedonia, his homeland (transcription: a.a[b.ba] ki-*šú ú-šé-bi*[*r-ma*] *ana* ᵏᵘʳ*Ma-ak-ka-du-nu* kur-*šú*; normalization: *tâmti ittīšu ušēbir-ma ana Makkadunu mātīšu*).[24]

The Chronicle's entries, quite standardly, are structured by origin and destination of military expeditions: from Babylonia to Lydia and from Lydia to Macedonia. However Macedonia is qualified and privileged by the appositional phrase *mātīšu*, "his own land" or "his homeland": *-šu* functions as a third-person singular, possessive pronominal suffix for the noun *mātu*, "country," "land." This is entirely unprecedented. In no other Chronicle, for a corpus extending over half a millennium, does the compound "homeland" (Sumerian kur-*šú*; Akkadian *mātīšu*) appear. The three other mentions of Macedonia in the Babylonian Chronicles appear without qualification.[25] This can be seen most clearly in the so-called Successor Chronicle, describing a similar journey to Macedonia four decades before Seleucus'. Here the Babylonian scribe describes the return home of Philip III Arrhidaeus, Alexander's successor, in 319/8: "He crossed over to Macedonia, but he did not come back" (*a-na* ᵏᵘʳ*ma-ak-ka-du-nu i-bir-ma ana* egir-*šú* nu gur-*ár*).[26] This Chronicle establishes no sentimental or ethnic link between Philip III and Macedonia; the land stands alone as a simple destination. Furthermore, we are told that king Philip "did not come back"

(Sumerian nu gur-*ár;* Akkadian *ūl itâr*), that is, did not return to Babylonia. The verb *târu*, "to come back," is used for journeys from abroad back to the point of departure, for example, a soldier returning from campaign or a merchant from foreign travel. The Successor Chronicle, notwithstanding the political developments following Alexander's conquests, retains the cuneiform genre's traditional geography, in which Babylon figures as the center of the world, from which the scribe's eye gazes out. In striking contrast, the Seleucus Chronicle, describing the founder-king's final years, recognizes Seleucus I's ethnicity and figures Macedonia as originary and ultimate destination.

The convergence of concept at this very moment (immediately after the victory at Corupedium) in Nymphis' history of a Greek colony on the Black Sea coast of Bithynia and the cuneiform clay tablet of Marduk's priests is extraordinary, like an echo trick of St. Paul's Cathedral or Golkonda. It is rare, if eloquent, testimony of culturally singular but imperially delocalized manifestations of official discourses. There can be no doubt that the shared figuration draws from authorized Seleucid proclamations.[27] For, as we will see, Seleucus was assassinated shortly after crossing the Hellespont and never made it home to Macedonia.[28] This means that the two historiographical traditions are not independently describing real and widely known events; rather, Seleucus I's publicized but unfulfilled ambition has simultaneously trickled, oblivious of failure, into the priest's reed and the historian's pen.

Homeward Bound! At some point in the absorption of Lysimachus' kingdom, probably immediately after the battle of Corupedium, Seleucus broadcast to his empire his desire to return home.[29] The statement reported by Nymphis and the Babylonian Chronicle has two elements: it insisted on the king's Macedonian ethnicity, and it projected a terminus for the king's travels/conquests. This is, as far as we know, the first and only explicit expression of a territorial aspiration by Seleucus Nicator. The plan did not espouse the incorporation of anything to the north, west, or south of Macedonia. There were to be no further conquests. East to west, the empire was to stretch from the diplomatically established boundary with Chandragupta's Mauryan kingdom right up to Seleucus' Macedonian homeland. This never-to-be-fulfilled spatial ambition should be understood as the official policy statement of the kingdom's natural boundaries in the period from the battle of Corupedium to the murder of Seleucus. Seleucus' empire was to lie within Alexander's. Its spatial ideology was explicitly enmeshed within the historical narrative of Seleucus' participation in Alexander's Persian campaign. The kingdom would be complete only when Seleucus returned to his point of departure. Empire and biography were to be coterminous:[30] routes as roots.

Seleucus never made it back to Macedonia. He was murdered just after landing in Europe by his ward Ptolemy Ceraunus (the "Thunderbolt"). Nymphis (via Memnon and Photius), again our most detailed narrative, reports that the murderer Ceraunus leapt on a horse, fled to Lysimachia, took the royal diadem, and presented himself to the army.[31] The Babylonian Chronicle seems to record an army revolt.[32] The extension of the empire to Macedonia was aborted; "Homeward Bound!" died with its king; Seleucid territory was prematurely foreclosed.

The assassination of Seleucus I was a profound crisis. Disasters accumulate. In Europe we find the founder-king murdered, his army abandoned, his assassin crowned and recognized.[33] In Ionia Ptolemaic forces won control of Miletus and probably much else farther south.[34] In the northwest Antigonus II Gonatas, the son of Demetrius Poliorcetes, the kings of Bithynia and Pontus, and powerful Greek cities formed an alliance against the Seleucid empire. That the *polis* members of this so-called Northern League struck coinage in the name of the vanquished Lysimachus indicates an assault on the legitimacy of Seleucid claims to this region.[35] Seleucid settlers in northern Syria (the region known as "the Seleucis") broke into revolt,[36] perhaps supported by Ptolemaic forces.[37] And to top it all, onto the stage burst tens of thousands of marauding Galatians, migrating from the Balkans.[38] If the precise details are in question, the overall impact is not: a near total succession crisis in the empire's western hemisphere.

Against the odds, Antiochus I, the son and viceroy of Seleucus I, confirmed his tottering rule over the kingdom. The new king raced from the Upper Satrapies to crush the revolt in Syria, perhaps driving Ptolemaic forces out of Damascus.[39] Patrocles, the Caspian navigator of Chapter 2, campaigned on Antiochus I's behalf in Asia Minor.[40] To secure his western border, Antiochus I was obliged to conclude a short-lived truce with his father's assassin, Ptolemy Ceraunus,[41] and then two more substantial peace treaties with Ptolemy II[42] and Antigonus II Gonatas. To win this latter peace, as we will see, Antiochus was obliged to renounce Seleucid claims to the Macedonian homeland. The crisis period can be best summarized in Nymphis' epigrammatic statement that, "In many wars Antiochus, the son of

Seleucus, though with difficulty and not in its entirety (εἰ καὶ μόλις καὶ οὐδὲ πᾶσαν), restored his paternal kingdom (ἀνασωσάμενος τὴν πατρῴαν ἀρχήν)."[43]

Periodization by monarch's death may seem an unadventurous methodology. But Seleucid rule was too young for the dynastic refrain "The king is dead, long live the king!" The assassination of Seleucus and the crises that concatenated around it ruptured and reformulated imperial practices and ideologies. However tragic the murder, its aftershocks demanded rich ideological experimentation. This inventiveness is most clearly attested in an important inscription from the Greek city of Ilium in honor of Antiochus I.[44] The decree's motivating clauses narrate Antiochus' crushing of rebels and restoration of peace in Syria and Asia Minor:

> Whereas in the beginning king Antiochus, son of king Seleucus, having succeeded to the kingdom (παραλαβὼν τὴμ βασιλείαν) and conducting a noble and honorable policy, sought to restore the cities throughout the Seleucis, which were beset by difficult circumstances because of those rebelling against the state, to peace and their former prosperity (τὴν ἀρχαίαν εὐδαιμονίαν), and (sought), by punishing as was right (καθάπερ ἦν δίκαιον) those who attacked the state, to recover his paternal rule (ἀνακτήσασθαι τὴμ πατρῴαν ἀρχήν); for which reason, both pursuing a laudable and just ambition (ἐπιβολῇ καλῇ καὶ δικαίᾳ) and having not only his Friends and the forces as his supporters in contending for the state, but (having) also the divine as his well-disposed helper (τὸ δαιμόνιον εὔνουν καὶ συνεργόν), he restored the cities to peace and the kingdom to its previous condition (τὴμ βασιλείαν εἰς τὴν ἀρχαίαν διάθεσιν κατέστησεν).[45]

Antiochus I's actions are legitimized repeatedly and in various ways: the defeat of enemies is righteous; Antiochus' ambition is laudable and just; he receives divine support and approval; he restores the kingdom to its former prosperity. It can hardly be doubted that the inscription reproduces the official discourse of the Seleucid court. Note, for example, that the historian Nymphis, quoted earlier, used a very similar phrase for Antiochus' succession (ἀνασωσάμενος τὴν πατρῴαν ἀρχήν). Indeed, the similarity of the decree's narrative and ideology to the great Behistun inscription of the Persian king Darius I—righteous defeat of insurgents, return to a preexisting order, god's assistance and authorization—may point to the influence of Achaemenid succession traditions on this half-Iranian former viceroy of the Upper Satrapies.

Most importantly, the decree inscribes a clear conception of a preexisting and heritable imperial space. Antiochus I succeeded to his father's throne *and* territory. The transition from father to son transformed the basis of the monarchy's legitimacy: a kingdom created by Seleucus would be inherited by the closed group of his biological successors. In the late 280s across the Hellenistic world, son succeeded father—Antiochus I in Asia, Ptolemy II in Egypt, and Antigonus II in Macedonia. The successful shift from first-generation charismatic rule to second-generation hereditary rule stabilized and fixed the east Mediterranean's geopolitical order for at least a century. Crucially, in the Seleucid kingdom the transformation of achieved kingship into assigned kingship was a spatial move: from achieved territory to assigned territory. Seleucus I Nicator had generated and delimited a spatial unit; Antiochus I Soter preserved and maintained it. Antiochus' response to the succession crisis determined this—the preservation of Seleucid territorial rule—as the prime function of the legitimate Seleucid monarch. All succeeding monarchs followed in his footsteps. That Antiochus I was able to inherit his father's enormous kingdom, albeit "with difficulty and not in its entirety," owed as much to the ideological work done to establish a sense of Seleucid territory as to the early and undisputed identification of an heir.

Antiochus I had been born and raised in the new world of conquered Asia; for the last decade he had reigned in the Upper Satrapies. This son of Sogdian Apame had never sailed the Aegean, hunted in the forests of Macedonia, gazed upon the Parthenon, or worshipped at Delphi. The accession of Antiochus I opens to the transformed horizons of second-generation colonialism, for whom Macedonia and Greece, Before Alexander, the Old World belonged to fireside yarns and history books. After the failure of Seleucus' Homeward Bound campaign, Antiochus I was responsible for a number of important spatial operations that closed and demarcated Seleucid territory in the west. The remainder of the chapter will examine the delimitation of the kingdom's western boundary, in the corner of the European mainland bordering the northeastern Aegean and the Black Sea, known as European Thrace.

European Thrace

Seleucid territory was bounded by diplomacy. The murder of Seleucus and the crisis that followed left it to Antiochus I to define the western edge of the Seleucid kingdom. In the early 270s the new king made peace with Antigonus II Gonatas, the new master of Macedonia.[46] Although no ancient source expressly outlines the treaty's provisions, there is no disagreement about what was entailed:[47]

>   (i) Antiochus renounced all claims to Macedonia.
>
> (ii) The north Aegean coast, formerly united under Lysimachus, was divided between the two kingdoms: all lands west of Abdera went to Antigonus and his Macedonian kingdom;[48] European Thrace, into which Seleucus I had crossed just before his murder, to Antiochus I and his descendants.
>
> (iii) The two kings were joined in a marriage alliance. Antiochus I gave his half-sister Phila, daughter of Seleucus I and Stratonice, to Antigonus Gonatas; she would be his only wife and the mother of his successor, Demetrius II. It is to be regretted that we have lost the wedding song composed by Aratus for the occasion.[49]

The Antiochus-Antigonus peace is the western counterpoint to the Treaty of the Indus, explored in Chapter 1. Just as the eastern boundary had been formed by withdrawal from the Hindu Kush, so the western boundary by the abandonment of Macedonia. It performed a similar spatial operation, exchanging a formal renunciation of territory for a mutually recognized and beneficial border in the context of friendly relations between kings of equal status bound by marriage. Like the Treaty of the Indus, again, the Antiochus-Antigonus peace retained an ideological stability right up to the reign of Antiochus III. The Seleucid kings never disputed the Antigonid kings' right to Macedonia, the Antigonids never attempted to expel the Seleucids from Europe,[50] and the dynastic alliance was renewed into the next generation by the marriage of Antigonus Gonatas' son by Phila, Demetrius II, to Stratonice, daughter of Stratonice and Antiochus I.[51]

The clearest indication of the treaty's continued salience for the Seleucid kingdom's official memory are the diplomatic exchanges between Rome and Antiochus III that followed the king's opening of military activities in Europe in the 190s. The great Seleucid monarch countered Roman accusations of illegitimate territorial expansion in the region with the argument that Thrace had always belonged to the Seleucid kings.[52] The foundation for this uninterrupted ancestral possession, so Antiochus III argued, was Seleucus I Nicator's victory over Lysimachus at Corupedium in 281. Antiochus invoked a principle for territorial title—"spear-won land"—that by itself should have given him a claim to all of Lysimachus' kingdom in Asia Minor, Thrace, *and* Macedonia.[53] That Antiochus III restricted his claims (and conquests) to Asia Minor and Thrace indicates his acceptance, from the first, of the continued authority and historical legitimacy of the territorial provisions of the Antigonid-Seleucid treaty.[54]

We have seen that Macedonia lay outside Seleucid imperial territories by the formal agreement of the second Seleucid monarch. Antiochus I's abandonment of his father's homeland produced an ideological demotion of the kingdom's western boundary. As opposed to Macedonia, no privileged element inhered in European Thrace to beckon back the kings like a pillar of fire; no king was born, died, or was buried there. Instead, Seleucid activities in European Thrace were limited to the intermittent defense of borders and reassertion of imperial control.

European Thrace in the Hellenistic period was politically fragmented. Following the murder of Seleucus and the mass Galatian invasion of the Balkan peninsula, the region was broken into the domains of Thracian chiefdoms, the newly established Galatian kingdom of Tylis, Greek *poleis* hugging the coastline,[55] and, from the reign of Ptolemy II, Egyptian ambitions in the north Aegean.[56] Seleucid dominance in the region was episodically enforced after the Antiochus-Antigonus treaty in each generation of Seleucid rule in the west. Antiochus I's successor, Antiochus II, won control of Cypsela[57] and the Gulf of Burgas in the course of the Second Syrian War (255–253).[58] The discovery at Cabyle of the king's royal bronze coins, struck at Sardis in Asia Minor, indicate a lengthy sojourn at this strategically located city and regional power on the great bend of the Tonzos river.[59] Antiochus II's army may also have razed Seuthopolis, capital of the Thracian dynast Seuthes III, near modern Kazanlak: archaeological evidence for the besiegers' use of stone-throwing artillery and the standardization of projectile size and shape are more appropriate to a Hellenistic royal army than a Galatian one.[60] About three decades later the pretender king Antiochus Hierax, younger son of Antiochus II and brother of the reigning Seleucus II, was killed in Thrace[61] in a last-ditch crack at legitimate kingship in this far-flung periphery of empire.[62] Seleucus II's son Antiochus III committed three summers to campaigning in Thrace[63] (196–194), refounding Lysimachus' eponymous capital, Lysimachia, as a base for his son Seleucus IV.[64]

The nature of Seleucid imperialism in European Thrace, characterized by strategic compromise and alternating abatement-intensification, demonstrates the region's acknowledged marginality. If the treaty-fixing of the western border with Antigonid Macedonia followed the Indian precedent, explored in Chapter 1, then the tremulous Thracian frontier more closely resembled Seleucid Central Asia, discussed in Chapter 2. Imperial garrisons appear to have been established in the coastal cities, forming a littoral network of Seleucid military nodes.[65] The Seleucid kings never attempted to sustain permanent control of the deep interior. Rather, they employed the Thracian nobility in a form of semiautonomous indirect rule. One of Polyaenus' stratagems, typical of his superficial analysis of supposed military tricks, illustrates this form of interaction for Antiochus II's Thracian campaign:

> Antiochus was besieging Cypsela, a Thracian city. He was accompanied by many Thracian aristocrats, led by Teres and Dromichaetes. Having decorated them with golden chains and silver-studded weapons he led them into battle. The men of Cypsela, when they saw men of their own race and language adorned with so much gold and silver, considered the men of Antiochus' army fortunate, threw down their weapons, went over to Antiochus, and became allies instead of enemies.[66]

The Thracian allies are under the immediate command of Thracian dynasts: the names Teres and Dromichaetes recall the famous kings of the Odrysian and Getaean kingdoms, respectively, and it has been suggested that this Teres was the son and successor of Seuthes III, named in the Seuthopolis inscription.[67] Behind the quasi-ethnographic characterization of Thracian nobles' love of glittering metal and swiftly changing loyalties it is not difficult to detect the kind of ritualized royal gift-giving, of high-status weaponry and sympotic vessels, which had established bonds of allegiance and expressed relations of political dependence in this region since Achaemenid times. Such practices explain the profusion of gold and silver vessels, often in burial contexts and of Achaemenid or Hellenistic form, in the Thracian archaeological record.[68] In addition to the integration of the baronial cavalry elite to the Seleucid cause, Antiochus II seems to have placed the administration of Thrace in the hands of a certain Adaeus, installed at Cypsela as a semi-independent Seleucid-aligned general of Thrace.[69] The overall picture is that the exercise of episodic Seleucid domination over Thrace was articulated through vassalage structures typical of the kingdom's treatment of its more marginal territories.[70]

The double morphology of the Seleucid "soft frontier" in European Thrace—garrisoned cities on the coast, a graduated zone of ritualized vassalage in the interior—was vulnerable to the reemergence of the long-standing opposition of Thracian/Galatian tribes and Greek cities. This not only rendered precarious the Seleucid hold on Thrace but also channeled official Seleucid discourse, at the outbreak of such tensions, toward the representational mode of nomad-city polarity. In Chapter 2 I argued that Demodamas of Miletus represented the Seleucid kingdom in Central Asia as the bulwark of civilization against aggressive and unsettled barbarity. Similarly, it seems that the contested western margin of Seleucid territory in European Thrace could be assimilated to the frontier of urban civilization. This is most evident in Antiochus III's treatment of Lysimachia. Lysimachus' eponymous capital had been burnt to the ground in a Thracian raid shortly before the Seleucid monarch's arrival.[71] Texts of the Polybian tradition report the steps Antiochus III took to refound the city: the king reerected the walls, ingathered the scattered citizens, and ransomed back the enslaved.[72] Antiochus III's actions in European Thrace echo perfectly the three-stage narrative pattern (royal foundation—nomadic destruction—royal refoundation) of his great-grandfather's achievements in Central Asia. Antiochus III, like Antiochus I, is depicted in the traditional Near Eastern model of builder-king and defender of the civilized life. Appian terms Lysimachia "a bastion," ἐπιτείχισμα, against the Thracian nomads;[73] the word implies a hostile surrounding environment.[74] In addition to the physical reconstruction of Lysimachia, Antiochus gave to the new inhabitants cattle, sheep, and agricultural equipment (βοῦς καὶ πρόβατα καὶ σίδηρον ἐς γεωργίαν ἐπιδιδούς).[75] This final act was a powerful symbol of the Seleucid monarchy's sponsorship of the settled, urban, agricultural way of life.[76] In particular, the royal gift of the plow functions as an archetypal gesture of cultural heroism:[77] Antiochus III at Lysimachia in European Thrace acts like Megasthenes' Dionysus in India.[78]

The ideological implication of Antiochus III's symbolic behavior—that Seleucid territory and civilization were coterminous—is supported by a late second-century cuneiform King List from Babylon.[79] The tablet records the murder of Seleucus I in the following terms: mu 31 ká[m] kin [1]Si lugal ina [kur]Ha-ni-i gaz, "Year 31, Month Ulûlu. Se(leucus I), the king, was killed in the land of Hana." In the first half of the second millennium the Hanaeans were a nomadic tribal confederacy based around the middle Euphrates, on the Syrian-Iraqi border.[80] In subsequent centuries Babylonian scribes decoupled the name "Hana" from its original ethnic or geographical referent and generically reapplied it to populations that, from the perspective of the Mesopotamian alluvium, were regarded as uncivilized hordes of nomadic barbarians.[81] It has been shown that the cuneiform scribes labeled

Alexander's invading army "Hanaeans" in hostile contexts only.[82] The Babylonian King List's use of this term for European Thrace categorized its inhabitants as a stereotypical enemy of the Mesopotamian monarchic order and center.[83] In this way the cuneiform tradition traces the ideological demotion of the western frontier after the Antiochus-Antigonus treaty. In the Seleucus Chronicle predating the treaty, Seleucus was returning *ana Makkadunu mātīšu*, "to Macedonia, his homeland." In the second-century King List, he was killed *ina Hani*, "in Hana," that is, in the barbaric margins beyond the Bitter Sea.

At its western boundary the Seleucid kingdom settled into the Achaemenid precedent:[84] an unstable, loosely structured, and territorially limited form of imperial buffer, subordinate to the administration and interests of the royal capital at Sardis, requiring intermittent reconquest from without.[85] Likewise, the Hellenizing tendencies of the Thracian elite and the involvement of Thracian populations in Seleucid colonial practices were anticipated in the late sixth century by the Thracian adoption of Persian artistic motifs and by the density of Thracian laborers in the Achaemenid heartland.[86] Despite Seleucus I's intentions, the imperial terrain composed by his son followed the defensive logic of an Asian power reaching into European Thrace to protect the Hellespontine Straits and secure its control of the east Aegean coast. The Seleucid kings established no new, eponymous city in Europe. Lysimachia and Agathopolis,[87] foundations of Lysimachus and his unfortunate son Agathocles, were never renamed.[88] The most westerly Seleucid foundation was a small island, named Antioch, floating just off the Propontic coast of Asia.[89] As we will see, this process of kneading the land of Macedonia out of the kingdom's imperial physiognomy aligned Seleucid territory ever more closely with traditional Mesopotamian and Iranian conceptual geographies.

CHAPTER **4**

Syria—Diasporic Imperialism

The territorial unit inherited and closed by Antiochus I was unlike anything yet seen in the ancient world. For, with Greece and Macedonia beyond the kingdom's western horizon, the Seleucid monarchs were sundered from their ancestral homeland. By contrast, the Seleucids' Mesopotamian and Achaemenid predecessors had shared an idealized concentric representation of world and empire, in which the rulers' ancestral homeland was considered geographically central, ethnologically normative, and culturally superior, and also served as the node of all axes of movement and conquest. Persian royal inscriptions, palatial art, and imperial rituals repeatedly reaffirmed this spatial model. In the tribute-bearing relief sculptures on Darius I's Apadana at Persepolis, for example, the subject nations faithfully parade inward to the Persian overlord at the center. King Xerxes' march to war was a sort of moving world map:[1] the chariot-borne king at the center was immediately preceded, surrounded, and followed by Persian cavalry, in front of and behind which, separated on each side by a gap of two furlongs, walked the mixed host of subject nations. In Chapter 2 we saw the centripetal discourse of Darius I's Suez Canal inscription: "I am a Persian. From Persia I seized Egypt. . . . Ships came from Egypt through this canal to Persia."[2] Such an ideological strategy—a consistent and recurring emphasis on the homeland's spatial centrality—was simply and spectacularly unavailable to the Seleucid dynasty.

The period from Homeward Bound's failure to the Antiochus-Antigonus peace was an ideological interregnum in which, to paraphrase Gramsci, the old had died and the new could not yet be born. But, after Antigonus' possession of Macedonia was officially accepted, the Seleucid dynasty developed a novel and sophisticated response to its "homelessness." Antiochus I and his immediate successors built up, on a foundation already laid by Alexander and Seleucus I, an ideology of diasporic imperialism.

The hermeneutic of diaspora is appropriate to the early Seleucid empire. It had been born from the expulsive trauma of Alexander's decade-long Asian campaign, which had deposited a strandline of Graeco-Macedonians across the Near East. Even if the first-generation Macedonian elite was in no sense a "victim diaspora," they had experienced, like the canonical Jewish and Armenian diasporas, a forced and irreversible separation from their birthland. Typical diasporic forms of social organization developed within the kingdom's colonies: minority self-segregation, a cultural orientation toward the land of origin, and close relations with other, non-Seleucid Graeco-Macedonian diaspora communities. The focus of this chapter will be the Seleucid court's development of a twofold diasporic ideology. First, it will show that the kingdom officially acknowledged, explained, and narrativized the externality of the Old World. Macedonia was never left behind; instead, it was an irrecoverable point around whose absence the early Seleucid rulers in part oriented themselves,[3] whose fragments and echoes were turned into deterritorialized cultural markers, and whose memory, invoked in hostile charges of decadence and assimilation, came to represent a moral location.[4] Second, it will explore how the Seleucids powerfully valorized their new home in Asia and reembedded their dynastic identity in northern Syria.

The "Seleucus Romance"

A natural departure point for an examination of the kingdom's official diasporic discourse is the Seleucid court's own narrativization of Seleucus I's failure to reach and conquer Macedonia. The ancient historians Appian, Diodorus Siculus, Justin, Libanius, and Malalas preserve parts of an encomiastic and novelistic biographical tradition of Seleucus I, the "Seleucus Romance."[5] Although the Romance was built up from different and distinct channels, its transparently legitimizing purpose indicates its major derivation from court-propagated historiography.[6] It seems likely that the biography achieved its final stable form during or after the reign of Antiochus III, but much earlier material is present. The Romance incorporates a set of omens, dreams, and oracles that predict both Seleucus I's rise to greatness and his murder in European Thrace and so evidently postdate the events of 281. These sacred utterances carry a specific spatial inflection that directly addresses and authorizes Seleucus' failure to incorporate Macedonia into his kingdom. That is to say, they are structured on the spatial opposition of Macedonia as place of Seleucus' origin versus Asia as place of his kingship.

Ultimately, as we will see, they depict Seleucus' abandoned Macedonian homeland as a forbidden space.

A religious prohibition on Seleucus' return home is most visible in two oracles reported by Appian. In the first, a young Seleucus, following Alexander into war against the Persians, consults the oracle of Apollo at Didyma "about his return to Macedonia" (περὶ τῆς ἐς Μακεδονίαν ἐπανόδου).[7] The choice of oracle is important: not only was Didyma the recipient of much royal Seleucid benefaction (see Chapter 2), but the dramatic date of the episode can be fixed at 334, when the cult's oracle miraculously revived to greet Alexander's liberating Macedonian army and to guarantee its successes farther east. In this way the oracle characterizes the *pothos* for Macedonia that Seleucus declared in the final year of his life as an early and continual concern. The oracle's hexameter reply is direct and clear:

> μὴ σπεῦδ᾽ Εὐρώπηνδ᾽· Ἀσίη τοι πολλὸν ἀμείνων.
>
> Do not hurry back to Europe; Asia will be much better for you.

Note that μὴ σπεῦδε, "Do not hurry," fits the context of Seleucus' questioning about home in the early days of Alexander's campaign. The heavy spondees of the opening half-line's prohibition and the fast dactyls of the closing phrase's encouragement reinforce the oracle's message. Moreover, the oracle has a clear geographic arrangement, with the two continents meeting at the middle of the line, divided by a Hellespontine sense-break. Indeed, it is by eliding Europe and Asia, in the literal attempt to combine the two, in the passage between, that Seleucus' good fortune turns sour. The cartography of this carefully crafted line semantically, metrically, and visually gives divine authorization to Seleucus' eastward trajectory, to his failure to return home, and to his kingdom's oriental setting.

The second oracular interdiction occurs several chapters later. At an unknown date and unspecified cult site in Asia Seleucus inquired "about his actual death" (περὶ αὐτοῦ τοῦ θανάτου).[8] He received the hexameter reply:

> Ἄργος ἀλευόμενος τὸ πεπρωμένον εἰς ἔτος ἥξεις·
> εἰ δ᾽ Ἄργει πελάσαις, τότε κεν παρὰ μοῖραν ὄλοιο.
>
> By avoiding Argos you will reach your appointed year;
> But if you should approach Argos, then you will perish before your time.

Accordingly, Seleucus investigated and shunned four places named Argos: in the Peloponnese, in Amphilochia (south of the Ambracian Gulf), in the

Ionian Sea (founded by Diomedes), and in Orestia (in Upper Macedonia). Metonymically, "Argos" seems to represent the Graeco-Macedeonian mainland, from which Seleucus had departed, as well as kingship in Macedonia: Argos in the Peloponnese and Argos in Orestia were each considered the original home of Macedonian royalty.[9] Seleucus is warned away from both landscape and rule in Europe. The prohibition "Avoid place X" is a well-known type, whose fulfillment demonstrates the inevitability of fate, the infallibility of oracular response, and the deficiency of human interpretation: ὅ τι δεῖ γενέσθαι ἐκ τοῦ θεοῦ, ἀμήχανον ἀποτρέψαι ἀνθρώπῳ.[10] Accordingly, Appian reports that Seleucus was murdered by his ward Ptolemy Ceraunus at an altar near Lysimachia called "Argos," erected by the hero Jason sailing to Colchis or the Argives en route to Troy.[11] In a theatrical, tragic scene, the king is stabbed in the back at the very moment the altar's name is revealed. Parallels abound: Herodotus' Cambyses, whose death in Ecbatana was predicted by the oracle of Buto, perished in the so-named minor Syrian town, not the Median capital;[12] Hannibal fulfilled his death oracle at Bithynian Libyssa, not, as expected, in his Libyan homeland;[13] as predicted, the emperor Julian fell at Phrygia.[14] This oracular genre is predicated on imperial expansiveness and the resulting geographic ignorance: homonymy kills the king. Taken together, the oracles indicate indisputable divine disapproval of Seleucid rule in Macedonia.

The form and location of Seleucus' assassination in the Romance tradition—sacrificing/sacrificed at an altar overlooking the Straits—comes to function as a perverted or tragic or ironic boundary ritual.[15] In Chapter 2 we saw how Demodamas' erection of altars to Apollo of Didyma on the Iaxartes river in Central Asia was a spatial gesture that delimited Seleucid sovereignty in the region. Similarly, according to the account of Pompeius Trogus, Alexander the Great had bracketed his Asian conquests with twelve altars at the Hellespont and two at the Hyphasis river.[16] Seleucus crossed the Straits and, like Alexander and Demodamas, sacrificed on the far bank of a watery boundary. Intended as a midway-sacrifice en route to Macedonia, "Argos" became an altar of spatial closure. The sacrifice of Seleucus neatly expressed the isomorphism of imperial space and founder-king.

The murder scene also resonates with two linked and in some sense paradigmatic Hellespontine deaths that identified the Straits between Europe and Asia as a threshold of dangerous transition and a not-to-be-joined fault line. First, epic sings that Protesilaus, the first of the Argives to make landfall in Asia, was immediately cut down by Trojan spear.[17] His tomb and cult site, clinging to the extreme edge of Europe near the site of Seleucus' assassination, came to symbolize the trauma of the intercontinental crossing.[18] Pliny the Elder and Quintus of Smyrna report that the trees in Protesilaus' sacred grove cyclically relived the hero's fate, growing up until, on "seeing" Troy across the Straits, they withered back.[19] Second, Herodotus writes that at the end of the Persian Wars Xanthippus, the father of the famed Athenian Pericles, nailed Artaÿctes to a plank on the rocky headland where Xerxes' engineers had lashed his bridge of boats to Europe in a vain attempt to unite the two continents. This Artaÿctes, the Persian governor of the Greek city of Sestos in the Thracian Chersonese (mod. Gallipoli peninsula), interpreted his own crucifixion as a punishment from Protesilaus, whose heroön the Persian nobleman had defiled.[20] To Demodamas' series of precedents for his Iaxartes' altars (Hercules, Dionysus, Cyrus, Semiramis, and Alexander; see Chapter 2), we can oppose a catalogue of the damned for Seleucus' murder on the Straits—the first Greek killed in the Trojan War and the last Persian killed in Xerxes' offensive; all three dead at the Thracian Chersonese.

The geography of forbidden return in the Seleucus Romance is devastatingly simple. Europe=death. Such an equation correlates remarkably well with traditional Babylonian conceptual geography; once again, Seleucid space seems to be nestling into a Near Eastern frame. Although death imagery was never consistent in Mesopotamia,[21] a significant tradition expressed the transition from life to death as a journey along the "Road of No Return" to the extreme west of the world, to the "Gate of Sunset."[22] Such imagery combined the Oceanic model, according to which a cosmic sea *(marratu)* encircled the continental landmass,[23] with the notion of a Styx-like river, the Hubur, across which the dead were ferried to the netherworld.[24] Seleucus' westward march out of Asia and across the Hellespont to his death in Europe fitted this scheme and, from the Babylonian perspective, further naturalized Macedonia's externality.

Alongside the oracular prohibitions discussed earlier, Appian recounts a dream narrative that is more complicated and allusive but altogether richer in imagery and stronger in symbolism:

[Seleucus'] mother saw in a dream that whatever ring (δακτύλιον) she should find she should give to Seleucus to wear, and that he would become king in that place where he should lose the ring (τὸν δὲ βασιλεύσειν ἔνθα ἂν ὁ δακτύλιος ἐκπέσῃ). She did find an iron ring, with an anchor engraved on it, and he lost this seal-ring (σφραγῖδα) in the Euphrates.[25]

Justin's epitome of Pompeius Trogus, reproducing the common Seleucus Romance tradition, adds that Seleucus' mother was instructed by Apollo, who had just impregnated her with Seleucus, to give to their son the seal-ring, engraved with an anchor, she would find in her bed when she awoke the next morning.[26]

Most obviously, Appian's narrative functions as an oneiric prediction of the geographic origin of Seleucus' royal power in Babylonia. A much-attested folktale motif uses a magic object to indicate a desired place: an arrow is shot to determine where to found a city or seek a bride or build a church; a coffin lands where a dead king is to be buried and his son to settle; a saint's bell falls at a place where a monastery should be established; a divining rod sinks where a tribe will settle.[27] But none of these tales involves loss. The Seleucus Romance account is very odd. In classical myth and international folklore, seal-rings act as *talismans du pouvoir*,[28] object-symbols for the acquisition of regal status, only by their discovery.[29] Conversely, the loss of a ring is, almost without exception, inauspicious, usually followed by punishment, madness, or death.[30] In the Seleucus Romance, therefore, how can Seleucus' *loss* of his seal-ring signify his future greatness? Recalling that Seleucus' seal-ring falls into the Euphrates and that its device is an anchor, it is tempting to interpret the loss of the ring as a symbolic "dropping anchor," by which Seleucus, adrift in Alexander's conquests, reembeds himself in Babylonia.[31] But I think we should accept that loss is one of the points of the tale. Seleucus' kingship can come only at the cost of what his seal-ring represents.

The magical significance of seal-rings is based on their close identification with their wearer.[32] All through antiquity the seal-ring served as a means of identification:[33] "the ring was pre-eminently a personal possession, we might say a part of the person."[34] In the Hellenistic period, they acquired dynastic and legitimizing significance.[35] Appian's narrative, quoted earlier, has Seleucus himself invest the anchor ring with his identity: given as a finger-ring (δακτύλιος) it has become his personal seal (σφραγίς) by the time it is lost. The young Seleucus received the ring from his mother as a departure gift when leaving Macedonia for the east;[36] it functions as a symbol and an embodiment of the Macedonia he has left behind. His mother's dream is explicit that Seleucus' ascent to kingly status in Babylonia requires a painful loss: the dropping of the ring into the Euphrates marks a necessary abandonment and renunciation of Macedonia. Seleucus' seal-ring is, unusually, made of iron. This heavy metal was used in oath-taking rituals at sea precisely because it would not resurface[37]—the ring's weight is acting as the objective correlative of irreversibility. Macedonia is lost for good.

That the ring can function this way in the Romance—as a symbol of motherland and its loss—can be confirmed by comparing Seleucus' *sphragis* to the "little gems" of the Hellenistic poet Posidippus. In some key respects, the prose narrative recorded by Appian resembles early Hellenistic *lithika,* or gemstone, poetry. The first and longest section of the Milan Papyrus, a recently edited ancient anthology of Hellenistic epigrams, consists of twenty such poems that form an unparalleled meditation on the cultural significance of finger-rings.[38] Functioning as a literary gem cabinet or an inventoried royal spectacle,[39] the poems linger on the delicacy and exquisite workmanship of the stones. As has been recognized, these qualities provide suitable programmatic metaphors for the poetics of epigram.[40] In addition to this self-reflexivity, the gems function as geographic symbols of the place from which they have been taken.[41] As a result, the epigrams can trace the journeys of individual seal-stones, much like the narrative in the Seleucus Romance. For example, one epigram follows a honey-stone's path from the mountains of Arabia to the neck of Niconoe in Alexandria.[42] A magnetically polarized stone is "torn from the roots" (ἀνερρίζωσεν) of Mount Olympus in Mysia.[43] In two particularly interesting cases the gems' travels encode and reflect the collapse of the Achaemenid kingdom: Darius' own blue-green gem, a "Persian stone" (Πέρσην . . . λίθον), now drapes the arm of a courtesan in Alexandria;[44] an enormous carnelian, presumably also now in Alexandria, is engraved with Darius and his chariot.[45] This *lithika* poetry manifests a recognized ability of seal-stones to embody a cultural and historical heritage and, thereby, to serve as the vehicle for its transmission. Moreover, their symbolism appears especially appropriate for themes of kingship, empire, and loss.

The sinking of the anchor ring recalls Seleucus' involvement in an episode toward the end of Alexander's life, when the great conqueror's diadem was blown into the Euphrates. We are told that, according to some historians, Seleucus leapt into the river to retrieve it and, in order to keep it dry, wrapped it around his head; this autocoronation was held to indicate his future kingship.[46] It is plausible that, in the Seleucus Romance, the two scenes on the Euphrates belong to a single status-transformation narrative moment, with Seleucus losing his seal-ring as he swam for the diadem[47]— one symbol for another, a kingdom for a home.[48]

Through oracular and oneiric warnings, therefore, the Seleucus Romance worked through the externality of Macedonia. If my interpretation of this court-propagated biography is valid, Seleucus' failure to incorporate his homeland into his kingdom was reinterpreted as the inevitable fulfillment of a divine prohibition. Such proscriptions on return to the "ancestral land" are a recognized *topos* within certain diasporic identities. Within some branches of Judaism, for instance, the ingathering to Zion is infinitely deferred and eschatological; the non-Messianic, politically achieved return is considered impious.[49] Some members of the modern Persian political diaspora refuse to sanction a return to Islamic Revolutionary Iran.[50] The Romance's divine warnings may have had iterative or secondary relevance for Antiochus III, during whose reign the Seleucids were expelled from European Thrace by the Romans—an experience of rediasporization that in the dynasty's historical memory did not so much succeed as echo back and forth with the original.[51]

The Seleucid Era

If the folktale-like stories of the Seleucus Romance functioned as a kind of retrospective rationalization of Homeward Bound's failure, the Seleucid king and court invented a more comprehensive and totalizing narrative technology for naturalizing Macedonia's externality: the Seleucid Era. The distinctive achievement of the reckoning system known as the Seleucid Era (SE) derived from two monarchic choices. First of all, the Seleucid Era was never the annual count of Seleucus I's sovereign kingship.[52] The era opened in 312 or 311, according to the Macedonian and Babylonian calendars, respectively,[53] when Seleucus returned to Babylon from Alexandria, soon after Ptolemy defeated Demetrius Poliorcetes at Gaza. Importantly, the Seleucid Era remained the official tally even after Seleucus took the diadem and began to rule formally as king. So, in the cuneiform King List from Babylon, we read the strange entry: mu.7.ká[m] *šá ši-i* mu.1.kám ⸢si-lu-ku⸣ lugal, "Year 7 (SE), that is the first year of Seleucus the king."[54] The reckoning remained six years in advance of Seleucus' regnal count: the Babylonian King List tells us that Seleucus I reigned for twenty-five years and died in 31 SE. Second and more important, at Seleucus' death in 281 his son and successor, Antiochus I, did not restart the calculation. According to the same Babylonian king-list, Antiochus I ruled from 32 SE to 51 SE;[55] his successors continued accordingly. During Seleucus I's reign the era could

in some sense be regarded as an annual count of, if not his sovereign kingship, then at least his independent rule. It is Antiochus I's decision that
marks the real innovation. In part, the reason for this continuity may have
been "a technical one" since Antiochus had already served as coregent in
the Upper Satrapies for a dozen years.[56] But such continuity of count was
entirely unprecedented and in no way necessary. Like Antiochus I, Ptolemy II Philadelphus had served as his father's coregent in Egypt, although
only for two years. Ptolemy II marked the beginning of his single rule with
the opening of his own regnal count but retrojected two years to the beginning of the coregency.[57]

These two decisions not to restart the clock, at the coronation of Seleucus
I and the accession of Antiochus I, gave the Seleucid Era's temporality a historically new texture. Previous chronological systems in the Near East had
included: year names, where a year was designated by an outstanding event
of the preceding twelve months, selected by royal authority and archived in
lists of date formulas (e.g., "the year when Enlil-bani made for Ninurta three
very large copper statues" or "the year when Naram-Sîn reached the sources
of the Tigris and Euphrates"); eponyms, also used in Greece (e.g., "in the
limmu-ship of Bēl-Dan, the herald of the palace" or "in the archonship of
Pythodorus"); and, most prominently, the regnal years of individual monarchs (e.g., "in the seventh year of king Nebuchadnezzar" or "in the fifth
year of king Philip [III]").[58] These systems recorded events, not dates, and
were geographically specific.[59] By contrast, time according to the Seleucid
Era, decoupled from the death-accession cycle, was transformed from being
concrete, immanent, and process linked into being abstract, homogeneous,
and transcendent. The Seleucid Era was a regular durational measure un-
constrained by the phenomenal order of things, objects, and events. It was
paratactic and endless, without high or low points, expansions, contractions,
or pulsations. All this was unprecedented. The Seleucid Era—the historical
invention of continuous, unbounded, abstract time—is, perhaps, the great
monument of the Seleucid kingdom. To this day the Yemenite Jewish community dates its documents and activities according to Seleucus I's return to
Babylon after the battle of Gaza,[60] and the invention engendered the copycat
eras of, among others, the Parthians, the kings of Pontus and Bithynia, of
Diocletian (still used by Egyptian Copts), of Zoroaster, as well as the Jewish
Era of Creation, the Christian Anno Domini, and the Islamic Hijrah.[61]

This little-heralded achievement was a highly politicized act.[62] The Seleucid Era established the chronological backbone along which the kingdom's

own history could be ordered. It framed the temporal parameters in which the kingdom lived forward and was understood backward. Seleucus' return to Babylon in 312/1 was established as the "Big Bang" from which the years descend. What was at stake in this demarcation? In 320 Seleucus had received the satrapy of Babylonia as an administrative assignment from a superior, sovereign authority. His return eight years later marked a new start—his rule was the result of personal bravery, military victory, and indigenous acknowledgment. Thereby, his state lay outside the authorizing structures of Alexander's kingdom. The chronological principle of the Seleucid Era (1 SE) figured Alexander's campaign as the background but not the genesis of the Seleucid kingdom. Such a profound rupture between Alexander's and Seleucus' kingdom also appears in Demodamas' narrative of Antiochus I's city-founding activities in Central Asia (see Chapter 2)—Alexander's settlements had been destroyed; years later new Antiochs are built in their stead. This contrasts markedly with the calendrical practice of Ptolemy I, who retroactively dated the start of his reign to the year of Alexander's death and chose for his coronation feast the very anniversary of Alexander's death.[63] The sundering of the Seleucid state from Alexander's expedition made it a kingdom born in Asia, not a conquest from without but an emergence from within. According to its 312/1 starting point, the kingdom expanded eastward and westward from Babylonia; counting from 1 SE made the conquest-narrative of the early Seleucid state traditionally concentric.[64] Against this Seleucid chronological principle, the anti-imperial Jewish literature generated by the Maccabaean revolt in the second century opened their narratives of the overweening kingdom with Alexander's invasion, thereby interpreting the dynasty as a hostile and short-lived presence in alien territory, a high tide that would recede.[65] Furthermore, the chronological system only ran forward. Before the Seleucid Era (BSE) was unthinkable in its own terms. Accordingly, Macedonia was not lost from Seleucid space—it was always already absent. Although never denying the Macedonicity of the dynasty,[66] the interpretative constraints of the official chronology made the Macedonian homeland anterior and exterior to the Seleucid kingdom *qua* political entity: one cannot lose what one never had. The Seleucid Era at the level of structuring principle operates homologically with the Romance's seal-ring story at the level of plot and symbol: the Seleucid kingdom begins without Macedonia in Babylon.

The Seleucid kingdom, like Lévi-Strauss' "hot society," had internalized its own historicity.[67] Seleucid time has much in common with the ideology of Seleucid space: a homogeneous, unstriated conceptual field that retained its uninterrupted legitimacy and coherence regardless of the shortcomings and failures of whoever happened to be ruling. Moreover, 1 SE did not represent a lost ideal to which Seleucus' descendants endeavored to return. Rather, it was the murder of Seleucus I and Antiochus I's accession that had bounded the kingdom and marked its high point, just as the Passion and the Resurrection of Christ are of greater theological importance than 1 AD.

Antiochus I's early reign, therefore, diplomatically and ideologically cast Macedonia out of the Seleucid kingdom. At the same time, a discrete though dependent spatial operation identified northern Syria as the kingdom's center and the dynasty's new homeland.

Royal Burial

The entombment of the founder-king's ashes was the immediate symbolic act in this recomposing of the imperial terrain. Seleucus, according to Nymphis, had proclaimed to his empire his desire to end his days in his Macedonian homeland; presumably, this also meant burial in the ancestral cemetery. By the treachery of Ptolemy Ceraunus neither ambition would be fulfilled. Appian reports what followed the assassination at the altar called Argos:

> Philetaerus, the dynast of Pergamum, purchased from [Ptolemy] Ceraunus the body of Seleucus for a large sum of money, burned it, and sent the remains to [Seleucus'] son Antiochus. The latter deposited them at Seleucia-by-the-Sea (Seleucia-in-Pieria), where he raised a temple over them, around which he established a *temenos;* the *temenos* is called the Nicatorium.[68]

The dead king's movements articulated a set of relationships and identities. By a double transfer—the body from Ceraunus to Philetaerus, the ashes from Philetaerus to Antiochus—Seleucus' remains were carried from European Thrace to northern Syria. The chain of handovers fixed the participants' profiles: Ptolemy Ceraunus as grasping assassin-pretender; Philetaerus as loyal eunuch-treasurer;[69] and Antiochus as legitimate heir. The political importance attributed to the possession and burial of the defunct monarch's remains had recently been demonstrated by Alexander's treatment of his vanquished Achaemenid opponent, Darius III,[70] and, perhaps more pertinently, by Ptolemy I's seizure of Alexander's funeral hearse on the road from Damascus.[71] Of course, throughout the ancient world the acceding king's burial of his predecessor was a regularized stage of monarchic succession, asserting smooth dynastic continuity. But the *mise au tombeau* of Seleucus I is of particular importance because it was the first ever Seleucid royal burial.

This interment was a spatializing act. The passage of Seleucus' ashes from Europe to northern Syria reversed the direction of the Corupedium and Homeward Bound campaigns. The journey obeyed the rhythmical oscillation of outward conquest and inward return. The conveyance of Seleucus' remains back to Syria, just like the ideological demotion of Thrace and the chronographic system of the Seleucid Era, established the European territories as the periphery of an Asian empire. The dead king, like Antiochus I, was turning his back on Macedonia. The burial at Seleucia-in-Pieria framed as the kingdom's salient temporal and spatial parameters in the west not Alexander's campaign out of Macedonia against Darius III but Seleucus' campaign out of Syria against Lysimachus. Accordingly, Seleucus' conquests at the barbaric northwestern periphery, his death, transportation back to Syria, and burial at Seleucia-in-Pieria become analogous to, say, Cyrus the Great's campaign against the Central Asian Massagetae, his death, transportation back to Persis, and burial at Pasargadae.[72]

The entombment of the founder-king in northern Syria was a deliberate selection. On the one hand, Seleucus was not gathered to his ancestors in the uplands of Macedonia. The burial emphatically privileged the new horizon of kingship and empire over the claims of ethnicity and birthland. On the other hand, Seleucus could have been buried anywhere in his vast kingdom, in newly conquered Anatolia (Ephesus or Sardis would have been suitable), or in Babylonia, where he lost his seal-ring and rose to power (Seleucia-on-the-Tigris was the obvious place), or in Iran (perhaps at Naqsh-i Rustam, royal cemetery of the Achaemenids). Antiochus I's choice of northern Syria—a land without significant precedent and associations—located here the empire's new geographical, dynastic, and ideological center. Like the eagles of Zeus, Antiochus, marching from the east, and the ashes of Seleucus, conveyed from the west, met at Seleucia-in-Pieria.

It seems reasonable to suppose that, as in so much else, Antiochus I established a normative model for Seleucid royal burial. Although the Nicatorium itself does not seem to have been expanded, like Alexandria's *Sōma*, into a dynastic mausoleum[73] (not least due to the Ptolemaic occupation of Seleucia-in-Pieria between 246 and 219), it is likely that northern Syria remained the dynasty's resting place. Aside from the dubious case of Antiochus II Theos,[74] only two other royal burials are in any way attested—those of Antiochus IV Epiphanes and Antiochus VII Sidetes. Antiochus IV died at Tabae, at or near modern-day Isfahan, in 164.[75] We learn from 2 Maccabees that the king's *syntrophos* Philip escorted the body (παρεκομίζετο δὲ τὸ σῶμα Φίλιππος),[76] to where we are not told. A cuneiform Astronomical Diary reports that in Tevet 164/3 (mid-December to mid-January), one calendar month after news of the king's death had been reported at Babylon, Antiochus IV's funeral cortege reached the city.[77] Although the escorting party is not named in our fragment, it would be hard to doubt that it was under the command of Philip. In 163 or 162, Philip reached Antioch-by-Daphne in northern Syria at the head of the late Antiochus IV's army, prompting Antiochus V Eupator and his guardian Lysias to abandon their siege of Jerusalem.[78] Pulling all this together, it seems that Philip conveyed the embalmed body of Antiochus IV from Iran, descending the Zagros massif into Babylonia and passing up the Euphrates to Antioch in Syria. Philip's control of the king's body may have been a significant legitimizing asset in his rivalry with Lysias. Our other case: Antiochus VII Sidetes, having been overcome by the Parthian army, perished on a battlefield in Media in 129 (see Chapter 6). Justin recounts the arrival of the king's body in Antioch-by-Daphne:

> In the meantime, the body *(corpus)*[79] of Antiochus, who had been killed by the king of the Parthians, having been sent back *(remissum)* in a silver casket *(in loculo argenteo),* arrived in Syria for interment *(ad sepulturam . . . pervenit).*[80]

King Antiochus VII was entombed at Antioch-by-Daphne: Justin observes that the pretender Alexander II Zabinas treated the corpse with such care that the Antiochians were sufficiently persuaded of his legitimacy. Although no ancient source locates a Seleucid mausoleum at Antioch—a contrast to Ptolemaic Alexandria—it is possible that the tomb in which Antiochus Sidetes was laid to rest may have performed this dynastic function.

So, the three attested Seleucid royal burials share a centripetal dynamic whereby the kings' remains are conveyed from distant provinces for burial in northern Syria—the gravitational pull of the heartland on ash and corpse. Further sources would, I believe, reinforce this pattern: a generation-by-generation parade of royal hearses somberly converging from across the empire for entombment in the Syrian Seleucis.

Biographical Toponymy

The northern Syrian landscape into which Seleucus' ashes were lowered and his dynasty alienated had undergone a comprehensive renaming. These new labels tightly bound the Seleucid house to northern Syria and thereby allowed Antiochus, after his father's assassination, to transfer affective ties and homeland associations (what Yi-Fu Tuan terms "topophilia"[81]) from Macedonia to the Seleucis.

By the time of Antiochus I's accession, two different toponymic systems had been laid on top of Syria's preexisting network of indigenous Semitic and imperial Persian onomastics (see Map 4). First, numerous settlements, both virgin colonies and refounded villages, were named after cities in Greece and Macedonia: Aenos, Amphipolis, Apollonia, Arethusa, Astacus, Beroea, Chalcis, Chaonia, Charadrus, Cyrrhus, Doliche, Europus, Gindaros, Heraea, Heraclea, Larisa, Maronea, Megara, Oropus, Perinthus, Tegea.[82] The north Syrian seaboard was named Pieria,[83] after the coastal region of Macedonia. The river Orontes, where it flowed by Apamea, was called the Axios, after the watercourse that passed the Macedonian capital, Pella, and debouched into the Thermaic Gulf.[84] It is immediately apparent that the majority of these names come from Macedonia, Thrace, and north-central Greece; one is Peloponnesian, none is Attic. In many cases it is impossible to differentiate between deliberate renamings, phonetic approximations, and errors of translation,[85] but this in no way negates the overall and sweeping transposition of Old World nomenclature onto the newly colonized territory of northern Syria. Second, several settlements were named after Seleucus himself, his father or son (Antiochus), his mother (Laodice), and his wife (Apame): Seleucia-in-Pieria, Antioch-by-Daphne (mod. Antakya in Turkey), Apamea-on-the-Axios, and Laodicea-by-the-Sea (mod. Latakia in Syria), which are collectively known as the Tetrapolis, as well as the smaller towns of Antioch-under-Libanus, Laodicea-by-Libanus, Seleucia-on-the-Belus, and Seleucia-on-the-Bay of Issus. The northwestern region of Syria, in which the Tetrapolis was located, was given the dynastic name Seleucis.[86]

The mapping of Syrian geography onto an Old World matrix was an appropriative and imperializing act of linguistic formalism. Such renaming of settlements was a panimperial monarchic gesture—to illustrate from the kingdom's wide landscape, Susa, at the foot of the Zagros mountains, was renamed Seleucia-on-the-Eulaeus; Alexandria-Eschate, in Central Asia, was refounded as Antioch-in-Scythia; and Tarsus, in Cilicia, was called Antioch-on-the-Cydnus. But northern Syria was exceptional. Here the density and concentration of Graeco-Macedonian, as opposed to Seleucid-dynastic, toponyms far exceeded that in the rest of the kingdom.[87] They were never used to the west, in Seleucid Asia Minor:[88] only across the Taurus mountains was the world sufficiently foreign to be named after home. East of the Euphrates, they were extremely unusual. Moreover, no regional landscape or geographic feature outside Syria was given a Graeco-Macedonian name.[89] In northern Syria alone were the population nodes joined to one another by a renamed contiguous, in-between territory.

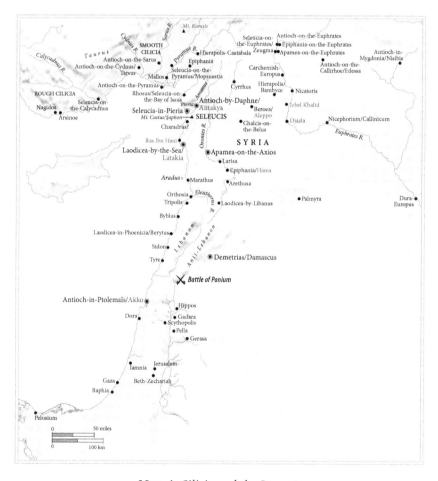

Map 4 Cilicia and the Levant.

Many scholars have argued that Seleucus intended by this semiotics of place to transform his kingdom's heartland into a New Macedonia.[90] According to this model, the renaming took place under Seleucus' auspices in the 290s and 280s, between the battle of Ipsus against Antigonus Monophthalmus and the Corupedium campaign against Lysimachus. During this period Lysimachus' trans-Aegean kingdom intervened between Seleucus and Macedonia, and the incorporation of the homeland had not become a declared ambition—an absence, in structural terms, not unlike the period following Seleucus' murder. Certainly, the redeployment of birthland toponymy is a well-paralleled diasporic phenomenon. To take just one example, it has been shown that first-generation Japanese and Punjabi immigrant communities in rural California each articulated the climate, soil, and topography of their new home according to supposed, and often wildly unlikely, resemblances to their respective birthlands and that this familiar toponymy forged strong collective identities among the diasporic communities and sentimental attachments to the new landscape.[91]

But the story—king Seleucus, separated from his homeland, reproduces Macedonia in Syria—is as incomplete as it is tidy; unfortunately, the situation is more stubbornly scruffy and confusing. Firstly, Seleucus' agency was not total. Northern Syria had experienced more than three decades of Macedonian domination before Seleucus began to incorporate the land into his kingdom. Antigonus Monophthalmus' pre-Ipsus colonizing projects in this region may have established much of the Graeco-Macedonian onomastic network.[92] In addition, some Old World names may have been generated bottom-up by newly settled, ethnically homogenous units of military veterans rather than imposed top-down by the king: for example, Syrian Larisa was populated by a regiment of cavalry from the homonymic Thessalian *polis*.[93] More critically, the argument ignores half of the picture. The colonies named after Seleucus and his family and the core region of Seleucis do not belong in this New Macedonia. The onomastic stratigraphy of Apamea, the Tetrapolis city astride the Orontes river, may give some indication of the occluded decisions and changing significations that elsewhere have faded out of the historical record. Before Alexander's invasion the site was occupied by a village called Pharnace, a Persian, not Semitic, name.[94] At some point a pre-Seleucid Macedonian military colony was installed and named Pella-on-the-Axios.[95] Finally, Seleucus I refounded the Macedonian colony of Pella as a city named Apamea. In other words, Seleucus turned a homonym of the Macedonian royal capital (Pella-on-the-Axios) into a dynastic eponym of his Sogdian wife, Apame; hardly New Macedonia. Furthermore, many of the Graeco-Macedonian toponyms may have particular biographical and thereby dynastic significance, now lost. For example, it is likely that the king named (Carchemish-)Europus and (Dura-) Europus after his hometown.[96]

The two new toponymic networks, Graeco-Macedonian and Seleucid-dynastic, cluster, overlap, and interweave one another, as well as the pre-Hellenistic nomenclature, where retained. It seems to me that this entanglement was precisely the point. The early Seleucids adopted a representational strategy that deliberately mixed the names of Graeco-Macedonian towns, dynastic family, and local geographical features: Seleucia-in-Pieria, Apamea-on-the-Axios, Antioch-by-Daphne, and so on. Seleucus' burial place resounds with this piling up of significations—Antiochus I buried his father in the Nicatorium, in Seleucia, in Pieria, in the Seleucis, in Syria. Seleucus, not his former homeland, is the organizing center of these compounds. Early Seleucid power was rooted in a constructed, freshly named landscape that telescoped into an indivisible whole elements of the founder-king's biography, birthland, and place of kingship. The renaming of northern Syria encoded by juxtaposition the physical fact of discontinuity, the translation from Macedonia to Asia. It was not a question of exchanging, like Aladdin's aunt, Old Macedonia for New. Instead, the former homeland was displaced, not reconstructed, by an altogether new kind of territory, into which the affective ties of natal origins *and* contemporary political realities could be embedded. The new toponymy illustrates the profound bifocality of diasporic consciousness, in which "living here" and "remembering there" coexist. Had the Homeward Bound campaign succeeded, the story would be very different. The new toponymy, even if some of the enunciative acts predate the Corupedium campaign, realized its full significance only from the accession of Antiochus I. It gained coherence in combination with Antiochus' treaty with Antigonus Gonatas, his continuation of Seleucus' regnal count (the Seleucid Era), and his burial of Seleucus in Seleucia-in-Pieria.

We can understand the purpose of such entangled onomastics by looking to the modern-day Jewish Chasidic communities of New York. These religious groupings are distinguished from one another by their allegiance to multigenerational dynasties of charismatic leaders, called rebbes. Chasidic conceptual geography is centered on the rebbe, each considered the spiritual leader of world Jewry, rather than on Israel or eastern Europe. The anthropologist Henry Goldschmidt has demonstrated that the landscape of

Chasidic New York—much like Seleucid Syria—is articulated according to three toponymic systems. The Chasidic communities recognize and use the American geographical categories New York, Brooklyn, Crown Heights, particular subway stations, street names, and so on. At the same time, each community is named after the Polish or Lithuanian town (e.g., Vitebsk) where its rebbes first established the dynastic court. Finally, regional Israeli toponymy is superimposed, above all to delineate Chasidic from non-Chasidic areas (e.g., "the Green Line," "the West Bank"). For Goldschmidt, the social function of these overlapping geographies is a profound valorization of the diasporic existence and the reterritorialization of the immigrant community in a new, nonautochthonous, dynastically conceived, and religiously legitimate homeland.[97] Analogously, the comprehensive and interwoven renaming of northern Syria authorized the new dwelling place. The Seleucids were here to stay.

The relocation of the dynastic homeland from Macedonia to northern Syria was an official and explicit ideological maneuver. This *translatio patriae* so successfully identified the ruling house with the Seleucis that, henceforth, northern Syria's geographical centrality for the kingdom and its ancestral primacy for the monarchs became unproblematic and assumed.

The homeland status of the Syrian Seleucis was reenunciated at the highest level by successive kings and senior members of the court right up to the dynasty's close. Two episodes in the fraught history of Seleucia-in-Pieria, burial place of Seleucus I, are illustrative. Seleucia had languished under an Egyptian occupying force since its capture by Ptolemy III in 246, during the Third Syrian War.[98] In 219, Antiochus III launched a successful campaign to conquer and reabsorb the city into his kingdom. According to Polybius' narrative, the king was prodded into this short operation by a speech of his doctor and adviser, Apollophanes, a Seleucian by birth. It would be foolish, argued Apollophanes, to attempt to conquer Coele Syria while permitting the continued occupation of Seleucia-in-Pieria, a city that was "the ancestress and, one could almost say, the sacred hearth of their own dynasty" (ἀρχηγέτιν οὖσαν καὶ σχεδὸν ὡς εἰπεῖν ἑστίαν ὑπάρχουσαν τῆς αὐτῶν δυναστείας).[99] This rhetoric of genesis and centrality surely derives from the kingdom's own spatial ideology and resonates with official Seleucid imagery and narratives.[100] ἀρχηγέτις, "ancestress," a religious epithet used for Athena, Aphrodite, and Artemis, recalls Apollo ἀρχηγέτης, "ancestor," Seleucus' supposed father.[101] More importantly, it is likely that Apollophanes' hearth image is intended to engage with a well-known episode in the Seleucus Romance. Among the numerous prophecies, oracles, and miracles that heralded Seleucus' future greatness Appian reports the following self-contained marvel: "In Macedonia a great fire burst forth on [Seleucus'] ancestral hearth without anybody kindling it" (ἐν Μακεδονίᾳ τὴν ἑστίαν αὐτῷ τὴν πατρῴαν, οὐδενὸς ἅψαντος, ἐκλάμψαι πῦρ μέγα);[102] Pausanias, who also narrates this incident, places it just before the departure of Alexander's expedition.[103] In the Romance, Seleucus' ancestral hearth is expressly located in Macedonia; in Apollophanes' speech, Seleucia is figured as the kingdom's dynastic hearth. The Macedonian hearth predicted the greatness that would become manifest in Syria. Even if the two uses are not equivalent—Seleucia-as-hearth is a metaphor for the city's foundational ideological primacy—side by side they encode the uprooting, then reembedding, of dynastic identity. This geographical transference is qualified by the limiting phrase σχεδὸν ὡς εἰπεῖν ("one could almost say"); Seleucia cannot entirely become the ancestral hearth. This not only serves to excuse the daringly figurative language but also represents the fragmentation and estrangement—the not-quite-ness—so typical of diasporic consciousness.

More than a century later, in summer 109, amid the general collapse of monarchic authority that now plagued the Seleucid empire's very heartland (see Chapter 8), Antiochus VIII Grypus or Antiochus IX Cyzicenus recognized the sovereign independence of Seleucia-in-Pieria.[104] A fragmentary inscription found at Paphos, in Cyprus, records this Antiochus' request that the Egyptian king Ptolemy X Alexander recognize the city's new status. Antiochus informs his Ptolemaic brother-in-law:[105]

> Now, being anxious to reward [the Seleucians] fittingly with the first [and greatest] benefaction, [we have decided that they be free] for all time . . . [thinking] that thus [our piety and generosity] toward our homeland will be most apparent ([νομίζοντες οὕτ]ως καὶ τὸ πρὸς τὴν πατρίδα | [εὐσεβὲς καὶ μεγαλομερὲς ἡμῶν] ἐκφανέστερον ἔσεσθαι).[106]

Although different restorations have been proposed to fill the inscription's lacunae, it is evident that the king represents Seleucia as, or as part of, his dynastic homeland.[107] According to the letter's logic, Antiochus' grant of freedom to the city is to be understood and advertised not as a desperate attempt to secure Seleucia's support in the current internecine conflict but as an act of devotion directed by the king toward his own homeland, his πατρίς. King Antiochus VIII or IX has applied to Seleucia-in-Pieria or, perhaps more widely, to northern Syria the very terms that Seleucus I, as refracted through Nymphis, used for Macedonia.

Moving outside the kingdom: it is well known that the Seleucid monarchs were most frequently identified by ancient Greek and Roman authors—from Polybius, Posidonius, and Appian to Athenaeus, Josephus, and Velleius Paterculus—as "kings of Syria," who reigned "in Syria."[108] These labels, once interpreted as hostile and damning designations that underscored Seleucid extra-Syrian territorial losses,[109] rather should be understood as expressions of the dynasty's own self-representation.[110] This is supported by a genealogical inscription from Miletus in Asia Minor, which identifies a certain Antigonus, son of Menophilus, as "admiral of Alexander, king of Syria" (ὁ γενόμενος ναύαρχος Ἀλεξάνδρου τοῦ Συρίας βασιλέως),[111] either Alexander I Balas or Alexander II Zabinas. The Seleucid admiral, a military commander of the highest echelon, places himself in the service of the "king of Syria."

The rooting of Seleucid monarchy within a Syrian homeland is not restricted to Greek and Roman traditions. Jewish sources on the Maccabaean revolt and subsequent national emancipation, both narrative historiography and apocalyptic revelation, reproduce this localization of Seleucid dynastic identity. For example, in 1 Maccabees, the Greek translation of a Hasmonaean royal chronicle originally composed in Hebrew,[112] Syria is recognized as a privileged and distinctly ancestral region of the much more extensive Seleucid kingdom. The numerous Seleucid royal journeys in 1 Maccabees are all, in fact, reducible to a triple typology: military campaigns and withdrawals between Syria and Judea; expeditions from Syria into the Upper Satrapies; and arrivals by ship on the Syrian littoral. In every case northern Syria functions as the origin or destination of travel. Moreover, the Syrian Seleucis is distinguished from the rest of the kings' imperial territory by the possessive and hereditary epithets "his own land" (τὴν γῆν αὐτοῦ),[113] "the land of his fathers" (τὴν γῆν τῶν πατέρων αὐτοῦ),[114] or, in the king's own voice, "our country" (τὴν χώραν ἡμῶν).[115] Compare this Hasmonaean chronicle's account of, say, Antiochus IV's march back "to Syria, his own land" with the report in the cuneiform Babylonian Chronicle, discussed in Chapter 3, that Seleucus I returned "to Macedonia, his own land" *(ana Makkadunu mātīšu):* two kings, parallel journeys, exchanged homes. The biblical book of Daniel's final eschatological vision, dating to 165 or 164, orients the political relations between the Ptolemaic and Seleucid houses along an axial Levantine geography centered on Judea: the Ptolemaic and Seleucid monarchs are thinly veiled as *meleḵ hannegev* ("king of the south") and *meleḵ haṣṣafôn* ("king of the north" or "king of Ṣaphon"), respectively.[116] Ṣaphon was, to the Greeks, Mount Casius at the mouth of the Orontes delta, by Seleucia-in-Pieria (see Map 4).[117] At the time of Daniel's composition,[118] the Seleucid kingdom still stretched eastward to the Zagros range and beyond. In an arresting synecdoche the author of Daniel 11 has represented the entire Seleucid empire through its core territory in northern Syria.

We have seen in Chapter 3 that Babylonian cuneiform sources echoed Seleucus I's official homeland pronouncements; similarly, they illustrate and construct the complex of ideological operations that followed his murder. The most important Akkadian text from Hellenistic Babylonia is the Borsippa Cylinder of Antiochus I, dating to 268; it is deeply influenced by official Seleucid ideology.[119] The cylinder is a small, barrel-shaped clay building inscription that was buried in the foundation of the Ezida, the temple of the god Nabû in Borsippa, about ten miles southwest of Babylon. It records, in his own first-person voice, Antiochus I's reconstruction of the temple and associated prayer for divine support.[120] In doing so, the text catches the dynastic translation midmove. The cylinder's opening lines immediately distinguish between the royal titles of Seleucus and Antiochus:

> Antiochus, the great king *(šarru rabû)* / the mighty king *(šarru dannu)*, king of the world *(šar kiššati)*, king of Babylon *(šar Bābili)*, king of lands *(šar mātāti)* / caretaker of Esagil and Ezida *(zānin Esagil u Ezida)*[121] / the foremost heir of Seleucus *(aplu ašarēdu ša Selukku)*, the king *(šarru)* / the Macedonian man *(Makkadunaya)*, king of Babylon *(šar Bābili)* / am I.[122]

These can be tabulated as shown in Table 1.

The reigning monarch's titulature far surpasses his predecessor's in degree and number of honors: father and son share no more than *šar Bābili* ("king of Babylon"). In itself, this is a standard trope of Mesopotamian "heroic priority."[123] Conspicuously, however, Seleucus alone is identified as *Makkadunaya* ("the Macedonian");[124] the classification corresponds to Seleucus I's Homeward Bound proclamation. But Antiochus does not bear this ethnic label. The cylinder recognizes that *Makkadunaya* possesses a salience for

Table 1. Royal titles in the Borsippa Cylinder

Seleucus I	Antiochus I
King	
	Great King
	Mighty King
	King of the World
	King of Lands
Macedonian	
King of Babylon	King of Babylon
	Caretaker of Esagil and Ezida
	Foremost heir of Seleucus

Seleucus that it does not for his son. In the passage from first- to second-generation rule we witness Macedonia sinking beneath the horizon. In such a formal and carefully written inscription the dramatic absence acknowledges more than Antiochus' half-Iranian ethnicity and Asian upbringing. It encodes the abandonment of Macedonia from Seleucid space. The royal inscription continues:

> When I decided to build Esagil and Ezida, the bricks for Esagil and Ezida I molded with my pure hands (using) fine quality oil in the land of Hatti (*ina* ^kur^*Hatti*), and for the laying of the foundation of Esagil and Ezida I brought (them) *(ubbil)*.[125]

King Antiochus has performed the ancient brick-making ceremony "in the land of Hatti" and then conveyed his ready-made mud bricks to Borsippa, presumably floating them down the Euphrates. ^kur^*Hatti* is an archaizing Akkadian word for northern Syria.[126] The Babylonian text has located the king's opening rituals in the Syrian Seleucis. This non-Babylonian setting and the subsequent royal journey are totally unparalleled in Mesopotamian building inscriptions, deviating from the centralizing tendencies typical of the genre's sacred geography and fundamentally unlike the dispatch to Babylon of unprocessed raw materials, like cedar trunks, from peripheral lands. Furthermore, when Antiochus' wife, queen Stratonice, is mentioned in the cylinder's concluding prayer, she is called *Astartanikku*;[127] this is a theophoric transliteration built on the north Syrian goddess Astarte, cognate with Babylonian Ishtar. Thus, the reigning king and queen are identified with and embedded in their north Syrian heartland. That the Borsippa

Cylinder, a cuneiform composition of priestly scribes buried at the foot of a Babylonian temple, should reproduce so exactly the Seleucid dynasty's *translatio patriae* suggests, once again, the wide dissemination and localized reinforcement of official Seleucid spatial ideology.

The Lost World

The dynastic displacement from Macedonia to Syria transformed official Seleucid notions of place, community, and identity. This development was not restricted to the reshaped landscape of northern Syria. Bound up with reconfiguring a new homeland was a reimagining of the ancestral and once familiar Old World. That is to say, the failure of Homeward Bound not only sundered the Seleucid house from Macedonia but also transformed the nature of successive kings' interactions with the southern Balkan peninsula. The metamorphosis of the dynasty's westward gaze can be most clearly demonstrated by a comparison of Seleucus I's European military campaign and euergetism to those of Antiochus III and Antiochus IV, respectively.

After Seleucus I's murder, Antiochus II Theos and Antiochus Hierax had campaigned in Europe, but, as we have seen in Chapter 3, their military activities were limited to traditional Seleucid possessions in Thrace. Antiochus III's war with Rome was the first attempt to expand Seleucid power into mainland territories since Seleucus I's aborted Homeward Bound campaign. Accordingly, Antiochus III's Greek campaign of 193–192 foregrounds to an unprecedented degree the later Seleucid monarchy's relationship to its land of origin.

At some point before 192 Menippus, Antiochus III's ambassador to Rome and Aetolia and, later, his military commander in Boeotia and Stratos,[128] dedicated on the sacred island of Delos a statue to "King Antiochus the Great, son of king Seleucus Callinicus, the Macedonian, his own savior and benefactor" ([Β]ασιλέα [μέγαν] | Ἀντίοχο[ν] | βασιλέως Σελεύκ[ου] | [Κ]αλλινίκου | [Μ]ακεδόνα | τὸν α[ὑ]το[ῦ] σωτῆρ[α] | [κ]αὶ ε[ὑ]ε[ργέ]την).[129] The official, programmatic inscription pronounced to an Old World audience Antiochus' identity as Macedonian, Μακεδών; the statue base constitutes, to my knowledge, the only extant use of this ethnic label in formal royal titulature for any of Seleucus I's successors. Its association with Antiochus III's mainland ambitions is evident. Menippus' dedication tactically redeployed a long overshadowed identity at this Panhellenic sanctuary to naturalize renewed Seleucid involvement in the western Aegean.[130] It is an important echo of Seleucus I's post-Corupedium proclamation of homesickness.

However, Antiochus III's campaign demonstrates a different set of values and priorities. In contrast to Seleucus I's campaign, Antiochus III's Greek expedition lacked any sense of a homeward return. Polybius and the historians who follow him reproduce in extended detail the opposed Roman and Seleucid claims and counterclaims of the "Cold War" diplomatic negotiation that preceded the military confrontation.[131] At no point did Antiochus III attempt to legitimize his presence in Europe by the organic entitlements of Macedonian ethnicity or homeland. Instead, the king's argumentation privileged Seleucus I's defeat of Lysimachus and the hereditability of spear-won land.[132] Furthermore, Seleucid forces never approached Macedonia proper. Livy recounts the transportation of king and army from the Hellespont into the Gulf of Pagasae in Thessaly, island-hopping Imbros to Sciathos to Pteleon.[133] Seleucid attention was exclusively focused on Central Greece's Aegean littoral—Chalcis on Euboea, Demetrias on the coast of Thessaly, and the storied pass of Thermopylae. Importantly, Antiochus and his Aetolian allies sponsored the wild claim to the throne of Macedonia of a certain Philip of Megalopolis.[134] In an obvious attempt to embarrass Philip V, the Antigonid ruler of Macedonia, the pretender Philip buried the Macedonian dead still lying on the battlefield of Cynoscephalae[135]—the Megalopolitan, not the Seleucid, enacted the responsibilities of Macedonian kingship. Indeed, Appian (following Polybius) reports that the Seleucid monarch represented Macedonia as the ancestral land of Philip of Megalopolis: not his own.[136]

Antiochus III's Greek campaign was a rashly opportunistic attempt to undercut the Roman Flamininus' 196 settlement of Greek affairs and thereby extend Seleucid influence into new regions. It was a war of expansion from Asia, not a war of return to Europe: the king did not attempt to turn an absence back into a loss in the manner of, say, Herzl's Zionism. Almost a century after Homeward Bound, the southern Balkan peninsula had been reduced to a proxy pawn of Great Power competition.

Let us move on to Antiochus III's son, Antiochus IV Epiphanes. Royal benefaction or donation was one of the more distinctive codes of interaction between territorial Hellenistic monarchies and independent Greek city-states: bilaterally, the *euergesia* of external kings gave symbolic expression to relationships of patronage or dependence and bore within themselves reciprocal obligations; globally, they participated in the competitive liberality and international ostentation of the multistate world order.[137] Seleucid euergetism in the Greek mainland never matched the levels of the Antigonid, Ptolemaic, or Attalid peer kingdoms.[138] Of the entire dynasty, only Seleucus I and Antiochus IV directed ideologically charged and meaningful acts of beneficence toward the *poleis* of central and southern Greece. Importantly, these two kings' gifts advertised markedly different cultural and political identities.

Soon after his victory over Lysimachus at Corupedium, Seleucus I had restored the island of Lemnus to Athens and received in return cult honors.[139] Such nesiotic assignments were a recurrent feature of the early Hellenistic period's geopolitics (see Chapter 6) and are of limited significance here. More interestingly, Athenian comic fragments indicate that Seleucus I donated a pair of Indian tigers to Athens;[140] it is likely that these beasts originated as a diplomatic gift of Chandragupta Maurya (see Chapter 1).[141] In his *Neaira* the comic poet Philemon humorously invoked the language of peer-polity gift exchange:

(A) Just as Seleucus sent the tigress here (δεῦρ'), which we have seen, we in turn ought to send back (ἀντιπέμψαι) to Seleucus some beast from us.

(B) A *trugeranos;* that animal doesn't exist over there (αὐτόθι).[142]

Since nothing more of the play survives, any interpretation of the joke is difficult. Certainly, the punch line exposes the actual imbalance between city-state and Asian empire: the Athenians are obliged to concoct an imaginary creature, the *trugeranos,* in order to reciprocate Seleucus' Indian wonder.[143] And at the very least, the donation of tigers to Athens bracketed the full expansiveness of Seleucus' domain, from the Hindu Kush to the Mediterranean. As the spatial opposition δεῦρ'-αὐτόθι, "here"-"there," demonstrates, Seleucus' faunal sensation deliberately advertised his kingdom's alien, eastern territories.

Almost a century and a half later, Antiochus IV Epiphanes' extraordinary generosity, earning even the admiration of Polybius,[144] framed a very different flavor of cultural dialogue between donor-king and recipient cities. On the Greek mainland, the king resumed the construction—abandoned since the fall of the Athenian tyrants—of the colossal temple to Zeus Olympius,[145] defrayed the cost of Megalopolis' city walls,[146] and funded a marble theater at Tegea;[147] in the Aegean, he erected an altar and statues on the island of Delos; on the western coast of Asia Minor he bestowed a golden table service on Cyzicus' Prytaneum,[148] and at Miletus his agents Timarchus and Heraclides built in his honor a new *bouleuterion*.[149] It is possible that Antiochus IV is the king to whom Pausanias attributes the gifts of the gilt bronze aegis on the south wall of the Athenian Acropolis, above the Theater of Dionysus,[150] and the "Assyrian" curtain in the Temple of Zeus at Olympia.[151] Antiochus IV's benefactions privileged the most prominent and exclusive markers of Old World classical Greek identity—civic government, theatrical performance, ancient sanctuaries. By continuing the work of the sixth-century tyrant Pisistratus at Athens and emulating the fourth-century Theban general Epaminondas at Megalopolis the Seleucid monarch jostled himself into an archaic and classical inheritance. Antiochus IV's mainland euergetism expresses an anxiety—a defensive, emphatic, public assertion of belonging.[152] Certainly, this was a function of distance: the territorial concessions that followed Antiochus III's defeat by Rome had rolled Seleucid space back across the Taurus mountains, detaching the kingdom from the Aegean world for the first time since the Corupedium campaign. Diaspora studies have long recognized that, as the mother-location becomes more distant, blurred, and indeterminate, so ideas of cultural distinctiveness, conservatism, and authenticity possess ever more salience to its colonial or diasporic populations.[153] Where the flamboyant exoticism of Seleucus I's tigers demonstrates the founder-king's assumed and confident Graeco-Macedonian identity, Antiochus IV's stereotypical Hellenism betrays the exaggerated compensation of a colonial Mimic Man.[154]

Father and son, Antiochus III and IV, manifest the transformation of the dynasty's official attitude to the Graeco-Macedonian mainland over the course of the third century: a waning of affective, homeland ties; a southward trajectory from Macedonia to central and southern Greece, from Macedonicity to Hellenicity; the preference for political sponsorship and euergetical performance over territorial possession; and the untroubled recognition of this region's existence outside the kingdom's territory.

This second part of the book has examined the closure of Seleucid territory in the west and the imperial structures and ideological figurations that followed from this. The formation of edge and center were, of course, synchronous, dialectically related processes. Seleucus' failure to incorporate his ancestral homeland transformed European Thrace into the kingdom's softly administered and ideologically demoted periphery. Antiochus I's coherent enterprise in diasporic fabrication—in the double sense of construction and invention—successfully and lastingly reembedded dynastic identity in the Syrian Seleucis. By the end of the succession crisis, Antiochus I ruled a landscape centered on northern Syria and bounded in the east and west by the Mauryan and Antigonid kingdoms.

The Kingdom of Asia

The bounding of Seleucid territory was an inhalation of Alexander's empire. The kingdom's first two rulers, Seleucus I and Antiochus I, generated a closed imperial space by shedding its latitudinal extremities. In each case, (claims to) lands were relinquished by bilateral peace treaty. The Seleucus-Chandragupta and Antiochus-Antigonus agreements were foundational, both as moment and process. The withdrawals, mirrored at east and west, figured the Seleucid empire as the Hellenistic world's middle kingdom, lying between the Mauryan and Antigonid states. They generated a related sense of regional centrality for the north Syrian core, toward which the imperial edges withdrew. The treaties, as we have seen, retained their territorial salience, framing a relatively stable spatial unit from the Hindu Kush to European Thrace, until the reign of Antiochus III at the end of the third century. Most importantly, the treaties also inaugurated the kingdom's long-term historical dynamic of centripetal retraction and established the authorized precedents and modes for later imperial withdrawals. So, when Antiochus III acknowledged the sovereign independence of Euthydemus' kingdom in Bactria in 206 (see Chapter 2) and signed Asia Minor over to Eumenes II in the Peace of Apamea in 188 (see Chapter 5), both withdrawals, at east and west, replayed and conformed to his ancestors' diplomatic matrix. The prototype peace treaties with India and Macedonia allowed later Seleucid kings in person to delimit anew Seleucid territory and the kingdom to adapt to its declining power with ideological coherence; the Seleucids did not throw sand against the wind. The practice clearly distinguished between royally authorized territorial renunciations and illegitimate acts of rebellion: that is to say, the negotiated diplomatic agreement with Euthydemus of Bactria could reshape official Seleucid space, whereas the de facto independence of insurgent Parthians could not. This model remained fairly constant throughout the third and second centuries. The history of official Seleucid territorial boundaries is no more than the movement of successive kings through this ideological structure.

One significant border had not been fixed in this way and would remain a focus of conflict for the empire's full lifespan—that with Ptolemaic Egypt. The cause lay in the unfulfilled division of Antigonus Monophthalmus' kingdom following the battle of Ipsus in 301: although the entire Levantine coast, with its wealthy Phoenician cities, had been awarded as a prize of war to Seleucus Nicator, its center and south were seized by Ptolemy I, and while Seleucus agreed not to fight a friend to whom he owed so much, he and his descendants retained their claims to rightful possession of the region.[1] Consequently, and in contrast to the diplomatically established borders to east and west, the Ptolemaic frontier in Syria was a zone of fierce, recurring dispute for two centuries, encouraged by a rift valley geography that eased north-south movement between the kingdoms. According to the empire's official ideology, the history of this southwestern border was simple: Seleucid sovereignty extended to the Sinai peninsula, but this remained unexercised until Antiochus III undid Ptolemy I's theft of Coele Syria and Phoenicia at the battle of Panium in 200.[2] But on the ground the situation was far messier. The Seleucid kings for most of the third century were obliged to accept a territorial division at the Eleutherus river (mod. Nahr el-Kalb), which runs westward into the Mediterranean through the Homs Gap, the depression between the coastal mountains of modern Syria and Lebanon.[3] To the north of the river's mouth, the Phoenician island city of Aradus (mod. Arwad) and its extensive *peraia* functioned as a Seleucid-affiliated buffer, leveraging its location to win various privileges from the Syrian kings.[4] Furthermore, the wartime incursions of Ptolemy II and III penetrated deep into the Seleucis,[5] garrisoning from the Third to the Fourth Syrian Wars, that is, between 246 and 219, Seleucia-in-Pieria, Seleucus I's royal foundation and burial place, and Ras Ibn Hani, a small settlement a few kilometers north of Laodicea-by-the-Sea.[6] And during the second century, after Antiochus III's conquest of Coele Syria and Phoenicia, the region was incorporated into the Seleucid empire only incompletely and fitfully,[7] retained the previous Ptolemaic weight standards and so commercial orientation,[8] and suffered periodic interventions from Alexandria.[9]

That a sense of coherent Seleucid space was born and configured by a series of managed retreats at its eastern and western peripheries, along with claimed but unheld territory to its south, gave a distinctive texture to its landscape. Hand in hand with the recognition of bilateral boundaries and external peer kingdoms came the insistence that all in-between territory—everything from the eastern to the western frontiers, including Coele Syria and Phoenicia—was Seleucid. Although the dynasty's effective exercise of political sovereignty was, of course, irregular, fragmentary, and of variable intensity, its spatial ideology flattened this into an uninterrupted territorial unity. The Ptolemaic empire, which developed its own sophisticated spatial ideology, offers itself as a useful contrast. Where the kings of Alexandria ruled over a maritime (coastal or nesiotic), segmented, and dispersed constellation of provincial enclaves, the Seleucid monarchs governed a contiguous, continental, "Oceanic" spatial unit. The difference between Ptolemaic and Seleucid levels of territorial coherence in part explains the official Ptolemaic habit of listing named provinces and the Seleucid kingdom's avoidance of such a discourse. So, in Theocritus' poetic *Encomium* to Ptolemy II Philadelphus, the Egyptian king "takes slices of" (ἀποτέμνεται) various coastal regions.[10] Interestingly, an inscription of Ptolemy III from Adoulis in Eritrea applies this segmentary list to his territorial conquests in the Seleucid empire in a manner quite unparalleled by any official Seleucid source.[11]

Seleucid imperial space was no horizonless expanse: as we have seen, an explicit and formal recognition of equal peer kingdoms distinguished the Seleucid kingdom from its "universalist" predecessors, Alexandrian, Achaemenid, and Neo-Assyrian. Parts I and II have examined the enormous ideological effort put into naturalizing the new eastern and western frontiers. But it should be recognized that, taken together, the kingdom's borders delimited a contiguous territorial whole. Although the unified landscape was the end result of a violent and agglomerative process, it was taken as the starting point for the kingdom's developed spatial ideology, like Wittgenstein's ladder, which one discards after climbing up. Did this imperial unit, this Seleucid space, have its own name? It has been argued very influentially that no term officially designated the Seleucid empire; in Greek inscriptions and historiography it was known simply as the king's *basileia* ("kingdom"), *archē* ("rule"), or *ta pragmata* ("the affairs").[12] Undeniably, the terminological variation indicates that a strictly juridical or constitutional name for the kingdom *qua* political entity was lacking. Even so, the bounded imperial landscape fitted into, made use of, and ultimately derived a legitimacy from established Near Eastern and Greek geographical concepts of coherent territorial blocks.

The spatial unit framed by Seleucus I, Antiochus I, and their agents corresponded to long-standing and influential Babylonian geographical traditions, attested by a unique cuneiform tablet giving a bird's-eye sketch of the earth's surface and various literary compositions.[13] In brief, the world was held to be a continental landmass, surrounded by a circular river or canal *(marratu)*, beyond which lay barbarian peripheral "regions" *(nagû)*. The Seleucid kingdom's promise of Oceanic roundability (Patrocles' *periplus*, the Caucasian canal, the Hellespont, the Aegean, the Persian Gulf),[14] the outlying barbarism of Central Asia and European Thrace, the latter's function as a peripheral *nagû*, and the centrality of the Fertile Crescent all correlate to standard Mesopotamian concentric world geography. The Babylonian name for the great Seleucid colony Antioch-by-Daphne, situated not far from the Mediterranean coast, was [uru]*an-tu-uk-ki-'a ana* ugu [id]*ma-rat*, "Antioch on the shore of the *marratu*."[15] What is new is that this formerly "universal" continental territory has been incorporated as but one unit, albeit the central one, of a much larger, multistate *oikoumenē*. Third-century Seleucid space approximates, matryoshka-like, the traditional Near Eastern model of a continent encircled by the Bitter Sea within the wider global framework of an updated Greek model of a world encircled by Ocean.

Of greater significance was the assimilation of Seleucid territory to the Greek concept of Asia. Alexander's campaigns and the conflicts that followed his death had given to "Asia" a political meaning and a bounded territorial connotation opposed to the Graeco-Macedonian mainland.[16] Although "king of Asia" was not authentic Achaemenid titulature,[17] Greeks and Macedonians had long used it as a designation for the Persian monarch.[18] Alexander's victories turned this loosely applied term into the conqueror's formally proclaimed royal title.[19] Later, the power-sharing agreements between Alexander's Successors recognized the "generalship of Asia" and the "generalship of Europe" as the two supreme military commands;[20] both territories were personified in the famous fresco series from Boscoreale.[21] It was this geopolitical concept of "Asia" that was employed by the Seleucid house (and various other groups) to designate the Seleucid political landscape. Greek texts dependent on Seleucid court historiography title Seleucus I Nicator and his successors "kings of Asia."[22] The road survey of the Seleucid kingdom mentioned by Strabo, Athenaeus, and Aelian (see Chapter Six), called the *Stations of Asia*, seems to have used the continental term in its full geopolitical significance.[23] In his negotiations with Rome Antiochus III deployed this sense of "Asia" to legitimize Seleucid possession of the Hellespont, Aeolis, and Ionia.[24] An inscription erected in Babylon by the *syntrophos* and future corpse conveyer Philip (see Chapter 4) honored Antiochus IV as, among other things, "savior of Asia" (σωτῆρος τῆς Ἀσίας);[25] "Asia" here must mean the Seleucid kingdom since only political entities or individuals could be the object of Hellenistic royal salvation.[26] In 145 Ptolemy VI, having driven Alexander I Balas out of Syria, was crowned with two diadems by the inhabitants of Antioch-by-Daphne as monarch of Asia and Egypt, i.e., the Seleucid and Ptolemaic kingdoms (δύο περιτίθεται διαδήματα, ἓν μὲν τὸ τῆς Ἀσίας, ἕτερον δὲ τὸ τῆς Αἰγύπτου).[27] The double diadem illustrates not only the correspondence of the Seleucid kingdom to Asia but also a developed sense of sovereign Seleucid territory independent of the king, much as James VI of Scotland was separately crowned James I of England in 1603.[28] The "diadem of Asia" phrase is used again of the pretender Diodotus Tryphon's autocoronation three years later (περιέθετο τὸ διάδημα τῆς Ἀσίας).[29] Jewish[30] and Babylonian[31] writings in Greek adopted the same terminology, while Roman propaganda turned the concept against Antiochus III.[32] The Seleucid empire was Asia.

The first half of the book has investigated the methods by which the Seleucid kingdom conceived its eastern and western peripheries. As a historically situated configuration generated by moments in the reigns of Seleucus I and Antiochus I, the notion of bounded Seleucid territory was a historicizing ideology. It required an official mnemonic tradition, expressed through court-generated discourses and royal behaviors, to identify, privilege, and pass on these particular acts and processes of delimitation. But "space is a practiced place":[33] the second half of the book will turn to the practices that enacted and realized this spatial ideology and to the principal agents and technologies that unfolded it—king and colony.

PART **III**

Movement

CHAPTER 5

Arrivals and Departures

Early July, 168 BCE; the second campaign season of the Sixth Syrian War between the Ptolemaic and Seleucid kingdoms. Eleusis, a dusty suburb in the Egyptian delta, to the east of the Ptolemaic capital; now the Seleucid army's main encampment. King Antiochus IV Epiphanes, newly crowned pharaoh and master of Lower Egypt, presses the siege of Alexandria.

On the horizon "ships of Kittim"[1] shake their sails to landfall. The Roman envoy, Caius Popilius Laenas, marches up to the Seleucid monarch, brusquely shrugs off the myth of diplomatic nicety, and thrusts a *senatus consultum* (senatorial decree) into the king's welcoming hand: end the siege! withdraw from Egypt! or make of Rome an enemy!

Antiochus, quite properly, seeks to consult with his advisors. Popilius Laenas, forbidding this, inscribes a circle around the king with his staff of office:[2] in there think about it and reply!

Mindful of Rome's victory over his father, Antiochus accedes to the demands, withdrawing from Egypt a few days later.[3]

The "Day of Eleusis," as this episode is known, has attracted to itself a profound significance. The historian Polybius paired Popilius' humiliation of Antiochus IV in Egypt with L. Aemilius Paullus' elimination of the Macedonian monarchy following the battle of Pydna as the original conclusion of his historical narrative of Rome's rise to Mediterranean dominance.[4] Modern historians have followed suit, seeing in the sand-circle a primary exhibition of the republic's willingness to humble the Hellenistic monarchs, the extension of a Roman protectorate over Ptolemaic Egypt, and the diplomatic efficacy of the mere threat of Roman displeasure.[5] Even if the episode's importance has been overplayed, there is no doubting that Antiochus IV's acquiescence acknowledged Roman superiority. But C. Popilius Laenas' specific action—tracing a circle around the king—meant much more than separating Antiochus from his advisors or forcing on him a quick decision. Popilius' gesture should be understood as a visual translation of his diplomatic message. For the circle in the sand actualized the possibilities and inhibitions of Seleucid space.

Rome's intervention in the Sixth Syrian War insisted on the independent territorial integrity of the Ptolemaic and Seleucid kingdoms; the *senatus consultum* demanded that Antiochus IV abandon his Egyptian conquests and return to the Seleucid realm. This senatorial modeling of separate spatial units, reinforcing the traditional multipolar Hellenistic world order, was sketched onto the Egyptian beach. Popilius Laenas' actions should be understood as a minatory spatial fable, laying out for the besieging king a set of options and their consequences. The logic seems to run as follows: Laenas' encircling of Antiochus Epiphanes, by a sort of symbolic reversal, restored the monarch to his kingdom; the king now stands within a bounded territorial unit that can only represent Seleucid territory. As long as Antiochus remains within this bounded territory, he retains an independent dominion without fear of Roman intervention. The king then determines the mode in which he steps out of the circle, crosses out of Seleucid space: either the monarch can march out of his kingdom in an expansionist war of appropriation and face the wrath of Rome, or he can publicly express his peaceful intent and amicably cross into an external, friendly territory without fear of conflict. As we have seen, chastened by his father's defeat by Rome at the battle of Magnesia, Antiochus Epiphanes chose, albeit in high dudgeon, to abandon Egypt and march back into Coele Syria, where he would unload his bile on Jerusalem. Laenas' circle orchestrated for king Antiochus a symbolic, perhaps even quasi-magical,[6] replay of his entry into Egypt, exchanging the first hostile path for the second peaceful one.

The Day of Eleusis represents, not C. Popilius Laenas' on-the-spot invention of a territorial architectonics suited to senatorial ambitions, but the manipulation of the Seleucid kingdom's own ideology of delimited space. Although in this case it is the Roman *legatus,* not the monarch, who bounds the kingdom, the sand-circle actualized legitimate and widely paralleled principles of Seleucid territoriality. This third part of *The Land of the Elephant Kings* examines the modes of Seleucid royal travel and the repertoire of actions by which the mobile kings could embody spatial claims, and articulate territory. The nature of our source material means that for these chapters we have only isolated historical moments to investigate; but by teasing them apart, reading them against one another, and standing back to look at the big picture we can reveal the underlying, structuring spatial logic.

Border Coronations

Seleucus I Nicator, by generating an imperial territory about himself, and his immediate successors, by campaigning only within the kingdom's boundaries, never had occasion to cross into their own kingdom. Things changed after the Roman defeat of Antiochus III, when the terms of the Apamea peace settlement demanded that senior royals reside as hostages in Rome. For the first time, Seleucid princes dwelt outside their kingdom, interrupting the practice of presuccession viceroyship, which had identified the heir and eased his inauguration. Accordingly, in the course of the second century numerous princes and pretenders to the Seleucid throne crossed into the kingdom from outside to claim their birthright. The homology of entry and accession underscores the legitimizing qualities of Seleucid space. The territory itself bequeathed to the king his diadem.

We are fortunate to possess an extended testimony of Antiochus IV's coronation at the threshold of Seleucid space. The constellation of events and people is as follows. At the close of 176 Seleucus IV, the successor of Antiochus III, was murdered by his vizier, Heliodorus.[7] The victim's first-born son, Demetrius, was held in Rome as a hostage, and the Senate refused to release him.[8] Demetrius' younger brother, Antiochus, though present in Syria, was a mere child. At the time of the assassination, Antiochus (IV Epiphanes)—the uncle of the Roman hostage Demetrius and his younger brother Antiochus, the younger sibling of Seleucus IV, and the youngest son of Antiochus III—was in Athens;[9] as the only unobstructed senior member of the dynasty he headed for Syria. Prince Antiochus, having sailed from Athens to Asia Minor, was escorted to the Seleucid border by the Attalid king, Eumenes II, and his brothers Attalus, Philetaerus, and Athenaeus. The events are narrated in an honorific decree passed by the Athenian Council, which was inscribed—following the prince's journey—in the agora at Athens, in the sanctuary of Athena Nicephorus at Pergamum (the fragmentary extant copy), and in the sanctuary of Apollo at Daphne, near Antioch in northern Syria.[10] The historical narrative runs as follows:

When Seleucus died [and since the calamity] invited this, as [Eumenes and his brothers] saw that the occasion was providing for them [an opportunity] to lay in store a favor as benefactors, they considered everything else to be of no relevance and placed themselves at his disposal, and accompanying him up to the frontiers of his own kingdom (μέχρι τῶν ὁρίων τῆς ἰδίας βασιλείας συμπροελθόντες), providing him with money and furnishing him with military forces, crowning him with the diadem along with the other suitable apparel (τῷ διαδήματι μετὰ τῆς ἄλλης κατασκευῆς κοσμήσαντες ὡς καθῆκεν), offering sacrifices and exchanging pledges of faith with each other with all good will and affection, in a memorable way they helped in restoring to his ancestral kingdom king Antiochus (συγκατέστησαν ἐπὶ τὴμ πατρῴαν ἀρχην τὸμ βασιλέα Ἀντίοχον).[11]

The inscription describes a journey and a status transformation. Antiochus processes as a prince in the entourage of Eumenes II until he reaches the boundary of Seleucid territory. This subordinate mode of travel amounts to a formal recognition of the terms of the Apamea peace treaty of 188, imposed by Rome on Antiochus III, by which all Seleucid territorial possessions in Asia Minor had been transferred to the Attalid kings of Pergamum. The journey physically acts out, both to the processing parties and to the witnessing communities along their path, Antiochus' acknowledged renunciation of all claims to this ancestral region. Whereas Seleucus IV had maintained throughout his reign an attitude of hostility toward the Attalid house, Eumenes' royal process unfolds a new era of friendly relations, confirmed by sacrifices and pledges at Antiochus' coronation. At the post-188 border of "his own kingdom" (τῆς ἰδίας βασιλείας) Antiochus was transformed from a prince into a king. According to a king-making *rite de passage,* Antiochus (the "ritual passenger," to use Victor Turner's term[12]) passed from one state to another by the adoption of the diadem, change of dress, and, presumably, appropriate gestures and acclamations.[13] These threshold rituals functioned as an elevation to power. Antiochus, now as *basileus,* proceeded to Antioch. Seleucid kingship and Seleucid territory were coterminous: Antiochus entered imperial space as the crowned and legitimate ruler.[14] Although Antiochus IV's threshold coronation was a ceremony without wide audience, the Athenian council's decree, publicly recited at festivals in Athens, Pergamum, and Daphne, advertised to a Seleucid and international world the prince's elevation. Indeed, the decree linguistically reperformed the ceremony, reserving to the end of the lengthy sentence, after we have processed to the border and witnessed the coronation, the title and name "king Antiochus."

Antiochus IV's accession, when the sons of Seleucus IV were still alive, was a coup. It fundamentally challenged the vertical, determinate system of hereditary rule and, despite his subsequent murder of Seleucus IV's younger son, Antiochus,[15] inaugurated the internecine quarreling that would tear the empire apart. For the next three decades two rival lines—the children and grandchildren of Seleucus IV and Antiochus IV, respectively—competed for control as their kingdom tottered. The bifurcation of the formerly exclusive primogeniture succession and the consequent competition between legacies brought to the fore the legitimating qualities of Seleucid territory.

The historical pattern was set by Seleucus IV's older son, Demetrius (I), who, soon after the death of his uncle, Antiochus IV, fled his captivity at Rome for Syria.[16] Polybius, having played a prominent role in organizing Demetrius' escape, narrates the thrilling story:[17] a disguised prince Demetrius slipped himself onto a Carthaginian pilgrimage vessel that was carrying the Roman Punic community's first fruits to Phoenicia; en route, in Lycia, he sent to the Senate to justify his actions;[18] we next learn that Demetrius made landfall at Tripolis, where he crowned himself with the diadem.[19] At Tripolis Demetrius "entered into the kingdom" (εἰς τὴν βασιλείαν εἰσῆλθε);[20] like Antiochus IV, Demetrius was raised to kingship only at the gates of empire—a transformation of status achieved by the spatial translation from Rome, via the sea, to the Seleucid littoral.[21] The Greek translation of the Hasmonaean dynasty's Hebrew chronicle, 1 Maccabees, reports with forceful and generalizing simplicity that Demetrius "arrived with a few men in a seaside city (εἰς πόλιν παραθαλασσίαν) and began to reign there (ἐβασίλευσεν ἐκεῖ)."[22] The sentence could apply to seven similarly structured but sketchily reported coastal coronations of Seleucid kings: Alexander I Balas, at Antioch-in-Ptolemaïs, in 153/2;[23] Demetrius II Nicator, in Cilicia, perhaps at Mallus, in 147;[24] Antiochus VII Sidetes, at Seleucia-in-Pieria, in 138;[25] and, amid the final dynastic agony, Antiochus IX Cyzicenus, probably at Seleucia-in-Pieria, in 113;[26] Demetrius III, again probably at Seleucia-in-Pieria, in 97;[27] Antiochus X Eusebes, at Aradus, in 95;[28] and perhaps Antiochus XIII Asiaticus, somewhere in Syria, in 69.[29]

The gateway harbors, between kingdom and sea, and the bilateral boundary, between peer states, both welded together and opposed discrete spatial units. In these nine cases (at least) the border of the Seleucid kingdom emerges as a site of metamorphosis, a *Zwischenraum*, that transformed princes into kings. As much as the edge of Seleucid territory demanded the threshold ritual, so the coronations themselves performed it into visibility, just as today's passport checks, immigration control, and luggage inspections give the nation-state border a spatial presence.[30] The boundary of Seleucid space was the exclusive *terminus a quo* for kingship. The prince neither became king before he entered Seleucid territory nor delayed his coronation to some later point after his arrival; rather, the status elevation occurred at the precise point of crossing. It is difficult to find a clearer demonstration of the dynasty's profound conception of territoriality.

Departing in Peace, Departing in War

In the ledgers of the kingdom royal arrivals are more common than royal departures. Yet specific instances of Seleucid kings leaving imperial territory again display the kingdom's official recognition of its boundaries. As Popilius Laenas had demonstrated so dramatically, the monarch's exit could play itself out in two modes, peace and war.

We know of two peaceful exits—Seleucus I's relations with Demetrius Poliorcetes on the Bay of Issus (mod. Gulf of Iskenderun) and Antiochus III's crossing of the Hindu Kush. In the diplomatic repositioning that followed the defeat of Antigonus Monophthalmus at Ipsus in 301, Ptolemy in Egypt allied with Lysimachus in Asia Minor, and Seleucus in Syria with the vanquished and stateless son of Antigonus, Demetrius Poliorcetes (see Chapter 3).[31] To secure their alliance, Seleucus married Stratonice, Demetrius' daughter by Phila, at the coastal town of Rhosus, in the Bay of Issus.[32] Plutarch preserves an account of their meeting and festivities:

> Demetrius set out from the sea-coast. . . . His wife Phila was already with him and, at Rhosus, he was met by Seleucus. Their exchanges were at once put on a royal footing and knew neither guile nor suspicion. First, Seleucus entertained Demetrius at his tent in the army camp (πρότερον μὲν Σέλευκος ἑστιάσας ἐπὶ σκηνῆς ἐν τῷ στρατοπέδῳ Δημήτριον), then Demetrius in his turn received Seleucus on board his thirteen-decker ship (αὖθις δὲ Δημήτριος ἐκεῖνον ἐν τῇ τρισκαιδεκήρει δεξάμενος). There were also amusements, long conferences with one another, and whole days spent together, all without guards or arms; until at length, Seleucus took Stratonice and went up in great state to Antioch (Σέλευκος τὴν Στρατονίκην ἀναλαβὼν λαμπρῶς εἰς Ἀντιόχειαν ἀνέβη).[33]

The balanced etiquette of Rhosus pivots on the identification of clearly distinct zones of authority, in which husband and father-in-law could each play the host: Seleucus' tent and Demetrius' ship—an obvious polarity of land and sea—function as separate sovereign spaces. On Demetrius' flagship, moored just off Seleucus' imperial territory, the founder-king was received as a guest. By his subordinate behavior, Seleucus recognized the spatial limits of his sovereignty. The marriage that concluded this performance of parity can be seen as a sort of boundary coronation, like those of Antiochus IV and his successors, discussed earlier: Stratonice, having been recognized as queen in this gateway harbor, entered the kingdom and marched in state up to Antioch-by-Daphne.[34] It may be fair to assume similar boundary-articulated behavior for other interdynastic marriages. A letter of Artemidorus from the Ptolemaic Zenon archive records that he and Apollonius escorted Berenice, daughter of Ptolemy II and soon-to-be second wife of Antiochus II, "up to the border" of the Seleucid kingdom (συμπεπορευμένοι τῇ βασιλίσσῃ ἕως τῶν ὁρίων), where, presumably, she was received in state by the Seleucid monarch or his representatives;[35] the participial phrase quoted here comes remarkably close to that of the Antiochus IV inscription, given earlier. 1 Maccabees and Josephus report that, just over a century later, Ptolemy VI escorted his daughter, Cleopatra Thea, by ship to the coastal city Antioch-in-Ptolemaïs, where he was welcomed by Alexander I Balas and the marriage celebrated "with great glory, in the manner of kings."[36] We learn from Jewish sources that the Hasmonaean High Priest Jonathan was summoned to join the celebration,[37] where he received honors from both kings (τῆς παρ᾽ ἀμφοτέρων ἀπέλαυσε τιμῆς),[38] recalling the balanced sovereignty of the Rhosus marriage. The process most likely took place in reverse for the marriage of Antiochus III's daughter, Cleopatra Syra, to Ptolemy V: the wedding occurred at Raphia, on the post-Panium boundary between the two kingdoms.[39]

The second known instance of a Seleucid monarch leaving Seleucid space in peace has already been discussed in some detail in Chapter 1. In about 206 Antiochus III marched his army over the Hindu Kush into northwestern India. Polybius, making use of a Seleucid court historian, reports that Antiochus "renewed his friendship with Sophagasenus, king of the Indians" (τήν τε φιλίαν ἀνενεώσατο τὴν πρὸς τὸν Σοφαγασῆνον τὸν βασιλέα τῶν Ἰνδῶν).[40] Unfortunately, we do not know by what procedures this *philia*, or diplomatic friendship, was reenacted. Certainly, the Seleucid monarch, recognizing the terms of the peace treaty between Seleucus I and Chandragupta, made no sovereign claims on Subhagasena's territory even though the Mauryan kingdom had disintegrated in the intervening century.[41] Antiochus' actions in northwest India stand in isolation from the rest of his great eastern expedition, which was characterized throughout by the king's insistence on his exclusive and legitimate sovereignty.

The renunciations of sovereignty by Seleucus I in the Bay of Issus and by Antiochus III in the Hindu Kush recognized that the monarchs had passed in peace beyond the horizon of legitimate Seleucid territory. This traditional boundary was acknowledged and rearticulated in war by the only two campaigns of imperial expansion ever launched by the Seleucid dynasty after the founder-king's reign—the Greek expedition of Antiochus III (192–191) and the Sixth Syrian War of his son Antiochus IV (170–168). In each case, the conquest of geographical regions beyond the circumscribed landscape of Seleucid space demanded creative rites of incorporation that both strongly distinguished these new possessions from the kingdom's inherited territorial unit and characterized their subordination to the Seleucid monarch in entirely novel ways.

In late 192 Antiochus III conquered Euboea, a narrow finger-island lying off the northern coast of Attica, which had never before been part of the Seleucid kingdom. According to a hostile tradition reported by Polybius and his redactors, in early 191 Antiochus established his base in the city of Chalcis and fell in love with and wedded the daughter of a wealthy local, Cleoptolemus.[42] Not only, Polybius grumbles, was the marriage morally unsuitable—the king was over fifty, his bride a mere teenager—but in addition Antiochus and his army frittered away the winter with drunken festivities and enervating debauchery while Rome gathered her resources and recruited allies. This *caprice d'ivrogne* narrative has been accepted without major challenge,[43] but the Polybian report disguises an unrecognized and quite extraordinary ritual of territorial absorption.[44]

The standing account is problematic. The accusations of a wasted winter are unfounded, for Livy's own narrative demonstrates that Antiochus and his army were busy throughout the season.[45] Far more importantly, the status of Antiochus' new Chalcidian bride is unclear. Antiochus III had married Laodice, daughter of Mithridates II of Pontus, immediately following his accession in 221, by whom he fathered Antiochus, Seleucus (IV), and Antiochus (IV).[46] She had accompanied him to Asia Minor in 196, where, at Iasus in Caria, she donated grain to fund the dowries of the city's poor daughters.[47] In 193, just over a year before Antiochus' supposed marriage to his Chalcidian girl-wife, the king had established a pan-imperial cult for Laodice, praising "the affection and care she shows in her life with us."[48] It is clear that Laodice survived her husband by at least a decade, for a Babylonian Astronomical Diary reports rumors of her death in 182,[49] and a manumission decree from Seleucia-on-the-Eulaeus/Susa "for the safety of" (ὑπὲρ . . . σωτερίας) the reigning Seleucus IV, his wife, his daughter, and "Laodice, the mother of the king" dates to 177/6.[50] We are faced with a conundrum: no Seleucid ruler is known to have engaged in polygamous marriage,[51] and nowhere, even in the most hostile sources, is such a charge hurled at Antiochus III; yet Polybius tells us that the Seleucid monarch married the daughter of an unknown private citizen of Chalcis at a time when queen Laodice was still living and newly honored with cult worship. Louis Robert, who identified the problem, proposed that Laodice was repudiated and later restored to royal dignity either by a regretful Antiochus or his successor and her son Seleucus IV,[52] but this is special pleading. In any case, it must be recognized that the Polybian narrative belongs to a propagandistic tradition that assimilated Antiochus III's invasion of Greece and trouncing by Rome (at Thermopylae!) to the Persian Wars' narratives of self-defeating eastern sensuality.[53] Furthermore, the account carries the imprint of Alexander's edge-of-empire love marriage to the teenage Rhoxane.[54] Having recognized the extant version as a propagandistic and literary distortion, we can reconstruct from its constituent elements an altogether stranger tale.

The king wedded the island. A fragment of Polybius, preserved by Athenaeus, and a passage in Appian's *Syriaca* report that the monarch "gave the girl the name Euboea" (ἔθετο δὲ καὶ τῇ παιδὶ ὄνομα Εὔβοιαν):[55] that is to say, the Seleucid king, soon after conquering Euboea, selected a young girl from the city of Chalcis, renamed her after the island, and married her. Such a manipulation of nomenclature transformed Cleoptolemus' daughter into a living symbol of the island. Thereby, her marriage to Antiochus III could function as a figuration of the island's political subordination and territorial absorption. Antiochus' marriage to "Euboea" should be understood, therefore, not as a love affair that demands our invention of unattested dynastic strife (the divorce of Laodice) but rather as the allegorical integration of the island into the king's sovereign domain. Although the form of this symbolic incorporation is, to my knowledge, unprecedented, the rite resonates with various traditions of political representation. First, a long-standing, indigenous Euboean iconography had generated a personification for their own island: a youthful, female "Euboea," signifying the political-geographical entity, appears on the coinage of the Euboean League (late fifth to early third centuries).⁵⁶ "Euboea" also appears as a dancing maenad, alongside fellow island-maenads "Delos" and "Lemnos," on a cup of the 440s by the Eretria Painter, now in Warsaw.⁵⁷ A second tradition, common to the representational vocabulary of both ancient Near Eastern and Mediterranean empires, figured subject lands and provinces as personifications. For example, early Achaemenid imperial art, from the palaces of Persepolis and the tombs of Naqsh-i Rustam, showed male personifications of each of the Persian empire's subject peoples, labeled and in ethnically distinctive clothing, either bearing tribute to the king or supporting his throne dais. These reliefs, in contrast to typical Mesopotamian and Egyptian imperial iconography, consistently represented the personifications of foreign lands as unfettered and dignified men, joined by sacral covenant in voluntary support of the king.⁵⁸ Personifications of conquered peoples would become a common feature of Roman imperial art, at least from late third-century Roman triumphs.⁵⁹ The sculpted reliefs from the Aphrodisias Sebastium, for instance, depict weak and submissive female provinces: in one scene a striding Claudius, sword in hand, tugs back the head of a prostrate Britannia, who struggles, pathetically, to save her dress from slipping down; in another Nero raises a collapsed Armenia, ready to embrace her to the imperial bosom.⁶⁰ In the Greek world, such personifications could breathe. During the fifth-century Athenian hegemony, female island personifications, in all probability including Euboea, had walked the Old Comic stage. For example, Eupolis' *Poleis* ("Cities") featured a chorus of women representing the Athenians' subject-allies; the few extant fragments suggest that the play explicitly enmeshed the discourses of imperial power and sexual relations (e.g., "And here's Chios—a beautiful one she is! . . . she takes orders wonderfully"⁶¹). The marriage of the island-women to Athens, perhaps personified as the male *dēmos*, plays a substantial role in the comedy's politics, where—as with the matrimony of Antiochus III and "Euboea"—"the relationship between the ideal ally and its putative leader (Athens) is portrayed much as the relationship between the ideal wife and her husband."⁶² Presumably, the chorus of Aristophanes' lost *Nēsoi* ("Islands") was also made up of female island personifications. Such personifications also appear on classical Athenian documentary reliefs, usually in *dexiōsis* with Athena or the personified Athenian *dēmos*.⁶³ In the Hellenistic period, the Seleucids' Ptolemaic neighbors offer a striking parallel to Antiochus' treatment of Euboea. Ptolemy II Philadelphus' famous grand procession at Alexandria, dated to some time in the 270s,[64] contained at its heart *tableaux vivants* of the kingdom's Greek subjects and allies rolling through the streets of Alexandria: "The city of Corinth, crowned with a golden diadem, was standing next to Ptolemy . . . this cart was followed by women who wore expensive robes and jewelry; they were called after (προσηγορεύοντο) the cities of Ionia and the rest of the Greek cities in Asia and on the islands."[65] The personifications are living women who, for the purpose of the parade, have been renamed after Ptolemy's imperial possessions. Antiochus IV's great parade at Daphne contained personifications of Night and Day, Earth and Heaven, Dawn and Midday;[66] the account is abbreviated—perhaps regions or cities were similarly represented.

Personification was the imperial imagination's simple way of embodying territorial conquest. The calm and respectful homosocial bond of Achaemenid art aside, the gendering of these personifications—no island is a man—encodes a political subordination and permits a whole range of sexual metaphor, from rape to wedlock. Whereas the Athenian and Roman provincial personifications deploy an overbearing and aggressive imperial sexuality, Antiochus III's "marriage" to his newly conquered province expressed a polite and honorable relationship entirely in line with the rhetoric of his Greek campaign.[67] Indeed, Plutarch reports that the king's wedding to "Euboea" encouraged the Chalcidians to support his interests most zealously.[68] The innovative island wedding, by which Antiochus III attempted to integrate Euboea into his imperial structure, marked it as a region floating outside bounded Seleucid territory. Whereas the king's earlier military activities in Asia Minor, the Upper Satrapies, and Thrace, all part of the sovereign landscape bounded by Seleucus I and Antiochus I, were officially considered *re*conquests of ancestral territory, the takeover of Euboea was the first act of imperial expansion in the established kingdom's history. As such, it required a unique form of subordination.

Two decades after Antiochus III's marriage to "Euboea," his third son and second successor, Antiochus IV Epiphanes, twice invaded Egypt. Peace had prevailed between the Ptolemaic and Seleucid houses for as long as Antiochus IV's sister, the queen dowager Cleopatra Syra, served as regent for her son Ptolemy VI Philometor. But at her death, power passed to the aggressive courtiers Eulaeus and Lenaeus, and rising bilateral tensions with the Seleucid kingdom coalesced into the Sixth Syrian War. In late 170, an inept Ptolemaic invasion of Coele Syria (lost to Antiochus III in 200, in the Fifth

Syrian War) was easily swept aside by Antiochus IV, who rolled his victorious armies onward into Egypt. Having besieged Alexandria unsuccessfully, in late summer 169 the Seleucid armies withdrew to the Levant. The following year, 168, Antiochus again occupied Egypt, besieging Alexandria for a second time, until obliged by Popilius Laenas' sand-circle ultimatum, discussed earlier, to withdraw.[69] Our understanding of Antiochus' two invasions is severely hindered by the loss of Polybius and the compression of Livy; a clear reconstruction of events is notoriously difficult. Even so, it is apparent that the Seleucid monarch deployed two distinct strategies for control of Egypt that each underscored the land's essential separateness from Seleucid territory.

Antiochus' first invasion (170–169) attempted to establish an informal hegemony over Egypt. When Ptolemy VI Philometor's younger siblings, Cleopatra II and Ptolemy VIII, were proclaimed kings of a rival court in Alexandria in summer 169, Antiochus IV claimed to be defending the interests of his nephew, Ptolemy VI Philometor, in what had become an Egyptian civil war: "His only motive was to assist the elder Ptolemy in securing the position that was his by right of inheritance."[70] It seems that an agreement between Antiochus Epiphanes and Ptolemy Philometor, negotiated by the philosopher and historian Heraclides Lembus,[71] left them as allies. Before an audience of mediating Greek envoys Antiochus acknowledged that Egypt belonged to Ptolemy VI, and the monarchs recognized one another as friends and allies (φίλος or *socius*).[72] It is probable that Antiochus IV usurped the position of guardian to exercise control of the kingdom.[73] The key point: despite his military superiority, Antiochus IV refrained from annexation and articulated his dominance of Egypt through the legitimate structures of a politically sovereign and spatially independent Ptolemaic kingdom.

At the beginning of 168 Ptolemy VI Philometor joined his siblings in Alexandria, and the three young Ptolemies now reconciled their differences into a unity government. Antiochus IV, deprived of his cipher, was provoked into a second invasion of an entirely different character and strategy. With the fig-leaf guardianship discarded, Antiochus embarked on a campaign of nakedly expansionist ambition and destructive aggression.[74] Our scrappy evidence indicates that the Seleucid king quickly secured the submission of the Egyptian *chōra* as the newly crowned pharaoh. We learn from Porphyry of Tyre, as preserved in Jerome's commentary on the biblical book of Daniel, that Antiochus "went up to Memphis and there received the crown in the

Egyptian manner" *(ascendit Memphim, et ibi ex more Aegypti regnum accipiens);*[75] the presence of "the Syrian tyrant" at Memphis was recalled long afterward.[76] A very interesting small papyrus fragment records an instruction of Antiochus IV, as sovereign of Egypt, to the Greek and Macedonian settlers of the "Crocodilopolite" nome, or district, in the Fayum.[77] This nome was usually termed "Arsinoïte"; its renaming suggests that Antiochus was attempting to transform the regional administration, perhaps even forging a new toponymy of Seleucid Egypt in avoidance of Ptolemaic dynastic names.[78] Probably at this time Antiochus IV struck bronze coins in his own name in Egypt.[79] In this second campaign, therefore, it appears that Antiochus attempted to formalize his military conquest into a sovereign kingship of Egypt. The coronation at Memphis is of the utmost importance. It indicates that Antiochus IV's sovereignty over Seleucid territory could not simply be extended to the Ptolemaic realm; rather, Egypt represented a discrete political landscape that demanded its own crown, much as, in 145 at Antioch-by-Daphne, Ptolemy VI would add the diadem of Asia to that of Egypt.[80]

The Sixth Syrian War—the second and final Seleucid attempt at imperial expansion after Seleucus I—expressed the official notion of territorially bounded kingship, first by Antiochus Epiphanes' guardianship and then by his coronation. Attributing motivation to the king, 1 Maccabees expresses this succinctly: "He thought to reign over the land of Egypt, so that he might have the dominion of two realms" (ὑπέλαβεν βασιλεῦσαι γῆς Αἰγύπτου, ὅπως βασιλεύσῃ ἐπὶ τὰς δύο βασιλείας).[81]

The exits and entrances of Seleucid kings (and queens) acted out the boundary of Seleucid territory; the threshold transformations enunciated the empire's spatial ideology. Like Popilius' sand-circle, the boundary coronations and imperial expansions, as well as the textual and symbolic practices that gave them voice, clearly distinguished between an interior landscape of legitimate hereditable sovereignty and an exterior world governed by friendly peers or hostile competitors. Equally, the absence of such ritualized behaviors—notably during the kings' expeditions into Lagid-occupied Coele Syria and the Parthian-dominated east—manifested Seleucid claims to rightful possession.

CHAPTER 6

The Circulatory System

The threshold movements of the Seleucid kings marked out the empire's edges; but Seleucid territory was more than a container. The formal demarcation of boundaries alone cannot produce, constitute, or maintain a sovereign political landscape.[1] This required, among other things, the integration of diverse regions and communities, the sedimentation of dynastic identity into Seleucid territory, and the configuring of the imperial space into administrative structures. Just as the kingdom's boundaries were articulated by royal travel, so the Seleucid monarchs took possession of their empire by journeying through it.

The mobility of the Seleucids' predecessors, the Persian Great Kings, was a central element in the dynamics of Achaemenid imperialism and in the ethnographic observations of Greek historians.[2] Although the rigidity and regularity of the Persian kings' migrations have been overplayed,[3] it is nonetheless apparent that the Achaemenid court journeyed between the great royal capitals of the Zagros mountains, the Iranian plateau, and the Mesopotamian alluvium in a flexible but seasonally ordered schedule of set-piece movements. Archaeological excavation and textual evidence has brought to light a built infrastructure of way stations, *paradeisos* gardens, and pavilion residences along the well-maintained Royal Roads—an architectural rhetoric suited to an imperial court passing en route from one great palatial complex to the next.[4] The archive of bureaucratic documents from Persepolis, known as the Fortification Tablets, offers ample testimony of the kind of local administrative machinery that would gear up to respond to the kings' arrival, temporary presence in, and departure from Persis, such as the ingathering of commodities to be consumed at the king's table or the lance-bearers' inspection of the Royal Road in advance of his advent.[5] In addition, the tablets indicate that the king, once in Persis, made further detours, independent of the seasonal migration, to places not located on the Royal Road; subordinates made their own tours and kept their own table.[6]

We must resist the temptation to treat Seleucid travel as an unconsidered survival of these Achaemenid imperial practices.[7] The Seleucid evidence deserves to be gathered and discussed in its own right. However, in reconstructing the intraimperial movements of Seleucid kings we face a double challenge. First, the two main sources from which we know of Achaemenid royal travel—Greek ethnographic descriptions and cuneiform palace archives—are missing from the Seleucid empire, and travel, in general, hardly deposits a material trace. As a result, the Seleucid court's mobility is attested only obliquely, from scattered, curt references to individual journeys in literary and epigraphic texts. Second, these matter-of-fact statements of atomized movement—"That day in the afternoon he went out from Babylon to Seleucia-on-the-Tigris";[8] "Seleucus crossed the Taurus with his army"[9]—themselves give little indication of the integrated, ideologically significant system of which they form part. In order to realize the importance of the phenomenon we are obliged to hypostatize type behind episode, structure beneath moment. It may be helpful to compare our evidence and method to *Following Piece*, a 1969 artwork by Vito Acconci. For twenty-three days, the performance artist would select and follow a stranger in Manhattan until she or he entered a building or private space, documenting the journey with photographs and notes. Then, immediately or after a break of a few hours, Acconci would pick and pursue another at random, recording as he went, and so on. The artist's data resemble what we have from the Seleucid empire—captured fragments of isolated journeys that at first can seem utterly random. But, taking Acconci's documentation as a full assemblage, we can identify beneath the apparently unordered crisscrossings of New York an underlying urban logic and shared pedestrian practices that generate about themselves a particular understanding of space. Acconci's performance, playing on the intersection of the random, spontaneous, and individual with the social, the regular, and the rule, parallels the historical operation at work here as, notebook in hand, we stalk Seleucid kings across Asia.

The mobility of the Seleucid kings cannot be underestimated as a daily reality of court life, as a central characteristic of monarchic identity, and as an important, if not the major, mechanism of imperial integration. Of the dynasty's first fourteen kings, from Seleucus I to Antiochus VII, ten died on campaign; only two, Antiochus II and Seleucus IV, died in their palaces (Antiochus V and Antiochus VI were infants and soon assassinated). We wait until Trajan for a Roman emperor who died in the field.[10] Take the impressive itinerary of Antiochus III, who ruled from 222–187: arriving from the Upper Satrapies at Antioch-by-Daphne for his accession (222); marching to Zeugma on the Euphrates and back for his marriage to Laodice (222); embarking on the expedition against the rebel Molon, taking in Babylonia and the satrapies by the Caspian Sea (222–220); the Fourth Syrian War against the Ptolemaic kingdom down the Levantine coast (219–217); the campaign against the pretender Achaeus across the Taurus to Sardis (216–213); another *anabasis* all the way to the Hindu Kush (212–206); the voyage to Arabia and Bahrain (205); further campaigning in Asia Minor (204–203); the victorious Fifth Syrian War against the Ptolemies into Coele Syria and Phoenicia (202–200); the voyage along the southern Anatolian coast of Cilicia, Pamphylia, Lycia, and Caria (199–197); campaigning in Thrace (196–194); the expedition into Greece (192–190); and a third *anabasis* into Media, concluding with his death in the lower Zagros (187).[11] Shorter reigns would make shorter lists, but, in most cases, no less motion.

It would be misleading to establish a typology of royal travels. Where indigenous priestly sources represent the kings' engagement with a local, often religious, concern as the express and unique motivation for royal movement, and where Greek and Latin historical narratives privilege large-scale military objectives, we must recognize that the dynasty's incessant journeying incorporated at the same time into its movements a whole range of military, administrative, and ceremonial functions, including participation in local cult, the consultation of oracles, city foundation, bureaucratic reorganization, tribute collection, inspection of defenses, diplomatic marriage, the defeat of pretenders, the suppression of rebellious movements, and interstate warfare.[12] Accordingly, the directionality and frequency of these movements are of far greater importance than any expressed "purpose." Maps 5 and 6 represent "traffic-flow lines" of royal travel across Seleucid territory: Map 5 covers the reigns of Antiochus I to Antiochus III (281–187), Map 6 Seleucus IV to Antiochus XII (187–84), after the ceding of Asia Minor and Bactria. These telescoped maps attempt to graphically and synchronically represent our total evidence of monarchic journeys, as reconstructed from our scarce and scrappy Greek, Latin, Akkadian, and Aramaic sources. Needless to say—and this deserves emphasis, given the state of our knowledge—the lines should be treated as incomplete and approximate reconstructions from narrative itineraries or studies of historical geography;

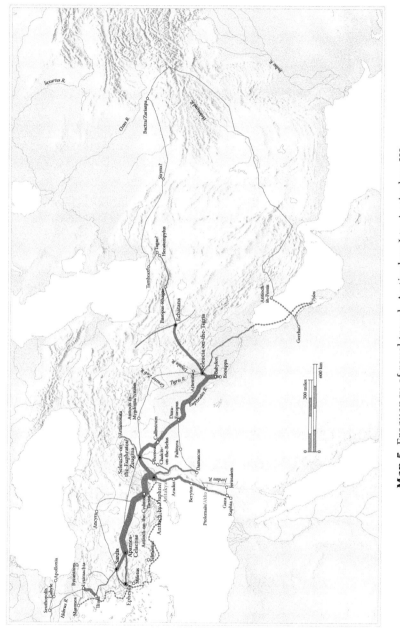

Map 5 Frequency of royal travel, Antiochus I to Antiochus III.

pretenders' journeys are not shown. The thickness of the traffic-flow lines represents the frequency of attested travel: for instance, the thinnest line on Map 5, running from Hecatompylus by the Caspian Sea to the Hindu Kush and around to Antioch-in-Persis, indicates that these regions were traversed by kings, as far as we know, only once (Antiochus III's second, great *anabasis*), whereas the thickest line, from Antioch-by-Daphne to Apamea-Celaenae in western Asia Minor, represents ten attested journeys for the period 281–187.

The traffic-flow lines show a dense if uneven network of monarchic circulation throughout Seleucid territory; the thickest lines demonstrate imperial priorities as well as the key arteries and nodes of travel. Map 5 shows that, for the first century of the established empire, an imperial backbone of movement extended out from northern Syria: an easterly route, following the Euphrates from Zeugma to Seleucia-on-the-Tigris, and then climbing the Diyala valley toward Ecbatana in the Zagros; and a westerly route, passing from Cilicia over the Taurus mountains and along the so-called Common Road to Apamea-Celaenae, Sardis, and Ephesus. The complexi-

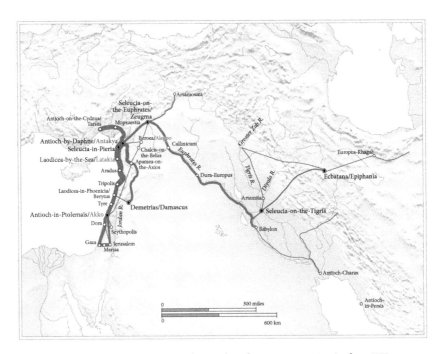

Map 6 Frequency of royal travel, Seleucus IV to Antiochus XII.

ties of Seleucid political, military, and colonial history in the third century can be broadly understood as a single "grand strategy"—the determined defense and consolidation of this roadway. Off this main artery spread secondary networks of travel that flesh out the imperial landscape, denoting the kings' periodic expeditions toward the borders of Seleucid territory, such as those into Armenia, Thrace, and Hyrcania. Note the maritime journeys of Antiochus III in the Mediterranean and Persian Gulf.

Map 6, representing the second century of Seleucid rule (187–84) and covering a reduced territory on account of military defeats, consequently displays higher route frequencies, such as twenty between Antioch-by-Daphne and the Phoenician city of Aradus. We notice immediately the refocusing of imperial attention on the coastal Levantine route, running from Cilicia at the edge of Asia Minor to Gaza on the borders of Egypt, the consequent emergence of Antioch-in-Ptolemaïs (mod. Akko) and Demetrias-Damascus as major nodes of travel, and the continuing importance of the Euphrates corridor.

For both maps, the thickness of line, representing iterations of monarchic presence along the *lieux de passage*, testifies either to actual density of imperial control (e.g., the Zeugma-Babylon and Antioch-Cilicia branches of the main third-century highway) or to the repeated royal will to impose it, such as the campaigns against Ptolemaic-held Coele Syria, rebels, and pretenders. Correspondingly, the thinness or absence of line correlates to the weakness of imperial control. The maps represent an attempt at visualizing Seleucid territory as a dynamic landscape of varying political density, as, to use Harvey's phrase, a "spacetime" of processes and motion,[13] rather than a smooth "inkblot" state of traditional, spatially absolute cartography.

The Sovereign Style

The multipurpose journeying of the Seleucid kings within their empire, as depicted on the maps, was constructed from a limited repertoire of mannered movements—departures from capital cities, arrivals at urban centers, and travel through the interurban landscape. Taken together, these movements were a form of royal progress that claimed to legitimately possess the landscape it traversed. I will investigate each of these forms of royal mobility in turn, pulling from the historical debris the most interesting fragments of evidence.

Departures

For some reason or other, the ancient world's departure ceremonies have received remarkably little attention. It seems that the Seleucid monarchs of the established empire inaugurated their lengthy campaigns with some kind of official pronouncement and parade. The stirring of a static, capital-based, and palace-residing court into a three-mile-an-hour government required that the empire be informed and the administrative patterns of court and departed city reconfigured. Entries in a range of texts, including the Astronomical Diaries from Babylon and 1 Maccabees from Judea, indicate that the departures were formalized moments of imperial ceremony: the time, place, and manner of a king's departure were made known to the imperial subjects. For example, the (fragmentary) Babylonian Astronomical Diary entry for 150 runs, "That month I he[ard . . .] *(alteme)* king Demetrius with twenty-five elephants and the troops . . . they went out from Antioch."[14] The verb *alteme*, "I heard," restored with confidence, indicates an official imperial declaration.[15]

The royal departure was a complex of considered political decisions. Polybius' narrative of Antiochus III's consultation with his Friends in 222, soon after his accession, illustrates how the campaign choices available to the newly crowned king—the nature of command (to lead or to delegate); the direction of march (against the rebel Molon in the Upper Satrapies or against the Ptolemaic occupation of Coele Syria)—explicitly identified policy priorities, privileged and overlooked particular regions of empire, and elevated or deflated the status of whichever courtier's recommendation was accepted or rejected.[16] Moreover, the Polybius passages suggest that departures on campaign were expected to follow closely on a king's accession, characterizing the new ruler as warrior-king, worthy successor, and protector of his legacy; almost all Seleucid kings opened their reigns with a campaign departure.[17]

What constituted these monarchic march-offs? Departure rituals are only sketchily known from Mesopotamia[18] or archaic and classical Greece. Thucydides gives a detailed picture of the *embatēria* (ship-boarding rituals) of the Athenian navy leaving for Sicily, including full civic participation, pious silence, vows, libations, and a paean;[19] vases depict sailors tossing garlands into the sea as their ship departs.[20] It seems that inter*polis* land campaigns were preceded by extispicy (the consultation of the innards of sacrificed animals) and propitiatory offerings directed to heroized virgins, such as the

Hyacinthides in Athens and the Leuctrides in Boeotia.[21] Up in Macedonia, Alexander the Great inaugurated his eastern adventure with a grand nine-day festival at Dion, the monarchy's traditional religious center, entertaining his army and the ambassadors from his Greek allies;[22] his subsequent victory over Persian forces at the Granicus river in northwestern Asia Minor was tied back to the sanctuary by the erection there of a statue group of the Macedonian fallen.[23] Rome offers more direct comparisons, for reasons of territorial expansiveness, campaign length, and forms of political leadership. Imperial departure ceremonies, or *profectiones,* functioned as a sort of reverse of their anticipated counterpart, the triumph: the departing consul or emperor sacrificed on the Capitoline Hill, contracted vows with the state gods (especially Jupiter), and was accompanied by the citizens to Rome's gates; at the *pomerium,* the city's sacred boundary, he changed from civilian into military clothes, i.e., from first citizen into commander-in-chief, and was escorted by the city's population for a long distance into the countryside.[24] From passages in the Roman historian Livy, it is clear that witnessing the *profectio* constituted a form of civic participation and prompted public recollection of similar departures and their triumphant returns.[25]

Our only firm indications for the character of Seleucid royal departures are brief entries in the Astronomical Diaries and 1 Maccabees that itemize the military force (the number of infantry, cavalry, elephants, and occasionally chariots),[26] and a distorted account in Justin's *Epitome,* almost certainly deriving from the late Hellenistic polymath Posidonius,[27] of Antiochus VII Sidetes' march out of Antioch on his ill-fated campaign (131–129) to reclaim the Upper Satrapies from the Parthians:

> Antiochus, thinking he should strike the first blow in the war, led out against the Parthians an army. . . . There was as much provision in it for luxurious living as for fighting a campaign; eighty thousand men at arms were attended by three hundred thousand camp-followers, most of whom were cooks and bakers. Certainly, there was so much silver and gold that even the common soldiers used hobnails of gold in their boots, and trod underfoot the substance people so love that they fight over it with cold steel. Cooking vessels, too, were of silver—as though they were proceeding to a dinner rather than to a war.[28]

Even if the description is molded by commonplace tropes of morally corrosive decadence (Gr. *tryphé*)—the accompanying *patisseurs,* the fancy footwear, the precious metals[29]—the passage illustrates more than a mere *topos*. The Seleucid king's leading out of his troops is, above all, a magnificent and enumerated spectacle of exit, combining military strength and extravagant display; as we will see, of Antiochus VII's and his predecessors' campaigns, the Seleucid king must always travel with full monarchic dignity and regal luxury. The splendor of the exodus turns the march to war into, in Kantorowicz's felicitous phrase, a victorious departure.[30] Although no mention is made of religious ritual, it is inconceivable that the march was unsanctified by sacrifice, libation, and prayer; certainly, we have explicit testimony of this if it is correct to see Antiochus IV's great Daphne festival of 166 as, at least in part, a departure ceremony for his eastern *anabasis*.[31] Justin's hostile tone indicates that Antiochus VII's departure, as strong an act of self-representation as the Roman emperor's *profectio*, offered itself as an occasion for political commentary, historical judgment, and the implicit comparison with other departures, especially in the later context of dynastic strife.

The Seleucid ceremonies of exit, concentrating military and ideological resources at a particular place and time, helped to configure the imperial territory. The rituals focused the landscape on major urban nodes and played an important part in developing the concept of royal capitals: most obviously Antioch-by-Daphne and Apamea-on-the-Axios, but also Sardis, Ephesus, Seleucia-in-Pieria, Seleucia-on-the-Tigris, and, in the dynasty's final decades, Antioch-in-Ptolemaïs and Demetrias-Damascus. By formally inaugurating imperial travels they also posited closing points, structuring the kings' reigns into delimited episodes of movement. That our sources increasingly use the language of "return" for royal movements into northern Syria reveals the departure ritual's power to centralize and privilege. By contrast, the kings' egress from a subject community, where he had paused only momentarily on his travels, was not a major imperial ceremony. Even if the local communities from which the king moved on would have marked his exit, just as they celebrated his entrance (see the section titled "Arrivals"), with acts of obeisance, this was a lesser and different phenomenon. Our sources clearly distinguish between temporary pauses on an itinerary and splendid ceremonies of new movement: for example, an honorific decree for Boulagoras of Samos reports that the honorand accompanied Antiochus II, midcampaign, from Ephesus to Sardis "when Antiochus shifted quarters" (ἀναζεύξαντος δὲ Ἀντιόχου).[32] The verb ἀναζεύγνυμι is used for the mundane breaking of camp or moving off from a temporary halting spot.

All royal travel was constituted by departure, but not every departure was a ceremonious exit.

By embarking on campaign, the Seleucid monarch evacuated the departure point of his sovereign presence and the courtly world that orbited it; monarchic absence was the inescapable result of itinerant kingship. The rupture, opened by the king's movement, was filled by delegation: for instance, Seleucus III, "entrusted the government to Hermias when he made an expedition over the Taurus mountains" into Asia Minor.[33] Such arrangements were explicitly focalized on the moving monarch: in the empire's bureaucratic discourse, officials were "left behind" when the king departed. From epigraphic evidence we know that the formal title of Zeuxis, Antiochus III's governor of cis-Tauric Asia Minor, was ὁ ἀπολελειμμένος ὑπὸ τοῦ βασιλέως Ἀντιόχου ἐπὶ τῶν ἐπιτάδε τοῦ Ταύρου πραγμάτων, "the man left behind by king Antiochus in charge of affairs on this side of the Taurus"; Antiochus VII Sidetes was honored at Antioch-in-Ptolemaïs by a First Friend and Chief Scribe of the army ἀπολελειμμένος ἐπὶ τῶν τόπων, "left behind in charge of the region."[34] Jewish narrative sources record that Antiochus IV marched out of Antioch-by-Daphne καταλιπών ("leaving behind") Andronicus[35] and Lysias.[36] The cuneiform Astronomical Diary for 274 furnishes an identical formulation in Akkadian, reporting that king Antiochus I "left behind *(umaššir)* his [. . .], his wife, and a famous official in Sardis" when he set out for Syria.[37] The terminology represents, in John Ma's words, "the king's absent authority and his having-been-there."[38] As far as we can tell, the epigraphic and literary sources, both Greek and Akkadian, use this language of delegation only for the Seleucid kings' departures from the major royal capitals (Antioch-by-Daphne, Sardis, and Antioch-in-Ptolemaïs) at the inauguration of great campaigns. That is to say, during periods of royal movement, the administrative physiognomy of Seleucid territory was constituted both by the itinerant center of the king's own body and the fixed substitutes he had left behind.

Arrivals

The Seleucid kings restlessly sought out interactions with their subjects, traveling to visit the peoples and settlements under their sovereignty. The reception of the itinerant Seleucid monarch into the kingdom's cities must have been one of the most frequent acts of empire; certainly they are better attested than royal departures. Arrival ceremonies, known in Greek as ἀπάντησις and in Latin as *adventus,* demonstrate a remarkably stable basic structure, from Mesopotamian to early modern kingship:[39] Antioch-by-Daphne's reception of Ptolemy III,[40] Pompey's freedman Demetrius,[41] and caliph abu-'Ubaidah[42] are strikingly similar. I will restrict myself to Seleucid material even if we are then without the artistic representations and heady orations of late antiquity.

The variegated sociopolitical landscape of the Seleucid empire meant that the kings arrived at all kinds of urban settlement, from *poleis* and temple-cities to forts and palatial complexes; furthermore, the Seleucid kings were welcomed into settlements which had remained uninterruptedly loyal to the dynasty and those which had voluntarily (re-)entered the imperial fold. In every example, the fundamentals of *apantēseis* appear identical; it was a common idiom. The ceremonial topography of Seleucid *apantēseis* functioned so as to incorporate the king into the city and, thereby, the city into the kingdom. The monarch, whose imminent arrival would easily have been made known to the settlement's authorities, was met on the road and escorted into the urban area. In other words, Seleucid kings were formally welcomed twice—once on approach to the settlement and again at its gates—graduating the entrance with marked stages of subordination and, for a short distance, integrating the local elite into the monarch's traveling entourage. This can be demonstrated by a couple of examples. A cuneiform Babylonian Chronicle from the reign of Seleucus III records that, to the king's younger brother, Antiochus (III), who was at this point viceroy of the Upper Satrapies, traveling in 224/3 from northern Syria to Seleucia-on-the-Tigris, [^{lú}gal].ukkin kur *u* ^{lú}un^{meš} kur *a-na* igi-*šú* è-*ú ni-gu-tu* [*ina* kur gar-*at*], "[The sat]rap of the land and the people of the land went out to meet him and a festival [was held in the land]."[43] A fragmentary text from Egypt, known as the Gurob Papyrus, records in Ptolemy III's own voice his takeover of the major north Syrian cities of Seleucia-in-Pieria and Antioch-by-Daphne in the course of the Laodicean or Third Syrian War (246–241). This Gurob Papyrus describes the Ptolemaic king's arrival and reception at these two Seleucid cities in some detail. Although the document derives from the Ptolemaic milieu, the cities' response to the invader's approach must have reproduced patterned actions regularly performed for their Seleucid monarchs, and the text's evident concern to depict a successful, consensual ritual allows it to be used as an ideal type of such receptions.[44] At Seleucia-in-Pieria, we are told, "the priests, the [magistrates, the] other citizens, the officers, and the soldiers were all wearing crowns and came to meet us at the harbor (ἐπὶ τὸν λιμένα συνήντησαν) . . . goodwill [toward us] and . . . into the city (εἰς τὴν πόλιν) [they escorted us]"; the fragmentary report goes on to narrate the offerings made on roadside altars within Seleucia proper and the honors awarded in the city's market (ἐν τῷ ἐμπορίῳ).[45] The scheme is repeated at Antioch-by-Daphne: "[After] this [we came] to Antioch. . . . Outside the gate (ἐκτὸς τῆς πύλης) [there came to meet] us the . . . satraps and the other officers [and soldiers], the priests, the board of magistrates, and [all the] young men [from] the gymnasium and the rest of the [crowd] . . . wearing [crowns], and they brought out all the sacred objects to the road in front of [the gate] (εἰς τὴ[ν] πρὸ [τῆς πύλης] ὁδόν)"; within the city offerings, presumably, were made outside each house (παρ' ἑκάστην οἰκία[ν]), and, toward sunset, Ptolemy entered Antioch's royal palace.[46] Note the numinous, quasi-religious atmosphere: the city's deities join in welcoming the arriving monarch. In each case, the monarchs' progress into the most privileged nodes of local power and identity—marketplace and palace in the Gurob Papyrus, assembly and temple in other documents[47]— enacted the settlement's integration.

If the departure ceremony organized the king's traveling army, as we have seen, then, inversely, the arrival ceremony schematized a city's population into demographic groups and official statuses. As the Gurob Papyrus demonstrates, in the king's presence the community formulated its corporate identity as an orderly and segmented population of subgroups.[48] At the same time, our sources assert that the king was welcomed in a festive, spontaneously joyful atmosphere: the arrival of Crown Prince Antiochus (III) at Seleucia-on-the-Tigris was celebrated by *nigûtu* (musical celebrations);[49] Antiochus IV was ushered into Jerusalem by High Priest Jason amid a blaze of torches and shouts;[50] for Ptolemy III at Antioch-by-Daphne, "some of them greeted us with their right hand (ἐδεξιοῦ[ντ]ο), while others . . . with applause and cheering (μετὰ κρότου καὶ κραυγῆς)."[51] These totemic acts of salutation, analogous to the insistence on genuinely felt emotion in civic honorific decrees, represented obeisance as voluntary, jubilant greeting. Accordingly, the warmth and splendor of the reception was considered an index of loyalty. For example, Ptolemy III exclaimed of his arrival at Antioch that "nothing pleased us so much as their enthusiasm" (οὐθενὶ οὕτως ἡδόμεθα ὡ[ς ἐπὶ τῆι] τ[ού]των ἐκτενείᾳ);[52] Antiochus III, writing to Ptolemaeus, son of Thraseas, the governor of Coele Syria, explained his benefactions to Jerusalem as fair reciprocation for, among other things, the generous welcome he had received in 200: "in as much as, when we came to their city, [the Jews] received us magnificently (λαμπρῶς ἐκδεξαμένων) and met us with their senate."[53]

The stylized Seleucid entrance—a slow, stately movement of socialized display and civic obeisance—was transactional. In addition to the sounds and ceremonies of official welcome, the sovereign extracted economic services from the settlement he had entered over and above the *basso continuo* of regular taxation. Simply put: the king and his army needed to be fed, an enormous expense. In the letter to his governor Ptolemaeus, just quoted, Antiochus III goes on to praise the Jews for ungrudgingly (ἄφθονον) supplying his soldiers and elephants. Similarly, Josephus reports that the high priest Hyrcanus admitted Antiochus VII into Jerusalem in 134 and ungrudgingly and zealously (ἀφθόνως . . . καὶ φιλοτίμως) supplied his army.[54] By welcoming the Seleucid sovereign, the settlement had acknowledged its role as an imperial resource, a constituent producing element of the Seleucid landscape; implicitly, this enormous economic burden was predicated on the king's mobility, the temporary impingement of a circulating imperial center. Further gifts were presented to the king, sometimes framed in the binding language of euergetistic reciprocation. In Babylon in 187, for instance, an elderly Antiochus III was awarded a thousand-shekel golden crown and a purple robe of Nebuchadnezzar II by the *kiništu*, the council of the main Esagil temple.[55] There was no comedy of refusing honors.

In return, the king's reception into the city was a privileged moment for benefaction and the confirmation or transformation of its status by royal grant; this was of particular importance for recently (re)acquired settlements. So, in 200, Antiochus III, having been well received and generously supplied by the inhabitants of Jerusalem, granted to the Temple an allowance for sacrifices in kind, support for rebuilding, tax exemptions for the temple staff and urban population, and governance in accordance with traditional religious laws;[56] at Teos in Asia Minor, in 203 or 197,[57] the same king pronounced in the city's assembly its sacredness, inviolability, and freedom from tribute;[58] it would be easy to accumulate parallels. This "surrender and grant" mode of interaction has been well studied as the king's juridical privilege and as a particular discursive formulation,[59] but its spatial inflection should be recognized. Even if such status fixings could also be arranged at distance by subordinates or embassies, nonetheless they were a central component of the king's arrival at and presence within certain communities. It is striking that the inscription announcing Antiochus III's consecration of the city of Xanthus, in southwest Anatolia, to the gods Apollo,

Artemis, and Leto—a great benefaction—was located on the very gateway through which, arriving from the coast, he would have entered the settlement.[60] Indeed, just as the reception rituals highlighted the king's visibility to his subjects, equally they put the city up for inspection by royal gaze. The first Tean decree for Antiochus III emphasizes the importance of the king's autopsy for securing support: Antiochus not only resided in the city (ἐπιδημήσας ἐν τῇ πόλει) but also gazed upon its public and private weakness (θεωρῶν ἐξησθενηκότας ἡμᾶς κα[ὶ] ἐν τοῖς κοινοῖς καὶ ἐν τοῖς ἰδίοις).[61] King and city locked eyes. The Seleucid monarch reformulated about his moving body the modalities of imperial subordination.

The city open and grateful, the king respectful and beneficent, the atmosphere joyful and sacred: this was the model script for royal arrival and reception projected by the central imperial organs.[62] But what of resistance? Time and again, Seleucid monarchs traveling within Seleucid territory would butt up against, indeed, would deliberately seek out cities or other population centers in the hands of external powers, insurgent pretenders, or emancipatory movements that, in the metonymic geography of arrival, had "closed their gates against the king."[63] Such a failure to enact the appropriate ceremonies of welcome was equivalent to rejecting the Seleucid king's claims to legitimate sovereignty: refusing *apantēsis* was, in itself, an act of rebellion. So, where reception and gifts were withheld, they were squeezed out by violent siege and punishments. The turbulent dynastic history and mercurial loyalties of Seleucid subjects offer many instances of forced arrival, of which I will offer only three examples. In 220, Antiochus III recovered the royal city Seleucia-on-the-Tigris from the rebel Molon. Polybius reports that the king's chief advisor, Hermias, imposed an enormous fine of 1,000 talents on the city, expelled its governing council,[64] and executed a large number of citizens; the king, in his turn, reduced the fine to 150 talents and conciliated the city.[65] Example two: Sardis, regional capital of Seleucid Asia Minor, had functioned as the governmental center and final bastion of the pretender Achaeus. Following a two-year siege, in 213 the same Antiochus captured the city and delivered it over to his soldiers for pillage and massacre.[66] We learn from contemporary inscriptions that the monarch extracted a large sum of money (a fine and a new 5 percent tax were imposed), billeted troops on the population, and took over the gymnasium; after a couple of months, following the city's petitioning and formal obeisance, the punishments were reduced and assistance given for civic reconstruction.[67] Example three: in 134 Antiochus VII Sidetes, having exhausted the inhabitants of Jerusalem by lengthy siege, compelled them to recognize his sovereignty, took hostages, exacted 500 talents as overdue tribute, and razed the walls;[68] according to Diodorus' account, presumably derived from Posidonius, the king wisely rejected his Friends' advice to annihilate the Jewish people or to renew the religious persecution launched by Antiochus IV. In these three cases each stage of *apantēsis* is played out in an involuntary, joyless mode: the city breached, not opened; its status demoted, not enhanced; money or tribute exacted, not offered. A court-derived narrative pattern emplots the reintegration of the conquered settlements into the imperial landscape through the king's refusal to countenance his advisor's harsher recommendations; imperial unity is an effect of the king's forgiving nature and μεγαλοψυχία, "greatness of soul."

A similar pattern emerges in the treatment of the semi-independent dynasts of the northern and eastern peripheries; our evidence derives mostly from Polybius' fragmentary account of Antiochus III's military interventions in the Upper Satrapies, following Molon's revolt, in 220, and during his second *anabasis*, 212–205. The Seleucid monarch's arrival at and successful siege of the regional capitals of Armenia (Arsamosata) and Hyrcania (Hecatompylus, Tambrax, and Sirynx) subordinated Xerxes and Arsaces II, respectively; Polybius' narrative puts particular emphasis on Antiochus' occupation of the royal palaces. The dynasts' defeats were formalized into vassalage agreements that acknowledged their integration into the Seleucid political landscape.[69] Take the treatment of Armenian Xerxes:

> The most trustworthy of Antiochus' friends advised him that, when he had once got the young man (Xerxes) in his hands, not to let him go, but, having taken control of the city, to bestow the sovereignty on Mithridates. The king, however, paid no attention to them and, having summoned the young man (Xerxes), ended the conflict and remitted the majority of money, which his father had still owed to him as tribute. Having received on the spot three hundred talents, a thousand horses, and a thousand mules with all their trappings, he restored to him his entire dominion, and by giving his sister Antiochis in marriage conciliated and attached to himself all the inhabitants of the district (πάντας τοὺς ἐκείνων τῶν τόπων ἐψυχαγώγησε), who considered that he had acted in a truly magnanimous and royal manner (μεγαλοψύχως καὶ βασιλικῶς).[70]

Evidently, the forced arrival is a form of ceremonial interaction as applicable to fortified palatial centers as it was to Greek and Near Eastern cities:

obeisance and the giving of tribute in coin and kind to the monarch, on the one hand, and a performance of kingly clemency, on the other, reabsorb the dynast and his Armenian territories into the empire. Diplomatic marriage secured the vassalage—a form of integration not possible for cities (except, perhaps, in symbolic form at Chalcis in Euboea; see Chapter 5).

Seleucid royal travel was covenantal and admonitory. The kings' movements through the imperial landscape, arriving at one subject settlement after another, consisted of repeated enactments of voluntary or forced subordination. The monarch's presence was temporary—the itinerant king arrived and left, arrived and left, arrived and left. Accordingly, the reception ceremonies insisted on the territorial distribution of the kingdom, embedding individual settlements into suprapoliad networks of continuous royal travel. Entrance and exit perforated boundaries: this traveling-through quality of the king's arrival, by itself, incorporated the settlements he visited into a contiguous, integrated imperial territory.

On the Road

We must not think of Seleucid royal travel as a set of asyndetic arrivals at settlement nodes. The kings journeyed through a continuous, interstitial landscape that was meaningful for imperial practice and ideology: the royal movements connected dots, making constellations of scattered points. This journeying was not only or primarily about getting anywhere; it was also a way of being somewhere, of inhabiting by traveling through.

Movement through the landscape was a process of political engagement, emitting sovereign claims throughout the traversed territory. This is recognized in Rome's treaty of friendship with John Hyrcanus of Judea, in which the Senate expressly forbade Antiochus IX Cyzicenus (or his father, Antiochus VII Sidetes) to march with his army through the territory of the Jews and their subjects.[71] There were various ways in which Seleucid claims over the nonurban landscape could be expressed by the mobile king, but such interstitial travel leaves few markers. Four brief examples can each be taken as instances of more common practices. One: in narrating Antiochus III's campaign into Hyrcania in 210 Polybius places the king's protection of the *qanāt* underground water tunnels, lying to the south of the Elburz mountains (and to this day a marvel), within the context of an earlier Achaemenid grant of five-generation-long usufruct; it is probable that the farming population appealed to Antiochus to reestablish the fiscal arrangement put in place by his Persian predecessors.[72] Accordingly, part of the Seleucid monarchs' engagement with the rural landscape involved their recognition of traditional privileges over natural resources and physiographic features. Two: we learn from Nicolaus of Damascus, via Josephus, that during his anti-Parthian *anabasis* of 131–129 Antiochus VII Sidetes set up a *tropaion*, a battlefield monument, on the bank of the river Lycus (mod. Greater Zab) in Assyria to commemorate his victory over the Parthian general Indates.[73] The Seleucid king's triumphant presence was marked on the landscape, making the battlefield a *lieu de mémoire*. The erection of battlefield trophies is attested elsewhere in the kingdom[74] and must have been widely practiced, sowing Seleucid territory with monuments of royal victories and so sedimenting dynastic identity directly into the rural topography. Three: in 220 Antiochus III ordered that the body of Molon, the defeated rebel, be impaled "in the most conspicuous place in Media" (κατὰ τὸν ἐπιφανέστατον τόπον τῆς Μηδίας); he was crucified on the path ascending into the Zagros.[75] This traditional kind of Near Eastern punishment (see the case of pretender Achaeus, later), publicly stripping away a rebel's charisma, invested the landscape with visible and deterring examples of legitimate monarchic sanction. Finally: it is likely that the Seleucid kings, much like their Achaemenid predecessors, received roadside submission from the local peasantry as they progressed.[76] Although such a mode of subordination is not explicitly attested for the Seleucid kingdom, this may be the meaning of Justin's assertion that every population (distinguished in the narrative from local dynasts) through which Antiochus VII marched in his Parthian campaign "came over to him."[77] All in all, Seleucid royal travel through interurban landscapes was as meaningful and transactional an interaction as city arrival, if differently calibrated.

More, in fact, is known of how the dynasty's kings traveled through the imperial territory than what exactly they did there. Seleucid monarchic progresses through the nonurban landscape maintained a mode of living that advertised the kings' monopoly of legitimate power and established the mobile royal encampment as the political, administrative, and ideological center of empire. Although evidence of this monarchic style has been dismissed as "superficial snippets concerning luxury,"[78] it is important to recognize that such forms and ceremonies emitted sovereign claims over the immediate landscape. The king traveled like a king should; ideally, palatial luxury was to be maintained from the victorious departure to the triumphant return.

When traveling through the imperial landscape or encamped outside resisting settlements, the Seleucid monarch resided in his tent. We learn much about the daily practices and ideological importance of the royal tent from Polybius' account of Antiochus III's capture of the pretender Achaeus in 214, at the siege of Sardis, the main Seleucid node in western Asia Minor.[79] Taken by stratagem in the middle of the night, Achaeus was brought into the king's tent and set on the ground bound hand and foot; Antiochus, too excited to sleep (ἐγρηγορώς) while the operation was under way, had dismissed his usual attendants (ἀπολύσας τοὺς ἐκ τῆς συνουσίας) and all but two or three of his bodyguards. The next morning, at dawn (ἅμα τῷ φωτί), the king's Friends gathered at his tent (συναθροιζομένων τῶν φίλων εἰς τὴν σκηνήν), according to the established routine (κατὰ τὸν ἐθισμόν), and were astonished to see on the floor the pretender they thought they were still besieging; the king's advisory council then met (καθίσαντος δὲ τοῦ συνεδρίου) to determine the appropriate punishment for Achaeus. Evidently, the royal tent functioned both as the king's nightly sleeping quarters, with full attendance of servants and guards, and the daylight location for the court rituals of audience and debate; presumably, the Friends arrived from their own, lesser tents. Such a spatial overlap of the monarch's daily-life routine and the court's public ceremonial precisely echoes the multifunctionality of built Hellenistic palaces.[80] In their meeting, Antiochus III and his advisors decided, first, to amputate Achaeus' extremities (ears, nose, tongue, lips, hands) and, after that, to cut off his head and sew it up in an ass' skin, and to impale (what was left of) his body on a stake.[81] The lopping of extremities, at least, appears to have taken place within Antiochus' tent, for Polybius reports that the main body of the Seleucid army found out about and rejoiced over Achaeus' capture and execution only after the punishments had been inflicted.[82] A clear spatial logic emerges. Like the Achaemenid kings' royal tent, which functioned as the symbolic center of the itinerant court and by its capture marked a transfer of power,[83] so Antiochus III asserted his monopoly of legitimate Seleucid kingship by humiliating and disfiguring in his royal tent the pretender who would oust him from it.[84]

The biblical book of Daniel offers a further interesting representation of the Seleucid royal tent. Daniel 11 closes with an "end of time" vision, where the Maccabaean author leaves the accurate historical ground of his *vaticinium ex eventu* (a description of past events in prophetic mode) to falsely predict the death of Antiochus IV before Jerusalem.[85] The author forecasts that the *melek ḫaṣṣafôn* ("king of Ṣaphon/the north"—Antiochus IV Epiphanes), having conquered all of Egypt, Libya, and Ethiopia, would return to the Levant, where "he shall pitch the tents of his palace *(wayiṭṭaʿ 'ohāley 'appadənô)* between the sea and the beautiful holy mountain; yet he shall come to his end with no one to help him."[86] The noun *'appeden* (with the pronominal suffix), a hapax legomenon in the Bible and notorious crux for ancient translators and commentators,[87] derives from the Old Persian *apadāna*, meaning "palace" or "throne hall"; the same word was applied to the Hellenistic palace at Seleucia-on-the-Tigris.[88] So, the Jewish apocalyptic metonymically represents the hostile presence of the Seleucid court and army before Jerusalem as a palatial tent-complex. Such a focalization foregrounds Antiochus IV's mobility, characterizing him as a restless monarch-in-motion, a seminomadic blemish on the holy landscape, as well as underscoring the palatial equivalence and ideological centrality of the king's campaign tent within the military encampment.

There is one final tent image. The Roman anecdotalist Aelian, describing how white swallows portend disaster, notes that the bird made its nest in <lost> of Antiochus VII during his Parthian campaign (131–129) and that, in consequence, the expedition failed and the monarch committed suicide;[89] the most plausible reconstruction is ἐν <τῇ σκηνῇ> αὐτοῦ, "in his tent."[90] If correct, the location of the swallow's nest in the royal tent of Antiochus VII makes this mobile palace once again the stage center of the kingdom and its fate.

The traveling king, residing and holding court in a mobile palace, maintained on campaign a palatial lifestyle. Of particular importance were opulent banquets hosted by the Seleucid king during his movements between successive city receptions. It appears that the monarch in some sense took possession of the interurban productive landscape through an ingathering and redistribution of local food resources. Campaign feasts belong to well-established Near Eastern and Macedonian traditions of monarchic banqueting, whose function in configuring royal exceptionalism and its service-providing legitimacy is widely recognized. The Seleucid campaign banquets, attended by the royal army, in-the-field bureaucrats, and native elites, should be considered as both vertical ceremonies of structured subordination and horizontal ceremonies of imperial solidarity. Just as the king's *apantēsis* refreshed and reformulated the monarchic-urban relationship, so the campaign feast was an occasion for strengthening ties and interactions with local, nonurban communities. Polyaenus preserves a fascinating account, perhaps derived from the Hellenistic historian Phylarchus, of Antiochus I's march against Damascus:

> Antiochus, wishing to gain control of Damascus, which was guarded by Dion, general of Ptolemy [II], announced to his army and to all the country around (τῇ στρατιᾷ καὶ τῇ χώρᾳ πάσῃ) that they should celebrate a Persian festival (Περσικὴν ἑορτὴν θαλιάζειν) and instructed all the hyparchs (ἅπασι τοῖς ὑπάρχοις) to contribute copious supplies in preparation. While Antiochus was celebrating with everyone, Dion slackened his guard, having learned about the luxury of the festival (τὴν τρυφὴν τῆς ἑορτῆς). But Antiochus instructed his army to take four days' worth of uncooked provisions and led them through the desert and over precipitous ways; having appeared unexpectedly (ἀπροσδοκήτως ἐπιφανείς), he captured Damascus.[91]

It is significant that Polyaenus, or his source, considered the festival "Persian." Certainly, Antiochus I, son of Seleucus I's Central Asian wife, Apame, and viceroy for more than a decade in the kingdom's Upper Satrapies, would have been familiar with Persian customs. But the ethnic label suggests more, that the Περσικὴ ἑορτή ("Persian festival") was similar to a distinctive category of royal banquet hosted by the Achaemenid kings.[92] Antiochus' feast, like those of his Persian predecessors, activated a local bureaucratic network of mid-to-low-rank administrators[93] and, presumably, royal magazines inherited from the Achaemenid empire.[94] The Seleucid banquet integrated both the mobile army and the local population (τῇ στρατιᾷ καὶ τῇ χώρᾳ πάσῃ) into an ideological performance of the king's role as greatest-giver and master of territory.

Tryphē as stratagem: against the expectations of the Ptolemaic commander of Damascus, Antiochus I's tactically deployed display of banqueting luxury in the early third century ensured rather than undercut his military victory. By contrast, when history had turned against the Seleucids, this same campaign decadence was identified as a cause of enervating military weakness. The accusations of the late Hellenistic scholar Posidonius, taken with a pinch of salt, shed further light on the nature of royal travel. In several surviving fragments, this Stoic from Apamea-on-the-Axios berated the wartime feasting of Antiochus I's great-great-great-great-grandson, Antiochus VII Sidetes, the dynasty's last great hope. We have already seen that he accused this monarch's ceremonial departure from Antioch-by-Daphne in 131 of more closely resembling a procession to supper than to battle.[95] A further quotation reports that, when Antiochus Sidetes was leading his troops into Media against the Parthian king Phraates II (131–129), "every day he organized receptions for large numbers of people" (ὑποδοχὰς ἐποιεῖτο καθ' ἡμέραν ὀχλικάς), from which his guests bore away enormous quantities of food and golden-bound crowns.[96] The repetition and regularity of these campaign feasts, even if somewhat exaggerated by Posidonius, point to a centralized network of redistribution and an institutionalized mode of interaction with rural populations[97]—all in all, a picture very similar to the Περσικὴ ἑορτή, "Persian festivals," six generations earlier. We are told that as Antiochus VII marched eastward toward Parthia he received the surrender of many eastern princes *(advenienti Antiocho multi orientales reges occurrere tradentes se regnaque sua)* and the defection of all peoples *(ad eum omnibus populis deficientibus);*[98] the gifting of crowns at the encampment banquets suggests that these receptions were the location for the ceremonies of reappointment and confirmations of status by which the regional elites were reattached to the Seleucid crown. Despite initial success, however, Antiochus VII was defeated and killed, his army massacred, his kingdom broken.[99] While all Syria mourned, the Parthian victor, Phraates, gloated an epitaph over Antiochus VII's corpse: ἔσφηλέν σε, Ἀντίοχε, θάρσος καὶ μέθη· ἤλπιζες γὰρ ἐν μεγάλοις ποτηρίοις τὴν Ἀρσάκου βασιλείαν ἐκπιεῖν, "Your boldness and drunkenness, Antiochus, caused your fall; for you expected to drink up the kingdom of Arsaces in huge cups."[100] More is at stake than the king's love of drink: the apophthegm, surely Posidonius' own formulation, identified the practical and ideological linkage between Seleucid monarchic campaigning and regal symposia.

θάρσος καὶ μέθη, boldness and drunkenness. Such a combination is physically manifested in one of the few surviving examples of monumental Seleucid art, the famous rock-cut Heracles at Behistun in the middle Zagros (see Figure 5). This sculptural ensemble was dedicated in 148 by a certain Hyacinthus on behalf of Cleomenes, commander of the Upper Satrapies.[101] Cut into the rock face above head height, the iconographic assemblage depicts a stocky, nude Heracles reclining in sympotic pose on a lion skin; in his left hand, he raises a large wine cup; his club rests off to one side; at his back, his bow leans against an olive tree and a pedimental stele records the dedication in Greek and Aramaic. The hero stretches out above a prominent *lieu de passage*—the main road from Seleucia-on-the-Tigris in Babylonia to Ecbatana in Media passes directly below, the wheel ruts still visible—and around the corner from Darius I's famous Behistun relief, rolled across the cliff face as if by a giant cylinder-seal, ten bound kings, one trampled underfoot, a triple enceinte of cuneiform, altogether a sharp contrast in spirit and style. Heracles, much revered in the Hellenistic Zagros,[102] appears here at banquet, resting as if en route between labors. Moreover, the low-relief stele in the background gives the sculptural group an imperial authority—not only does the dedicatory inscription make direct use of the kingdom's administrative titulature (ἐπὶ τῶν ἄνω σ[ατρ] απειῶν) and calendrical system (ἔτους δξρ', μηνὸς Πανήμου, šnt . . .), but the pedimental stele also recalls the epigraphic form in which the Seleucid kings erected their letters and instructions in the region.[103] This sympotic Heracles, a type often depicted on Near Eastern graves, here seems to function as an archetype of Seleucid "tryphic" conquest, as an imperial idealization of luxurious travel. Certainly, Alexander the Great and his court had identified Heracles as an ancestral model for the Conqueror's eastern exploits. The so-called Vulgate historical sources on Alexander wonder at his rolling symposium through Carmania, in which he took possession of this Iranian region while reclining at banquet:[104] royal travel as *kōmos*. The

Figure 5 Tryphic Heracles, Behistun, Iran.

Behistun Heracles shows us that two decades before Antiochus VII's failed expedition and in anticipation of Phraates' epitaph, the territorialization of Seleucid power in Media was indeed figured ἐν μεγάλοις ποτηρίοις, "in huge cups."

Like their Persian predecessors, the Seleucid monarchs appear to have traveled frequently with their children and wives. In part, this public display of the family unit functioned as an advertisement of family *pietas* and a guarantee of dynastic continuity.[105] In part, it seems that the accompanying Seleucid queens created gender-appropriate ties with the subject populations; for instance, Laodice, wife of Antiochus III, funded dowries for the poor daughters of Iasus, a city in Caria.[106] In part, the familial entourage functioned as an administrative resource to be deployed when occasion demanded. We have seen that Antiochus III, having captured Arsamosata in Armenia, married his sister Antiochis to its ruler, Xerxes; Antiochis would later do away with this Xerxes on her brother's orders.[107] The same king joined one of his daughters (μίαν τῶν ἑαυτοῦ θυγατέρων) to Demetrius, the son of Euthydemus, ruler of Bactria.[108] It is likely that the daughter of Demetrius II, whom her uncle Antiochus VII had brought with him in his ill-fated campaign against Phraates II *(filiam Demetrii, quam secum Antiochus advexerat)*,[109] would have been employed in a similar vassalage marriage had the expedition succeeded. The unmarried princesses in the entourage were used to organize the imperial territory and to establish vassalage or peer relations with local dynasts or independent rulers. Accompanying princes participated as army commanders and, occasionally, as regional viceroys: for example, Antiochus III appointed his son Seleucus (IV) as viceregent over Lysimachia and the Seleucid territories in Thrace.[110]

For the Seleucid monarchs restlessly crisscrossing their empire, a further, contrasting characteristic was added to the palatial luxury of their intercity movements: in the kingdom's ideology of travel, as expressed by court historiography and artistic production, the landscape's difficult terrain was elevated into a kind of trial to be overcome, from which the monarch emerged as an adventuring hero. The stubborn, opaque environments of the empire's complex topography can be reduced to two kinds of wilderness space—desert and mountain. In the Polyaenus passage discussed earlier, Antiochus I led his army from their great Persian feast to Damascus "through the desert and over precipitous ways" (διά τε ἐρημίας καὶ ἀτραπῶν παρακρήμνων).[111] Antiochus III's campaign against the Parthian king Arsaces II obliged him to traverse the great wasteland south of the Elburz mountains. According to Polybius' account, almost certainly deriving from an official Seleucid campaign narrative,[112] the Parthian king considered the desert too harsh an environment for Antiochus even to dare to lead his army across (οὐ τολμήσειν ἔτι δυνάμει τηλικαύτῃ διεκβαλεῖν), especially due to lack of water (μάλιστα διὰ τὴν ἀνυδρίαν). But the Seleucid king, having heroically protected the ancient water supplies from Parthian destruction, made it through the desert (διανύσας τὴν ἔρημον) to Hecatompylus.[113] Deserts in earlier Near Eastern kingship narratives function much as "the forest" into which the hero ventures in European folktale.[114] Crossing the desert from one settlement or inhabited zone to another in itself constitutes a kind of victory—the boundary-crossing king successfully links together imperial regions.

Ascending from desert to mountain: on his march against the Parthian dynast Antiochus III was obliged to cross into Hyrcania by the difficult terrain of Mount Labus (τήν τε δυσχέρειαν τῶν τόπων). The king defeated both the hostile landscape and its brigandlike inhabitants. By royal will, Antiochus drove a roadway across the mountain, transforming a δυσχέρεια, "harsh landscape," into a τόπος εὔβατος, "accessible terrain," passable for phalanx and pack train.[115] The Seleucid king then swept aside the mountain dwellers, who, by barricading the narrow defile, had thought to further strengthen nature's own defenses.[116] A monument erected in Antioch-by-Daphne half a century later offers a strikingly direct figuration of king as mountain-vanquisher. According to the late antique Antiochene orator Libanius, who can be trusted for his hometown's sights, the cities of Cilicia commissioned for Antiochus IV Epiphanes, in thanks for defeating brigands and securing trade routes in the Taurus mountains, a bronze statue group of the king having subdued or tamed a bull (ἵστατο χαλκοῦς ταῦρον κεχειρωμένος).[117] Both episodes place the ideology of Seleucid mountain travel squarely within a long-standing Mesopotamian (and thus alluvial) tradition. The driving of roads through dangerous ranges had been considered a paradigmatic act of heroic campaigning in both Assyro-Babylonian epic and historiography: the prologue to the Gilgamesh epic began its summary of the hero's career with his opening of passages through the mountains,[118] and Neo-Assyrian campaign narratives insisted on their kings' conquest of mountains.[119] The iconography of the Epiphanes-bull group finds its direct compositional antecedents in an age-old Mesopotamian repertoire of heroes wrestling with bulls and other monsters. Of course, the very name Taurus, meaning "bull" in Greek, demanded the visual pun, but the tradition of figuring mountains as bulls goes far back.[120] Appian's aetiology for depictions of Seleucus I with bull horns surely rationalizes similar mountain-conquest imagery: "He was of such a large and powerful frame that once, when a wild bull was brought for sacrifice to Alexander and broke loose from its ropes, Seleucus held him alone, with nothing but his hands, for which reason his statues are ornamented with horns."[121]

In sum, the Seleucid kings took possession of and expressed their sovereignty over their empire's intersettlement landscape by, on the one hand, establishing their encampment as the kingdom's palatial center and, on the other hand, by exploring, dominating, and taming the wilderness landscapes. The monarchs proclaimed their sovereignty over whichever territory they inhabited in these modes: during invasions of, for example, Ptolemaic-occupied Coele Syria or rebellious Hyrcania, the style of travel by itself formulated the claims of Seleucid kingship. When these monarchs advanced, so did their territorial claims; they stimulated the land, accredited themselves by it, and thereby created the scene of their rule.

Royal Roads

The journeys of the Seleucid kings through the imperial territory were canalized along major axes of communication. Seleucid roadways and road infrastructure are of major importance as the material manifestation of royal movements, as instruments of territorial integration, and as a disciplinary mechanism for bodies and space. Our evidence for Seleucid "Royal Roads" is, inevitably, uneven and scant, but it is intriguing.

At an interregional scale, it is clear that the Seleucid kings repeatedly followed certain extended roadways. Map 5's great western arc, from Antioch-by-Daphne to Apamea-Celaenae, Sardis, and Ephesus corresponds to the "Common Road" (κοινὴ ὁδός) "constantly used by all who travel eastward from Ephesus."[122] As early as the fourth century, this southern route, passing below the central Anatolian salt plateau, had overshadowed the more ancient Persian Royal Road described by Herodotus, which arched north of the desert.[123] As described by the geographer Artemidorus in the first century, the road, traveling "from Ephesus to Carura, a boundary of Caria towards Phrygia, via Magnesia[-on-the-Maeander], Tralleis [formerly Seleucia-on-the-Maeander], Nysa, and Antioch[-on-the-Maeander], is a journey of 740 stadia; and from Carura, the journey in Phrygia, though Laodicea, Apamea, Metropolis, and Chelidonia. . . ."[124] The number of major Seleucid colonies along this route is immediately apparent; several smaller fortresses or outposts protected the passes.[125] Moreover, these settlements were understood to be linked elements sitting on a coherent interregional artery of travel that ran from the Aegean to northern Syria: for instance, the Common Road entered and exited Laodicea-on-the-Lycus through gates named "Ephesian" and "Syrian," respectively, after the road's termini, not the city's more immediate neighbors. So, successive third-century Seleucid kings pursued an imperial strategy of densely distributing a colonial and military network—large colonies in the fertile plains, smaller garrisons at restricted bottlenecks—along their most frequented westward roadway (see Chapter 7). Repeated royal travel along this route (see Map 5) confirmed and consolidated its imperial function; equally, the road, with its precedents, its colonies, and the opportunities these offered for the kinds of city-king interactions described earlier, channeled westward royal movement along it. Other similarly colonized and canalizing imperial roadways include the Euphrates transit route,[126] the Diyala rise from the Tigris to Ecbatana,[127] and the great Khorasan Highway extending from Media, south of the Elburz range, into Central Asia; all are described in the early Parthian itinerary of Isidore of Charax.[128]

The Seleucids maintained parts of the Persian imperial network of Royal Roads, improving key sections and overlooking redundant ones. Seleucid milestones indicate the kingdom's interest in upkeeping and measuring the empire's roadways. Two have been found in Persis, the former Achaemenid heartland, and one more, perhaps, in Lydia. A fragmentary opisthographic milestone found somewhere near Marvdasht, about ten kilometers from Persepolis, records in large Greek letters distances of sixty stades in one direction and twenty stades in the other; the stone block itself was a piece of the destroyed parapet of the Persepolis terrace. The milestone should be dated to the end of the fourth century or the first half of the third, according to standard orthography.[129] The second opisthographic milestone was excavated at Pasargadae from an early third-century archaeological context on the Tall-i Taxt fort, the seat of the Seleucid garrison. This stone, again fragmentary, recorded in Greek, with an Aramaic summary, two distances from or to Pasargadae in different directions (presumably, the route from Persepolis through Pasargadae up into Media).[130] Finally, a milestone from the Cayster valley in western Asia Minor, giving distances from Sardis and Ephesus in stades, may be Seleucid.[131] It is unclear from these milestones how widespread and systematic was the measurement of roads, but the short distances suggest that they would have been erected at frequent intervals.[132] As for the upkeep of these routes, a corvée labor force in Seleucid employ is attested from third-century Asia Minor; it is likely that such workforces were used by the imperial administration for maintaining the roadways.[133] But not all roads were preserved. In 254/3, Antiochus II sold a landed estate near Cyzicus in northwestern Asia Minor to his recently divorced queen Laodice. As recorded in an inscription from Didyma, the purchased land was delimited to the north by "the Royal Road that leads to the river Asepus" and to the west by "the ancient Royal Road that leads to Pannucome"; this latter, "ancient" roadway had been plowed up by local farmers—two non-Greek inhabitants of Pannucome, an indigenous village, were needed to point out its former course to the Seleucid hyparch.[134] The Laodice inscription reveals that, while a distinct category of Royal Road (ὁδὸς βασιλική) was recognized by the Seleucid administration, the kingdom had allowed certain of these routes to fall into disrepair, at least at its far western periphery.[135]

The Seleucid sponsorship of roads and their measurement was closely connected to the royal ideology of movement and territory. Its importance to the early Seleucid imaginary is shown in Megasthenes' *Indica*. This ethnography, contemporary with the Persis milestones and engaging closely with Seleucid state formation (see Chapter 1), attributed similar policies to the royal bureaucracy of India: the Mauryan *agoranomoi*, among other responsibilities, "build roads and place pillars every ten stades, showing the turnoffs and distances" (ὁδοποιοῦσι δέ, καὶ κατὰ δέκα στάδια στήλην τιθέασι τὰς ἐκτροπὰς καὶ τὰ διαστήματα δηλοῦσαν);[136] furthermore, a Royal Road extended from the capital, Palimbothra, to the western edge of India, its distance measured (καταμεμέτρηται γὰρ σχοινίοις).[137] When the Mauryan king Sandrocottus moves through his kingdom, he travels by means of these roadways in a highly ritualized progress, characterized by his entourage's booming sonic presence and monopolization of the road surface: "The roadway is fenced off (περιεσχοίνισται δ' ἡ ὁδός), and it is death for anyone to come within the circle of women (the king's bodyguards); they are preceded by drummers and bell-carriers."[138] Moreover, the Seleucid sponsorship of road measurement was part of a broader imperial exercise in generating, ordering, and deploying spatial knowledge. Although we know of no Seleucid Domesday Book, the borders of at least some estates and cities were registered in imperial archives: a description of Laodice's estate, mentioned earlier, was filed with the "royal records" at Sardis;[139] a boundary stone from the city of Aegae in the Aeolis explicitly records that its territory was measured and marked "on the order of king Antiochus [II]" (συντάξαντος βασιλέως Ἀντιόχου);[140] sundials from the Seleucid colony at Aï Khanoum, in northeastern Bactria, show that the settlement could be geographically and astronomically located.[141] And so on. The milestones applied to the major axes of movement a regular and abstract unit of distance, the stade. Such milestones were new to the Near East: there are no Assyrian or Achaemenid parallels; Alexander had his bematists, but no public markers. By locating a point in relation to two others, these Seleucid monuments generated around themselves a dynamic sense of passing-through: their abstract language of distance is a nonlocalized one of mobility, connectedness, and interregionality. Such a rationalization of Seleucid territory also functioned as an imperial rhetoric, characterizing the Seleucid kings as "scientific" rulers, clutching the measuring stick and transforming an exotic and largely unfamiliar landscape into a knowable geographical entity.[142]

The anthropological and archaeological disciplines are increasingly recognizing roads and trails as built places in their own right, infused with the activities that took place along them and effectively shaping or reproducing the experience of movement.[143] The imperial roadways functioned as mechanisms of territorial integration, binding together settlements and satrapies. Repeated royal movements achieved a degree of structural homology and cultural identity among the linked points.[144] Paths produce regular actions: travel along these roads recalled dynastic precedents; imperial memories, mapped onto the terrain, were triggered by the roadways' imposed spatial moves, explicitly in the case of specific juridical privileges for cities (where precedent was a dominant mode of imperial bureaucracy), implicitly in other circumstances. Walking the same path was a way of emulating, of stalking great models. For example, Demodamas' altar-founding activities on the Iaxartes were held to repeat those of Dionysus, Hercules, Semiramis, Cyrus, and Alexander (see Chapter 2).[145] As we have seen, the "tryphic" Heracles at Behistun functioned as a heroic antetype for royal travel along the roadway. Antiochus III's great eastern *anabasis*, following in the footsteps of Seleucus I and "renewing" the Indus Treaty (see Chapter 1), was anticipated and celebrated by reviving the founder-king's coin types;[146] the same Antiochus' arrival at Ecbatana recalled in Polybius' account the journeys of Alexander, Antigonus, and Seleucus.[147]

Kings at Sea

While the vast majority of Seleucid royal travel took place along the road-ways of Asia, on occasion the monarchs took to the sea. Our kings sailed two contrastingly configured maritime worlds—an open, unclaimed east Mediterranean and an imperialized Persian Gulf.

Royal voyages in the east Mediterranean, the Babylonian "Upper Sea," de-lineated a continental coastline; in Chapter 2 we explored the bounding func-tion of naval voyages. Although the Seleucids held brief control of certain islands—Lemnus, gifted to Athens following its capture by Seleucus I;[148] Cy-prus, returned by Antiochus IV soon after its betrayal by Ptolemy Macron;[149] Aradus, granted autonomy in the mid-third century and fully integrated into a coastal *peraia*;[150] Antioch-in-the-Propontis, of which nothing is known be-sides its name[151]—they made no pretensions to maritime sovereignty. Recall that Seleucus I was received in the Gulf of Issus onto Demetrius Poliorcetes' flagship (see Chapter 5) and that various Seleucid princes, arriving in north-ern Syria by sea to claim their throne, took the diadem only after they had disembarked (again, Chapter 5). Furthermore, Laodice, daughter of Seleu-cus IV, was conveyed to Perseus, her husband, by a magnificent Rhodian, not Seleucid, flotilla;[152] no island league was assembled under Seleucid suzer-ainty, no ship imagery was struck onto royal coinage, and, to our knowledge, no Seleucid prow monuments were erected in sanctuaries or palaces.[153]

Where we find Seleucid royal voyages in the Mediterranean, during the reigns of Seleucus II and Antiochus III, they consist of the limited deployment of naval power to secure control of important coastal settlements. Justin tells us that Seleucus II prepared a large fleet, presumably at Ephesus, against the cities that had sided with Ptolemy III in the Third Syrian, or Laodicean, War.[154] Although tempests soon scattered his armada and almost drowned the king, Seleucus' intention must have been to win back the port cities of Asia Minor from the sea. Such a strategy was pursued by Antiochus III in his *reconquista* of Asia Minor in 199–197: the king led a coastal sweep from northern Syria to the north Aegean, mopping up harbor by harbor the Ptolemaic possessions in Cilicia, Pamphylia, Lycia, and Caria, while a coordinated hinterland cam-paign, under the command of his general Zeuxis, progressed westward along the Common Road.[155] These rare royal voyages along the Anatolian coast con-structed the imperial territory in an enclaval, littorary manner. Put another way, the absorption, attempted or achieved, of the Ptolemaic provinces of Asia Minor demanded a Ptolemaic-type technique of conquest; by contrast, Zeuxis' land campaign conformed to traditional Seleucid road-based movements.

A different use of the eastern Mediterranean emerged in the dynasty's final, internecine agony. Kings, princes, and pretenders hopped from one port to another along the Cilician, Syrian, or Phoenician coastline: the pretender Diodotus Tryphon, for instance, escaped from besieged Dora to Antioch-in-Ptolemaïs[156] and then to Orthosia, north of Tripolis;[157] Demetrius II fled by ship from, perhaps, Seleucia-in-Pieria to Tyre.[158] Such voyages belong in the context of the increasing importance of the Levantine corridor (see Map 6) and the fragmentation of territorial control among competing claimants (see Chapter 8), but they represent nothing more than the escapes, outmaneuvers, and surprise descents that characterized the myopic tactics of this period's continuous dynastic warfare.

The Persian Gulf, the Babylonians' "Lower Sea," makes for a different story (see Map 7). Until quite recently, with the exception of the small colony of Icarus on the Kuwaiti island of Failaka, the region had been thought not to fall within the Seleucid kingdom or even the wider Hellenistic

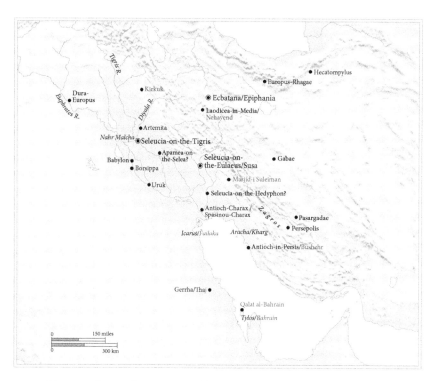

Map 7 The Arab-Persian Gulf, Mesopotamia, and western Iran.

cultural zone.[159] The discovery in northern Bahrain of a late second-century Greek inscription recording the dedication of a shrine to the Dioscuri by Cephisodorus, "general of Tylos (Bahrain) and the Islands" (στρατηγὸς Τύλου καὶ τῶν Νήσων), has overturned these assumptions.[160] Although Cephisodorus dedicated the sanctuary on behalf of Hyspaosines, the first king of Characene (the gateway region for Babylonia, where the Shatt el-Arab debouches into the Gulf), this ruler had been appointed satrap by Antiochus IV and broke away as an independent ruler only in the final years of his life (127–124);[161] early Characenian kingship is characterized throughout by the continuation of Seleucid forms, language, and administration.[162] Accordingly, it is all but certain that Cephisodorus' administrative archipelago "Tylos and the Islands"—presumably Bahrain, Failaka, Tarut, and Kharg—was a preexisting Seleucid district. The inscription attests the presence of a Seleucid station on northern Bahrain, headed by a *stratēgos* and staffed by a colonial garrison; the archaeological evidence concurs.[163] And so, in contrast to its Mediterranean strategy, it seems that the Seleucids maintained in the Gulf a militarized island network and, necessarily, a specialized infrastructure of dockyards and deep-water anchorages to support the *cursus maritimi*. The only Seleucid king known to have sailed the Gulf is Antiochus III. His presence in the Gulf is attested from a letter of Antioch-in-Persis[164] and a condensed account of a naval expedition in Polybius. According to the historian, the Seleucid king headed to the Arabian spice capital, Gerrha, now identified with the Thaj oasis, where he granted the inhabitants their freedom and received as a gift enormous amounts of silver and incense; from there "he sailed to the island of Tylos and then sailed back for Seleucia" (ἐποίει τὸν πλοῦν ἐπὶ Τύλον τὴν νῆσον καὶ ἐποίει τὸν ἀπόπλουν ἐπὶ Σελευκείας).[165] Antiochus' Gulf voyage was very different from those in the Mediterranean. First, crisscrossing the open waters instead of hugging the coast did not construct a linear edge: in fact, throughout antiquity the absence of nucleated settlements on the Arabian mainland and the persistent landward threat from nomadic Bedouin of the interior meant that the principal nodes of travel were the offshore islands.[166] In contrast to the east Mediterranean voyages, therefore, Antiochus III was able to integrate a noncontiguous constellation of isolated points in a nonlinear fashion: bypassing, reversing, circling. Second, the new Bahrain inscription indicates that Antiochus was visiting and, perhaps, consolidating a Seleucid military outpost on Tylos. Without the threat of peer-kingdom competition in the Gulf, the king's voyage expressed the claims of Seleucid sovereignty over the islands and the waters. Finally, the nesiotic province merged into the Seleucid mainland, forming an indivisible, interpenetrated whole: in an unbroken journey Antiochus sailed from Bahrain to the upstream capital, Seleucia-on-the-Tigris.[167] In contrast to its western edge along the sands and cliffs washed by the Mediterranean, in the Gulf Seleucid sovereignty spilled out to sea.[168]

Parades and Parodies

Victorious departures, grand arrivals, palatial tents, luxurious banquets, and Royal Roads make sovereign travel. The significance of this style of journeying in embodying legitimate territorial rule is highlighted by its travestying counterparts: the king in chains or in retreat. The historical trajectory of the Seleucid kingdom makes these all too common. In the second half of the second century three captive Seleucid kings were driven in chains through the imperial landscape in a parodic subversion of legitimate royal travel. In 138, Demetrius II, having been captured by the Parthians, was paraded as a prisoner through the cities of the east *(traductus per ora civitatium populis, qui desciverant, in ludibrium favoris ostenditur)*;[169] the mockery was intended (note *ludibrium*). Eusebius reports that the king received the moniker "Seripides,"[170] a diminutive built on the Aramaic for a bound prisoner *('swr):* "the little chained one." Sixteen years later, Alexander II Zabinas, having attempted to melt down the golden Nike of Antioch-by-Daphne, was apprehended at Posidium on the Syrian coast and led in chains (δεδεμένος ἐπανήγετο) to the camp of Antiochus VIII Grypus, his dynastic competitor.[171] At the close of the dynasty, in 88/7, Demetrius III Eucaerus was captured by Straton, the ruler of Beroea, Aziz, the phylarch of the Arabs, and Mithridates Sinaces, the Parthian satrap of Mesopotamia, and sent together with the war booty to Mithridates II (τὸν [Δημήρτιον] μὲν τῷ Μιθριδάτῃ τῷ τότε βασιλεύοντι Πάρθων ἔπεμψαν).[172] These parades of chained kings were public spectacles of dispossession; before the eyes of the empire's subjects they undercut the kings' charisma and advertised the transfer of effective power.

Our narrative sources build up peripeteic tableaux of defeated kings, disorderly flights, royal panic, scattered companions, and unmonarchic dress. So, the shipwreck of Seleucus II's great armada cast onto the beach nothing but the king's naked body *(nudum corpus)* and a few of his companions; "he fled in panic to Antioch" *(trepidus Antiochiam confugit)*.[173] After the defeat of his navy at Myonnesus, Antiochus III in complete panic (πάμπαν ἐξεπλάγη) fled from Lysimachia; in an inversion of the language, ceremonies, and emotions of departure and arrival rituals, the city's inhabitants "accompanied him in his flight with lamentations, together with their wives and children" (συμφεύγοντας μετ' οἰμωγῆς, ἅμα γυναιξὶ καὶ παιδίοις), while the king paid them no attention (ὑπερεώρα).[174] With only 500 men, Alexander I Balas fled to Abae in Arabia, where he was decapitated by the Arab sheikh Zabdiel[175] or, by another account, murdered by his own officers.[176] The retreat of Antiochus IV Epiphanes from defeat in Persia offers the best-attested withdrawal narrative.[177] In particular, the Jewish author of 2 Maccabees delights in the most lurid and grotesque details of the persecutor's death throes. The fugitive king, having lost most of his army and beating a shameful retreat, was convulsed by bowel pains and thrown from his chariot; now carried in a litter, his body was devoured from the inside by worms; the stench of his decaying flesh became so overwhelmingly putrid that the soldiers could no longer bear him forward. Such worm deaths ("phthiriasis"[178]) were standard divine punishments for impious rulers,[179] but Antiochus Epiphanes' retreat is in addition a parodied progress, inverting the constituent elements of sovereign travel: his unmajestic fall in place of stately movements, his malodor in contrast to incense-wafted arrivals and sweet-smelling kings,[180] the avoidance of his presence rather than enthusiastic reception, and the resisted mobility—Antiochus' chariot hurls him off, his litter cannot be carried—that literally grounds the king to a halt.

A subgroup of retreat involves the king disguising his identity and skulking off road. Polyaenus reports that the founder-king, Seleucus I, having been defeated by some unspecified barbarians, presumably in the Taurus mountains, fled toward Cilicia. In order to escape recognition, "he pretended to be an armor-bearer" (ὁπλοφόρος εἶναι προσεποιήσατο) and dressed in the appropriate clothes; only when he came upon the major part of his army did he put back on his royal garb (τὴν βασιλικὴν στολὴν ἀναλαβών).[181] If Seleucus I's disguise, ending in success, ultimately illustrated his derring-do and Odyssean cunning, like Charles II of England in the tree, then the failed escapes of Demetrius II merely iterated his capture. King Demetrius, prisoner of the Parthians, twice tried to flee his gilded captivity in Hyrcania; with the assistance of his loyal courtier Callimander, who had traveled through the deserts in Parthian clothes, the king made his escapes, presumably hiding himself beneath a similar costume.[182] The wilderness spaces were used as a mask to disappear behind rather than a trial to overcome.

Disguised kings were the antithesis of the sovereign mode of travel's insistence on royal visibility.

Seleucid kings scurrying in retreat or paraded in chains were deterritorialized; withdrawing their sovereign claims from the imperial territory, they did not own the landscape through which they moved. The forms of movement, even the king's wardrobe, determined the modes of imperial interaction. The contrast between legitimate royal progress and its travestying doubles was as dramatic as that between, say, hunting and poaching: two apparently similar uses of space that distinguished the former's ownership and the latter's transgression by the style of mobility.

Evaluating Kings

The attestations of Seleucid royal journeys out of which this chapter's reconstructions have been developed are, at their most basic level, evidence of how people spoke and wrote about the Seleucid kings. In the narrative imaginations of the court, its subjects, and its peers, Seleucid rulers were always on the move; it is impossible to overemphasize how frequently the kings appear en route. A couple of examples: Ilium's honorific decree for Antiochus I establishes as its chronological reference point the king's passage over the Taurus mountains;[183] similarly, Smyrna located the time of its sympolity with Magnesia-on-the-Maeander in reference to Seleucus II's crossing the same range in the opposite direction.[184] Samos honored its local notable Boulagoras for following Antiochus II when he moved from Ephesus to Sardis.[185] In 2 Maccabees, the (forged) testamental final letter of Antiochus IV has the king report, "I suffered an annoying illness on my way back from Persia."[186] The Mesopotamian temple scribes were obsessed with royal mobility. The monthly Astronomical Diaries regularly recorded the kings' movements, with an increasingly fine calibration the closer to Babylon: from "That month I heard as follows: king Antiochus marched victoriously through the cities of Meluhha"[187] to "On 13th he entered Borsippa. On 14th . . . to the ziqqurat of Ezida . . . That day in the afternoon he went out from Babylon to Seleucia-on-the-Tigris."[188] Even the famous cuneiform cylinder from Borsippa, discussed in Chapter 4, recording Antiochus I's reconstruction of the Ezida temple, foregrounds the king's journey from northern Syria to Babylonia: "the bricks for Esagil and Ezida I molded with my pure hands (using) fine quality oil in the land of Hatti, and for the laying of the foundation of Esagil and Ezida I brought them *(ubbil).*"[189]

Numismatic evidence, too, depicts monarchs in motion. Amazingly, on some royal silver and bronze campaign issues the facial hair of certain Seleucid kings grows from clean-shaven jowls or short stubble to a fully grown and pointed beard: for instance, the coinage struck during Seleucus II's anti-Parthian campaign depicted him with a short curly beard at Nisibis in northern Mesopotamia, a slightly fuller, pointed beard at Susa in Elymaïs, and a long, pointed beard at Ecbatana in Media; the coins struck along Antiochus IX Cyzicenus' journey from western Cilicia to Antioch-by-Daphne present a clean-shaven youth slowly growing out a full beard.[190] The royal image transformed with the landscape: lengthening facial hair on these coins, presumably struck for military pay, were an iconographic marker of the king's spatial and temporal progress.

This language of Seleucid space, focalized on the traveling monarch, wove itself into various official and indigenous discourses; we find no valorization of a king's stationary presence or motionless tranquility. Accordingly, royal travel became an index for evaluating rulers. Good kings were in the saddle, energetically roaming their territories, seeking out interactions in a blaze of personal bravery and regal pomp; conversely, bad kings were immobile, lazy, and slothful, prisoners of their palaces, wallowing amid idle pleasures and crass pursuits. Thus, the criticisms of, say, Seleucus IV,[191] Demetrius I,[192] Alexander I Balas,[193] and Antiochus IX Cyzicenus[194] were framed around their (supposed) inertia.

Given the expansiveness of Seleucid territory and the irregular rhythms of travel, knowledge of the kings' location and direction was of obvious practical necessity; but our contemporary sources go above and beyond this. Why such emphasis on royal mobility? What was the function of this strategy of representation? In part, the answer may lie in the language of displacement, peregrination, and journeying that rose to a general prominence in the Hellenistic period.[195] More directly, traveling kings were integral to a coherent and specifically Seleucid system of kingship ideology and governmental practices.

At the root of Seleucid kingship was an extreme degree of centralization on the king's person, and, as a result, at the heart of itinerant monarchy was an absolute insistence on the transformative effects of the king's appearance in a landscape. If royal arrivals among a population or within a settlement reformulated imperial structures, then the glowing presence of the king's charismatic body strengthened bonds of loyalty. Polybius' account of Antiochus III's campaign against the rebel Molon repeatedly show that the monarch's face, viewed by soldiers and peoples, lies at the center of his kinghead's unique legitimacy. Where imperial armies under the delegated leadership of Seleucid generals failed to defeat or win over Molon's troops, the king in person could achieve victory. So, Antiochus' courtier Epigenes advised the young ruler that "it was of the first importance that the king proceed to the spot and be present at the actual theater of events; for thus either Molon would not dare to disturb the peace, once the king himself was before the eyes of the people (τοῦ βασιλέως παρόντος καὶ τοῖς πολλοῖς ἐν ὄψει) with an adequate force, or, if in spite of this he ventured to persist in his project, he would very soon be seized by the populace and delivered up to the king."[196] Having reached the Tigris, the king was advised that, if he marched into the region of the Apolloniatis (formerly Sittacene in eastern Mesopotamia), the population would resume their allegiance and join him (πρόσκλισιν τῷ βασιλεῖ τῶν κατὰ τὴν Ἀπολλωνιᾶτιν χώραν ὄχλων).[197] In the eventual confrontation between the armies of Antiochus III and Molon, the rebel's left wing defected to the royal army as soon as they came in sight of the king (ἅμα τῷ συνιὸν εἰς ὄψιν ἐλθεῖν τῷ βασιλεῖ).[198] Similar principles are attested eight decades later, in the context of Demetrius II's anti-Parthian expedition. Josephus informs us that the Seleucid colonial population of the Upper Satrapies had been continually dispatching ambassadors to the king, promising to join him if he appeared among them (οἱ ταύτῃ κατοικοῦντες Ἕλληνες καὶ Μακεδόνες συνεχῶς ἐπρεσβεύοντο πρὸς αὐτόν, εἰ πρὸς αὐτοὺς ἀφίκοιτο, παραδώσειν μὲν αὐτοὺς ὑπισχνούμενοι).[199] It is significant that, as presented, the structures of Seleucid sovereignty in this region could be reactivated only by the personal appearance of the king; as in the case of Molon's revolt, neither subordinates nor regional administrators are effective substitutes for the king's body.

The immediate and profound impact of the Seleucid monarchs' presence on the imperial landscape was framed in quasi-religious forms. As we have seen, the ritualized incorporations of royal arrival ceremonies were marked by sacrificial offerings, the opening of temples, and prayers. Even if Seleucid kings did not reproduce a single religious paradigm, in the manner of the late antique *adventus'* Jesus-into-Jerusalem model,[200] royal movement and arrival were not without salvific resonance: note the kings hailed as "Savior" and the claims of order restored. Above all, the sudden appearances of Seleucid monarchs were considered as or as equivalent to *epiphaneiai.*[201] This is explicit for Antiochus IV, the first Seleucid ruler to take the epithet *Epiphanēs* ("Manifest"); according to Appian, Antiochus earned the sobriquet for literally being seen as the legitimate king following Seleucus IV's assassination (ὅτι τῆς ἀρχῆς ἁρπαζομένης ὑπὸ ἀλλοτρίων βασιλεὺς οἰκεῖος ὤφθη).[202] The title was strongly associated with Seleucid kingship—in contrast to the Ptolemaic kingdom, where only Ptolemy V took this epithet, it was used of at least nine Seleucids (Antiochus IV, Alexander I, Antiochus VI, Alexander II, Antiochus VIII, Seleucus VI, Antiochus XI, Antiochus XII, and Philip I);[203] moreover, its late second-century deployment by Graeco-Bactrian, Anatolian, and Parthian dynasties was in emulation of this markedly Seleucid practice.[204] Such insistence on the charismatic force of royal visibility drew from earlier traditions. Late classical and Hellenistic *polis* discourse assimilated visibility to the recognition of concentrated political capital, clearly shown in the numerous Hellenistic honorific decrees that claimed to "make manifest" (the key verb is φαίνεσθαι) city leaders or benefactors, as well as the honoring *dēmos*, in the most conspicuous civic or sacred locations.[205] Alongside this, an ancient and widespread Near Eastern religious discourse asserted that the gods directed a portion of their blinding heavenly brilliance (known in Mesopotamia as *melammu, šalummatu*, or *namrīru*) into legitimate kings, who in turn emitted a quasi-divine brightness;[206] first-millennium cuneiform royal inscriptions attribute victory on campaign and in battle to a king's personal *melammu*, in a way not dissimilar to the battlefield appearance (ὄψις) of Antiochus III.

One way to conceive of the Seleucid kingdom is not as a static geography of regional core and increasingly graduated periphery but as a system of imperial structures that could manifest centrality around the moving monarch. The Seleucid king functioned as a glowing center of mass that, circulating through Seleucid territory, pulled toward itself from across and beyond the empire imperial resources, troops, ambassadors, officials, and vassals at the same time as it pumped out commands, envoys, delegates, and armies. The Seleucid empire was a kind of politico-territorial configuration that could be operated only by continuous royal movement. In contrast to, say, the high Roman empire, the Seleucid kingdom failed to develop systems for effectively manifesting the monarch's absent authority. Coins, inscriptions, statues, bureaucracy, envoys, decrees, court literature, rumors, and much more all helped to represent and constitute imperial power, it is true, but none of these accommodated sufficient charismatic or sovereign force to operate in the absence of the king's occasional revivifying presence. Seleucid kingship was a restless battle against time. The royal presence worked like the slowly dissipating wake of a boat. Regions had to experience its impact again before all traces had disappeared, before an imperial necrosis severed all links and the peripheries dropped away: recall the Graeco-Macedonian settlers of the Iranian plateau, sending envoy after envoy, begging to be visited by the king.[207] And so, much like real roads through a landscape, the pathways of imperial power could become overgrown and indistinct without recurring activity in the prescribed directions. Although the Seleucid kingdom displays an, at times, astonishing capacity for even the most neglected of these paths to be rejuvenated—observe Antiochus III's second *anabasis* up to the Hindu Kush—ultimately the empire would prove too vast and unmanageable. Within its far-flung frontiers, the inescapable correlate of a systematic insistence on the king's presence was the far more typical condition of the king's absence.

This chapter has argued for the significance of specific modes of royal travel in articulating the Seleucid political landscape and, generally, for the material and symbolic importance of movement in constructing territorial identities. But we must acknowledge two fundamental lacks. First, it is to be greatly regretted that we have nothing but passing hints on the movements of Seleucid officials. The empire was more than its ruler even if the ideology of Hellenistic monarchy, as refracted through all kinds of contemporary evidence, exclusively focalized narrative agency on the kinghead. It is likely that, much as in the Achaemenid and Roman empires,[208] secondary circuits of royal representatives, such as regional viceroys, satraps, or governors, articulated particular units of the political landscape in the king's absence; we get some sense of this from the cuneiform Astronomical Diaries, whose entries record the journeying of the satrap of Babylonia and sometimes lesser officials into and around the triangle of Babylon, Borsippa, and Seleucia-on-the-Tigris. Except for the particular demands of warfare or embassy, these lower-order circuits, operating within the circumscribed responsibilities of Seleucid administrative geography, would have lacked the boundary-perforating quality of royal movements. And so, a more comprehensive set of evidence would figure an imperial territory dominated by the brilliant orbit of the king's glowing presence but also swarming with the localized epicycles of royal officials. Second, the sheer scarcity of evidence has demanded a synchronic approach; there is simply not enough information to examine in detail the transformations in meaning of kings' travels over the empire's almost two and a half centuries. Certainly, the empire shrank, new routes and nodes rose to prominence (compare Maps 5 and 6), and internecine conflicts fragmented sovereignty, but the scattered indices do not suggest a major revolution in royal mobility until the city-based kinglets of the dynasty's very final years (see Chapter 8).

Movement enacts relations between differentiated positions and thereby gives shape to spaces. In a famous essay Michel de Certeau, gazing down from the 110th floor of the World Trade Center, concluded that it was not his panoptic vision that most effectively represented the space of New York but rather its pedestrians, linking together urban facts by walking and thereby generating the idea of the city.[209] Similarly, the overlapping and intertwined paths of Seleucid kings enunciated their provincial landscape, transforming locales or regions into a continuous imperial territory. Seleucid royal travel molded a landscape haunted by the echo of the kings' footsteps and banquets, encysted with display punishments, bejeweled with *tropaia*, and veined by roadways and trails. All in all: a territory imminent with the memories or potential of imperial presence.

PART IV

Colony

CHAPTER **7**

King Makes City

The Seleucid kings pinned their empire into place with colonial settlements. It is a historical commonplace, and rightly so, that the dynasty's most transformative and historically significant undertaking was its establishment of new urban foundations across the Hellenistic Near East.[1] The walls of these colonies have loomed high over our journey so far—from Megasthenes' Indian ethnography and Demodamas' Central Asian anthropology to the fabrication of the Syrian Seleucis and the ritualized receptions of itinerant kings. They manifest, like nothing else, the intense physicality of Seleucid power, the extraordinary effort put into opening and ordering Seleucid territory. Colonization was a continuous theme of Seleucid kingship, in both the practical actions of individual monarchs and the legitimizing discourses that enunciated them. The scale of these urbanizing activities is breathtaking, far outpacing those of the Ptolemaic and Antigonid neighbors in number and importance[2] and prompting in ancient and modern historians the bureaucratic recoil into lists. So, Appian estimates that Seleucus I Nicator founded sixteen Antiochs, five Laodiceas, nine Seleucias, three Apameas, and one Stratonicea in addition to more than twenty cities named after Greek *poleis* (if anything, an understatement).[3] Many more were established by Antiochus I, Antiochus II, Seleucus IV, and Antiochus IV and a few others by Seleucus II, Antiochus III, Demetrius II, and Demetrius III. Eighty-seven Seleucid settlements have been counted west of the Euphrates, in Asia Minor and Syria;[4] a further thirty-five at least were founded between the Euphrates and Sogdiana.[5] Maps 8 and 9 illustrate these colonial foundations by reign. As we will see, the colonies varied widely in their origin, size, internal composition, and evolution, ranging from small forts *(phrouria)* through sub*polis* settlements *(katoikiai)* to sprawling cities; several of these settlements were physically expanded or abandoned, juridically demoted or promoted.

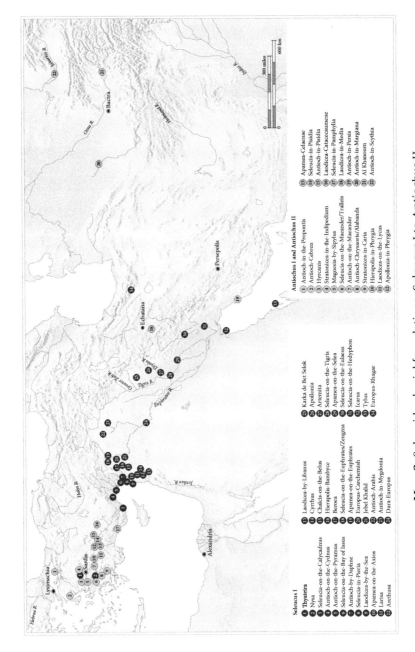

Map 8 Seleucid colonial foundations, Seleucus I to Antiochus II.

Seleucus I

1. Thyatera
2. Nysa
3. Seleucia-on-the-Calycadnus
4. Antioch-on-the-Cydnus
5. Antioch-on-the-Pyramus
6. Seleucia-on-the-Bay of Issus
7. Antioch by-Daphne
8. Seleucia-in-Pieria
9. Laodicea-by-the-Sea
10. Apamea-on-the-Axios
11. Larisa
12. Arethusa
13. Laodicea-by-Libanus
14. Cyrrhus
15. Chalcis-on-the-Belus
16. Hierapolis-Bambyce
17. Beroea
18. Seleucia-on-the-Euphrates/Zeugma
19. Apamea-on-the-Euphrates
20. Europus-Carchemish
21. Jebel Khalid
22. Antioch-Arabis
23. Antioch-in-Mygdonia
24. Dura-Europus
25. Karka de Bet Selok
26. Apollonia
27. Artemita
28. Seleucia-on-the-Tigris
29. Apamea-on-the-Selea
30. Seleucia-on-the-Eulaeus
31. Seleucia-on-the-Hedyphon
32. Icarus
33. Tylus
34. Europus-Rhagae

Antiochus I and Antiochus II

1. Antioch-in-the-Propontis
2. Antioch-Cebren
3. Hyrcanis
4. Stratonicea-in-the-Indipedium
5. Magnesia-by-Sipylus
6. Seleucia-on-the-Maeander/Tralleis
7. Antioch-on-the-Maeander
8. Antioch-Chrysaoris/Alabanda
9. Stratonicea-in-Caria
10. Hierapolis-in-Phrygia
11. Laodicea-on-the-Lycus
12. Apollonia-in-Phrygia
13. Apamea-Celaenae
14. Seleucia-in-Pisidia
15. Antioch-in-Pisidia
16. Laodicea-Cataccaumene
17. Seleucia-in-Pamphylia
18. Laodicea-in-Media
19. Antioch-in-Persis
20. Antioch-in-Margiana
21. Ai Khanoum
22. Antioch-in-Scythia

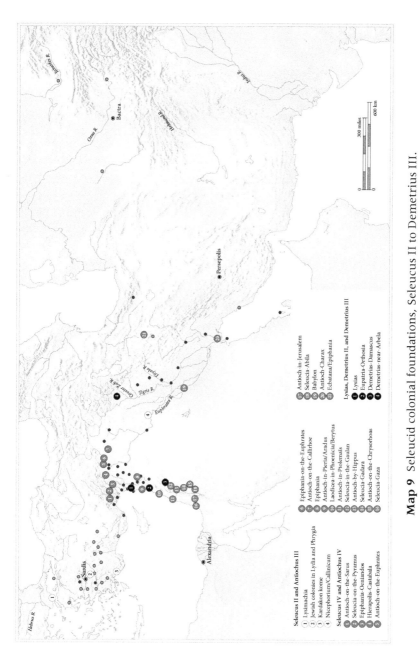

Map 9 Seleucid colonial foundations, Seleucus II to Demetrius III.

Seleucus II and Antiochus III
1 Lysimachia
2 Jewish colonies in Lydia and Phrygia
3 Kardakon kome
4 Nicephorium/Callinicum

Seleucus IV and Antiochus IV
5 Antioch-on-the-Sarus
6 Seleucia-on-the-Pyramus
7 Epiphania-Oeniandos
8 Hierapolis-Castabala
9 Antioch-on-the-Euphrates

Epiphania-on-the-Euphrates
Antioch-on-the-Callirhoe
Epiphania
Antioch-in-Pieria/Aradus
Laodicea-in-Phoenicia/Berytus
Antioch-in-Ptolemais
Seleucia-in-the-Gaulan
Antioch-by-Hippus
Seleucia-Gadara
Antioch-on-the-Chrysorhoas
Seleucia-Gaza

Antioch-in-Jerusalem
Seleucia-Abila
Babylon
Antioch-Charax
Ecbatana/Epiphania

Lysias, Demetrius II, and Demetrius III
Lysias
Eupatria-Orthosia
Demetrias-Damascus
Demetrias-near-Arbela

Whereas thematic investigations of Seleucid urbanism have tended to focus either on the complicated question of Hellenization, in which the colony is held to be both location and cause of cultural change within the kingdom, or on the rather bloodless questions of autonomy and juridical status, this part of the book will approach the foundations primarily as a phenomenon of space.

Facts on the Ground

The spatial impact of Seleucid colonization on the Near East was profound. It can be observed at three levels, situating us over the continental expanse of Seleucid Asia, at a finer-grained regional perspective, and finally in the newly laid boulevards of the Antiochs and Seleucias.

Toward a General Pattern

The externality of Macedonia granted to the early Seleucid kings the Promethean freedom to compose about themselves their imperial territory. Although no ancestral bonds elevated one part of empire over another, Seleucid colonies were not of course evenly distributed in a regularized mesh of settlement. Rather, the location of colonial foundations was a royal choice that deliberately selected or bypassed particular regions of empire and thereby generated both preferential zones and internal peripheries. On a panimperial scale two discrete spatial patterns of colonization emerge, unfurling over the dynasty's course: densely settled panels and linear hinges.

Seleucus I quickly and radically reoriented the urban physiognomy of the Near East. For the most concentrated foci of early Seleucid colonial activities, as can be seen on Map 8, were the lower-middle Tigris river and its affluents and the coastline and hinterland of northern Syria. These two areas had languished in the imperial interstices under the Achaemenid kings, who had concentrated their power on the inherited Zagros and Euphrates capitals of Ecbatana, Susa, and Babylon and on the new Persian palace-cities of Pasargadae and Persepolis; and it is sufficiently clear that by the end of the reign of Alexander the Great Babylon was stabilizing into something like a capital. Accordingly, Seleucus I's founding activities in both new areas constituted a relocation of imperial gravity away from long-established cores to traditionally marginal zones. It is important to recog-

nize that this reorientation was a strategic, top-down intervention, a deliberate rebooting of the landscape; as we will see, this newness is repeatedly
emphasized in official colonizing discourses.

The urban development of the lower-middle Tigris in the pre-Seleucid
first millennium had been hindered by naval inadequacy despite the forced
settlement of transplanted populations into the region by the Persian
kings.[6] In contrast to the Euphrates, mostly fed by regular seasonal snow-
melt from the Anatolian plateau, the Tigris receives several rainfall tributaries along its entire left flank.[7] To regulate the consequently turbulent,
flood-prone riverflow and to facilitate irrigation the Achaemenids or their
agents constructed, perhaps seasonally, numerous weirs from bank to bank
but at the expense of waterborne travel;[8] at such times ships were unable
to cruise the Tigris, which was separated by these barriers from the Persian
Gulf.[9] Alexander had cleared these weirs on his return from the east in
324,[10] but the river's communicative potential was first realized only by
Seleucus Nicator's construction of his great eponymous capital city, Seleucia-
on-the-Tigris, on an unoccupied site near Opis, in the final decade of the
fourth century.[11] Seleucia was located about thirty kilometers south of
modern Baghdad at the unexploited intersection of a number of overland
and freshwater routes: at the northernmost point of navigability on the
Tigris, making the city a gateway settlement for Arabian and Indian maritime trade and for Seleucid dominion over the Gulf;[12] at the mouth of the
Nahr Malcha ("Royal Canal"), which flowed from the Euphrates north of
Babylon into the Tigris, thereby linking Seleucia to western Babylonia,
Syria, and ultimately the Mediterranean;[13] and at the approach to the Zagros mountains, the Iranian plateau, and Central Asia through the Diyala
valley. The excavation of an enormous harbor in the city's southeastern
corner, protected from the flow of the Tigris by an L-shaped mole still visible in aerial photographs,[14] and of a landing area for the Nahr Malcha
along the city's southern edge provided secure maritime structures.

Seleucia-on-the-Tigris was, in the language of urban studies, a "primate
settlement" and the highest-ranking focus for the region's central institutional transactions,[15] as the 30,000-plus excavated administrative seal impressions *(bullae)* attest.[16] Even so, it was supported by an integrated system
of second-tier foundations. Seleucus I established several downstream settlements on the lower stretches of the Tigris, Eulaeus, Hedyphon, and Pa-
sitigris rivers, at or slightly inland from where they debouched into the
Gulf: we know of Seleucia-on-the-Hedyphon, Seleucia-on-the-Eulaeus,

Seleucia-on-the-Erythraean-Sea, and Apamea-on-the-Selea (see Maps 7 and 8). It is likely that Seleucus I improved access from the sea to Seleucia-on-the-Eulaeus, the former Elamite and Persian capital Susa, by canalizing the Eulaeus river.[17] An archipelago of Seleucid military settlements in the Persian Gulf—Icarus (Failaka), Tylus (Bahrain), and perhaps Tarut (Seleucid name unknown)—was fully incorporated into this network.[18] Inland toward the Zagros we find the important colony of Artemita, 500 stades from Seleucia up the Diyala valley,[19] and farther to the north Karka de Bet Selok (mod. Kirkuk).[20] Imperial urbanization continued in the mid-second century under Antiochus IV, who refounded the inundated Alexandria-Charax as Antioch-Charax,[21] and Demetrius II, who established a Demetrias somewhere near Arbela (mod. Arbil) in northern Iraq.[22] As we would expect, the cuneiform evidence from Babylon shows that the preexisting indigenous Euphrates settlements were pulled into the urban network and hierarchy that developed around Seleucia-on-the-Tigris.

For similar reasons as the middle Tigris, northern Syria had failed to develop any major urban centers following the Neo-Assyrian conquest of the Iron Age Aramaean and Neo-Hittite states:[23] even though the Euphrates river comes closest to the Mediterranean in northern Syria, forming the great bend of the Fertile Crescent, the coastline lacked any natural anchorage or good harbor between Cilicia and the Phoenician island-city of Aradus. Worse, the mouth of the Orontes, the main Syrian river, is one of the most difficult mooring points along the shore.[24] The coast's lack of shelter had not posed a problem for small Bronze or Iron Age trading vessels, which could be dragged onto the beaches of Ugarit and Al Mina, but deeper-hulled classical and early Hellenistic ships were obliged to dock at the more southerly Phoenician harbors. These cities, operating in a semiautonomous and mutually beneficial vassalage for their inland imperial suzerains, provided sufficient Mediterranean access for as long as the entire Levantine coast was subject to a single imperial authority (i.e., during the Neo-Assyrian, Achaemenid, and Alexandrian periods). However, the political fragmentation that followed Alexander's death ruptured this unity, leaving the good harbors south of the Eleutherus river to Ptolemy I and the difficult coastline of northern Syria to Seleucus I.

Seizing the bull by its horns, in the very first years of the third century Seleucus founded the four great cities of the so-called Tetrapolis—Seleucia-in-Pieria and Laodicea-by-the-Sea on coastal sites, Antioch-by-Daphne and Apamea-on-the-Axios in the Orontes valley (see Maps 4 and 8). There are numerous indications that these foundations were conceived as an integrated, cohesive unit, from the sibling status attributed to them by Strabo (ἐλέγοντο ἀλλήλων ἀδελφαί, "they were called siblings of one another")[25] and struck onto their late second-century coinage (ΑΔΕΛΦΩΝ ΔΗΜΩΝ, "brother peoples"),[26] the grant of citizenship collectively to Antioch-by-Daphne, Seleucia-in-Pieria, and Laodicea-by-the-Sea by the Ionian city Teos,[27] their similar urban plans and almost identical insula size,[28] and their interwoven foundation narratives.[29] Artificial, well-protected, deepwater harbors were excavated at the coastal cities of Seleucia-in-Pieria and at Laodicea-by-the-Sea, instantly providing northern Syria with an unprecedented maritime infrastructure; the late antique scholar Libanius tells us that the harbor at Seleucia was cut out of solid rock at enormous expense.[30] In each case, the port was the primary urbanistic unit, determining the layout of the surrounding city construction.[31] Antioch-by-Daphne, paired to Seleucia as Athens to the Piraeus, was constructed a mere 120 stades to the east—a half-day's journey for a healthy man laden with goods.[32] Together they formed a gateway to Syria and beyond. Laodicea and Apamea do not form such a natural pairing—the vine-draped ridge of Mount Bargylus hinders inland access—but still the Orontes near Apamea could be reached by the Seleucobelus pass. Furthermore, the specific imperial or capital functions that had been gathered into Seleucia-on-the-Tigris were distributed here between the group of Tetrapolis cities: Apamea served as the kingdom's military headquarters, stud, and elephant base and guarded access to the Orontes valley from the Ptolemaic south; Laodicea and Seleucia had clear mercantile and naval purposes; Antioch seems quickly to have developed administrative concentration.[33] The Tetrapolis colonial square was supported by a matrix of smaller urban settlements, both new or recently founded colonies and expanded Syrian towns, at regular, approximately one-day intervals along the coastline (Seleucia-on-the-Bay of Issus, Heraclea-on-the-Sea, Charadrus), the Orontes valley (Seleucia-on-the-Belus, Laodicea-by-Libanus, Antioch-under-Libanus, Larisa, Arethusa), and the roads to the Euphrates (Chalcis, Beroea, Cyrrhus). Royal-sponsored urbanization of this region continued into the late second century, infilling the landscape with Lysias, Antioch-in-Pieria, Epiphania (mod. Hama), and Demetrias (mod. Damascus).

The middle Tigris and northern Syria formed the two great panels of Seleucid colonial settlement. In each case, Seleucus I created entirely new city networks based upon the interactions of existing overland routes with newly developed naval infrastructure. The construction of two artificial harbors on the Syrian coastline was a truly significant intervention into the Near Eastern landscape that, viewed at an imperial scale, successfully transformed the arc of the Fertile Crescent into the colonized keystone of empire, allowing an unprecedented unification of the Mediterranean and Mesopotamian worlds. The wisdom of concentrating colonization on these two regions is evident from their flourishing post-Seleucid afterlives: in the very shadow of Seleucia-on-the-Tigris, in the so-called Capital District,[34] Parthian, Sasanid, and Arab kings constructed their great urban centers of Ctesiphon, Vologesias, Veh-Ardashir, and Baghdad, and northern Syria remained a vigorous center of urban civilization throughout Roman and Late Antique times.

Between and beyond these colonial panels the early Seleucid monarchs, especially Seleucus I's first two successors, Antiochus I and Antiochus II, founded long chains of freshwater settlements along the major roadways (the Common Road from Ionia to northern Syria; the trans-Euphratene route; and the Khorasan highway from Media to Central Asia) and secondary axes: extended horizontal lines of colonization, with new foundations beaded along alluvial valleys or over passes. The duration of Seleucid rule in each region saw continual urban infilling of these trunk and branch ways with additional settlements and the expansion of existing ones. A hierarchy of colonial settlement emerges: schematizing for clarity, cities were founded along the primary axes, smaller settlements (called *katoikiai*) along the secondary axes, and garrisoned fortresses (called *phrouria*) at bottleneck passes or where the terrain could not sustain a larger colony.[35] As a result of the distribution of economic, administrative, and social functions appropriate to each colony, large city foundations, with a high number of higher-order functions each of large range, were much less frequent than the scattered *katoikiai* and *phrouria*, with lower-order functions each of a smaller range. For example, along Asia Minor's Common Road, as we have seen in Chapter 6, the key artery between the Aegean and northern Syria, Seleucus I founded Nysa, Antiochus I or II established Seleucia-Tralleis (a refoundation), Antioch-on-the-Maeander, Apamea-Celaenae, Hierapolis-in-Phrygia, Laodicea-on-the-Lycus, Laodicea-Catacecaumene, and probably Tyriaeum; these cities are separated from one another by on average *c.* forty kilometers. Secondary routes headed off northward toward the Troad, Mysia, and the Thracian Chersonese and southward toward Caria and Pisidia. One axis, for instance, departing from the western end of the Common Road for Mysia in the north, received several colonies from Seleucus I and Antiochus I—Magnesia-by-Sipylus, Hyrcanis, Agatheira, Thyateira, and Stratonicea-in-the-Indipedium (see Map 3). Of these all were *katoikiai* but the last (a city, as its dynastic name suggests); they are separated from one another by *c.* fifteen kilometers on average. Small fortresses are also known to have dotted the landscape;[36] Josephus, for example, records a letter of Antiochus III to his official Zeuxis establishing garrisons of Babylonian Jews "in the fortresses and most important places" of Lydia and Phrygia.[37] The evidence for the regions east of Syria is scrappier (less epigraphy, less Rome), but a similar picture emerges. On the trans-Euphratene road Seleucus I established the fort-city twin of Seleucia-on-the-Euphrates (Zeugma) and Apamea-on-the-Euphrates as well as the military garrisons at Jebel Khalid (ancient name unknown) and Dura-Europus (see Maps 4 and 8). As in Asia Minor, further colonies were established by Seleucus I's successors—Callinicum by Seleucus II,[38] the twin cities of Epiphania-on-the-Euphrates and Antioch-on-the-Euphrates by Antiochus IV, and the fort of Djazla (ancient name unknown);[39] furthermore, important archaeological work has shown that at some point in the mid-second century the *phrourion* of Dura-Europus was physically expanded into an orthogonally planned settlement and perhaps juridically promoted.[40] Less is known about the Khorasan highway, the main west-east route from the Zagros mountains to Central Asia, but at the very least Seleucus I founded Europus-Rhagae (mod. Rey) and, perhaps, Laodicea-in-Media (mod. Nehavend) and Apamea-in-Media, and Antiochus I, as viceroy of the Upper Satrapies, Antioch-in-Margiane (mod. Merv), Achaïs-in-Margiane, Antioch-in-Scythia (mod. Khodjend), and probably Aï Khanoum (ancient name unknown).[41] There were certainly numerous other colonies and forts, such as a fort under the command of a certain Thoas near modern Kermanshah in the central Zagros[42] or Sirynx in Hyrcania, besieged by Antiochus III.[43]

Where the topography is known, it is evident that the settlements were sited directly on the transit routes: Antioch-on-the-Maeander[44] and the twin Seleucia-on-the-Euphrates (Zeugma) and Apamea controlled the major bridges over their respective rivers; at Dura-Europus local geological features required the ancient traveler to pass via a gorge through the very heart of the colony immediately below the citadel (see later); Kampyr Tepe and Termez protected crossings of the Oxus; Aï Khanoum guarded the access from Bactria to the badlands of Badakhshan, where today Afghanistan, Pakistan, Tajikistan, and China rub shoulders. The functions of these roadway colonies clearly were to protect, channel, and rigorously oversee movement, to maintain the empire's unity by linking the two great colonial panels to one another and to their peripheries, and to shield the imperial territory from the jealous encroachment of rival kingdoms and the savage howls of barbarians.

Whereas Seleucus I's colonial panels had relocated the Near Eastern centers of gravity and emphasized naval communications, the settlement hinges followed ancient arteries of overland travel and made use of long-established regional capitals. The global pattern is one of change at the center, continuity at the margins. So the Seleucids readily inherited the major Achaemenid satrapal centers of Bactra, Persepolis, and Ecbatana in the east and Sardis and the more recently founded Lysimachia in the west. When Antiochus III reestablished the razed Lysimachia in the early years of the second century (see Chapter 3) and Antiochus IV refounded Ecbatana as Epiphania three decades later, father and son were confirming more than transforming the pre-Seleucid urban landscape. Sardis may be typical of these inherited satrapal capitals; it is certainly the best excavated. With the relatively minor exceptions of royal support in the building of the enormous Artemis temple and for limited reconstruction following the defeat of the pretender Achaeus (see Chapter 6), the Seleucid kings effected little change to the city's urban fabric—as far as we know it was not renamed, not moved to a new site, not redesigned or rationalized, not provided with new fortifications, not expanded to incorporate new inhabitants.[45]

Recoding the Regional Landscape

The two extensive panels of northern Syria and the middle Tigris and the hinges to their sides constitute Seleucid colonialism at the continental scale. Equally significant transformations were wrought at the regional and local levels. Alien colonizers were introduced (typically Macedonian, Greek, and southern Balkan, but on occasion Jewish and Iranian)[46] and indigenous populations were transferred from old settlements to new ones; land in the immediate vicinity of new foundations was segmented and redistributed; and regional settlement patterns were profoundly altered.

The movements of indigenous populations from their homes to newly founded towns and cities were both lateral shifts within the same alluvial plains and vertical descents from hillsides or peaks to valley floors. Such interventions, belonging to an age-old Near Eastern imperial strategy of population transfer, were either forced synoecism (urban amalgamation) or metoecism (urban relocation) or some combination of the two.[47] Several are known from literary sources. For example, Seleucia-on-the-Calycadnus in Cilicia (mod. Silifke) was a synoecism of the coastal cities of Hermia, Holmi, and Hyria,[48] as were Antioch-on-the-Maeander and Nysa of various Asia Minor settlements.[49] As for metoecism, Strabo reports that Antiochus I moved the Phrygian inhabitants of hilltop Celaenae down to his new foundation of Apamea on the banks of the Marsyas river,[50] and several sources report that after the battle of Ipsus in 301 Seleucus I transferred the inhabitants of Antigonia, the new urban foundation of his vanquished opponent Antigonus Monophthalmus, to his own Antioch-by-Daphne and/or Seleucia-in-Pieria.[51] Babylonian sources also attest these practices: it appears that Antiochus I, as Crown Prince, relocated the Macedonian population in Babylon to the new capital Seleucia-on-the-Tigris;[52] a heavy tax (miksu dannu) was imposed on Babylon, perhaps intended to encourage such migration.[53] Where we have no literary or epigraphic record, site excavation has revealed the third-century abandonment or precipitous decline of certain indigenous settlements, indicating either forced synoecism/metoecism or economic and administrative outcompetition from a nearby colony. For example, Ebla (mod. Tell Mardikh) suffered from the nearby establishment of Chalcis-on-the-Belus;[54] four towns on the lower Orontes (Al Mina, Sabouni, and two anonymous sites in the foothills behind modern Soueidia) disappeared at or shortly after the foundation of Seleucia-in-Pieria.[55] Clearest of all is the round, concentrically walled Achaemenid fort of Kohna Qala on the left bank of the Oxus, which was completely abandoned at the founding of Seleucid Aï Khanoum less than two kilometers to its southwest[56] (see Figure 6). We should assume that similar reorganizations occurred throughout the mostly unexcavated imperial expanse. The foundation accounts of Antioch-by-Daphne give a legitimizing symbolism to these translations of center: when Seleucus I, soon after his victory at Ipsus in 301, was sacrificing at Antigonia, the eponymous capital of the vanquished Antigonus Monophthalmus, an eagle swooped down, snatched up the thigh meat from the altar, and carried it off to the future site of Antioch-by-Daphne.[57]

All of this is rather thin and gives little indication of the devastating trauma of forced dislocation known from the other Successor states: so resistant were the Ephesians to Lysimachus' intended metoecism that he resorted to flooding them out of their old homes;[58] two letters of Antigonus

Monophthalmus to the Ionian city of Teos, concerning his (interrupted) plan to synoecize the *polis* with neighboring Lebedus, indicate that the city's authorities raised several excuses and administrative hurdles in an attempt to delay their uprooting;[59] an inscription from the Ptolemaic colony of Arsinoe in Cilicia shows that the neighboring ancient Samian city of Nagidos had objected to the foundation and disputed the territorial arrangements.[60] Such (ineffectual) indigenous hostility no doubt was com-

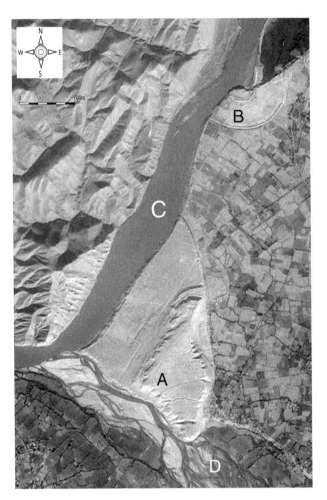

Figure 6 Satellite image of the Dasht-i Qala plain. Note (a) Aï Khanoum, (b) Kohna Qala, (c) Oxus/Amu Darya river, and (d) Kokcha river; see Figure 14.

mon. Even so, it is sufficiently clear that the Seleucid kings relocated the built apparatus of regional and local government off the mountains and across the plains, eliminating or overshadowing preexisting centers of power and forging an entirely new landscape of authority. The Seleucid programs of resettlement must have brought about a brutal reordering of social, economic, and ideological structures as well as the overlaying of local, preconquest perceptions of landscape with a sense of place organized by the new regime.[61] So, the panorama view of the wind-gutted girdle of Achaemenid-period Kohna Qala from the battlements of Aï Khanoum (see Figure 6) must have functioned as a spatial-historical point of reference, the empty bulb of an hourglass, periodizing the transition from Persian to Seleucid rule.[62] This could well have been a frequent experience: "A ruin's a stubborn architectural style." In other places, the Seleucids actively erased traces of the regional centers that preceded them. Seleucus I, according to Libanius, obliterated (ἠφάνισεν) Antigonia;[63] according to Malalas, he razed it to its foundations (κατέστρεψε τὴν Ἀντιγονίαν πόλιν πᾶσαν ἕως ἐδάφους) and transferred its construction materials to Antioch-by-Daphne.[64] Mud bricks of Nebuchadnezzar II, from Opis or the so-called Median Wall, were used in the construction of Seleucia-on-the-Tigris' theater,[65] perhaps suggesting something similar. Destruction by incorporation: this requisitioning of building material cut costs and memories. We are dealing with a technology of forgetting, with exorcisms of the pre-Seleucid terrain.[66]

In addition to these population transfers, the provision of agricultural estates (called *klēroi*) to colonial settlers in the environs of a new foundation meant that the region's fertile lands had to be reallocated. Parchments from the Euphratene colony of Dura-Europus and Antiochus III's letter, quoted by Josephus, concerning the installation of Jewish colonists in Lydia and Phrygia show that settlers were given a variety of plots with different agricultural and horticultural functions—grain cultivation, orchards, vineyards, and gardens[67]—meshing together in new ways a network of productive topographies. For reasons of market and residency it seems that the majority of these *klēroi* were located in the immediate vicinity of the new colony. Archaeological field survey in eastern Bactria discovered dozens of farmsteads and agricultural estates in the Dasht-i Qala plain around Aï Khanoum, graduating in the two kilometers beyond the colony's walls from a relatively dense semiurban zone to a more scattered semirural zone, following the lines of roadways and canals.[68] More striking, perhaps, are old aerial photographs of Damascus (Demetrias), which show the segmentation of lands to the city's north into rectangular *klēroi* of exactly the same dimensions and, presumably, date as the city blocks of the Hellenistic urban plan. Roman centuriation, not following the insulae, is visible to the south. There appear to be similar field divisions around Hellenistic Beroea (mod. Aleppo).[69] Much of this fertile territory would have been cultivated, if not as intensively, before the establishment of Seleucid colonies. By necessity, the indigenous peasantry would have been dispossessed of their estates and, if they remained on site, reduced to a form of dependent labor for their colonial masters.[70] It is hard to overemphasize the extent to which the sudden reallocation of productive lands would have destroyed the traditional routines of daily life and threatened the livelihood of much of the rural population.

If the parcelization of the fertile land surrounding a colony reshaped the boundaries of fields and the obligations of peasants, the Seleucid state coordinated landscape modifications of a more radical kind. Wherever archaeological surveys have been conducted in the vicinity of a Seleucid colony, Hellenistic canalization programs have been uncovered. So, a substantial extension of the cultivated zone, based on new lateral canal construction, took place in the lower Diyala plain behind Seleucia-on-the-Tigris.[71] Hellenistic canals have been identified in the Amuq valley above Antioch-by-Daphne;[72] we know from Roman-period inscriptions of the civic repair in 73/4 CE of Antioch's "Fuller's Canal"[73] and of the Roman army carrying out further works.[74] Survey in eastern Bactria showed that the preexisting irrigation channels running off the Kokcha river above Aï Khanoum were expanded and supplemented, opening several thousand new hectares for agricultural exploitation.[75] New Seleucid canals have been identified around Seleucia-on-the-Eulaeus, formerly Susa,[76] where two Parthian-era Greek epigrams honor a certain Zamaspes for renovating the channels.[77] Pliny reports the canalization of the Margus river beside Antioch-in-Margiane,[78] which is called "well-watered" in the itinerary of Isidore of Charax.[79] All in all, it seems that the Seleucid kings and their agents pursued a deliberate policy of canalization and agricultural intensification. This practice may be mythically encoded in a passage, probably dating back to the Seleucid period, of the obscure and almost unreadable Imperial-period poem, *Cynēgetica:*[80] the poet tells how the personified river Orontes, the main river of northern Syria, having fallen in love with the water nymph Meliboea and rushing forward to unite with her, threatened to inundate Pella (an earlier name for Apamea; see Chapter 4); at the request of the city's ruler, Archippus, Heracles—a well-established stand-in for Seleucid monarchs (see Chapter 6)—heroically channeled the waters northward along their present course.[81] If the aetiology represents Seleucid hydraulic regulation, we will see in Chapter 8 that the invention of a Bronze Age past for Apamea is significant in other respects. The excavation of irrigation channels was not the only transformation of a colony's district. Ancient geographers and modern excavation attest to Antiochus I's construction of an enormous wall at the Merv oasis in Turkmenistan, within which he founded Antioch-in-Margiane, to protect this island of watered orchards as much from blowing sand as nomadic hordes[82] (see Figure 7): the impact on agriculture and demography may well have been dramatic. Perhaps the "Wall of Seleucus," which appears in Babylonian texts, performed a similar function.[83]

The transfer of populations, distribution of lands, and construction of irrigation channels all were the deliberate interventions of willful sovereignty. The results of survey archaeology have revealed the seismic and systemic knock-on effects of these colonial acts.[84] The emerging picture is, by any standards, astonishing: the foundation of new cities in the colonial panels produced population explosions, intensification of agriculture and

Figure 7 Section through the city wall of Antioch-in-Margiane (Merv), Turkmenistan. Note the nested walls of (a) Antiochus I, (b) the Parthians, and (c) the Sasanids; for location of section, see Figure 11.

irrigation, and, in some places, the complete restructuring of Achaemenid and Iron Age patterns of local settlement size and distribution.

This is most apparent in the two colonial panels. Early Seleucid northern Syria experienced a "great dispersion." A recently conducted, methodologically sophisticated survey of the Amuq basin, the agricultural plain above Antioch-by-Daphne, shows that the valley enjoyed a remarkably stable settlement structure from the early Bronze Age to the late Achaemenid period, despite conquests, migrations, and the development of new agricultural technologies. For these three pre-Seleucid millennia settlement had been concentrated at tell sites, usually surrounded by walls and moats; two of these, the twin mounds of Tell Tayinat and Tell Atchana at the top of the valley, together functioned as the stable center of regional power. A radical transformation took place with the foundation of Antioch-by-Daphne at the Amuq's base in the early third century. Each and every traditional center of urban life in the Bronze and Iron Ages (the nucleated tells) was suddenly and completely abandoned. In their place appear, on the one hand, Antioch, dwarfing all other settlements in the Amuq and more extensive in the third century than previously thought,[85] and, on the other hand, hundreds of small, unwalled sites dispersed across the plain. Furthermore, settlement moved into the hills for the first time, to an elevation of about 500 meters (the limit for olive cultivation) and building materials generally switched from mud brick to stone and wood. Overall settlement density rapidly increased, in terms of the number of settlements and total occupied area, continuing until its peak in the late Roman period. Accordingly, the foundation of Antioch-by-Daphne reordered the demography, economy, and society of the Amuq valley and the social and economic systems that governed it; this new settlement pattern continued to early Islamic times.[86] We see similar results in the Homs region of the middle Orontes, where around Laodicea-by-Libanus (located at Tell Nebi Mend, the site of Bronze Age Qadesh) habitation shifted from walled tells to numerous new and unfortified settlements.[87] In the northern (Seleucid) Beqa' valley in Lebanon the Hellenistic-period settled area and population are three times those of the preceding Persian period, and 80 percent of Hellenistic sites lack an earlier occupation.[88]

The middle Tigris, our other colonial panel, produces equally striking if differently directed results. A survey of the Diyala basin—the land behind Seleucia-on-the-Tigris—demonstrated that the region was a backwater under the Neo-Babylonian and Achaemenid kings: no important towns are mentioned in the cuneiform record, and the economy may have been pre-dominantly pastoral. By contrast, the Seleucid and Parthian periods, whose ceramic profiles unfortunately could not be distinguished at the date of survey, saw an explosive urban development of the Diyala region. Most of the basic innovations in settlement and irrigation were introduced at this time. The area of built-up settlement increased an astonishing fif-teenfold from Achaemenid times, accompanied by a shift from villages and small towns to much larger urban agglomerations.[89] As we have already seen, this nucleation was made possible by extensive canalization work.

The colonial hinges demonstrate the significant, if less revolutionary, impact of Seleucid colonization. In the Khuzestan plains around Seleucia-on-the-Eulaeus, the former Elamite and Achaemenid capital of Susa, un-der the Seleucid kings settlement shifted away from the rain-watered Za-gros foothills to the base of the citadel along the banks of newly excavated canals, but the Seleucid and Parthian periods were not ones of major pop-ulation growth.[90] We have seen that in the Hellenistic Dasht-i Qala, the east Bactrian plain stretching twenty kilometers to the northwest of Aï Kha-noum, the urban center shifted a short distance from the 25-hectare semi-circular Achaemenid fortress of Kohna Qala to the new 135-hectare colony of Aï Khanoum.[91] Other regions of Hellenistic Bactria, however, seem to have experienced drastic reductions of population.[92]

Each valley tells its own story, and the surveys are too few by far to al-low comprehensive conclusions. Future research may well complicate the picture. But it seems fair to say that settlement discontinuity and expan-sion are more apparent in the colonial panels, where whole populations seem conjured from the ground, than in the colonial hinges. In every case the establishment of a new Seleucid foundation functions as the source of rippling changes throughout the entire productive landscape; such multi-plier effects are well known and studied from other ancient colonizing em-pires, say Roman Gaul[93] or the Neo-Assyrian Jazirah.[94] The establishment of Seleucid colonies, to a greater or lesser extent depending on situation, deterritorialized then reterritorialized the regional and local landscapes of empire, like the pieces of a shaken kaleidoscope settling into a new order.

Cities of Order

All of this becomes meaningful solely in terms of the new urban founda-tions, radiating out their influences and reorganizing their hinterlands. It will be helpful to divide the variety of new Seleucid foundations into two basic types—the small, ungeometric fortified settlement and the large, grid-planned city. The distinction is, in Gramscian terms, between the former's architecture of dominance (giving control of the physically coercive forms of rule) and the latter's additional political aesthetics of hegemony (providing the nonviolent construction of a normative, imperial reality).[95]

Of the former only a few sites have been in any way excavated or studied—the peak fort on Mount Karasis in Cilicia, Jebel Khalid and early Dura-Europus on the middle Euphrates, the square enclosure at Icarus in the Gulf, and perhaps Kakul,[96] Termez,[97] and Kurganzol[98] in Bactria. The Euphratene *phrouria* share a basic topographic separation between a citadel (the seat of the garrison leader) and the houses of the Graeco-Macedonian settlers *(klērouchoi)* clustered at its base[99] (see Figures 8 and 9).

The acropolis at each site is occupied by an administrative building or "governor's palace."[100] The careful excavation of Jebel Khalid's citadel indi-

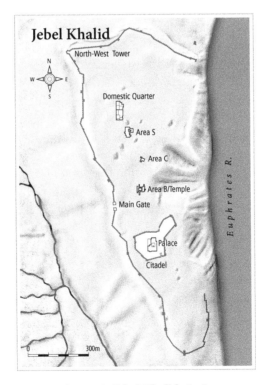

Figure 8 Jebel Khalid, Syria.

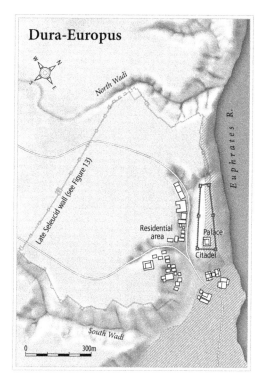

Figure 9 Early Seleucid Dura-Europus, Syria.

cates that this palace functioned as the settlement's redistributive, administrative center (coinage, food, and weaponry were stored there) and the setting for sympotic entertainments and various rituals of garrison solidarity.
The strongly fortified acropolis at Jebel Khalid was entered by a single narrow entrance, at Dura-Europus, via three narrow gateways, each overlooked
by a tower. The Seleucid fort high on Mount Karasis in Cilicia shows a similar bifocal topography, between a lower garrison and an upper administrative and banqueting center, accessed through two well-defended gateways[101]
(see Figure 10).

It is probable that the pattern, petrifying the fixed hierarchy of a military
community, would have been found elsewhere in the kingdom; certainly,
dedicatory and honorific inscriptions from other, unexcavated sites attest to
a corresponding two-tier organization of officers and soldiers. Other than
this, however, the small military settlements seem to have few architectural or urbanistic principles in common besides a basic concern for defense

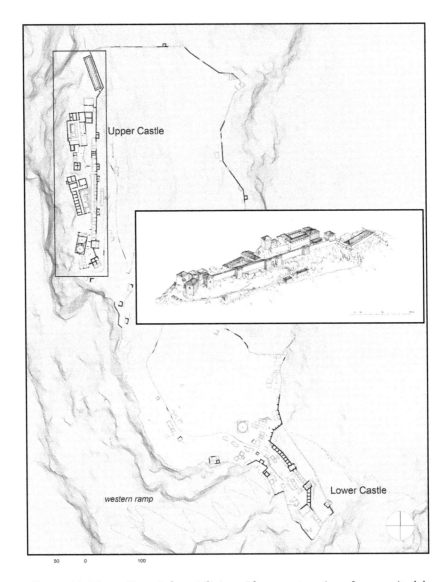

Upper Castle

western ramp

Lower Castle

50   0   100

Figure 10 Mount Karasis fort, Cilicia, with reconstruction of upper citadel.

and surveillance. They display little that would be out of place under earlier or later regimes.

The grandiose, orthogonal cities of the Seleucid kingdom, by contrast, manifest a distinct and instantly recognizable imperial urbanism (see Figure 11). Those sites whose layouts have been uncovered by excavation or inferred from aerial photography and modern street plans display a regimented geometric uniformity that, in its replication and formalism, is without precedent in the Near East.[102] Its fundamental characteristics are simple. The new city, roughly rectangular in shape, was cut across by a grid of rigidly linear roads, intersecting at right angles and at regular intervals. It is evident from a number of these colonies that certain streets, aligned with the city's gates, formed wider, preferential axes of movement that segmented as much as united the urban space;[103] Hellenistic and Roman inscriptions from Seleucid colonies in Asia Minor, as from other sites, term these *plateiai*.[104] This grid delineated and enclosed urban modules of city blocks, which varied in size across the kingdom. At Seleucia-on-the-Tigris, Seleucus I Nicator's first foundation, these stretched an enormous 140 meters by 70 meters, the largest ever constructed in the ancient world, each divided into eight square housing units by the second century.[105] The north Syrian Tetrapolis cities, with the exception of Seleucia-in-Pieria, shared common city-block dimensions of approximately 112 meters by 58 meters;[106] those of Demetrias are 110 meters by 55 meters;[107] of Beroea 120 meters by 45 meters; of Apamea-on-the-Euphrates 105 meters by 38 meters;[108] of Jebel Khalid 90 meters by 35 meters;[109] of Dura-Europus (in its second, orthogonal period) 70 meters by 35 meters. All the blocks have an approximate 2:1 proportionality and are oriented north-south, with their long sides at east and west. Regardless of whether this indicates a common architect, as has been proposed for the Tetrapolis cities,[110] at the very least it suggests a shared conception of how a large colony should be shaped. Hellenistic and early imperial inscriptions from Seleucid colonies in Syria and Asia Minor term the city blocks either *amphoda* or *plintheia*,[111] again terms attested elsewhere;[112] as we will see, these blocks could be named. Public areas, such as *agorai* and temples, were incorporated into the grid, taking up a particular number of city-block modules: the meeting points of streets, so important in Roman cities, were never the basis of the urban plan. Fortification walls, winding over the most suitable contours independent of the street grid, typically enclosed enormous and well-defended acropoleis at the cities' edges:[113] such an arrangement, recalling that of the *phrouriai*, discussed earlier, allowed the citadel to dominate and separate itself from the city.[114] Furthermore, as we will see in detail in Chapter 8, the more important cities contained extensive palace quarters that were in some way distinguished and isolated from more accessible civic areas. Finally, it is worth identifying a subgroup of these planned cities, including Beroea (mod. Aleppo), Antioch-in-Margiane (mod. Merv), and Demetrias (mod. Damascus): these constituted expansions of indigenous, nonorthogonal settlements into large, planned colonies; the pre-Seleucid city was incorporated unchanged into the new colonies as a distinctive urban quarter.[115]

This much is evident from the city plans. Although a good part of this urban fabric is familiar from the so-called Hippodamian city planning of classical Greece[116]—the palatial districts are the major exception—it has a different significance in the context of Seleucid state formation and in the colonial environment of the Near East. The implementation of a standard urban formula across the far-flung, polyglot, and culturally diverse empire had the obvious pragmatic advantages—easily built, easily learned, easily distributed—demanded by the sheer magnitude of the Seleucid colonial project. In other words, the early Seleucid court generated for its architects

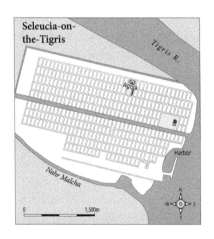

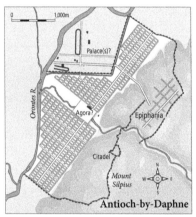

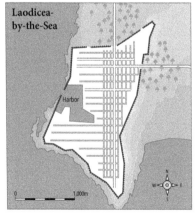

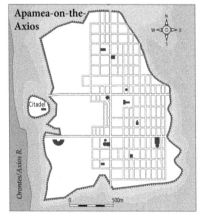

and their workforces a set of operating assumptions for city construction and therefore the liberty to work without constant recourse to a distant and wandering central authority.[117] The consistent geometric logic of these urban spaces, in no way privileging local over outsider knowledge, was effortlessly legible, to use James Scott's term, and, as a result, ideally suited to an immigrant population and an itinerant court.[118] The abstract simplicity of urban plans also turned the city blocks into a kind of easily exchanged, aggregated, or fragmented unit, convenient for distribution among a colonial community.[119]

At the same time, the cities' orthogonality formed part of the ideological matrix of government. It appears that colonists and newcomers were

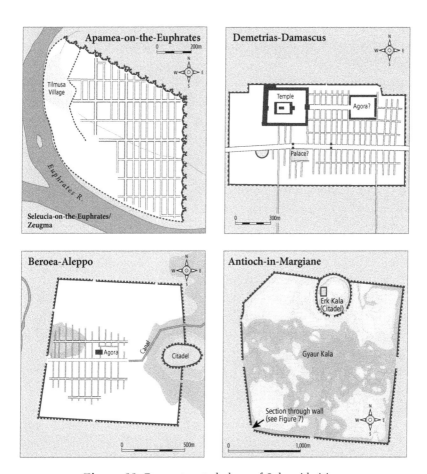

Figure 11 Reconstructed plans of Seleucid cities.

assigned by the state to prescribed communal affiliations and spatial locations. An interesting example is the request of king Seleucus IV in 186 that the magistrates and overseer *(epistatēs)* of Seleucia-in-Pieria grant citizenship to a certain Aristolochus, loyal servant to the reigning king, his older brother (Antiochus), and his father (Antiochus III); the city's secretary *(grammateus)* was instructed to generate a civic identity for Aristolochus by enrolling him in the deme Olympieus and the tribe Laodicis.[120] A special case, no doubt, but it reveals the dynastically and religiously named political categories into which colonial citizens were slotted. Similarly, individuals could be categorized in spatial terms by urban module. So, the military responsibilities of the citizens of Hellenistic Stratonicea-in-Caria, for example, were organized according to the urban grid plan, with the residents of particular *amphoda*—identified in reference to shrines, roads, and monuments—assembled into units and attached to numbered towers of the city wall.[121] Likewise, the laborers who repaired Antioch's "Fuller's Canal" in 73/4 CE were recruited *kata plintheia,* by city block. Almost 200 of these blocks were involved, identified by name in two fragmentary inscriptions: most have Greek or Macedonian eponyms—e.g., the *plintheia* of Demades, of Apollas son of Seleucus; three have Persian names—the *plintheia* of Bagadates, of Pharnaces the gymnasiarch, and of Damasaphernes/Damas son of Saphernes; one is Thracian—the *plintheion* of Athenaeus son of Bithys; four are called after religious associations—e.g., the *plintheion* of the Cerauniasts, honoring Zeus Ceraunus of Seleucia-in-Pieria; and one is named after a deity, Zeus Soter. It is most probable that these city-block names refer not to their contemporary inhabitants but to their most ancient proprietors and so offer evidence of these quarters' founding population;[122] the presence of Persian residents is particularly intriguing. What is key is that the relevant divisions of civic infrastructure are the individual modules of the Seleucid urban plan. As a further example, an inscription from 175 records the civic authorities of Laodicea-by-the-Sea conceding the property rights over an *amphodon* to the cult of the Egyptian deities Sarapis and Isis located there.[123] Lest it be thought that such forms of governmentality were restricted to the empire's western hemisphere, we should note the (sadly truncated) reference in the cuneiform Astronomical Diary for 145 to a census (*minûtu,* "counting") of the Babylonians, administrators, and colonists (Akkadian *puliṭū* for Greek πολῖται) at Babylon and Seleucia-on-the-Tigris.[124] It is clear, even from this scanty evidence, that the regular grid plans of Seleucid cities functioned as a homogenizing technology of government, a simplification indispensable to the emerging kingdom's statecraft. In other words, the Seleucid colony created an urban terrain with precisely the standardized characteristics that would be easiest to assess and manage.

The easy-to-master city, in the twin sense of comprehension and control, has long been the dream of autocrats and empire builders: Baron Haussmann's transformation of Paris under Napoleon III is the *locus classicus* in urban studies for the identification of wide boulevards and regularized plans with civic discipline and government surveillance.[125] Even if the Seleucid kingdom lacked the governmental and disciplinary capacity or ambition of the modern liberal or imperial state, in the wildly mercurial world of dynastic and international politics it was crucial that it maintain political and military control over independent-minded cities. We have already seen that the colonies were dominated from the first by large walled citadels[126] (see Figure 11). These continued to be built: amid the dynastic agony in the late second century Antiochus IX constructed an oppressive citadel, later razed by the Roman general Pompey, in Apamea-on-the-Axios.[127] But in addition to this vertical architecture of fortification, the flat, orthogonal plans opened the cities up to the free movement of military violence, providing little opportunity for escape or spatial camouflage: the one disadvantage Aristotle identified in the "new" rectilinear plan for self-governing *poleis*—that, while elegant, they could more easily be penetrated and conquered by a hostile force—was precisely what made it attractive to Seleucid monarchs.[128] We see this dynamic in action during the failed revolt of the inhabitants of Antioch-by-Daphne against Demetrius II Nicator *c.* 145. According to Josephus and Diodorus Siculus, each presumably following Posidonius, the fleeing Antiochians were unable to hide from the king's mercenaries and were slaughtered in the streets.[129] Seleucid Antioch was no Casbah of Algiers.

The most interesting, albeit nebulous, characteristic of these regularly planned Seleucid colonies is the sociopolitical effect of their *esprit géométrique*. Put another way, it seems likely that these new cities, with their grandiose scale, visual regimentation, orderly proportions, extended vistas, framed squares, and insistent uniformity, were intended as manifestations of the kings' awesome power and aesthetic expressions of legitimate authority. The Seleucid cities stood in architectural contrast to the preexisting and coexisting indigenous urban centers, which vastly outnumbered them. While all the colonies had large pre-Hellenistic settlements in their vicinity offering themselves up for comparison, the opposition is most striking where the unrectilinear indigenous settlement was incorporated at the edge of the new one, thereby producing an old town–new town dyad. This was the case for at least Antioch-in-Margiane, Beroea-Aleppo, Demetrias-Damascus, Apamea-Celaenae,[130] and perhaps, in an incipient sense, Antioch-in-Jerusalem, where the new foundations refocused the towns, placed newcomers at the center, and so marginalized the existing inhabitants.[131] In his stimulating study of New Delhi, constructed as the new capital of British India in the first half of the twentieth century next to what then became Old Delhi, Stephen Legg has illustrated the various ways in which the division between the old and the new towns served as an iconic representation of the Raj's self-claimed progressive ethos; the twin cities represented, respectively, boulevards-galis, health-disease, order-disorder, and, inevitably, white-brown.[132] While the Seleucid state did not profess *avant la lettre* a commitment to Enlightened social transformations, its cities' orthogonal plans demonstrably broke with the past in favor of what Aristotle called the "modern style" (τὸν νεώτερον τρόπον):[133] the straight roads of Aï Khanoum as much as the view from its battlements to abandoned Kohna Qala (see Figure 6 in this chapter and Figure 14 in Chapter 8) ordered the recent past into distinct periods. Urban plans, like the milestones explored in Chapter 6, advertised the Seleucid monarchy's "scientific" credentials as the marriage of reason to power.

The Ideology of Colonialism

Hand in hand with the transformations wrought on the ground by the Seleucid colonial project were a set of court-propagated discourses which gave them narrative form and ideological interpretation. The founding of colonies was made a central characteristic of Seleucid royal identity, in which the king emerged as a civilizing hero and master architect. We see this in the colonies' names, narrative accounts of their foundation, and the secondary urbanism that saw their continued development and expansion.

Names

The bestowal of a city name was the most formal and direct method for coding the colonial act, a baptism of place, prescribing conformity upon land, settlers, and administration. As we saw in Chapter 4, in reference to the north Syrian Seleucis, the imperial labeling made use of two new onomastic systems: town names borrowed from the Graeco-Macedonian mainland and dynastic names derived from Seleucus I's immediate family. We will not explore here the Old World toponymy, which is more typical of second-tier or satellite settlements than of the major orthogonal foundations, often the Hellenized misunderstanding of preconquest Semitic names (e.g., Megara from Ma'ara or Pella from Pahil),[134] in some cases of pre-Seleucid date,[135] and very infrequent outside northern Syria; accordingly, the focus will be the dynastic names.

While the king's bestowal of a name was of itself an Adamic act of possession, Seleucid colonial onomastics are remarkable for their repetitive, unvaried, formulaic quality. For the first century and a half only five names were used (Seleucus, his father/son, Antiochus, his mother, Laodice, and his wives, Apame and Stratonice); from the reign of Antiochus IV to the dynasty's collapse a couple of new epithets (Epiphania, Eupatria) and names (Demetrius, Lysias) were added. Specification was provided by combining one of these dynastic names with a prominent landscape feature, such as a river, mountain, or region, in some cases relabeled, in others not. Accordingly, the empire was dotted with settlements called *dynastic name*-in/on-*landscape feature:* Seleucia-on-the-Tigris, Antioch-in-Persis, Laodicea-by-the-Sea, and so on. This is a spatial discourse predicated on the controlled deployment of geographic knowledge and the identification of the imperial terrain with the ruling dynasty.[136] Much like the orthogonal city plan, this onomastic system was a kind of institutionalized uniformity that functioned so as to standardize the vastness of empire and to smooth out regional distinctions. The nomenclature was infinitely repeatable, allowing, even encouraging, the colonial infilling we witness right up to the kingdom's close (see Maps 8 and 9). The replicability of name is figured in the famous and influential statue of *Tychē* ("Fortune"), created for Antioch-by-Daphne by Eutychides of Sicyon in the early third century. Unlike earlier images,[137] Eutychides' included specific references to Antioch's local topography: in a geographical allegory, the mural-crowned goddess sat on rocks that represented Mount Silpius and rested her feet on the personified Orontes river.[138] This was a visual formula that would be reproduced throughout the ancient world simply by switching out the name of the waterway or mountain. It is no coincidence that it emerges in a Seleucid court milieu alongside its onomastic equivalent.

The ideological significance attributed to this naming formula is shown by its consistent use throughout the empire. Whenever the Seleucid kings refounded a city, they renamed it with their dynastic toponymy, in this way preferring to mark themselves off from recent precedent than appear as the rightful heirs of empire. So, the Achaemenid capitals of Susa and Ecbatana were refounded as Seleucia-on-the-Eulaeus by Seleucus I and Epiphania by Antiochus IV, respectively. As we have seen in Chapter 2, several of Alexander's colonies in Central Asia, after destruction by nomadic razzia, were rebuilt and retitled by Antiochus I,[139] including Alexandria-in-Margiane as Antioch-in-Margiane and Alexandria-Eschate as Antioch-in-Scythia. Antiochus IV rebuilt Alexander's colony at the mouth of the Tigris, Alexandria-Charax, under his own name, Antioch-Charax.[140] In fact, it seems that no Seleucid foundation continued officially to use a pre-Seleucid name with the explicable exceptions of Babylon and Lysimachia: the former functioned as the origin point of the kingdom;[141] the latter legitimized Seleucid claims to European Thrace (see Chapter 3). This Seleucid onomastic practice was far from the standard solution to the Successor kingdoms' dearth of legitimacy: Lysimachus had refounded Antigonia-Troas as Alexandria-Troas; the Antigonids firmly slotted themselves into Macedonia's preexisting Argead royal tradition; the Ptolemies based themselves in Alexandria-by-Egypt and portrayed themselves as the Conqueror's heirs;[142] even the Parthians emphasized their Achaemenid connections, returning to Seleucia-on-the-Eulaeus its former name, Susa.[143] In contrast to their peers, Seleucid nomenclature quite deliberately framed their colonial enterprise as something new. Although much would have remained of the earlier cities physically and demographically, court-derived naming patterns chose to portray a specific image—the Seleucid monarch forging, not inheriting, an empire.

That the colonies' names were formulaic did not make them meaningless. This is most evident in the marriage of Antiochus III to Laodice, daughter of the king of Pontus in northern Asia Minor. According to Polybius, the Seleucid king met his intended at the twin foundations of Seleucia-on-the-Euphrates and Apamea-on-the-Euphrates. The reason for this location is not immediately apparent—it lies neither at the edge of Seleucid territory, as Rhosus for the marriage of Seleucus I and Stratonice[144] and Antioch-in-Ptolemaïs for that of Alexander I Balas and Cleopatra Thea,[145] nor on the most direct route of travel from the Pontic kingdom. As Amélie Kuhrt and Susan Sherwin-White suggested, the explanation must lie, at least in part, in the dynastic nomenclature.[146] Seleucia-on-the-Euphrates was named after Seleucus I, Apamea-on-the-Euphrates after his Iranian wife Apame. The paired settlements were linked by a bridge, the major crossing of the Euphrates, giving the sobriquet Zeugma. Zeugma derives from the verb ζεύγνυμι, used of yoking, bridging, and joining in marriage. Accordingly, in a symbolic replay of Seleucus' wedding to Apame, Antiochus III, coming from Seleucia, met his Iranian wife Laodice, coming from Apamea, at "Marriage." The wedding of Alexander Balas, of the Seleucid family, to Cleopatra Thea, of the Ptolemaic family, at Antioch-in-Ptolemaïs may have had similar symbolism.[147] A more explicit example: Antioch-in-Persis' letter to Magnesia-on-the-Maeander, an ancient city in Asia Minor, to be discussed in more detail in Chapter 8, narrates Antiochus I's request to the Ionian *polis* for the dispatch of colonists to the new foundation in the Gulf; according to the letter, Antiochus was "eager to increase our *polis,* since it was named after him" (φιλοτιμο[υ]μένου ἐπα[υξ]ῆσαι τὴμ πόλιν ἡμῶν οὖσαν αὐτοῦ ἐπώνυμον).[148] The eponymy binds the king's reputation to the colony's prosperity.[149]

In sum, the colonial nomenclature tied the Seleucid settlement program directly to the royal family and projected an image of geographical control and colonial fecundity. Like the battlefield *tropaia* and roadside milestones discussed in the previous chapter, the baptisms of place were ways of marking the territory as Seleucid.

Foundation Narratives—The King's Tale

Foundation narratives or *ktiseis,* a literary genre that recounted the creation and peopling of a new city, are a much more complex kind of ideological fashioning. Fragments of official court foundation narratives survive for seven Seleucid colonies: each of the Syrian Tetrapolis, Kirkuk, Seleucia-on-the-Tigris (all established by Seleucus I), and Lysimachia (refounded by Antiochus III). In addition, a few curt lemmata in classical geographers and encyclopaedists and an inscription from Babylonia are all colored to a greater or lesser extent by legitimizing *ktisis* discourse. From the general shipwreck of Hellenistic literature this flotsam teases with what might have been; foundation narratives may well have taken as central a place in Seleucid court literature as the colonizing act in Seleucid imperial practice. Needless to say, the extant accounts should be taken, not as an accurate or direct record of the actual, mechanical, sweaty building work, but as literary, ideologically motivated meditations on the goals and expectations of colonization.

The foundation narrative of Seleucia-on-the-Tigris, in chapter fifty-eight of Appian's *Syriaca,* our most extended history of the Seleucids, comes as close as we can to the official court representation of the colonizing process. The foundation account appears within a ten-chapter excursus on the rise, reign, and demise of Seleucus I;[150] as we have seen, much of this material, including the omens, dreams, and oracles examined in Chapter 3, derives from court-propagated historiography. Furthermore, Appian's narrative is free of the local, civic accretions that fastened onto the foundation accounts of the Syrian colonies (see Chapter 8), a fact partly to be explained by the Parthian curtain that descended across the trans-Euphratene provinces from the 140s; although this political boundary was by no means culturally impermeable,[151] it makes it much more likely that Appian made use of an early Hellenistic tradition preserved in the libraries of Rome or Alexandria. Moreover, various internal features of the narrative point to an early date.[152] It is worth telling the tale in full:

They say that when the Magi were ordered to indicate the propitious day and the hour of the day for beginning the foundations of Seleucia-on-the-Tigris, they lied about the hour, not wishing to have such a stronghold (ἐπιτείχισμα) built against them. While Seleucus was in his tent waiting for the appointed hour, and the army, in readiness to begin the work, stood quietly until Seleucus should give the signal, suddenly, at the more auspicious moment (κατὰ τὴν αἰσιωτέραν ὥραν), supposing that someone had ordered them, they leapt to the task with such alacrity that none of the heralds were able to restrain them. When the work had been completed, Seleucus, being troubled, asked the Magi about the city, and they, having first secured a promise of impunity, replied, "O king, that which is fated (τὴν πεπρωμένην . . . μοῖραν), for better or worse, neither man nor city can change; for there is a destiny (μοῖρα) for cities just as for men. It seems good to the gods that the city endure for ages (χρονιωτάτην), having its origin at this hour. For we altered the fated time, fearing lest the city should be a stronghold against us. But destiny is stronger than knavish Magi or an unsuspecting king. Accordingly, heaven (τὸ δαιμόνιον) announced the more auspicious hour to the army: it is permitted that you be made aware of this, so that you no longer suspect us of artfully deceiving you (τεχνάζειν). For you yourself, the king, were presiding over the army, and you had given the instruction to wait; and the army, most obedient to you in all dangers and toils, could not be restrained even when you gave the order to stop; but they sprung forward, not just a part of them but all together, their officers with them, supposing that they had been ordered. And indeed the order had been given: that is why they did not obey even you when you restrained them. For what can be stronger in human affairs than a king, if not a god? The god overcame your intention and gave directions about the city in our place (ἡγεμόνευσέ σοι τῆς πολεως ἀντὶ ἡμῶν), being hostile to us and to all the people round about. For how can our affairs prosper with a more powerful people settled beside us? For your city was born with fortune (γέγονε σὺν τύχῃ) and it will grow great (μεγιστεύσει) and enduring. As for you, confirm your pardon to us, who erred in fear of losing our own prosperity." The king was pleased with what the Magi said and pardoned them.[153]

The story performs a number of functions. Fundamentally, the entire account takes for granted and reinforces the assumption that the foundation of a colony will firmly embed Seleucid rule; this is the source of the priests' fear. The Magi term Seleucia an ἐπιτείχισμα, "stronghold," used of a military presence in alien territory,[154] closely identifying the new city with effective imperial control. To rule is to found colonies. Second, the narrative recognizes, if schematically, the new kingdom's distinct ethnic identities and local environments and effects a reconciliation of the conquered to the conquerors and the Macedonians to Asia. The participating groups pivot on the person of Seleucus—the Graeco-Macedonian army excavates the foundations, the Magi indicate the auspicious moment, and king Seleucus translates the ritual expertise of the latter into monarchic instruction for the former. The Magi, despite their Persian associations, in this text are clearly identified with nearby Babylon and Chaldaean wisdom[155] and given the rituals pertinent to that tradition: while Greek colonial divination was chiefly concerned with identifying the right location,[156] the selection of the single, propitious moment on which the city's entire future depended is a well-known feature of Mesopotamian city-building rituals.[157] Deceitful Magi are a trope of Greek historiography.[158] By tale's close, in a resolution of sorts, the Magi acknowledge their subordination and receive Seleucus' magnanimous forgiveness. Third, the passage dramatizes and legitimizes the realignment of imperial centrality from the Euphrates to the Tigris and of political control from the Achaemenids to the Seleucids. The miracle at Seleucia both guarantees the city's prosperity and celebrates a *translatio imperii*. The phrase used by Appian's Magi to refer to the inescapability of fate, τὴν πεπρωμένην μοῖραν, is found in Herodotus 1.91.1, where it is Delphi's justification for Cyrus' victory over pious Croesus, king of Lydia: the same destiny that led to Persia's replacement of Lydia now demands Seleucia's replacement of Babylon. Heaven has thrown its weight behind the new rulers and their new city. Accordingly, in a neat reversal, the Magi's interpretative role is displaced from heralding the appropriate moment to interpreting the miracle, and, as a result, the priests themselves move from condemning the city by inauspicious timing to confirming its future fortune; a curse has become a blessing.[159] Finally, Appian's account is emphatically monarchist, both in giving to Seleucus' instructions and interrogations narrative centrality and in the pious political theology delivered by the Magi—who but a god is stronger than the king? Even this unnamed divinity is molded after the king's persona: the army, awaiting Seleucus' instruction, receives instead an order from heaven, an unmediated theophany, without disguise or symbol, without physicality or image, entirely limited to the command the king should have given.

The other foundation narratives are later, briefer, and of uncertain provenance, and so more difficult evidence for an examination of official Seleucid colonizing discourse. They can be treated quickly. The accounts of the Syrian Tetrapolis (Antioch-by-Daphne, Seleucia-in-Pieria, Apamea-on-the-Axios, and Laodicea-by-the-Sea) focus on king Seleucus' identification of appropriate locations, by eagle divination or hunt, and on his laying out of the urban plan through symbolic gestures. So, for Libanius, Antioch-by-Daphne was founded where an eagle, its flight followed on horseback by Seleucus' son Antiochus, dropped the sacrificial meat it had snatched up from an altar in Antigonia. Around this splatter zone, Seleucus I stationed his Indian elephants at intervals, where the towers of the city wall would be constructed, and marked out the streets with wheat:[160] the first gesture allegorized the defensive strength of the new city and embraced the full geographical extent of the imperial territory;[161] the second, as in the foundation of Alexandria-by-Egypt, signified hopes for the city's fecundity and prosperity.[162] Seleucus settled there nearby populations, including the inhabitants of Antigonia, and those of his army who chose to remain.[163] The king then dedicated and beautified the suburb of Daphne after his horse stumbled on Apollo's golden arrow while out hunting.[164] The hunt motif appears again in Malalas, a sixth-century CE Christian chronicler from Antioch, who writes that Seleucus marked out the walls of Laodicea-by-the-Sea with the dripping blood of a wild boar he had speared on the chase; Apamea was outlined with the blood of a sacrificed bull and goat.[165] While hunting was an important arena for the display of the personal prowess and bravery expected of Macedonian and Hellenistic kings, the particular significance of the bloodlines remains obscure.[166] In sum, the Tetrapolis narratives place Seleucus I in the narrative driving seat, figure him as chief architect, and mask planning as spontaneity and forethought as revelation in order to give the new settlements the blessing of divine approval.

The sixth-century CE Syriac Christian chronicle of Karka de Bet Selok contains a more down-to-earth account of the refounding of Assyrian Kirkuk. According to this narrative, Seleucus raised new walls, constructed sixty-five towers *(purqᵉsē)*, and opened two great gateways, one of which was named after its architect, a certain Totay. The king enlarged the city, divided it into seventy-two straight streets, and placed a splendid palace at its center. He then settled five extended families *(šarbātā)* in the city, providing them with farmlands and vineyards on a tax-free basis.[167] What emerges, once again, is the absolute agency of the Seleucid monarch and his profile as architect-king.

Finally, Livy and Appian, taking their material from Polybius, describe Antiochus III's refoundation of Lysimachia in European Thrace in terms that can derive only from official Seleucid pronouncements:[168] the king, arriving victorious from the east, reerected the walls, ingathered the scattered citizens, and ransomed back the enslaved; to the inhabitants, Antiochus awarded cattle, sheep, and agricultural equipment. As we saw in Chapter 3, the reconstruction in general and the gift of the plow in particular characterize the Seleucid monarch as an urbanizing culture hero. Lysimachia, like Seleucia-on-the-Tigris in the initial perspective of the Magi, is an ἐπιτείχισμα, "stronghold," that serves to confirm and represent Antiochus' revitalization of Seleucid sovereignty in European Thrace.

The chief characteristic of these official representations of the colonial enterprise is the Seleucid king's monopolization of agency, a distortion that was achieved by suppressing predecessors, subordinates, and partners. Seleucid colonization was deliberately marked off from recent precedents, much as the Seleucus Romance and the Seleucid Era sundered the founder-king from his Macedonian homeland and Alexander's campaigns (see Chapter 3). As we have seen, the Seleucid kings renamed most of the Achaemenid and Alexandrian settlements they colonized[169] and demolished Antigonus Monophthalmus' eponymous capital in northern Syria. Indeed, divine authorization is given to such rupture in Malalas' account of the founding of Antioch-by-Daphne: when Seleucus asked the priest Amphion for a sign to be given whether he ought to rebuild Antigonia or "found another city in another place" (κτίσαι πόλιν ἄλλην ἐν ἄλλῳ τόπῳ), an eagle, sweeping down from heaven, carried away the sacrificial offering to the new site of Antioch-by-Daphne on Mount Silpius.[170]

Without doubt, the construction of dozens of new colonies across the Near East was the hard work of battalions of architects, stonemasons, bricklayers, unskilled laborers, and so on under the guidance of royal administrators. But official foundation narratives obscured the role of these subordinates and employees.[171] We can see this in a couple of examples. Antiochus III's letter to Zeuxis, concerning the planting of 2,000 Jewish families in Lydia and Phrygia, carefully leaves to his subordinate the handling of all logistical and administrative challenges, while preserving for himself the ultimate decision-making and founding role.[172] Passages in various ancient sources suggest that Dura-Europus, the famous Seleucid foundation on the middle Euphrates, was established, not by Seleucus I Nicator, but his by nephew Nicanor, the governor of Mesopotamia.[173] However, it was Seleucus I who was identified as the colony's formal founder and honored with cult in this capacity.[174] Indeed, a sculpted relief from the Parthian-period temple of the Gadde, dated to year 470 of the Seleucid Era (159 CE), should be considered a figuration of the king's founding of Dura-Europus. Three figures are portrayed, each identified by a label in Palmyrene Aramaic (see Figure 12): on the left stands the dedicant, Hairan bar Malikou bar Nasor, wearing a priestly tiara and holding a large palm branch; in the center, wearing a diadem and holding a scepter on a throne flanked by eagles, sits a bearded Olympian Zeus-like deity, identified as Dura's Gad (Palmyrene *gd*), a tutelary deity much like *Tychē;* standing on the right, dressed in Hellenistic military costume, with a scepter and diadem, and extending a laurel crown over the Gad of Dura, is Seleucus Nicator. This second-century CE relief almost certainly depended on a Hellenistic model.[175] So, as far as we can tell, in Dura-Europus' and the empire's official version, governor Nicanor falls into shadow of his uncle-king. Moreover, settlements' promotions to *polis* status could originate within the communities as requests to the king.[176] Accordingly, it is likely that several urban foundations attributed to the Seleucid dynasty were established in practice by subordinates and administrators, who subsequently have dropped out of the historical record.

The third suppressed agents are certain long-established Old World cities that joined as partners in the creation or consolidation of Seleucid settlements. Magnesia-on-the-Maeander offers our strongest case. The geographer Strabo bluntly states that the ancient Ionian city colonized the Seleucid foundation of Antioch-in-Pisidia (ταύτην δ' ᾤκισαν Μάγνητες οἱ πρὸς Μαιάνδρῳ);[177] an inscribed letter, most probably from this Antioch to Magnesia-on-the-Maeander, recalls their kinship.[178] A letter from Antioch-in-Persis, inscribed at Magnesia-on-the-Maeander, reported that Antiochus I had asked Magnesia to dispatch a colony of settlers (ἀποικίας) to this new foundation on the Iranian coast of the Gulf and that the *polis*, "having passed a splendid and glorious decree and having offered prayers and sacrifices, sent men sufficient in number and distinguished in excellence,

Figure 12 Temple of the Gadde relief, Dura-Europus, Syria.

striving to join in increasing the *dēmos* of the Antiochians";[179] the verb συναυξῆσαι, "to join in increasing," emphasizes the collaboration of king and city (see Chapter 8). A similar involvement in Seleucid colonization is implied in a very fragmentary inscription from Nagidos in Cilicia.[180] A decree from Samos speaks of the citizens of Antioch-on-the-Maeander as "kinsmen," and it is possible that this indicates Samian involvement in the colony's foundation.[181] Once again, these collaborators do not appear in the official Seleucid record.

The Seleucid kings' monopolization of narrative agency magnified their colonial achievements and elevated them into founder-heroes. In general, the political history of the Hellenistic period demonstrates time and again that the foundation of eponymous cities was a symbolic proclamation of legitimate kingship, by both Alexander's Successors (e.g., Cassandria, Lysimachia, Antipatria, Pleistarchia, Antigonia, Ptolemaïs, and all the Antiochs and Seleucias) and breakaway Seleucid governors (e.g., Artaxias of Armenia's Artaxata,[182] Eucratides of Bactria's Eucratidia,[183] and Hyspaosines of Mesene's Spasinu-Charax[184]). More specifically, Seleucid court literature generated mythical and historical prototypes for this *roi bâtisseur* type. We have seen, in Chapter 1, that Megasthenes' *Indica,* contemporary with Seleucus' colonial activities and strongly aligned with Seleucid interests, developed a model of heroic city foundations for Dionysus and Indian Heracles that considered royal urbanism the key to the country's unconquerability and developed civilization. Similarly, Berossus, the Babylonian priest who dedicated his autoethnographic *Babyloniaca* to Antiochus I and used his narrative to establish the local parameters and appropriate behavior to which his Seleucid masters should conform,[185] gave particular attention to Nebuchadnezzar II's rebuilding and beautification of Babylon.[186] In this light it is striking that an inscription, apparently found near Babylon, hailed Antiochus IV in the linked roles of "savior of Asia and founder of the *polis*" (σωτῆρος τῆς Ἀσίας καὶ κτίσ[του] τῆς πόλεως);[187] one wonders whether the hostile assimilation of Antiochus IV to Nebuchadnezzar II, prevalent in Jewish sources from the Maccabaean revolt, reinterprets a positive identification promoted by the Seleucid court.[188] The ultimate representation of the kings' unique role in the colonial act is religious: founder-cults were established in Seleucid colonies and modeled on the honors awarded to archaic *ktistai*. This was a widespread practice[189] that telescoped the entire colonial process into the individual royal honorand.

Secondary Urbanism

Colonies were created; various cities celebrated their dates of birth,[190] and we have seen that the hour of foundation is the dramatic heartbeat of Seleucia-on-the-Tigris' *ktisis*. But the Seleucid colonial program was not limited to planting new colonies and moving on. For in addition to establishing settlements, the Seleucid kings expanded, beautified, and promoted certain of those founded by their ancestors.

These fortunate cities were turned into display pieces of cumulative dynastic benefaction and continuing royal commitment to urban development. Antioch-by-Daphne was constructed by Seleucus I as a walled settlement on the Orontes' right bank at the foot of Mount Silpius, under the present-day souk (see Figure 11).[191] This original foundation was extended in two directions: the river's island was built up as a new city quarter by Seleucus II[192] and walled by Antiochus III,[193] with bridges to connect the districts, and on the mountain slope above the original settlement Antiochus IV constructed a new quarter called Epiphania.[194] Furthermore, the dynasty bestowed various public buildings and works on Antioch. Libanius, stating that "each king took careful thought to hand on enhanced the city which he had received," lists without further detail street-paving, fountains, temple and theater construction.[195] From other sources we are able to attribute the following: Antiochus III and Antiochus IX/X each established libraries; Antiochus IV constructed a *bouleuterion*, a temple to Capitoline Jupiter,[196] an aqueduct,[197] and perhaps the colossal bust of Medusa, known as the Charonion;[198] and Demetrius I built a new palace.[199] Similar cumulative royal practice must lie behind Strabo's statements that Stratonicea-in-Caria was adorned by the kings with lavish improvements (ἐκοσμήθη . . . κατασκευαῖς πολυτελέσιν ὑπὸ τῶν βασιλέων),[200] and that Seleucus and all his successors took great concern over Seleucia-on-the-Tigris (καὶ γὰρ ἐκεῖνος καὶ οἱ μετ' αὐτὸν ἅπαντες περὶ ταύτην ἐσπούδασαν).[201]

An alternative form of secondary urbanism was the physical reconfiguration and juridical promotion of a colony. Take the case of Dura-Europus. Whereas the original Yale-French archaeological team believed that the settlement's grid-plan and associated constructions had been established at foundation, new excavation and review of earlier work has shown that there were in fact two distinct urban phases. Dura-Europus had been founded as a small *phrourion*, with dwellings clustered around the foot of the commanding citadel (see Figure 9). At some point in the mid-second century, the settlement was replanned and massively expanded: an orthogonal street grid was put in place, along with new fortifications, gateways, the agora, the temples of Zeus Megistos and Artemis, and the civic archives (Figure 13).

This was not an expression of Europus' organic growth, even if the settlement had flourished in its first century and a half. Rather, the restructuring can only have been a top-down political decision of the central power; without doubt the expansion was motivated by both the commercial opportunities offered by the newly conquered harbors of Phoenicia and the security concerns prompted by Parthian conquests in the east.[202] Like Europus, the fortress of Icarus, constructed in the early third century on Failaka island, had two clear Seleucid phases, sandwiching a brief period of indigenous rule: most likely during the reign of Antiochus III, the original settlement was reconstructed—routes of access were altered, it was expanded to the north, and a moat was excavated.[203] Whether or not these alterations are to be associated with the extremely worn inscription found in the

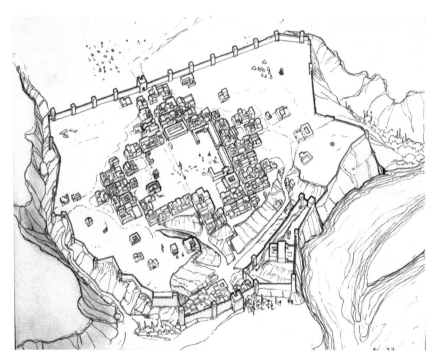

Figure 13 Late Seleucid Dura-Europus, Syria.

fort,[204] a letter from an unnamed Seleucid monarch to his official Icadion, in this document the king seems concerned to encourage agricultural exploitation and for this purpose awards tax-exemption and hereditary leasehold on the farmed land; quite clear is the verb συνοικισθῆναι, "to be synoecized," which suggests some kind of imperially sponsored repopulation or ingathering of settlers.[205] It is possible that Jebel Khalid has a similar history.[206]

The expansions and reconstructions of Seleucid colonies required demographic reinforcement, and so the Seleucid monarchs orchestrated episodic immigration to boost their colonies' populations. The letter of Antioch-in-Persis to Magnesia-on-the-Maeander, cited earlier, reports that Antiochus I requested that the Ionian city dispatch settlers; the worthy Magnesians were to bolster an already existing colony, not establish a new one. We have seen, above, that Antiochus III repopulated Lysimachia. Seleucid kings sponsored secondary colonization to Antioch-by-Daphne—Cretans under Antiochus II, and Aetolians, Cretans, and Euboeans under Antiochus III.[207]

The settlements' dynastic names and foundation narratives presented the Seleucid colonial program as the reification of monarchic will: king makes city. Continued royal interest in the foundations' vitality demonstrated to a colonial and imperial audience the kings' cumulative, dynastic agency and their effective commitment to molding imperial territory.

CHAPTER 8

City Makes King

The Colonial Response

Up to now we have been working along the grain of monarchic ideology. But grids fail. Behind Baron Haussmann saunters the flâneur. There is a slippage between what the Seleucid colonies meant for their planners and how they were lived by their residents: while the kings attempted to forge an empire in their own image, local, messy, traditional behaviors and ideas frustrated Seleucid power and domesticated Seleucid space. Such assertions of the vernacular were most motivated, observable, and unsurprising for indigenous communities in revolt: for instance, the Jewish Maccabees of the 160s moved as much against the new urban topography of Hellenized Jerusalem as against Antiochus Epiphanes, playing out their conflict between the high places of Temple and Acra.[1] But assertions of local, city identity are visible throughout the empire, not necessarily in opposition to the Seleucid dynasty but always at a certain distance from its claims. We can explore this in three ways: the zoning of major Seleucid colonies into palatial and civic areas; the civic communities' development of nonroyal foundation narratives; and the cities' own coin iconography and nomenclature.

Palace-City Zoning

The itinerant nature of Seleucid monarchy, explored in Part III, demanded a network of palatial residences to appropriately, if temporarily, house the king on his travels. Several palaces are explicitly attested in literary sources, both at the major imperial capitals (the Syrian Tetrapolis, Seleucia-on-the-Tigris, Babylon[2]) and at smaller regional centers (Apamea-Celaenae in Phrygia,[3] Mopsuestia in Cilicia[4]). A late third-century inscription from

Seleucia-on-the-Eulaeus (formerly Susa, in Elymaïs) honors the daughter of an official "in charge of the palace of the king" (ὁ ἐπὶ τῆς αὐλῆς τοῦ βασιλέως),[5] in all likelihood a fairly standard post. Moreover, archaeological excavation independently has uncovered Seleucid palaces at Jebel Khalid[6] and Dura-Europus[7] on the Euphrates, at Aï Khanoum on the Oxus,[8] and perhaps at Mount Karasis in Cilicia.[9] The fairly random nature of this textual, epigraphic, and material record, pointing to the existence of palaces at such relatively insignificant sites as Mopsuestia and Jebel Khalid and at such geographically distant ones as Phrygian Apamea and Bactrian Aï Khanoum, implies the spread of a dense matrix of palace complexes across the full breadth of the Seleucid kingdom. It would be fair to assume that in the monarchs' absence—as we saw, the more typical condition of itinerant kingship—the palaces would have served as the seat of the satrap or garrison commander. (We may wonder whether the evident dangers of handing over this architecture of legitimate authority to subordinates were mitigated by a set of taboo spaces for exclusive royal use, like an empty throne or unoccupied chambers, but there is no evidence.) All of these residence complexes were housed in Seleucid cities and colonies; the spatial relationship between palace and city should be understood as manifesting and molding the development of urban and royal identities and associated modes of city-king communication.[10] We will see that, as the Seleucid colonies' ground plans materialized certain themes of imperial ideology, so the emergence within these cities of marked and distinguishable royal zones can be seen to have literally circumscribed the kings' agency and control.

The two basic types of new Seleucid colony identified in Chapter 7—the small, fortified *phrourion* and the large, orthogonal city—show two different modes of urban-palace integration, which we can call the "citadel model" and the "forbidden city model." It must be acknowledged, however, that lack of excavation and the randomness of what we have limits us to an almost but not quite overwhelming degree; it is very possible that future discoveries will transform our understanding of this question. The first mode can be handled swiftly; like the kings we need not honor the forts with a lengthy sojourn. We have seen that the military settlements seem to have been characterized by a topographical separation between a high walled acra and a settlement cluster at its base. At Dura-Europus, Jebel Khalid, and Mount Karasis, the palace or banqueting center lay within the well-defended citadel, separate and to a degree detachable from the lower settlement (see Figures 8–10). Walls and height easily achieved a clear zoning into palatial and residential areas.

The large Seleucid colonies, on the other hand, present a much more interesting interaction of royal and urban spaces. Our clearest evidence comes from Aï Khanoum, the much-discussed but only partially excavated colony at the kingdom's far eastern periphery on the Afghan-Tajik border (see Figure 14).[11] The triangle of Aï Khanoum is divided almost equally into an upper city or acropolis at the southeast and an urban and administrative area below it to the northwest. This lower city was traversed by a main north-south boulevard, on either side of which lay the prominent public buildings of theater, temple, arsenal, and public baths; the gymnasium and *heroön* of Cineas lay to the west of this principal road. The city's palatial complex sprawled over the southwestern corner of the urban plateau, between the main road and the bank of the Oxus river. This royal quarter was accessed off the north-south boulevard through grandiose propylaea, or gateways, erected between about 280 and 250, consisting of a double prostyle in antis portico more than 31 meters long and 24 meters wide; in a second building phase, dating to the early second century and the post-Seleucid Graeco-Bactrian monarchy, the entrance portico on the side of the main street was doubled in length and number of columns; the palace was also enlarged. Managing the gradient, a flight of fifteen steps (a ramp in the second phase) then descended into a long, 29-meter-wide esplanade of beaten earth, framed to north and south by high mud-brick walls.[12] At the end, a pebble-paved path led off to the palace; visitors would access the palace's great peristyle courtyard through a further propylon. It is likely that the palace was accessed by another, less-monumentalized roadway to the south of the public sanctuary, probably for the carts which provisioned the administration and residents, but it is obvious which is the privileged entrance. Furthermore, the palatial buildings follow their own axial alignment, clearly at odds with that of Aï Khanoum's main boulevard, public buildings, and private houses; this would have been visible from the city's acropolis. The main road's enormous propylaea, only slightly smaller than Mnesicles' entrance to the Athenian Acropolis, marks and generates a threshold between two clearly distinct zones of colonial life and public expression. Regardless of whether passage through the gateway was physically restricted, the monumentality of the construction dramatized the movement through, emphasized the separateness of what lay beyond, and no doubt produced in the urban community self-regulated patterns of circulation. On the esplanade itself the high walls to right and left canalized movement toward the palace and prevented any visual perception of the city's more civic areas. The effect of all this was to mark out the palace as a discrete entity within the urban area—to use a more provocative term, a forbidden city.

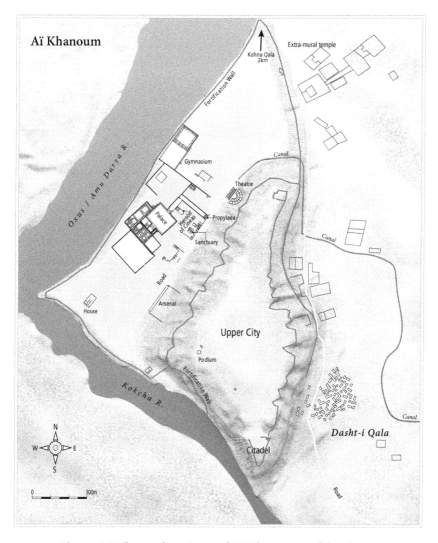

Figure 14 Plan and environs of Aï Khanoum, Afghanistan.

Much less is known of the more central and significant colonies of
Seleucia-on-the-Tigris and Antioch-by-Daphne (see Figure 11). It seems
that the royal palace at Seleucia-on-the-Tigris, known by the Old Persian
loanword *apadāna* in Akkadian sources,[13] was situated at the northern
edge of the city, where one finds the main archive building, evidence of
dynastic cult, and an Achaemenid-style column base. This palace location
is a very common feature of earlier Babylonian and Assyrian urbanism,
usually explained by the direction of the most pleasant wind, the physical
centrality of city temples, and defensive requirements. It can be observed
at Sargon II's Dur-Sharrukin (modern Khorsabad), Ashurnasirpal II's
Kalhu (modern Nimrud), and, most relevantly, Nebuchadnezzar II's Babylon.[14] It has been suggested that Seleucia's palatial area, complete with
paradeisos garden, was isolated from the rest of the city by a wall or canal.[15]
Certainly, since Seleucia-on-the-Tigris was constructed on a level plain,
the palatial complex must have been incorporated into the city rather than
set above it. Presumably, as at Aï Khanoum, access would have been marked
in a way that contributed to a sense of urban zoning. Similarly, almost
nothing is known of the Seleucid palace(s?) at Antioch-by-Daphne. At least
from the reign of Seleucus II the main palatial area probably lay on the
Orontes island, which, like Aï Khanoum's forbidden city, had a different
axial alignment to the rest of the city; certainly, this is where the Roman-
period palaces were located.[16] Josephus reports, in a passage to which we
will return, that Demetrius I locked himself away in a *tetrapyrgion* palace he
had built not far from Antioch;[17] perhaps this describes a renovation of the
Seleucid palace on the Orontes island. Accordingly, our best guess is that
the Seleucid palatial complex lay beside the lower city of Antioch, separated
from the rest of the urban area by the canalized Orontes and Antiochus III's
island wall[18] and accessed via river crossings.

This is not much to go on. But in the few large, orthogonal colonies for
which we have any evidence at all it seems that the Seleucid palace was incorporated into the body of the city, occupying an entire and substantial
urban district on the same ground level as the rest of the settlement and toward its edge. The kind of spatial separation achieved in the "citadel model"
by topography was manufactured in the "forbidden city model" by the
construction or manipulation of canalizing thresholds (propylaea, walls,
bridges). It is important to recognize that this urban relationship derives
from neither the Macedonian nor the Persian traditions: the Macedonian
palaces of Philip II and his Antigonid successors at Aegae (Vergina), Pella,

and Demetrias were set in an intermediate, somewhat ambiguous position, on panoramic terraced platforms above their respective cities but below the fortified citadels;[19] the Persian palatial hypostyles at Pasargadae, Persepolis, and Susa formed the dominating center and raison d'être of these Achaemenid capitals.[20] Rather, the Seleucid pattern seems closest to the more ancient Neo-Babylonian conception of palace-city configuration. At Babylon, for example, the palatial complex constructed by king Nabopolassar in the seventh century lay at the northern edge of the city, part within and part outside the city's walls; it was separated from the urban area by the Lībil-hengalla canal to its south and by the Euphrates to its west, thereby forming its own semi-island;[21] the major road artery linking the palace to the city and the Esagil temple at its core, known as the Ay-ibūr-šabû, was a route of exceptional religious and monarchic importance and monumentalized accordingly.[22] Several of these features, individually or together, are found in the three major Seleucid colonies just examined. This is no surprise: Babylon was Seleucus' original power base, and he had taken up residence in the palace of Nabopolassar; the cuneiform Astronomical Diaries attest to the palace's continued use by his successors—indeed, in the late fourth or early third century it seems to have undergone a Greek-style renovation, complete with a stuccoed peristyle courtyard at its core;[23] and certain of Babylon's urbanistic features were reproduced at Seleucia-on-the-Tigris, the first and in some ways paradigmatic Seleucid colony.[24]

The quantity and quality of this archaeological evidence, however, allows conclusions that can be only tentative. To better understand the colonies' spatial semiotics (the routes of circulation, points of interaction, forbidden or accessible terrains, architecturally dramatized entrances and exits) as well as more phenomenological concerns (habit, repetition, comfort, and their opposites[25]) we turn to our literary sources. Narratives of royal impropriety are particularly helpful, as it is of course behavioral infractions that make visible the transgressed boundaries and their policing. Hellenistic historiography has provided us with a polarity of royal behavior vis-à-vis the palace-city configuration. It seems that the relationship between the two zones was an arena of constant negotiation for thinking through the respective interactions of royal power and civic identity.

King Demetrius I, son of Seleucus IV, who in 161 had slipped from Rome to his birthright after the death of Antiochus IV, quickly lost popular and military favor in Syria. Josephus attributes this to his arrogance (ὑπερηφανία) and general unpleasantness (δυσέντευκτος), which were most clearly manifested in the fortified *tetrapyrgion* palace he occupied near Antioch-by-Daphne.[26] A *tetrapyrgion* was, as its name indicates, a four-towered fortified palatial complex, somewhat like a square medieval castle; our best excavated example comes from the Antigonid city of Demetrias in the Bay of Pagasae in Thessaly, where, at some point in the reign of Philip V, the formerly undefended peristyle courtyards of the royal palace were given exterior walls and corner towers and incorporated into an extended citadel area.[27] Josephus emphasizes that the palatial architecture overly restricted accessibility and ruptured the king's relationship with the urban community: Tiberius-like, Demetrius "locked himself away" (ἀποκλείσας); "he admitted nobody" (οὐδένα προσίετο); he failed to perform appropriately his monarchic duties (περὶ τὰ πράγματα ῥάθυμος ἦν καὶ ὀλίγωρος).[28] Accordingly, when Demetrius was challenged by Antiochus IV's supposed son, Alexander I Balas, the people of Antioch favored the pretender.[29]

If Demetrius I withdrew too far, his predecessor, Antiochus IV, got too close. Antiochus IV's actions in Antioch-by-Daphne were considered so bizarre that his divine epithet *Epiphanēs*, "(God) Manifest," was playfully refashioned—a weapon of the weak—to *Epimanēs*, "Insane."[30] Polybius, as quoted or paraphrased in Athenaeus and Diodorus Siculus, lists various examples of the king's oddness; the hostile content and tone may derive from Polybius' sources, either the circle around Demetrius I, for whom Antiochus IV was an illegitimate usurper,[31] or from the pen of Ptolemy VIII Physcon, for whom Antiochus IV was an invader.[32] They take two directions. On the one hand, the king, who had been held a hostage in the Latin capital for a decade, emulated things Roman—wearing a toga, establishing gladiatorial games at Daphne,[33] outfitting some of his forces in Roman armor,[34] and constructing at Antioch a temple to Capitoline Jupiter.[35] On the other hand, and more germane to this discussion, the king repeatedly and inappropriately crossed from the palatial to the civic sphere of Antioch. Antiochus' transgressions, too often dismissed as idle invention or meaningless gossip, actually bring to life the urban zoning, of which the city's inhabitants would have been socially aware. Time and again the king collapsed the spatial distinction between palace and city. For instance, we are told that Epiphanes would "slip out" of the palace (ἀποδιδράσκων;[36] ὑπάγων λάθρᾳ[37]) and "aimlessly wander" with a couple of companions through the city (ἀλύων[38]), often wearing civilian, not royal, garb:[39] the old and universal folktale motif of the disguised king may lie in the background.[40] He would spend hours chatting with craftsmen or metalworkers and would drink with ignoble foreign visitors to Antioch; our sources insist on the language of social descent—κατέβαινεν ("he came down"),[41] συγκαταβαίνων ("stooping"),[42] συγκαταρριπτεῖν ("to throw down together").[43] Moreover, Antiochus, though uninvited, would lead revels to private banquets and symposia:[44] the partiers either were struck dumb with fear or took to their heels on account of τὸ παράδοξον, the strangeness of it all.[45] It is also alleged that the king was a candidate in elections for the civic magistracies of *agoranomos* and *dēmarchos*, drumming up support for his candidacy in the city's agora,[46] although this should probably be connected in some way to his encouragement of local government (he constructed a *bouleuterion* for Epiphania, his new suburb).[47] A final set of transgressions focuses on Antiochus' disturbance of the spatialized logic of royal euergetism. Ptolemy VIII, as quoted by Athenaeus, recounts that the Seleucid king used to roam about the public streets of Antioch (ἐν ταῖς δημοσίαις ὁδοῖς) tossing out coins to passersby and announcing, "To whomever *Tychē* gives, let him take" (τίνι ἡ τύχη δίδωσι, λαβέτω).[48] Note that the phrase "public streets" requires a clear sense of urban zoning, opposing itself to identifiably nonpublic, royal ones (for which we should think, perhaps, of something like the esplanade at Aï Khanoum). The king's invocation of *Tychē* not only draws attention to the frivolous and deliberately arbitrary mode of benefaction but also allows Antiochus to playact the colony's civic personification. At other times, according to the Polybian narrative, the king gave gifts of knuckle bones, dates, money, and other "unexpected gifts" (δωρεὰς ἀπροσδοκήτους); these were awarded even to people he had never seen before (οὓς μὴ ἑωράκει ποτέ).[49] Random gifts and unknown beneficiaries: the king's activities do not sustain a social relationship between two socially defined personalities but rather undercut the key political function of the traditional benefactions-for-honors exchange, namely, the transformation of unidirectional monarchic power over a city into a dialogue in which the civic authorities could claim some control.[50] Instead, the entire city of Antioch becomes the butt of one-sided monarchic jest. The culmination of Antiochus IV's transgressions is an episode that pulls together the king's overstepping of urban thresholds, collapsing of hierarchy, and parodying of well-ordered benefaction:

He also used to bathe in the public baths (τοῖς δημοσίοις βαλανείοις), when they were full of common people (δημοτῶν), having jars of the most precious ointments brought in for him; and on one occasion, when someone said to him, "How blessed you are, you kings, to use such scents and smell so sweet!" he answered nothing at the time, but the next day, when the man was having his bath, he came in after him and had a huge jar of the most precious ointment, called *stactē,* poured over his head, so that all the bathers jumped up and rolled themselves in it, and by slipping in it created great amusement, as did the king himself (ὡς πάντας ἀναστάντας κυλίεσθαι ⟨τοὺς⟩ λουομένους τῷ μύρῳ καὶ διὰ τὴν γλισχρότητα καταπίπτοντας γέλωτα παρέχειν, καθάπερ καὶ αὐτὸν τὸν βασιλέα).[51]

Just as Antiochus roamed the city's streets, so he visited the public baths; there is an implied contrast with the more suitable palatial alternative. Furthermore, the king responded to a fellow bather's praise of monarchic luxury with yet another misunderstanding of the euergetistic economy: a vast vat of precious *stactē* is upturned over the commoner's head in an act of clownish excess and physical comedy. Indeed, the scene climaxes in a dramatic and total casting off of socially prescribed identities. King and townspeople, indistinguishable now in nudity and scent, unite in a bawdy glissade. It is a minicarnival of wild, utopian equality, negating social distance, debasing court ceremony, and blurring outlines to dissolution.

Antiochus IV Epiphanes' behavior amounts to the misappropriation of things and spaces. His capricious drollery confounds the urban audience, producing *aporia* in place of a coregulated obeisance, a powerless disgust instead of a choreographed encounter. Antiochus' invasions of Antioch can be counterposed to Demetrius I's removal. Together their respective failures split the colony into its dialectic poles—the discrete but ceremonially linked royal and civic zones of bathhouses, roadways, clothing, offices, banquets, and populations. These can be mapped onto the enclosed, modular units of urban terrain discussed earlier.

Foundation Narratives—The City's Tale

Running parallel to the delineation of a nonroyal urban zone within a colony was the settlement's production of a nonroyal account of its origins. We have seen in Chapter 4 that formal Seleucid time, manifested in the dynastic Seleucid Era, started in 312/311. A host of other measures and discourses worked to ignore what came before. As far as we can reconstruct (see Chapter 7), official foundation narratives asserted newness and lack of precedent— the colonies have no mythic ancestry; in some sense *Tychē* minds the gap. But over the course of the Hellenistic period certain Seleucid colonies, both major and minor, generated alternative, civic accounts of their foundation: ancient, nondynastic *ktistai* (founders) were resurrected or invented; an Old World undergirding was fabricated; Seleucid rule was historicized and thereby demoted.

In Asia Minor, where the first three Seleucid monarchs synoecized already existing communities, it appears that the citizens chose to honor the eponymous heroes of the constituent former settlements. Strabo reports that the inhabitants of Nysa, Seleucus I's colony on the banks of the Maeander, considered the Lacedaemonian Athymbrus their founder.[52] Similarly, certain quasi-municipal coins of imperial-period Antioch-on-the-Maeander, founded by Antiochus I as a synoecism of Symmaethos and Cranaos, carried on their reverse an image of a man with the legend *Kranaos Antiocheōn,* clearly the eponymous founder of the presynoecized Cranaus.[53] Both cities, despite having attested cults to their actual Seleucid creators, asserted an older, nobler identity.[54]

While the existence of pre-Seleucid settlements allowed the Maeander colonies to show off their pre-Seleucid founders, it is striking that the major Tetrapolis cities of the Syrian Seleucis do the same. For archaeological investigation has made it sufficiently clear that these north Syrian dynastically named colonies were new urban centers without pre-Seleucid strata: a small Macedonian military garrison, going by the name Pella, may have been established by Alexander or Antigonus at the site of Apamea-on-the-Axios, but that is it.[55] Accordingly, if we look closely at the foundation narratives for Antioch-by-Daphne, contained in the late antique sources Libanius, *Oration* 11 and Malalas, *Chronographia* 8, it is possible to see alongside the legitimizing court tale, discussed earlier, the invention of a proudly independent civic one: the two traditions ripple across the narrative surface, disputing possession. Libanius' account reinterprets Seleucus Nicator's foundation of Antioch in two ways. First, the Seleucid colonization is but one episode in successive waves of Greek immigration.[56] The original settlement on the site is established by the primordial hero Triptolemus, leading Argives in search of Io; they are joined by Cretans, brought by Casus, then by the Cyprian fleet escorting the daughter of Salaminus to her marriage with Casus, and finally by some of the Heraclidae. In each case the wondrous beauty of the land so enchanted the traveling heroes that they never returned home. Second, Seleucus' actions are placed in the context of repeated bestowals of benefaction on the community by rulers of Asia. The urban area is built up by the standard succession of eastern imperial powers: the

Assyrian queen Semiramis, the wife of the Persian king Cambyses, and Alexander the Great, who constructed the fountain house "Olympias," a shrine of Zeus Bottiaeus, and the citadel.[57] Malalas has a garbled version of the same, only adding a mountaintop shrine founded by the hero Perseus.[58] This account of Antioch's prehistory was already well-enough established to be recorded, in its rudiments, by Strabo in the Augustan period.[59] Pushing us back even earlier, the ear of wheat on Antioch's second-century quasi-municipal diobols may well allude to Triptolemus, inventor of agriculture, as it already does on fifth-century coinage from nearby Tarsus.[60] So, various elements of Antioch's tale work to play down or undercut the role of Seleucus and the authority of his kingdom. Antioch's origins are cast back to the most archaic beginnings of civilization. Successive stages of settlement, as superimpositions, not conquests, sew a wide supra-Seleucid kinship network for the city. Seleucus' activity is limited to precisely the characteristic a civic community would favor—royal benefaction: the settlement, formed by autonomous, self-directed colonization from the Greek world, receives individual public or religious buildings from monarchs who have limited agency over the city.

Moving to Apamea-on-the-Axios, it was argued in Chapter 7 that the self-contained local myth of Heracles' canalization of the river Orontes, preserved in [Oppian]'s *Cynēgetica,* is of Hellenistic date and encodes Seleucid hydraulic improvements in the city's plain.[61] What is instructive for our purposes here is that the heroism takes place in an invented mythical past. In Homeric diction the tale tells how Archippus, ruler of divine Pella (Ἀρχίππῳ δ' ἑτάρῳ, Πέλλης ἡγήτορι δίης),[62] called upon the assistance of his companion Heracles and how, as a result of Heracles' labor, cattle now graze around the tomb of Memnon, son of Dawn.[63] Pella was the Macedonian military colony established in the late fourth century by Antigonus Monophthalmus or Alexander, expanded by Seleucus I into the city of Apamea. The Hellenistic mythographer has simply transformed the settlement's pre-Seleucid name into a Bronze Age one. Archippus, the ἡγήτωρ, "commander," of mythic Pella, is more difficult to identify. The name may belong to the Macedonian official who physically established the settlement, like Nicanor at Dura-Europus (see Chapter 7) or Cineas at Aï Khanoum (see later), now reframed in mythic terms;[64] or the name Archippus, literally "commander of horse," may be a playful reference to Seleucid Apamea's function as headquarters of the empire's cavalry force and its commander, the *hipparchos.*[65] In either case, it is clear that out of the raw materials of real-world Seleucid Apamea—its first Macedonian foundation and military purpose—our poet has crafted a city-based tale entirely in independence of the Seleucid dynasty.

It must be acknowledged that most of the evidence for these non-Seleucid foundation narratives from the empire's western hemisphere is of Roman date, but similar claims were already prominent in the local historiography and erudite poetry of the third and second centuries.[66] For instance, the recently discovered Salmacis epigram from Halicarnassus, dating to the late second century, makes a good parallel for Libanius' Antioch narrative. The inscription, listing the city's five mythical founders (Bellerophon, Cranaus, Endymion, Anthes, and one more in connection to Ariadne—all from the Greek mainland or Crete), shows that Old World oecistic stratigraphies were very much a phenomenon of learned and proud Hellenistic civic identity.[67] It is certainly suggestive that Euphorion of Chalcis, who directed the library of Antioch-by-Daphne during the reign of Antiochus III, composed an *Inachos,* named after the father of Io; perhaps this treated the city's mythical foundation.[68]

While such literary fabrications do not survive from the Upper Satrapies, as these regions submitted neither to Rome nor its scholars, third-century inscriptions from Antioch-in-Persis on the Gulf coast of Iran and Aï Khanoum in eastern Bactria reveal that even these far-flung foundations attempted to take control of their past, to compose their own non-Seleucid histories.

I have already invoked the inscription from Antioch-in-Persis several times; let us now look at it in more depth. In the last decade of the third century, the ancient Ionian city of Magnesia-on-the-Maeander, following an earlier epiphany of its patron goddess, Artemis Leucophryene ("Of the White Brow"), and an oracle from Delphi, dispatched at least twenty teams of sacred ambassadors *(theōroi)* across the Greek world.[69] Bearing attestations of Magnesia's antiquity and her benefactions, the envoys were to request recognition for Artemis' festival games of the privileged "crowned" rank and for the *polis* of inviolate status *(asylia).*[70] More than sixty responses survive, inscribed on the west stoa of Magnesia's Sacred Agora.[71] We can follow the journey of one team, made up of Demophon, Philiscus, and Pheres, into the distant Upper Satrapies on the trail of Antiochus III. They caught up with him, returning with his elephants from the Hindu Kush, at Antioch-in-Persis (συμμείξαντες ἐν Ἀντιοχείᾳ τῆς Περσίδος).[72] Antiochus consented to recognize the "crowned" games and graciously promised to instruct the officials in charge of his kingdom's affairs "in order that the cities in their turn also recognize" the promotion.[73] In due course Antiochus III's brief, generic letter was inscribed in prominent first place alongside those of kings Attalus I, Ptolemy IV, and Philip V as well as the Greek *koina* in Magnesia's agora.[74] Such a diplomatic exchange would correspond to the glowing center model of itinerant Seleucid kingship, outlined in Chapter 6, but for the preservation of two further responses, for the mission of Demophon, Philiscus, and Pheres did not end with the king's agreement. On a subsequent day these Magnesian ambassadors carried the same request before the civic authorities of Antioch-in-Persis, the Seleucid colony where the king was momentarily residing. The city's lengthy reply, inscribed alongside other city decrees on the western stoa's rear wall, runs as follows:

> When Heraclitus son of Zoes was priest of Seleucus (I) Nicator and Antiochus (I) Soter and Antiochus (II) Theos and Seleucus (II) Callinicus and king Seleucus (III) and king Antiochus (III) and his son king Antiochus, in the first half-year, resolutions of a sovereign meeting of the assembly which were handed in by Asclepiades son of Hecataeus and grandson of Demetrius, the secretary of the council and the assembly, on the third of the waning month of Pantheus. Resolved by the assembly on the motion of the prytaneis. The Magnesians-on-the-Maeander, being kinsmen (συγγενεῖς) and friends of our *dēmos*, and having performed many distinguished services for the Greeks from among those pertaining to glory, formerly, when Antiochus (I) Soter was eager to increase our *polis*, since it was named after him, and sent an embassy to them about (the sending of) a colony (ἀποικίας), they, having passed a splendid and glorious decree and having offered prayers and sacrifices, sent men sufficient in number and distinguished in excellence, striving to help in increasing the *dēmos* of the Antiochians; as they are preserving their goodwill toward all the Greeks (πρὸς ἅπαντας τοὺς Ἕλληνας) and wishing to make public that they are admitting deserving men to a share in the libations, sacrifices, and other religious honors, when an oracle was rendered to them, they proclaimed it throughout all Greece (κατὰ πᾶσαν τὴν Ἑλλάδα), celebrating for the ancestress of their city sacrifices, a festival, a truce, and a "crowned" competition to be held every five years, musical, gymnastic, and equestrian, returning just thanks to their benefactress; and they sent as ambassadors to our *dēmos* Demophon son of Lycideus, Philiscus son of Philius, and Pheres son of Pheres, who, having come before the council and the assembly, handed over a decree from the Magnesians and,

having renewed their kinship and friendship, spoke at length about the epiphany of the goddess and the services which the Magnesians provided to many of the Greek cities (πολλαῖς τῶν Ἑλληνίδων πόλεων) and invited us to recognize the games, which they celebrate for Artemis Leucophryene, as "crowned," in accordance with the oracle of the god. The *dēmos*, honoring the same gods (τοὺς κοινοὺς θεούς) as the Magnesians, and wishing to increase its goodwill toward its kinsmen, and since many other *poleis* have previously decreed [the same things . . .] thinks it necessary before anything else not to overlook any opportunity for displaying to each individual privately and to everyone publicly the zeal which it continuously shows for the interests of the Magnesians. With good fortune, [it is resolved] by the council and the *dēmos* to praise the Magnesians for their piety toward the gods and their friendship and goodwill toward king Antiochus and the *dēmos* of the Antiochians, and because they make good use of their advantages and of the prosperity of their *polis* they will preserve their ancestral constitution, and (it is resolved) that the priests shall pray to all the gods and goddesses that their constitution remain with the Magnesians for all time in good fortune, and (it is resolved) to recognize the sacrifice, the festival, the truce, and [the games as "crowned" and "isopythian"], the musi[cal, gymnastic, and equestrian events which the Magnesians] celebrate [for Artemis Leucophryene].[75]

The remainder of the inscription, increasingly fragmentary, awards gifts to the Magnesian envoys and confirms standard civic privileges on future victors at Artemis Leucophryene's games. Appended to Antioch-in-Persis' decree, like to many others,[76] is a list of geographically clustered colonies which also responded favorably to Demophon, Philiscus, and Pheres:

Similar decrees were passed by:

Seleucia-on-the-Tigris
Apamea-on-the-Selea
Seleucia-on-the-Erythraean Sea
Seleucia-on-the-Eulaeus
Seleucia-on-the-[Hedyphon]
[- -]
[- -]
An[tioch-on-the-?]
Al[exandria-on-the-?]
[- -]

Finally, returning to the west, the *theōroi* secured a further response from king Antiochus, eldest son of the reigning but absent Antiochus III, who probably governed the empire's western hemisphere during his father's *anabasis*.[77] This Antiochus, noting that Antiochus III was the principle objective of the Magnesians' mission (οἱ παρ' ὑμῶν πεμφθέντες πρὸς τὸν πατέρα), visibly occluded himself behind his father:

> Since my father has had from the beginning the friendliest attitude to your *dēmos* and has given his approval, and wishing myself to follow his policy, I approve the honors you have voted for the goddess and in the future I shall try to follow the example of my father in increasing these [in whatever respects] you invite me or I myself think of.[78]

The letter is inscribed beneath Antiochus III's on the same block.

These three responses to the Magnesian team represent the geographical and typological distribution of authorized power within the Seleucid empire: the itinerant monarch; his son and coregent, probably based in and in some sense representing the north Syrian heartland; and the provincial colonial foundations—king, core, and colony. Prince Antiochus' echoing, referential language evidently serves to reinforce a dynastic solidarity and viceregal loyalty; note that less than a decade had passed since the suppression of viceroy Achaeus' revolt. By contrast, the decree of Antioch-in-Persis carves out for itself an independent domain. The imperial context is relegated to the wings. One would never guess from the decree that Antiochus III was at that moment residing in the colony (surely a great honor): rather, the monarch appears but twice and in minor roles, taking his seat beside his eldest son and the deceased royal ancestors in the decree's dating formula and, as the recipient, along with Antioch-in-Persis, of the Magnesians' praiseworthy friendship. In place of or in addition to the political space of the Seleucid empire, the Antiochians locate themselves within an extended landscape of Hellas (κατὰ πᾶσαν τὴν Ἑλλάδα) and a supra-Seleucid community of Greek cities.[79] The fascinating account of Magnesia's dispatch of additional settlers at the request of Antiochus I establishes a kinship dynamic of metropolis and city colony alongside the imperial framework of king and royal foundation: emphatically, the citizens of Antioch and Magnesia worship the same gods. The original, royal foundation of the settlement is not even mentioned. Furthermore, Antioch-in-Persis' decision to recognize the crowned games is motivated by the precedent of "many other *poleis*," not of Antiochus III;[80] the contrast with the response of Antiochus the son is striking. It is likely that the other colonies' decrees did similar work: proudly, if anxiously, asserting before a Panhellenic audience a discrete civic identity and Hellenic cultural community functioning both beyond and beneath Seleucid monarchy.[81]

Aï Khanoum, the large royal foundation at the intersection of the Oxus and the Kokcha rivers, locates itself within a similar non-Seleucid world. One of the more spectacular discoveries from the site was an inscribed stone block, dating to the early third century, found in the *pronaos* of the city's *heroön*.[82] It carried two inscriptions. First, an epigram in elegiac couplets:

> ἀνδρῶν τοι σοφὰ ταῦτα παλαιοτέρων ἀνάκει[τα]ι
>
>   ῥήματα ἀριγνώτων Πυθοὶ ἐν ἠγαθέαι·
>
> ἔνθεν ταῦτ[α] Κλέαρχος ἐπιφραδέως ἀναγράψας
>
>   εἵσατο τηλαυγῆ Κινέου ἐν τεμένει.

These wise sayings of more ancient and well-known men
are set up in most holy Pytho;
Clearchus, having copied them down carefully there,
set them up, shining from afar, in the *temenos* of Cineas.[83]

The second inscription consists of the five closing maxims of the canonical list of 147 apophthegmata of the Seven Sages, known in full from an inscription at Miletoupolis and from a list preserved by Stobaeus; another small fragment gives part of maxim forty-eight. It is clear that the full list was preserved on a stone stele standing above Clearchus' epigram.[84] The epigram describes Clearchus' 5,000-kilometer journey from Delphi, Greece's geographical and religious heart, to this Seleucid colony at world's edge. ἔνθεν . . . Κινέου ἐν τεμένει: Aï Khanoum is geographically fixed with reference to "most holy Pytho," the sanctuary's ancient, Homeric name; the maxims "shine from afar" (Pindaric τηλαυγῆ). Moreover, the Seleucid colony is temporally located in relation to the wise men of yore: the comparative παλαιοτέρων, "more ancient," contrasts with the Seleucid present.[85] So, at the very least, the two inscriptions orient Aï Khanoum's community to a place and era beyond the bounds of Seleucid space and time. But they do even more work. The Sages' maxims are part of the baseline *paideia* of the Hellenistic world. One would expect them to be erected, like those of Miletoupolis, in the city's gymnasium, the standard colonial center of Hellenic education; Aï Khanoum's enormous gymnasium contained other inscriptions and pedagogical material. The city's main temple or the palace courtyard could have been alternative display spaces (see Figure 14 for locations). Instead, by some process now lost to us, the authorities of Aï Khanoum arranged for Clearchus' epigram and the Delphic maxims to be inscribed in the *temenos*, or sacred burial enclosure, of Cineas. This Cineas, entombed at the heart of the city beneath a Macedonian-style *heroön*, was the colony's on-the-ground founder, its *oikistēs*;[86] as we have already seen, cities founded "by" Seleucid kings were established in fact by imperial officers in the monarch's name and according to his instructions. The location of the maxims in Cineas' *heroön* deliberately ties this nondynastic *oikistēs* with Delphi, thereby constructing *après coup* a traditional Greek colonial bond to Delphic Apollo, *archēgetēs* of new settlements. In sum, Clearchus' monument, in content and site, is emphatically non-Seleucid: an assertion of a more distant authority, more local identity, and more ancient practice than the official Seleucid court versions of founder-king acting on a land without history.

Coins and Names

The expression of an independent colonial identity, visible in urban zoning and articulated in foundation accounts, also found expression in coinage and names.

Three kinds of coinage coexisted in the Seleucid kingdom—royal coinage, struck in precious metals and bronze with official imperial types at mints throughout the kingdom; autonomous bronze coinage, a privilege awarded to certain cities or populations by the king,[87] distributed locally in their name and types; and quasi-municipal coins, in bronze and occasionally silver.[88] This third type, on which we will focus, appears at Tyre in Phoenicia during the reign of Antiochus III, shortly after his conquest of Coele Syria in the Fifth Syrian War:[89] the city's mint, while retaining the royal portrait as the obverse type, replaced the standard and long-used Seleucid reverse types (e.g., Apollo, anchor, elephant) with symbols of local relevance (e.g., a palm tree, the club of the city's god Melqart-Heracles, the prow or stern of a galley). Under Antiochus IV and his successors, almost twenty other cities in Cilicia, Syria, Phoenicia, and northern Mesopotamia, the majority new colonies or Seleucid refoundations, struck quasi-municipal coins.[90] From the reign of Antiochus VII, Antioch-on-the-Cydnus (Tarsus) even operated two entirely separate workshops, one for the production of the standard royal, the other for the quasi-municipal coinage.[91] Accordingly, these cities' coinage combined the approved portrait of the reigning Seleucid monarch on the obverse with an independent city-specific image and often city name on the reverse. They should be regarded as the negotiated meeting point of imposed royal iconography and civic self-representation.

Much like the city-based foundation narratives, discussed earlier, several cities and refounded, dynastically named colonies in Phoenicia and Cilicia adopted types that emphasized their long-established, pre-Seleucid religious and cultural traditions (see Figure 15). Local Levantine deities appear as the reverse-types at Byblus (Cronos-El[92] and Isis-Pharia[93]) and at Laodicea-in-Phoenicia, the refounded Berytus (Ba'al-Berit[94]). In Cilicia, the god Sandan and his altar appear at Antioch-on-the-Cydnus,[95] the refounded Tarsus, and Athena Margarsia at Antioch-on-the-Pyramus,[96] near Mallus. In Syria, coin reverses from early first-century Demetrias, the refounded Damascus, depict Atargatis[97] and Hadad.[98] Importantly, these local-deity types were shown in poses or styles that emphasized an archaic, non-Greek iconographic tradition—Byblus' Cronos-El is a six-winged Phoenician deity; Antioch-on-the-Cydnus' Sandan stands astride a horned and winged Neo-Hittite lion; Demetrias' Hadad is a rigidly frontal Syrian *agalma* with small bulls to either side. Furthermore, all of the Phoenician cities and refoundations, with the exception of Tripolis, used the Phoenician alphabet on the reverse. This indigenous script asserted a linguistic and historical culture beneath and beyond the Seleucid state. For instance, in a fascinating onomastic hybrid of dynastic colonial title and pre-Seleucid local identity, the reverses of the quasi-municipal coinage of Berytus, refounded as Laodicea-in-Phoenicia, carried the legend *ll'dk' 'm bkn'n*, "[belonging] to Laodicea, mother of Canaan":[99] Seleucid colonialism gets reframed in indigenous mode as a claim to ancient regional superiority.[100] Similarly, the entirely new foundations of northern Syria also put on display their particular civic identity: the thunderbolt at Seleucia-in-Pieria,[101] referring to the local cult of Zeus Ceraunius/Baal Ṣaphon; Poseidon, dolphins, and boat imagery at Laodicea-by-the-Sea,[102] alluding to the city's maritime function; armor, a panther, and a thyrsus at Apamea-on-the-Axios,[103] invoking the colony's military role and its cult of Dionysus. Earlier I suggested that Antioch-by-Daphne's use of an ear of wheat on its quasi-municipal diobols makes reference to the colony's fabricated founder, Triptolemus.[104]

On two sides of the same coin: the imagery and idea of empire, city cult and character. Such a combination both promoted a distinctive urban

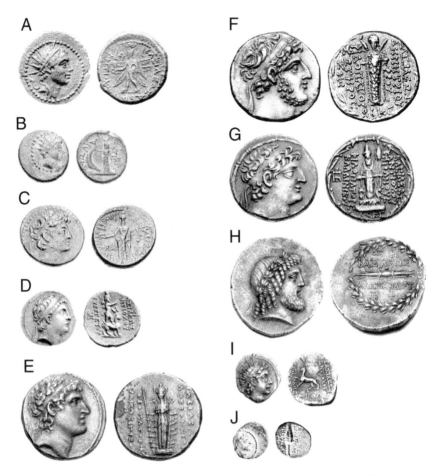

Figure 15 Seleucid quasi-municipal coinage: (a) Byblus, bronze; obv.
Antiochus IV, rev. Cronos-El; (b) Byblus, bronze; obv. Antiochus VI, rev.
Isis-Pharia; (c) Laodicea-in-Phoenicia/Berytus, bronze; obv. Demetrius II, rev.
Ba'al-Berit; (d) Antioch-on-the-Cydnus/Tarsus, silver drachm; obv. Antiochus
VII, rev. Sandan; (e) Mallus, silver tetradrachm; obv. Alexander I, rev. Athena
Magarsia; (f) Demetrias/Damascus, silver tetradrachm; obv. Demetrius III,
rev. Atargatis; (g) Demetrias/Damascus, silver tetradrachm; obv. Antiochus
XII, rev. Hadad; (h) Seleucia-in-Pieria, silver tetradrachm; obv. Zeus, rev.
thunderbolt; (i) Apamea-on-the-Axios, silver hemidrachm; obv. Antiochus
VI, rev. panther; (j) Antioch-by-Daphne, silver diobol; obv. Seleucus VI, rev.
ear of wheat.

identity and expressed it in an exclusively Seleucid context;[105] it is, in some sense, a numismatic analogy of the urban zoning examined earlier. The quasi-municipal coinage recognized a discrete civic space of self-representation, which would grow in size as dynastic squabbling further and further eroded the authority of the king.[106]

In one short series of quasi-municipal coins, struck during the short reign of Alexander II Zabinas, the Seleucid refoundation of Laodicea-in-Phoenicia briefly reverted to its precolonial name: the Phoenician legend on the reverse read *lbyrt 'm bkn'n* ("[belonging] to Berytus, mother of Canaan"); the dynastic name Laodicea was restored immediately after Zabinas' fall.[107] Such variation on an official medium suggests not only that city names were significant but also that civic agency could be expressed in the avoidance or manipulation of the officially imposed onomastic monotony.[108] Obviously, this is most apparent in the refoundations of preexisting settlements, whose original names reappear either immediately after the removal of Seleucid power or much later under its Roman, Parthian, or even Arab successors. For example, the Seleucid refoundations of Antioch-Chrysaoris and Seleucia-Tralleis in Caria returned to their original names of Alabanda and Tralleis immediately after Antiochus III's defeat at Magnesia.[109] Likewise, after the Parthian conquest, Seleucia-on-the-Eulaeus reemerges as Susa,[110] Epiphania as Ecbatana,[111] Artemita as Chalasar,[112] and Europus as Dura.[113] This suggests, exactly as we would expect, the continued local use throughout the period of the kingdom's dominance of a settlement's pre-Seleucid, nondynastic name.[114] Such an assumption is epigraphically confirmed in the case of Laodicea-in-Phoenicia, where members of the city's diaspora in the Aegean are identified by the ethnic *Bērutios* at the same time as the dynastic, colonial name Laodicea appears on the settlement's coins and formal documents.[115] One wonders whether the emergence of sobriquets for entirely new foundations, such as Zeugma for Seleucia-on-the-Euphrates or Kibōtos for Apamea-Celaenae,[116] represents a similar colonial resistance to the imperial baptism of the landscape.[117]

The emerging picture is one of determined civic self-fashioning in the Seleucid colonies, increasing throughout the third and second centuries: we witness a delineation of palatial zones, articulations of corporate pasts, and efforts to make the urban community visible and accessible to the imagination.[118] These manifestations open a space for the Seleucid colony as a self-consciously independent site of authority and so establish its population as an active and participatory agent in and amid the dynastic politics of the kingdom's decline.

Dynastic Strife and Urban Revolt

The mid-second century—ὅτε σκάπτρων ἦλυθ' Ἄρης Συρίην, "when a war of scepters came to Syria"[119]—marks a turning point in the kings' interaction with their major colonies. Antiochus IV Epiphanes' invasion, coup, and murder of his reigning nephew, all backed by the Attalid house of Pergamum (see Chapter 5), fractured the line of legitimate dynastic succession and generated decades of violent squabbling between rival rulers, manipulated by Parthia, the Attalid, Cappadocian, and Ptolemaic peer kingdoms, and the Roman republic. Moreover, the kingdom's territorial losses—to Graeco-Bactria and Parthia in the east, to Pergamum in the west, and to various insurrectionary movements in the north and the south—compounded the corrosive impact of this almost unceasing conflict. Pretender challenges to monarchic monopoly, from within the royal family and the administrative elite, were nothing new. But the revolts of an Achaeus in cis-Tauric Asia Minor or a Molon in the Upper Satrapies were the breakings away of cohesive provincial blocks at some distance from the imperial heartland. Reincorporation of these territorial units was relatively unproblematic: the renewal by campaign of the discarded bonds of dependency between king and governor. Third-century colonial revolts in the dynastic heartland were similarly a function of royal absence and in any case ephemeral.[120] The intradynastic competition of the kingdom's closing decades was qualitatively different—the protagonists were confronting one another within a smaller frame and competing over a handful of dynastic centers. As a result, the imperial heartland of northern Syria and Cilicia was shattered into a mosaic of discontiguous, mutually hostile zones (for places, see Map 4). In this way, the late second- and first-century Seleucid rump resembles, say, classical or Hellenistic Ionia, fought over and broken up by competing powers. The dynamics of territorial frontiers—a mercurial political landscape, loyalties auctioned to the highest bidder, proxy conflicts between cities or classes—have telescoped into the core, but unlike the grasping disputes over Ionia, these late Seleucid kinglets had no securely held base from which to gather strength or exploit resources. And so, amid this toil for possession of an accursed inheritance, the Seleucid colonies emerged as not only a prize to be wooed but also a source of semistable authority in a broken world.

It is hard to tell a story of fragmentation. The narrative details are labyrinthine and disputed, dependent on inadequate literary accounts and incomplete numismatic data (magistrates' countermarks, die usage and output, Seleucid Era dates, etc.). But in brief: there were three successive dynastic conflicts pitting senior and cadet branches against one another— the line of Seleucus IV (Demetrius I, Demetrius II, Antiochus VII) against that of his younger brother Antiochus IV (Antiochus V, Alexander I, Antiochus VI) between 164 and 125; the line of Demetrius II (Seleucus V, Antiochus VIII) against that of his younger brother Antiochus VII (Alexander II, Antiochus IX) between 125 and 96, each branch descending from Cleopatra Thea, wife to both brothers; and finally the five male children of Demetrius II's son Antiochus VIII (Seleucus VI, Antiochus XI, Philip I, Demetrius III, Antiochus XII) and Philip I's son Philip II disputed possession between themselves and the line of Antiochus IX (Antiochus X, Antiochus XIII) between 96 and 64, when Pompey's provincialization of Syria puts Hellenistic historians out of their misery.[121] To illustrate the difficulties: between 121 and 97 the half-brothers Antiochus VIII and Antiochus IX threw one another out of Antioch-by-Daphne four or five times, each thereby having several separate, short, insignificant reigns in the city; there are at least five different chronological reconstructions.[122] The response of the great historian Édouard Will, simply to omit from the dynastic stemma of his magisterial work the regnal dates for all kings after Antiochus IX, is entirely understandable.[123]

Within this bewildering *courte durée* flurry it is nonetheless possible to observe certain key developments in king-colony interactions. The most fundamental emergence into the historical record are explicit statements that the inhabitants of the major colonies—Antioch-by-Daphne above all, but also Seleucia-in-Pieria, Laodicea-by-the-Sea, Antioch-in-Ptolemaïs, and Demetrias-Damascus—were able to manifest their opinion, favorable or (more typically) hostile, toward particular monarchs. So, we are told that Alexander II Zabinas was greatly loved by the masses of Laodicea-by-the-Sea (διαφερόντως ὑπὸ τῶν πολλῶν ἠγαπᾶτο);[124] in 110/09, in the midst of the civil war between Antiochus VIII and Antiochus IX, the *dēmos* of Laodicea-in-Phoenicia (Berytus) dedicated on Delos a statue of Antiochus VIII as their savior and benefactor.[125] Conversely, we see the inflamed hatred, ἀπέχθεια or μῖσος, of the kingdom's subjects or the cities' masses for Demetrius I,[126] Alexander I Balas,[127] and Demetrius II,[128] as well as hostile actions against several others.

Such capacity for (dis)approval produced entirely new forms of communicative interaction between the urban residents and the monarchs or dynastic representatives. For the first time, core colonial populations appear as quasi-independent corporate entities to be wooed and won over by the ruler. Three forms stand out—persuasion, benefaction, and aggression. For the first, the paratactic accumulation of 2 Maccabees 13:26 can be taken as standard: when the inhabitants of Antioch-in-Ptolemaïs were indignant at the agreement the young Antiochus V had made with the Jews, the king's regent, Lysias, "ascended the speaker's platform, made the best possible defense, persuaded them, appeased them, gained their good will, and broke camp for Antioch" (προσῆλθεν ἐπὶ τὸ βῆμα Λυσίας, ἀπελογήσατο ἐνδεχομένως, συνέπεισεν, κατεπράυνεν, εὐμενεῖς ἐποίησεν, ἀνέζευξεν εἰς Ἀντιόχειαν).[129] Another example: after Ptolemy VI had turned against his creature Alexander I Balas, he gathered the Antiochians into an assembly (συναγαγὼν τοὺς Ἀντιοχεῖς εἰς ἐκκλησίαν) and persuaded them to receive as their king Demetrius II (πείθει δέξασθαι τὸν Δημήτριον αὐτούς), assuring the crowd that, should Demetrius attempt anything improper, he himself would come to their defense.[130] In each case, official pronouncement is not sovereign; instead, a submerged dialogue takes place between the king or regent, present and visible within the colony, and the anxieties or expectations of an urban audience, who exist as an entity capable of withdrawing consent. Second, we see kings' attempts to buy cities' or communities' loyalty by granting a privileged status and/or exemptions from various imperial burdens. Typically, this occurs at distance, to secure civic loyalty in the monarch's absence, so its standard mode of expression is epistolary. But in contrast to the royal letters of the flourishing third- and early second-century kingdom, directed exclusively at imperial officials and cascading down successive bureaucratic levels in willful disregard of subject populations,[131] these address and so recognize the independent existence of urban communities. Compare, for instance, Antiochus III's provisions and benefactions to the Jerusalem Temple in a letter concerning the Jews but addressed to his governor ("King Antiochus to Ptolemaeus, greetings"),[132] with the promised grants of Demetrius II "to the *ethnos* of the Jews"[133] or of Antiochus VII "to Simon the priest and ethnarch of the Jews and to the entire *ethnos*."[134] In the kingdom's closing decades grants of coinage rights or autonomy or *asylia* or tax exemption march inward on all sides, in the high-lands of Judea, up the Phoenician coast, across Cilicia, and ultimately right into the kingdom's heartland, where Seleucia-in-Pieria, the very burial place of the kingdom's founder, received its autonomy in 109/8 and Demetrias-Damascus, base of Demetrius III, Laodicea-by-the-Sea, and Apamea-on-the-Axios were declared holy and inviolate in the 80s or 70s.[135] 1 Maccabees 10, narrating Demetrius I's attempt to win over the Hasmonaean dynast Jonathan by surpassing Alexander Balas' benefactions, tears away the mask of kingly generosity to expose the general context for all these grants: a bidding war between Seleucid rivals, selling off the kingdom's resources and territorial integrity for the short-term gain of hollow victories. Third, kings could attempt to compel obedience through destruction of a city's property or physical assaults on the urban community itself: Alexander I Balas plundered the agricultural hinterland of Antioch-by-Daphne;[136] Demetrius II burned down the homes of the rebellious Antiochians;[137] Antiochus XI and Philip I sacked Mopsuestia to avenge the killing there of Seleucus VI, their older brother.[138]

Urban populations, on their part, were able to reify their hostility to kings in various ways. If the hated monarch were present in the city, the inhabitants could aggressively march on the palace. These boundary crossings were revolutionary acts of political self-definition, reversing the proper direction of formal interaction between urban zones. The best-attested instance of such an assault is the uprising of Antioch-by-Daphne against Demetrius II in 145. We are told that tens of thousands of inhabitants gathered in the city's center (ἐπισυνήχθησαν οἱ ἀπὸ τῆς πόλεως εἰς μέσον τῆς πόλεως),[139] seized weapons, and besieged the palace (περιστάντες τοῖς βασιλείοις αὐτοῦ τρόπῳ πολιορκίας).[140] Having been fought off by Demetrius' Jewish mercenaries, who hurled missiles at them from the palace roofs, the Antiochians surrendered to the king (παραδοῦναι αὐτοὺς τῷ Δημητρίῳ).[141] The language is that of reconciliation between discrete and opposed entities. Half a century later, Seleucus VI, according to Appian the most tyrannical (τυραννικώτατος) of the dynasty's kings, found himself besieged and burnt to death in his palace by the residents of Mopsuestia in Cilicia.[142] Alternatively, the colony could seek to expel the ruler: in the mid-second century, Justin reports that the Cappadocian prince Oropheres, the exiled brother of Ariarathes V, entered upon a pact with the Antiochians *(inita cum Antiochiensibus pactione)* to dethrone Demetrius I; the Antiochians then received support from the kings of Egypt, Pergamum, and Cappadocia.[143] Similarly, in 67/6 the Antiochians collectively decided, albeit unsuccessfully, to banish Antiochus XIII (συνεβούλευον ἐκ τῆς πόλεως μεταστήσασθαι).[144] Hostility to absent kings could be manifested by closing the city's gates and refusing entry: in this way Seleucia-in-Pieria rejected Alexander II Zabinas[145] and Antioch-in-Ptolemaïs Tigranes of Armenia.[146] Or the city could entrust itself to a new ruler: Cleopatra Thea feared that Seleucia-in-Pieria would hand itself over to the rebel Diodotus Tryphon;[147] Damascus called in the Nabataean ruler Aretas III;[148] the Antiochians replaced Demetrius II with the pretender Alexander II Zabinas;[149] eventually they called in Tigranes of Armenia.[150]

Cuneiform evidence attests similar manifestations of colonial hostility in the dying days of imperial rule in Babylonia. In contrast to the Syrian heartland, where there were too many Seleucid kings, for the most part this landscape did not have any, and so, from the death of Antiochus IV in 164, the disintegration and multiplication of Seleucid authority played out among senior imperial officials, Parthian invaders, and emancipated Elamite and Characenian monarchs.[151] Stability was not restored until the 120s, under the reign of Mithridates II. The Astronomical Diaries, as the contemporary, eyewitness accounts of indigenous priests, set us gazing out from a window of the Esagil temple onto urban conflicts generated by Seleucid decline. For instance, in 163, in the chaotic aftermath of Antiochus IV's death, we are told that the Seleucid colonists of Babylon (Akkadian ^{lú}pu-li-$ṭa$-nu for Greek πολῖται), together with their wives and children, fled the city for the *chōra* (Sumerian edin), where they were harassed by the "governor of the king" ($^{lú}ša$-kin_7 *šá* lugal), a supraregional command identified with Antiochus V's regent Philip[152] or the rebel Timarchus.[153] This may have been an attempt to compel urban obedience. Within Babylon itself, the priest reported that the city's administrator (^{lú}pa-hat e^{ki}, probably the colony's *epistatēs*[154]) and a senior military official (^{lú}gal ^{giš}kak = *rab sikkati*) hunkered down in the royal palace, fearful of entering the city streets[155] on account of the king's governor and the (indigenous) population (un^{meš});[156] perhaps a palace siege, like those of Antioch and Mopsuestia (see earlier). At the end of the same month, the Seleucid satrap of Babylonia fled from Seleucia-on-the-Tigris, the regional capital, presumably from a hostile urban environment.[157] Accordingly, we seem to have a spatialized conflict between, on the one hand, the suprasatrapal royal governor and the indigenous population in control of the public streets of Babylon and the hinterland and, on the other, the city's authorities, corralled in the palace, and the colonists, in flight beyond its walls. Moreover, the colonial population of Seleucia-on-the-Tigris, like those in Syria, was able to formally reify its collective political hostility. So, in 141, the year of Mithridates I's conquest, our astronomer-priest reports that the citizens of Seleucia-on-the-Tigris set up a public curse against the Parthian general Antiochus (*ár-rat . . . gar-ú*) on the grounds that he had made common cause with Elamite marauders; they then plundered his personal possessions.[158]

In the troubled twilight of the Seleucid kingdom the relationship between kings and colonies had been turned inside out. Where urban communities, like the lay congregation of a Catholic priest, had once been an audience before whom the kings represented their power and by which that power could be made manifest, they now formed a public sphere (in Habermas' sense, loosely[159]) with which royal figures negotiated, by which they were monitored, and from which they deduced at least part of their legitimacy. How had this public sphere developed?

We can quickly discard the systematic bias of our literary sources, which, reproducing the typical elite disdain (fear) of the urban mob, reduces it to a violent, mutable, rank-scented rabble.[160] Rather, as numerous studies of ancient and early modern crowd behavior have emphasized, there is good evidence that the urban riot was a self-conscious, disciplined, goal-oriented attempt to rectify perceived injustices.[161] Seleucid colonial riots remain obscure and varied, and with our current evidence it is impossible to develop in any sophisticated way a typology of urban violence in regard to its composition, causes, and triggers. Nonetheless we are able to put at least some faces to the crowd and to identify a few of the institutional kernels around which colonial opposition could precipitate. It is clear that, despite borrowed names and governmental organs, the internal dynamics of Seleucid colonies are fundamentally not those of Old World *poleis*. Immediately striking is that several anti-king uprisings seem to have been orchestrated by imperial or civic elites, taking sides in (and advantage of) dynastic conflicts. For example, Hierax and Diodotus, who had been appointed by Alexander I Balas as cogovernors of Antioch-by-Daphne,[162] incited the Antiochians to revolt against his rival Demetrius II (ἀνέσεισαν τοὺς Ἀντιοχεῖς πρὸς ἀπόστασιν).[163] The distinguished leaders (ἀξιόλογοι ἡγεμόνες—an inexact title) Antipater, Clonius, and Aeropus caused Laodicea-by-the-Sea to revolt from Alexander II Zabinas.[164] Similarly, individual citizens, addressing the massed citizenry, were able to provoke righteous indignation against Seleucid monarchs—during the reigns of Demetrius II (τοῦ δὲ πλήθους ἀθροισθέντος, καὶ πολλῶν λεγόντων)[165] and of Antiochus XIII Asiaticus (τῶν Ἀντιοχέων τινὲς . . . ἀνέσειον τὰ πλήθη καὶ συνεβούλευον);[166] Demaenetus of Antioch-in-Ptolemaïs is identified by Josephus explicitly as a demagogue.[167] It is likely that formal representative organs and informal associations within the Syrian colonies provided the setting for the political discussion and opinion formation that underlay the mass actions discussed earlier.[168] We hear of, on the one hand, governing assemblies and councils of Greek or Macedonian type[169] and, on the other, of dining clubs,[170] religious guilds,[171] gymnasia, and presumably various other military and artisanal groupings,[172] all of which may have functioned somewhat like eighteenth-century coffee-houses in anticipating behind closed doors the political criticism that would later break into the open.[173] Furthermore, the colonial populations demonstrated a remarkably resilient loyalty to the royal house. Dynastic legitimacy is a recurring concern—the inhabitants of Syria requested from Ptolemy VIII Physcon a king of Seleucid stock (τινὰ τῶν ἐκ τοῦ Σελεύκου γένους παραδῷ αὐτοῖς);[174] the Larisans were devoted to the royal line (τοῖς ἀπὸ Σελεύκου τοῦ Νικάτορος βασιλεῦσι γεγονότας συμμάχους);[175] the pretender Alexander II Zabinas won the favor of the Antiochians by displaying appropriate, if unfelt, care over the remains of Antiochus VII Sidetes.[176] The conservatism of the colonial population comes through most clearly in the Antiochians' support for Andriscus, the supposed son of the Antigonid king Perseus, defeated by Rome; in 149 the assembled crowd demanded that Demetrius II either restore Andriscus or abdicate if he were unable or unwilling to be a king (δεῖν . . . παραχωρεῖν τῆς ἀρχῆς τὸν Δημήτριον, εἰ μήτε δύναται μήτε βούλεται βασιλεύειν):[177] this mid-second-century colonial crowd was clinging to ideals, now outdated, regarding the capacity and proper behavior of royalty.[178]

But by the dynasty's last gasps royal authority had been hollowed out to the point of its explicit rejection by colonies. A first harbinger: In 151/0, immediately after Alexander I Balas' victory over Demetrius I, the major colonies Seleucia-in-Pieria and Antioch-by-Daphne began to strike coinage without the royal portrait and with the entirely novel legend ΑΔΕΛΦΩΝ ΔΗΜΩΝ, "of the brother peoples," instead of the standard title and name of the ruler:[179] sovereignty was manifested in the cities' inhabitants and their corporate identities; the king was simply ignored.[180] In the mid-80s, Philip I Philadelphus managed to seize Demetrias-Damascus during the absence of Antiochus XII Dionysus, its ruler and his brother. Although this had been achieved with the connivance of the city's garrison commander,

Milesius, Philip tried to make it seem as though he had taken Damascus through the fear he inspired (τῷ παρ' αὑτοῦ φόβῳ βουληθεὶς δοκεῖν παραλαβεῖν τὴν πόλιν).[181] In response to this claim, he became an object of suspicion and was locked outside the walls.[182] Philip's boast had constituted a discursive reminiscence, an impotent attempt to turn back the clock to a time of royal dominance. His expulsion was a self-conscious assertion by the Damascene public of its capacity to select its own ruler; city to king—being weak, seem so! A final example: Endangered by the Hasmonaean aggression of the Judean ruler Alexander Jannaeus, the people of Antioch-in-Ptolemaïs had begged the assistance of the Ptolemaic prince Ptolemy IX Lathyrus, who was ruling Cyprus after being driven from Alexandria by his mother, Cleopatra III. The demagogue Demaenetus persuaded the inhabitants to abrogate the offer: it was better to run the risk of battle with the Jews alone than to accept open servitude (φανερὰν . . . δουλείαν) by handing themselves over to a despot (δεσπότῃ παραδόντας αὑτούς).[183] We don't need a king. In the utter demoralization of the land the repudiation of kingship is absolute and revolutionary.

The historical texture of these dying paroxysms was not driven by the claimants to Seleucus' throne, whose failings and failures are interchangeable; at night all cats are gray.[184] Rather, it derives its pattern from the kind of imperial space generated by Seleucus I. As was argued in Chapter 7, in the formation of the imperial heartland of the Syrian Seleucis, state functions had been distributed among the major Tetrapolis colonies and then, after the conquest of Coele Syria, extended down the Levant to Antioch-in-Ptolemaïs and Demetrias-Damascus.[185] Such an absence of a "primate" settlement—a generally recognized single imperial capital with exclusive responsibilities and privileges—was both useful for an itinerant court and unproblematic as long as the reigning monarch monopolized legitimate kingship. But the appearance of rival claimants to the throne within the same region changed everything. Now the political landscape offered no single, dominant city to occupy and therewith to subordinate the rest of the kingdom. Now the coexistence of several authorized residences permitted the multiplication of the royal persona. The result: a hydralike landscape of rival principalities centered upon those colonies which the sojourns of the great rulers of the dynasty's past had invested with sufficient royal dignity. It was a crisis impossible to reverse. Accordingly, Seleucid dynastic conflict was spatialized in a very different way to, say, contemporaneous Ptolemaic rivalries, where the dominance of Alexandria and the unifying channel of the Nile prevented a similar territorial fragmentation despite an equally fractious and incapable ruling family.[186]

The overall picture, then, is of a late second- to early first-century systemic and accelerating breakdown in king-colony interactions and settlement networks in Syria. Various new forces filled the interstices left by diminished authorities. Piracy and brigandage abounded, attested in both literary sources and the new built architecture of security that developed in rural areas, where farmsteads were fortified and towers of retreat constructed.[187] Subordinate colonies attempted to rework the urban hierarchies established at foundation; for example, the men of Larisa fought against dominant Apamea,[188] the outpost of Lysias succeeded in breaking away.[189] Aradus managed to destroy its rival Marathus (mod. Amrit) on the mainland.[190] By a process now lost to historical record a host of settlements, individually or as groups, fell under the control of petty potentates.[191] We hear of Zoilus, tyrant of the coastal sites Strato's Tower and Dora;[192] of Strato ruling Beroea in Cyrrhestica and of Dionysius, son of Heracleon, at a different time ruling Beroea, Heraclea, and Hierapolis-Bambyce;[193] of Ptolemy, son of Mennaeus, at Chalcis-under-Libanus;[194] of Silas, a Jew, holding the stronghold of Lysias on the Orontes;[195] of Cinyrus at Byblus;[196] of Dionysius at Tripolis;[197] of Demetrius at Gamala in the Galilee;[198] and so on. The onomastics suggest a mix of enfranchised imperial officials and local adventurers.[199] Furthermore, the weakening of central royal authority had permitted nomadic Arab chieftains to push farther into Syria and to dominate sedentary communities;[200] these figures emerge as significant allies and protectors in the dynastic conflicts. For instance, Alexander I Balas entrusted his son Antiochus (VI) to the Arab Yamlik-Iamblichus,[201] with whose assistance Diodotus Tryphon later captured Chalcis-on-the-Belus.[202] After his defeat on the banks of the river Oenoparas, Balas was welcomed and decapitated by another Arab dynast, Zabdiel-Diocles.[203] Antiochus X Eusebes was killed while fighting for Laodice, queen of the Arab Samenians;[204] the regal name perhaps indicates some kind of marriage alliance between the Seleucid monarch and a lord of tents.[205] Philip II's attempt on the Seleucid throne was sponsored by Aziz, his rival Antiochus XIII's rule by Sampsigeramus of Emesa, deep ancestor of the Severans; the two dynasts ultimately planned to do away with their ciphers and divide Syria between them.[206] Similarly, frequent Arab incursions into the Babylonian alluvium are attested in cuneiform sources.[207] And then, of course, we see the better-known and -attested expansion of the Hasmonaean, Ituraean, and Nabataean kingdoms.

As a result, the north Syrian political landscape, soon to be provincial-ized by Pompey in 64, was shattered into a mosaic of small and mutually hostile statelets. And, despite Rome's greater capacity to regulate land-scapes and channel civic ambitions productively, the colonial fault lines of northern Syria were never completely smoothed over. In 194 CE, in the aftermath of Pertinax' assassination, Syria would again splinter its loyal-ties between contestants for an imperial throne—Antioch-by-Daphne and Berytus for Pescennius Niger, Laodicea-by-the-Sea and Tyre for Septimius Severus.[208] And as I write this, I cannot fail to note that Syria, once more victim of its spaces and its leaders, descends into urban revolt, political fragmentation, and dynastic collapse. Thus the dead annex the living; to paraphrase Calvino, the victors over enemy sovereigns are made the heirs to their long undoing.

Conclusion

The people of Syria put up with him:
as long as someone stronger doesn't come along.
And what "Syria"? It barely comes to half;
what with little kingdoms, with John Hyrcanus,
with the cities that are declaring their independence.

It seems the realm once began, the historians say,
at the Aegean and went right up to India.
From the Aegean right up to India! Patience.
Let's have a look at those puppets,
the animals he's brought us.

Cavafy, Antiochus the Cyzicene (unfinished)[1]

    The Seleucid empire developed a set of official discourses and imperial behaviors that gave expression to territory: a spatial unit was bounded and explored, settled and progressed through, configured and withdrawn from. Throughout, the focus of discussion has fallen largely on the writings, actions, and movements of the rulers and their court. This privileging of the imperial apex, a deliberate top-down approach given the book's central concerns, of course does not do justice to all the other actors and countervailing processes of Seleucid history. While concentrated historical agency is a function of the distribution of power within the empire, the institutions of which were organized to transmit and implement royal will,[2] it is also a fiction of the monopolizing court rhetoric which legitimized these (and interests us), as well as the Roman-period sources' own investment in an image of centralized, determining leadership. For the Seleucid kings did not have it all their own way. We are obliged in closing to confront the inconsistencies, objections, and heterotopias that undermined Seleucid space and left to Antiochus IX, the puppeteer, barely half of Syria.

It would, of course, be nonsense to propose a fundamental dichotomy between ideology and practice, but, in a very real sense, the empire's technology of provincial control was inadequate, even detrimental, to its elaborated territorial claims. That is to say, cogenerated with Seleucid territory were the fault lines along which it fractured. We have seen much of this already. The kingdom's birth in diplomatic retreat set a precedent for authorized and repeated territorial renunciations. The selection and development of northern Syria as the off-center imperial heartland unbalanced the empire and, especially after the loss of Asia Minor, marginalized the Upper Satrapies. An insistence on the significance, symbolic and practical, of the monarch's mobile presence was undermined by the sheer expansiveness of the land and by competing demands for royal intervention; governors-in-revolt filled the breach. The segmentation of the imperial territory into delimited satrapies or suprasatrapal commands, well armored with palace, mint, and soldiers and in the grip of royal relatives or top-rank courtiers, gave to the territorial blocks an incipient centrality and so eased their emancipation from Seleucid authority. The failure to produce or privilege a primate city had devastating consequences for the kingdom's political unity in its closing decades.

Alongside these weaknesses in the architecture of the kingdom, which are in any case merely the flip side of its strengths, we encounter among subject peoples and rivals the development of alternative ideologies of territory that could face down Seleucid claims and explicitly oppose the inalienable rights of ancestral land to the sovereign claims of empire. A full analysis of such responses is a project in its own right, but a sampling gives some sense of the terms in which this opposition could be framed. Clearest of all is the confrontation between Antiochus VII Sidetes and the Jewish High Priest Simon, as reported in 1 Maccabees. Antiochus Sidetes, determined to reassert control over Judea, sent a set of demands to Simon:

> You are holding Jaffa and Gazara and the Acra of Jerusalem, cities of my kingdom (πόλεις τῆς βασιλείας μου). You have devastated their territory, you have done great damage to the land, and you have seized control of many places in my kingdom (τόπων πολλῶν ἐν τῇ βασιλείᾳ μου). Now then, hand over the cities which you have seized, and the tribute of the places you have seized beyond the borders of Judea. If you do not, give me five hundred talents of silver for them and another five hundred talents for the destruction you have caused and for the tribute of the cities. If you do not, we are coming against you in war.[3]

Simon brusquely responded:

> We have neither taken foreign land (γῆν ἀλλοτρίαν) nor seized another's property (ἀλλοτρίων), but only the inheritance of our fathers (τῆς κληρονομίας τῶν πατέρων ἡμῶν), which at one time had been seized unjustly by our enemies. Now, since we have the opportunity, we are holding firmly the inheritance of our fathers.[4]

The two narratives are irreconcilable, and the leaders uncompromising: only force will determine which wins out (in the short term the king, in the long term the priest). The territorial concept of *Eretz Yisrael*, the promised "land of Israel," had a central place in second-century Jewish thought:[5] the Hasmonaean rebels were equipped for their rebellion with a powerful and inherited ideology of space. But in contrast to the explicitly biblical language of Ben Sira, Daniel, Jubilees, 1 Enoch, and so on, the exchange in 1 Maccabees strikingly recalls official Seleucid discourse, especially the debate between Antiochus III and L. Lentulus at Lysimachia in 196: the Seleucid monarch had defended his activities in Asia Minor and Thrace with precisely the arguments used by Simon—repossession of an illegally occupied patrimony.[6] The manipulation of such language by a subject people in revolt speaks both to the successful penetration of Seleucid spatial ideology and to the weakness of its historicizing claims before deeper ancestral memories and God-given legitimacy.

Such an oppositional, indigenous cultural space can also be found in second-century Persia. Although we lack comparable access to developed Persian notions of homeland,[7] the coins of the breakaway *frataraka* ("leader," "governor") dynasty proudly display Achaemenid onomastics, iconography, and religious sites. The degree and the date of the *frataraka*'s political independence are still matters of discussion,[8] but it cannot be doubted that their coin types were modeled on the Great Kings' funerary reliefs from Naqsh-i Rustam and treasury reliefs from Persepolis.[9] Furthermore, the dynasts bear the title *prtrk' ZY 'LHY'*, an Aramaic rendering of the Middle Persian, *frataraka ī bayān* ("*frataraka* of the gods"); the *bayān* may be either the deceased Achaemenid kings or Zoroastrian divinities.[10] At about the same time as these coins were struck, a new and very large building was constructed on the southwestern edge of the Persepolis terrace from architectural fragments of the old and long-abandoned palaces—a literal reconstruction of an Achaemenid space.[11] Altogether, it seems that the *frataraka*, much like the Hasmonaeans, legitimized their rebellion and subsequent rule over the old Persian heartland through an appeal to the sacred images and places of the glory days before Alexander, Seleucus, and his descendants.[12] Lori Khatchadourian has recently suggested a similar movement in Armenia, where Artaxias I appeals to Yervandid ancestry and Urartian inscriptional and building traditions in his break from Seleucid rule.[13]

There is one other conceivable—and very strange—appeal to a pre-Hellenistic territorial tradition. According to Pompeius Trogus, the rebel Timarchus, Antiochus IV's governor of the Upper Satrapies and recognized by the Senate as an opponent of Demetrius I, was considered *Medorum rex,* "king of the Medes";[14] on his coins he took the title *basileus megas,* breaking with a century and a half of Seleucid custom to associate himself with older, eastern titulature.[15] It is just possible that Timarchus' revolt from the Seleucids was articulated as a revival of the long-defunct Median monarchy.

The emancipatory movements of the Hasmonaeans and Timarchus, although localized eruptions within Seleucid territory, received explicit support from the Roman Senate, for the great republic in the west repeatedly undermined Seleucid space, rolled back the kingdom's borders, and arbitrated its territorial disputes. In addition to the backing it gave to the rebellions, the Senate directly recomposed the Seleucid imperial landscape—such acts of spatial dominance included the Peace of Apamea, where cis-Tauric Asia Minor was lopped off,[16] and the consequent debate over Pamphylia's fate;[17] the sand-circle of Popilius Laenas;[18] and the prohibition on Seleucid troops marching through Judea.[19] Rome's delineation of Seleucid borders publicly undercut the authority of the kings and became the rhetorical object of Roman self-fashioning as space-maker.

The Seleucid empire fell apart, as things do—internal failures and others' successes, inevitability and chance. The epithets of kinglets accumulated, reechoing because the core was hollow. The diadem became a wreath of flies. When at last the lots were shaken and the world divided, the kingdom's west fell to Rome, and its east to Parthia; Seleucid space and the ideologies that challenged it can seem nothing but a game of substituted corpses. But the Seleucid empire was not a dead end, a mere place holder between Alexander and Rome. For if historical significance is to be measured by transformations of the anterior and the longevity of their survival, then we can identify three areas in which the Seleucid spatial contribution was of major long-term importance.

First, the Seleucid court fixed Greek and Roman geographical and ethnographical conceptions of the farther east for several centuries. Megasthenes and Patrocles retained their authority over the now impossibly distant Ganges and Caspian; the whole Iranian zone of the fourth-century CE *Tabula Peutingeriana*, from Demodamas' *Ara Alexandri* on the Iaxartes river to the road measurements through Carmania, seems to derive from Seleucid intelligence.[20]

Second, Seleucid monarchy became one of the major models and sources of legitimacy for the kingdoms that succeeded it. Everywhere we see the manifest preservation of Seleucid governing structures, administrative personnel, provincial hierarchies, the Era, and so on.[21] Ideologically charged Seleucid symbols, like Apollo's anchor, were used by Hyspaosines of Characene,[22] Euthydemus I of Bactria,[23] the Kamnashkirids of Elymaïs,[24] the Parthians,[25] and even Alexander Jannaeus of Judea.[26] Kinship with or authorization from the Seleucid dynasty were cherished and advertised—1 Maccabees twice draws attention to the purple robe and golden clasp granted to the Hasmonaeans;[27] similarly, the relief at Hung-e Azhdar/Nauruzi in Elymaïs may depict Demetrius II proclaiming a local dynast's legitimate right to rule;[28] most spectacular of all is the sculptural gallery of Seleucid ancestors at Commagenian Antiochus I's *hierothesion* of Nemrud Dağı.[29] In almost every case, the image of Seleucid kingship was adopted, not effaced; I suspect that its importance as a precedent for post-Hellenistic kingship (and Roman imperialism) will come to be as recognized as the Achaemenid model for the Hellenistic world.

Finally, the Seleucid empire transformed the political geography of the Near East and shaped its broad outlines right up to the Arab conquests, in other words, for almost a millennium. The kingdom was responsible for the development of the Common Road through Asia Minor and the north Syrian routes to the Euphrates, as well as the further unification of the northern and southern Levant. Furthermore, it is sufficiently clear that Seleucid provincial boundaries and subdivisions anticipated those of several of the independent kingdoms that succeeded it, from Commagene[30] to Mesene,[31] and post-Apamea Pergamum[32] to Diodotid Bactria.[33] More importantly, the concentration of colonial settlements and imperial bureaucracy in the two great panels of northern Syria and the middle Tigris established these areas as the Near East's lasting cores of urban civilization and imperial power. And while a sense of an east-west polarity had long existed in the Greek world, this bicentrality of Seleucid territory and its formal division by Seleucus I and his immediate successors into the domains of the king and the general-commander of the Upper Satrapies, respectively,[34] helped to generate the fundamental spatial characteristic of the following centuries: the *divisio orbis,* or great partition, of the east Mediterranean and west Asia into Roman-Byzantine and Parthian-Sasanid spheres. Indeed, the transformation of the middle Euphrates from a line of communication within a single political unit into the frontier zone between two hostile empires was a Seleucid creation, first emerging briefly with the revolt of Molon in the late third century[35] and then continuously after the Parthian conquest of Babylonia in 141. The Seleucids bequeathed to Rome both their core Syrian territory and their Euphrates frontier with Parthia.[36] Henceforth, the dominant power in the Mediterranean would be sundered from the worlds of the Tigris and Iran. This geopolitical separation of "west" from "east," obtaining in the ancient world from at least the first century and subsequently fixing the boundaries of modern academic disciplines, was an effect of a specifically Seleucid imperial space and not the inevitability we might otherwise be tempted to assume.

The Seleucid elephant, hamstrung and weary of time, expired in winter 64/3 BCE after a journey of two and a half centuries. Its successor regimes—Rome, Parthia, and the Hasmonaeans among them—each have their own tales of territory, yet remained indebted in various ways to Seleucid space-making: reordering the bones, reshaping the flesh, and crafting new creatures for the bestiary of antiquity.

APPENDIX

NOTES

GLOSSARY

REFERENCES

ACKNOWLEDGMENTS

INDEX

On the Date of Megasthenes' *Indica*

At the basis of any interpretation of Megasthenes' *Indica* are two fundamental and related questions. Who sent him to India? When did he go? It has long been argued that Megasthenes was the envoy of Seleucus I Nicator to the court of Chandragupta in the years immediately following the Treaty of the Indus;[1] this is the historical framework that I use. But in an important intervention, published in *Classical Philology* in 1996, A. B. Bosworth argued that Megasthenes' embassy to Chandragupta in fact took place a decade and a half earlier, in 319/8.[2] Professor Bosworth's argument has been accepted by Duane Roller in his reedition (and now standard version) of the Megasthenes fragments for *Brill's New Jacoby* (*BNJ* 715).[3] This entails a reevaluation of the historical context and cultural meaning of the *Indica*. For this revisionist dating, Megasthenes is describing a world where Alexander's death is recent, the Mauryan empire is nascent, king Porus still rules over the Indus valley, and Eumenes and Antigonus are competing for control of the Upper Satrapies. Megasthenes appears as a contemporary of Nearchus and Onesicritus, not Hecataeus of Abdera. He belongs in the satrapal court of Sibyrtius in Arachosia, not the royal court of Seleucus in Babylon and Syria. And so his *Indica*, while engaging with the post-Alexander world in which Seleucus would triumph, tells us little about the specific ethnographic concerns of the early Seleucid empire because it was completed when Seleucus was a mere subordinate of Antigonus or a refugee in Ptolemaic Alexandria.

Bosworth's argument focuses on two of the *testimonia* for Megasthenes' career: Arrian, *Indica* 5.3 (T2b) and *Anabasis* 5.6.2 (T2a). In a passage noting the size and number of India's rivers, a trope of Greek ethnographic writing, Arrian admits Megasthenes' knowledge of the extraordinary number of navigable Indian rivers in addition to the Ganges and the Indus, "but not even Megasthenes, so far as I can see, traversed much of the land of the Indians, although more than the companions of Alexander, the son of Philip. For he says that he kept company with Sandrocottus, the greatest king of the Indians, and with Porus, who was even greater than him (συγγενέσθαι γὰρ Σανδροκόττῳ λέγει, τῷ μεγίστῳ βασιλεῖ Ἰνδῶν, καὶ Πώρῳ ἔτι τούτου μείζονι)." This is the unemended reading of Arrian, *Indica* 5.3, which Bosworth prefers.[4] Megasthenes claimed to have visited both Chandragupta and Porus, and, since Porus was assassinated *c.* 318, Bosworth concludes—on the basis that Megasthenes made only one visit to India—that his mission must have predated that year.

Bosworth's second main point is that Arrian, *Anabasis* 5.6.2, identifies Megasthenes as an associate of Sibyrtius, the satrap of Arachosia: "Megasthenes, who associated with Sibyrtius, the satrap of Arachosia (ὃς ξυνῆν μὲν Σιβυρτίῳ τῷ σατράπῃ τῆς Ἀραχωσίας), frequently says[5] that he visited Sandrocottus, king of the Indians." Certain details of Sibyrtius' career in the early Successor period are known.[6] He had been appointed satrap of Arachosia and Gedrosia by Alexander in 324 and retained this posting in the Babylon and Triparadisus settlements. He joined the satrapal confederacy against Pithon[7] but was afterward targeted by Eumenes and would have been condemned to death.[8] He was reconfirmed in his command by Antigonus in 316, who assigned him the most turbulent of the Silver Shields to be used up on suicide missions.[9] Thereafter, he drops out of the historical record as Diodorus' major source, Hieronymus of Cardia, turns his attention westward.

Combining these two *testimonia*, Bosworth suggests that Megasthenes traveled on a single mission to Chandragupta and Porus as envoy of Sibyrtius in 319/8 and that his *Indica* was published around 310, more than half a decade before Seleucus I's ceding of the Indus lands to the Mauryan state. The embassy's traditional dating and association with Seleucus are due to "a natural tendency among scholars to retroject the importance of Seleucus"[10] and a convenient but groundless conflation of the only known ambassador to Chandragupta, Megasthenes, with the only known diplomatic agreement, between Chandragupta and Seleucus in 304/3.[11]

Bosworth's argument is a sophisticated reappraisal of Megasthenes' historical context, as is to be expected from a scholar of such rigor and insight. But in what follows, I hope to show that an analysis of the *testimonia* and fragments of Megasthenes' *Indica* cannot support the revisionist thesis and requires the restoration of the traditional dating. Inevitably, this means responding directly to the specific arguments of Bosworth's 1996 *Classical Philology* article, as it was this piece alone which overturned the former consensus. I trust, nonetheless, that my comments will be taken in the spirit of admiration with which they are composed.

The *Testimonia*

Even if we were to accept the manuscript reading of Arrian, *Indica* 5.3 (T2b συγγενέσθαι γὰρ Σανδροκόττῳ λέγει, τῷ μεγίστῳ βασιλεῖ Ἰνδῶν, καὶ Πώρῳ ἔτι τούτου μείζονι), that would in no way invalidate the traditional dating: a younger Megasthenes could well have visited Porus before 318 and Chandragupta more than a decade later, when the Mauryan empire extended into the Indus basin, and there is indeed evidence for frequent visits (see below). But various scholars have justly regarded the manuscript reading of Arrian, *Indica* 5.3, with its superlative-comparative combination, as doubtful: if Chandragupta were the greatest of Indian kings, how could there be a greater? Accordingly, Lassen considered the reference to Porus a scribal interpolation,[12] while Schwanbeck emended the final clause to "καὶ Πώρου ἔτι τούτῳ μείζονι," which was adopted in Roos' Teubner edition: that is, Megasthenes kept company with Chandragupta, the greatest king of the Indians, "who was still greater than Porus."[13] Bosworth suggests that the manuscript's paradoxical comparison may derive from Arrian's "penchant for rhetoric" and identifies parallels in Appian and Thucydides (though none in Arrian),[14] but these do not hold water.[15]

Of more weight than the passage's stylistic difficulties is the historical problem of considering Porus a greater monarch than Chandragupta.[16] Bosworth argues at length that "in a specific historical and psychological context" Megasthenes would have represented Porus as Chandragupta's superior; this is the key argument for his antedating of the *Indica*.[17] It is certainly true that Porus played a prominent propagandistic role in the narration of Alexander's Indian campaign in the literary and numismatic record.[18] No other former enemy was granted such honors or territorial rule. The settlements of Babylon and Triparadisus, acknowledging the limits of Macedonian imperial reach, confirmed him in his position.[19] Nonetheless, the Alexander Historians are unanimous in emphasizing the unprecedented size and superior power of the Ganges-based kingdom of the Nandas. Their 20,000 cavalry, 200,000 infantry, 2,000 war chariots, and 3,000–4,000 elephants far outstripped the army Porus had been able to muster.[20] Although the fantastically exaggerated numbers clearly serve an apologetic function, both for the mutiny on the Hyphasis and Alexander's abandonment of further eastward conquest, they reveal undeniable Greek perceptions of the preeminence of the kingdom of the Gangetic plain.

Bosworth suggests that the historical context for Porus' superiority, as asserted in the transmitted reading, is an early stage of Chandragupta's rise, when the Nanda kingdom had collapsed and the Mauryan was still nascent: "Prior to [the conquest of the Indus valley] Chandragupta's domains were in the Ganges valley, and, however rich and populous they may have been, they could have been viewed as inferior to the lands under Porus."[21] But Megasthenes' ethnographic statements do not permit such a reading. Far from depicting Porus' superiority, the Indus ruler does not appear once in the extensive extant fragments. More to the point, the Ganges basin and its Mauryan capital city are the superlative examples in India time and again. For example, "The largest city in India is called Palimbothra in the land of the Prasii, where the river Erannoboas flows into the Ganges. The Ganges is the largest river."[22] The city itself was Heracles' most magnificent urban foundation.[23] Palimbothra's population, the Prasii, is the most distinguished *ethnos* in India.[24] The region has the largest tigers.[25] Chandragupta's army camp is 400,000 strong, almost double what the wildest fantasies of the Alexander Historians assigned to the Nanda kingdom.[26] It is difficult to conceive how Megasthenes' ethnography would have represented Porus as Chandragupta's superior when the latter possessed the most enormous army, resided on the greatest river, led the most distinguished tribe, and inhabited the most magnificent city.

Finally, the reference to Porus in the phrase under discussion (καὶ Πώρῳ ἔτι τούτου μείζονι) makes little sense within its immediate textual context. Arrian's point in *Indica* 5.3 is geographical: though Megasthenes had visited but a fraction of India, he had traversed more than Alexander, his army, and his historians.[27] Consequently, it makes excellent sense for Arrian to introduce Chandragupta in this context since it was in Megasthenes' visit to the Mauryan kingdom that he far surpassed the most eastward penetration of Alexander's *anabasis*. The testamentary function of this information is demonstrated by the epexegetical γάρ in the phrase συγγενέσθαι γὰρ Σανδροκόττῳ λέγει. In contrast, the reference to Porus in no way sustains Arrian's point about Megasthenes' eastward travel and exploration beyond Alexander because Alexander and his army had met Porus, and Porus' kingdom lay well to the west of Chandragupta's.

Accordingly, it seems that the manuscript reading of Arrian, *Indica* 5.3 is flawed on stylistic, semantic, and contextual grounds; the unemended passage cannot be a faithful representation of Megasthenes and so is inadequate foundation for a redating of Megasthenes' *Indica*. It is likely that the text is corrupt: all extant manuscripts of Arrian's *Indica* were copied, directly or indirectly, from a single twelfth- or thirteenth-century manuscript, Vindobonensis gr. 4 (A), badly faded by damp. A fourteenth-century scribe (A²) carelessly rewrote over the old traces, with the result that several glosses have been absorbed into the text and wrong case endings are used.[28] The most economic explanation of the various difficulties remains that of Lassen, namely, that the Indus king was interpolated by an Alexander-focused scribe, for whom an *Indica* without Porus would have been unimaginable.[29]

Bosworth's second main point, insisting on Megasthenes' connection to Sibyrtius, for which our only source is Arrian, *Anabasis* 5.6.2 (T2a ὃς ξυνῆν μὲν Σιβυρτίῳ τῷ σατράπῃ τῆς Ἀραχωσίας), is correct and salutary. Arrian is absolutely clear that Megasthenes was associated with Sibyrtius, and the ethnographer's embassy to Chandragupta appears in this context.[30] But this is not necessarily evidence in support of the antedating, for nothing about Megasthenes' Sibyrtius connection invalidates the traditional dating of his *Indica*.

In order to distance Megasthenes from Seleucus Nicator, Bosworth downplays the significance of the *testimonium* in Clement of Alexandria (T1). The passage, *Stromata* 1.72.4–5, written around 200 CE, is worth quoting in full:

> The Jewish people are the oldest of all these by far, and they had a written philosophy long before philosophy existed amongst the Greeks, as the Pythagorean Philon shows, not to mention Aristobulus the Peripatetic and many more (so that I do not waste time mentioning them by name). Most conspicuously, Megasthenes, the writer who lived with Seleucus Nicator (ὁ συγγραφεὺς ὁ Σελεύκῳ τῷ Νικάτορι συμβεβιωκώς), writes as follows in the third book of his *Indica*: "Everything, however, mentioned about nature by the ancients is also said by philosophers outside Greece, by the Brachmanes among the Indians and by those called the Jews in Syria."

Clement here directly quotes Megasthenes' *Indica* and identifies the ethnographer by his association with Seleucus I Nicator. The verb συμβιόω denotes a close cohabitation rather than a mere synchronism; this is confirmed by several other passages in Clement.[31] The verb is used by other authors to describe the cohabitation of a husband, a resident concubine, and a wedded couple.[32] Clement clearly means that Megasthenes actually lived in the court of Seleucus, a stronger association than the ξυνῆν Σιβυρτίῳ of Arrian, *Anabasis* 5.6.2. Dihle has demonstrated Clement's wider familiarity with Megasthenes. In the Alexandrian's discussion of Indian philosophy in *Stromata* 1.71.3, alone among comparative lists, he includes both Brachmanes and Sarmanai.[33] The two are often paired in Megasthenes' ethnography and almost certainly derive from the Mauryan collective term for Brahmanic and non-Brahmanic ascetics, *bramanaśramaṇanam*.

Other, admittedly more ambiguous, *testimonia* need to be brought into discussion; where there is evidence for dating, they support the traditional over the revisionist thesis. Pliny, *Naturalis historia* 6.17.58 (T8), concludes his description of the unusual climactic and astronomical phenomena of India with an account of the country's discovery and exploration, a passage we encountered in Chapter 2:

> Thus it has been opened up not only by the armies of Alexander the Great and the kings who succeeded him, Seleucus and Antiochus and the commander of their fleet Patrocles, who even sailed around the Hyrcanian and Caspian Sea *(cirumvectis etiam in Hyrcanium mare et Caspium Seleuco et Antiocho praefectoque classis eorum Patrocle)*, but also by other Greek authors who spent time with the Indian kings, such as Megasthenes and Dionysius, who was sent by [Ptolemy II] Philadelphus *(Dionysius a Philadelpho missus)* to report on the manpower of these people.

This passage is organized around an opposition between military expedition and diplomatic embassy: India was revealed on the one hand by the armed forces of Alexander, Seleucus, and Antiochus and on the other hand by the missions of Megasthenes and Dionysius. Unfortunately, Pliny does not directly state who sent Megasthenes; our ethnographer hangs awkwardly between Patrocles, commissioned by Seleucus and Antiochus, and Dionysius, sent by Philadelphus. What would be the most natural reading of this passage? The first two Seleucid corulers, Seleucus I and Antiochus I, are contained in the historically false ablative absolute claim that they sailed with their admiral, Patrocles, in his Caspian explorations; identifying them, or Seleucus I alone, as Megasthenes' sponsor would require an awkward repetition. That Megasthenes follows Patrocles, representative of Seleucus and Antiochus, and precedes Dionysius, who alone is qualified by his Ptolemaic sponsor, suggests that the sense of Seleucid commission continues for Megasthenes. At any rate, there is no named monarch or power in addition to Alexander, Seleucus, Antiochus, and Ptolemy. Sibyrtius is not mentioned.

Like Philadelphus' Dionysius, the *Indica* author Deimachus is virtually unknown (*BNJ* 716). Nonetheless, he is paired with Megasthenes in Strabo 2.1.9 (T2c): "For they were sent to Palimbothra—Megasthenes to Sandrocottus and Deimachus to Amitrochates his son—as ambassadors." Amitrochates is Chandragupta's son Bindusara. It is universally accepted that Deimachus was Antiochus I Soter's ambassador to the Mauryan court. I would suggest that Strabo, or his source Eratosthenes, has established a generational succession here. Just as we have the set Amitrochates-Deimachus-Antiochus I, so we have Chandragupta-Megasthenes-Seleucus I. It should be observed, à propos the earlier discussion, that Megasthenes is known as the envoy to Chandragupta, not to Porus.

More strongly, a statement of Pliny, not included among Jacoby's *testimonia*, should be added to the discussion, for it explicitly links Seleucus I and the geographic or ethnographic description of India. Having observed that the Hyphasis river marked the terminus of Alexander's eastward journey, Pliny, *Naturalis historia* 6.17.63, notes that the land beyond, right up to the city of Palimbothra, was explored for Seleucus Nicator: *reliqua inde Seleuco Nicatori peragrata sunt. Seleuco Nicatori* is a dative of advantage. That is to say, Seleucus commissioned the exploration of the Gangetic heartland of the Mauryan kingdom. No explorer is named as Seleucus' agent, but Megasthenes is the only known possibility.

Can Arrian, *Anabasis* 5.6.2, and the other *testimonia* agree? How can Megasthenes have "associated with" Sibyrtius and "lived with" Seleucus? There are at least three possibilities. First, Megasthenes could have begun his career with Sibyrtius and then transferred to Seleucus.[34] The revisionist dating insists on a single, limited period of diplomatic activity by Megasthenes. But Seleucus surely would have made use of a regional expert with specialized knowledge of India in his diplomatic relations with Chandragupta. Indeed, Megasthenes is quoted in Arrian, *Anabasis* 5.6.2, as πολλάκις δὲ λέγει ἀφικέσθαι παρὰ Σανδράκοττον, where the adverb can be taken as naturally with ἀφικέσθαι as with λέγει.[35] Frequent visits to the foreign court are a priori probable for a well-informed ambassador, and such statements would authorize textual claims of autopsy. Second, Sibyrtius may have retained Arachosia when Seleucus Nicator extended his rule over the Upper Satrapies; his campaign against Chandragupta Maurya was predicated on the stability of the Central Asian provinces. It is not unfair to consider, as several have suggested, the transformation of Sibyrtius from semi-independent satrap to recognized subordinate of Seleucus.[36] Accordingly, Megasthenes may well have been Seleucus' agent while associating with Sibyrtius. A third possibility has been raised by Irfan Habib and Vivekanand Jha. Since Arachosia was one of the territories ceded to Chandragupta in the peace of 304/3 (see Chapter 1), Sibyrtius may have been retained as a regional governor within the Mauryan Empire. They note, "His border territory, doubtless with its large body of Macedonian and Greek settlers, was a natural base for Megasthenes' journeys to Chandragupta's court."[37] It is significant that in the Greek translation of Ashoka's Twelfth Edict, found at Kandahar in Arachosia, the last two sentences concerned with the functions of officials *(dhamma-mahāmātas)* have been omitted "as if these had no relevance to the local administration of Arachosia,"[38] perhaps demonstrating a more autonomous status for this region. Indeed, the later use of Greek governors is known from the *yavanarāja* ("Greek chief") of Rudradaman's Junagarh inscription.[39]

The above analysis of the *testimonia* should have demonstrated that Arrian, *Indica* 5.3 (T2b) does not contradict the traditional, Seleucid dating for Megasthenes, not least since unresolvable difficulties remain with the manuscript reading. The Sibyrtius association of Arrian, *Anabasis* 5.6.2 (T2a), is important but must be paired with the Seleucus connection for a fair reconstruction of Megasthenes' career; there are several possible scenarios. Clement of Alexandria (T1) and the unused Pliny passage confirm Megasthenes as Seleucus' agent. For further insight into the date of Megasthenes' *Indica* we must shift our gaze from the *testimonia* to the fragments.

The Fragments

It is tempting to suggest, with Andrea Primo, that Megasthenes' *Kulturgeschichte* and description of contemporary, Mauryan India, with its focus on urbanization, imperial bureaucracy, and kingship (see Chapter 1), better fit the city-building royal Seleucid court than the satrapal world of Sibyrtius.[40] In addition, the ethnography's apologetic tendency (Chapter 1, again) makes sense only after the Treaty of the Indus. We have already seen that Megasthenes left no doubt as to the fluvial, faunal, political, and military superiority of Chandragupta's Gangetic kingdom. A couple of passages from the *Indica*, on India's political unity and on Nebuchadnezzar II of Babylon, give more explicit support for the traditional dating.

The revisionist thesis requires the division of northern India, at the time of Megasthenes' embassy, between the kingdom of Porus in the Indus basin and the nascent kingdom of Chandragupta on the Ganges: "There were two great dynasts at either extremity of India and between them a colorful blend of autonomous peoples and minor kings."[41] We would expect to find traces of such a dyarchy in Megasthenes' text. In fact, the overall impression given by the *Indica*'s fragments is of a single, unified, relatively centralized, northern Indian kingdom ruled by Chandragupta from the royal capital of Palimbothra, with no differentiation of polity between the Indus and Ganges basins. As has already been noted, Porus does not make one appearance in the fragments, and there is not a single contrast between different Indian kingdoms despite comparisons of the Indus and Ganges valleys. Rather, India operates as a cohesive political-geographical unit within Megasthenes' ethnography. The legendary early Indian kingdoms of Dionysus and Heracles form a spatial block coextensive with all India.[42] This is important, for Megasthenes' detailed Indian prehistory provides an effective prototype for the developed Mauryan empire (and its territorial claims), not for a north Indian dyarchy. A diadochy of kings, ruling India in a single line, runs for 153 generations from Dionysus to Chandragupta,[43] and Dionysus' cultural legacy still influences the forms of Mauryan kingship.[44] In other words, the hour-glass shaped narrative draws attention to the heroic emergence of unified Indian monarchy and demonstrates this period's aetiological function for the developed Mauryan state. Even though there are a couple of references to other kings and autonomous cities, as Bosworth observes,[45] these seem either to be embedded as vassals within the Mauryan state or to belong to the historical line of Chandragupta's predecessors. For instance, that Chandragupta is called "king of the Prasii"[46] does not imply that the Mauryan state was nascent and not yet an imperial formation.[47] Ashoka, Chandragupta's grandson and ruler of the Mauryan empire at its greatest extension, takes the equivalent title *rājā Māgadhe*, the Magadhan king, in his Bairat Edict.[48] For the Mauryan kingdom, much like the Achaemenid and Seleucid, incorporated preexisting royal and urban entities and identities into its overarching imperial formation.[49]

More importantly, Megasthenes' report of a Royal Road extending from Chandragupta's capital, Palimbothra, to the western frontier of India is evidence of Mauryan control of the Indus basin.[50] This cannot be ignored since, as we saw in Chapter 6, the Mauryan construction, measurement, and use of such roadways are of distinct interest to the ethnographer.[51] Furthermore,

Megasthenes' Royal Road, running from Palimbothra to the western edge of India, functions in the same historiographical or ethnographic tradition as Herodotus' and Ctesias' descriptions of the Persian Royal Road, from Sardis to Susa and from Ephesus to India, respectively;[52] in each case, the imperial roadway links center to periphery or periphery to periphery as an expression of territorial sovereignty. Palimbothra functions as the point from which Indian geographical distance is now measured.[53]

The extension of Chandragupta's kingdom to the Indus basin is confirmed by Megasthenes' freakish geography. Megasthenes followed his Indographic predecessors in populating India with mouthless, pygmy, one-eyed, feet-inverted, dog-eared, prominent-upper-lipped, and ear-dwelling tribes (see Chapter 1). However, in what I have argued is a reflection of the centripetal spatial modalities of Mauryan imperial ideology, these peoples are now geographically placed on the peripheries of the kingdom and travel to Palimbothra to be displayed before Chandragupta.[54] The home of the Astomoi, at the source of the Ganges,[55] located by Megasthenes in the northwestern mountains,[56] implies Mauryan territorial control of this region.

The second set of fragments confirms the traditional dating in a different way. Megasthenes is the first Greek author to discuss the great Neo-Babylonian conqueror and builder Nebuchadnezzar II.[57] In a company of pre-Alexandrian conquerors, including the Ethiopian king Tearcon, the Scythian Idanthyrsus, the Egyptian Sesostris, and the Assyrian Semiramis, Nebuchadnezzar of Babylon is singled out for the highest praise. Megasthenes tells us that he is more esteemed among the Chaldaeans (παρὰ Χαλδαίοις) of Babylonia than even Heracles, whom he outstripped in bravery and deeds (τῇ ἀνδρείᾳ καὶ τῷ μεγέθει τῶν πράξεων).[58] This is the only non-Indian indigenous opinion offered in the surviving fragments of Megasthenes' *Indica*. Nebuchadnezzar is figured as a great conqueror of the west, who levied troops, conquered Iberia and Libya right up to the Pillars of (his inferior) Heracles, and resettled the subdued populations on the eastern coast of the Black Sea.[59] By introducing Nebuchadnezzar with such prominence, the *Indica* made a radical innovation within the Greek ethnographic tradition, bypassing Herodotus' and Ctesias' great Mesopotamian queens, Nitocris and Semiramis, in favor of this new representative of Babylonian imperialism. Such praise for Nebuchadnezzar makes little sense in a Sibyrtian context: for what reason would the satrap of Arachosia's envoy heap such praise on a long-dead Babylonian king, who had never, to our knowledge, yet surfaced in Greek literature? and what could Megasthenes, up in the mountains of Sibyrtius' Hindu Kush, know of Chaldaean opinion? By contrast, the Megasthenic Nebuchadnezzar perfectly fits into a Seleucid court context. Seleucus had risen to power as satrap of Babylon, which he held with the good opinion of the Chaldaeans.[60] Babylonia was the undisputed core of Seleucus' empire at precisely the time when, according to the traditional chronology, Megasthenes was engaging in his Mauryan diplomacy.[61] Megasthenes' praise of Nebuchadnezzar prefigures subsequent identifications of the Seleucid rulers with this greatest of Neo-Babylonian kings: Berossus, who dedicated his autoethnographic *Babyloniaca* to Seleucus I's son and coruler Antiochus I, presented Nebuchadnezzar as the ruler to emulate;[62] the famous Borsippa Cylinder of Antiochus I, a cuneiform building inscription, gave the Seleucid king the precise titles of Nebuchadnezzar II;[63] Antiochus III, visiting Babylon shortly before his death, was formally presented with Nebuchadnezzar's kingly robe at the New Year *akītu* festival.[64]

In a problem of this kind, some speculation is unavoidable. While Megasthenes must certainly have had some relationship with Sibyrtius of Arachosia and may possibly even have visited Porus, the overall weight of the *testimonia* privilege his close connection to Seleucus. Furthermore, the *Indica*'s account of the general superiority of the Ganges basin, Mauryan control of the Indus region, and the prominence of Nebuchadnezzar II of Babylon makes it difficult for his diplomatic activity and ethnographic writing to be situated in a Porus-dominant, pre-Seleucid context. Indeed, it is striking that a work so frequently cited by post-Seleucid scholars should not once be used as an authority for Porus or appear to have left a trace in the Alexander Historians; most significant is the absence of Megasthenes' seven-tier caste system, which made such an impact on later readers.[65] Indeed, certain passages in the *Indica* give the impression of Megasthenes' critical reading of the published accounts of Onesicritus and Nearchus.[66] The best explanation for Megasthenes' historical context and textual choices remains the traditional dating.

Notes

Introduction

1. For discussion and plan of the Karasis fort, see Radt 2011 and Chapter 7, pp. 201–202.
2. *AD* -273 B Rev. 30–32.
3. 1 Macc. 6:43–46 with Joseph. *AJ* 12.373–374 and *BJ* 1.41–45.
4. Plut. *Demetr.* 25.4–9 and Mor. *Prae. ger. reip.* 823c–e; Athen. *Deipn.* 6.261b; see p. 279n44.
5. Kosmin 2013b; see also Alonso Troncoso 2013 and Iossif and Lorber 2010.
6. Libanius *Or.* 11.90.
7. Lucian, *Zeuxis* 11; Steph. Byz. s.v. Βοῦρα (see Bieńkowski 1929: 148).
8. *Suda* s.v. Σιμωνίδης (Μάγνης Σιπύλου).
9. Cn. Octavius: Polyb. 31.2.11 with Cic. *Phil.* 9.4 and Plin. *HN* 34.5.24 (a very confused account); Eleazar Avaran: 1 Macc. 6:43–46 with Joseph. *AJ* 12.373–374 and *BJ* 1.41–45.
10. Henceforth, all dates are BCE unless otherwise qualified.
11. See, e.g., Grainger 2010: 416; Will 1966: 1.262–290; Tarn 1966: 4; Rostovtzeff 1941: 1.429–430.
12. Tarn 1966: 4.
13. Note that interpretations of the Ptolemaic kingdom are moving away from *dirigiste,* strong-state models; see, e.g., Manning 2010.
14. E.g., Capdetrey 2007; Shipley 2000: 293–307.
15. The Briant *oeuvre* and Kuhrt and Sherwin-White 1993 have been enormously important in uncovering this debt.
16. E.g., Bingen 2007: 59–60; Austin 1986: 456–457; Gruen 1985: 259; Bickerman 1938: 7; Bevan 1902: 1.57.
17. Kuhrt and Sherwin-White 1993. *Topoi* 4 (1994) offers a range of critical scholarly responses to this work; I have found Briant 1994 particularly instructive.
18. Ma 2002.
19. Capdetrey 2007.
20. Primo 2009.

21. The bibliography is enormous. See, e.g., Lefebvre 1991; Certeau 1984; Foucault 1986; Harvey 2001 and 2009; Feld and Basso 1996; Gregory 1994; Said 2000; Soja 1989; Tuan 1974 and 1977; Warf and Arias 2009; Helms 1988; Streicker 1997.

22. E.g., Smith 2003.

23. E.g., Thonemann 2012; Malkin 2011; Horden and Purcell 2000.

24. E.g., Thalmann 2011; Selden 1998.

25. E.g., Nicolet 1988; see Purcell 1990 review.

26. For discussion and plans, see Chapters 7 and 8.

27. Tens of thousands of these "bullae," often stamped with official seals, have been excavated from public and private archives in Seleucia-on-the-Tigris; see Invernizzi 2004, Rostovtzeff 1932, and Aperghis 2004: 154–156. They are of invaluable assistance in the reconstruction of Seleucid glyptic art and taxation systems.

28. The Diary tablets, now held in the British Museum, have been edited and translated by Abraham Sachs and Hermann Hunger, in their *Astronomical Diaries and Related Texts from Babylonia* (Vienna, 1988–1996), abbreviated in this book as *AD.*

29. The Chronicle tablets, also at the British Museum, are in the process of being reedited and translated by Irving Finkel and Robert van der Spek as *Babylonian Chronicles of the Hellenistic Period,* abbreviated in this book as *BCHP;* they are published online with commentary at www.livius.org/cg-cm/chronicles/chron00.html. Older editions include Grayson 1975 and Glassner 2004.

30. The most important corpora are Rougemont's *Inscriptions grecques d'Iran et d'Asie centrale* (London, 2012), abbreviated in this book as *IGIAC;* de Rossi's *Iscrizioni dello estremo oriente Greco* (Bonn, 2004), abbreviated as *IEOG;* Dittenberger's *Orientis Graeci Inscriptiones Selectae* (Leipzig, 1903), abbreviated as *OGIS;* Welles' *Royal Correspondence in the Hellenistic Period* (London, 1934), abbreviated as *RC;* and the epigraphic appendix to John Ma's *Antiochus III and the Cities of Western Asia Minor* (Oxford, 2002), abbreviated as Ma. Up-to-date bibliography can be found by year and lemma in the annual *Supplementum Epigraphicum Graecum,* known as *SEG.*

31. We are fortunate to possess the illustrated and invaluable numismatic catalogues of Arthur Houghton and Catherine Lorber, *Seleucid Coins: A Comprehensive Catalogue. Part 1: Seleucus I through Antiochus III* (London, 2002), and Arthur Houghton, Catherine Lorber, and Oliver Hoover, *Seleucid Coins: A Comprehensive Catalogue. Part 2: Seleucus IV through Antiochus XIII* (London, 2008).

32. Zechariah 4:6.

33. They are not found, for instance, in Primo's 2009 survey of historiography produced by or about the Seleucids; see Kosmin 2009.

34. The fragments of the lost Greek historians were collected by Felix Jacoby in his magisterial *Die Fragmente der griechischen Historiker* (Berlin, 1923–), abbreviated as *FGrHist.* The work is being reedited, extended, and translated

into English by *Brill's New Jacoby,* or *BNJ,* under the direction of Ian
Worthington; it can be found at http://referenceworks.brillonline.com.

35. See Lebreton 2005: 656–657.

36. For discussion of the natural resources and agricultural productivity of each
region, see Aperghis 2004: 35–86 and Cary 1949, with bibliography. For
Anatolia, see Mitchell 1993 and Magie 1950, and for the Iranian world, Frye
1984.

37. Potts 1999: 10–42.

38. This section is intended as historical scene setting for the book's abundantly
documented chapters, so here, except for direct quotations, I will not include
references to our ancient sources and modern scholarship. In brief, the
invaluable, if dated, overview of all Hellenistic political history is Will 1966.
The more outstanding Seleucid kings have earned for themselves monographs: Mehl 1986 on Seleucus I, Schmitt 1964 on Antiochus III, Mørkholm
1966 and Mittag 2006 on Antiochus IV, and Fischer 1970 on Antiochus VII.
Ehling 2008 is a remarkably clear narrative of the dynasty after Antiochus IV.

39. Just. *Epit.* 17.2.2: *victor victorum;* similar sentiments in App. *Syr.* 61 and Arr.
Anab. 7.22.5.

40. Polyb. 31.2.11.

1. India—Diplomacy and Ethnography at the Mauryan Frontier

1. Especially in the fragments of Hieronymus of Cardia, main source for the
Successor Wars; see Hornblower 1981.

2. See, e.g., Herrenschmidt's 1976 demonstration that in Old Persian inscriptional formulae the word *būmiš* designates at the same time "empire" and
"earth." For further attestations of the universal, all-encompassing claims of
the Achaemenid kingdom one could look to Persian imperial art, palatial
architecture, royal rituals, *paradeisos* gardens, demands of earth and water,
and much else (Briant 2002).

3. The cache of Akkadian documents found at Tell el-Amarna represents the
developed international system of the mid-fourteenth century during the
reign of Amenhotep IV (Akhenaten); see Cohen and Westbrook 2000. The
Great Powers' club consisted of Egypt, Mittani, Babylonia, and Hatti, with
the independent kingdoms of Arzawa (southern Anatolia) and Alashiya
(Cyprus). Numerous vassal states appear. Interestingly, the archive plots the
transformation of Assyria from vassal of Mittani to Great Power.

4. These can be observed most clearly in the assigning of responsibilities at
Babylon and Triparadisus and in various subsequent episodes of peer
recognition. For example, the Peace of 311 declared that "Cassander is to be
stratēgos of Europe until the Alexander born of Rhoxane comes of age;
Lysimachus is to be master of Thrace, and Ptolemy of Egypt and the cities
bordering on it in Libya and Arabia; Antigonus is to have command over all
Asia; the Greeks are to be autonomous" (Diod. Sic. 19.105.1).

5. See Rigsby 1996.

6. E.g., the dossier for the "crowned games" of Artemis Leucophryene at Magnesia-on-the-Maeander, discussed in Chapter 8.

7. E.g., the Rhodian earthquake (Polyb. 5.88–90).

8. Just. *Epit.* 15.4.11–12. For the date I follow Skurzak 1964, Lauffer 1956: 43, and Schwarz 1972: 91. Breloer's suggestion (1941: 175) of 308/7 does not permit sufficient campaigning time in Central Asia. Schmitt 1964: 66 and Schober 1981: 140–146 prefer 303.

9. I.e., ruling both the Gangetic and Indic basins. Chandragupta's conquest of northwestern India remains obscure. On Chandragupta's rise to power, see Yardley, Wheatley, and Heckel 2011: 275–291, with bibliography. Porus and Taxiles had been recognized by the settlement of Triparadisus (Diod. Sic. 18.39) in 321/0. In 318, Porus was assassinated by Eudamus, who subsequently abandoned his Indian responsibilities to join the satrapal coalition against Pithon, taking with him 120 elephants (Diod. Sic. 19.14.8). This evacuation of Macedonia's Indian possessions no doubt created a power vacuum into which the new Gangetic empire could expand, perhaps *c.* 312 (Habib and Jha 2004: 17). Capdetrey 2007: 39–48 has suggested that Seleucus' campaign was defensive, not expansionist, aimed at limiting Chandragupta's expansion into the Central Asian satrapies rather than at conquering into India.

10. The occasional spelling "Androcottus" tends to follow words ending in *sigma;* the loss of the initial *sigma* from the start of this unusual name would be a simple scribal error, known as haplography. Of course, *Andr-* would have been familiar as the first part of a male Greek name.

11. Just. *Epit.* 15.4.20 (*sic adquisito regno Sandrocottus ea tempestate qua Seleucus futurae magnitudinis fundamenta iaciebat Indiam possidebat,* "Sandrocottus, having gained the throne in this way, took possession of India at the time when Seleucus was laying the foundations of his future greatness") synchronizes the formation of the Mauryan kingdom with the beginnings of Seleucus' own imperial greatness: the very word order frames Seleucus' achievements within Chandragupta's.

12. Plut. *Al.* 62.4. The trope of the youthful encounter with the previous generation's great ruler is familiar (e.g., Galba and Augustus; Alexander and the Persian envoys). Ptolemy I's history of Alexander should be considered as an extended account of this type.

13. Plut. *de laude ipsius* 10 (542d).

14. Plut. *Al.* 62.4.

15. Some South Asian scholars have argued for a decisive "national" victory, thereby fashioning a prototype of the twentieth-century's anticolonial struggle (see Thapar 2002a: 16–17). Oddest of all is Senarat Paranavitana's 1971 monograph, *The Greeks and the Mauryas.* Paranavitana, former professor of archaeology at Ceylon University, claimed to have had "the good fortune to discover documents written in Sanskrit which give the Indian version of the events narrated by Greek and Roman historians, and also embody

accounts of personages and events not dealt with in these sources. These documents are of such a unique character, and the manner of their preservation and their discovery so unusual, that the skepticism which greeted the announcement of their existence is quite understandable" (5). The inscriptions recount in lengthy, novelistic detail Chandragupta's noble and courageous capture of the Macedonian king. Paranavitana "translates" as follows: "Anantayogya, the son of Calukya Nikatora, heard that Calukya Nikatora had been taken prisoner, and came to the Suvarṇṇakuḍya kingdom from the Suriya kingdom. He decided that it was not possible to release his father by hostile action. Therefore he gave an undertaking to cede to Candragupta the Suvarṇṇakuḍya kingdom, the Gandhāran kingdom, the Takṣaśila kingdom, the Sugdha kingdom, the Paropaniṣadha kingdom, the Suvāsta kingdom and the Sindhu kingdom, and also to give to Candragupta the princess Suvarṇṇākṣi, the daughter of Calukya Nikatora, and having contracted the treaty on these terms with Candragupta, returned to the Suriya kingdom. Calukya Nikatora returned to the Suriya kingdom with the force of elephants given him by Candragupta, obtained victory in the great battle fought at a place named Ipsus, made the kingdom of Suriya an empire, reigned and died in due course" (39). Needless to say, Paranavitana's work is complete invention. The account is replete with historical inaccuracies (such as, here, Seleucus' pre-Ipsus Syrian kingdom and epithet) and Greek words and names have been Sanskritized from their English forms. The popular Indian comic book, *Travellers to India: Megasthenes* (New Delhi, 2010), appears to take its framing narrative from Paranavitana's fabrication; I owe my cherished copy to my editor, Sharmila Sen.

16. App. *Syr.* 55 is the only source to mention Seleucus' crossing the Indus, but there is no reason to doubt it.
17. Just. *Epit.* 15.4.21; App. *Syr.* 55; Strabo 15.2.9.
18. Tarn 1966: 100; Schmitt 1964: 66 n.4, and with caution Schober 1981: 156–183, based on Strabo 15.2.9 (using Eratosthenes).
19. Mookerji 1928: 12 and Foucher 1942: 208, based on Plin. *HN* 6.20.78 and the discovery in Kandahar of two royal edicts issued by Chandragupta's famous grandson, Ashoka, confirming Mauryan possession of Arachosia, at least by the mid-third century; as Will 1966: 1.266 observes, in the absence of evidence of later Mauryan expansion and with friendly relations maintained between the two kingdoms (see later), the most economical explanation is that Seleucus ceded the region of Kandahar, but the state of our evidence obliges caution. Strabo 15.1.10 notes that much of Aria passed from Macedonian into Indian hands. Aelian's reference (*NA* 16.16) to Ἀριανοὶ οἱ Ἰνδικοί may indicate a Mauryan presence.
20. Plut. *Alex.* 62.4; Strabo 15.2.9; Strabo 16.2.10 mentions that the 500 war elephants were stabled at Apamea-on-the-Axios in northern Syria. Diod Sic. 20.113.5 gives 480 at the battle of Ipsus (301), Plut. *Demetr.* 28.6 400. Although the immense size of the elephant force has raised doubts (notably Tarn 1940: 84–89, whose arguments have been dismissed by Trautmann

1982: 269), it is by no means impossible. If Megasthenes is to be believed, all elephants had passed into royal ownership since Alexander's invasion. Kautiliya's *Arthashastra,* an Indian handbook of good governance dating back in part to the Mauryan kingdom, contains a canonical list of eight royal elephant forests. Trautmann 1982 points to medieval parallels: Mahmud of Ghazna had 1,300 elephants in his muster of 1023 CE, his son Mas'ud almost 400 more less than a decade later; in 1311 CE the eunuch general Malik Kafur brought more than 600 to Delhi as spoils of his southern expedition.

21. As Siebert 1967: 47 has pointed out, it is more likely that a daughter or niece of Seleucus is unknown to us than an Indian wife. In this context ἐπιγαμία or κῆδος are certainly more personal and real than an abstract and legal *ius conubii* (Yardley, Wheatley, and Heckel 2011: 295 *contra* Thapar 1961: 20 and Coloru 2009: 142–143).

22. A couple of parallels exist for this practice. Darius had offered Alexander the hand of his eldest daughter, Barsine-Stateira after Issus, with all Achaemenid territories east of the Euphrates as dowry (Arr. *Anab.* 2.25.1). Ptolemy III married Berenice II, heiress of Cyrene, who brought him the territory as a dowry (see Ogden 1999: 80). Antiochus II married Ptolemy Philadelphus' daughter Berenice, whose epithet was φερνοφόρος, "dowry-bringer" (Porphyry *BNJ* 260 F43 = Jer. *in Dan.* 11:6). The Ptolemies claimed that Antiochus III had given his daughter Cleopatra Syra to Ptolemy V Epiphanes with Coele Syria as dowry.

23. Just. *Epit.* 15.4.21: *Seleucus conpositisque in oriente rebus in bellum Antigoni discendit.*

24. For a detailed geographical description, see Foucher 1942: 186–188. The region has functioned historically as a sort of eastern Coele Syria.

25. Seleucus adopted the diadem of kingship in the year 305/4; the earliest Babylonian document dated by Seleucus' reign is one of 16 April 304 (Parker and Dubberstein 1942: 18). This was almost two years after the coronation of Antigonus and almost six years after the murder of Alexander IV, posthumous son of Alexander the Great; see Gruen 1985: 258. Diod. Sic. 20.53.4 explicitly connects Seleucus' military activity in the Upper Satrapies to his taking the diadem (οἱ λοιποὶ δυνάσται ζηλοτυπήσαντες ἀνηγόρευον ἑαυτοὺς βασιλεῖς, Σέλευκος μὲν προσφάτως τὰς ἄνω σατραπείας προσκεκτημένος). Schober 1981: 143–146 places the adoption of the royal title before Seleucus' Indian expedition, but the connection may be supported by numismatic evidence: the earliest coinage to bear Seleucus' name and title celebrates, above all, his involvement in India (Houghton and Lorber 2002: 3).

26. Crossing a border river to engage in battle is a standard narrative trope of attempted imperial expansion (see Hartog 1988: 57). In Herodotus, for example, Croesus crossed the Halys to fight the Persians, Cyrus the Araxes to meet the Massagetae, Darius the Ister to enter Scythia, and Xerxes the Bosphorus to subjugate the Thracians.

27. The Treaty of the Indus finds parallels in Parthian-Chinese diplomacy of the second and first centuries. Here, too, a shared and unprivileged peripheral

zone was divided up, gifts exchanged, and regular contacts opened between culturally unfamiliar peers; see Leslie and Gardiner 1982.

28. See later and Wiesehöfer 1998: 230. Indian mahouts lived with the Seleucid elephant force at Apamea-on-the-Axios in northern Syria; although *Indos* came to be the generic term for elephant rider, Aelian's insistence (*NA* 11.25) that elephants understood only the Indian language implies a certain amount of ethnic exclusivity in the profession; see Sick 2002: 135.

29. Strabo 2.1.9. Amitrochates is Chandragupta's son Bindusara. His name in Greek sources derives from his throne name, Amitraghata ("slayer of foes") or Amitrakhada ("eater of foes"); see Habib and Jha 2004: 20. Three works of Deimachus (*BNJ* 716) are known by title only: an Indian ethnography, a tactical handbook, and an ethical tract (Περὶ εὐσεβείας); see Schwarz 1969 for a discussion of these works. Eratosthenes condemned Deimachus as the most untrustworthy of all Indian ethnographers, which is quite a claim (Strabo 21.9.1).

30. Liverani 2001.

31. See Briant 2002: 388–421.

32. Phylarchus *FGrHist* 81 F35b = Ath. 1.18d–e.

33. Plin. *HN* 16.32.135. Pliny is discussing here the transplantation of trees from their original habitat rather than the importation of already processed incense.

34. Ath. 14.652f–653a. Schwarz 1969: 295 rather uncautiously takes this as evidence of the Hellenization of intellectual life at the Mauryan court.

35. See Godelier 1999, who, in a criticism of the influential gift-giving theory of Mauss 1954, observed the importance of inalienable goods/services/people in gift-giving contexts and, therefore, the ambivalence of the gift-exchange relationship: it aims both at solidarity by sharing and at superiority by establishing an inequality.

36. Polyb. 11.34.11–12.

37. Thapar 1961: 190.

38. Polyb. 11.34.11; Strabo 15.2.9.

39. Polyb. 8.23. For Antiochus III in Armenia, see Kuhrt and Sherwin-White 1993: 190–197.

40. Polyb. 11.34.1–10. For Antiochus III in Bactria, see Holt 1999: 127–130 and Coloru 2009: 177–186.

41. For the place of the Treaty of the Indus and the Indian elephant in official Seleucid historiography and iconography, see Kosmin 2013b.

42. Plut. *Demetr.* 28–29; Diod. Sic. 21.1.5.

43. See Kosmin 2013b.

44. Plut. *Demetr.* 25.5–9 and Mor. *Prae. ger. reip.* 823c–e; Phylarchus *FGrHist* F19 = Ath. 6.261b. The date of the toast turns on the absence of Cassander (d. 298/7) and the presence of Antigonus (d.301): accordingly, a date of 302 (Hauben 1974) must explain the absence of Cassander; a date of 290s (Gruen 1985: 260) must explain the presence of Antigonus. 302 is a more persuasive date: Cassander's absence can be explained by his weakness in 302; Demetrius

officially recognized his opponents after Ipsus (not least in marrying his daughter Stratonice to Seleucus); and Seleucus' elephants would hardly be mocked after the battle. Gruen 1985: 260 objects, in addition to the absence of Cassander, that the anecdote is an excursus and that Agathocles would not have impressed the other dynasts before his conquest of Corcyra in 299 or the marriage of his daughter to Pyrrhus in 295. These do not hold: Agathocles' war with Carthage would have been unmissable; its failure and the restriction of his rule to Sicily explain the mockery of "the Sicilian nesiarch."

45. Megasthenes could well have been qualified from his earlier association with Sibyrtius, Macedonian satrap of Arachosia, 325–316/5 (*BNJ* 715 T2a = Arr. *Anab.* 5.6.2); see Appendix.

46. Tarn 1940: 86.

47. Hellenistic historiography and ethnography have suffered more than most; see Schepens 1997.

48. Dihle 1984: 93–97.

49. Josephus, Clement of Alexandria, and Eusebius were naturally drawn to the prominence of Nebuchadnezzar II and to Megasthenes' paralleling of Jewish and Brahmanical wisdom. The paradoxographical or natural historical traditions (Phlegon, Antigonus of Carystus, Aelian, Plutarch, and Pliny) preserved, no doubt secondhand, various *thaumata*.

50. The *Indica*'s "fragments" were first collected by Schwanbeck, in his monograph of 1846 (translated for the Indological audience without significant change by McCrindle in 1876), then by Felix Jacoby, as #715 of his extraordinary *Fragmente der griechischen Historiker*. Jacoby was unable to write the commentary for the *Indica* before his death. This task has been completed recently by Duane Roller (*BNJ* 715), who has accepted, in my view incorrectly, Bosworth's 1996 antedating; see the Appendix. A comparison of Schwanbeck and Jacoby/Roller demonstrates the latters' greater caution. *FGrHist/BNJ* must be used carefully; see Bowersock 1997 and Humphreys 1997: 211 on the danger of denying authorial rights to "secondary" (i.e., extant) authors in order to restore authorship to a lost writer. In this light, see Muntz 2012 on Diodorus Siculus' own authorial craft in describing India.

51. *BNJ* 264; see Murray 1970: 166–168. Diodorus' epitome of Hecataeus suffers from the Sicilian's pride in having visited Egypt himself; he was "not averse from giving the impression that the whole was the result of his own researches" (Murray 1970: 145). India offered no danger of such claims.

52. *BNJ* 715 F3 = Clem. Al. *Strom.* 1.72.4: ἐν τῇ τρίτῃ τῶν Ἰνδικῶν ὧδε γράφει . . . The reference to a fourth book in F1a = Joseph. *AJ.* 10.227 (καὶ Μεγασθένης δὲ ἐν τῇ δ' τῶν Ἰνδικῶν μνημονεύει) is almost certainly in error. Jacoby emended the Δ to A, but an abbreviated δευτέρᾳ seems more likely. Brunt 1980: 487 has observed, "[N]umbers are particularly liable to textual corruption, and since in any individual case the author himself may have carelessly cited the wrong book, we need a fair number of such book references to provide reciprocal confirmation . . . Implicit faith in all book references is thus unwarranted."

53. *BNJ* 715 F4 = Diod. Sic. 2.38.3–2.39.5; F12 and F13a = Arr. *Ind.* 7.1–9.8.

54. Cole 1967: 4. The subject fits most naturally with accounts of autochthonous peoples, as here, where historical origins cannot be external to the land. Accordingly, we find theories of cultural origins in the Atthidographers Philochorus (*FGrHist* 328 F2a-b, F93–98) and Cleidemus (*FGrHist* 323 F5a, F7), in Arcadian local historians (Paus. 8.1.4–6), and in Hecataeus of Abdera (*BNJ* 264 F25 = Diod. Sic. 1.10–98).

55. *BNJ* 715 F12 = Arr. *Ind.* 7.2 (trans. D. Roller, with changes; applies to all of Megasthenes' translations in this chapter); cf. F4 = Diod. Sic. 2.38.3. Muntz 2012: 32–34 has argued that Arrian's account is closer to Megasthenes' original than Diodorus'.

56. Especially Hdt. 4.17–19.

57. *BNJ* 715 F12 = Arr. *Ind.* 7.3–4.

58. *BNJ* 715 F4 = Diod. Sic. 2.38.3.

59. *BNJ* 715 F12 = Arr. *Ind.* 7.5–9. F4 = Diod. Sic. 2.38.5–6 preserves a parallel account.

60. See Saunders 2001 and Cole 1967. I deliberately exclude from Megasthenes' fragments the account of F4 = Diod. Sic. 2.38.2, which merely reproduces and abbreviates Diod. Sic. 1.8. This alternative account of human progress as an accumulation of technological advances on a gradualist continuum of inventive process starkly contradicts Megasthenes' actual *Kulturgeschichte*: naturalistic vs. euhemeristic, anonymous vs. heroic, gradual and accumulative vs. episodic and momentous, discovery vs. benefaction, and ultimately democratic vs. royal.

61. Cole 1967: 162: Hecataeus of Abdera shifts the scene of cultural creation to the palace and the court, "and thereby the beginnings of human culture are made over in the image of Ptolemaic Egypt." Sacks 1990: 71 counts almost seventy occurrences of this narrative pattern in Diodorus Siculus' first six books: they include Osiris, Uranus, Hesperus, the daughters of Atlas, Heracles, Theseus, Zeus, Minos, Aeneas, Demeter, Phorbas, Halia, Orion, Hephaestus, and many more; see also Sartori 1984.

62. Henrichs 1999: 237.

63. *BNJ* 715 F4 = Diod. Sic. 2.38.5.

64. *BNJ* 715 F4 = Diod. Sic. 39.1 and F13a = Arr. *Ind.* 8.4.

65. *BNJ* 715 F4 = Diod. Sic. 39.1 and F13b = Arr. *Ind.* 8.6.

66. For other instances of Heracles as civilizing hero and city founder, see Lacroix 1974. In the standard Greek tradition, Heracles removes the dangers faced by travelers in order to open up the world. In Megasthenes, his civilizing activities close it.

67. *BNJ* 715 F4 = Diod. Sic. 2.39.3.

68. Udayin, son of Ajatashatru, moved the capital from Rajagrha, the setting of the First Buddhist Council, to Pataliputra; see Schwarz 1972: 88.

69. *BNJ* 715 F17 = Arr. *Ind.* 10.2.

70. *BNJ* 715 F18b = Strabo 15.1.36. F18a = Arr. *Ind.* 10.5–6 preserves a parallel account.

71. In Arrian's parallel account, the wall has sixty-four gates (*BNJ* 715 F18a = Arr. *Ind.* 10.6).

72. Waddell 1903: 21–23.

73. Recorded in Arrian's parallel account: *BNJ* 715 F18a = Arr. *Ind.* 10.6.

74. *BNJ* 715 F31 = Strabo 15.1.50–52: the *astunomoi,* operating within the royal capital, are collectively concerned with the upkeep of public works, markets, harbors, and temples and also divided into six groups of five officials each for the control and oversight of craftsmen, foreigners, births and deaths, retail trade, artisanal production, and taxation, respectively. The activities of the officials who are responsible for foreign visitors are described in detail: assigning lodgings, forwarding the possessions of the dead, looking after the sick, and burying the dead. This may reflect the actual logistics behind Megasthenes' diplomatic presence at Pataliputra.

75. Hdt. 3.98.3. Concurrent settled and nomadic populations are found elsewhere in Herodotus: Scythians (4.18, 53), Libyans (4.186, 191), and Persians (1.125); see Briant 1982b: 13.

76. *BNJ* 715 F19b = Strabo 15.1.41.

77. *BNJ* 715 F19a = Arr. *Ind.* 11.11.

78. *BNJ* 715 F33 = Strabo 15.1.60.

79. Hdt. 4.46.2–3.

80. Hartog 1988: 202.

81. *FGrHist* 156 F72 = Eustath. *ad Dionys.* 669.

82. Diod. Sic. 19.94–100; see the interesting discussion of Bosworth 2002: 187–209.

83. Diod. Sic. 2.1.5.

84. Bosworth 2002: 195–196.

85. Curt. 7.8.8–9.2.

86. Briant 1982b: 19–20.

87. E.g., Ephorus (*BNJ* 70 F147 = Strabo 10.4.8: [ὁ Ῥαδάμανθυς] πρῶτος τὴν νῆσον ἐξημερῶσαι δοκεῖ νομίμοις καὶ συνοικισμοῖς πόλεων καὶ πολιτείαις) synchronizes city foundation and law giving. Philochorus' Cecrops founded cities, held the first census, established the earliest cults, and invented weapons and armor (*FGrHist* 328 F94 = Strabo 9.1.20, F95 = Schol. Pind. *Ol.* 9.70, F97 = Macrob. *Sat.* 1.10.22). Perhaps closest to the Megasthenic *Kulturgeschichte* is Schol. Eur. *Or.* 1646: Πελασγὸς ὁ Ἀργεῖος . . . ἐλθὼν εἰς Ἀρκαδίαν θηριώδεις ὄντας τοὺς ἀνθρώπους εἰς τὸ ἡμερώτερον μετέβαλε καὶ πόλιν ἔκτισεν, ἣν Παρρασίαν ὠνόμασεν.

88. As portrayed by Pl. *Prt.* 322b; Diod. Sic. 1.8.2–6; Polyb. 6.5.5; Lucr. 5.982–1010.

89. See Cole 1967.

90. Pl. *Prt.* 322b; Pl. *Leg.* 3.681a; Thuc. 1.2 (city fortification, implicitly). Other models associated the birth of the city with the absence of individual or household self-sufficiency (Pl. *Resp.* 2.369b; Arist. *Pol.* 1252a–1253a) and the centralizing tendency of primitive monarchy (Polyb. 6.5; Lucr. 5.1108–1109).

91. Arist. *Pol.* 1285b, 1310b; see Nagle 1996: 158–159. We should consider the influence on Aristotle's doctrine of kingship of contemporary developments in Macedonia; see, among others, Kelsen 1937.
92. Diod. Sic. 15.72.4; Paus. 8.27.1. Still the most striking architectural feature of Messene is the fortification wall.
93. As demonstrated by the Spartan policy of *dioikismos,* applied to, e.g., Mantinea in 385.
94. Hatzopoulos 2011; Demand 1990: 151–155.
95. Indeed, Alexander's speech to mutinying Macedonian troops at Opis (Arr. *Anab.* 7.9.1–5) depicted Philip II as a comprehensive monarchic culture-hero of the Megasthenic order; see Bosworth 1988: 109. Philip's civilizing activities, according to his son, centered on city foundation and transformed a militarily vulnerable Macedonia into a geopolitical master. Despite ethnographic commonplaces (mountains to plains, skins to clothes) and rhetorical elaboration, the speech contains details specific to the Macedonians and may be genuine in substance; see Hammond and Griffith 1979: 657–660, Bosworth 1988: 111–113, and Nagle 1996. Curtius' version of the speech (10.2.23) also refers to Philip and cultural transformation.
96. Kosmin 2013d: 198–200; Primo 2009: 58–59.
97. *Contra* Bosworth 2003, who sees the *Indica* as "a justification of Macedonian rule in India and an implicit encomium of the men who created it" (318) and "full-blooded justification of aggrandisement" (320). The logic of the *Kulturgeschichte* and the space of India (see later) do not permit such an interpretation.
98. Michel de Certeau (1986: 68; 1984: 116) has observed, of Montaigne's *On Cannibals* and de Léry's *Historia,* the power of ethnography to compose and distribute places through narrative procedures of delimitation ("bornage") and focalization; see Giard 1991.
99. Cf. the Ionian accounts of the Nile rejected by Hdt. 2.15. Arr. *Anab.* 4.22.6 counts Taxiles among "the Indians on this side of the river Indus."
100. *BNJ* 709; see Chapter 2 on royal-sponsored *peripli.*
101. For Herodotus' Indian geography, see Puskás 1983. Strangely, Herodotus reorients the Indus, so it flows from west to east.
102. Hdt. 3.94–106, 4.44.
103. *FGrHist* 688 F45 = Phot. *Bibl.* 72.5: in a clear analogy with Egypt and the Nile, Ctesias claims habitable India is watered by the Indus since rainfall is unknown.
104. Lenfant 2004: cxxxviii. It has been frequently suggested that the great desert is the Thar, separating modern Pakistan from Rajasthan (e.g., Puskás 1983: 207).
105. The nature of the Indian monarch's relationship to the Persian Great King is not unambiguous. Are the gifts (*FGrHist* 688 F45 = Phot. *Bibl.* 72.47) he offers a mark of subservience or a diplomatic practice of an independent king? Lenfant 2004: cxl–cxli has persuasively shown that, since the Royal Road in

the *Persica* runs right to the Indus (F33), the area was considered part of the Achaemenid empire and the king of the Indians a vassal ruler.

106. *FGrHist* 688 F45 = Phot. *Bibl.* 72.23.

107. *FGrHist* 688 F45 = Phot. *Bibl.* 72.41.

108. Caution demands that, where explicit attribution is lacking, the Indian geography of the lost Alexander Historians be reconstructed from historical campaign narratives and not theoretical geographical passages, which are more prone to contamination by later, better-informed sources (not least Megasthenes).

109. The major development is rumor of the Gangetic basin and the Nanda kingdom; in addition, Onesicritus (*BNJ* 134 F12 = Strabo 15.1.15 and F13 = Pliny, *HN* 6.22.81) knew of Sri Lanka ("Taprobane") and lauded the utopian kingdom of Musicanus, in the southernmost part of the country (*BNJ* 134 F22 = Strabo 15.1.21–24 and F24 = Strabo 15.1.34).

110. Although *Hiⁿduš* frequently appears as a destination in the Fortification Tablets, we do not know the satrapy's capital (although the Bhir Mound at Taxila is the most likely site) or the name of a single satrap; see Fleming 1993.

111. Murray 1972. Pearson 1960: 13: "It is noteworthy that the historians of Alexander made no effort to revolutionize geographical knowledge; their object, on the whole, was to make new discoveries harmonize with what was known and believed"; Romm 1992: 94: "[R]eports from the edges of the earth tended to assume the forms molded for them long before."

112. Dihle 1984: 89–91 has shown that the Achaemenid concept of India (the Indus and its tributaries) was revived in later antiquity, within the framework of the Parthian and Sasanid empires. This is the India visited by St. Thomas in the apocryphal Acts and in the account of Mani's voyage from Mesopotamia to India.

113. *BNJ* 715 F6b = Arr. *Ind.* 3.7–8.

114. *BNJ* 715 F9a = Arr. *Ind.* 5.2.

115. *BNJ* 715 F6c = Strabo 15.1.11.

116. The move from the Indus to the Ganges resembles a shift from the Ionian to the Herodotean conception of the Nile (Hdt. 2.15–17).

117. *BNJ* 715 F6c = Strabo 15.1.11.

118. Seleucia-on-the-Tigris was also situated on a major river and embraced by a canal; see Theophylactus Simocatta, *Histories* 5.6 and Plin. *HN* 5.26.90 with Gullini 1967: 144 and 1968–1969: 40.

119. *BNJ* 715 F23a = Arr. *Ind.* 15.7.

120. *BNJ* 715 F13a = Arr. *Ind.* 9.1–8; F13b = Plin. *HN* 6.20.76; F13c = Phlegon, *Mir.* 33; F13d = Plin. *HN* 7.2.29.

121. *BNJ* 715 F26 = Plin. *HN* 6.22.81. According to Pliny, Megasthenes called the island's inhabitants Palaeogoni, perhaps indicating their ancient birth. Onesicritus (*BNJ* 134 F13 = Plin. *HN* 6.22.81) had already observed that Taprobane's elephants were larger and more belligerent.

122. *BNJ* 715 F27a = Strabo 2.1.9; F27b = Strabo 15.1.57. Unlike Ctesias, Megasthenes does not combine human and animal anatomies.

123. Megasthenes would, no doubt, be relieved to know that the Astomoi are included in the *Barrington Atlas of the Greek and Roman World,* p. 6 E3.

124. *BNJ* 715 F27b = Strabo 15.1.57.

125. *BNJ* 715 F27b = Strabo 15.1.57. The passage responds to the expectation that populations will be transported to Palimbothra.

126. Ael. *NA* 13.25. The passage almost certainly derives from Megasthenes: the king is unnamed, but the royal stabling of horses and elephants directly parallels *BNJ* 715 F31 = Strabo 15.1.52.

127. On this travel tale, see Graf 1993, Winston 1976, and Brown 1955.

128. Diod. Sic. 2.60.2.

129. The passage shows familiarity with Megasthenes' *Indica:* the identification of Palimbothra as the royal capital, the city's distance from the coast, the king's good relations with Greeks. Moreover, Iambulus' claim (Diod. Sic. 2.60.4) to improve on existing accounts of India, while a stock assertion, at least implies knowledge of such works.

130. Romm 1992.

131. See later for Mauryan imperial space; on the capacity of indigenous traditions to model Greek ethnographers' basic conceptions of space and time, see Moyer 2011: 42–83.

132. The country's climate and hydrology (fifty-eight navigable rivers and two monsoon inundations), described in book one of the *Indica,* result in two annual harvests (*BNJ* 715 F9a = Arr. *Ind.* 4.2–5.2, F4 = Diod. Sic. 2.36.4–5, F8 = Strabo 15.1.20); the αὐτοματίζοντες καρποί, "spontaneously growing fruits," also support the population (F4 = Diod. Sic. 2.36.5). Famine is consequently unknown in India. Megasthenes goes to great length to refute claims of external contact or conquest. No Indian army or colony ever exited the homeland (F14 = Arr. *Ind.* 9.12, F4 = Diod. Sic. 2.38.1 and 2.39.4).

133. *Contra* Bosworth 2003, who, based on his controversial backdating of the *Indica* (see Appendix), argues that the *Kulturgeschichte* were "totally inappropriate for the Seleucid court" (312) because they emphasized the uniqueness of Alexander's Indian conquests. But, among other things, this ignores the ethnography's consistent privileging of the Gangetic basin as India's true heartland, where Dionysus and Heracles performed their civilizing works but which Alexander never reached.

134. Megasthenes counted 118 ethnically distinct peoples in India (*BNJ* 715 F12 = Arr. *Ind.* 7.1).

135. Zambrini 1985: 825.

136. Zambrini 1985: 824, discussing *BNJ* 715 F19a = Arr. *Ind.* 12.5 and F4 = Diod. Sic. 2.38.7.

137. Ashoka makes no mention of such entities in his inscriptions; see Thapar 1961: 121–122.

138. *Contra* Zambrini 1985: 782, 825 and Murray 1972: 208.

139. Temporal distance: e.g., Hesiod's Golden Age, Plato's Atlantis, ancient Athens, and ideal future foundations; geographical distance: e.g., Homer's Ethiopians, Abii, and Phaeacians, Theopompus' Meropis, Euhemerus' Panchaea, Hecataeus' land of the Hyperboreans, and Iambulus' Islands of the Sun.

140. Strabo 7.3.6 recognized this ethnographic subset of the utopian genre. Note that the basic geometry of circular space explains the size of the world's margins.

141. The indicative present tense, "prétend rendre compte d'une réalité contemporaine, mais suggère en même temps un univers coupé du temps" (Lenfant 2004: cxxxviii).

142. *BNJ* 715 F4 = Diod. Sic. 2.35.3, 2.36.4, F8 = Strabo 15.1.20.

143. *BNJ* 715 F4 = Diod. Sic. 2.36.2.

144. *BNJ* 715 F4 = Diod. Sic. 2.36.1, 2.38.1.

145. *BNJ* 715 F4 = Diod. Sic. 2.39.5, F16 = Arr. *Ind.* 10.8, F32 = Strabo 15.1.54.

146. *BNJ* 715 F4 = Diod. Sic. 2.40–2.41, F19a = Arr. *Ind.* 11–12, F19b = Strabo 15.1.39–49.

147. *BNJ* 715 F32 = Strabo 15.1.53–54.

148. In an odd footnote Droysen 1878: 3.22 n.1 claimed that Euhemerus may have been sent by Cassander as ambassador to the court of Chandragupta. This entirely unsubstantiated suggestion points out, in fact, the important difference between Megasthenes' *Indica* and Euhemerus' *Hiēra Anagraphē*, that is, between the real world of India and the imaginary and incredible island Panchaea.

149. Several generations after Dionysus and Heracles some of the cities became democracies (*BNJ* 715 F4 = Diod. Sic. 2.38.7, 2.39.4).

150. *BNJ* 715 F4 = Diod. Sic. 2.35.3, 2.36.6; F19a = Arr. *Ind.* 11.10; F19b = Strabo 15.1.40.

151. Thieves are executed (*BNJ* 715 F31 = Strabo 15.1.51). Perjurers have their hands and feet cut off; those who maim others lose their hand and receive in addition the injury they inflict; and those who blind or cripple craftsmen are put to death (*BNJ* 715 F32 = Strabo 15.1.54).

152. *BNJ* 715 F19b = Strabo 15.1.48.

153. *BNJ* 715 F32 = Strabo 15.1.55. It is difficult not to recall the Successor period's cluster of conspiracies, which resulted in the assassination of, among others, Meleager, Perdiccas, Alexander IV, Philip III Arrhidaeus, Heracles (son of Barsine), Olympias, and eventually Seleucus Nicator himself. Alexander's death, too, was quickly (correctly?) the object of suspicion.

154. The loss of India as a land for utopian speculations seems to have been compensated in part by the relocation of ideal states into the world of Ocean. Gabba 1981: 55–59 has demonstrated the emergence of far-off islands as privileged sites for this genre (as well as paradoxography), as they combined with greatest efficiency isolation, atemporality, and the self-contained perfection of a total system; moreover, the postulate of the outbound and

return voyage, that is, the utopia's emplotment at the center of a travel account, empowered the text to speak from elsewhere and ensured the strangeness of the picture in a manner quite opposed to Megasthenes.

155. Hartog 1988: 324.

156. In some respects, Hecataeus' *Aegyptiaca* similarly neutralized kingship as a marker of otherness. But this was achieved by inscribing Ptolemy within the dynastic history of Egyptian rulers rather than naturalizing the monarchic institution per se.

157. *BNJ* 715 F11a = Strabo 15.1.6–7; F11b = Arr. *Ind.* 5.4–7 preserves a parallel, though less detailed, fragment.

158. Observed by Kuhrt and Sherwin-White 1993: 97. Note that the references to the Macedonians or Alexander in these catalogues are intrusions, unlikely to derive from Megasthenes, as Duane Roller has observed (*BNJ* 715 F11 comm.); similarly, the inclusion of Heracles in a list of foreign conquerors directly contradicts Megasthenes' explicit account of Heracles as an autochthonous culture-hero and Dionysus as sole invader.

159. Semiramis' expedition had been described in Ctesias' *Persica,* where it was modeled on Xerxes' invasion of Greece (*FGrHist* 688 F1b = Diod. Sic. 2.16–19); Nearchus mentioned her disastrous return through the Gedrosian desert (*BNJ* 133 F3a = Arr. *Anab.* 6.24.2, F3b = Strabo 15.1.5). Megasthenes' account of an invasion abandoned on account of the queen's death may be modeled on Alexander's Arabian expedition, aborted by his passing in Babylon. In asserting the failure of Sesostris' expedition, Megasthenes may have been rejecting Hecataeus of Abdera's claim in the *Aegyptiaca* that pharaoh Sesoösis had overcome and brought civilization to India (Diod. Sic. 1.55.2–4). King Idanthyrsus appears in Herodotus as the nephew of transgressive Anacharsis (Hdt. 4.76) and interlocutor with Darius I (Hdt. 4.126–127). His conquest of all Asia up to Egypt appears to be Megasthenes' creation.

160. Arrian's abbreviated list omits these kings, but there is no indication that they are interpolated into Strabo's version. Megasthenes' discussion of Nebuchadnezzar is well attested by Josephus and Eusebius. Tearcon is Pharaoh Taharqa, last of the twenty-fifth (Kushite) dynasty. In a cross-reference to Megasthenes, his expedition appears in Strabo 1.3.21 as an instance of unfamiliar history. Manetho merely gives his regnal years (*FGrHist* 609 F64: γ´ Τάρκος ἔτη ιη´). Taharqa had waged war against Sennacherib during the reign of Hezekiah, saving Jerusalem from the Assyrian yoke (2 Kings 19:9; Isaiah 37:9). Nebuchadnezzar II of Babylon, greatest of the Neo-Babylonian kings, rebuilt Babylon, destroyed the Jerusalem Temple, and deported the Jews. Megasthenes' choice of Nebuchadnezzar as representative of Babylonian monarchy bypassed the great builder-queens of historiographical tradition, Nitocris and Semiramis. That Megasthenes came to know of Nebuchadnezzar is no great surprise, given the Babylonian context of the early Seleucid court (see Appendix). But Taharqa is more startling. From where did Megasthenes derive his information? The combination of

these two monarchs in this passage most plausibly suggests Jewish influence. Megasthenes' interest in Jews is shown by *BNJ* 715 F3a = Clem. Al. *Strom.* 1.15.72.5, where he parallels the Brahmans in India with the Jews in Syria; Megasthenes' observation was picked up by Clearchus of Soli (F69 M; 6 W. Joseph. *Ap.* 1.22). Large Jewish diaspora communities existed within the Seleucid kingdom in the core regions of Babylonia and Syria. Not only are Taharqa and Nebuchadnezzar prominent foreign kings in the Hebrew Bible, but they also appear, as here, in the context of imperial conquest.

161. *BNJ* 715 F13a = Arr. *Ind.* 8.11–12.

162. *BNJ* 715 F13a = Arr. *Ind.* 8.10. For Heracles' associations with the sea and its creatures, see Lacroix 1974: 47–53.

163. Theophr. *de lapidibus* 36. According to Caley and Richards 1956: 4, "[i]nternal evidence indicates that the treatise was written near the end of the fourth century B.C."

164. The pearl swarm's absolute dependence on the king may derive from Aristotle's account of the monarchism of bee society (Arist. *Hist. an.* 624a).

165. E.g., Xen. *Cyr.* 5.1.24, where Cyrus' innate kingliness is compared with the queen bee, whom the drones willingly obey and follow; see Pomeroy 1984.

166. Note that pearls were closely associated with the domineering ambitions of the late Roman Republic's Big Men: at his triumph of 61 Pompey exhibited thirty-three pearl crowns and a pearl portrait of his own face; Suetonius (*Iul.* 47) writes that Caesar, according to malicious gossip, invaded Britain *spe margaritarum* ("in the hope of pearls") and gave his mistress Servilia an extravagant pearl (*Iul.* 50). More relevantly, in a famous anecdote indicating the identification of pearls with eastern monarchy and female rule, Cleopatra VII dissolved and drank one of her enormous pearl earrings at a banquet for Antony; the other was cut in two and dedicated by Augustus in the Pantheon (Plin. *HN* 9.35.119–121). Pliny writes that the pearls were a possession handed down from one generation of kings of the east to the next: *utrumque possedit Cleopatra, Aegypti reginarum novissima, per manus orientis regum sibi traditos* (Plin. *HN* 9.35.119); see Flory 1988. Interestingly, Marco Polo reports that the kings of the Malabar coast (the same region as Megasthenes' Pandaean kingdom) wore a necklace of 108 pearls, which was handed down from one generation of kings to the next.

167. For example, Jewsiewicki 1989 on the Belgian Congo.

168. In contrast to, e.g., Onesicritus, according to whom the gymnosophist Mandanis, speaking through a chain of three interpreters, equated the act of translation to pure water flowing through mud (*BNJ* 134 F17a = Strabo 15.1.64). Greenblatt 1991: 131–135 has persuasively argued that imperializing, possessive ethnography depends on the effacement of strong affinities, echoes, structural parallels.

169. According to Buddhist legend, Ashoka executed ninety-nine of his brothers, but this may be explained by the tendency in Buddhist texts to demonize preconversion Ashoka in order to stress the transformation wrought by *dhamma;* see Habib and Jha 2004: 21.

170. Thapar 1961: 180.
171. For a discussion of concentric Indian geography derived from the Sanskrit Puranas, see Minkowski 2010.
172. Robert 1958a: 17 observes that the edict's phrase λῶιον καὶ ἄμεινον is a formulaic oracular response to consultants. The ἀποχὴ τῶν ἐμψύχων recalls Pythagorean ideas (Robert 1958a: 15–16). Ashoka's *dhamma* is translated as εὐσέβεια (see Schlumberger 1958: 5–6). Schwarz 1969: 298–301 has suggested that the περὶ εὐσεβείας of Antiochus I's Indian ambassador, Deimachus, may reflect the developing importance of *dhamma* at the Mauryan court. More generally, Pugliese Carratelli 1953 has demonstrated the similarities between Ashokan *dhamma* and the politico-ethical theory of Hellenistic kingship.
173. *Dhamma* is represented by the substantive adjective and hafel participle *qšyṭ' mhqšṭ*, both deriving from the verbal stem *qšṭ*, "to be truthful" (cf. Daniel 2:47; 4:34). Old Persian loanwords include *pati-zbāta* (to ban), **frabasta* (controlled), *ʰuᵛpatạyasti* (obedient), *mazišta* (older). Note that *'f zy* is an Aramaic provincialism. For detailed linguistic discussion, see Dupont-Sommer 1958.
174. Schlumberger 1958.
175. Thapar 1961: 7.
176. Thirteenth Major Rock Edict 9 (Shahbazgarhi version).
177. *Majjhima Nikāya* 93, quoted in Habib and Jha 2004: 134.
178. Thirteenth Major Rock Edict 17–18.
179. On the *yojana* in Indian geography, see Minkowski 2010: 13.
180. Second Major Rock Edict 1 (Kalsi version).
181. Note that Prakrit dialectal differences between the Mauryan Gangetic heartland and its northwestern periphery explain the variations between, e.g., *raja*, used in the Indus region, and *laja*, used in eastern India; see Thapar 2002b: 6–7 for brief discussion.

2. Central Asia—Nomads, Ocean, and the Desire for Line

1. Diplomatic relations between the Near East and China opened only in the first century, between the Arsacid and Han courts. The first great history of China, Ssu-ma Ch'ien's *Shih-chi*, derives its description of western Asia in chapter 123 from the personal account of Chang Ch'ien, sent on a mission to the Yüeh-chih nomads by Emperor Wu, from *c.* 138–125. Leslie and Gardiner 1982 suggest that the account's geographical pair *Li-kan/T'iao-chih* of the distant west should be identified as Seleucia-on-the-Tigris and Antioch-by-Daphne, respectively, splitting the syllable *kan* down the middle. Pulleyblank 1999, however, identifies *Li-kan* and *T'iao-chih* as Hyrcania and Seleucia-on-the-Tigris. Chinese historian Martin Kroher, in correspondence, cautions that the phonological changes are too obscure and the far western geography too thoroughly mythologized for positive identifications.
2. The most detailed discussion remains Schober 1981: 145–151.

3. Diod. Sic. 18.17.1–9; see Coloru 2009: 130–134.

4. Wolski 1960: 113–115.

5. Even after his grubby victory over his rival Eumenes at Gabiene, Antigonus had not felt strong enough to replace Stasanor and Oxyartes, the established satraps in Bactria and Parapamisadae; Diod. Sic. 19.48.1–2.

6. Not Sophytes, as previously thought. It is a Greek rendering of the Indian name Subhuti; another Sophytos, son of Naratos and perhaps a descendant of our numismatically attested one, appears on a second-century acrostic funerary epigram from Kandahar (*IGIAC* 84). The most recent examination of the coins, based on a new hoard found at Aqtcha, suggests that Sophytos exercised his power in Bactria, not Arachosia, and between *c.* 315 and *c.* 305, not *c.* 305 and *c.* 290 (Bopearachchi and Flandrin 2005: 195–201 and Coloru 2009: 139–141 *contra* Bernard, Pinault, and Rougemont 2004: 301–311).

7. See Coloru 2009: 136; Holt 1988: 96–97; Fuÿe 1910: 289–292; Bellinger 1962: 67; though note the caution of Grenet and Rapin 1983: 378 n.28.

8. Just. *Epit.* 15.4.11–12: *principio Babyloniam cepit; inde auctis ex victoria viribus, Bactrianos expugnavit. transitum deinde in Indiam fecit;* Oros. 3.23.44: *Bactrianos novis motibus adsurgentes perdomuit.* See Yardley, Wheatley, and Heckel 2011: 273–274.

9. Capdetrey 2007: 42, for example, observes the striking contrast with the Upper Satraps' hostile and suspicious attitude towards Pithon, Eumenes, and Antigonus.

10. Capdetrey 2007: 44.

11. Wolski 1960: 113–115.

12. Ogden 1999: xiii.

13. Plin. *HN* 6.23.93.

14. Strabo 11.10.2; Plin. *HN* 6.16.47.

15. Plin. *HN* 6.16.48.

16. App. *Syr.* 57. Although Appian attributes this list of foundations to Seleucus Nicator, we know in one case (Achaïs) that Antiochus was responsible (Plin. *HN* 6.16.48) and can fairly assume his role in others: Seleucus I remained the senior reigning king during this period of Antiochus' viceroyship.

17. For example, Strabo 11.10.2 and Plin. *HN* 6.16.47 describe the enormous circuit wall constructed around the Merv oasis by Antiochus. This has now been located; see Košelenko, Bader, and Gaibov 1995 and my Chapter 7. The earliest strata of Khodjend (Alexandria-Eschate/Antioch-in-Scythia) are Seleucid; see Negmatov 1986.

18. Archaeological survey and excavation have identified nearly forty early Seleucid sites in Afghanistan, Turkmenistan, and Uzbekistan. Aï Khanoum is the most important and duly famous; see Chapters 7 and 8. Maracanda (Afrasiab-Samarkhand) was refortified with enormous walls (Rapin and Isamiddinov 1994; Grenet 2004/5: 1056–1058); Antiochus' defenses continued to function, with modification, well into the thirteenth century. The enormous Oxus temple at Takht-i Sangin is almost certainly a royal-

sponsored construction of this period (Litvinskiy 2010a: 14; Litvinskiy 2010b; Litvinskiy, Vinogradov, and Pičikjan 1985; for bibliography, see Mairs 2011: 24–25). The small Alexandrian fort at Kurganzol, in southern Uzbekistan, was reconstructed, after a short abandonment, in the early Seleucid period (Sverchkov 2008 and 2009). Hellenistic material has now been found at Termez (Leriche and Pidaev 2007). It is possible that Panjikant, east of Samarkhand on the Zarafshan river, was another Antioch: a fragmentary Middle Persian inscription, on a wall otherwise inscribed in Sogdian and Kushan-Bactrian (Hephthalite), reads –*t*]*ywky*. In an unpublished letter to comrade Iranianists in St. Petersburg, Henning suggested that this could stand for "Antiocheia" (quoted in Frye 1967: 34).

19. Agriculture is made possible in this region by irrigation alone. Excavation has revealed the evolution of sophisticated systems of irrigation, the so-called BMAC, or Bactria-Margiana Archaeological Complex, long predating the arrival of Near Eastern or European imperial forces (see Baumer 2012: 104–121 and Kuz'mina 1976). Hellenistic Bactria witnessed the digging of new canals and consequent extension of cultivated land; see Chapter 7.

20. See Holt 1999: 29–37.

21. Apame: *IDidyma* 480; Antiochus: *OGIS* 213 = *IDidyma* 479 = *BNJ* 428 T3.

22. *BNJ* 428 T2 = Plin. *HN* 6.16.49.

23. Wolski 1947: 23–24. Robert 1984b: 467–472 dismisses Pliny's phrase as a general reference to Demodamas' entire career. On the basis of the mention of Milesian military service in the decree honoring Apame (*IDidyma* 480), Robert backdates Demodamas' activities in Central Asia to the first period of Seleucus I's involvement (307–304). For Robert 1984b: 470, Apame enthusiastically supported the Milesian soldiers serving with Seleucus because they were campaigning in her birthplace. However, Milesian mercenaries could have been involved in any of Seleucus' campaigns before 299/8 (the date of the inscription, see earlier), including the battles for Babylonia, the conquest of western Iran, the Indian campaign, or the battle of Ipsus, and there are surely countless reasons for Apame's good treatment. The force of Pliny's gloss should be recognized.

24. *BNJ* 428 F2 = Plin. *HN* 6.16.49.

25. Pliny's manuscripts read *demonas, dein onas, deviona, dęmones,* and *dęmona,* but Harduin's emendation *Demodamas* is universally accepted. The Milesian appears in book 6's list of authors; he is also referenced in an entry of Stephanus of Byzantium's *Ethnica* (s.v. Ἄντισσα) for a city in India (unlisted in *BNJ*).

26. Arr. *Anab.* 5.29; Diod. Sic. 17.95.1–2; Curt. 9.3.19; Plut. *Al.* 62.7–8; Metz Epit. 69; Just. *Epit.* 12.8.16. In the Vulgate tradition, the altars were at the center of a gigantic camp. Strabo 3.5.5 suggests that Alexander's altars were in deliberate emulation of Heracles and Dionysus. It was noted in Chapter 1 that Chandragupta Maurya and the kings of the Prasii piously celebrated their territorial expansion by sacrificing on these altars whenever they crossed the Hyphasis.

27. Just. *Epit.* 11.5.4. Although these Hellespontine altars may be an invented doublet, bracketing Alexander's empire, the account underscores the act's symbolic meaning.
28. Oikonomides 1988.
29. Sall. *Jug.* 19.3; Polyb. 3.39.2.
30. *Tabula Peutingeriana* segment 11; see Bosio 1983: 116–117. A total of five *arae* on the map mark its edges: one on the Iaxartes *(Ara Alexandri)*, two on the Hyphasis *(Hic Alexander Responsum accepit. Usque quo Alexander)*, and two in Africa *(Arae Philenorum fines Affricae et Cyrenensium)*. In Ptol. *Geog.* 5.9.15, the Iaxartes' altar is also considered Alexander's.
31. Will 1966: 1.268 and Tarn 1940: 91 are surely correct that Antioch-in-Scythia (the tenth Antioch listed by Stephanus) can only be the rebuilt Alexandria-Eschate (App. *Syr.* 57). The *Tabula Peutingeriana* places the names "Alexandria" and "Antioch" side by side to the south of the Iaxartes ("Araxes"). See Cohen 2013: 250–255.
32. *FGrHist* 239 §108 under the date 328/7: ᾠκίσθη δὲ πρὸς Τανάι πόλις Ἑλληνίς. Egyptian Alexandria is the only other of Alexander's foundations to be included (§106).
33. For details see Bosworth 1995: 19. Briant 1978: 74 observes that the population of Cyropolis was shifted to Alexandria-Eschate. Alexander's reverence for Cyrus is well attested in the Vulgate tradition: for example, he is said to have rewarded the Ariaspians of Drangiana with special privileges for the aid they had given Cyrus on his eastern campaign (Curt. 7.3.1–3); see Kosmin 2013a: 674–675.
34. Strabo 11.11.4.
35. Ptol. 6.12.5; Steph. Byz. s.v. Κύρου πόλις; Amm. Marc. 23.6.59. Benveniste 1943–1945 suggests that this form may correspond to the Old Persian *Kuruš-kaθa*, "city of Cyrus," making Cyropolis a translation and Cyreschata a transcription.
36. Note that the Branchidae, Didyma's priests, had been exiled to Sogdiana by Darius or Xerxes. Almost one and a half centuries later they were massacred by Alexander; for sources and bibliography, see Parke 1985 and Hammond 1998.
37. *IDidyma* 480.
38. Gifts: *IDidyma* 424 (*OGIS* 214; *RC* 5; *SEG* 41 952). Restoration of Canachus' Apollo: Paus. 1.16.3, 8.46.3.
39. *IDidyma* 479 (*OGIS* 213); see Haussoullier 1902: 34–48.
40. Hammond 1998: 339 with n.2, with reference to Pičikjan 1991.
41. See Robert 1965: 209 n.1.
42. On the identification of the dedicator, see Robert 1968: 421–457; on the settlement, see Chapter 7; on Clearchus' inscription, see Chapter 8.
43. *SEG* 31 1381; *IGIAC* 95; *IEOG* 311. Note that almost fifty fragments of bone flutes have been recovered from the temple (Litvinskiy 2010b: 35).
44. This functions somewhat like the bracketing of the Nile and Maeander in the name Neilomandros, attested on a sixth-century vase from Naucratis in Egypt; see Thonemann 2006. Pičikjan suggested that the identification of the

Oxus with the Marsyas-Maeander was a result of obvious hydrological similarities between the two rivers: their gold-bearing properties, narrow depths, and abundant reeds, from which flutes are still today whittled (Litvinskiy, Vinogradov, and Pičikjan 1985: 110). However, Bernard 1987 has convincingly shown that Pičikjan has confused characteristics of the Pactolus and Maeander and that reeds grow on most Central Asian rivers. He proposes, instead, that the cult of Marsyas was brought to the Oxus by colonists from the Maeander valley, more precisely, from Apamea-Celaenae. On reeds, the Maeander valley, and river cult, see Thonemann 2012: 57–75.

45. We know that Pliny used Demodamas (see the earlier Iaxartes altar passage), who appears in Book 6's list of authors. Certainly, a common source lies behind the description of Antioch-in-Margiane/Merv in Plin. *HN* 6.16.47 and Strabo 11.10.2; Kuhrt and Sherwin-White 1993: 83 have plausibly proposed Demodamas. Wolski 1984: 13–14 has suggested Pliny's accounts of Antiochus' refoundations derive from Demodamas. There is no known suitable alternative author.

46. Antioch-in-Margiane: Plin. *HN* 6.16.47, Strabo 11.10.2; Achaïs-in-Margiana: Plin. *HN* 6.16.48; Antioch-in-Aria: Plin. *HN* 6.23.93. If we follow Tarn 1940: 89–94, we can add Khodjend (Alexandria-Eschate/Antioch-in-Scythia) and perhaps Termez (Alexandria/Antioch/Demetrias).

47. Baumer 2012: 210, 284–285; Gardiner-Garden 1987: 46–47; Wolski: 1960; Tarn 1940: 91.

48. Note the doubts of Holt 1999: 29 and Coloru 2009: 148.

49. Holt 1999: 129. Primo 2009: 133–135 suggests that a Seleucid court historian lies behind Polybius' account of Antiochus' actions in Bactria; certainly, Polybius' depiction of Antiochus' courageous leadership in battle against Euthydemus' cavalry portrays the Seleucid monarch as an ideal warrior king.

50. Polyb. 11.34.4–5.

51. Tarn 1966: 82, 117 interpreted Euthydemus' observation of the nomadic menace as thinly veiled blackmail. He takes the verb προσδέχωνται to imply that Euthydemus would call in the nomads. Walbank 1957–1979: 2.313, however, shows that here προδέχεσθαι means only "to be attacked by" (cf. Polyb. 2.68.8, 3.42.5).

52. On the Graeco-Bactrian kings' marching in Seleucid footprints, see Coloru 2009 and Holt 1999. Note that an altar was erected by a certain Heliodotus on behalf of the Graeco-Bactrian king Euthydemus and his son Demetrius in a sacred grove of Zeus near modern Kuliab, about ninety kilometers north of the Oxus river and Aï Khanoum (see Bernard, Pinault, and Rougemont 2004: 333–356); it does not seem to function as a spatial boundary.

53. Inevitably for a rebel prince, the space he claims to protect is not the specific demarcated territory of the Seleucid kingdom but a vague and neutral χώρα, "land," free from the connotations of imperial sovereignty.

54. Briant 1982b: 35–40 observes that Hellenic and Babylonian discourses on the barbarism of mountain dwellers and steppe nomads articulate, within a dominant mode of repulsion and disgust, a common series of identity traits.

55. Holt 1989: 52–58; Bernard 1990: 20–25. Some Scythians were settled in military colonies in Babylonia and Syria; see Briant 1982b: 198–199. Central Asian nomads were integrated into the Achaemenid army: Bactrians, Sogdians, and Sacas fought side by side at Gaugamela (Arr. *Anab.* 3.8).

56. Anthropology has recognized a wide range of symbiotic relations in modern Afghanistan, ranging from moneylending and seasonal labor to regional communication and warfare; see, e.g., Dupree 1975. For comparison, see Arsen'ev's 1990 study of the sub-Saharan Sahel zone.

57. Henkelman 2011a; Briant 1982b: 81–112, 198–226.

58. Most obviously in Simonides of Magnesia's epic poem and the monumental art celebrating Antiochus I's victory over marauding Galatians at the Elephant Battle (Lucian, *Zeuxis;* Steph. Byz. s.v. Βοῦρα). "Papyrus Hamburgensis de Galatis" (Lloyd-Jones and Parsons 1983: 459–460 (#958)) preserves a verse account of the opposition of a Hellenistic monarch to Galatian soldiers; the king has been identified as Antiochus I, Attalus I, Antigonus Gonatas, or Ptolemy II; see Primo 2009: 102–103. Lloyd-Jones 2005: 59 (#454C) has convincingly assigned to the Seleucid court poet Euphorion of Chalcis a new papyrus fragment on the Gigantomachy: perhaps, like the Altar of Zeus at Pergamum, a celebration of royal order and its victory over barbaric chaos; see Primo 2009: 100.

59. *BNJ* 712 T2 = Plut. *Demetr.* 47.4; see Capdetrey 2007: 30.

60. *BNJ* 712 T1 = Diod. Sic. 19.100.5. If he is to be restored as the indirect object of the verb *paqādu* ("to entrust") in the cuneiform Chronicle's account of Antigonus Monophthalmus' invasion, he took up residence in the Babylonian palace - *BCHP* 3 Rev. 8–9: *ana muh²-hi²* [Patrocles²] *ina lìb-bi* [- -] *ip-qid* ("he entrusted the palace² to [Patrocles]").

61. *BNJ* 712 F4a = Strabo 2.1.17.

62. Patrocles advised against Seleucus' good treatment of his prisoner Demetrius Poliorcetes, son of Antigonus Monophthalmus (*BNJ* 712 T2 = Plut. *Demetr.* 47.4).

63. *BNJ* 712 T4 = Phot. *Bibl.* 224 (Memnon) p. 227a 4. See Chapters 3 and 4 on the murder of Seleucus I and Antiochus' succession. Primo 2009: 77–78, 186–187, 230–232 persuasively argues that Patrocles' memoirs lie behind Diodorus' account of Seleucus' return to Babylon and the subsequent Antigonid invasion (Diod. Sic. 19.90–92) and Plutarch's account of his treatment of Demetrius (Plut. *Demetr.* 47–51).

64. *BNJ* 712 T3a = Plin. *HN* 6.17.58; F4c = Plin. *HN* 2.67.167–168.

65. Patrocles' trustworthiness: *BNJ* 712 T5a = Strabo 2.1.2, T5b = Strabo 2.1.6. Most important is F1 = Strabo 2.1.6, where Patrocles claims to have been given Alexander's very own geographical report, kept secure in the Babylonian treasury. This statement not only buttresses Patrocles' observations with the Conqueror's authority; it also highlights the close relationship between geographical survey, monarchic authority, and royal legitimacy.

66. Tarn 1901: 13 n.5 notes that Strabo's use of the definite article (*BNJ* 712 F8a = Strabo 11.6.1: τὸν ὑπὸ τῶν Ἑλλήνων γνωριζόμενον περίπλουν τῆς

θαλάττης ταύτης -"the *periplus* of this sea that was known by the Greeks" implies that Patrocles' was the only well-known published account of the Caspian. Certainly, Greek or Macedonian control of the Caspian region was never again so strong.

67. Hdt. 4.42–44.

68. Hdt. 4.44.

69. For a detailed study of Darius' canal, see Tuplin 1991. The badly preserved Hieroglyphic stelae also record, albeit in local idiom, the linking of Egypt and Iran.

70. Under Nearchus, whose account of the voyage is preserved in the second half of Arrian's *Indicē* (Nearchus *BNJ* 133).

71. Under Androsthenes of Samos and Archias. Note that Dion 1977: 181–183 suggests that Pytheas, the famed explorer of Europe's northern seas, had been commissioned by Alexander in connection with his western-oriented Last Plans.

72. Arr. *Anab.* 7.16.1–3. Note that Alexander's πόθος, "desire," for peripleutic exploration semantically and syntactically parallels Darius' *kāma* in the Suez inscription, quoted earlier. On the strategic and political significance of naval exploration for Alexander, see Dion 1977: 175–177.

73. Neumann 1884: 182; Tarn 1901: 13.

74. Surviving *peripli* include those of Hanno of Carthage, [Scylax], Nearchus, Arrian, and the anonymous author of the Red Sea voyage.

75. Hartog 1988: 343.

76. Eratosthenes' citations suggest at least two voyages, along the western and southern coasts of the Caspian (*BNJ* 712 F8a = Strabo 11.6.1). The ships were probably constructed in the southwestern corner of the Caspian, where pine and fir were available.

77. *BNJ* 712 F4a = Strabo 2.1.17; F8a = Strabo 11.6.1; F4d = Arr. *Anab.* 7.16.4; F7a = Strabo 11.6.2; F7b = Strabo 11.7.1; F7d = Curt. 6.4.19; F7g = [Arist.], *De mundo* 393b; F7h = Mela 3.5.38; F8b = Plin. *HN* 6.13.36.

78. *Tabula Peutingeriana* segment 11; see Bosio 1983: 116–117.

79. Thomson 1948: 127–129.

80. Hecataeus *BNJ* 1 F18a/302c = Schol. ad Ap. Rhod. *Argon.* 4.259 is ambiguous.

81. Hdt. 1.203.1; see Casson 1918–1919.

82. Arist. *Meteor.* 354a3–4.

83. Certainly, Alexander was not decided on the question, and sent Heraclides to determine the nature of the Caspian. Nonetheless, according to Plut. *Alex.* 44.1–2, he "conjectured that in all probability it was a stagnant overflow from Lake Maeotis" (εἴκασε τῆς Μαιώτιδος λίμνης ἀνακοπὴν εἶναι). Moreover, important episodes in his *anabasis* depend on the lake model. According to Arr. *Anab.* 4.15.4–5, Pharasmanes, king of the Chorasmians, claimed that his kingdom bordered Colchis on the Black Sea. The flattering identification of the Iaxartes with the Tanaïs required continuous land north of the Caspian, between the Hindu Kush and the Black Sea, through which the river could flow (see Strabo 11.7.4). Polyclitus even gave proofs that the Caspian was

enclosed: *FGrHist* 128 F7 = Strabo 11.7.4: Πολύκλειτος δὲ καὶ πίστεις προσφέρεται περὶ τοῦ λίμνην εἶναι τὴν θάλατταν ταύτην—ὄφεις τε γὰρ ἐκτρέφειν καὶ ὑπόγλυκυ εἶναι τὸ ὕδωρ ("Polyclitus offers proofs that this sea is a lake— for it supports serpents and the water is sweetish"). For detailed discussion, see Gardiner-Garden 1987: 28–33.

84. Diod. Sic. 18.5.2–6.3; see Hornblower 1981: 80–87.

85. Diod. Sic. 18.5.4: "Next to these are Aria, Parthia, and Hyrcania, by which the Hyrcanian Sea, a detached body of water, is surrounded (δι' ἧς συμβαίνει περιέχεσθαι τὴν Ὑρκανίαν θάλατταν, οὖσαν καθ' αὑτήν)."

86. The north-south mirroring of geographic models emerged with the Presocratic interest in the opposition of hot and cold temperatures. The most famous example is Herodotus' claim that if Hyperboreans, "Men beyond the North Wind," existed, so must Hypernotians, "Men beyond the South Wind" (Hdt. 4.36.1); see Romm 2010: 217. The theory of a zero-latitude equator from the Pillars of Hercules to the Himalayas ("Imaos") was first expounded explicitly by Dicaearchus of Messana (F110 (Wehrli) = Agathemerus, *Geographiae informatio,* prooem. 5); see Keyser 2001: 365–368, Pédech 1976: 97–100, and Thomson 1948: 134–135.

87. *BNJ* 712 F4a = Strabo 2.1.17; F4b = Strabo 11.11.6.

88. *BNJ* 712 T3b = Plin. *HN.* 6.17.58.

89. Neumann 1884: 180 and Tarn 1901: 18 suggest that the Roman encyclopaedist in error represented Patrocles' hypothetical proposition as a historical journey. This invented voyage was cited in the mid-sixteenth century as evidence for the feasibility of a northeast passage to China. The Spanish ambassador to Elizabethan England, Jehan Scheyfve, wrote to the bishop of Arras of the Willoughby-Chancellor venture on 10th April 1553, "they will follow a northerly course, and navigate the Frozen Sea *(Mare Congelatum)* towards the country of the great Cham (i.e., Khan) of China, or the neighbouring countries. The English opine that the ancients passed by that sea and joined the Ocean, as Pliny and others wrote: and they believe the route to be a short one" (quoted by Taylor 1932: 214).

90. The western Scythian and Sarmatian nomads of Europe are found "on the right as one sails in (εἰσπλέοντι)," the eastern Scythians "on the left" (*BNJ* 712 F7a = Strabo 11.6.2); elsewhere, the Dahae of Central Asia are "on the left as one sails into the Caspian Sea" (F7b = Strabo 11.7.1). The nomadic populations and the geographical distances of the western seaboard were described and measured from north to south (F5e = Strabo 11.4.2–4, F8a = Strabo 11.6.1, F8b = Plin. *HN* 6.13.36), those of the southern coast from west to east (F8a = Strabo 11.6.1, F8b = Plin. *HN* 6.13.36), and the eastern ones from south to north (F6a = Strabo 11.11.5, F8a = Strabo 11.6.1, F8b = Plin. *HN* 6.13.36).

91. *BNJ* 712 F4c = Plin. *HN* 2.67.167–168.

92. Dion 1977: 218: "Accomplir une circumnavigation de cette ampleur, ou même seulement en être réputé capable, étaient une manière de se signaler au monde comme le souverain légitime des territoires qu'elle eût enveloppés."

93. Compare the fabrication of Pytheas of Marseilles, a rough contemporary, who claimed to have sailed the northern border of Europe, from the Pillars of Hercules to the Tanaïs river, πᾶσαν τὴν παρωκεανῖτιν τῆς Εὐρώπης ἀπὸ Γαδείρων ἕως Τανάιδος (Strabo 2.4.1); Pytheas' invention, unlike Patrocles', was disputed.

94. It is unlikely that the Greeks knew of the Aral Sea. The distinction between "Hyrcanian" and "Caspian" seas refers to different parts of the Caspian coastline, much as "Aegean" and "Ionian" for the Mediterranean, *contra* Casson 1918–1919; see Hamilton 1971: 110–111.

95. Bosworth 1980: 373; Gardiner-Garden 1987: 13 n.46; Holt 1988: 12 n.7 suggest a lower, Caspian branch of the Oxus in historical times. Tarn 1901: 10–13 dismisses such a possibility, observing that Alexander, who saw the southern Caspian, neither founded a town at its supposed mouth nor sent an expedition to search for the mouth. Bernard (in Rapin 1992: 298 n.1203) concludes that the archaeological evidence is insufficient to support the existence of a true riverway. For a discussion of the findings of the Soviet archaeological mission in Chorasmia, see Callieri 1999: 37–42.

96. *BNJ* 712 F4d = Arr. *Anab.* 7.16.3–4, F5c = Plin. *HN* 6.17.52, F5d = Solinus 19.4–5, F6a = Strabo 11.11.5, F6b = Strabo 11.7.4, F8a = Strabo 11.6.1, F8b = Plin. *HN* 6.13.36.

97. *BNJ* 712 F6a = Strabo 11.11.5. It is interesting that Patrocles measures in Persian parasangs. Tarn 1901: 15 argued that this indicates that the information was hearsay, deriving from "Persian-speaking folk of some sort." Gardiner-Garden 1987: 43 suggested that, since Patrocles did not sail to the mouths of the rivers, the measurement came from either Alexander's or Demodamas' inland march from the Oxus to the Iaxartes. Of course, the use of parasangs could be a literary choice; the unit is found in Herodotus, Xenophon, and Arrian.

98. *BNJ* 712 F6b = Strabo 11.7.4.

99. *BNJ* 712 F5a = Strabo 11.7.3; F5b = Strabo 2.1.15.

100. *BNJ* 712 F5b = Strabo 2.1.15. The great Roman Pompey, who campaigned against the Albanians between Colchis and the Caspian Sea in 66, revived the notion of an Indian–Black Sea trade route. Plut. *Pomp.* 32–37 states that Pompey did not reach the Caspian; Plin. *HN* 6.17.51 notes that Caspian water was brought for him to drink, a gesture recalling Persian monarchs.

101. Houghton and Lorber 2002: # 283A.

102. Other dedications honored the river, including a relief of the fight between Heracles and Silenus and an ivory hippocampess (see Litvniskiy and Pičikjan 1995). The river's holiness was recognized in the distant west, where Dionysius Periegetes wrote (746–747) ἔπι γαῖα / Σουγδιάς ἧς ἀνὰ μέσσον ἑλίσσεται ἱερὸς Ὦξος.

103. Arist. *Meteor.* 358a18–30; Strabo 11.7.4 suggests that the identification was a flattery to present Alexander as conqueror of Asia entire; note that the Gazetteer of 324/3 (Diod. Sic. 18.5.4) and the *Marmor Parium* (*FGrHist* 239 §108)

call the Iaxartes "Tanaïs." Hamilton 1971 argues that the equation of the rivers was a genuine geographical belief.

104. Plut. *Alex.* 44.1–2.

105. Plin. *HN* 6.11.31.

106. Demonstrated by Neumann 1884: 183–185, supported by Callieri 1999: 35.

107. Ptolemy II reopened (or, according to some sources, completed) Darius' canal. The canal is mentioned in the Pithom Stele; see Tuplin 1991: 238.

108. Note that the late Hellenistic scholar Posidonius, from Apamea-on-the-Axios, paralleled the "isthmus" between the Black and Caspian Seas to that between the Mediterranean and Red Seas (*FGrHist* 87 F101a (F206 Edelstein/ Kidd) = Strabo 11.1.5).

109. 2 Macc. 5:21: ὁ Ἀντίοχος . . . οἰόμενος ἀπὸ τῆς ὑπερηφανίας τὴν μὲν γῆν πλωτὴν . . . θέσθαι. Note that the overreaching works of Antiochus IV are, like those of Seleucus I, still in the planning phase.

110. See Romm 1992: 10–26.

111. Aristides 26.10.

112. Aristides 26.102.

113. It is uncertain when the Rampart of Alexander/Sadd-i Yajuj va Majuj was first built, as it is extremely difficult to date a structure of raw clay; most likely it is Sasanian (see Nokandeh et al. 2006).

114. Quran, *Sura* 18.

115. *Sikandar Nāma* 36.25–28 (trans. Capt. Wilberforce Clarke).

3. Macedonia—From Center to Periphery

1. Diod. Sic. 21.1.5; App. *Syr.* 55. Appian includes in Seleucus' share inland Phrygia (Φρυγίας τῆς ἀνὰ τὸ μεσόγειον); it is unclear what geographical region is intended.

2. Ptolemaic control of the south Syrian coast reproduced Pharaonic Egypt's traditional buffer strategy of Levantine defense as well as the conflicts such a policy tended to generate with the dominant Anatolian, Syrian, or Mesopotamian power, in this case the Seleucid empire; see Liverani 2001.

3. *IDidyma* 424; *OGIS* 214; *RC* 5; *SEG* 41 952. For Seleucus' relationship to Apollo of Didyma, see Chapter 2.

4. Ptolemy's alliance with Lysimachus against Seleucus resembles that of Ptolemy, Lysimachus, Seleucus, and Cassander against Antigonus in 301 and that of Ptolemy, Antipater, and Craterus against Perdiccas in 320.

5. Plut. *Demetr.* 51.

6. Agathocles' widow, Lysandra, Lysimachus' son, Alexander, the chief administrators, and the military commanders eagerly defected to Seleucus (Paus. 1.10.3–4; Just. *Epit.* 17.1). Memnon *BNJ* 434 F1 5.7 reports cities in revolt. Polyaenus, *Strat.* 8.57 mentions a pro-Seleucus party at Ephesus (τῶν σελευκιζόντων τὰ τείχη καταβαλλόντων καὶ τὰς πύλας ἀνοιγόντων).

7. Memnon *BNJ* 434 F1 5.7.

8. A battle in the plain of Corus is commemorated in the grave stele of the Bithynian noble Menas (*IIznik* 751; *IKios* 98; *SEG* 36 1149). Since the epigram celebrates Menas' smiting of men from Thrace and Mysia (both districts of Lysimachus' kingdom) the monument has been connected to the campaign of 281; see Dintsis 1986: 117 with bibliography. Bevan 1902: 1.323 and Mehl 1986: 295–296, however, suspect that the inscription may refer to a later conflict between Bithynia and Pergamon.

9. The battle of Corupedium fits Mehl's categories of "spear-won land": the enemy was defeated, the battle took place on the enemy's own territory, the conquered land was permanently occupied; see Mehl 1980–1981: 173–181. This was the argument used by his great-great-grandson Antiochus III in negotiations with Rome (Polyb. 18.51.4–6; Liv. 34.58.4–5; App. *Syr.* 6).

10. I am indebted to the discussion of these sources in Briant 1994 even if my conclusions are rather different.

11. *BNJ* 432. For discussion of Nymphis and his relationship to the Seleucid house, see Primo 2009: 109–117.

12. In two passages, *BNJ* 434 F1 7.3 and 16.3, Memnon mentions Nymphis by name; in the second he is called expressly ὁ ἱστορικός. It is unclear whether Memnon used Nymphis' local history and general history concurrently; certainly, the Heracleote history was better known in later antiquity.

13. Codex 224 of Photius' *Bibliotheca* covers the period from 364/3 to Julius Caesar. For Photius and his epitomizing method, see Desideri 1967: 367–374, who observes Photius' preference for histories of the east before Roman dominion.

14. Primo 2009: 109–117 has argued that Nymphis was one source for the stabilized encomiastic biography of Seleucus I, known as the "Seleucus Romance" (see Chapter 4).

15. Memnon *BNJ* 434 F1 8.1.

16. See Plato's definition, Pl. *Cra.* 420a: πόθος αὖ καλεῖται σημαίνων οὐ τοῦ παρόντος εἶναι ἀλλὰ τοῦ ἄλλοθί που ὄντος καὶ ἀπόντος. Whitmarsh 2011: 139–176, examining the role of *pothos* in the Greek novel, has observed that such declarations of longing create a space for narrative potentiality—an absence to be remedied, a crisis to be resolved, a journey to be undertaken.

17. Ehrenberg 1938: 54–61; Montgomery 1965: 192–203. Note the caution, to me unpersuasive, of Bosworth 1980: 62 as to whether this *pothos* goes back to Alexander.

18. See Briant 1994: 464.

19. Arr. *Anab.* 5.27.6 (the speech of Coenus on the Hyphasis river): πόθος μὲν γονέων ἐστίν . . . πόθος δὲ γυναικῶν καὶ παίδων, πόθος δὲ δὴ τῆς γῆς αὐτῆς τῆς οἰκείας. Coenus' triple use of *pothos* here has been interpreted by Ehrenberg as "an explicit and tart repartee to the king's favourite phrase" (Ehrenberg 1938: 54). For analysis of this mutiny, see Roisman 2012: 32–40.

20. Diod. Sic. 18.7.1: οἱ ἐν ταῖς ἄνω καλουμέναις σατραπείαις κατοικισθέντες Ἕλληνες ὑπ' Ἀλεξάνδρου, ποθοῦντες μὲν τὴν Ἑλληνικὴν ἀγωγὴν καὶ δίαιταν. . . .

21. E.g., Hom. *Od.* 4.596; Hdt. 1.165.3; Xen. *Anab.* 6.4.8.
22. Paus. 1.16.2.
23. For a description of the genre see Glassner 2004: 3–114 and Spek 2008: 277–287.
24. Glassner 2004: 250–252 (#33); *BCHP* 9; Del Monte 1997: 197–200. Note that a "transcription" of a cuneiform text lays out each sign, both Akkadian syllables (in *italicized* type) and Sumerian logograms (in roman type); a "normalization" of the text translates the Sumerian logograms into Akkadian words and renders the whole line into grammatical Akkadian. For example, on this tablet the word for "sea" is written in Sumerian logograms and so transcribed in roman type as "a.ab.ba" and normalized in italicized type as the Akkadian noun *tâmti*.
25. *BCHP* 1 Rev. 13: ᵏˡᵘʳ*ma-ak-ka-du-nu*, "Macedonia." The context is unclear. *BCHP* 3 Obv. 32: mu.bi ᴵ*Pi-líp-ip-i ina* ᵏᵘʳ*ma-ak-ka-du-nu ba-*[*ši?*], "That year, Philip was [present?] in Macedonia." The final verb is not clear; it may be a form of *mâtu,* "to die." In any case, Macedonia is not qualified as Philip's homeland. *BCHP* 3 Obv. 27, the Successor Chronicle, is discussed below.
26. *BCHP* 3 Obv. 27. Smith read, not egir-*šú* nu gur-*ár,* but egir-*šú-nu* gur-*ár,* "he returned after them," taking the <nu> as part of an Akkadian third-person plural pronominal suffix rather than a freestanding Sumerian logogram, meaning "not." This is a valid reading of the sign but makes little historical sense. In either case, the earlier argument is not affected. Del Monte 1997: 183 supports van der Spek's reading, which is used here.
27. *Contra* Kuhrt 2002: 24, who seems to regard the Chronicle's identification of Seleucus' foreignness as a delegitimizing step.
28. Memnon *BNJ* 434 F1 8.2; App. *Syr.* 62–63; Paus. 1.16.2; Just. *Epit.* 17.2.4.
29. Appian describes another official policy statement, concluding his account of Seleucus' transfer of his wife Stratonice to his son Antiochus with a speech (App. *Syr.* 61). Seleucus, having assembled the army (τὴν στρατιὰν συναγαγών), expounded on his achievements and the extent of his empire (κατελογίζετο μὲν αὐτοῖς τὰ ἔργα τὰ ἑαυτοῦ καὶ τὴν ἀρχήν, ὅτι δὴ μάλιστα τῶν Ἀλεξάνδρου διαδόχων ἐπὶ μήκιστον προαγάγοι) and observed the difficulties for an old man of ruling such an expansive territory (διὸ καὶ γηρῶντι ἤδη δυσκράτητον εἶναι διὰ τὸ μέγεθος). The passage shares with the Nymphis-Chronicle proclamation, proposed earlier, an official status, a focus on Seleucus' advanced age, and an explicitly spatial understanding of imperial governance.
30. Just. *Epit.* 17.1.12 observes, albeit in a criticism of Seleucus' and Lysimachus' pre-Corupedium *cupiditas imperii,* this interdependency of identity and imperialism: *quippe cum orbem terrarum duo soli tenerent, angustis sibi metis inclusi videbantur vitaeque finem non annorum spatio, sed imperii terminis metieban-tur* ("For although the two between them had the world in their hands, they felt themselves confined and restricted within narrow bounds, measuring

the terms of their lives not by the passage of years but by the extent of their empires").

31. Memnon *BNJ* 434 F1 8.3. Other, briefer accounts: Plut. *Mor.* 555b; Paus. 1.16.2, 10.19.7.

32. Grayson read *BCHP* Rev. 3–4: [. . .]^{meš} ta ^{lú}érin^{meš} [. . .]/*si-hi ana muh-hi-šú is-hu-u* [. . .^{iti}]Sig iti.bi ta u_4 [. . . kám], "the [*plural noun*] of/with the troops [. . .] revolted against him. In the month of Siwan, that very month, from the [. . .]th day. . . ." Van der Spek proposes: [. . .]^{meš} ta ^{lú}érin^{meš} [. . .]/*si-hi ana muh-hi-šú is-hu-u*[-*ma* ga]z-*šú* iti.bi ta u_4 [. . . kám], "the [general]s with th[eir?] troops rebelled against him and [*personal name*] killed him." He suggests that the passage refers to Ptolemy Ceraunus' murder of Seleucus; as he notes, it is odd that no mention is made of Antiochus' succession.

33. Ceraunus married his half-sister and Lysimachus' widow, Arsinoe (Memnon *BNJ* 434 F1 8.7); he was recognized by Pyrrhus of Epirus (Just. *Epit.* 17.2.13–15) and sought alliance with his half-brother Ptolemy II (Just. *Epit.* 17.2.9–10). It seems that even Antiochus I was obliged to make peace with, and thereby recognize, his father's murderer (Just. *Epit.* 24.1.8: *pacem cum Antiocho facit*).

34. The *Syrischer Erbfolgekrieg* (the term is from Otto 1931) or Carian War (from Tarn 1926). Despite the doubts of Grainger 2010: 76–78, Huß 2001: 261–262 n.60, and Mastrocinque 1987–1988 and 1993, which are invalidated in part by identifying the honorand of the Ilium inscription *OGIS* 219 as Antiochus I and not Antiochus III (see n.44, this chapter), it is clear that Ptolemy II gained some of his Asia Minor possessions during or shortly after the disintegration of Lysimachus' kingdom, if without major battle; see Meadows 2008 and 2012, with updated bibliography. Miletus' shift from the Seleucid to the Ptolemaic orbit is concisely expressed by the Delphinium stephanephorate lists. In *IMilet* 123; *Syll.*[3] 322 the eponymous official for 280/79 is Antiochus son of Seleucus, i.e., Antiochus I. The entry for the following year, 279/8, reads Ἀντήνωρ Ξενάρους· ἐπὶ τούτου ἐδόθη ἡ χώρα τῷ δήμῳ ὑπὸ τοῦ βασιλέως Πτολεμαίου. Ptolemy II has granted some land to Miletus, presumably from local royal estate formerly belonging to the Seleucid house. The land gift is mentioned again in Ptolemy II's letter to Miletus, *IMilet* 139; *RC* 14. By at least 278 Halicarnassus (Frost 1971) and Myndus (*SEG* 1 363) had passed into Ptolemaic hands (see Tarn 1926: 155), but perhaps even before Seleucus' death. A dated decree from Termessus, honoring the Ptolemaic governor (not, as previously thought, Pamphyliarch), Philip, son of Alexander, a Macedonian, points to Ptolemaic rule here in 280 (Robert 1966a: 53–57; Meadows and Thonemann 2013). Lycia, however, is unlikely to have been under earlier Seleucid control. Ultimately, with our present epigraphic record, it remains unclear precisely which of the Lagid conquests in Asia Minor, as given by Theoc. *Id.* 17, belong to the period before the Corupedium campaign, to the *Syrischer Erbfolgekrieg*, or to the First Syrian War.

35. Memnon *BNJ* 434 F1 9–15 describes Heraclea Pontica's alliance or coopera-
    tion with Byzantium, Chalcedon, Teos, Cieros, Mithridates of Pontus,
    Nicomedes of Bithynia, and Antigonus Gonatas. Further members, from
    evidence of posthumous Lysimachus coins, included Cyzicus, Parion, Istros,
    and Odessus (Seyrig 1958). The Northern League remained in existence for a
    long time. For example, in the mid-third century Nicomedes of Bithynia
    entrusted his young sons to Antigonus Gonatas, Ptolemy II, Byzantium,
    Heraclea Pontica, and Cius (Memnon, *BNJ* 434 F1 14.1): this shows a clear
    desire to resist Seleucid power; see Avram 2003.
36. *OGIS* 219 4–7; *Ilion* 32: ἐζήτησε τὰς μὲν πόλεις τὰς κα(τὰ) τὴν Σελευκίδα,
    περιεχομένας ὑπὸ καιρῶν δυσχερῶν διὰ τοὺς ἀποστάντας τῶν πραγμάτων, εἰς
    εἰρήνην καὶ τὴν ἀρχαίαν εὐδαιμονίαν καταστῆσαι, τοὺς δ' ἐπιθεμένους τοῖς πρά(γ)
    μασιν ἐπεξελθών. On the date of *OGIS* 219 (*Ilion* 32) see n.44, this chapter.
    Newell 1941: 51–54 identifies Series II at Carrhae and the coins of Antiochus
    I struck at Edessa as emergency issues to combat this dangerous rebellion.
    Notably, the iconography on these coins is warlike and seems to emphasize
    Antiochus' legitimacy. A one-time minting of royal bronzes at Dura-Europos
    may also belong in this context; see Bellinger 1948 and Kosmin 2011.
37. Droysen 1878: 3.256 n.1 took *OGIS* 219 7; *Ilion* 32 (τοὺς δ' ἐπιθεμένους τοῖς
    πρά(γ)μασιν ἐπεξελθών) to indicate an attack by Ptolemaic military forces. In
    his commentary (*OGIS* 219 n.7) Dittenberger disagreed. Tarn 1926: 156
    argues, I think correctly, that the inscription indicates two different groups—
    those rebelling from within the kingdom (ἀπὸ . . . τῶν πραγμάτων) and those
    attacking it from outside (ἐπὶ . . . τοῖς πράγμασιν). Jones 1993: 78 supports
    Droysen and Tarn. Note that, despite the situation in Asia Minor, Antiochus I
    remained in Syria initially.
38. Just. *Epit.* 24.4–25.2.
39. Polyaenus, *Strat.* 4.15. This passage is discussed in Chapter 6.
40. Memnon *BNJ* 434 F1 9.1 (= Patrocles *BNJ* 712 T4).
41. Just. *Epit.* 24.1.8.
42. The peace is mentioned in *IMilet* 139.
43. Memnon *BNJ* 434 F1 9.1; *contra* Mastrocinque 1993: 30, who considers this a
    summation of Antiochus I's entire reign.
44. Scholarly opinion has swung toward dating the decree to the very early years
    of Antiochus I's reign, between 278 and 274; see Ma 2002: 254–259, Jones
    1993, Strobel 1996: 245–246, Orth 1977: 61–72, and Robert 1966b: 175.
    Piejko 1991 and Mastrocinque 1983: 67 argue for a date in the reign of
    Antiochus III.
45. *OGIS* 219 2–12; *Ilion* 32; *SEG* 49 1752 trans. Jones 1993: 75, with changes.
46. Just. *Epit.* 25.1.1: *inter duos reges, Antigonum et Antiochum, statuta pace cum in
    Macedoniam Antigonus reverteretur . . .* The peace treaty may be mentioned in
    the Ilium inscription, described earlier: *OGIS* 219 13–14; *Ilion* 32: ταῖς
    πόλεσιν τὴν εἰρήνην κατεσκεύασεν.
47. Delev 2003: 113–114; Carney 2000: 179–183; Welles 1970: 478; Seibert 1967:
    33–34; Will 1966: 1.109; Tarn 1913: 168.

48. Tarn 1913: 168 n.3. Note that this placed the Antigonid-Seleucid boundary a little to the east of the pre-Philip II Macedonian-Thracian one.
49. Suda s.v. Ἄρατος.
50. The only Antigonid monarch whose activities in Thrace are in question, Philip V, targeted Aetolian and Ptolemaic interests. The Antigonid and Seleucid kingdoms never clashed over this territory, even during Antiochus III's war with Rome (see Chapter 4). Also, note that Philip V's justification for occupying Lysimachia, formerly part of the Aetolian League (Polyb. 15.23.8), specious though it may be, was not that the land belonged to his kingdom but that he was protecting the inhabitants from the Thracian barbarians (Polyb. 18.4.5–6); an inscription from Dion, with new fragments restored by Pandermalis 1981: 285–286, records Philip's treaty with the city (*SEG* 38 603).
51. Carney 2000: 183–185.
52. App. *Syr.* 6; Polyb. 18.51.4–6; Liv. 34.58.4–5.
53. Polyb. 18.51.4: εἶναι μὲν γὰρ ἐξ ἀρχῆς τὴν δυναστείαν ταύτην Λυσιμάχου, Σελεύκου δὲ πολεμήσαντος πρὸς αὐτὸν καὶ κρατήσαντος τῷ πολέμῳ πᾶσαν τὴν Λυσιμάχου βασιλείαν δορίκτητον γενέσθαι Σελεύκου. Liv. 33.40.6: *sed qua Lysimachi quondam regnum fuerit, quo victo omnia quae illius fuissent iure belli Seleuci facta sint, existimare suae dicionis esse.* For a discussion of the concept "spear-won land," see Mehl 1980–1981.
54. Grainger 1996: 342 observes that Antiochus III's reconquests in European Thrace, by not acquiring Abdera, left an unclaimed space between the Seleucid kingdom and Antigonid Macedonia. As in the Hindu Kush, he respected the territorial boundaries of Seleucid sovereignty.
55. The best surveys of this confusing period are Delev 2003 and Mihailov 1961.
56. See Avram 2003; Delev 2003: 114–117; Bagnall 1976: 159–162. The Adoulis inscription of Ptolemy III (*OGIS* 54) includes Thrace among the territories conquered from the Seleucids.
57. Polyaenus, *Strat.* 4.16.
58. *I.Bulg.* I² 388 3–5: - -]ς τεταγμέ/[νος στραταγὸς ὑπὸ τοῦ βασιλέος Ἀν]τιόχου ἐπ' Ἀ/[πολλωνιάταις . . . or, for Avram 2003, ἐπ' Ἀ/[στικῆς], a Thracian region abutting Apollonia. For the identification of king Antiochus as Antiochus II, see Mihailov (commentary on *IBulg.* I² 388) and *BE* 63 (1950) n.141, Avram 2003, and Emilov 2005: 327–328. According to Mihailov (*IBulg.* I² 350), the letter-forms better belong to the mid-third century than the early second century. The presence of Antiochus II's army at Cabyle (see later) suggests that he would have controlled the Black Sea harbors. It is supposed that the Seleucid general, though based in or near Apollonia, gave military assistance to both Apollonia and Mesambria and that the honors decreed in Mesambria were displayed in Apollonia.
59. The Seleucid bronzes, after much use, had been countermarked by the local authorities and so entered into local circulation as an approved currency alongside the locally minted coins (see Youroukova 1982; Psoma, Karadima, and Terzopoulou 2008: 227–228). It is a well-known principle in numismatic

studies that bronze coins are rarely widespread outside the frontiers of the state (*polis* or kingdom) in whose name they have been struck and entered into circulation. Emilov 2005 has claimed that a fragmentary inscription, now in the Yambol Museum, mentions Antiochus II's support for the city against the Galatian enemy (*SEG* 55 741).

60. See Nankov 2008: 41–43, with references.

61. Polyb. 5.74.4–6; Ael. *NA* 6.44.1–8; Euseb. *Chron*. I. p. 253 (ed. Schoene). Note that Just. *Epit*. 27.3.9–11, preserving a different tradition, states that Hierax was killed by bandits in Alexandria.

62. Some of Hierax' tetradrachms seem to have been struck at the Lysimachia mint; see Boehringer 1993.

63. See Grainger 1996.

64. Polyb. 18.51.7; Liv. 33.38.10, 33.40.6, 33.41.4; App. *Syr*. 1.

65. Under Antiochus II Seleucid garrisons are attested at Cypsela (Polyaenus, *Strat*. 4.16) and Apollonia (*IBulg*. I² 388); under Antiochus III at Lysimachia (Liv. 37.31.1–2), Aenos, and Maronea (Liv. 37.33.1). Antiochus III "either controlled or was allied with every Greek city from Maroneia to Byzantion" (Grainger 1996: 342). Antiochus II appointed a (regional?) governor over Apollonia, in the Gulf of Burgas on the Black Sea (*IBulg*. I² 388).

66. Polyaenus, *Strat*. 4.16.

67. *SEG* 42 661; *IBulg*. III² 1731.

68. See Zournatzi 2000 and Ebbinghaus 1999. For example, the Panagyurishte treasure is generally considered a gift, securing and manifesting loyalty, of Lysimachus to the Thracian dynast Seuthes III.

69. Psoma, Karadima, and Terzepoulou 2008: 231–238. Adaeus struck a local bronze coinage in the Apollo/tripod type of Antiochus II's Sardis mint but bearing his own (untitled) name. He was executed by a Ptolemy in the course of the Third Syrian ("Laodicean") War; see Trogus, *Prol*. 27 with Buraselis 1982: 119–151.

70. Such integration of peripheral areas under a *stratēgos*-dynast can be paralleled to the interactions of, e.g., Antiochus IV with Artaxias of Armenia, Demetrius II with Hyspaosines of Mesene, and Alexander I Balas with Jonathan of Judea; see Capdetrey 2007: 117–130.

71. Liv. 33.38.10–14: *desertam ac stratam prope omnem ruinis*.

72. Liv. 34.58.4–5; App. *Syr*. 1. The treaty between Lysimachia and a king Antiochus, who promises tax exemption and garrison-free status, probably belongs in this context (Piejko 1988b; Frisch and Taşliklioğlu 1975: 101–106). Gauthier and Ferrary 1981, pointing to Antiochus III's garrisoning of Lysimachia and the ruinous state of the city, have identified the king as Antiochus I or II.

73. App. *Syr*. 1.

74. Similarly, Philip V justified his occupation of Lysimachia in 202 as a protection against the Thracians: his troops were a guard, not a garrison (Polyb. 18.4.6).

75. App. *Syr.* 1. On this passage Gauthier and Ferrary 1981: 329 state "on ne peut douter qu'il remonte lui aussi à Polybe." Piejko 1988b: 164 considers, without argument, σίδηρον a corruption of σῖτον.

76. Bickerman 1935 compared Antiochus III's actions at Lysimachia to his "charter" for Jerusalem in 200, as reported by Joseph. *Ant.* 12.138–144. In addition to certain tax exemptions and royal sponsorship of Temple sacrifices, the Seleucid monarch promised to gather back the scattered population and rebuild the destroyed city. However, we should note that the Jerusalem community received no farming implements from the king: in this nonmarginal place Antiochus' ideologically salient actions emphasized his piety toward the Jewish God rather than his protection of urban civilization and agriculture.

77. Georges Dumézil made much of the symbolism of the plow in the construction of his *idéologie tripartie;* for detailed discussion, see Belier 1991.

78. Megasthenes *BNJ* 715 F12 = Arr. *Ind.* 7.1–9: Dionysus founded cities, taught agriculture, dispensed seeds, and introduced the plow; see Chapter 1.

79. Sachs and Wiseman 1954.

80. See Buccellati 1988.

81. Kuhrt 2002: 14–16; Del Monte 2001: 144–147 and 1997: 7–8; *Reallexikon der Assyriologie s.v.* "Hana"; Kupper 1957: 44–46. For example, the Neo-Assyrian *Sargon Geography* A, a text mapping out the quasi-mythical empire of Sargon of Akkad, identified Hana as a vast region to the distant northwest of Akkad bordering the Cedar Mountain; see Horowitz 1998: 67–95.

82. Kuhrt 2002: 25–27. There are four uses of Hana in total: for Alexander's invading troops, in the hostile Dynastic Prophecy (Grayson 1975: #3, iii 9 and 17); for Ptolemy III's army, "who do not fear the gods," in the Babylonian Chronicle describing the Third Syrian War (*BCHP* 11 Obv. 6, 11 and Rev. 7, 13); and for the land in which Seleucus is murdered, in the Babylonian King List discussed here. Our final example, the "Alexander Chronicle" (*BCHP* 1), is the most complicated due to its extremely lacunose nature and dating difficulties. It refers both to Alexander's troops as Hanaeans (Obv. 6) at a period when Darius III still seems to be alive and then to [klur]*Ma-ak-ka-du-nu,* "the land of Macedonia," (Rev. 13) for a period late in Alexander's reign, when he is recognized as legitimate king. In conversation, Paul-Alain Beaulieu has pointed to the assonance between Hana and Yavana, "Greek."

83. See Kuhrt 2002: 27.

84. The extent of Persian control of Thrace ("Skudra") has been debated. I find convincing the arguments of Balcer 1988 that Achaemenid direct rule extended to the coastal regions alone, *contra* Hammond 1980. That "Skudra" and the "Skudrians" appear in Achaemenid inscriptions and reliefs at Persis does not indicate that Thrace was a satrapy: Cameron 1973 has demonstrated (from the Elamite versions' use of the personal plural marker) that these represent ethnic groups, not provinces or satrapal organizations.

85. Antiochus II in the 250s, Antiochus Hierax in the 220s, and Antiochus III in the 190s.

86. Balcer 1988: 7 suggests that Skudrians may have formed the largest nonindigenous ethnic group in Persis. The Odrysian and Macedonian kingdoms seem to have owed much of their development to the mechanisms of secondary-state formation catalyzed by the governing structures of Persian rule (on secondary-state formation see Parkinson and Galaty 2007 and Brown 1986); it appears that the Hellenistic powers' involvement in Thrace failed to transform Thracian society as dramatically.

87. See Cohen 1995: 81–82.

88. Contrast with Antiochus I's actions in Central Asia; see Chapter 2. Mehl 1986: 318 suggests that, before his assassination, Seleucus I intended to rename Lysimachia as he had renamed Antigonia. This is plausible.

89. Plin. *HN* 5.32.151; *Tabula Peutingeriana* 11. Cohen 1995: 131 identifies the founder as Antiochus I or possibly Antiochus II.

4. Syria—Diasporic Imperialism

1. Briant 2002: 183, examining Hdt. 7.40–41.

2. Old Persian inscription DZc.

3. Edson 1958 demonstrates that the Seleucid dynasty was frequently represented from outside as Macedonian, particularly in sequence-of-empire contexts.

4. This is very prominent in the Vulgate historiographical tradition on Alexander the Great. In his own narrative account of Alexander's expedition, Ptolemy I was eager to emphasize his commitment to traditional Macedonian virtues; see Bearzot 1992.

5. Primo 2009: 29–35; Fraser 1996: 37–46.

6. Primo 2009: 33–34.

7. App. *Syr.* 56.

8. App. *Syr.* 63.

9. App. *Syr.* 63: ὅθεν οἱ Ἀργεάδαι Μακεδόνες. On Macedonian royal genealogy and myths of ancestry, see Hatzopoulos 2006: 52.

10. Hdt. 9.16.4: "What has been destined to happen by god, no man can evade by contrivance"; see, e.g., Kirchberg 1965: 30–32. Note that Hdt. 6.80 narrates the Argos-error of the mad Spartan king Cleomenes, fulfilling a Delphic oracle to conquer Argos by burning a grove of Argos instead of the *polis*.

11. App. *Syr.* 63.

12. Hdt. 3.64.4.

13. Plut. *Flam.* 20.3–4; App. *Syr.* 11.

14. Amm. Marc. 25.3.9.

15. "Argos," of course, prompts associations with Athenian tragedy and its common tragic motif of the perverted sacrifice.

16. Just. *Epit.* 11.5.4.

17. *Cypria* F17 = Paus. 4.2.7; Hyg. *Fab.* 103.

18. Hence the hero's propitiation by Alexander: Arr. *Anab.* 1.11.5.

19. Plin. *HN* 16.44.238; Quint. Smyrn. 7.408–411.

20. As often, Herodotus uses an ancient hero to unite the Persian and Trojan Wars; see Boedeker 1988: 42 and Desmond 2004: 31–33.

21. See Katz 2005.

22. Katz 2005: 71–72; Bottéro 1983: 191–192. The heavenly bodies associated with the gods Shamash (the sun) and Ishtar (the planet Venus) sank below the western horizon. Katz 2005: 78 suggests that the myth text of Ishtar/Inanna's descent to the netherworld was recited at Venus' setting.

23. Note that the north Syrian city of Antioch-by-Daphne was termed by the priest-scribes of Babylon ^{uru}an-tu-uk-ki-'a ana ugu ^{id}ma-rat, "Antioch on the shore of the *marratu*" (*AD* -155 A Upper Edge, *AD* -149 A Rev. 3–4, *AD* -143 C 6, and *BCHP* 12 Rev. 12, with Del Monte 1997: 90–91). Seleucia-in-Pieria may appear once (*AD* -149 A Rev. 6–7) as ^{uru}se-lu-ke-'-a-a $š\acute{a}$ ana muh-hi ^{kur}p[i$^?$ . . .] x x x ^{id}ma-rat-tu_4, "Seleucia which is against the land of Pi[eria$^?$] x x x the *marratu*"; see Del Monte 1997: 91–94 for this and other options.

24. George 2003: 499–500; Horowitz 1998: 93–103, 325–330. Gilgamesh, model of monarchic heroism, passed by Mount Mashu, home of the Scorpion-Men, traversed all twelve leagues of the Region of Darkness, and continued through the Grove of Gem-Bearing Stones until he reached the Alewife Siduri dwelling on Ocean's shore, from which he was ferried by Urshanabi across the "Waters of Death" *(mê mūti)* to the uncharted region where the gods had settled the flood hero Uta-napishti (Tablet 10).

25. App. *Syr.* 56; trans. H. White, with changes.

26. Just. *Epit.* 15.4.3–6.

27. Thompson 1958: Motif D1314.

28. Vilatte 1990: 9–10.

29. See the comprehensive discussion in Jones 1877. E.g., Plato's Gyges of Lydia (Pl. *Resp.* 359d–360c; see Gernet 1968: 109–112), Theseus diving for Minos' ring (Bacchyl. 17.67–90, Paus. 1.17.2–3, Hyg. *Poet. astr.* 2.5).

30. Thompson 1958: Motif D860ff. A single example will suffice: the slipping from his finger of Hadrian's seal-ring was considered an omen of his death (SHA, *Had.* 26.7).

31. The symbolic marriage of the Venetian doge to the sea was ritualized by the casting of a ring into the Adriatic; see Reinach 1906: 206–219.

32. See Rosenberger 1995.

33. E.g., Soph. *El.* 1223: Electra recognizes Orestes by their father's ring. Men. *Epit.* 503–504: the ring serves as a pledge.

34. Versnel 1977: 37.

35. Plantzos 1999.

36. Just. *Epit.* 15.4.6: *Laodice anulum Seleuco eunti cum Alexandro Magno ad Persicam militiam, edocto de origine sua, dedit.*

37. See Hdt. 1.165 on the Phocian oath and [Arist.] *Ath. Pol.* 23.5 and Plut. *Arist.* 25.1 on the Delian League oath. The ritualized throwing down of an object was used in oath-taking to confirm the absolute irreversibility of the decision

being made. For examples and discussion of such rites, see Burkert 1996: 174–175, Faraone 1993: 79 n.74, and Jacobson 1975.

38. Bing 2005, Kuttner 2005, Hunter 2004, Smith 2004, Schur 2004.
39. Kuttner 2005: 145 compares Posidippus' *lithika* to Callixenus' description of Ptolemy II's *pompē*.
40. Kuttner 2005: 144–153 and Bing 2005.
41. Bing 2005: 128–130.
42. *Milan Papyrus* AB 7.
43. *Milan Papyrus* AB 17.
44. *Milan Papyrus* AB 4.
45. *Milan Papyrus* AB 8.
46. App. *Syr.* 56; Arr. *Anab.* 7.22.
47. Although the two scenes are narrated separately by Appian, it is easily enough apparent that his *Syriaca* reproduces only an abbreviated and segmented version of the Romance.
48. Additionally, the Seleucus Romance's narrative may allude to Herodotus' famous account of the ring of Polycrates, tyrant of Samos (Hdt. 3.40–41). Having been advised by Pharaoh Amasis of Egypt to avoid the envy of the gods by casting away his most precious possession, whose loss would most grieve him, Polycrates sailed out to sea and publicly threw overboard his seal-ring. But the ring returned in the belly of a fish gifted to Polycrates by a fisherman and so condemned the unfortunate tyrant. Despite the prohibition of his prescient daughter, Polycrates sailed to Asia and was treacherously murdered by the Persian satrap Oroetes (Hdt. 3.125). Herodotus' account serves as a suitable intertext for the Seleucus Romance. In both cases, the *loss* of a ring, rather than its recovery, successfully secures rule; pain and kingship are distinctively combined. Like Polycrates, Seleucus ignored heaven-sent warnings, overambitiously crossed to the neighboring continent, and was treacherously murdered. Seleucus' ring was not, of course, returned to him, but if the ring represents home, Seleucus' crossing of the Hellespont functions as a similar kind of deadly return. Seleucus is condemned by the same narrative structure: ring composition.
49. Boyarin and Boyarin 2003: 101–107; Davies 1982: 82.
50. Graham and Khosravi 1997: 118–119.
51. According to Lib. 11.119, Antiochus III settled Aetolians, Cretans, and Euboeans in Antioch-by-Daphne. Libanius represents as an act of colonization what is self-evidently the flight and exile of pro-Seleucid political factions following Rome's victory over Antiochus III.
52. Bickerman 1944: 73. Note Bickerman's caution: "Why Seleucus placed in 311–0 the beginning of his Babylonian kingdom, we are unable to say" (76).
53. Savalli-Lestrade 2010: 58; Bickerman 1944: 74–75.
54. Sachs and Wiseman 1954. Olmstead 1937: 4 and Bickerman 1944: 75 n.11 incorrectly interpreted this calendrical synchronism as Year 7 of Alexander IV = Year 1 of Seleucus. This is impossible; see Sachs and Wiseman 1954: 205 n.1. Note that the Babylonian King List mentions only those rulers who used

the royal title and so mentions a six-year reign for the child-king Alexander IV and no reign for Antigonus; see Boiy 2000.

55. Sachs and Wiseman 1954: Obv. 9: [m]u.32.kám ¹an a šá ¹si lugal mu 20 in.ag.

56. Hallo 1984–1985: 145; Bickerman 1944: 73.

57. Porphyry *BNJ* 260 F2.2 with Grzybek 1990: 115–134; note that a calendar reform for demotic texts in 267 retrojected the regnal year. Savalli-Lestrade 2010: 57–61 contrasts the chronological choices made by Antiochus I and Ptolemy II.

58. See Hallo 1988.

59. Feeney 2007: 9–13.

60. As I saw in Yemenite manuscripts auctioned as part of the Valmadonna Trust Library at Sotheby's (New York) in 2009. The era was used by the Syriac Church until the twelfth century.

61. Hallo 1988: 175; Bickerman 1980: 71–77.

62. While Savalli-Lestrade 2010: 61, in an essay devoted to early Hellenistic dating systems, has recognized it as "vraiment révolutionnaire," more general works on ancient chronology either briefly acknowledge its importance (Feeney 2007: 139) or pass over it with scarcely a comment (Clarke 2008). For comparison, see Thonemann's thrilling 2005 exposition on the political significance of Demetrius Poliorcetes' interventions in the Athenian calendar, religious and secular.

63. See Hölbl 2001: 21–22; Grzybek 1990: 90, 96–97; Samuel 1962: 11–19. Note that demotic scribes continued to count Ptolemy I's regnal year from his assumption of the diadem. A newly discovered inscription from Caunus in Lycia (Marek 2006: #4) is dated to the fifteenth year of a king Antigonus; were this Monophthalmus and not Gonatas or Doson, it would suggest that the Diadoch began to date his rule from the death of Alexander's half-brother Philip III Arrhidaeus in 317/6.

64. The difference between a historical origin in Alexander's expedition and in 312/1 BCE is not unlike that for Roman origins between the Trojan War and the foundation of the city of Rome.

65. Daniel 8 (prophecy of the goat and ram) and 11 (the prophecy of kings); 1 Macc. 1:1. Portier-Young 2011 has demonstrated that one of the functions of Jewish apocalyptic literature of the Hellenistic period was to assert that God, not the Gentile king, was the master of time.

66. See Edson 1958.

67. See Gell 1992: 23–29.

68. App. *Syr.* 63.

69. According to Ctesias, eunuchs were entrusted with the conveying of deceased Achaemenid kings back to the Persian heartland (*Pers.* 9, 13); see Briant 2002: 275. Philetaerus conforms to this traditionally sanctioned role.

70. Arr. *Anab.* 3.22.6; Just. *Epit.* 11.15.15; see Kosmin 2013a: 674–675.

71. Erskine 2002; Badian 1968: 186–188; Schubert 1914: 180–189. Alexander's entombment in Alexandria, to be joined by Ptolemy and his descendants, cast the new dynasty of Egypt as Alexander's successors; Theocritus'

encomium to Ptolemy II Philadelphus seats the deceased Ptolemy I Soter beside Alexander (*Id.* 17.18), echoing on Olympus the physical juxtaposition in the Alexandrian royal mausoleum.

72. Hdt. 1.214; Ctesias *Pers.* 9.

73. A large, early Hellenistic, Doric peripteral (6 by 12) temple at Seleucia-in-Pieria has been identified as the Nicatorium. The temple-tomb, located on a spur of the southern Amanus, dominated the sea entrance to Seleucia-in-Pieria to the immediate northwest and overlooked the Orontes delta to the south. Beneath the cella a flight of steps leads to a wide adyton, now too overgrown to be entered. This feature is typically associated with heroa, like the two at the Seleucid colony of Aï Khanoum in northeastern Bactria; Canepa 2010, with caution, and Hannestad and Potts 1990: 116. There is no evidence of postconstruction expansion or additions. The preservation was too slight and the excavation too hasty for anything more to be concluded.

74. It has been proposed by Praschniker and others that the Belevi Mausoleum in western Asia Minor was the final resting place of king Antiochus II Theos, who died in nearby Ephesus in 246 (Praschniker and Theuer 1979: 109–120). This is certainly a possibility. However, it should be emphasized that the tomb's architectural scheme and decorative motifs date to the last third of the fourth century. If the mausoleum did indeed house the remains of Antiochus II, this was a secondary reuse of a monument originally intended for a regional Big Man, perhaps Darius III's admiral Memnon of Rhodes, Alexander's Lydian satrap Menander, or, at a stretch, king Lysimachus (Praschniker and Theuer 1979: 118–119). Accordingly, the form and location of the Belevi Mausoleum cannot be taken as evidence of regular Seleucid royal burial. The exceptional political context of the Third Syrian War—rival courts at Ephesus and Antioch-by-Daphne polarized around the divorced queen Laodice and her successor, queen Berenice, respectively; Ptolemy III's invasion and occupation of northern Syria—would have militated against the conveyance of Antiochus II's body to Antioch or Seleucia-in-Pieria.

75. Polyb. 31.9.3; Porphyry *BNJ* 260 F56. Tabae has been identified with Gabae (Isfahan) or at least placed in its vicinity (Mørkholm 1966: 171 n.17). Gera and Horowitz 1997: 250 n.71 prefer a location in Media, near Ecbatana. For a full discussion, see Schmitt 2000.

76. 2 Macc. 9:29.

77. *AD* -163 C$_2$ 17–18: . . .lú$^{me\check{s}}$ *it-t]i* adda *šá* lugal gin$^{me\check{s}}$-*ni it-ti* [. . .]/ . . .]-*sa-at šá* ^{I}an a *šá* ^{I}an $^{he-pí}$ *ina* [. . .], "those who] came [wit]h the corpse of the king, with [. . .]/which Antiochus (V/IV) the son of Antiochus (IV/III) "BROKEN" in [. . .]." Note that "BROKEN" $^{(he-pí)}$ indicates that the diary's source tablet was damaged at this point.

78. 1 Macc. 6:55–63; 2 Macc. 13:23–26; Joseph. *Ant.* 12.379–386.

79. Antiochus VII's body had been embalmed. Similarly, in the Astronomical Diary quoted earlier, adda, the Sumerian logogram for Akkadian *pagru*

("corpse"), indicates that Antiochus IV had not been cremated. Although it is possible that royal Seleucid funerary practices had shifted from cremation to inhumation, in both these cases local Persian custom may have determined the treatment of the kings' bodies.

80. Just. *Epit.* 39.1.6.

81. Tuan 1974.

82. For discussion of each settlement, see Cohen 2006.

83. Attested from the settlements Seleucia-in-Pieria, Antioch-in-Pieria, Heraclea-in-Pieria, and, perhaps, the Babylonian Astronomical Diary *AD* -149 A Rev. 6–7, which locates Seleucia-in-Pieria *ana muh-hi* ᵏᵘʳ*p*[i? . . .], "against the land of Pi[eria?]."

84. The appellation "Axios" for the Orontes is attested by Apamea's quasi-municipal coins, dating to the reign of Antiochus IV, the fifth-century ecclesiastical historian Sozomen. 7.15, and the modern Arabic name for the river, Nahr al-Asi; see Cohen 2006: 99–100; Hollis 1994: 158; Honigmann and Schmitt 1939.

85. For example, Frézouls 1977: 226 has suggested that Syrian Megara derives from a simple Hellenization of Semitic Ma'ara and Pella from Pihil.

86. The Seleucis is twice mentioned in third-century epigraphy, *OGIS* 219 4–5 and *OGIS* 229 1 and 12. A second-century inscription from Delos, *ID* 1544, honors king Demetrius I or II's satrap of the Seleucis (σατράπης [ἐπὶ τῆς Σελ]ευκίδος). In a lengthy discussion, Musti 1966: 61–81 claimed that "Seleucis" was the name for Seleucus I's entire imperial territory before the battle of Corupedium on the basis of two pieces of evidence: (i) third-century CE coins of Nicopolis, which Musti places in Cilicia, located the city in the Seleucis (Νεικοπολειτῶν Σελευκίδος); (ii) App. *Syr.* 55 reports that among the territories Seleucus I acquired was "so-called Seleucid Cappadocia" (Καππαδοκίας τῆς Σελευκίδος λεγομένης). The argument does not hold: (i) Nicopolis, often confused with Issus, was located in Syria, not Cilicia (Ptol. *Geog.* 5.7.4; Strabo 14.5.19; *CIL* III Suppl. 1, 6703); the coins are evidence of the traditional understanding of the Seleucis as northern Syria; (ii) Seleucus never occupied all of Cappadocia; Appian's adjective merely distinguishes the part incorporated into the Seleucid kingdom from that which retained its independence.

87. The dynastic toponyms will be discussed in Chapter 7.

88. Cohen 2006: 26.

89. A possible exception is Antioch-in-Mygdonia, formerly Nisibis; see Cohen 2013: 62–67.

90. Capdetrey 2007: 62–65; Sève-Martinez 2003: 233; Musti 1966: 91–92; Bickerman 1938: 79; Rostovtzeff 1941: 1.479.

91. Leonard 2001. The Syrian situation is even more striking: in contrast to these immigrant populations in California, the Syrian landscape had been known for centuries to Greek traders and mercenaries, who had no doubt made use of the well-developed local toponymy; see Lane Fox 2008.

92. Grainger 1990: 31–42.

93. Diod. Sic. 33.4a; see Grainger 1990: 39. We should not necessarily accept this claim as genuine fact. Of course, the logic can be reversed: a variegated population of settlers gradually unifying their identity around their town's Old World homonym. Nonetheless, Diodorus' account demonstrates that such popular onomastic practices were conceivable.

94. Eustathius on Dionysius Periegetes 918: ποτὲ μὲν κώμη οὖσα καὶ Φαρνάκη καλουμένη.

95. Strabo 16.2.10: ἐκαλεῖτο δὲ καὶ Πέλλα τοτὲ ὑπὸ τῶν πρώτων Μακεδόνων.

96. Steph. Byz. s.v. Ὠρωπός claims that Seleucus Nicator was born at Oropos in Macedonia. But there was no Oropos in Macedonia; the Macedonian town Europus must be meant (see Grainger 1990: 4–5; Kosmin 2011: 98–99).

97. Goldschmidt 2000.

98. The Gurob Papyrus of the Third Syrian War (*BNJ* 160) records an official and propagandistic Ptolemaic narrative, in the king's own voice, of Ptolemy III Euergetes' unopposed arrival and warm reception in Seleucia-in-Pieria; see Chapter 6.

99. Polyb. 5.58.4.

100. Brown 1961 proposed that Polybius' source for this speech, as well as for his earlier account of the fall of overweening Hermias and for the geographical description of Seleucia-in-Pieria, was a historical work composed by Apollophanes himself; see also Primo 2009: 48.

101. Marinoni 1972: 594–595 places particular emphasis on Apollophanes' use of sacral language here.

102. App. *Syr.* 56. Appian sandwiches the miracle between Seleucus' consulting Apollo's oracle at Didyma in 334 and his mother's dream before his birth.

103. Paus. 1.16.1.

104. On the identification of this king Antiochus, see Ehling 2008: 77–80 and Wilcken 1894.

105. Antiochus VIII Grypus married Cleopatra Tryphaena; Antiochus IX Cyzicenus married Cleopatra IV—both Cleopatras were younger sisters of Ptolemy X Alexander.

106. *OGIS* 257 11–16; *RC* 71.

107. Wilhelm 1898: 213–214 persuasively argues that a reference to local, civic patriotism (i.e., the Seleucians devotion to their own homeland) would have been "überflüssig, ja unpassend" in this context, *contra* Paton 1890: 283. In the Hellenistic kingdoms such proclamations of citizens' loyalty were figured as *eunoia* directed toward the rulers and their house. See Muccioli 2006b, which compares this inscription to Cleopatra VII's adoption of the epithet *philopatris*.

108. Polyb. 2.71.4, 5.34.6, 10.40.7, 28.1.3, 28.20.6, 28.20.7, 31.11.8, 39.8.5; Posidonius 87 F29 = Ath. 8.333b; App. *Syr.*; Ath. 5.211a (see Braund 2000); Joseph. *AJ* 13.253, 13.270; Vell. Pat. 1.10. Also epigraphic: see, e.g., the Greek translation of the Roman piracy law of 101 (*IDelphes* III 4, 37; *IKnidos* 31; *SEG* 51 1517), mentioning τοὺς βασιλεῖς τοὺς ἐν Συρίᾳ βασιλεύοντ[ας.

109. Bickerman 1938: 4–6.

110. Ma 2002: 8.

111. *IMilet* 422; *SEG* 37 992; see Herrmann 1987: 183–185 and Chaniotis 1987.
112. The book consciously resembles Samuel and Kings. Based on the syntax and evidence of mistranslations it is generally accepted that the original was written in Hebrew; see Williams 1999: 1–2 and Dancy 1954: 1–4.
113. 1 Macc. 1:24, 13:24.
114. 1 Macc. 10:55, 10:67.
115. 1 Macc. 10:52, 15:4.
116. Daniel 11:5–6, 8–9, 11, 13–15, 25, 40.
117. Eißfeldt 1932: 30–48 and Seyrig 1939: 296.
118. Daniel 10–12 is generally recognized as a *vaticinium ex eventu,* a description of past and present events in the form of an earlier prophecy, in order to authorize these claims as divinely revealed; see Millar 1997: 96–98. Since Porphyry, it has generally been agreed that the author of Daniel 10–12 wrote between 168 and 164, i.e., after Antiochus IV's second campaign against Egypt and before his death in Persia.
119. Kosmin 2014c.
120. Kuhrt and Sherwin-White 1991.
121. Esagil is the Sumerian name for Bel-Marduk's temple in Babylon, Ezida for Nabû's temple in Borsippa.
122. Borsippa Cylinder 1.1–6.
123. On the reigning king's "heroic priority" in Mesopotamian royal discourse, see Tadmor 1999: 56.
124. *Contra* Sève-Martinez 2003: 234; Ma 2003: 189; Briant 1994: 461–463; Kuhrt and Sherwin-White 1991; Bickerman 1938: 7. It is clear that *Makkadunaya* refers to Seleucus and not Antiochus. The ethnic label lies between Seleucus' name and the bound-form title *šar Bābili* ("king of Babylon"), which has already been used for Antiochus.
125. Borsippa Cylinder 1.6–13.
126. Zadok 1985: 157; *Reallexikon der Assyriologie* iv.2/3 *s.v.* "Hatti"; Kuhrt and Sherwin-White 1991: 72.
127. Borsippa Cylinder 2.26; see Kosmin 2014c.
128. Grainger 1997: 105 s.v. Menippos.
129. *IG* XI.4 1111; *OGIS* 239.
130. I am grateful to Aneurin Ellis-Evans for observing, in correspondence, that the similar and roughly contemporary dedication to Antiochus III from Pergamum (*OGIS* 240; *IPerg* 182) does not use the Macedonian ethnic; see also Bielfeldt 2010: 144 n.89.
131. See Badian 1959.
132. Mehl 1980–1981.
133. For discussion of Antiochus' route, see Grainger 2002: 195.
134. Liv. 35.47.
135. Liv. 36.8.3–4; App. *Syr.* 16.
136. App. *Syr.* 13.
137. The bibliography on Hellenistic euergetism is extensive: see, e.g., Gauthier 1985. Bringmann and von Steuben 1995 fully catalog known Hellenistic

royal benefactions. For sophisticated anthropological treatments of formal gift-giving, see Mauss 1954 and Godelier 1999.

138. For summary, see Habicht 1989 (reprinted in English as Habicht 2006: 155–173).

139. Phylarchus *FGrHist* 81 F 29 = Ath. 6.254f-255a; see Primo 2009: 118–121.

140. Bringmann and von Steuben 1995 #20. Alexis, *Pyranos,* F 204; Philemon, *Neaira,* F 47 (Kassel and Austin) Habicht 1989: 7 argues that, since Alexis speaks of a tiger (ὁ Σελεύκου τίγρις) and Philemon of a tigress (τὴν τίγριν, see earlier), Seleucus sent a pair.

141. Note that Megasthenes had described a tame Prasian tiger (*BNJ* 715 F21a = Strabo 15.1.37).

142. Philemon, *Neaira,* F 47 (Kassel and Austin).

143. Robert Cioffi, expert on faunal exotica, has suggested that the *trugeranos* should be understood as a (fictional) hybrid bird, half *trugōn* (turtledove) and half *geranos* (crane).

144. Polyb. 26.1.10–11; Liv. 41.20.5–9.

145. Bringmann and von Steuben 1995 #24. Liv. 41.20.8; Gran. Lic. 28.11; Vell. 1.10.1; Polyb. 26.1.11; Vitr. 7.pref.15.7; Strabo 9.1.17; Anth. Pal. 9.701f.

146. Liv. 41.20.6. Bringmann and von Steuben 1995 #55.

147. Liv. 41.20.6. Bringmann and von Steuben 1995 #56. Tegea, an Arcadian *polis* of limited importance, is a surprising recipient of royal benefaction. Perhaps Antiochus IV was honoring the birthplace of Telephus, mythic ancestor of his Pergamene allies.

148. Liv. 41.20.7. Bringmann and von Steuben 1995 #240.

149. Bringmann and von Steuben 1995 #283; see Herrmann 1965b.

150. Paus. 5.12.4. Bringmann and von Steuben 1995 #23. Callaghan 1981 identifies the king as Epiphanes' father, Antiochus III.

151. Paus. 5.12.4. Bringmann and von Steuben 1995 #60. It has been suggested by Olympia's excavators that this παραπέτασμα was the sacred curtain looted by Antiochus IV from the Temple in Jerusalem in 167; see Pelletier 1955. Although the hypothesis will remain unverifiable, the reconstruction coheres with the king's cultural crusading in Judea, where he rededicated the Jerusalem Temple to Zeus Olympius.

152. Gruen 2000 has identified behind the second-century *Kulturpolitik* of the Attalid kings of Pergamum a not too dissimilar desire to overcome parvenu status and humble origins.

153. See, e.g., Gupta and Ferguson 1992: 9–13.

154. On Mimic Men, where to be Anglicized is not the same thing as to be English, see Bhabha 1994: 85–92.

Interlude—The Kingdom of Asia

1. Diod. Sic. 21.1.5; Polyb. 5.67.8, 28.20.7; App. *Syr.* 55; Paus. 1.6.8; Plut. *Demetr.* 30.1. For a short time, Tyre and Sidon remained in the hands of Demetrius Poliorcetes.

2. See, e.g., the arguments of Antiochus IV to the Greek ambassadors in the Sixth Syrian War (Polyb. 28.20.6).

3. Strabo 16.2.12; see Grainger 2010: 45; Gera 1998: 3–10; Bagnall 1976: 11–13; Seyrig 1950: 31–35. Like Demodamas' altar, the Eleutherus riverbank was marked with a successive imperial epigraphy of great conquerors: Ramses II, Esarhaddon, Nebuchadnezzar II, an unknown Hellenistic ruler, Caracalla, Sultan Barquq, and Napoleon III; see Maila Afeiche 2009. A dedication in the name of Ptolemy IV, found near the river, reasserted the Ptolemaic border following the Egyptian victory over Antiochus III at Raphia (*SEG* 38 1571; Salamé-Sarkis 1986).

4. Duyrat 2005. For example, according to Strabo 16.2.14, Aradus was allowed to profit from receiving the kingdom's exiles during the War of the Brothers; see Rigsby 1996: 11.

5. For Ptolemy II, see Davesne and Yenisoğancı 1992 and Winnicki 1991; for Ptolemy III, see Chapter 6.

6. Polyb. 5.58.10, 5.60.1. For Ras Ibn Hani, see Cohen 2006: 124–126 and Rey-Coquais 1978.

7. See, e.g., the Heliodorus stele (Cotton and Wörrle 2007; Jones 2009; *SEG* 57 1838).

8. Houghton, Lorber, and Hoover 2008: xviii–xx; Aperghis 2004: 233–234. A privileged site for understanding the transition from Ptolemaic to Seleucid rule is the Persian and Hellenistic administrative building (PHAB) at Tel Kedesh, located near the Hula valley in northern Israel; see Herbert and Berlin 2003.

9. Grainger 2010: 337–402; Van 't Dack et al. 1989. The defunct Eleutherus frontier still was recognized by Jonathan (1 Macc. 11:7, 12:30) and Antony (Joseph. *AJ* 15.95).

10. Theoc. *Id.* 17.86.

11. *OGIS* 54. In lines 6–8 Ptolemy III lists the provinces inherited from his father (Egypt, Libya, Syria, Phoenicia, Cyprus, Lycia, Caria, and the Cyclades islands) and in lines 13–20 those won by his own conquest or subordinate to his rule (the lands this side of the Euphrates, Cilicia, Pamphylia, Ionia, the Hellespont, Thrace, Mesopotamia, Babylonia, Persis, Media, and the lands up to Bactriane).

12. Bickerman 1938: 3–7. Bickerman contrasts the "personal" monarchies of the Seleucid and Ptolemaic houses, where the imperial territories supposedly found no coherence outside the person of the monarch, with the "national" Macedonian monarchy of the Antigonids.

13. See Horowitz 1988 and 1998: 96–105, 325–330. The most important sources are the so-called *Babylonian Map of the World,* the *Bilingual Creation of the World,* (Standard Babylonian) *Gilgamesh* tablet 10, and the *Sargon Geography.*

14. Horowitz 1988: 156 observes that the term *marratu* is written with the determinative [id], used to designate rivers and canals; the *Babylonian Map of the World* avoids *tâmtu,* "sea." [id]*marratu* is eminently suitable for a geographical boundary that would include the Oxus river and the Caucasian canal.

15. *AD* –155 A Upper Edge; *AD* –149 A Rev. 3–4; *AD* –143 C 6; *BCHP* 12 Rev. 12; see Del Monte 1997: 90–91.

16. Muccioli 2004 and 2006a.

17. Fredricksmeyer 2000: 137.

18. E.g., Xen. *Hell.* 3.5.13; Aristobulus *BNJ* 139 F51b = Strabo 15.3.7 reports that the epitaph on Cyrus' tomb at Pasargadae called him "king of Asia"; Arr. *Anab.* 3.25.3 narrates that Bessus, in the autumn of 330, assumed the upright tiara and called himself "king of Asia."

19. In an *anagoreusis* ceremony held shortly after his victory at Gaugamela (331), Alexander sacrificed to the gods, bestowed gifts on his friends, guaranteed the freedom of the Greeks, and was publicly proclaimed "king of Asia" (Plut. *Al.* 34.1); see Muccioli 2004: 109–111 and Fredricksmeyer 2000. Goukowsky 1978: 1.175 has unpersuasively relocated this episode to 324. The Lindos Chronicle (*BNJ* 532 F2 §38) records a dedication from Alexander "lord of Asia" (βασιλεὺς Ἀλέ[ξ]ανδρος . . . κύριος γε[ν]όμενος τᾶς Ἀσίας). According to Curt. 6.6.6 Alexander adopted Darius' signet ring for dispatches in Asia, while retaining his own for dispatches in Europe.

20. Antigonus Monophthalmus was appointed στρατηγὸς τῆς Ἀσίας at the settlement of Triparadisus in 321; Eumenes was appointed στρατηγὸς αὐτοκράτωρ τῆς Ἀσίας by Polyperchon in 318. Antipater, appointed στρατηγὸς τῆς Εὐρώπης by Alexander in 334, was succeeded by Polyperchon in 319 and his rival Cassander in 317. For full details, see Bengtson 1937–1952: 1.94–127.

21. Smith 1994.

22. Polyb. 5.67.10; Joseph. *AJ* 12.119, 13.119; App. *Syr.* 1, 12, 60; Tertull. *De an.* 46.6; Malalas 8.198.

23. Ath. 11.500d; Strabo 15.1.11; Ael. *NA* 17.17; see Tarn 1951: 55, 153.

24. App. *Syr.* 1: Ἑλλησποντίους ἐπῄει καὶ Αἰολέας καὶ Ἴωνας ὡς οἷ προσήκοντας ἄρχοντι τῆς Ἀσίας, ὅτι καὶ πάλαι τῶν τῆς Ἀσίας βασιλέων ὑπήκουον; see also Polyb. 18.40a, 51.

25. *IEOG* 103; *OGIS* 253; *SEG* 36 1274. The doubts of Sherwin-White 1982: 65–66 over provenance have been partially answered by a recently discovered Babylonian Chronicle fragment; see Spek 2009: 107–108.

26. Nock 1972: 720–735.

27. Joseph. *AJ* 13.113; also 1 Macc. 11:13 (καὶ εἰσῆλθε Πτολεμαῖος εἰς Ἀντιόχειαν καὶ περιέθετο τὸ διάδημα τῆς Ἀσιάς).

28. Ptolemy VI even introduced a double regnal era, adding a separate Seleucid count to his Ptolemaic one; see Chauveau 1990.

29. 1 Macc. 13:32.

30. 1 Macc. 8:6, 11:13, 12:39, 13:32; 2 Macc. 3:3; 4 Macc. 3:20; Joseph. *AJ* 12.119, 13.119.

31. A fragment of Berossus' *Babyloniaca* (*BNJ* 680 F9a = Joseph. *Ap,* 1.145), an autoethnographic history of Babylonia written in Greek and dedicated to Antiochus I (see Kosmin 2013d), calls Cyrus the Great "king of Asia."

32. Roman rhetoric depicted a vainglorious Antiochus III as a new Xerxes, attempting to extend his vast Asian empire into Europe. This association was reinforced by armed conflict at Thermopylae and in the maritime terms of the Peace of Apamea (see Part III). Note that, if Catullus 66 accurately renders the geopolitical terminology of Callimachus' *Coma Berenices*, then we may see in the line *is haud in tempore longo / captam Asiam Aegpti finibus addiderat* (35–36) a Ptolemaic redeploying of the Seleucid concept of Asia.

33. Certeau 1984: 117.

5. Arrivals and Departures

1. The Romans-Daniel 11: 30.
2. Walbank 1957–1979: 3.405 argues that Laenas was clutching a *vitis* (Polybius: κλῆμα) rather than a mere traveler's walking stick.
3. Classical tradition: Polyb. 29.27.1–10; Liv. 45.12.3–8; Diod. Sic. 31.2; App. *Syr.* 66; Just. *Epit.* 34.3.1–4; Cic. *Phil.* 8.23; Vell. Pat. 1.10.1; Val. Max. 6.4.3; Porphyry *BNJ* 260 F50 = Jer. *in Dan.* 11:29–30; Plut. *Mor.* 202f; Jewish tradition: Daniel 11:30; Egyptian tradition: prophecy of *Hor* (see Ray 1976: 14–20).
4. Polyb. 3.3.8.
5. E.g., Will 1966: 2.320–325; Briscoe 1969: 49. Note the caution of Morgan 1990.
6. Circle tracing was a widespread technique of ancient magic used for, among other things, protection against demons, thaumaturgy, rain magic, and debt obligations; see Goldin 1963 and Cameron 1928.
7. App. *Syr.* 45; Jerome, *in Dan.* 11:21. 2 Macc. 3:37–40 hints at the murder.
8. Polyb. 31.11.
9. App. *Syr.* 45; note that by the time of the Athenian decree (immediately below) statues of Antiochus (IV) already stand in the agora.
10. *OGIS* 248; *IPerg* 160; *SEG* 15 757. Fränkel 1890–1895: 160, *editor princeps*, proposed that the decree was passed by the citizens of Antioch-by-Daphne. Holleaux 1900 demonstrated that this was impossible for a number of reasons and identified the decree as Athenian.
11. *OGIS* 248 9–23; *IPerg* 160; trans. Austin 2006: 370, with changes.
12. Turner 1969: 94–95.
13. For discussion of diadem ritual, see Ritter 1965: 132–134.
14. Zambelli 1960: 377–380 has suggested that Antiochus Epiphanes' accession was celebrated by annual *charisteria* festivals: the cuneiform Hellenistic King List from Babylon (Sachs and Wiseman 1954: Rev. 9–10) reports that Seleucus IV died in Ulûlu 137 SE = September 175 BCE; the honorific inscription erected by Philip in Babylonia (*OGIS* 253), quoted in the Interlude, mentions *charisteria* celebrations during the Macedonian calendar month Hyperberetaios, which corresponds to the Babylonian Ulûlu. Despite the attractions of this hypothesis, the King List is confused about Antiochus

IV's accession and cannot be used in this way: not only does it suggest that
Seleucus IV died a natural death (Sumerian nam.gar) and that Antiochus IV
was Seleucus IV's son rather than younger brother, but also the cuneiform
signs (Rev. 9: *ana* igi) may mean that Antiochus's reign began either "before"
(reading *ana* igi as *ina mahri*) Ulûlu or, more plausibly, that the lemma
needed "to be checked" (reading *ina* igi as *ina amāri*).

15. This reconstruction derives from Bevan 1902: 2.126; it has been supported by
Will 1966: 2.305–306, Zambelli 1960: 365–371, and Mørkholm 1966: 43–50
contra Aymard 1953.

16. For full historical discussion, see Volkmann 1925: 380–391 and Ehling 2008:
122–130.

17. Polyb. 31.11–15. Walbank 1957–1979: 3.478 has observed that Polybius' use
of the present tense in relation to Carthage at 31.12.12 indicates a composition before 146; Polybius probably wrote his account soon after the events
took place.

18. Zonaras 9.25.

19. 2 Macc. 14:1; Zonaras 9.25; Joseph. *AJ* 12.389; Justin. *Epit.* 34.3.9; Porphyry
BNJ 260 F32, 14; 1 Macc 7:1 has for Tripolis only a "seaside town" (πόλιν
παραθαλασσίαν).

20. Joseph. *AJ* 12.389.

21. Although the intrigue at Rome demanded secrecy and obfuscation, it is
worth noting that Demetrius' silent and anonymous travel are entirely
characteristic of *rites de passage*'s intermediate, transitional stage; see Turner
1969: 106–107.

22. 1 Macc. 7:1.

23. 1 Macc. 10:1 (κατελάβετο Πτολεμαΐδα, καὶ ἐπεδέξαντο αὐτόν, καὶ ἐβασίλευσεν
ἐκεῖ); Joseph. *AJ.* 13.35; Diod. Sic. 31.32a. In fact, Alexander I Balas made
two journeys into the Seleucid kingdom. First, Attalus II placed the young
Alexander under the care of Zenophanes, a local dynast in Rough Cilicia;
Diod. Sic. 31.32a reports that, like Eumenes II for Antiochus IV, Attalus
crowned Alexander Balas with the diadem. Second, Alexander sailed for
Antioch-in-Ptolemaïs, from where his reign began. For full discussion, see
Volkmann 1925: 403–412 and Ehling 2008: 145–153.

24. 1 Macc. 10:67, Joseph. *AJ* 13.86. For full discussion, see Ehling 2008:
154–164.

25. 1 Macc. 15:10; Joseph. *AJ* 13.222 (πέμπει πρὸς αὐτὸν Κλεοπάτρα, καλοῦσα
πρὸς αὑτὴν ἐπί τε γάμῳ καὶ βασιλείᾳ). For full discussion, see Ehling 2008:
185–189. Note that the letter sent by Antiochus Sidetes, while still based in
Rhodes, to Simon in 1 Macc. 15:2–9 suggests that the Seleucid prince had
taken the royal title before landing in Syria. This is possible but cannot be
trusted: the letter lists a series of privileges and grants, including tax
remission and the right to mint coins, for which the Jewish Chronicler would
have wished to give as great an authority as possible.

26. Joseph. *AJ* 13.272. For discussion, see Ehling 2008: 217.

27. Joseph. *AJ* 13.370; see Ehling 2008: 234–240, who notes that although Demetrius III established himself at Damascus, which he renamed Demetrias, he took the diadem immediately upon his arrival at the Syrian coast.
28. Joseph. *AJ* 13.367: Ἀντίοχος ὁ Εὐσεβὴς καλούμενος παραγενηθεὶς εἰς Ἄραδον καὶ περιθέμενος διάδημα.
29. App. *Syr.* 49; Justin. *Epit.* 40.2.2. Antiochus XIII's unfortunate sojourn in Sicily, on his journey from Rome to Syria, is vividly described in Cic. *Verr.* 2.4.61–68; see Downey 1951.
30. On the reification of the state as a tangible object by way of its material effects, see Harvey 2009: 260–283.
31. Plut. *Demetr.* 31.2; Just. *Epit.* 15.4.23–24; Paus. 1.9.6.
32. See *OGIS* 10; *IEph* 1453, where the marriage is reported in celebration to Ephesus.
33. Plut. *Demetr.* 32.1–3; trans. Perrin, with changes. Malalas 8.98, writing more than seven centuries later, also records Seleucus meeting Demetrius Poliorcetes and Stratonice at Rhosus but represents them as hiding in the city (ἥντινα ηὗρεν ὁ Σέλευκος ἐν Ῥώσῳ κρυπτομένην μετὰ Δημητρίου τοῦ πατρὸς αὐτῆς).
34. It is possible that Rhosus was refounded by Seleucus I as Seleucia-on-the-Bay-of-Issus, perhaps in commemoration of the festivities and marriage that took place there; see Cohen 2006: 136–139.
35. *PCairoZen* II 5925.
36. Joseph. *AJ* 13.82; 1 Macc. 10:57–58 (quotation from 58).
37. 1 Macc. 10:60; Joseph. *AJ* 13.83.
38. Joseph. *AJ* 13.83.
39. Liv. 35.13.4: *Antiochus rex, ea hieme Raphiae in Phoenice Ptolemaeo regi Aegypti filia in matrimonium data. . . .*
40. Polyb. 11.34.11.
41. Thapar 1961: 197–217.
42. Polyb. 20.8; Liv. 36.11.1–2, 36.17.7; Plut. *Phil.* 17.1; Plut. *Flam.* 16.1–2; App. *Syr.* 16; Diod. Sic. 29.2 (locating the episode, in error, at Demetrias).
43. Seibert 1967: 60–61; Schmitt 1964: 11–12; Bickerman 1938: 25; Will 1966: 2.204–206.
44. See Kosmin 2014a.
45. Liv. 36.5–11; see Grainger 2002: 220. Walbank 1957–1979: 3.76 suggests that the episode may be modeled on the legend of Hannibal's stay in Capua.
46. Polyb. 5.43; see Seibert 1967: 60.
47. *Ilasos* 4; *OGIS* 237; Ma #26. For bibliography and discussion, see Ma 2002: 196–198, 329–335.
48. The establishment of the cult is known from three inscriptions: from Nehavend (*IGIAC* 66–67; *IEOG* 277–278; *SEG* 50 1387) and Kermanshah (*IGIAC* 68; *IEOG* 271–272) in Iran and from Phrygia (*OGIS* 224; *RC* 36–37; *SEG* 50 1103); see Robert 1949: 5–22.
49. *AD* -181 Rev. 7–12.

50. *SEG* 7.2; *IGIAC* 14; *IEOG* 191; see Robert 1949: 25–29. Grainger 2002: 219 n.30 unjustly doubts the restoration, which is based on well-known formulae used at Susa, and presumes that Laodice was dead by the time of the new marriage. For resolving a possible contradiction between the Astronomical Diary and Susan manumission, see Savalli-Lestrade 2005b.
51. Bickerman 1938: 24.
52. Robert 1949: 25–29, supported by Aymard 1949: 327–339.
53. For the identification of Antiochus III as a new Xerxes, see Plut. *Comp. Cat. Mai. et Arist.* The Seleucid court, in its turn, seems to have represented the conflict with Rome as a renewed Trojan War; see Primo 2009: 93–94 on Hegesianax' *Troica*.
54. Arr. *Anab.* 4.19; Curt. 8.4.23–30; Plut. *Alex.* 47. Both episodes turn on the political unimportance of the bride, her youth and unsurpassed beauty, and the criticisms the marriage provoked.
55. Polyb 20.8.2; App. *Syr.* 20: Antiochus returned to Ephesus μετ' Εὐβοίας τῆς νεογάμου (τοῦτο γὰρ αὐτὴν ὠνόμαζεν).
56. *LIMC* s.v. "Chalkis and Euboia"; Picard 1979: 168–171; Wallace 1956. A nymph Euboea appears in myth as the daughter of Boeotian Asopus, pursued by Poseidon, and rooted in the sea (Diod. Sic. 4.72; Nonnus, *Dion.* 42.411; Eust. *Il.* 2.536–537; [Scymnus] 567–570).
57. *ARV*² 1243, 58; *LIMC* s.v. "Euboia II."
58. Root 1979: 131–161.
59. In 211, Marcellus opened his triumph with an allegorical painting of Syracuse made prisoner (Liv. 26.21); in 187 M. Fulvius Nobilior displayed a similar image of Ambracia (Liv. 38.43.9).
60. For photographs, descriptions, and commentary, see Smith 1987. Other examples include: a cycle of conquered peoples in the Porticus ad Nationes (Plin. *HN* 36.5.39); Scipio Asiaticus, the Roman victor over Antiochus III, paraded 134 *oppidorum simulacra* in his triumphal procession of 188 (Liv. 37.59.3); a set was carried in Augustus' funerary procession and perhaps displayed afterward (Dio Cass. 56.34.2; Tac. *Ann.* 1.8.4).
61. Eupolis, *Poleis* F246 (Kassel and Austin).
62. Rosen 1997: 154.
63. Lawton 1995: Messana (#66) and Salamis (#120).
64. For the difficulties of dating more precisely Philadelphus' *pompē*, see Thompson 2000: 381–388. Foertmeyer 1988 has argued from the astral symbols displayed in the procession that it was held between December 275 and February 274.
65. Ath. 5.201d–e. Rice 1983: 103–106 suggests that Corinth's prominence, traveling before the other cities and diademed, represents the Corinthian League that Ptolemy I Soter had tried, unsuccessfully, to refound in 309/8.
66. Polyb. 30.25.15.
67. On the official court language behind Antiochus III's Greek policy, see Primo 2009: 90–95; Walsh 1996: 359–361; Schmitt 1964: 96–99.

68. Plut. *Flam.* 16.1–2.
69. For narrative reconstruction, see Grainger 2010: 272–308, Mørkholm 1966: 66–95, Will 1966: 2.311–325, Swain 1944. The Babylonian Astronomical Diary for the month Ab 169 reports that "Antiochus the king marched triumphantly through the cities of Meluhha" (*AD*-168 A Obv. 15); see Gera and Horowitz 1997: 242–243. Meluhha, originally referring to the Indus valley, was used in the first millennium as an archaizing term for Egypt; see Potts 1982. For Akkadian texts' deployment of archaizing geographic terms in general, see Tigay 1983: 181–186.
70. Diod. Sic. 31.1; see also Liv. 44.19.8, 45.11.1, 45.11.8–10.
71. Suda s.v. Ἡρακλείδης Ὀξυρυγχίτης.
72. Polyb. 28.23.4. Indeed, an Egyptian grain order, dating to this first invasion, records the dispatch of barley "to the army camp with the king" (εἰς τὸ μετὰ τοῦ βασιλέως στρατόπεδον), not the more typical "to the king's camp" (εἰς τὸ τοῦ βασιλέως στρατόπεδον). Skeat, who published this papyrus, identifies the king as Ptolemy VI Philometor but the camp as that of Antiochus IV, concluding that "the expression perfectly exemplifies the ambiguous position of Philometor who, while nominally retaining his sovereignty over Egypt, was really little more than a prisoner, helpless in the power of his adversary" (Skeat 1961: 111).
73. Mørkholm 1966: 84; Aymard 1952 persuasively argues, *contra* Otto 1934: 54–56, that Antiochus followed no established or recognized Macedonian procedure.
74. Destruction noted by Porphyry *BNJ* 260 F49a = Jerome, *in Dan.* 11:24. *PTebt* 781, dated about 164, speaks of a temple of Ammon in the Fayum that was sacked by Antiochus' soldiers.
75. Porphyry *BNJ* 260 F49a = Jerome, *in Dan.* 11:24. Porphyry, like Josephus, conflated the two campaign seasons of the Sixth Syrian War, meaning that Otto 1934 placed the coronation in 169. On the grounds that Antiochus IV represented himself as the protector of Philometor throughout 169, Hampl 1936: 34–39, Swain 1944, and Grainger 2010: 306, whose chronology I follow, persuasively relocate the coronation to 168, the second campaign season. The whole event has been doubted by Mørkholm 1966: 79–83, Aymard 1952, and Volkmann 1959; Bevan 1927: 285 suggested that Epiphanes arranged the coronation "not as an expression of his real political purpose, but for the fun of the thing." For full discussion and bibliography, see Blasius 2007.
76. Dio Chrys. *Or.* 32.101; see Lewis 1949.
77. *PTebt* 698: Βασιλέως Ἀντιόχου προστάξαντος· τοῖς ἐν τῷ Κροκοδιλοπολίτη κληρού[χοις]. . . .
78. See Swain 1944: 87 and Groningen 1934. It may be significant that Arsinoe II, after whom Ptolemy II named the nome, had been married to Seleucus I's murderer, Ptolemy Ceraunus.
79. The coins are of Egyptian fabric; see Mørkholm 1966: 81 n.69 and 92 and Houghton, Lorber, and Hoover 2008: #1497–1498.

80. Joseph. *AJ* 13.113; 1 Macc. 11:13.
81. 1 Macc. 1:16.

6. The Circulatory System

1. On the notion of "political landscape," see Smith 2003.
2. For a general discussion of the Greek and Near Eastern evidence, see Tuplin 1998; for a synchronic analysis of the ideology and political meanings of Achaemenid peregrination, see Briant 1988.
3. Tuplin 1998: 71, noting that crisis or wartime moments disrupt the patterns; Cambyses, for example, established his base at Memphis for several years.
4. See, e.g., the recent excavations at Qaleh Kali (Potts et al. 2007).
5. Henkelman 2010; cf. Ael. *NA* 15.26, where the inhabitants of the Zagros received the order to sweep the Royal Road from Ecbatana to Persis of scorpions before the king's departure.
6. Henkelman 2010.
7. See Horden and Purcell 2000: 130 on countering the impression of unproblematic continuity of Peloponnesian road networks: "[W]hat matters in assessing the communications of the area is not the fate of particular routes but the relative significance of each part in the workings of the whole."
8. *AD* -187 A Rev. 18.
9. Polyb. 5.40.5.
10. Observed by Bickerman 1938: 13.
11. For full details, see Schmitt 1964.
12. Details later. Alexander Balas consulted the oracle of Apollo Sarpedonius in Cilicia: Diod. Sic. 32.10.2. For comparison, Chang 2007 brilliantly explores the political and symbolic multivalency of Qing-dynasty imperial tours between Beijing and Jiangnan.
13. Harvey 2009: 133–165.
14. *AD* -149 A Rev. 7–9: itu bi *a[l-te-me* . . .] / [. . .] ᴵ*De-meṭ-ri* lugal ki 25 am-si^{meš} *u* ^{lú}erín^{meš} [. . .] / [. . .] x *lu u'*] ta ^{uru}*An-ti-ke-'a* è^{meš}-*ma* [. . .]. Other examples: *AD* -249 Rev. 6; 1 Macc. 6:28.
15. From *šemû* (*š* appears as *l* before dentals in Standard Babylonian phonology). The verb is used elsewhere in the Astronomical Diaries for official proclamations of royal deaths (*AD* -253 Obv. A$_1$10, B$_1$6 (of Statonice), *AD* -245 A Rev. 5 (of Antiochus II), *AD* -181 Rev. 7–12 (of Laodice)), imperial victories (*AD* -183 A Rev. 11–12 (commander of Susa), *AD* -168 A Obv. 14–15 (Antiochus IV in Egypt), *AD* -164 B Obv. B15, C13–14 (Antiochus IV in Gulf or Armenia), *AD* -156 A Rev. 18–20 (unidentified fighting, perhaps related to Seleucia-on-the-Tigris)), and for instructions delivered by letter to the citizens of Babylon (*AD* -155 A Rev. 12–17).
16. Polyb. 5.41.6–5.42.9; 5.49.
17. Note that, according to Just. *Epit.* 35.1.1, Demetrius I thought this necessary: *Demetrius occupato Syriae regno novitati suae otium periculosum ratus ampliare fines regni et opes augere finitimorum bellis statuit.*

18. (Standard Babylonian) *Gilgamesh* 4.212–231 has the officers and young men of Uruk mob Gilgamesh as he and Enkidu depart, repeating to him the blessing that the elders spoke at the beginning of the tablet. For Sargonic royal progresses, see Foster 1980.
19. Thuc. 6.32; see Jordan 2000.
20. Burkert 1985: 266.
21. Burkert 1985: 267.
22. Arr. *Anab.* 1.11.1–2; Diod. Sic. 17.16.3–4.
23. Arr. *Anab.* 1.16.4; Plut. *Al.* 16.16; Vell. Pat. 1.11.3–5; Plin. *HN* 34.8.64.
24. Lehnen 2001.
25. Feldherr 1998: 9–12.
26. E.g., 1 Macc. 6:28: "The king gathered his friends, commanders of his forces, and those in charge of the cavalry; and mercenaries joined him from the other kingdoms and the islands of the sea. And the number of the force was one hundred thousand footmen, twenty thousand horsemen, and thirty-two elephants exercised in battle. He marched . . ."
27. Compare Justin's passage with Posidonius F54 (Edelstein-Kidd) = Ath. 4.176b–c, on the Apameans' decadent march to war against the Larisans, and F61a and b = Ath. 12.540b–c, on Antiochus VII's campaign banquets, discussed later.
28. Just. *Epit.* 38.10.1–4; trans. J. Yardley, with changes.
29. On *tryphē* in Hellenistic historiography, see Bernhardt 2003, Cozzoli 1980, and Passerini 1934. Bernhardt 2003: 199–202 has shown how lack of moderation in food and drink was considered a first-order index of decadence. For example, Smindyrides of decadent Sybaris was accompanied to Sicyon, for the famous wooing of Cleisthenes' daughter Agariste, by 1,000 cooks and fowlers (Ath. 12.541b–c, Ael. *VH* 12.24). The expensive shoes and silver cooking vessels of Sidetes' army are well paralleled (see Bernhardt 2003: 209–217).
30. Kantorowicz 1944: 219.
31. The *pompē,* described by Polyb. 30.25.3–19, is generally seen as a propagandistic attempt to represent the king's withdrawal from Egypt (following P. Laenas' sand-circle) as a victory and to surpass Aemilius Paullus' games at Amphipolis: Polyb. 30.25–26; Diod. Sic. 31.16; see Mittag 2006: 282–295; Walbank 1996; Kuhrt and Sherwin-White 1993: 220–221; Völcker-Janssen 1993: 222–224; Geller 1991; Bunge 1976; Mørkholm 1966: 96–101. But the festival also sits easily alongside the *profectio* passages in the Astronomical Diaries, 1 Maccabees, and Justin, just discussed —the display and enumeration of soldiers and weapons, expensive costumes and banquetware before an eastern expedition directly parallel the description of Antiochus VII's departure from Antioch, quoted earlier. It is evident that the parade brought together before the eyes of the world the dazzlingly diverse force with which Antiochus Epiphanes would head east.
32. *SEG* 1 366 l.10. Cf. the departures of Antiochus IV, in 2 Macc. 9:2, and Lysias, regent of Antiochus V, in 2 Macc. 13:26.

33. Polyb. 5.41.2: ὁ δὲ Ἑρμείας ἦν μὲν ἀπὸ Καρίας, ἐπέστη δ ἐπὶ τὰ πράγματα Σελεύκου τἀδελφοῦ ταύτην αὐτῷ τὴν πίστιν ἐγχειρίσαντος, καθ' οὓς καιροὺς ἐποιεῖτο τὴν ἐπὶ τὸν Ταῦρον στρατείαν. There are numerous other attestations: e.g., Antiochus III, departing from Sardis, established Zeuxis as viceroy over the cis-Tauric region (see Ma 2002: 123–130); Antiochus IV entrusted Syria to Andronicus when he marched into Cilicia (2 Macc. 4:31) and to Lysias when he headed into the Upper Satrapies (Joseph. *AJ* 12.367).
34. Landau 1961 (*SEG* 19 904; 53 1821).
35. 2 Macc. 4:31.
36. Joseph. *AJ* 12.295.
37. *AD* -273 B Rev. 29; see Del Monte 1997: 27–28.
38. Ma 2002: 54.
39. Achaemenid: Briant 2002: 183–193 and 1988; Attalids: Robert 1985 and 1984a; Rome: Ando 2000: 207–252 and Millar 1977: 3–53; Byzantium: MacCormack 1981; medieval and early modern: Buc 2001: 37–40, Bak 1990, and Geertz 1985.
40. See the Gurob Papyrus (*BNJ* 160), discussed later.
41. Plut. *Cat. Min.* 13.
42. See Donner 1981: 128–155.
43. *BCHP* 12 Rev. 14–15.
44. On the legitimizing function of ritual-in-text, see Buc 2001.
45. *BNJ* 160 II.25—III.30.
46. *BNJ* 160 III.35–47; cf. Robert 1984a: 480–484, who has argued, in his study of *OGIS* 332 (*IPerg* 246; *SEG* 34 1251), concerning Attalus III's victorious return to Pergamum, that the king was first welcomed at the Asclepium in the *chōra* (παρεγένετο εἰς Πέργαμον) and then again at the city gates (παραγίνηται εἰς τὴν πόλιν ἡμῶν). Robert 1985: 471–480 observed that the extramural reception was considerably more lavish.
47. Assembly: First Tean Decree for Antiochus III and Laodice III (Ma #17 17; *SEG* 41 1003 1); temple: Antiochus III in Ecbatana (Polyb. 10.27.12).
48. To the numerous classifications of the Gurob Papyrus we can add the simpler schematizations from Jerusalem, where Antiochus III was met by the city's *gerousia* (Joseph. *AJ* 12.138), Antiochus IV by the high priest and the city dwellers (2 Macc. 4:22), and Antiochus VII by Hyrcanus (Joseph. *AJ* 13.250).
49. *BCHP* 12 Rev. 14–15. Cf. *AD* -245 B Obv. 3–5, very fragmentary, where *nigûtu* and a feast seem to be offered to a royal prince; see Del Monte 1997: 47–48.
50. 2 Macc. 4:22.
51. *BNJ* 160 III.41.
52. *BNJ* 160 III.44.
53. Joseph. *AJ* 12.138.
54. Joseph. *AJ* 13.250.
55. *AD* -187 A Rev. 11.
56. Joseph. *AJ* 12.138–141; see Bickerman 1935.
57. See Ma 2002: 260–265.

58. Ma #17; *SEG* 41 1003 1. Compare Attalus I's refusal to personally address the Athenian Assembly (Polyb. 16.25–26; Liv. 31.15.2).

59. The former by Bickerman 1935, the latter by Ma 2002.

60. Ma #22; *TAM* 2.266; *OGIS* 746. Le Roy 1986 has persuasively argued that the famous sacred law from Xanthus' Letoön, prohibiting (among other things) the bearing of weapons and the Macedonian *kausia* hat within the sanctuary, should be understood as a response to the presence of Antiochus III and his army, defending the temple complex against occupying Seleucid troops: an attempt to channel the occupiers' movements away from its sacred center.

61. Ma #17 11–13; *SEG* 41 1003 1.

62. See, e.g., the royal narratives of Joseph. *AJ* 12.138 and Gurob Papyrus (*BNJ* 160).

63. E.g., Liv. 33.20.5: *Coracesium praeter spem clausis portis tenebat eum*. The behavior and language were also traditionally Mesopotamian, where years could be named *šattu ša edil bābi*, "the year of the closure of the gates"; see Beaulieu 1997 and Oppenheim 1955: 76–78.

64. The *peliganes*, an institution of Macedonian origin. Polybius' text gives, in error, *Adeiganes*; see Roussel 1942–1943: 31–32; on the institution, see Hatzopoulos 2006: 89–90.

65. Polyb. 5.54.9–11.

66. Polyb. 7.18.9.

67. For narrative and discussion, see Ma 2002: 61–63; inscriptions Ma #1–3; *SEG* 39 1283–1285.

68. Diod. Sic. 34/35.1.5; Joseph. *AJ* 13.246.

69. Xerxes of Armenia: Polyb. 8.23; Arsaces II of Parthia: Polyb. 10.27–31 and Just. *Epit.* 41.5.7 (*in societatem eius adsumptus est*). Antiochus III's earlier successes against Artabazanes of Media Atropatene surely have a similar structure: Polyb. 5.55.10.

70. Polyb. 8.23.

71. Joseph. *AJ* 13.262: ἵνα τε τοῖς στρατιώταις τοῖς βασιλικοῖς μὴ ἐξῇ διὰ τῆς χώρας τῆς αὐτῶν καὶ τῶν ὑπηκόων αὐτῶν διέρχεσθαι. On the dating of this Roman treaty with Hyrcanus to the reign of Antiochus IX, see Giovannini and Müller 1971.

72. Polyb. 10.28; Briant 2001 and 1984: 67; Kuhrt and Sherwin-White 1993: 79–89; note the caution of Tuplin 2008: 111.

73. Joseph. *AJ* 13.251. Note that Shayegan 2011: 152–153 has identified Josephus' Indates with Indupanē of the Babylonian Astronomical Diaries, which is plausible, and with a certain Sindād, who, according to the tenth-century Isfahani geographer Ḥamza, ruled in the Gulf region "in ancient times," which is less plausible; on Ḥamza Eṣfehānī and his sources, see Pourshariati 2007.

74. Plin. *HN* 6.28.152: Numenius, general of Mesene, erected a double-trophy to Zeus and Poseidon at the Straits of Hormuz; for historical and geographical context, see Kosmin 2013c: 67–70.

75. Polyb. 5.54.6–7: πρὸς αὐταῖς ἀνεσταύρωσαν ταῖς εἰς τὸν Ζάγρον ἀναβολαῖς. For comparison, note that Alexander ordered that Bessos, murderer of Darius III and pretender to the Achaemenid throne, be displayed to the right of the road along which the Macedonian army would march (Arr. *Anab.* 3.30.3) and that Cyrus the Younger displayed the mutilated bodies of criminals beside the major roads of his province (Xen. *Anab.* 1.9.13: πολλάκις δ᾽ ἦν ἰδεῖν παρὰ τὰς στειβομένας ὁδοὺς καὶ ποδῶν καὶ χειρῶν καὶ ὀφθαλμῶν στερομένους ἀνθρώπους).

76. On the Achaemenid case, see Briant 1988: 256–257. According to Plut. *Artax.* 5.6, the female rural population similarly interacted with Artaxerxes II's wife, Stateira, who traveled through the countryside in an open carriage.

77. Just. *Epit.* 38.10.6

78. Edelstein and Kidd 1989: 299.

79. Polyb. 8.15–21, especially 8.20.8–8.21.6.

80. See Nielsen 1994.

81. For precedents and parallels see Proosdij 1934. According to 2 Macc. 7:4, Antiochus IV inflicted a similar punishment on the first of the Seven Pious Brothers. The sewing up of Achaeus' head in an ass skin is unusual, however, and does not seem to be drawn from the established Near Eastern repertoire of somatic sanctions. Hdt. 1.214.4, where Tomyris, queen of the Massagetae, deposits the head of the defeated Cyrus the Great in a wineskin filled with blood, offers the only direct parallel. Fleischer 1972–1975 related the humiliation to the myth of Marsyas, in which the satyr was flayed by Apollo for having deigned to challenge his musical supremacy. Fleischer argues that the famous Hellenistic Apollo-Marsyas statue-group was in origin a Seleucid work, representing Antiochus III's defeat and punishment of Achaeus: the satyr and Achaeus shared both strong Phrygian associations (Achaeus took the diadem at Laodicea-in-Phrygia, amid his family estates) and hybristic ambitions against their legitimate overlords. Ehling 2007 has connected the punishment to Achaeus' horsehead coinage type, unpersuasively. The end of Achaeus provided the prototype for Ovid's curse in *Ibis* 299.

82. Polyb. 8.21.4.

83. The *locus classicus* is Alexander's capture of Darius III's tent after the battle of Issus, in 333; see Briant 1988: 269, reading Curt. 3.11.23: *ita tradito more, ut victorem victi regis tabernaculo exciperent.*

84. It is generally accepted (Ma 2002: 61; Fleisher 1972–1975; Proosdij 1934) that the form of Achaeus' punishment (with the exception of the head in an ass' skin) derives from Achaemenid precedents. Darius I's famous Behistun inscription records the punishment of various rebels in stock terms. For example, Darius writes that the Median usurper Fravartish was "bound and brought to me" *(agarbiya ānayatā abiy mām);* "I cut off his nose and ears and tongue and I gouged out one eye" *(adamšaiy utā nāham utā gaušā utā hazānam frājanam utāšaiy 1 cašam avajam).* Darius then reports that Fravartiš "was held bound at my palace gate" *(duvarayāmaiy basta adāriya),* where "the entire

army looked upon him" *(haruvašim kāra avaina)*, before being impaled at Ecbatana *(pasāvašim Hagmatānaiy uzmayāpatiy akunavam)* (DB 2.73–78). Sagartian Ciçataxma received an identical punishment, being disfigured at Darius' palace gateway and then impaled at Arbela (DB 2.85–90). Note that Antiochus III's mutilation of Achaeus within the royal tent echoes Darius' palace setting (expressed by the locative *duvarayā*, "at the palace gate/ courtyard"); yet again, the Seleucid king's tent functions as palace. Cf. Phraates II's display in his palace of Pitthides/Pittit, his mutilated Elamite enemy, to the envoys from Seleucia-on-the-Tigris (Diod. Sic. 34/35.19); on the possible redating of this episode to the reign of Mithridates II, see Shayegan 2011: 119–120.

85. Daniel 11:40–45. For a review of some old interpretations of this prophecy, see Montgomery 1927: 464–470.

86. Daniel 11:45.

87. LXX Daniel 11:45 skips over the word; Theodotion transliterated unaccented εφαδανω. Jerome (Jer. *in Dan.* 11:44–45) delivers a lengthy excursus on the meaning of *'appƏdnô*, disagreeing with Porphyry's identification of a locale "Apedno," between the upper Tigris and the upper Euphrates; certain Christians had suggested an Apedno near Emmaus, in Judea; Jerome himself proposed a compound of θρόνου αὐτοῦ.

88. *AD* -86 Flake 11 terms the palace at Seleucia-on-the-Tigris *ᵉap-pa-dan* rather than the more typical Akkadian *ekallu* (usually written with Sumerian logograms as é.gal); see Stolper 2007.

89. Ael. *NA* 10.34.

90. Hercher 1858: xxxvii. The same omen had befallen Alexander of Epirus a line before (Ael. *NA* 10.34: ἐν δὲ τῇ Ἀλεξάνδρου τοῦ Πύρρου παιδὸς σκηνῇ χελιδὼν νεοττεύουσα).

91. Polyaenus, *Strat.* 4.15. Since Droysen 1878: 3.256 n.1, most have placed this incident in the Syrian War of Succession or the First Syrian War (see Chapter 3), although Grainger 2010: 86 suggests Antiochus III. Antiochus I's conquest of the city was quickly undone; see Bagnall 1976: 12–13.

92. Henkelman 2011b has shown, in a brilliantly argued study, that the Achaemenid rulers regularly hosted extravagant feasts in the royal *paradeisoi*, conspicuous for the number and variety of animals sacrificed and termed *šip* in Elamite, and that the phenomenon survived the fall of the Achaemenid dynasty: the carefully arranged banquet held by the Macedonian satrap Peucestas at Persepolis for Eumenes' army and local Persian nobles (Diod. Sic. 19.22.1–3) conformed to the traditional type.

93. On *hyparchoi* see Capdetrey 2007: 258–260.

94. Such resource centers are attested from the early Hellenistic period: according to Arist. [*Oec.*] 2.2.38=1353a, Alexander's financial officer Antimenes obliged the satraps to replenish the storehouses along the Royal Roads (τούς τε θησαυροὺς τοὺς παρὰ τὰς ὁδοὺς τὰς βασιλικάς) following the established custom (κατὰ τὸν νόμον τὸν τῆς χώρας); he would sell the contents to armies moving

without the king; see Groningen 1933: 202–204 for commentary; on
Antimenes see Berve 1926: 2.44–45 (#89).

95. Just. *Epit.* 38.10.4.

96. Ath. 12.540b–c = Posidonius F61a (Edelstein-Kidd).

97. Note that, according to Justin 38.10.8, the burden of supplying an offensively
behaved royal army encouraged the cities to defect back to Phraates II.

98. Just. *Epit.* 38.10.5–6.

99. For narrative and analysis of the campaign, see Fischer 1970.

100. Ath. 10.439d–e = Posidonius F63 (Edelstein-Kidd).

101. *IGIAC* 70; *IEOG* 27: ἔτους δξρ', μηνὸς Πανήμου, Ἡρακλῆν Καλλίνικον Ὑάκινθος
Πανταύχου ὑπὲ[ρ] τῆς Κλεομένου τοῦ ἐπὶ τῶν ἄνω σ[ατρ]απειῶν σωτηρίας. The
Aramaic inscription is almost entirely illegible but began (like the Greek) *šnt*
.., "In the year . . ." On the influence of Iranian sculptural technique,
especially the rupestral relief and the use of the flat rather than claw chisel,
see Callieri 2007: 111–112 and Colledge 1979: 228–229.

102. Heracles was worshipped at the Karafto caves in the northern Zagros (*IGIAC*
75); excavations at Masjid-i Solaiman uncovered a Hellenistic bas-relief of
Heracles at banquet; another at Tang-i Shimbar in the Bakhtiari mountains:
Ghirshman 1975 suggests that this Hellenistic Heracles should be considered
a syncretism of the Greek figure with Artagnes/Verethragna, the Iranian
war deity. Note that there is also evidence of a Heracles cult at the Seleucid
garrison on Failaka island in the northern Gulf (Connelly 1989).

103. E.g., *IGIAC* 66, *IEOG* 277 (Antiochus III's organization of an empire-wide
cult for his wife Laodice, from Nehavend, ancient Laodicea).

104. Diod. Sic. 17.106.1; Curt. 9.10.24–29; Plut. *Al.* 67; Arr. *Anab.* 6.28.1–4.

105. For example, in the mid-190s Themison made a dedication at Aegae "for the
safety of the great king Antiochus and Antiochus the son and queen Laodice
and the children" (Ma #20; *SEG* 49 1493). Ma 2002: 287 observes that παιδία
rather than τέκνα is used for "the children," advertising familial tenderness.
The dedication "implies the presence on the expedition of all, or most of, the
royal family" (Ma 2002: 82).

106. *IIasos* 4; Ma #26. Cf. the Achaemenid queen Stateira receiving gifts from
peasant women (Plut. *Artax.* 5.6).

107. John of Antioch *FGH* IV. p. 557 = Exc. De ins. p. 9; see Kuhrt and Sherwin-
White 1993: 191 for an instructive Neo-Assyrian analogy.

108. Polyb. 11.39. The partitive genitive implies that several daughters accompanied the Seleucid king.

109. Just. *Epit.* 38.10.10.

110. Polyb. 18.51.8; App. *Syr.* 3; Liv. 33.40.6.

111. Polyaenus, *Strat.* 4.15.

112. Primo 2009: 132–135; Walbank 1957–1979: 2.232.

113. Polyb. 10.28.

114. See Liverani 2004: 90–91 and Talmon 1966.

115. Polyb. 10.29.

116. Polyb. 10.30.

117. Lib. *Or.* 11.123.

118. (Standard Babylonian) *Gilgamesh* 1.37–44; see George 2003: 92–94.

119. For instance, Shalmaneser III boasts, "I crossed over Mounts Namdanu and Merhisu. I smashed out with copper picks rough paths in rugged mountains which rose perpendicularly to the sky like points of daggers" (Shalmaneser III A.0.102.2 41–42).

120. See, e.g., Karahashi 2004 and Root 1979: 303–308.

121. App. *Syr.* 57.

122. Strabo 14.2.29. On the so-called Common Road see French 1998: 21–22; Syme 1995: 3–23; Debord 1985: 346–349; Ramsay 1890: 27–43.

123. On the Persian Royal Road see Briant 2012; Syme 1995: 3–23; Calder 1925; Ramsay 1890: 27–43. In contrast to the southerly "Common Road," the northern one bears all pre-Hellenic names—Satala, Sardis, Pessinus, Gordium, Ancyra. As Syme 1995: 18 observed, this proves only that the Seleucid kings were unable to win and hold the northern route, not that the southern route was unimportant before Alexander: for instance, Alcibiades, en route to the court of Artaxerxes, was assassinated at Melissa, a village on the southern road between Synnada and Metropolis (Plut. *Alc.* 37–39).

124. Strabo 14.2.29.

125. Liv. 37.56.3: *castella ad Maeandrum amnem.* The Seleucid-allied dynast Olympichus held the fort at Petra near Labraunda, overlooking the road between Mylasa and Alinda (Ma 2002: 116).

126. Comfort and Ergeç 2001; Chaumont 1984.

127. Masson 1850.

128. *BNJ* 781 F2 = *Mans. Parth.*

129. *IGIAC* 64; *SEG* 45 1879; *IEOG* 247; Callieri 1995: 65–73.

130. *IGIAC* 65; *SEG* 45 1880; *IEOG* 248; Stronach 1978: 161–162; Callieri 1995: 75–77.

131. *SEG* 47 1624; *IEph* 3601. The abbreviation B AA appears on the top corners of each side of this opisthographic milestone. Thonemann 2003: 96 proposes, only to reject, β(ασιλευόντων Ἀ(ντιόχου καὶ) Ἀ(ντιόχου), i.e., the joint reign of Antiochus III and his son Antiochus (209–193), in favor of β(ασιλεύοντος) Ἀ(ττάλου) αʹ, i.e., the first year of Attalus II or III (159/8 or 138/7). Note that "k(ing) A(ntiochus) son of A(ntiochus)" is also a possibility, for Antiochus II.

132. Tomaschek 1883 suggested that Seleucid itineraries or cartography lie behind the Persian and Carmanian road measurements on the *Tabula Peutingeriana.*

133. οἱ ἐργαζόμενοι appear, receiving rations or supplies from the royal treasury (βασιλικόν), in an inscription found near Aegae in the Aeolis, dated by its *editor princeps* Malay to the reign of Antiochus I; see Malay 1983; *SEG* 53 1363.

134. *OGIS* 225; *IDidyma* 492; *RC* 20; *SEG* 37 878. For an illustrated geographical discussion of the location and extension of Laodice's estate, see Hasluck 1910: 127 and Wiegand 1904: 274–280.

135. In this case, it seems that the coastal route across the Granicus plain to Cyzicus had been preserved; the inland Persian road to Dascylium had not; see Hasluck 1910: 127.
136. *BNJ* 715 F31 = Strabo 15.1.50.
137. *BNJ* 715 F6c = Strabo 15.1.11.
138. *BNJ* 715 F32 = Strabo 15.1.55.
139. *OGIS* 225 23–24; *RC* 18; *IDidyma* 492; *SEG* 37 878.
140. Herrmann 1959: 4–6 (#2); *SEG* 19 720.
141. Veuve 1982.
142. A useful comparison is Edney 1997, who has investigated the intersection between Britain's surveying and cartographic endeavors in India and the extension and legitimization of its imperial control.
143. See Snead, Erickson, and Darling 2009; Gates 2006; O'Hanlon and Frankland 2003; Parmentier 1987: 109–116.
144. Parmentier 1987: 109.
145. Demodamas *BNJ* 428 F2 = Plin. *HN* 6.16.49.
146. Houghton and Lorber 2002: 354–361.
147. Polyb. 10.27.
148. Phylarchus *FGrHist* 81 F29 = Ath. 6.254f-255a.
149. Polyb. 27.13, 29.27.9–10; 2 Macc. 10:12–13. Note that Demetrius I tried to buy the island off its Ptolemaic governor Archias for 500 talents, but the plot was detected (Polyb. 33.5).
150. Aradus and the Aradian *peraia* used a local chronological era, beginning in 259, on its autonomous coinage. The first datable coinage comes from the reign of Seleucus II, during the Third Syrian War in 243/2, but it is likely that undated autonomous coinage circulated earlier; see Duyrat 2005: 223–238.
151. Plin. *HN* 5.32.151; *Tabula Peutingeriana* 11.1. Cohen 1995: 131 identifies the founder as Antiochus I, or possibly Antiochus II.
152. Polyb. 25.4.9–10: by the terms of the Apamea treaty the Seleucid king could not sail his own fleet beyond Cape Sarpedonium, a correspondence to the putative terms of the Peace of Callias between Athens and Persia.
153. Cf. the Antigonid ship or prow monuments at Samothrace and the palace at Demetrias (Rice 1993: 245–247).
154. Just. *Epit.* 27.2.1–2.
155. For narrative, see Ma 2002: 86–90.
156. Charax of Pergamum *BNJ* 103 F29 = Steph. Byz. s.v. Δῶρος.
157. 1 Macc. 15:37.
158. Just. *Epit.* 39.1.8; Joseph. *AJ* 13.268.
159. Salles 1987: 75; Potts 1990: 2.22.
160. Gatier, Lombard, and al-Sindi 2002; Kosmin 2013c.
161. For the dates of Hyspaosines' satrapal and monarchic rule, see Schuol 2000; Nodelman 1960; Bellinger 1942.
162. Kosmin 2013c: 70–73.

163. Kosmin 2013c: 64–65, with bibliography.
164. *IGIAC* 51; *OGIS* 231; *IEOG* 250; *IMagn* 18; *RC* 31.
165. Polyb. 13.9.5.
166. Potts 1978: 29–32.
167. Strabo 16.1.9 reports that Seleucia-on-the-Tigris was located at the northernmost point of navigability on the Tigris.
168. Antiochus IV (*AD* -164 C 13–14; Plin. *HN* 6.28.147) and Demetrius I/II (*BM* 34433) were also active in the Gulf, but there is no evidence of voyages.
169. Just. *Epit* 36.1.5. The capture of Demetrius II and his nobles, presumably the *philoi*, is reported in the Astronomical Diary for 138 (*AD* -137 A Rev. 8–10) and in 1 Macc. 14:3. On the *anabasis* of Demetrius II, see Dąbrowa 1999 and Shayegan 2003.
170. Euseb. *Chron.* 1.256 = *BNJ* 260 F32.16.
171. Diod. Sic. 34/35.28.2; Just. *Epit.* 39.2.6. Note the alternative account of Joseph. *AJ* 13.269, where Alexander II Zabinas was defeated and killed in battle; see Ehling 2008: 214 for discussion.
172. Joseph. *AJ* 13.386.
173. Just. *Epit.* 27.2.2–5.
174. App. *Syr.* 28.
175. 1 Macc. 11.16–17; Joseph. *AJ* 13.116.
176. Diod. Sic. 32.10.2.
177. Polyb. 31.9; 1 Macc. 6:4; 2 Macc. 9:1–12; Joseph. *AJ* 12.354.
178. Africa 1982.
179. E.g., Pheretima of Cyrene (Hdt. 4.205), Cassander (Paus. 9.7.2–4), Sulla (Plut. *Sull.* 36.3), Herod Agrippa (*Acts of the Apostles* 12.19b-23), and Galerius (Lactant. *de mort. pers.* 33).
180. On Alexander's sweet scent, see Plut. *Alex.* 4.2.
181. Polyaenus, *Strat.* 4.9.6.
182. Just. *Epit.* 38.9.4–9. The Parthian-style beard of Demetrius II has sprouted its own body of scholarship: see, e.g., Iossif and Lorber 2009: 105–106, Ehling 2008: 206–207, and Mittag 2002: 389–398. Mittag 2002 has suggested that Phraates II's supposed "release" of Demetrius II, narrated by Just. *Epit.* 38.10.7, 11, was in fact a third and successful escape, although note the doubts of Shayegan 2003 and 2011: 143–145, who identifies a developed "hostage policy" of the Arsacid kings.
183. *OGIS* 219 12; *IIlion* 32: νῦν τε παραγενόμενος ἐπὶ τοὺς τόπους τοὺς ἐπιτάδε τοῦ Ταύρου.
184. *OGIS* 229 1–2; *IMagnSipylos* 1: ἐπειδὴ πρότερόν τε καθ᾽ ὃν καιρὸν ὁ βασιλεὺς Σέλευκος ὑπερέβαλεν εἰς τὴν Σελευκίδα.
185. *IG* 12, 6 1 9–11; *SEG* 1 366: ἀποδημήσας τὴν μὲν ἀρχὴν εἰς Ἔφεσον, ἀναζεύξαντος δὲ Ἀντιόχου συνακολουθήσας ἕως Σάρδεων.
186. 2 Macc. 9:21: ἐπανάγων ἐκ τῶν κατὰ τὴν Περσίδα τόπων.
187. *AD* -168 A Obv. 14–15 (reporting Antiochus IV's invasion of Egypt in the Sixth Syrian War).

188. *AD* -187 A Obv. 13, 18.
189. Borsippa Cylinder 1.8–13; see Kosmin 2014c.
190. Iossif and Lorber 2009.
191. Jer. *in Dan.* 11:20.
192. Joseph. *AJ* 13.35–36.
193. Liv. *Per.* 52; Just. *Epit.* 35.2.2.
194. Diod. Sic. 34/5.34.
195. Selden 1998.
196. Polyb. 5.41.8–9.
197. Polyb. 5.51.8.
198. Polyb. 5.54.2. On this passage in the broader context of visibility and royal power, see Hekster and Fowler 2005: "The battlefield is an obvious locus for royal visibility" (13).
199. Joseph. *AJ* 13.185.
200. Kantorowicz 1944.
201. Note that *epiphanēs* and *epēkoos* were divine epithets especially prominent in the archaic and classical Greek east (Pfister 1927: 306).
202. App. *Syr.* 45. Mittag 2006: 128–139 has emphasized the astral symbolism adopted by Antiochus IV, especially the radiate crown.
203. On the use and significance of the title, see Platt 2011: 142–146.
204. Pfister 1927: 307–308.
205. Bielfeldt 2010.
206. Cassin 1968: 65–82.
207. Joseph. *AJ* 13.185.
208. Henkelman 2010; Millar 1977: 28–53. Hekster and Fowler 2005: 14 compare the English royal circuit and secondary assize system.
209. Certeau 1984: 91–110.

7. King Makes City

1. E.g., Cohen 1978, 1995, 2006, and 2013; Mueller 2006: 1–3; Walbank 1992: 133–140; Seyrig 1968: 53–63; Rostovtzeff 1941: 1.472–502.
2. Cohen 2006: 34 observes that the Ptolemies carried out very little colonization in their southern half of Syria. The contrast between Seleucid and Ptolemaic urbanization in Syria is well demonstrated by the results of the archaeological survey of the Beqa' valley in Lebanon (Marfoe 1978). From the battle of Ipsus (301) until the Fifth Syrian War (202–200) the Beqa' was split between Seleucid occupation in the very north and Ptolemaic in the south; in the middle lay an unpopulated no man's land. Marfoe 1978: 631–638 observed that the Seleucid Beqa' was far more densely settled and intensively developed than its Ptolemaic southern reaches. Similarly, recent excavations have shown that Ptolemaic (third-century) Beirut saw little building activity and no major changes in the occupation of the site; by contrast Seleucid (second-century) Beirut was a period of busy expansion,

with considerable change in the ceramic assemblage; see Perring 2001–2002.

3. App. *Syr.* 57.
4. Cohen 1995 and 2006.
5. Cohen 2013.
6. Carians from western Asia Minor and Eretrians from the Greek island of Euboea were forcibly moved by early Persian monarchs; see Grosso 1958. It was once thought that the Neo-Babylonian king Nebuchadnezzar II had settled Jews, deported from Jerusalem, on the lower-middle Tigris. However, recently published Neo-Babylonian texts from al-Yahudu ("Jews' town") have conclusively shown that the Jews were settled in southern Babylonia (the Nippur-Kesh-Karkara triangle); see Pearce 2011: 270.
7. Adams 1981: 3–7.
8. Arr. *Anab.* 7.7.7; Strabo 16.1.9. Quite unfairly this irrigation technology was regarded by the Alexander Historians as a symptom of Persian military decadence; see Briant 1986, 1999, 2002: 719–721, 2006, 2008.
9. Strabo 15.3.4 τῶν ποταμῶν μὲν οὐ δεχομένων τὰ ἐκ τῆς θαλάττης.
10. Arr. *Anab.* 7.7.7; Strabo 16.1.9. Perhaps a seasonal operation; see Briant 2008.
11. The *terminus post quem* for the foundation of Seleucia is the Antigonid retreat from Babylonia in 308. The *terminus ante quem* is Seleucus' westward march against Antigonus Monophthalmus in 301; see Cohen 2013: 163, Invernizzi 1991: 180, Marinoni 1972: 616–621, Le Rider 1965: 30–31, and McDowell 1935: 53 (for the numismatic evidence). Hadley 1978 argues for a post-301 date, unpersuasively.
12. Strabo 16.1.9; see Polyb. 13.9.5, with Chapter 6, for Antiochus III's voyage from Tylos to Seleucia-on-the-Tigris.
13. Both waterways are mentioned in the city's full Akkadian name: ᵘʳᵘ*Se-lu-ke-ʻa-a šá a-na muh-hi* ⁱᵈidigna *u* íd lugal, "Seleucia, which is on the Tigris and the Royal Canal"; see, e.g., *AD* -181 Rev. 9–11.
14. The harbor of Seleucia appears in Astronomical Diaries as *ka-a-ri* ᵍⁱˢm[áᵐᵉˢ] / *šá ina* ⁱᵈidigna, "the harbor of ships in the Tigris" (*AD* -132 B Rev. 19–20).
15. For these terms see Blanton 1976: 251–258.
16. Invernizzi 2004; Aperghis 2004: 154–156; Rostovtzeff 1932.
17. See the argumentation, with ancient references, of Le Rider 1965: 263–267. On commercial traffic between Seleucia-on-the-Tigris and Seleucia-on-the-Eulaeus (formerly Susa), see Le Rider 1965: 299.
18. See Kosmin 2013c.
19. Strabo 16.1.17; Isidore of Charax *BNJ* 781 F2 = *Mans. Parth.* 2; Plin. *HN* 6.26.117.
20. This Seleucid foundation is known from the late antique Syriac Chronicle of Karka de Bet Selok; for translation and commentary, see Pigulevskaja 1963: 39–47.
21. Plin. *HN* 6.27.138; see Cohen 2013: 109–117.

22. Strabo 16.1.4; see Cohen 2013: 97–98.
23. Grainger 1990: 7–29; Seyrig 1968; Lund 1993 and 2003: 255–256.
24. Seyrig 1968: 61.
25. Strabo 16.2.4.
26. For details and discussion, see Chapter 8.
27. Ma #18 90–104; Herrmann 1965a; *SEG* 41 1003 II. For the offer of isopolity see Herrmann 1965a: 79–84 and Gauthier 1985: 169–175. The absence of Apamea is unexpected; Herrmann 1965a: 81 suggests that Seleucus I's Sogdian wife Apame, unlike his mother, Laodice, did not qualify among the *Macedonian* royal ancestors and so among the ἐπώνυμοι πόλεις τῶν τοῦ βασιλέως προγόνων mentioned in l.95 of the inscription.
28. Balty 1991: 214–220; Ward-Perkins 1974: 20; Leblanc and Poccardi 1999: 124–126; Peters 1983; Sauvaget 1934: 107.
29. Lib. *Or.* 11.85–104; Malalas 8.191–203; see later discussion.
30. Lib. *Or.* 11.263: τέτμηται δὲ ὑπὲρ ἡμετέρας τοσούτῳ χρυσῷ λιμὴν ἐκ πέτρας γενόμενος.
31. Seleucia-in-Pieria: Honigmann 1921. Polyb. 5.59.7 reports that the emporia and a suburb lie beside the harbor. Laodicea-by-the-Sea: Sauvaget 1934.
32. Lib. *Or.* 11.41. Strabo 16.2.7 says that the journey could be completed within a single day.
33. Grainger 1990: 58–60; Sève-Martinez 2004: 22–29.
34. Oates 1968: 7–8.
35. Capdetrey 2007: 160–161; on the importance of agricultural territory for colonial development, see Briant 1978.
36. Liv. 37.56.3: *castella ad Maeandrum amnem.* The garrisoned fort of Palaemagnesia is mentioned in *OGIS* 229 93–94; *IMagnSipylos* 1. The Seleucid-allied dynast Olympichus held the fort at Petra near Labraunda, overlooking the road between Mylasa and Alinda; see Ma 2002: 116.
37. Joseph. *AJ* 12.147. Antiochus III also established a colony of Iranian Cardacians in Lycia; see later discussion.
38. Cohen 2013: 77–79.
39. This site, on the middle Euphrates between Jebel Khalid and Dura-Europus, has only recently been surveyed; it has been dated to the Seleucid period (Napoli 2000).
40. Details later. We do not know who established Anthemusia and Ichnae, the other Euphratene colonies mentioned in the itinerary of Isidore of Charax *BNJ* 781 F2 = *Mans. Parth.* 1; see Cohen 2013: 57–61, 76–77.
41. Holt 1999: 36–37 has shown that the period of Antiochus I's viceregency in the Upper Satrapies, 294–281, accounts for 37 percent of all stray bronze coins from the site. Only nine possibly pre-Seleucid bronzes have been recovered from the whole settlement; they may in fact be Seleucid.
42. *IGIAC* 68; *IEOG* 271–272.
43. Polyb. 10.31.
44. Strabo 13.4.15; Plin. *HN* 5.29.108.

45. Ratté 2008. In fact, Gauthier 1989: 151–170 has argued that Sardis did not juridically become a *polis* until the brief period of Pergamene rule between 226 and 222, attributing a series of autonomous coins to these years.

46. The Seleucid kings intentionally relocated a (broadly speaking) ethnically uniform group of people from its ancestral or long-established home to a foreign and unfamiliar region of the empire; this is over and above immigration from the southern Balkan peninsula. A very fragmentary inscription from Nagidos in Cilicia (Jones and Russell 1993: 297–304) records the response to a request by Seleucus I or Antiochus I to send colonists to one of the newly founded Antiochs (specification lost). Similarly, Antiochus I asked Magnesia-on-the-Maeander to dispatch settlers to Antioch-in-Persis, i.e., from Ionia to the Persian Gulf (*IMagn* 61; *OGIS* 233; *IEOG* 252; Curty 1995: #46a). Pliny the Elder's description of the same king's Central Asian foundation of Antioch-in-Margiane as *Syriana* (Plin. *HN* 6.16.47) may indicate the settlement of a predominantly Syrian or north Mesopotamian colonial population. A force of Persians, under the command of a certain Omanes, is attested at the Seleucid fort of Palaemagnesia during the reign of Seleucus II (*OGIS* 229; *IMagnSipylos* 1 105–106); the force had probably been settled there by Antiochus I (Cohen 1995: 225–226). During his second *anabasis,* Antiochus III organized the relocation of 2,000 Jewish households from Mesopotamia and Babylonia to *katoikiai* in Lydia and Phrygia (Joseph. *AJ* 12.147–153). An inscribed letter of Eumenes II suggests that the same Antiochus may also have established near Telmessus on the Lycian coast of Asia Minor a colony of Cardacians, central Iranian tribesmen who had fought and lost at Raphia (Segre 1928; *BE* 1980: 455–458 (#484); Wörrle 1979; Magie 1950: 1026; Rostovtzeff 1941: 2.645–648), but it is possible that this was an Achaemenid colony (*SEG* 53 1706). Even with this scanty documentation, we can recognize an early and continued Seleucid practice of population transfer, differently expressed but fundamentally similar to the forced migrations of the Neo-Assyrian, Neo-Babylonian, and Achaemenid kingdoms.

47. See Demand 1990 on urban relocation in archaic and classical Greece.

48. Plin. *HN* 5.27.93 reports that the coastal village of Hermia was moved inland to Seleucia; Strabo 14.5.4 says the same of Holmi and Steph. Byz. s.v. Σελεύκεια of Hyria. Tscherikower 1927: 39 quite sensibly identified Seleucia-on-the-Calycadnus as a synoecism of at least these three settlements; see Cohen 1995: 369–371.

49. Antioch-on-the-Maeander: Plin. *HN* 5.29.108 reports a synoecism of Symmaethos and Cranaus. Nysa: Strabo 14.1.46 reports a synoecism of Athymbrus, Athymbradus, and Hydrelus.

50. Strabo 12.8.15; see the first report of the Apamea-Celaenae survey (Summerer, Ivantchik, and von Kienlin 2011).

51. Antioch-by-Daphne: Strabo 16.2.4; Lib. *Or.* 11.92; Malalas 8.199–201. Seleucia-in-Pieria: Diod. Sic. 20.47.5–6.

52. *BCHP* 5 Rev. 6–9; cf. Paus. 1.16.3.
53. *BCHP* 5 Rev. 10.
54. Mazzoni 1991; Mehl 1991: 104.
55. Lund 1993: 34–36; Duyrat 2005: 224.
56. Gardin 1998: 45–58.
57. Lib. *Or.* 11.85–88; Malalas 8.200. Malalas 8.199 gives an almost identical account of the foundation of Seleucia-in-Pieria: an eagle snatched the sacrificial victim from Seleucus I, sacrificing on Mount Casius, and dropped it on the future site of Seleucia.
58. Strabo 14.1.21.
59. *RC* 3–4; *Syll.*3 344; *SEG* 56 1248.
60. *SEG* 52 1462; see Bencivenni 2003: 299–331 and Jones and Habicht 1989. Chaniotis 1993 sensitively demonstrates that this opposition is manifested in the very terminology used by the Nagidians to describe the new Ptolemaic colony.
61. See Smith 2003: 167–170 on similar Urartian policies in the plain of Ararat.
62. See Gardin 1998: Plate IXb.
63. Lib. *Or.* 11.92.
64. Malalas 8.201.
65. Invernizzi 1966: 58.
66. As a comparison, note that Antigonus Monophthalmus' instructions for the synoecism of Lebedus and Teos included, for the construction of the new city, the reuse of Tean roof tiles by the Lebedian colonists (*RC* 3 16; *Syll.*³ 344: [ᾠόμεθα δὲ] δεῖν καὶ τὰστέγας τῶν οἰκιῶν ἀποδοθῆναι τοῖς Λεβεδίοις); by giving Tean building materials to Lebedian citizens Antigonus surely intended to combine and replace presynoecic identities. Additionally, the law code of Cos was to be imposed on the newly synoecized community. See Ager 1998 on the local history of Lebedus in the Hellenistic period and Connor 1985 on the wider associations of house and city razing.
67. *PDura* 15; Joseph. *AJ* 12.147–153; see Cohen 1978: 45–70 and Kosmin 2011: 100. Thonemann 2009: 377 discusses the estate of Crateuas, the first attested land grant with such tripartite productive composition.
68. Gardin 1998: 41–58.
69. Dodinet, Leblanc, Vallat, and Villeneuve 1990. Note that such divisions of *chōra* land into geometrically regular parcels following the city grid are known from the Greek colonies of Chersonesos in the Black Sea and of southern Italy; see Carter 2006 and Guy 1995. On the Seleucid refoundation of Damascus, see Cohen 2006: 242–245. Paestum, similarly, experienced two parcelizations, first Greek, then Roman; see Delezir and Guy 1988.
70. Briant 1978: 68–69 has proposed a persuasive concentric model, whereby the ring of land closest to the Seleucid colony was divided into settlers' *klēroi* and enjoyed a certain juridical and social contiguity to the urban center, while the zone beyond that remained in the hands of the preconquest communities and at greater cultural and administrative distance; obviously Briant's

model, as a geometric ideal type, deliberately underplays the stubborn messiness of contour, fertility, and accessibility.

71. Adams 1965: 58–69.

72. Casana 2003.

73. *SEG* 35 1483; Feissel 1985.

74. *SEG* 35 1522; *IGLS* 1131–1140; see Berchem 1985 and Millar 1993: 86–89.

75. Gardin and Genetelle 1976.

76. Wenke 1975–1976: 94–112.

77. *IGIAC* 11–12; *IEOG* 213–214; *SEG* 7 12–13.

78. Plin. *HN* 6.16.46–47.

79. Isidore of Charax *BNJ* 781 F2 = *Mans. Parth.* 14: ἐντεῦθεν Μαργιανή . . . ἔνθα Ἀντιόχεια ἥ καλουμένη Ἔνυδρος. It has been suggested from excavation that water would have entered the city by canal (Zavyalov 2007: 316), as at Seleucia-on-the-Tigris and Aï Khanoum.

80. [Oppian], *Cynēgetica* 2.100–158. Hollis 1994 suggested as source of this passage Euphorion of Chalcis, librarian of Antiochus III and resident of Apamea; see also Bernard 1995: 354, 380.

81. For a discussion of the mythic geography and its connections to Macedonian Pella see Hollis 1994 and Bernard 1995: 355–366.

82. Plin. *HN* 6.16.47, Strabo 11.10.2. Solinus 48.3 and Martianus Capella 6.691, mentioning the wall, erroneously name the colony Seleucia. Archaeological excavation has identified Antiochus I's wall confusingly with, not the so-called Wall of Antiochus but the Giljakin-Čil'burž,; see Košelenko, Bader, and Gaibov 1995 and 1997: 133–135.

83. *AD* -133 B Rev. 19: bàd *šá* ¹*Si-lu-ku* lugal; another possible reference in "Demetrius and Arabia fragment" 6: bà]d⁇ *ša* ¹*Si-lu-ku*.

84. For a general discussion of Hellenistic survey archaeology, see Alcock 1994 and Alcock, Gates, and Rempel 2003.

85. Casana 2003: 292–295 (the evidence was gathered from recent rescue excavations).

86. Casana 2003.

87. The major settlement shift was first dated to Roman times (Philip et al. 2002), but subsequent research demonstrated a Hellenistic context (Philip et al. 2005).

88. Marfoe 1978: 623–624.

89. Adams 1965: 63–64. The proportion of the settled area consisting of villages and small towns declined from 62 percent in the Achaemenid period to 30 percent in the Seleucid and Parthian eras. Settlement size expanded from an average of 3.5 hectares in the Isin-Larsa period (the apogee of population and settlement in earlier antiquity) to 8.8 hectares, but it is also possible that urban densities were reduced as a result of Hellenistic city planning.

90. Wenke 1975–1976: 105–112.

91. Gardin 1998: 38–58, 109–114, 144–145.

92. Gardin 1998: 162.

93. Woolf 1998: 107–129.
94. Kühne 1994.
95. For the distinction between the concepts "hegemony" and "dominance," outlined in Gramsci's *Prison Notebooks,* see, e.g., Portier-Young 2011: 11–27 and Mitchell 1990.
96. Gardin 1998: 46.
97. Leriche and Pidaev 2007.
98. Sverchkov 2008 and 2009.
99. Kosmin 2011: 99–102; Leriche 2003a.
100. Jebel Khalid: Clarke 2002; Dura-Europus: Downey 1986.
101. Radt 2011.
102. See Rante 2008, Castagnoli 1971, and Lampl 1968.
103. At least Aï Khanoum, Seleucia-on-the-Tigris, Dura-Europus (in its second phase), Apamea-on-the-Euphrates, Apamea-on-the-Axios, and Antioch-by-Daphne. For general discussion see Peters 1983; Lauter 1986: 65–84; Lawrence 1957: 196–197. On the recent archaeological discoveries of Hellenistic Syria, see Leriche 2003b.
104. See Robert 1937: 531–534. Sauvaget 1941: 46 notes that the wide road in Aleppo (Hellenistic Beroea) is called al-Balât, doubtless from Greek *plateia.* On the very variable terminology for city streets and blocks, see Hennig 2000.
105. Hopkins 1972: 28–35.
106. Leblanc and Poccardi 1999; Grainger 1990: 48–49; Feissel 1985: 91–92; Downey 1961: 70; Sauvaget 1934.
107. Sauvaget 1949: 353–357.
108. Abadia-Reynal and Gaborit 2003: 150; Desreumaux, Gaborit, and Caillou 1999: 75–84.
109. Clarke et al. 2008: 68–69.
110. Downey 1961: 54; Balty 1969: 34.
111. *Amphoda*—Stratonicea-in-Caria: *IStrat* 1003–1004; Wilhelm 1909: #158 (with discussion, 183–187); Laodicea-by-the-Sea: Roussel 1942–1943 (*IGLS* 1261; *SEG* 55 1641); *plintheia*—Antioch-by-Daphne: Feissel 1985 (*SEG* 35 1483).
112. See Hennig 2000.
113. Such irregularity may lie behind Pliny's description of the walls of Seleucia-on-the-Tigris as having the outline of an eagle spreading its wings (Plin. *HN* 6.26.122).
114. Rante 2008; Grainger 1990: 61–62.
115. Sauvaget 1941: 33–53; Herrmann, Kurbansakhatov, and Simpson 2001: 14–22.
116. It is unclear for what precisely Hippodamus was responsible. The bibliography on Hippodamus' contribution and orthogonal planning in Old World and colonial Greece is extensive; see, e.g., Stefanidou-Tiveriou 2000; Cahill 2002: 3–21; Fehr 1979; Vallet 1976; Wycherley 1967.
117. The Alfredian burhs of Anglo-Saxon England offer a good comparison; see Lilley 2009: 42–46.

118. See Arist. *Pol.* 1330b26–27 for a brief discussion of "old-fashioned" urban-
     ism, which made it difficult for strangers to make their way around
     (δυσείσοδος . . . τοῖς ξενικοῖς) and for assailants to explore (δυσεξερεύνητος
     [τοῖς] ἐπιτιθεμένοις). James Scott usefully compares the spatial function of
     such higgledy-piggledy cities to the linguistic function of a difficult dialect:
     both remain stubbornly unfamiliar to nonlocals and state administrators;
     see Scott 1998: 53–54.
119. Cf. Scott 1998: 58 on Chicago.
120. *IGLS* 1183; Holleaux 1942: 200–251.
121. Wilhelm 1909: 183–187 (#158); Robert 1937: 531–534. A new inscription
     from Stratonicea, Şahin 2008 #31, gives a further *amphodon*-based watch
     post, bearing the markedly Seleucid symbol of the elephant. On the civic
     organization of Stratonicea-in-Caria, see Bremen 2000 and Şahin 1976.
122. Feissel 1985: 100–102. The fact that each *plintheion* is charged with the
     upkeep of the canal for the future suggests a stable eponymy. Such a practice
     is attested elsewhere: at Hadrian's refoundation of Jerusalem, for example,
     the names of the first seven *amphodarchs* remained attached to the seven
     amphoda (Chron. Pasch. (ed. Dindorf) p. 474 12–15: καὶ ἐμέρισεν τὴν πόλιν εἰς
     ἑπτὰ ἄμφοδα, καὶ ἔστησεν ἀνθρώπους ἰδίους ἀμφοδάρχας, καὶ ἑκάστῳ ἀμφοδάρχῃ
     ἀπένειμεν ἄμφοδον· καὶ ἕως τῆς σήμερον εἰς τὸ τοῦ ἀμφοδάρχου ὄνομα ἕκαστον
     ἄμφοδον χρηματίζει). Similarly, parchments from Dura-Europus and Avro-
     man indicate that Seleucid agricultural *klēroi* retained the names of their
     owners at the original distribution several centuries after alienation; see
     Kosmin 2011: 100 and Minns 1915.
123. Roussel 1942–1943; *IGLS* 1261; *SEG* 55 1641.
124. *AD* -144 Obv. 36–37: *mi-nu-tú* [. . .*š*]*á* ᴸᵘᵉki.meš ᴸᵘ̂ir meš lugal [x x ᴸ]ᵘ*pu-li-ṭe-e šá
     ina* eki *u* ᵘ[ru]*Se-lu-ke-'a-a i-man-nu-ú.* Note that Shayegan 2011: 62–63
     considers this, incorrectly, a muster of troops. Contrast this census, where
     the population is divided into three separate social groups, with the Arsacid
     census of 106, which was "a counting of the peoples of all lands" (*mi-nu-tú šá*
     unmeš kur.kurmeš *gab-bi*) without (recorded) distinction (*AD* -105 B Upper
     Edge 2).
125. See Scott 1998: 58–63, for a brief introduction and Clark 1999: 23–78 for a
     brilliant discussion of Haussmanization, Parisian urban modernity, and the
     critical (e.g., Manet) or supportive (e.g., Pissarro) artistic responses. Cf.
     Purcell 2005: 262–263: "[L]ike most forms of *geometria,* the chequerboard
     plans of ancient cities are instruments of social control."
126. See Grainger 1990: 61–62.
127. Joseph. *AJ* 14.38.
128. Arist. *Pol.* 1330b21–27.
129. Joseph. *AJ* 13.135–141; Diod. Sic. 33.4.
130. Recent survey evidence has shown that the Hellenistic acropolis of Apamea-
     Celaenae, on the hill Üçlerce, was the location of the Achaemenid-period
     settlement; see Ivantchik, Belinskiy, and Dovgalev 2011.

131. Compare the Norman treatment of Anglo-Saxon burhs; see Lilley 2009: 151.
132. Legg 2007.
133. Arist. *Pol.* 1330b23–24; similarly, Heraclides Criticus (*BNJ* 369A F1.1) attributes the untidiness of Athens' streets to their antiquity (κακῶς ἐρρυμοτομημένη διὰ τὴν ἀρχαιότητα).
134. Frézouls 1977.
135. Recall Seleucus I's renaming of Pella-on-the-Axios as Apamea; see Chapter 4.
136. As Thonemann 2012: 24–25 emphasizes, the selection of the appropriate landscape feature—e.g., Antioch-on-the-Maeander and not -under-Mycale or -in-Caria—was "a positive choice, a conscious decision to categorise a city in one way rather than another."
137. Matheson 1994. The earliest statue of *Tychē*, that of Bupalus of Chios at Smyrna, according to Paus. 4.30.6, to the sixth century BCE.
138. For a discussion of the iconography, symbolism, and reception of Antioch's *Tychē*, see the comprehensive monograph of Meyer 2006.
139. App. *Syr.* 57 lists two colonies, Alexandropolis in India and Alexandreschate in Scythia, supposedly founded by Seleucus Nicator ἐς τιμὴν Ἀλεξάνδρου τοῦ βασιλέως, "in honor of king Alexander." Neither holds up on inspection: Alexandreschate was refounded by Antiochus I as Antioch-in-Scythia, and no colony could have been founded in India after the Treaty of the Indus; see Errington 1976: 163–164.
140. Plin. *HN* 6.27.139.
141. For the ideological function of Babylon, see Capdetrey 2007: 25–28; for the name of Antiochus IV's refoundation, see Leschhorn 1984: 243–245.
142. See Errington 1976: 156–169.
143. Wolski 1966; Shayegan 2011; see *IGIAC* 11–12, with commentary.
144. Plut. *Demetr.* 32.1–3; Malalas 8.98.
145. Joseph. *AJ* 13.82; 1 Macc. 10:57–58.
146. Kuhrt and Sherwin-White 1993: 15.
147. Joseph. *AJ* 13.82; 1 Macc. 10:57–58.
148. *IGIAC* 53 15–16; *IEOG* 252; *OGIS* 233; *IMagn* 61.
149. Such a sentiment is found elsewhere: e.g., *SEG* 39 1426 10, where the Ptolemaic governor Thraseas wished to make Cilician Arsinoe worthy of its name (βουλόμεθα τὴν πόλιν ἀξίαν τῆς ἐπωνυμίας ποιεῖν).
150. App. *Syr.* 54–64.
151. See, e.g., the Parthian history of Apollodorus of Artemita (*BNJ* 779).
152. Seleucus' eldest son, Antiochus, plays no part, in contrast to the Tetrapolis narratives, which affirm the elevation of Antiochus to coruler; there is genuine Chaldaean religious content and local color (see later); and certain phrases and ideas parallel early third-century Seleucid inscriptions—compare in particular the helpful but unnamed δαιμόνιον of App. *Syr.* 58 with the δαιμόνιον εὔνουν καὶ συνεργόν of *OGIS* 219 11–12 (*Illion* 32).
153. App. *Syr.* 58; trans. H. White, with changes.

154. Typically the word refers to garrisoned strongholds in enemy landscapes; for example, it is used of Athenian fortresses in Eretria (Thuc. 8.95.6), Aegina (Xen. *Hell.* 5.1.2), and the Chersonese (Dem. 8.66).

155. Persian names and religious titles appear regularly in temple prebend lists and administrative documents of early Seleucid Babylon; see Boiy 2004: 294 and Stolper 2006.

156. Malkin 1987: 92–113.

157. Lackenbacher 1982: 130. Esarhaddon's refoundation of Babylon is the most famous example. Recensions A, B, and C of Esarhaddon's Babylon inscription, assigning great prominence to the astrologers, record the specific astronomical configurations which signaled the arrival of the propitious time to begin the work. Further divinatory procedures (extispicy, lecanomancy) are performed in recensions A, B, and D; see Cogan 1983.

158. Most famously in Darius' accession narrative, Hdt. 3.65. Interestingly, very similar language is used in an inscription from Labraunda (*ILabr* 3), recording the attempt of the Carian priest to deceive Seleucus II.

159. The Hebrew Bible offers the closest comparison I can find. Numbers 22–24 recounts that the holy man Balaam, commissioned by the Moabites to curse the children of Israel, newly arrived from Egypt, instead blesses them three times and predicts their prosperity in the land, after experiencing a theophany. The story is discussed in Greek by Philo, *Life of Moses,* where Balaam is labeled a *magos,* and Joseph. *AJ* 4.102–130. The Balaam narrative is the only place in the Bible where a foreign seer/diviner/magician is the source of true prophecy and a blessing.

160. Lib. *Or.* 11.85–90.

161. See Kosmin 2013b, where it is argued that the use of elephants in this way marked the culminating justification of Seleucus I's Treaty of the Indus with Chandragupta Maurya.

162. Foundation of Alexandria-by-Egypt: Arr. *Anab.* 3.2.1–2; Strabo 17.1.7; Plut. *Alex.* 26.5–9; see Fraser 1972: 3–4 (with n.4).

163. Lib. *Or.* 11.91–92. The pre-Hellenistic populations will be discussed in Chapter 8.

164. Lib. *Or.* 11.94.

165. Malalas 8.203. Malalas' narrative contains accounts of virgins being sacrificed by Seleucus at the foundations of cities, who then receive worship as the city *Tychē*. These *Tychē* sacrifices are found throughout Malalas' universal history, whenever cities are established, from Adam to Justinian. Garstad 2005 has persuasively argued that they derive from a Christian polemical history composed in Antioch in the late fourth century. On the Christian agenda of Malalas more generally, see Liebeschuetz 2004. On Malalas' likely source, Pausanias of Antioch, see Garstad 2011.

166. I can find no Greek or Near Eastern precedent or parallel.

167. Syriac text: Moesinger 1878: 2.63 and Bedjan 1890: 2.507–511; French translation: Pigulevskaja 1963: 46–47. This grant of tax-free *klēroi* is virtually

identical to that offered by Antiochus III to the Jewish colonies in Lydia and Phrygia (Joseph. *AJ* 12.147–153). On Karka de Bet Selok, see Cohen 2013: 98–100.

168. Liv. 34.58.4–5; App. *Syr.* 1.

169. An assertion of Seleucid superiority may lie behind Pliny's contrast between Alexander's eponymous foundation in Aria and Antiochus I's reconstruction of the larger (forty stades vs. thirty), more beautiful, and more ancient *(multoque pulchrius sicut antiquius)* city of Artacabene (Plin. *HN* 6.23.93).

170. Malalas 8.199.

171. Exceptionally, Antioch-by-Daphne's strong local identity preserved the names and accounts of four of its architects, Attaeus, Perittas, Anaxicrates (Tzetz. *Chil.* 7.118 176–180), and Xenaius (Malalas 8.100).

172. Joseph. *AJ* 12.147–153.

173. Isidore of Charax *BNJ* 781 F2 = *Mans. Parth.* 1; Plin. *HN* 6.26.117; Malalas 8.198; see Rostovtzeff 1938. It is possible, of course, that Isidore's lemma should be emended from *Nicanor* to *Nicator*, as in Seleucus I Nicator—confusion between the two names is found in App. *Syr.* 57; see Chaumont 1984: 90.

174. *PDura* 25, a deed of sale from 180 CE, is dated by the Roman consuls, the regnal years of the emperors, the Seleucid Era, and four eponymous priesthoods. Separate priesthoods exist for Zeus, Apollo, the cults of the *progonoi* (the official dynastic cult of the Seleucid dynasty), and Seleucus I Nicator alone. That is to say, Seleucus I appears twice: once with his dynasty and once by himself. His separate cult can be only for the king in his capacity as founder of Dura-Europus *(ktistēs);* see Kosmin 2011: 96–97.

175. Rostovtzeff 1939: 292–293.

176. As attested by an inscription from Tyriaeum, a town in Lycaonia (Jonnes and Ricl 1997; *SEG* 47 1745), and the narrative of the Hellenizing Jews in 2 Maccabees 4; see Kennell 2005.

177. Strabo 12.8.14.

178. *IMagn* 80 12–13: τή[ν τε συ]γγ[έ]νειαν καὶ τὴν οἰκ[ε]ι[ό]τητα [κα]ὶ φ[ιλίαν τὴν ὑ]πάρχουσ[αν] τ[ῆ]ι πόλει [τῶν] Ἀντ[ιοχ]έων [π]ρὸς [τὴ]ν πόλιν τὴν [Μ]αγνήτω[ν]. Curty 1995: #46b.

179. *IEOG* 252 17–20; *OGIS* 233; *IMagn* 61.

180. *SEG* 43 998; Jones and Russell 1993: 297–304

181. *IG* 12, 6 1 6. Habicht 1957: 242–252, especially 250. Curty 1995: 61–63 and Patterson 2010: 147–149 each try to explain away the kinship as mythical convenience, through the river-god Maeander and through Aeolus, respectively. Thonemann 2012: 25 tidily suggests that the Samian kinship can be explained by the just-mentioned inscription from Nagidos (*SEG* 43 998)—the Nagidians, descendants of Samian founders, were headed to Antioch-on-the-Maeander.

182. Plut. *Luc.* 31.3–4; Diod. Sic. 31.17a.

183. Strabo 11.11.2.

184. Plin. *HN* 6.27.138.

185. Kosmin 2013d.

186. Berossus *BNJ* 680 F8a = Joseph. *Ap.* 139–141. Indeed, the builder-king figures strongly in Babylonian and Assyrian monarchic ideology; see Lackenbacher 1982: 64–130.

187. *IEOG* 103; *OGIS* 253; *SEG* 36 1274.

188. The identification of Antiochus I with Nebuchadnezzar was deliberately promoted by the Babylonian priest Berossus and by the cuneiform Borsippa Cylinder; see Kosmin 2014b. Antiochus III received the robe of Nebuchadnezzar II at the *akītu* festival of 187 (*AD* -187 A Rev. 11).

189. It is attested at Antioch-by-Daphne (Cohen 2006: 81) and Seleucia-in-Pieria (App. *Syr.* 63) in northern Syria, at Dura-Europus on the middle Euphrates (Kosmin 2011: 96–97), at Seleucia-on-the-Tigris in Babylonia (Nuffelen 2001), and at Nysa, Hyrcanis, Thyateira, Antioch-on-the-Maeander, and Apollonia-in-Caria in Asia Minor (Habicht 1956: 105–107 and Debord 2003: 282–284). Note that many of these cults survived the extinction of the Seleucid dynasty (Chankowski 2010). On the cult of Zeus Seleucius, see Nock 1928: 41–42 and Fraser 1949 (with *TAM* 5.2: 309 and 332 (#901)).

190. Schmidt 1910: 1139–1140.

191. For a general account of Antioch's urban development, see Downey 1961: 41–132.

192. Strabo 16.2.4.

193. Lib. *Or.* 11.119. This compromise between Strabo and Libanius was proposed by Müller 1839: 54 and followed by Förster 1897: 120.

194. Strabo 16.2.4; Malalas 8.205.

195. Lib. *Or.* 11.124–125.

196. Liv. 41.20.9.

197. The name of Antiochus' architect, Cossutius, was scratched onto the plaster wall of this aqueduct (*IGLS* 825).

198. Malalas 8.205.

199. Joseph. *AJ* 13.36.

200. Strabo 14.2.25. The kings are unnamed but presumably Seleucid: the city passed at some point in the third century to the republic of Rhodes, although briefly falling under the control of Philip V *c.*200–197 (Liv. 33.18.22). In 167 the Romans granted its freedom and autonomy; see Cohen 1995: 268–273.

201. Strabo 16.1.5.

202. For Seleucid Dura-Europus, see Kosmin 2011. The recently discovered letter of the Attalid king Eumenes II, granting *polis* status to the Seleucid military colony of Tyriaeum in southeastern Phrygia, gives some indication of how such promotions may have been negotiated, phrased, and awarded. The project may even have been initiated by Antiochus III. For the constitutional changes and role of Eumenes, see Savalli-Lestrade 2005a and 2003: 20–22, Bencivenni 2003: 333–356, and Jonnes and Ricl 1997.

203. Gachet and Salles 1993; Gachet 1990; Callot 1989 and 1990.

204. *IEOG* 421/422, *SEG* 56 1844. Several dates have been proposed for the letter, based on the almost illegible Greek numbers on line 44. Piejko 1988a: 114–116

and Jeppesen 1989: 83–92 date the letter to Seleucus II's reign, Roueché and Sherwin-White 1985: 17–19 to Antiochus III's.

205. Lines 23–24 (ed. Jeppesen) = 24–25 (ed. Roueché and Sherwin-White). Note for comparison that Leriche 2003b: 133 has raised the possibility that Apamea-on-the-Axios had been founded as a powerful citadel and subsequently expanded.

206. Berlin 2012.

207. Briant 1982a. Antiochus III's immigrants are likely to have been exiles and refugees from his failed war against Rome.

8. City Makes King

1. The location of Seleucid Jerusalem's Acra, the walled citadel, is one of the most disputed topics in the city's (ancient) topography; see Decoster 1989 with bibliography.

2. See below for details.

3. Liv. 35.15.3, 6.

4. Joseph. *AJ* 13.368.

5. *SEG* 7.4; *IGIAC* 7; *IEOG* 183.

6. Clarke 2002.

7. Downey 1986.

8. Rapin 1992.

9. Radt 2011.

10. See Hatzopoulos 2001, for whom "the relation of the palace to the capital city is no more and no less than the sensible image of the relation of the king to the citizen body" (193).

11. For full bibliography, see Cohen 2013: 225–244 and Mairs 2011: 26–29 and 2013: 7. Note that the main elements of the urban plan were already in place when the city passed out of Seleucid hands in the mid-third century and that, in any case, secessionist Graeco-Bactrian royal ideology appears to parade in the footsteps of its former masters (see Coloru 2009).

12. Guillaume 1983.

13. *AD* -86 Flake 11.

14. Invernizzi 1993: 243–244.

15. Held 2002: 228–236. Excavation has uncovered a canal, flanked by banks of baked bricks, in total more than 35 meters wide, running west to east through the center of the city and dividing it into two equal halves; subsurface prospection has revealed a further canal, 4.5 meters wide, flanking the city to the north and west. This confirms literary descriptions: Theophylactus Simocatta, *Histories* 5.6: ἡ δὲ τρίτη διαρρεῖ τῆς Σελευκείας ἐχόμενα καὶ εἰς τὸν Τίγριν εἰσβάλλει καὶ δίδωσι τῷ πολίσματι δυσμαχωτάτην ἀσφάλειαν, ταῖς λαγόσι τῶν ὑδάτων ὥσπερ στεφάνῃ ἕρκους τινὸς τὸ ἄστυ κατοχυρώσασα; Plin. *HN* 5.26.90: *scinditur enim Euphrates a Zeugmate DLXXXXIIII p. circa vicum Masicen et parte laeva in Mesopotamiam vadit, per ipsam Seleuciam circaque eam praefluenti infusus Tigri.*

16. Q. Marcius Rex constructed "the old palace" there during the reign of king Philip II, according to Malalas 9.225; the palaces of Gallienus and Diocletian were located on the island.
17. Joseph. *AJ* 13.36.
18. Lib. *Or.* 11.119; see Hoepfner 2004.
19. Kottaridi 2011; Hatzopoulos 2001; Nielsen 1997: 140–148.
20. Boucharlat 2001.
21. It had long been thought, on the basis of Herodotus' assigning of Babylon's palace and temple tower to different banks (Hdt. 1.181) that the course of the Euphrates had shifted east in Achaemenid times, either as the unintended consequence of Neo-Babylonian riverbank building work or as a deliberate diversion engineered by Xerxes; see George 1992: 355–356. But it has been shown by Rollinger 1993: 148–166 that the archaeological data cannot sustain this hypothesis and by Spek 1995: 467–477 that the Euphrates channel certainly was in its Neo-Babylonian position during the reign of Antiochus I; for subsequent bibliography, see Boiy 2004: 66, 78–79.
22. George 1992: 1–29.
23. Greek roof tiles and antefixes and high-quality painted plaster and stucco work, which belong to the late fourth century if we can date by stylistic comparison, were excavated on the site; see Boiy 2004: 9, 93–94 and Koldewey and Wetzel 1931–1932.
24. Invernizzi 1993.
25. For an enchanting phenomenological study of intimate, domestic space, see Bachelard 1958.
26. Joseph. *AJ* 13.35–36.
27. See Marzolff 1996: 154–158 and Batziou-Efstathiou 2002: 22–25. On *tetrapyrgia* generally, see Peschlow-Bindokat 1996.
28. Joseph. *AJ* 13.36.
29. For details, see Ehling 2008: 145–153.
30. Ath. 10.439a; Ath. 5.193d. On such everyday forms of resistance, see Scott 1985. As a parallel, note that in contemporary Jewish sources the name of the great Neo-Babylonian monarch and Seleucid prototype Nebuchadrezzar ("Nabû, protect the crown prince!") was reworked to the more familiar Nebuchadnezzar ("Nabû, protect the mule!"); see Selms 1974.
31. Mørkholm 1966: 184.
32. In the Sixth Syrian War (see Mittag 2006: 335); *BNJ* 234 F3 = Ath. 10.438d–f.
33. For doubts, see Carter 2001.
34. Polyb. 30.25.
35. Liv. *Per.* 41.
36. Polyb. 26.1.1 = Ath. 5.193d.
37. Diod. Sic. 29.32.
38. Polyb. 26.1.1 = Ath. 5.193d.1; Diod. Sic. 29.32.
39. Polyb. 26.1a.2, 26.1.5; Diod. Sic. 29.32; cf. Philip V at Argos (Polyb. 10.26.1–2).
40. See, e.g., Walsh 1975 and Blacker 1990.

41. Polyb. 26.1a.1.
42. Polyb. 26.1.3.
43. Diod. Sic. 29.32.
44. Diod. Sic. 29.32.
45. Diod. Sic. 29.32; Polyb. 26.1a.2, 26.1.4.
46. These offices are usually understood as Hellenized versions of the Roman offices of aedile and tribune; this is not necessary.
47. Malalas 8.205; see Bielfeldt 2010: 192–193.
48. *BNJ* 234 F3 = Ath. 10.438d–f.
49. Polyb. 26.1.9.
50. Ma 2002: 179–242.
51. Polyb. 26.1.12–14.
52. Strabo 14.1.46. The hero appears on Nysa's coinage during the reigns of Marcus Aurelius and Maximinus; see Leschhorn 1984: 234 n.6.
53. Robert 1958b.
54. Such a duality of mythic-historical founders is paralleled for various Greek cities: the archaic colonies Taras, Croton, and Abdera, for example, honored eponymous heroes alongside their actual oecists; for Malkin 1998: 210–221 this phenomenon functioned as self-enhancement, boosting the colonies' claims to antiquity and land. On occasion, this double founding was engineered: Polyaen. *Strat.* 6.53 reports that Hagnon, the Athenian oecist of Amphipolis, brought with him the bones of the hero Rhesus. Aphrodisias, too, honored both descendants of its historical synoecizers as well as Bellerophon and Ninus; see Chaniotis 2009. For a general account of early imperial Asia Minor foundation accounts, see Strubbe 1984–1986.
55. See Chapter 4 for details.
56. See the detailed discussion of Saliou 1999–2000.
57. Lib. *Or.* 11.47–76.
58. Malalas 8.119.
59. Strabo 16.2.5.
60. See Houghton, Lorber, and Hoover 2008: #2306 (under Antiochus VIII Grypus), #2372 (under Antiochus IX Cyzicenus), #2422 (under Seleucus VI). On Triptolemus as founder of Tarsus, see Scheer 1993: 273–282 and 2005: 226–230.
61. Bernard 1995 and Hollis 1994.
62. [Oppian], *Cynēgetica* 2.114.
63. [Oppian], *Cynēgetica* 2.100–158.
64. Proposed by Bernard 1995: 359.
65. Proposed by Hollis 1994: 159.
66. Most cities' assertions of fabricated mythical origins are attested from the Roman imperial era, not least in connection to Hadrian's Panhellenion (Heller 2006). For Hellenistic precedents, see Weiß 1984: 188–194.
67. *SEG* 54 1070; see Isager 1998 for the *editio princeps;* Bremmer 2009 and Gagné 2006 have discussed the relationship between the sixty-line poem and Halicarnassian cult.

68. Saliou 1999–2000: 360–361.

69. For teams and destinations, see the composite list in Kern 1901: 500–504; see also Parker 2004.

70. On "crowned" or *stephanitic* festival rank, see Slater and Summa 2006: 279–282; on *asylia*, see Rigsby 1996.

71. *IMagn* 16–87; see Thonemann 2007 and Rigsby 1996.

72. Antioch-in-Persis has been identified with modern Bushehr. Coinage indicates the likely presence of a cavalry detachment.

73. *IMagn* 18; *RC* 31; *OGIS* 231; *IEOG* 250; *IGIAC* 51.

74. For an up-to-date description of the Sacred Agora, see Bingöl 2006.

75. *IMagn* 61; *OGIS* 233; *IEOG* 252; *IGIAC* 53; Curty 1995: #46a; trans. Austin 2006: 342–344, with changes.

76. Such lists are attached to the decrees of Calydon (*IMagn* 26), the *koinon* of the Acarnanians (31), Same on Cephallonia (35), Megalopolis (38), the Achaeans (39), Sicyon (41), Corcyra (44), Paros (50), Mytilene (52), Clazomenae (53), Laodicea-on-the-Lycus (59), and Gortyn (65).

77. I am persuaded that the junior Antiochus was not present with his father in Antioch-in-Persis: the Magnesian decree taken before Antiochus III was separately brought to the son (ἀπέδωκαν καὶ τὸ πρὸς ἐμὲ ψήφισμα), who does not feature in the narratives of Antiochus III's great, second *anabasis*. In the voice of Antiochus IV, 2 Macc. 9:23 reports Antiochus III's appointment of a successor and coruler during one of his eastern expeditions.

78. *IMagn* 19 15–24; *OGIS* 232; *RC* 32; *IEOG* 251; *IGIAC* 52.

79. Even if the Antiochians are echoing here the language of the Magnesians' decree, it is their decision to use this terminology that is significant.

80. In his own letter (*IMagn* 18; *OGIS* 231; *RC* 31; *IEOG* 250; *IGIAC* 51) the Seleucid king had promised to arrange recognition from his subjects; the colony's letter makes no mention of this. Contrast this with, for example, the response of Chalcis on Euboea (*IMagn* 47), which noted that their recognition followed Philip V's instruction: οἱ στρατ]ηγο[ὶ] εἶπαν [περὶ ὧν ὁ] βασιλεὺς Φίλι[π]πος ἐγρα[ψ]εν τῆι βουλῆι κ[αὶ τῶι] δήμ[ωι] περὶ [Μ]αγνήτων τῶν ἐπὶ Μαιάνδρωι . . .

81. On a similar "independent tone" in Magnesia's originating documents for the Leucophryenea, see Sumi 2004: 80–82.

82. On the architecture, building history, and small finds of the *heroön*, see Bernard 1967 and Bernard, Le Berre, and Stucki 1973: 85–102.

83. *IGIAC* 97; *IEOG* 382; *SEG* 52 1514; Robert 1968.

84. The inscriptions have benefited from the brilliantly wrought commentary of Louis Robert, who, in a fine piece of detective work, identified the epigram's author with the famous Peripatetic philosopher and pupil of Aristotle, Clearchus of Soli (Robert 1968: 421–457). Note that Robert's identification and date have been challenged, though unpersuasively, by Lerner 2003–2004; see Rougemont's commentary in *IGIAC* 97.

85. For a similar contrast between the age of Alexander and heroic/archaic Greece, see, e.g., Plut. *De Alex. fort.* 343a8.

86. Bernard 1967: 310–312; Robert 1973: 217. A libation conduit, leading from the *cella* to the crypt, is evidence of the institutionalization of cultic honors for the city's founder; see Canepa 2010: 8.

87. See, e.g., 1 Macc. 15:6, where Antiochus VII gives the Jews permission to strike their own coins.

88. For typology, see Mittag 2006: 182–198. It is important to recognize that there is no direct correlation between juridical status and coinage kind. Royal, autonomous, and quasi-municipal coinages were minted concurrently at Antioch-in-Ptolemaïs (see Seyrig 1962: 25–32 with Houghton, Lorber, and Hoover 2008), Ascalon (*BMC* (Palestine) 105 #7), and Antioch-on-the-Cydnus, formerly Tarsus (see Cox 1950: 46–51 with Houghton, Lorber, and Hoover 2008). Antioch-by-Daphne and several Phoenician cities struck both quasi-municipal and royal types.

89. It is possible that Antiochus III was restoring an old privilege that the city had received under Ptolemy V; see Hoover 2004: 486–487.

90. See Mørkholm 1965 and 1966: 124–130; Schwartz 1982.

91. Houghton, Lorber, and Hoover 2008: 359.

92. Houghton, Lorber, and Hoover 2008 #1443–1444, #1822, #2044, #2099.

93. Houghton, Lorber, and Hoover 2008 #2021.

94. Houghton, Lorber, and Hoover 2008 #1825, #2100, #2185–2186.

95. Sandan: Houghton, Lorber, and Hoover 2008 #1778, #1895, #2058, #2161, #2287, #2289; Sandan altar: Houghton, Lorber, and Hoover 2008 #2057, #2159–2160, #2284–2286, #2288.

96. Houghton, Lorber, and Hoover 2008 #1896, #1998, #2059–2060.

97. Houghton, Lorber, and Hoover 2008 #2450, under Demetrius III Eucaerus (97/6–88/7).

98. Houghton, Lorber, and Hoover 2008 #2471–2472, under Antiochus XII Dionysus (87/6–83/2).

99. Laodice was the mother of the colony's founder, Seleucus IV, but it is likely that "mother" is meant in the sense of "metropolis." Houghton, Lorber, and Hoover 2008 # 2250–2251; see Sawaya 2004, Arnaud 2001, and Roussel 1911.

100. Similarly, Tyre presented itself on its quasi-municipal coinage as *lṣr 'm ṣdnm* ("of Tyre, mother of the Sidonians"); Sidon responded with the legend *'m kmb 'p' kt ṣr* ("mother of Cambe, Hippone, Citium, and Tyre"). Hoover 2004: 292 has suggested that the royal portrait on the obverse could be seen to offer imperial legitimization to this battle for ancestral primacy. Note that seal impressions from the Hellenistic administrative center at Tel Kedesh in northern Israel contain similar bilingual titles; one official Tyrian seal combines the Seleucid- and Tyrian-Era dates with Phoenician and Greek scripts (Ariel and Naveh 2003: 64–70).

101. Houghton, Lorber, and Hoover 2008 #1425, #1798, #2172, #2239, #2317.

102. Houghton, Lorber, and Hoover 2008 #1430–1431, #1806–1808.

103. Houghton, Lorber, and Hoover 2008 #1803–1804, #2012; on the thyrsus, see Houghton 1992: 123–124.

104. Houghton, Lorber, and Hoover 2008: #2306, #2372, #2422.
105. See Marcellesi 2004: 88–89; Hoover 2004: 487; Andrade 2009: 34–57.
106. Hoover 2004: 492–497 has shown that after the reign of Alexander I Balas, when Ptolemaic influence was reasserted in Coele Syria, the quasi-municipal coinage in Phoenicia was used to constrain the depiction of the Seleucid king on the obverse, showing neither radiate crowns nor extraneous epithets.
107. Houghton, Lorber, and Hoover 2008 #2252.
108. Compare Benjamin 1999: 519 on reformist proposals for the normalization of Parisian street names.
109. For details, see Cohen 1995: 248–250 (Alabanda) and 265–268 (Tralleis).
110. *IGIAC* 3, 11–12; *IEOG* 218, 213–214; *SEG* 7.1, 12–13. Note that the city also bore the Parthian dynastic name Phraata, perhaps from the reign of Phraates IV.
111. See Tscherikower 1927: 176 and Mørkholm 1966: 116–117.
112. Isidore of Charax *BNJ* 781 F2 = *Mans. Parth.* 2.
113. Isidore of Charax *BNJ* 781 F2 = *Mans. Parth.* 1. A fragmentary cuneiform tablet, scooped up with nearby river mud being collected to manufacture bricks for the Atargatis temple, discusses a field in the district of ^{uru}Da-$[m]$ a-ra^{ki} (city of Dawara); in Late Babylonian postvocalic m is consistently replaced with w (Westenholz 2007: 284–285), and so, in time, the weak consonantal Dawara would resolve into Dūra. The name is generic, meaning "wall" or "fortress." Accordingly, if Dawara or Dūra was indeed a pre-Macedonian town in the region, the emergence of this appellation in the Parthian period is a return to a pre-Seleucid name; see Kosmin 2011: 98–99.
114. Note that the Astronomical Diaries from Babylon, throughout the period of Seleucid dominance in Elymaïs, use the ancient, Middle Babylonian name of Susa, ^{uru}múš.šéš^{ki}, the civic form of the old Elamite goddess Inshushinak; see Labat 1988: #102. Diary entries call Antioch-in-Mygdonia by its pre-Seleucid name, Nisibis, spelled syllabically as ^{uru}na-ṣi-bi-in (*AD* -111 B Obv. 6).
115. *IDelos* 1520 (dating to 153/2), *IDelos* 2593 (144/3), *Delphes* 24 I.II (128/7); cf. the use of Laodicea on an honorific inscription on Delos for king Antiochus VIII (*IDelos* 1551; Roussel 1911) and the possible use in a Phoenician inscription from Umm el-'Amed, from 132/1, during the reign of Antiochus VII (the phrase *bplg l'dk* in the dedicator's genealogy could mean either "from the district of Laodicea" (Meyer 1931: 4–5) or "from the family grouping of L'dk" (Dunand and Duru 1962:181–184); note that coins from Laodicea-in-Phoenicia, unlike this inscription, spell the dynastic name with an open (aleph) ending, *l'dk'*.
116. On possible interpretations of Kibōtos, see Cohen 1995: 284–285.
117. Tarn 1966: 12–13 drew attention to what he called colonial nicknames; though see the caution of Cohen 2013: 352–359.
118. Cf. Bielfeldt 2010, a brilliant study of civic self-manifestation at Attalid Pergamum.
119. From the epitaph of the Ptolemaic officer Apollonius, who fought in the Judean-Syrian-Egyptian war of 103–101; see Clarysse 1989.

120. The earliest instance is the revolt of the Syrian Seleucis during the War of Syrian Succession after Seleucus I's assassination (*OGIS* 219 4–7; *Ilion* 32); for details, see Chapter 3. This occurred in the probable context of Ptolemaic invasion and a mere two decades after soldiers had been settled in the new colonies. It should probably be considered more a mutiny than a developed colonial revolt. The *apantēsis* ceremonies described in the Gurob Papyrus, according to which the colonial populations of Seleucia-in-Pieria and Antioch-by-Daphne welcomed Ptolemy III, should be considered a staged rite of surrender, not a revolt; for a discussion of ritualized royal receptions, see Chapter 4. More germane are the attempts by Seleucid queens to instigate righteous and indignant outrage on their behalf from colonial populations: at the outset of the Third Syrian War queen Berenice, widow of Antiochus II, appealed for the pity and assistance of the Antiochians (Polyaenus, *Strat.* 8.50) and was granted a bodyguard of Galatian mercenaries; Seleucus II's aunt Stratonice tried to bring Antioch-by-Daphne to revolt (Agatharchides *BNJ* 86 F20a = Joseph. *Ap.* 1.206–208). Finally, the rebel viceroy Achaeus attempted first to lead an army into Syria during the absence of Antiochus III (Polyb. 5.57.4) and second, while Antiochus III was still besieging Sardis, to escape to Syria and stir up revolt there (Polyb. 8.17). For a discussion of the political role of the colonial populations of Alexandria and Antioch-by-Daphne in the third century, see Mittag 2000.
121. For details, sources, and bibliography, see Ehling 2008.
122. Newell 1918: 92–110; Bellinger 1949: 87; Houghton 1993; Hoover 2007; Houghton, Lorber, and Hoover 2008.
123. Will 1966: 2.446.
124. Diod. Sic. 34/35.5.22.
125. *IDelos* 1551; *SEG* 42 740 bis. The context is the dynastic conflict between Antiochus VIII Grypus and his half-brother Antiochus IX Cyzicenus; see Moore 1992.
126. Joseph. *AJ* 13.35.
127. Joseph. *AJ* 13.108.
128. Diod. Sic. 33.4a.
129. 2 Macc. 13:26.
130. Joseph. *AJ* 13.114.
131. Ma 2002: 148: "[M]uch of the ideological effect of [the Pamukçu stele] resides in the fact that it is not directly addressed to the subjects: its effect is to display the mechanism of order transmission and implementation. The administrative dossier is not converted into a direct act of communication with the ruled, but simply displayed in monumental form: king speaks to official, official speaks of official, without ever consulting or addressing the party finally concerned."
132. Joseph. *AJ* 12.138.
133. 1 Macc. 10:25.
134. 1 Macc. 15:1.

135. For dates and details, see Ehling 2008; Sartre 2001: 379–380; Bickerman 1938: 153; Kahrstedt 1926: 75–85. The grant of *asylia* by an unspecified "king Antiochus" to the Zeus temple at Baetocaece (*IGLS* 4028; *OGIS* 262; *RC* 70; *SEG* 32 1446) may well belong in this context; see Rigsby 1996: 505.
136. Joseph. *AJ* 13.116.
137. Joseph. *AJ* 13.139.
138. Porphyry *BNJ* 260 F32.26 = Eusebius, *Chronographia* 117.1–124.5 (Karst).
139. 1 Macc. 11:45.
140. Joseph. *AJ* 13.135–137.
141. Joseph. *AJ* 13.138–141; cf. 1 Macc. 11.46–51.
142. Joseph. *AJ* 13.368; cf. the less reliable App. *Syr.* 69, where the king is killed in a gymnasium.
143. Just. *Epit.* 35.1.3.
144. Diod. Sic. 40.1a.
145. Diod. Sic. 34/5.28.1.
146. Joseph. *AJ* 13.420.
147. Joseph. *AJ* 13.222.
148. Joseph. *AJ* 13.392.
149. Joseph. *AJ* 13.267; Just. *Epit.* 39.1.3–5.
150. Joseph. *AJ* 13.419; Just. *Epit.* 40.1–3; App. *Syr.* 48; Strabo 11.14.15.
151. For a political narrative constructed from the cuneiform data, see Shayegan 2011: 60–168 and Boiy 2004: 162–180.
152. *BCHP* 14 comm. 7.
153. Boiy 2004: 163–164.
154. Boiy 2010 and 2004: 204–206; Spek 1986: 80.
155. The Sumerian phrase sila uru, Akkadian *sūqāti āli,* may be an equivalent of Antioch's δημόσιαι ὁδοί (Ath. 10.438d–f).
156. *AD* -162 Rev. 14–15.
157. *AD* -162 Rev. 16–17.
158. *AD* -140 C Rev. 29–34. For a discussion of later instances of the colony's independence, see Hopkins 1972: 153–158 and Goodblatt 1987.
159. Habermas 1962.
160. See, e.g., Diod. Sic. 31.40a, 34/5.28.1. Note that Sève-Martinez 2004: 35 curiously has suggested, like Fraser 1972: 115–131 on Egyptian Alexandria, that urban violence increased from the mid-second century as a result of demographic changes in the city's population, namely, the increase of indigenous commercial and artisanal groups at the expense of the original Graeco-Macedonian military settlers.
161. Mazzarella 2010; Barry 1993; Davis 1973; Thompson 1971; Rudé 1964. This concern for legitimacy and fairness was termed by E. P. Thompson 1971, in a famous article on eighteenth-century English food riots, the "moral economy of the crowd."
162. Diod. Sic. 33.3.

163. Diod. Sic. 32.9c; see also Joseph. *AJ* 13.111.
164. Diod. Sic. 34/35.22.
165. Diod. Sic. 31.40a.
166. Diod. Sic. 40.1a.
167. Joseph. *AJ* 13.330.
168. For comparison, note that Davis 1973: 89 has argued that existing organizations—confraternities, festive youth societies, units of militia, craft groupings—provided the basis for sixteenth-century French religious riots.
169. For attestations and bibliography, see Ehling 2008: 72–76.
170. In his denunciation of Syrian colonial luxury Posidonius (F62a and b [Kidd] = Ath. 12.527e–f and 5.210e–f) speaks of dining clubs called "Grammateia," possibly designated by letters in the manner of college fraternities in the United States, where citizens would spend much of their day.
171. See, e.g., the *plintheia* of Cerauniasts or of Zeus Soter at Antioch-by-Daphne (Feissel 1985) or the association of Serapis and Isis worshippers at Laodicea-by-the-Sea (Roussel 1942–1943).
172. Discussed earlier; see Wilhelm 1909: 183–187 (#158); Robert 1937: 531–534.
173. Compare the antidemocratic sympotic groups of late fifth-century Athens. On this note, it should be observed that the many horrors of civil war, merely glanced at in our sources, can only have exacerbated internal class and ethnic tensions within Seleucid Syria. Unfortunately, the imprecision of our sources' social terminology greatly hinders any investigation of this. But we should ask, does the support of the *plēthos* or *polloi* for a particular candidate imply the elite's opposition? Are "the Syrians"—in a phrase like "Antiochus son of Antiochus Pius ruled with the support of the Syrians (τῶν Σύρων ἑκόντων)" (App. *Syr.* 49)—the indigenous population, the colonial residents, or both? Certainly, the appearance in literary sources of Aramaic or Phoenician sobriquets for rival kings indicates a political evaluation in indigenous idiom well-enough established among colonial elites to reach, presumably, Posidonius—Alexander I "Balas," from *b'l*, "ruler"; Demetrius II "Seripides," from *srp,* "chained"; Alexander II "Zabinas," from *zbn,* "purchased." At least in the case of Alexander I Balas, his popularity in Judea and his unpopularity among the Greek or Hellenized populations of the coastal cities were directly correlated. The Byzantine historian Jordanes reports anti-Semitic disturbances in Antioch in 88/7, perhaps to be connected to the war between Philip I and Demetrius III (*Romana* 81: *Ptholomeus, qui et Alexander, ann. X. quo regnante multa Iudaeorum populus tam ab Alexandrinis quam etiam ab Antiochensibus tolerabat*); see Heinemann 1931: 7 and Bickerman 1951: 131–132 on the riot and O'Donnell 1982 on Jordanes and his method. The internal conflict at Babylon in 163, discussed earlier, seems to oppose the colonists and the indigenous population, but a Seleucid official leads each side. Overall interactions of ethnicity, class, religion, and political engagement must have been intense, complex, and unstable but remain—alas!—basically unknowable.
174. Joseph. *AJ* 13.267.

175. Diod. Sic. 33.4a.

176. Just. *Epit.* 39.1.6.

177. Diod. Sic. 31.40a.

178. Compare Seleucid colonial conservatism with the riot of 203 in Alexandria (Polyb. 15.31–32), where the crowd demanded that the boy-king Ptolemy V Epiphanes take appropriate action against his regent Agathocles; see Barry 1993 and Świderek 1980: 110–111. The English "church and king" riots of the Napoleonic Wars show a similar political conservatism.

179. Houghton, Lorber, and Hoover 2008: 227; see Grainger 1990: 157 and Kahrstedt 1926: 81. The coins' legend perhaps should be connected with the statement in Strabo 16.2.4 that the Tetrapolis cities "were called siblings of one another because of their concord" (ἐλέγοντο ἀλλήλων ἀδελφαὶ διὰ τὴν ὁμόνοιαν).

180. Other, smaller colonies struck an idealized, unidentifiable royal portrait and omitted the legend altogether; see Seyrig 1955: 105–106.

181. Joseph. *AJ* 13.388.

182. Joseph. *AJ* 13.388.

183. Joseph *AJ* 13.330; Kahrstedt 1926: 75 identifies a "demokratische Partei" within the city.

184. Cavafy, Ἀς φροντιζαν 23–28: Θ'ἀπευθυνθῶ πρὸς τὸν Ζαβίνα πρῶτα / κι ἂν ὁ μωρὸς αὐτὸς δὲν μ' ἐκτιμήσει, / θὰ πάγω στὸν ἀντίπαλό του, τὸν Γρυπό. / Κι ἂν ὁ ἠλίθιος κι αὐτὸς δὲν μὲ προσλάβει, / πηγαίνω παρευθὺς στὸν Ὑρκανό. / Θὰ μὲ θελήσει πάντως ἕνας ἀπ' τοὺς τρεῖς.

185. *Pace* Sève-Martinez 2004: 30–32, who suggests that Antioch-by-Daphne came to dominate northern Syria during the reign of Antiochus IV. Certainly, the city was expanded and developed by Antiochus IV, but the dynastic conflicts after his reign, in particular the Ptolemaic sponsorship of the pretenders Alexander, increased the importance of Antioch-in-Ptolemaïs and maintained the importance of Seleucia and Apamea.

186. Challengers to the king or queen of Alexandria were directed toward the separate territorial entities of Cyrenaica or Cyprus; the territorial unity of the core remained unbroken. After Cyrene was bequeathed to Rome in 96 and Cyprus was made a province in 58 claimants, such as the famous Cleopatra VII, fled either to the Thebaïd or to Syria. For full details, see, e.g., Hölbl 2001:179–256.

187. The evidence is clearest for the desert borders of southern Syria; see Braemer, Dentzer, Kalos and Tondon 1999.

188. Posidonius F54 [Kidd] = Ath. 4.176b–c.

189. Joseph. *AJ* 14.40.

190. For details and bibliography, see Duyrat 2005: 254–256.

191. See Ehling 2008: 258–259; Sartre 2001: 381–383; Hölscher 1903: 83–85.

192. Joseph. *AJ* 13.324.

193. Joseph. *AJ* 13.384; Strabo 16.2.7. The relationship between the two dynasties remains unclear; see Bellinger 1951: 59–60.

194. Strabo 16.2.10; see Jones 1931: 265–266.
195. Joseph. *AJ* 14.40.
196. Strabo 16.2.18.
197. Joseph. *AJ* 14.39.
198. Joseph. *AJ* 13.394.
199. See Grainger 1997.
200. See Dentzer 1999; Altheim and Stiehl 1964: 1.139–158; Dussaud 1955; Kahrstedt 1926: 86–94; note the cautions of Macdonald 2003 and Graf 2003.
201. 1 Macc. 11:39; Joseph. *AJ* 13.131; Diod. Sic. 33.4a.
202. Diod. Sic. 33.4a.
203. 1 Macc. 11:17 (Zabdiel); Diod. Sic. 32.10 (Diocles).
204. Joseph. *AJ* 13.371; Steph. Byz. s.v. Σαμηνοί. On manuscript variations and the possible, though in my eyes unlikely, identification of this queen with Laodice Thea Philadelphos, daughter of Antiochus VIII and wife of Mithridates Callinicus of Commagene, see Ehling 2008: 241 n.1057 and 260 n.1225 and Shayegan 2011: 314 n.912.
205. See Ehling 2008: 241.
206. Diod. Sic. 40.1a–b.
207. For references, see Boiy 2004: 180–181 and Del Monte 1997: 133–134. The data are tabulated in Shayegan 2011: 207. There are only two notices of successful resistance to what was, from the urban perspective, Arab brigandage—*AD* -118 A Obv. 22 and *AD* -111 B Rev. 11–12.
208. For narratives see Herodian 2 and 3, Dio Cass. 74 and 75, SHA *Pesc. Nig.* The victorious Severus subordinated Antioch to Laodicea (Herodian 3.6.9), but its dignity was quickly restored; see Butcher 2003: 101–102.

Conclusion

1. Mendelsohn 2009: 7.
2. How history makes history makers is, of course, an old chestnut. For a bracing and thoroughly enjoyable discussion, see Sahlins 2004: 125–194.
3. 1 Macc. 15:28–31.
4. 1 Macc. 15:33–35.
5. Mendels 1987.
6. Polyb. 18.50.4–52.5; Liv. 33.39.3–41.4; Diod. Sic. 28.12; App. *Syr.* 2–3; see Grainger 2002: 90–97.
7. Certain Achaemenid royal inscriptions attest a strong sense of homeland territoriality. E.g., DPd §2 *iyam dahạyāuš Pārsa tayām manā Auramazdā frābara hayā naibā uvaspā umartiyā* ("This land of Persia, which Ahuramazda bestowed on me, is good, is possessed of good horses, is possessed of good men"); DNa §51–53 *mām Auramazdā pātuv hacā gastā utāmaiy viθam utā imām dahạyāum* ("May Ahuramazda protect me from evil as well as my house and this land")—the near-deictic pronoun *ima-* refers to what is near to the speaker in space and time and what is on earth as opposed to in heaven, so

in this case Fars/Persis. Lincoln 2008 has emphasized the theological significance of the land of Persia in these inscriptions.

8. On the meaning of *frataraka,* see Wiesehöfer 1991. Polyaenus, *Strat.* 7.40 describes the massacre of 3,000 Seleucid colonists in Persis by Oborzos, who appears on the *frataraka* coinage as Wahbarz. In favor of a second-century "late" date: Alram 1986: 162–164; Wiesehöfer 1994: 101–136, 2011, 2013; Callieri 2007: 115–146; Potts 2007; and Haerinck and Overlaet 2008. In favor of a third-century "early" date: Houghton, Lorber, and Hoover 2008: 213–215 (which reorders the sequence of rulers on the basis of overstrikes, opening the line with the Achaemenid-named Ardaxšīr (Artaxerxes) and not, as was traditional, Baydād) and Curtis 2010: 379–394.

9. Note that the towerlike structure before which the *fratarakā* seem to pray on several coin reverses is most likely the Achaemenid-period Zendan-i Suleiman at Pasargadae or the Kaba-i Zardusht at Naqsh-i Rustam; see Potts 2007.

10. Wiesehöfer 2011; Callieri 1998. It is unlikely that they are the Seleucid kings. Note that Sasanid inscriptions distinguish between *bay,* used for kings (equivalent to θεός), and *yazd,* used for Zoroastrian deities; see Back 1978: 281 and 283. It is unclear whether such a distinction holds already in the second century; see Panaino 2003.

11. The area of Palace H has not been fully excavated; see Tilia 1972: 243–316 and Callieri 2007: 133. Note that Hellenistic-period column capitals, imitating Achaemenid types, have been found at Tomb-e Bot in the Lamērd valley, southern Fars; see Chaverdi 2002.

12. The parallel between the Hasmonaean and *frataraka* insurgencies is made explicit in 2 Maccabees; see Kosmin forthcoming.

13. Khatchadourian 2007. Note that Parthian appeals to the Achaemenid territorial inheritance, such as Artabanus II/III's 35CE threat to recover the *veteres Persarum ac Macedonum terminos* (Tac. *Ann.* 6.31), seem to have post-dated the Seleucid collapse by several decades and been inspired by the claims of Mithridates VI Eupator; see Fowler 2005 and Shayegan 2011.

14. Trog. *prol.* 34. Timarchus was recognized by the Roman Senate, but Diod. Sic. 31.27a.1 is damaged right at the place where we would learn the phrasing of the *senatus consultum.* It has been restored as Τιμάρχῳ ἕνεκεν αὐτῶν <ἐξεῖναι> βασιλέα εἶναι by Niese 1900: 501 n.5 and Τίμαρχον ἕνεκεν αὐτῶν βασιλέα εἶναι by Bevan 1902: 2.194. For a discussion of Timarchus' revolt, see Ehling 2008: 125–127.

15. Houghton, Lorber, and Hoover 2008: 141–143.

16. Polyb. 21.45; Liv. 38.38; Diod. Sic. 29.10; App. *Syr.* 38–39. On the territorial terms of the treaty, see, e.g., McDonald 1967 and Magie 1950: 757–764.

17. Polyb. 21.46.11; Liv. 38.39.17: *de Pamphylia desceptatum inter Eumenem et Antiochi legatos cum esset, quia pars eius citra pars ultra Taurum est, integra res ad senatum reicitur.* The Senate's decision is unstated, but in 169 a Pamphylian embassy appeared at Rome to renew its friendship with the republic, so at

least before this date they received their independence; see Magie 1950: 1158–1159.

18. For a full discussion, see Chapter 5.
19. Joseph. *AJ* 13.262.
20. Potts 1989: 581; Tomaschek 1883.
21. E.g., Artabanus II's letter to Susa/Seleucia-on-the-Eulaeus, overriding the colony's constitution (*SEG* 7 1; *IGIAC* 3; *IEOG* 218).
22. Le Rider 1959: 231.
23. Holt 1999: 131–132.
24. Hansman 1990.
25. Invernizzi 2007: 172–173 (on a Seleucid-anchor metope from Parthian Nisa); Sellwood 1980: 102–103.
26. Meshorer 1982: 61–62.
27. 1 Macc. 11:58, 14:43; on the Hasmonaean deployment of their Seleucid connections, see Rajak 1996.
28. Invernizzi 1998, though see the doubts of Shayegan 2011: 105–108.
29. For sculptural details, see Messerschmidt 2000: 41–43; for the significance, see Facella 2005.
30. Diod. Sic. 31.19a.
31. [Lucian], *Longaevi* 16.
32. Allen 1983: 76–98.
33. Coloru 2009: 157–173.
34. On the general command of the Upper Satrapies, see Bengtson 1937–1952: 2.78–89.
35. Polyb. 5.48.16 shows that Molon managed to extend his power right up to Dura-Europus; on Seleucid Dura-Europus and Molon's revolt, see Kosmin 2011.
36. On the Euphrates between Parthia and Rome, see Millar 1993: 33. As Millar observes, the river's border role was clearly symbolized in 1 CE when Caius, Augustus' grandson and adopted son, met the Parthian king Phrataces on an island in its stream, followed by banquets on each bank (Vell. Pat. 2.101).

Appendix

1. E.g., Primo 2009: 54–55; Capdetrey 2007: 42; Habib and Jha 2004: 18; Karttunen 1997: 72; Kuhrt and Sherwin-White 1993: 93–97; Thapar 1987: 32–33; Dihle 1984: 76; Frye 1984: 153–154; Zambrini 1982: 71; Murray 1972: 208; Schwanbeck 1846: 11–23.
2. Bosworth 1996, developing Bosworth 1995: 242–244 and Brown 1957: 12–15; see also Bosworth 2003.
3. Also Yardley, Wheatley, and Heckel 2011: 294.
4. Also Brown 1957: 13.
5. Or, "says that he frequently visited"; see below.
6. See Heckel 2006: 248–249.

7. Diod. Sic. 19.14.6.

8. Diod. Sic. 19.23.4.

9. Diod. Sic. 19.48.3. Note that Roisman 2012: 16 argues that this derives from a recurring narrative pattern in Hieronymus—the historian's uncovering of hidden ulterior motives.

10. Bosworth 1996: 118.

11. Bosworth 1996: 114.

12. Lassen 1827: 44.

13. Schwanbeck 1846: 22. Several scholars have had difficulties with Schwanbeck's sentence structure: Timmer 1930: 5–6; Brown 1957: 13; Bosworth 1996: 114. Certainly, one would prefer καὶ Πώρου μείζονι. The τούτῳ seems unnecessary and may derive from Schwanbeck's desire to emend case endings and not words.

14. Bosworth 1996: 115 n.9, listing App. *Prooem.* 45 and *Celt.* 1.9; Thuc. 1.21.2.

15. For each of these parallels—where a power, population, or war is identified as "greater than the greatest"—the superlative refers (explicitly or implicitly) to something external and not coextensive with the comparative. So, App. *Prooem.* 45 declares that the history of Rome is greater than the greatest of *earlier* histories (i.e., Macedonia). Similarly, the Germans of App. *Celt.* 1.9 are even "larger than the largest" of, implicitly, those we know about from other parts of the world. Finally, in Thucydides 1.21.2 (Bosworth's "ultimate model" for Arrian) there is a contrast between the "real" exceptionality of the Peloponnesian War and the acknowledged tendency to exaggerate a current conflict during the fighting and ancient ones afterward. Unlike these supposed parallels, in Arr. *Ind.* 5.3 there is an identity of group ("the Indians") between the comparative and superlative and thus an open contradiction: Chandragupta is the greatest king among the Indians; Porus is a greater king among the Indians.

16. Already noted by Schwanbeck 1846: 22.

17. Bosworth 1996: 115–117.

18. See, e.g., Holt 2003.

19. Babylon: Diod. Sic. 18.3.1–3; Curt. 10.10.1–4; Arr. *Succ.* 1.5–7; Just. *Epit.* 13.4; Oros. 3.23.6–13. Triparadisus: Arr. *Succ.* 1.29–38; Diod. Sic. 18.39; Oros. 3.23.20–23; Just. *Epit.* 13.8.10.

20. Diod. Sic. 17.93.2; Arr. *Anab.* 5.25.1; Plut. *Al.* 62; Curt. 9.2.3. The *periēgēsis* of Diod. Sic. 18.6 identifies the Gangaridae as the greatest *ethnos* of India. If this passage derives from Hieronymus of Cardia, as seems likely (see Hornblower 1981: 80–87), then we have a Diadoch-era attestation that the Ganges state was considered greater than the Indus state.

21. Bosworth 1996: 116.

22. *BNJ* 715 F18a = Arr. *Ind.* 10.5. Direct comparison of the Indus and the Ganges is found in F9a = Arr. *Ind.* 4.2 and F9b = Strabo 15.1.35, where the Ganges is the largest river in the world.

23. *BNJ* 715 F4 = Diod Sic. 2.39.3.

24. *BNJ* 715 F18b = Strabo 15.1.36.

25. *BNJ* 715 F21a = Strabo 15.1.37.

26. *BNJ* 715 F32 = Strabo 15.1.53.

27. Arrian again emphasizes how little of India was explored by Megasthenes at Arr. *Ind.* 7.1 (= *BNJ* 715 F12).

28. Chantraine 1952: 12–19 and Bosworth 1980: 38–41.

29. Lassen 1827: 44.

30. Note, however, that we must not overplay Sibyrtius' importance. We learn from Diod. Sic. 19.14.6 that Sibyrtius joined the army of Upper Satraps against Pithon of Media, under the command of Peucestas. Sibyrtius contributed the smallest force of the entire coalition, 1,000 infantry and 610 cavalry. This compares with Peucestas' 10,000 Persian archers and slingers, 3,000 infantry, and 1,000 cavalry; or the 1,500 infantry and 700 cavalry of Tlepolemus, satrap of Carmania; or the 1,200 infantry and 400 cavalry from Parapamisadae; or Stasander of Aria and Drangiane's 1,500 infantry and 1,000 cavalry; or, above all, the 300 infantry, 500 cavalry, and 120 elephants of Eudamus. Having fallen foul of Eumenes, he was considered weak enough to be put on trial; Eumenes sent horsemen into Arachosia to seize his baggage (Diod. Sic. 19.23.4; see Bosworth 2002: 122). Sibyrtius was reinstated by Antigonus after the Second Battle of Gabiene and received a thousand of the most turbulent Silver Shields to use up on campaign (Polyaenus, *Strat.* 4.6.15; Diod. Sic. 19.48.3–4; Plut. *Eum.* 19.2). This in itself is an indication of the satrap's limited ambitions, as Antigonus had no fear that Sibyrtius would use the Silver Shields to pursue his own agenda or emulate Pithon (Bosworth 2002: 164).

31. Clement. *Paed.* 2.54.2, 3.41.3; *Strom.* 2.142.1, 3.86.1; see Bosworth 1996: 114.

32. *LSJ* s.v. συμβιόω. Dem 18.250, 266; Isoc. 15.97.

33. Dihle 1984: 78.

34. Bosworth 1996: 123 in fact suggests this.

35. *Contra* Bosworth 1996: 117–118; see Brown 1957: 15.

36. Primo 2009: 54–55; Capdetrey 2007: 42; Heckel 2006: 249; Billows 1990: 432–433; Brown 1957: 15.

37. Habib and Jha 2004: 18.

38. Habib and Jha 2004: 33; see Thapar 1987: 23.

39. Habib and Jha 2004: 29.

40. Primo 2009: 55.

41. Bosworth 1996: 127.

42. *BNJ* 715 F12 = Arr. *Ind.* 7.1; F4 = Diod. Sic. 2.38.3, 2.39.2. The south Indian kingdom of Pandya is the exception that proves the rule, as its political independence is so clearly expressed in mythic terms: Megasthenes tells us that Heracles, the *Indica*'s second cultural hero, sired a host of sons but only one girl, the eponymous Pandaea, to whom he assigned the "exceptional kingdom," *praecipuo regno*, (*BNJ* 715 F13b = Plin. *HN* 6.76), where the natural processes of birth and death were accelerated (*BNJ* 715 F13a = Arr. *Ind.* 9.1, 8

and F13c = Phlegon, *Mirabilia* 33). Moreover, it is possible that Heracles' award of 500 war elephants to his daughter, Pandaea (*BNJ* 715 F13a = Arr. *Ind.* 8.7), in the context of his gift of independent territory, functions as some kind of prototype for Chandragupta's identical gift to Seleucus at the peace negotiations of 304/3.

43. *BNJ* 715 F14 = Arr. *Ind.* 9.9.
44. E.g., the "Bacchic" hunt (*BNJ* 715 F32 = Strabo 15.1.55), the king's entourage (F33 = Strabo 15.1.58).
45. Bosworth 1996: 124.
46. *BNJ* 715 F18b = Strabo 15.1.36.
47. *Contra* Bosworth 1996: 124.
48. Habib and Jha 2004: 24.
49. I am grateful to Professor Nayanjot Lahiri, of the University of Delhi's History Department, for emphasizing this point in personal correspondence.
50. *BNJ* 715 F6c = Strabo 15.1.11. The number is explicitly derived from Megasthenes, in contrast to a smaller figure given by Patrocles; see Biffi 2005: 156.
51. *BNJ* 715 F31 = Strabo 15.1.10; *BNJ* 715 F32 = Strabo 15.1.55.
52. Hdt. 5.52–53; *FGrHist* 688 F33.
53. See *BNJ* 715 F6c = Strabo 15.1.11: μέχρι Παλιβόθρων . . . μέχρι Παλιβόθρων.
54. *BNJ* 715 F27b = Strabo 15.1.57.
55. *BNJ* 715 F27b = Strabo 15.1.57.
56. *BNJ* 715 F4 = Diod. Sic. 2.37.4, 2.37.6.
57. *BNJ* 715 F3b = Joseph *AJ* 10.227; F1b = Euseb. *Chron.* 1.29.
58. *BNJ* 715 F3b = Joseph *AJ* 10.227; F 11a = Strabo 15.1.6.
59. *BNJ* 715 F3b = Joseph *AJ* 10.227; F1b = Euseb. *Chron.* 1.29; F11a = Strabo 15.1.6.
60. Diod. Sic. 19.55.7; Diod. Sic. 19.91.1–2; App. *Syr.* 54.
61. Furthermore, we have already seen, in Clement of Alexandria, *Stromata* 1.15.72.5 (T1), that Megasthenes paralleled the Jews of Syria and the Brahmans of India. A cultural interest in Jewish learning and a geographical knowledge of Syria make far better sense for a Babylonian, Seleucid context than an Arachosian, Sibyrtian one.
62. See Kuhrt 1987: 56.
63. See Kosmin 2014c.
64. *AD* 2 -187 A Rev. 11.
65. *Contra* Bosworth's identification of Megasthenes "as a contemporary of men like Onesicritus and Nearchus, writing at much the same time as them" (Bosworth 1996: 127).
66. Megasthenes radically altered the shape of India, rotating the landmass clockwise, so what had been considered by Ctesias, Onesicritus, and Nearchus as its length is now its width (*BNJ* 715 F6b = Arr. *Ind.* 3.7–8). Nearchus had mentioned reports of the supposed Indian expeditions of Semiramis and Cyrus (*BNJ* 134 F24 = Strabo 15.1.34); Megasthenes rejected these as unhistorical (*BNJ* 133 F3b = Strabo 15.1.5; F 3a = Arr. *Anab.* 6.24.2). Where

the Alexander Historians narrate the self-immolation of the Indian sage
Calanus as an event they witnessed and from the perspective of the awe-
struck Macedonian army, Megasthenes records the retrospective critical
judgment of the Indian sages (*BNJ* 715 F34a = Strabo 15.1.68): "The inescapable conclusion seems to be that Megasthenes knew no more about this
incident than he read in Onesicritus' book" (Brown 1960: 134). Nearchus
had claimed to have seen the skins of the famed gold-digging ants in the
Macedonian camp (*BNJ* 133 F8a = Arr. *Ind.* 15.4); Megasthenes that he knew
of them by *akoē* alone (*BNJ* 715 F23a = Arr. *Ind.* 15.4).

Glossary

In this brief glossary, as throughout the book, I have followed a simplified and inconsistent transliteration system. By and large, I have preferred Anglicized or Latinate versions of ancient names, places, and terms and have dispensed with most diacritical marks; quotations are the major exception. My primary concern has been ease of reading.

For the glossary, I have selected the individuals, terms, institutions, and texts which are both significant for the book's arguments and perhaps unfamiliar to readers from one of the academic disciplines intruded upon. Only those ancient locations with modern and differently named successors are listed. The definitions are intended to be short, useful, and germane to the Seleucid empire and nothing more.

1 Maccabees   Greek translation of the lost Hebrew chronicle of the Hasmonaean royal house, narrating the emancipation of Judea from the Seleucid empire between 175 and 134.

2 Maccabees   epitome of Jason of Cyrene's lost five-volume history of the Maccabaean revolt, composed in Greek, narrating the Jewish persecution and rebellion from the reign of Seleucus IV to the Maccabaeans' defeat of Seleucid general Nicanor in 161.

Achaeus   Seleucid relative, general of Seleucus III, viceroy of Antiochus III in cis-Tauric Asia Minor, recovering territories from Attalid control; from 221 to 213 a separatist king in Asia Minor until captured at Sardis and mutilated by Antiochus III.

amphodon, plural *amphoda*   Greek term for rectangular city block in grid-planned Hellenistic cities; equivalent to *plintheion*.

anabasis   Greek term for a military campaign from the Mediterranean coast into, for Xenophon and Alexander, the eastern provinces of the Achaemenid empire and, for Seleucid kings, their own Upper Satrapies.

Antigonus I Monophthalmus   Alexander's satrap of Phrygia and the dominant
Successor after the assassination of Perdiccas in 321, driving Seleucus I from
Babylonia in 315; he was defeated and killed at the battle of Ipsus in 301.

Antigonus II Gonatas   son of Demetrius I Poliorcetes, claiming the Macedonian throne after defeating the invading Galatians, r. *c.* 277/6–239.

Antioch-by-Daphne   modern Antakya, in Hatay province of Turkey (see Map 4).

Antioch-in-Margiane   modern Merv, in southeastern Turkmenistan (see Map 2).

Antioch-in-Ptolemaïs   modern Akko, in northern Israel (see Map 4).

Antioch-in-Scythia   modern Khodjend, formerly Leninabad, in the Fergana
valley of northern Tajikistan (see Map 2).

Antioch-on-the-Cydnus   ancient and modern Tarsus, in the Mersin province
of southern Turkey (see Map 4).

apadāna   Old Persian term for hypostyle palace, characteristic of Achaemenid
architecture and also, rather surprisingly, found at Seleucia-on-the-Tigris.

Apame   first wife of Seleucus I, mother of Antiochus I, daughter of the Sogdian
dynast Spitamenes, who incited the Sogdian insurgency against Alexander the
Great.

apantēsis   Greek term for an urban community's choreographed reception of an
arriving king or dominant figure, parallel to Latin *adventus*.

Aradus   tiny island city of Phoenicia, 800 by 500 meters, modern Arwad in
northern Syria, lying opposite modern Tartus and ancient Marathus
(see Map 4).

Ashoka   known to the Greeks as Piodasses (from his title Priyadarshin), third
major ruler of the Indian Mauryan empire (r. *c.* 269–232), son of Bindusara;
famed for his promotion of Buddhism and *dhamma* following the bloody
conquest of the state of Kalinga in eastern India.

Astronomical Diaries   Akkadian cuneiform records of dated astronomical and
meteorological phenomena and political events, compiled at Babylon's Esagil
temple.

asylia   immunity from seizure or inviolability, granted to certain temples and
cities by political powers, as protection from the depredations of war.

Babylonian Chronicles   Akkadian cuneiform historiographical lists of dated
political or religious events, composed in a sober third-person voice at Babylon's Esagil temple.

Bactra   also known as Zariaspa, probably modern Balkh, near Mazar-e Sharif in
northern Afghanistan (see Map 2).

Beroea   ancient Halab, modern Aleppo, in northwestern Syria (see Map 4).

Berossus' *Babyloniaca*   autoethnographic account of Babylonian myth and
history, preserved only in later quotation, composed in Greek from Babylonian
literary accounts and perhaps oral traditions by the priest Berossus (Bēl-rē'ûšu,
"Bel is his shepherd") and dedicated to Antiochus I.

Bindusara   known to the Greeks as Amitrochates (from his title Amitraghata/
Amitrakhada), second ruler of the Indian Mauryan empire (r. *c.* 298–272), son
of Chandragupta.

Borsippa Cylinder   barrel-shaped building inscription composed in Akkadian cuneiform and deposited in the foundations of the Ezida temple in Borsippa (see Map 7), recording in his own voice Antiochus I's reconstruction of the temple; dated to 27 March 268.

Chandragupta   known to the Greeks as (S)andracottus, conqueror of the Gangetic kingdom of the Nandas and founder of the Indian Mauryan empire (r. *c.* 322–298).

Characene   geographic and political region at the mouth of the Tigris-Euphrates, also known as Mesene and "the district of the Erythraean Sea," emancipated from the Seleucid empire by its satrap Hyspaosines *c.* 127 (see Map 7).

cis-Tauric Asia Minor   the Seleucid provincial ensemble in Asia Minor, between the Aegean Sea and the Taurus range (see Map 3).

Coele Syria and Phoenicia   official Seleucid term for the southern Levant, including Lebanon, modern Israel, the Palestinian territories, and western Jordan, taken from the Ptolemies by Antiochus III in the Fifth Syrian War.

Common Road   main trunk road across Asia Minor, from Ionia to northern Syria, developed and colonized by the Seleucid kings (see Map 3).

Conference of Triparadisus   agreement in Coele Syria, immediately following the assassination of the Macedonian regent Perdiccas in 321, which reassigned the satrapies of Alexander's empire and awarded Babylonia to Seleucus (I) Nicator.

Daniel   prophetic and apocalyptic book of the Hebrew Bible, composed in Hebrew and Aramaic, taking its final form in 165 toward the end of Antiochus IV's persecution.

Darius III   unfortunate final occupant of the Achaemenid throne (r. 336–330), defeated twice by Alexander at Issus (333) and Gaugamela (331), then killed in flight by his Bactrian satrap Bessus.

Day of Eleusis   Roman legate Popilius Laenas' humiliation of Antiochus IV in summer 168, demanding that he withdraw from Egypt and end the Sixth Syrian War.

Demetrias (in Syria)   ancient and modern Damascus in Syria (see Map 4).

Demetrius I Poliorcetes   son of Antigonus Monophthalmus, father of Seleucus I's second wife, Stratonice, and under Seleucid house arrest for the final years of his life.

diadem   headband worn as monarchic attribute, like a crown, by Hellenistic kings.

Didyma   ancient sanctuary of Apollo, a little south of Miletus, recipient of extensive Seleucid benefaction (see Map 3).

Diodotus Tryphon   Seleucid general who fought against Demetrius II in the name of Antiochus VI, son of Alexander I Balas, and then in his own right from 142/1; he was captured and executed in 138.

Ecbatana   ancient capital of Media, refounded by Antiochus IV as Epiphania, modern Hamadan, beneath Mount Alvand in western Iran (see Map 7).

Elymaïs   ancient Elam, modern Khuzestan, in southwestern Iran (see Map 7).

Erythraean Sea   modern Arab-Persian Gulf and Indian Ocean.

Esagil   "Temple of the Raised Head" in Sumerian, the major sanctuary of Babylon, sacred to Marduk, the major Babylonian deity.

ethnos   Greek term for ethnically distinctive population group, e.g., Jews and Prasii.

euergetism   modern scholarly term for the practice of external powers or internal elites voluntarily bestowing benefactions on communities, typically in exchange for civic gratitude and honors.

European Thrace   the corner of the European mainland, approximate to European Turkey and Bulgaria, bordering the northeastern Aegean, Hellespont, Propontis, and Black Sea (see Map 3).

Europus-Rhagae   modern Rey, near modern Tehran, in north-central Iran (see Map 7).

Ezida   "True Temple" in Sumerian, the sanctuary of the Babylonian scribal deity, Nabû, in the city of Borsippa, southwest of Babylon.

frataraka **dynasty**   indigenous rulers of Fars/Persis, known almost exclusively from their numismatic output, first appearing in either the early third century or, more probably, the early second century.

Galatians   "barbarian" Celtic populations, some invading the Greek mainland in the early third century, others settling in central Asia Minor, later "Galatia."

Gurob Papyrus of the Third Syrian War   fragmentary papyrus text, found at Egyptian Gurob, narrating in his own voice Ptolemy III's conquest of Cilicia and the Seleucis in 246.

Hasmonaean dynasty   Jewish high priests and kings descended from Mattathias of Modein, leaders of the Jewish Maccabaean revolt against the Seleucid empire, ruling Judea between 165 and 37.

heroön   sanctuary, often burial site, typically located within city walls, for cultic celebration of legendary heroes and historical founders.

Hyphasis river   modern Beas, flowing from the Indian Himalayas into the Sutlej river of the Punjab (see Map 2).

Iaxartes river   modern Syr Darya, rising in the Tian Shan mountains and flowing through Uzbekistan and Kazakhstan into the Aral Sea; identified by pre-Seleucid Greek geography with the Tanaïs River (see Map 2).

Icarus   modern Failaka island, Kuwait, at the head of the Persian Gulf (see Map 7).

Justin's *Epitome*   imperial-period Latin epitome of the forty-four book universal *Philippic Histories*, concentrating on the Hellenistic kingdoms, composed by Pompeius Trogus, an Augustan-period Romanized Gaul.

katoikia, **plural** *katoikiai*   a Hellenistic colonial foundation with some but not all of a *polis'* civic institutions.

Khorasan highway   ancient trade route from Babylonia to Bactria, passing up the Diyala valley into the Zagros mountains and south of the Caspian Sea and Elburz range to the oasis cities of Central Asia (see Maps 2 and 7).

klēros, **plural** *klēroi*   agricultural estates granted to settlers, known as *klēros*-holders *(klērouchoi),* typically from royal land.

koinon, plural *koina*   Greek term for a commonwealth or federation of urban communities, such as the Aetolian and Achaean leagues on the Greek mainland.

ktisis, plural *ktiseis*   foundation of a colony by a *ktistēs;* also the literary narrative of the foundation.

Laodicea-by-the-Sea   modern Latakia, in northern Syria (see Map 4).

Laodicea-in-Media   modern Nehavend, south of Hamadan, in western Iran (see Map 7).

Laodicea-in-Phoenicia   ancient and modern Beirut, central Lebanon (see Map 4).

Lysimachus   Macedonian general of Alexander and, after his death, king of Thrace, Asia Minor, and Macedonia; defeated and killed by Seleucus at the battle of Corupedium in 281.

Maccabaean revolt   Jewish rebellion against the Seleucid empire, breaking out in 167 in response to Antiochus IV's persecution and over the next decades winning semiautonomy for Judea.

Marduk   also Bel, main deity of Babylonia; identified with Greek Zeus.

marratu or *^{id}marratu*   the "bitter sea," first-millennium synonym for *tâmtu,* the Akkadian term for the ocean thought to encircle the continental landmass.

Meluhha   Sumerian name for distant geographic region, perhaps the Indus valley; used in Hellenistic cuneiform texts for Egypt.

Memnon   imperial-period local historian of Heraclea Pontica, using third-century historian Nymphis; books 9 to 16 are substantially preserved by the Byzantine patriarch Photius.

Molon   Seleucid satrap of Media, who rebelled against newly acceded Antiochus III in 222, advancing into Babylonia and up the Euphrates; defeated and mutilated by Antiochus III in 221.

Nebuchadnezzar II   second king of the Neo-Babylonian empire (r. 605–562), rebuilder of Babylon, destroyer of Jerusalem, son of Nabopolassar.

Ocean   the waterway, similar to the Babylonian *marratu,* believed to encircle the continental landmass in early Greek thought.

oikoumenē   Greek term for the inhabited world.

Oxus river   modern Amu Darya, flowing from the Wahkan Corridor in the Pamir mountains along the Afghani-Tajik and Uzbek-Turkmen borders and into the Aral Sea (see Map 2).

Parthians   the nomadic Parni, who, on occupying the Seleucid satrapy of Parthia in the mid-third century, adopted the province's name; expanded into Seleucid Upper Satrapies and Babylonia under Mithridates I (r. *c.* 171–138) and subsequently into a great empire.

Pataliputra   capital of Mauryan empire, known to the Greeks as Palimbothra, modern Patna, in Bihar province, India (see Map 2).

Peace of Apamea   agreement of 188, following Roman defeat of Antiochus III at the battle of Magnesia, by terms of which the Seleucid empire ceded European Thrace and cis-Tauric Asia Minor, surrendered its elephants, reduced its fleet, and paid a vast war indemnity.

peliganes Macedonian term for corporate group of city councilors, equivalent to Greek *bouleutai*.

peraia the mainland coastline controlled by, and typically facing, an island polity.

Perdiccas Macedonian general and, after Alexander's death in 323, regent of the Macedonian empire until assassinated in 321.

philos, plural *philoi* Greek term, literally "friend," used for a king's councilors and courtiers; increasingly stratified over the course of the Hellenistic period.

phrourion, plural *phrouria* Greek term for fort.

plateia Greek term for the wide street of planned Hellenistic *polis*, often aligned with city gates.

polis, plural *poleis* Greek term for a city possessing the institutions of internal self-government.

Polybius second-century Megalopolitan historian of the Hellenistic world, leading politician of Achaean league, hostage at Rome 167–150; of his forty-book history, covering the years 220 to 146, books 1 to 5 survive intact and the rest in excerpts.

pompē Greek term for religious procession.

Posidonius late second- and first-century Stoic polymath from Apamea-on-the-Axios, later settled at Rhodes; composed a history in fifty-two books, continuing Polybius down to the mid-80s.

profectio Latin term for grand military departure.

Ptolemy Ceraunus son of Ptolemy I and his third wife, Eurydice, daughter of the Macedonian regent Antipater; ward of Seleucus I and his murderer.

qanāt underground aqueduct, used in Iran.

Seleucia-on-the-Calycadnus modern Silifke, in the Mersin province of southern Turkey (see Map 4).

Seleucid Era (SE) the annual count of the Seleucid dating system, introduced by Seleucus I, with year 1 as 312 or 311 in the Babylonian and Macedonian calendars, respectively.

Seleucis sometimes "Syrian Seleucis," official Seleucid term for the imperial heartland of northern Syria, location of the Tetrapolis (see Map 4).

Seleucus Romance lost encomiastic biography of Seleucus I Nicator, quoted or paraphrased in later sources.

senatus consultum resolution of the Roman Senate.

stratēgos, plural *stratēgoi* literally "general," Greek term for the military and administrative commander of a Seleucid satrapy.

Stratonice daughter of Demetrius Poliorcetes, second wife of Seleucus I, then first wife of his son Antiochus I.

syntrophos literally "foster brother," Greek term for a high-ranking Seleucid courtier.

Takht-i Sangin sanctuary fortified temple, sacred to the Oxus river, constructed in the early Seleucid period on northern bank of the Amu Darya, in Tajikistan (see Map 2).

Tanaïs river   modern Don, flowing into the Sea of Azov, identified by classical Greek geographers as the western part of the Iaxartes.

Tetrapolis   the collective term for Seleucia-in-Pieria, Antioch-by-Daphne, Laodicea-by-the-Sea, and Apamea-on-the-Axios, Seleucus I's four primary colonial foundations in northern Syria (see Map 4).

tetrapyrgion   Greek term for a well-defended rectangular palace, with a tower at each corner.

theōros, plural *theōroi*   Greek term for a sacred envoy or ambassador, announcing oracular pronouncements or the celebration of games.

Thracian Chersonese   modern Gallipoli peninsula, the western coast of the Hellespont, in European Turkey (see Map 3).

Tigranes II   Artaxiad king of Armenia, son-in-law of Mithridates VI of Pontus, absorbed Seleucid territorial rump in 83 until forced to withdraw from Syria by Roman commander Lucullus in 69.

Timarchus   *philos* of Antiochus IV, appointed satrap of Media, rebelled against Demetrius I, who defeated and killed him in 160.

tryphē   Greek term for luxurious or splendid living; decadence if condemned.

Tylos   modern Bahrain (see Map 7).

Upper Satrapies   the collective term for the Iranian and Central Asian provinces of the Seleucid empire.

Zeuxis   Antiochus III's governor of cis-Tauric Asia Minor.

References

Abadia-Reynal, Catherine and Justine Gaborit. 2003. "Le développement urbain en Syrie du Nord: Étude des cas de Séleucie et Apamée de l'Euphrate," in Maurice Sartre (ed.), *La Syrie hellénistique* (*Topoi* Suppl. 4): 149–169. Paris.

Adams, Robert. 1965. *Land behind Baghdad: A History of Settlement on the Diyala Plains.* Chicago.

———. 1981. *Heartland of Cities: Surveys of Ancient Settlement and Land Use on the Central Floodplain of the Euphrates.* Chicago.

Africa, Thomas. 1982. "Worms and the Death of Kings: A Cautionary Note on Disease and History," *CA* 1: 1–17.

Ager, Sheila. 1998. "Civic Identity in the Hellenistic World: The Case of Lebedos," *GRBS* 39: 5–21.

Alcock, Susan. 1994. "Breaking Up the Hellenistic World: Survey and Society," in Ian Morris (ed.), *Classical Greece: Ancient Histories and Modern Archaeologies:* 171–190. Cambridge.

Alcock, Susan, Jennifer Gates, and Jane Rempel. 2003. "Reading the Landscape: Survey Archaeology and the Hellenistic *Oikoumene*," in Andrew Erskine (ed.), *A Companion to the Hellenistic World:* 354–372. Oxford.

Allen, R. 1983. *The Attalid Kingdom: A Constitutional History.* Oxford.

Alonso Troncoso, Víctor. 2013. "The Diadochi and the Zoology of Kingship: The Elephants," in Víctor Alonso Troncoso and Edward Anson (eds.), *After Alexander: The Time of the Diadochi (323–281 BC):* 254–270. Oxford.

Alram, Michael. 1986. *Iranisches Personennamenbuch IV. Nomina propria iranica in nummis.* Vienna.

Altheim, Franz and Ruth Stiehl. 1964. *Die Araber in der alten Welt.* Berlin.

Ando, Clifford. 2000. *Imperial Ideology and Provincial Loyalty in the Roman Empire.* Berkeley.

Andrade, Nathaniel. 2009. "Imitation Greeks": Being Syrian in the Greco-Roman World (175 BCE–275 CE). Dissertation. University of Michigan, Ann Arbor.

Aperghis, Gerassimos. 2004. *The Seleukid Royal Economy: The Finances and Financial Administration of the Seleukid Empire.* Cambridge.

Ariel, Donald and Joseph Naveh. 2003. "Selected Inscribed Sealings from Kedesh in the Upper Galilee," *BASOR* 329: 61–80.

Arnaud, Pascale. 2001. "Beirut: Commerce and Trade 200 BC–AD 400," *Aram* 13: 171–191.

Arsen'ev, V. 1990. "Les formes historiques des interactions entre nomades et agriculteurs dans la savane du Niger," in H.-P. Francfort (ed.), *Nomades et sédentaires en Asie centrale:* 26–30. Paris.

Austin, M. 1986. "Hellenistic Kings, War, and the Economy," *CQ* 36: 450–466.

———. 2006. *The Hellenistic World from Alexander to the Roman Conquest: A Selection of Ancient Sources in Translation.* 2nd edition. Cambridge.

Avram, Alexandru. 2003. "Antiochus II Théos, Ptolémée Philadelphe, et la Mer Noire," *CRAI* 147: 1181–1213.

Aymard, André. 1949. "Du nouveau sur Antiochos III d'après une inscription grecque d'Iran," *REA* 51: 327–345.

———. 1952. "Tutelle et usurpation dans les monarchies hellénistiques," *Aegyptus* 32: 85–96.

———. 1953. "Autour de l'avènement d'Antiochos IV," *Historia* 2: 49–73.

Bachelard, Gaston. 1958. *La poétique de l'espace.* Paris.

Back, Michael. 1978. *Die sassanidischen Staatsinschriften.* Liège.

Badian, Ernst. 1959. "Rome and Antiochus the Great: A Study in Cold War," *CP* 54: 81–99.

———. 1968. "A King's Notebooks," *HSCP* 72: 183–204.

Bagnall, Roger. 1976. *The Administration of the Ptolemaic Possessions outside Egypt.* Leiden.

Bak, János (ed.). 1990. *Coronations: Medieval and Early Modern Monarchic Ritual.* Berkeley.

Balcer, Jack. 1988. "Persian Occupied Thrace (Skudra)," *Historia* 37: 1–21.

Balty, Janine. 1969. *Apamée de Syrie. Bilan des recherches archéologiques 1965–1968.* Brussels.

Balty, Jean-Charles. 1991. "L'urbanisme de la tétrapolis syrienne," in Evangelos Arabatzes (ed.), *Ο Ελληνισμος στην Ανατολη:* 203–229. Athens.

Barry, William. 1993. "The Crowd of Ptolemaic Alexandria and the Riot of 203 BC," *EMC* 37: 415–431.

Batziou-Efstathiou, Anthi. 2002. *Demetrias.* Athens.

Baumer, Christoph. 2012. *The History of Central Asia I.* Volume 1, *The Age of the Steppe Warriors.* London.

Bearzot, Cinzia. 1992. "Πτολεμαῖος Μακεδών. Sentimento nazionale macedone e contrapposizioni etniche all'inizio del regno tolemaico," in Marta Sordi (ed.), *Autocoscienza e rappresentazione dei popoli nell' antichità:* 39–53. Milan.

Beaulieu, Paul-Alain. 1997. "The Fourth Year of Hostilities in the Land," *Baghdader Mitteilungen* 28: 367–394.

Bedjan, Paul. 1890–1897. *Acta martyrum et sanctorum.* Paris.

Belier, Wouter. 1991. *Decayed Gods: Origin and Development of Georges Dumézil's "idéologie tripartie."* Leiden.

Bellinger, Alfred. 1942. "Hyspaosines of Charax," *Yale Classical Studies* 8: 52–67.

———. 1948. "Seleucid Dura," *Berytus* 9: 51–67.

———. 1949. "The End of the Seleucids," *Transactions of the Connecticut Academy of Arts and Sciences* 38: 51–102.

———. 1951. "The Early Coinage of Roman Syria," in P. Coleman-Norton (ed.), *Studies in Roman Economic and Social History:* 58–67. Princeton.

———. 1962. "The Coins from the Treasure of the Oxus," *ANS MN* 10: 51–67.

Bencivenni, Alice. 2003. *Progetti di riforme costituzionali nelle epigrafi greche dei secoli IV–II A.C.* Bologna.

Bengtson, Hermann. 1937–1952. *Die Strategie in der hellenistischen Zeit. Ein Beitrag zum antiken Staatsrecht.* Munich.

Benjamin, Walter. 1999. *The Arcades Project* (ed. Rolf Tiedemann; trans. Howard Eiland and Kevin McLaughlin). Cambridge, MA.

Benveniste, E. 1943–1945. "La ville de Cyreschata," *Journal asiatique* 234: 163–166.

Berchem, Denis van. 1985. "Le port de Séleucie de Piérie et l'infrastructure logistique des guerres parthiques," *Bonner Jahrbücher des rheinischen Landesmuseums* 185: 47–87.

Berlin, Andrea. 2012. Review of Heather Jackson and John Tidmarsh, *Jebel Khalid on the Euphrates. III. The Pottery. BMCR* 2012.10.09.

Bernard, Paul. 1967. "Deuxième campagne de fouilles d'Aï Khanoum en Bactriane," *CRAI* 111: 306–324.

———. 1987. "Le Marsyas d'Apamée, l'Oxus et la colonisation séleucide en Bactriane," *Studia Iranica* 16: 103–115.

———. 1990. "Alexandre et l'Asie centrale: Réflexions à propos d'un ouvrage de F. L. Holt," *Studia Iranica* 19: 20–38.

———. 1995. "I. Une légende de fondation hellénistique: Apamée sur l'Oronte d'après les *Cynégétiques* du pseudo-Oppien; II. Paysages et toponymie dans le Proche Orient hellénisé," *Topoi* 5: 353–408.

Bernard, Paul (ed.). 1973. *Fouilles d'Aï Khanoum I.* Paris.

Bernard, Paul, Marc Le Berre, and Rolf Stucki. 1973. "Architecture: Le téménos de Kinéas," in Paul Bernard (ed.), *Fouilles d'Aï Khanoum I:* 85–102. Paris.

Bernard, Paul, Georges-Jean Pinault, and Georges Rougemont. 2004. "Deux nouvelles inscriptions grecques de l'Asie central," *JS:* 227–356.

Bernhardt, R. 2003. *Luxuskritik und Aufwandsbeschränkungen in der griechischen Welt.* Stuttgart.

Berve, Helmut. 1926. *Das Alexanderreich auf prosopographischer Grundlage.* Munich.

Bevan, Edwyn. 1902. *The House of Seleucus.* London.

———. 1927. *A History of Egypt under the Ptolemaic Dynasty.* London.

Bhabha, Homi. 1994. *The Location of Culture.* London.

Bickerman, Elias. 1935. "La charte séleucide de Jérusalem," *Revue des études juives* 100: 4–35.

———. 1938. *Institutions des Séleucides.* Paris.

———. 1944. "Notes on Seleucid and Parthian Chronology," *Berytus* 8: 73–83.

———. 1951. "Notes on the Greek Book of Esther," *Proceedings of the American Academy for Jewish Research* 20: 101–133.

————. 1980. *Chronology of the Ancient World.* Southampton.

Bielfeldt, Ruth. 2010. "Wo nur sind die Bürger von Pergamon? Eine Phänomenologie bürgerlicher Unscheinbarkeit im städtischen Raum der Königsrezidenz," *IstMitt* 60: 117–201.

Bieńkowski, Piotr. 1928. *Les Celtes dans les arts mineurs gréco-romains.* Krakow.

Biffi, Nicolà. 2005. *L'estremo oriente di Strabone: Libro XV della Geografia.* Bari.

Billows, Richard. 1990. *Antigonos the One-Eyed and the Creation of the Hellenistic State.* Berkeley.

Bing, Peter. 2005. "The Politics and Poetics of Geography in the Milan Posidippus. Section One: On Stones," in Kathryn Gutzwiller (ed.), *The New Posidippus: A Hellenistic Poetry Book:* 119–140. Oxford.

Bingen, Jean. 2007. *Hellenistic Egypt: Monarchy, Society, Economy, and Culture.* Edinburgh.

Bingöl, Orhan. 2006. "Die Agora von Magnesia am Mäander," in Wolfram Hoepfner and Lauri Lehmann (eds.), *Die griechische Agora:* 59–65. Mainz.

Blacker, Carmen. 1990. "The Folklore of the Stranger: A Consideration of a Disguised Wandering Saint," *Folklore* 101: 162–168.

Blanton, Richard. 1976. "Anthropological Study of Cities," *Annual Review of Anthropology* 5: 249–264.

Blasius, Andreas. 2007. "Antiochos IV. Epiphanes. Basileus und Pharao Ägyptens? Porphyrios und die polybianische Überlieferung," in Stefan Pfeiffer (ed.), *Ägypten unter fremden Herrschern zwischen persischer Satrapie und römischer Provinz:* 75–107. Frankfurt.

Boedeker, Deborah. 1988. "Protesilaos and the End of Herodotus' 'Histories,'" *CA* 7: 30–48.

Boehringer, Christof. 1993. "Antiochus Hierax am Hellespont," in Martin Price, Andrew Burnett, and Roger Bland (eds.), *Essays in Honour of Robert Carson and Kenneth Jenkins:* 37–47. London.

Boiy, Tom. 2000. "Dating Methods during the Early Hellenistic Period," *JCS* 52: 115–121.

————. 2004. *Late Achaemenid and Hellenistic Babylon.* Leuven.

————. 2010. "Between the Royal Administration and Local Elite: The *pāḫātu* in Hellenistic Babylonia as *epistates?*," *Anabasis* 1: 49–57.

Bopearachchi, Osmund and Philippe Flandrin. 2005. *Le portrait d'Alexandre le Grand. Histoire d'une découverte pour l'humanité.* Mayenne.

Bosio, Luciano. 1983. *La Tabula Peutingeriana: Una descrizione pittorica del mondo antico.* Rimini.

Bosworth, A. B. 1980. *A Historical Commentary on Arrian's History of Alexander.* Volume I, *Commentary on Books I–III.* Oxford.

————. 1988. *From Arrian to Alexander. Studies in Historical Interpretation.* Oxford.

————. 1995. *A Historical Commentary on Arrian's History of Alexander II. Commentary on Books IV–V.* Oxford.

————. 1996. "The Historical Setting of Megasthenes' *Indica*," *CP* 91: 113–127.

————. 2002. *The Legacy of Alexander: Politics, Warfare, and Propaganda under the Successors.* Oxford.

———. 2003. "Arrian, Megasthenes and the Making of Myth," in Juan López Férez (ed.), *Mitos en la literatura griega helenística e imperial:* 299–320. Madrid.

Bottéro, Jean. 1983. "Les morts et l'au-delà dans les rituels en accadien contre l'action des 'revenants,'" *Zeitschrift für Assyriologie und vorderasiatische Archäologie* 73: 153–203.

Boucharlat, Rémy. 2001. "The Palace and the Royal Achaemenid City: Two Case Studies—Pasargadae and Susa," in Inge Nielsen (ed.), *The Royal Palace Institution in the First Millennium BC: Regional Development and Cultural Interchange between East and West:* 113–123. Aarhus.

Bowersock, Glen. 1997. "Jacoby's Fragments and Two Greek Historians of Pre-Islamic Arabia," in Glenn Most (ed.), *Collecting Fragments—Fragmente sammeln:* 173–185. Göttingen.

Boyarin, Daniel and Jonathan Boyarin. 2003. "Diaspora: Generation and Ground of Jewish Identity," in Jana Braziel and Anita Mannur (eds.), *Theorizing Diaspora: A Reader:* 85–118. Malden.

Braemer, Frank, Jean-Marie Dentzer, Michael Kalos, and Philippe Tondon. 1999. "Tours à noyau chemisé de Syrie du sud," *Syria* 76: 151–176.

Braund, David. 2000. "Athenaeus, *On the Kings of Syria*," in David Braund and John Wilkins (eds.), *Athenaeus and His World: Reading Greek Culture in the Roman Empire:* 514–522. Exeter.

Breloer, B. 1941. *Alexanders Bund mit Poros: Indien von Dareios zu Sandrokottos.* Leipzig.

Bremen, Riet van. 2000. "The Demes and Phylai of Stratonikeia in Karia," *Chiron* 30: 389–401.

Bremmer, Jan. 2009. "Zeus' Own Country: Cult and Myth in the *Pride of Halicarnassus*," in Ueli Dill and Christine Walde (eds.), *Antike Mythen: Medien, Transformationen und Konstruktionen:* 292–312. Berlin.

Briant, Pierre. 1978. "Colonisation hellénistique et populations indigènes: La phase d'installation," *Klio* 60: 57–92.

———. 1982a. "Colonisation hellénistique et populations indigènes II. Renforts grecs dans les cités hellénistiques d'Orient," *Klio* 64: 83–98.

———. 1982b. *État et pasteurs au Moyen-Orient ancien.* Paris.

———. 1984. *L'Asie centrale et les royaumes proche-orientaux du premier millénaire (c. VIIIᵉ–VIᵉ siècles avant notre ère).* Paris.

———. 1986. "Alexandre et les 'Katarraktes' du Tigre," in Jean-Marie Pailler (ed.), *Mélanges offerts à Monsieur Michel Labrousse:* 11–22. Toulouse.

———. 1988. "Le nomadisme du Grand Roi," *Iranica Antiqua* 23: 253–273.

———. 1994. "De Samarkand à Sardes et de la ville de Suse au pays des Hanéens," *Topoi* 4: 455–467.

———. 1999. "*Katarraktai* du Tigre et *muballitum* du Habur," *Nabu* 1999–12.

———. 2001. "Polybe X.28 et les qanāts: Le témoignage et ses limites," in Pierre Briant (ed.), *Irrigation et drainage dans l'Antiquité: Qanāts et canalisations souterraines en Iran, en Égypte, et en Grèce:* 15–40. Paris.

———. 2002. *From Cyrus to Alexander: A History of the Persian Empire* (trans. Peter Daniels). Winona Lake.

———. 2006. "Retour sur Alexandre et les *katarraktes* du Tigre: L'histoire d'un dossier *(première parte),*" *Studi ellenistici* 19: 9–75.

———. 2008. "Retour sur Alexandre et les *katarraktes* du Tigre: L'histoire d'un dossier *(suite et fin),*" *Studi ellenistici* 20: 155–218.

———. 2012. "From the Indus to the Mediterranean: The Administrative Organization and Logistics of the Great Roads of the Achaemenid Empire," in Susan Alcock, John Bodel, and Richard Talbert (eds.), *Highways, Byways, and Road Systems in the Pre-Modern World*: 185–201. Oxford.

Bringmann, Klaus and Hans von Steuben. 1995. *Schenkungen hellenistischer Herrscher an griechische Städte und Heiligtümer.* Berlin.

Briscoe, John. 1969. "Eastern Policy and Senatorial Politics 168–146 BC," *Historia* 18: 49–70.

Brown, Stuart. 1986. "Media and Secondary State Formation in the Neo-Assyrian Zagros: An Anthropological Approach to an Assyriological Problem," *JCS* 38: 107–119.

Brown, Truesdell. 1957. "The Merits and Weaknesses of Megasthenes," *Phoenix* 11: 12–24.

———. 1960. "A Megasthenes Fragment on Alexander and Mandanis," *JAOS* 80: 133–135.

———. 1961. "Apollophanes and Polybius, Book 5," *Phoenix* 15: 187–195.

Brown, W. Edward. 1955. "Some Hellenistic Utopias," *Classical Weekly* 48: 57–62.

Brunt, Peter. 1980. "On Historical Fragments and Epitomes," *CQ* 30: 477–494.

Buc, Philippe. 2001. *The Dangers of Ritual: Between Early Medieval Texts and Social Scientific Theory.* Princeton.

Buccellati, Giorgio. 1988. "The Kingdom and Period of Khana," *BASOR* 270: 43–61.

Bunge, J. 1976. "Die Feiern Antiochos' IV. Epiphanes in Daphne im Herbst 166 v. Chr. Zu einem umstrittenen Kapitel syrischer und judäischer Geschichte," *Chiron* 6: 53–71.

Buraselis, Kostas. 1982. *Das hellenistische Makedonien und die Ägäis.* Munich.

Burkert, Walter. 1985. *Greek Religion. Archaic and Classical* (trans. John Raffan). Oxford.

———. 1996. *Creation of the Sacred: Tracks of Biology in Early Religions.* Cambridge, MA.

Butcher, Kevin. 2003. *Roman Syria and the Near East.* London.

Cahill, Nicholas. 2002. *Household and City Organization at Olynthus.* New Haven.

Calder, W. 1925. "The Royal Road in Herodotus," *CR* 39: 7–11.

Caley, Earle and John Richards. 1956. *Theophrastus: On Stones.* Columbus.

Callaghan, P. 1981. "The Medusa Rondanini and Antiochus III," *BSA* 76: 59–70.

Callieri, Pierfrancesco. 1995. "Une borne routière grecque de la région de Persépolis. Remarques additionnelles de M. Paul Bernard," *CRAI* 139: 65–95.

———. 1998. "A proposito di un'iconografia monetale dei dinasti del Fārs post-achemenide," *Ocnus* 6: 25–38.

———. 1999. "L'esplorazione geografica dell'Iran in epoca ellenistica e romana: Il contributo della documentazione archeologica," *Ocnus* 7: 31–43.

————. 2007. *L'archéologie du Fars à l'époque hellénistique*. Paris.

Callot, Olivier. 1989. "Failaka à l'époque hellénistique," in T. Fahd (ed.), *L'Arabie préislamique et son environnement historique et culturel*: 127–143. Leiden.

————. 1990. "Les monnaies dites 'Arabes' dans le nord du Golf arabo-persique à la fin du IIIe siècle avant notre ère," in Yves Calvet and Jacqueline Gachet (eds.), *Failaka. Fouilles françaises 1986–1988. Matériel céramique du temple-tour et épigraphie*: 221–240. Lyon.

Cameron, A. 1928. "Two Parallels," *CR* 42: 127.

Cameron, George. 1973. "The Persian Satrapies and Related Matters," *JNES* 32: 47–56.

Canepa, Matthew. 2010. "Achaemenid and Seleucid Royal Funerary Practices and Middle Iranian Kingship," in Henning Börm and Josef Wiesehöfer (eds.), *In commutatio et contentio: Studies in the Late Roman, Sasanian, and Early Islamic Near East in Memory of Zeev Rubin*: 1–21. Düsseldorf.

Capdetrey, Laurent. 2007. *Le pouvoir séleucide: Territoire, administration, finances d'un royaume hellénistique, 312–129 av. J.-C*. Rennes.

Carney, Elizabeth. 2000. *Women and Monarchy in Macedonia*. Norman.

Carratelli, Giovanni. 1953. "Asoka e i re ellenistici," *PP* 8: 449–454.

Carter, Joseph. 2006. "Towards a Comparative Study of *Chorai* West and East: Metapontion and Chersonesos," in Pia Bilde and Vladimir Stolba (eds.), *Surveying the Greek Chora: The Black Sea Region in a Comparative Persepctive*: 175–206. Aarhus.

Carter, Michael. 2001. "The Roman Spectacles of Antiochus IV Epiphanes at Daphne, 166 BC," *Nikephoros* 14: 45–62.

Cary, Max. 1949. *The Geographic Background of Greek and Roman History*. Oxford.

Casana, Jesse. 2003. From Alalakh to Antioch: Settlement, Land Use, and Environmental Change in the Amuq Valley of Southern Turkey. Dissertation. University of Chicago, Chicago.

Cassin, Elena. 1968. *La splendeur divine. Introduction à l'étude de la mentalité mésopotamienne*. Paris.

Casson, Stanley. 1918–1919. "Herodotus and the Caspian," *Annual of the British School at Athens* 23: 175–193.

Castagnoli, Ferdinando. 1971. *Orthogonal Town Planning in Antiquity* (trans. Victor Caliandro). Cambridge, MA.

Certeau, Michel de. 1984. *The Practice of Everyday Life* (trans. Steven Rendall). Berkeley.

————. 1986. *Heterologies: Discourse on the Other* (trans. Brian Massumi). Minneapolis.

Chang, Michael. 2007. *A Court on Horseback. Imperial Touring and the Construction of Qing Rule, 1680–1785*. Cambridge, MA.

Chaniotis, Angelos. 1987. "Ein neuer genealogischer Text aus Milet," *Epigraphica Anatolica* 10: 41–44.

————. 1993. "Ein diplomatischer Statthalter nimmt Rücksicht auf den verletzten Stolz zweier hellenistischer Kleinpoleis (Nagidos und Arsinoe)," *Epigraphica Anatolica* 21: 33–42.

————. 2009. "Myths and Contexts in Aphrodisias," in Ueli Dill and Christine Walde (eds.), *Antike Mythen: Medien, Transformationen und Konstruktionen:* 313–338. Berlin.

Chankowski, Andrzej. 2010. "Les cultes des souverains hellénistiques après la disparition des dynasties: Formes de survie et d'extinction d'une institution dans un contexte civique," in Ivana Savalli-Lestrade and Isabelle Cogitore (eds.), *Des rois au prince: Pratiques du pouvoir monarchique dans l'Orient hellénistique et romain:* 271–290. Grenoble.

Chantraine, Pierre. 1952. *Arrien, l'Inde.* Paris.

Chaumont, Marie-Louise. 1984. "Études d'histoire parthe: V. La route royale des Parthes de Zeugma à Séleucie du Tigre d'après l'itinéraire d'Isidore de Charax," *Syria* 61: 63–107.

Chauveau, Michel. 1990. "Un été 145," *Bulletin de l'institut français d'archéologie orientale* 90: 135–168.

Chaverdi, Ali-Reza. 2002. "Recent Post-Achaemenid Finds from Southern Fars, Iran," *Iran* 40: 277–278.

Clark, Timothy. 1999. *The Painting of Modern Life: Paris in the Art of Manet and His Followers.* Princeton.

Clarke, Graeme. 2002. "The Governor's Palace, Acropolis," in *Jebel Khalid on the Euphrates: Report on Excavations 1986–1996, Mediterranean Archaeology: Meditarch Supplement Series* 1: 25–48. Sydney.

Clarke, Graeme, Heather Jackson, Ted Nixon, Wendy Reade, John Tidmarsh, and Robert Thornley. 2008. "Jebel Khalid: The 2006 Season," *Meditarch* 21: 59–78.

Clarke, Katherine. 2008. *Making Time for the Past: Local History and the Polis.* Oxford.

Clarysse, W. 1989. "The Epitaph of the Officer Apollonios, Cairo inv. 9205," in E. Van't Dack, W. Clarysse, Getzel Cohen, J. Quaegebeur, and J. Winnicki, *The Judean-Syrian-Egyptian Conflict of 103–101 B.C.:* 84–88. Brussels.

Cogan, Mordechai. 1983. "Omens and Ideology in the Babylon Inscription of Esarhaddaon," in Hayim Tadmor and Moshe Weinfeld (eds.), *History, Historiography, and Interpretation: Studies in Biblical and Cuneiform Literatures:* 76–87. Jerusalem.

Cohen, Getzel. 1978. *The Seleucid Colonies: Studies in Founding, Administration, and Organization.* Wiesbaden.

————. 1995. *The Hellenistic Settlements in Europe, the Islands, and Asia Minor.* Berkeley.

————. 2006. *The Hellenistic Settlements in Syria, the Red Sea Basin, and North Africa.* Berkeley.

————. 2013. *The Hellenistic Settlements in the East from Armenia and Mesopotamia to Bactria and India.* Berkeley.

Cohen, Raymond and Raymond Westbrook (eds.). 2000. *Amarna Diplomacy: The Beginnings of International Relations.* Baltimore.

Cole, Thomas. 1967. *Democritus and the Sources of Greek Anthropology.* Ann Arbor.

Colledge, Malcolm. 1979. "Sculptors' stone-carving techniques in Seleucid and Parthian Iran, and Their Place in the 'Parthian' Cultural Milieu: Some Preliminary Observations," *East and West* 29: 221–240.

Coloru, Omar. 2009. *Da Alessandro a Menandro: Il regno greco di Battriana*. Pisa.

Comfort, Anthony and Rifat Ergeç. 2001. "Following the Euphrates in Antiquity: North-South Routes around Zeugma," *Anatolian Studies* 51: 19–49.

Connelly, Joan. 1989. "Votive Offerings from Hellenistic Failaka: Evidence for Herakles Cult," in T. Fahd (ed.), *L'Arabie préislamique et son environnement historique et culturel*: 145–158. Leiden.

Connor, W. 1985. "The Razing of the House in Greek Society," *TAPA* 115: 79–102.

Cotton, Hannah and Michael Wörrle. 2007. "Seleukos IV to Heliodoros: A New Dossier of Royal Correspondence from Israel," *ZPE* 159: 191–205.

Cox, Dorothy. 1950. "The Coins," in Heity Goldman (ed.), *Excvations at Gözlü Kule, Tarsus I: The Hellenistic and Roman Periods*: 38–83. Princeton.

Cozzoli, Umberto. 1980. "La τρυφή nella interpretazione delle crisi politiche," in *Tra Grecia e Roma. Temi antichi e metodologie moderne*: 133–145. Rome.

Curtis, Vesta. 2010. "The Frataraka Coins of Persis: Bridging the Gap between Achaemenid and Sasanian Persia," in John Curtis and St. John Simpson (eds.), *The World of Achaemenid Persia: History, Art and Society in Iran and the Ancient Near East*: 379–394. London.

Curty, Olivier. 1995. *Les parentés légendaires entre cités grecques*. Geneva.

Dąbrowa, Edward. 1999. "L'expédition de Démétrios II Nicator contre les Parthes (139–138 avant J.-C.)," *Parthica* 1: 9–17.

Dancy, John. 1954. *A Commentary on 1 Maccabees*. Oxford.

Davesne, Alain and Veli Yenisoğancı. 1992. "Les Ptolémées en Séleucide: Le trésor d'Hüseyinli," *RN* 34: 23–36.

Davies, William. 1982. *The Territorial Dimension of Judaism*. Berkeley.

Davis, Natalie. 1973. "The Rites of Violence: Religious Riot in Sixteenth-Century France," *Past and Present* 59: 51–91.

Debord, Pierre. 1985. "La Lydie du nord-est," *REA* 87: 345–358.

———. 2003. "Le culte royal chez les Séleucides," in Francis Prost (ed.), *L'Orient méditerranéen de la mort d'Alexandre aux campagnes de Pompée. Cités et royaumes à l'époque hellénistique*: 281–308. Rennes.

Decoster, Koen. 1989. "Flavius Josephus and the Seleucid Acra in Jerusalem," *ZDPV* 105: 70–84.

Del Monte, Giuseppe. 1997. *Testi dalla Babilonia ellenistica*. Pisa.

———. 2001. "Da 'barbari' a 're di Babilonia': I Greci in Mesopotamia," in Salvatore Settis (ed.), *I Greci. Storia, cultura, arte, società III. I Greci oltre la Grecia*: 137–166. Pisa.

Delev, Peter. 2003. "From Corupedion to Pydna: Thrace in the Third Century," *Thracia* 15: 107–120.

Delezir, Jean and Max Guy. 1988. "Les conditions géographiques du site et du terroir de Paestum étudiées d'après des images de satellites (Landsat TM et Spot)," in *Poseidonia-Paestum. Actes du 27ᵉ Congrès "Magna Grecia"*: 463–470. Tarento.

Demand, Nancy. 1990. *Urban Relocation in Archaic and Classical Greece: Flight and Consolidation*. Norman.

Dentzer, Jean-Marie. 1999. "L'espace des tribus arabes à l'époque hellénistique et romaine: Nomadisme, sédentarisation, urbanisation," *CRAI* 143: 231–261.

Desideri, Paolo. 1967. "Studi di storiografia eracleota," *SCO* 16: 366–416.

Desmond, William. 2004. "Punishments and the Conclusion of Herodotus' *Histories*," *GRBS* 44: 19–40.

Desreumaux, Alain, Justine Gaborit, and Jean-Sylvain Caillou. 1999. "Nouvelles découvertes à Apamée d'Osrhoène," *CRAI* 143: 75–105.

Dihle, Albrecht. 1984. *Antike und Orient*. Heidelberg.

Dintsis, Petros. 1986. *Hellenistische Helme*. Rome.

Dion, Roger. 1977. *Aspects politiques de la géographie antique*. Paris.

Dodinet, M., J. Leblanc, J.-P. Vallat, and F. Villeneuve. 1990. "Le paysage antique en Syrie: L'exemple de Damas," *Syria* 67: 339–367.

Donner, Fred. 1981. *The Early Islamic Conquests*. Princeton.

Downey, Glanville. 1951. "The Occupation of Syria by the Romans," *TAPA* 82: 149–163.

———. 1961. *A History of Antioch in Syria: From Seleucus to the Arab Conquest*. Princeton.

Downey, Susan. 1986. "The Citadel Palace at Dura-Europos," *Syria* 63: 27–37.

Droysen, Johann. 1878. *Geschichte des Hellenismus*. 2nd edition. Hamburg.

Dunand, Maurice and Raymond Duru. 1962. *Oumm el-'Amed. Une ville de l'époque hellénistique aux échelles de Tyr*. Paris.

Dupont-Sommer, André. 1958. "L'inscription araméenne," *Journal asiatique*: 19–35.

Dupree, Louis. 1975. "Settlement and Migration Patterns in Afghanistan: A Tentative Statement," *Modern Asian Studies* 9: 397–413.

Dussaud, René. 1955. *La pénétration des Arabes en Syrie avant l'Islam*. Paris.

Duyrat, Frédérique. 2005. *Arados hellénistique. Étude historique et monétaire*. Beirut.

Ebbinghaus, Susanne. 1999. "Between Greece and Persia: Rhyta in Thrace from the Late 5th to the Early 3rd Centuries B.C.," in Gocha Tsetskhladze (ed.), *Ancient Greeks, West and East*: 385–426. Leiden.

Edelstein, Ludwig and Ian Kidd. 1989. *Posidonius*. Cambridge.

Edney, Matthew. 1997. *Mapping an Empire: The Geographical Construction of British India, 1765–1843*. Chicago.

Edson, Charles. 1958. "Imperium Macedonicum: The Seleucid Empire and the Literary Evidence," *CP* 53: 153–170.

Ehling, Kay. 2007. "Der Tod des Usurpators Achaios," *Historia* 56: 497–501.

———. 2008. *Untersuchungen zur Geschichte der späten Seleukiden (164–63 v. Chr.): Vom Tode des Antiochos IV. bis zur Einrichtung der Provinz Syria unter Pompeius*. Stuttgart.

Ehrenberg, Victor. 1938. *Alexander and the Greeks* (trans. Ruth Fraenkel von Velsen). Oxford.

Eißfeldt, Otto. 1932. *Baal Zaphon, Zeus Kasios und der Durchzug der Israeliten durchs Meer*. Halle.

Emilov, Julij. 2005. "The Galatians and Cabyle. A Fragmentary Inscription and Its Context," *Studia Archaeologica Universitatis Serdicensis* Suppl. 4: 324–332.

Errington, Malcolm. 1976. "Alexander in the Hellenistic World," in Ernst Badian (ed.), *Alexandre le Grand: Image et réalité:* 137–179. Geneva.

Erskine, Andrew. 2002. "Life after Death: Alexandria and the Body of Alexander," *G&R* 49: 163–179.

Facella, Margherita. 2005. "Φιλορώμαιος καὶ Φιλέλλην: Roman Perception of Commagenian Royalty," in Olivier Hekster and Richard Fowler (eds.), *Imaginary Kings: Royal Images in the Ancient Near East, Greece and Rome:* 87–103. Munich.

Faraone, Christopher. 1993. "Molten Wax, Spilt Wine and Mutilated Animals: Sympathetic Magic in Near Eastern and Early Greek Oath Ceremonies," *JHS* 113: 60–80.

Feeney, Denis. 2007. *Caesar's Calendar: Ancient Time and the Beginnings of History.* Berkeley.

Fehr, Burkhard. 1979. "Kosmos und Chreia: Der Sieg der reinen über die praktische Vernunft in der griechischen Stadtarchitektur des 4. Jhs. v. Chr.," *Hephaistos* 2: 155–185.

Feissel, Denis. 1985. "Deux listes de quartiers d'Antioche astreints au creusement d'un canal (73/74 après J.-C.)," *Syria* 62: 77–103.

Feld, Steven and Keith Basso (eds.). 1996. *Senses of Place.* Santa Fe.

Feldherr, Andrew. 1998. *Spectacle and Society in Livy's History.* Berkeley.

Fischer, Thomas. 1970. *Untersuchungen zum Partherkrieg Antiochos' VII. im Rahmen der Seleukidengeschichte.* Tübingen.

Fleischer, Robert. 1972–1975. "Marsyas und Achaios," *JOÄI* 50: 103–122.

Fleming, David. 1993. "Where Was Achaemenid India?," *Bulletin of the Asia Institute* 7: 67–72.

Flory, Marleen. 1988. "Pearls for Venus," *Historia* 37: 498–504.

Foertmeyer, Victoria. 1988. "The Dating of the Pompe of Ptolemy II Philadelphus," *Historia* 37: 90–104.

Förster, Richard. 1897. "Antiochia am Orontes," *Jahrbuch des kaiserlichen deutschen archäologischen Instituts* 12: 103–149.

Foster, Benjamin. 1980. "Notes on Sargonic Royal Progress," *JANES* 12: 29–42.

Foucault, Michel. 1986. "Of Other Spaces" (trans. Jay Miskowiec), *Diacritics* 16: 22–27.

Foucher, Alfred. 1942. *La vieille route de l'Inde de Bactres à Taxila.* Paris.

Fowler, Richard. 2005. "'Most Fortunate Roots': Tradition and Legitimacy in Parthian Royal Ideology," in Olivier Hekster and Richard Fowler 2005: 125–155.

Fränkel, Max. 1890–1895. *Altertümer von Pergamon VIII: Die Inschriften von Pergamum.* Berlin.

Fraser, Peter. 1949. "Zeus Seleukeios," *CR* 63: 92–94.

———. 1972. *Ptolemaic Alexandria.* Oxford.

———. 1996. *Cities of Alexander the Great.* Oxford.

Fredricksmeyer, Ernst. 2000. "Alexander the Great and the Kingship of Asia," in A. B. Bosworth and E. Baynham (eds.), *Alexander the Great in Fact and Fiction:* 136–166. Oxford.

French, David. 1998. "Pre- and Early-Roman Roads of Asia Minor: The Persian Royal Road," *Iran* 36: 15–43.

Frézouls, Edmond. 1977. "La toponymie de l'orient Syrien et l'apport des éléments Macédoniens," in T. Fahd (ed.), *La toponymie antique:* 219–248. Leiden.

Frisch, P. and Z. Taşliklioğlu. 1975. "New Inscriptions from the Troad," *ZPE* 17: 101–114.

Frost, Frank. 1971. "Ptolemy II and Halicarnassus: An Honorary Decree," *Anatolian Studies* 21: 167–172.

Frye, Richard. 1967. "The Significance of Greek and Kushan Archaeology in the History of Central Asia," *Journal of Asian History* 1: 33–44.

———. 1984. *The History of Ancient Iran.* Munich.

Fuÿe, Allotte de la. 1910. "Monnaies incertaines de la Sogdiane et des contrées voisines," *RN* 14: 281–333.

Gabba, Emilio. 1981. "True History and False History in Classical Antiquity," *JRS* 71: 50–62.

Gachet, Jacqueline. 1990. "Un habitat du IIe siècle av. J.-C. dans la forteresse de Failaka," in Yves Calvet and Jacqueline Gachet (eds.), *Failaka. Fouilles françaises 1986–1988. Matériel céramique du temple-tour et épigraphie:* 167–191. Lyon.

Gachet, Jacqueline and Jean-François Salles. 1993. "Failaka, Koweit," in Uwe Finkbeiner (ed.), *Materialien zur Archäologie der Seleukiden- und Partherzeit im südlichen Babylonien und im Golfgebiet:* 59–85. Tübingen.

Gagné, Renaud. 2006. "What Is the Pride of Halicarnassus?," *CA* 25: 1–33.

Gardin, Jean-Claude. 1998. *Prospections archéologiques en Bactriane orientale (1974–1978) III. Description des sites et notes de synthèse.* Paris.

Gardin, Jean-Claude and P. Genetelle. 1976. "Irrigation et peuplement dans la plaine d'Aï Khanoum, de l'époque achéménide à l'époque musulmane," *Bulletin de l'École française d'Extrême-Orient* 63: 59–110.

Gardiner-Garden, John. 1987. *Greek Conceptions on Inner Asian Geography and Ethnography from Ephoros to Eratosthenes.* Bloomington.

Garstad, Benjamin. 2005. "The *Tyche* Sacrifices in John Malalas: Virgin Sacrifice and Fourth-Century Polemical History," *ICS* 30: 83–135.

———. 2011. "Pausanias of Antioch: Introduction, Translation, and Commentary," *Aram* 23: 669–691.

Gates, Jennifer. 2006. "Hidden Passage: Graeco-Roman Roads in Egypt's Eastern Desert," in Elizabeth Robertson, Jeffrey Seibert, Deepika Fernandez, and Marc Zender (eds.), *Space and Spatial Analysis in Archaeology:* 315–322. Calgary.

Gatier, Pierre-Louis, Pierre Lombard, and Khalid al-Sindi. 2002. "Greek Inscriptions from Bahrain," *Arabian Archaeology and Epigraphy* 13: 223–233.

Gauthier, Philippe. 1985. *Les cités grecques et leurs bienfaiteurs.* Paris.

———. 1989. *Nouvelles inscriptions de Sardes II.* Geneva.

Gauthier, Philippe and Jean-Louis Ferrary. 1981. "Le traité entre le roi Antiochos et Lysimacheia," *Journal des savants:* 327–345.

Geertz, Clifford. 1985. "Centers, Kings, and Charisma: Reflections on the Symbolics of Power," in Sean Wilentz (ed.), *Rites of Power: Symbolism, Ritual, and Politics since the Middle Ages:* 13–38. Philadelphia.

Gell, Alfred. 1992. *The Anthropology of Time: Cultural Constructions of Temporal Maps and Images.* Oxford.

Geller, Markham. 1991. "New Information on Antiochus IV from Babylonian Astronomical Diaries," *BSOAS* 54: 1–4.

George, Andrew. 1992. *Babylonian Topographical Texts.* Leuven.

———. 2003. *The Babylonian Gilgamesh Epic: Introduction, Critical Edition and Cuneiform Texts.* Oxford.

Gera, Dov. 1998. *Judaea and Mediterranean Politics 219 to 161 BCE.* Leiden.

Gera, Dov and Wayne Horowitz. 1997. "Antiochus IV in Life and Death: Evidence from the Babylonian Astronomical Diaries," *JAOS* 117: 240–252.

Gernet, Louis. 1968. *Anthropologie de la Grèce antique.* Paris.

Ghirshman, R. 1975. "Un bas-relief parthe de la collection Foroughi," *Artibus Asiae* 37: 229–239.

Giard, Luce. 1991. "Michel de Certeau's Heterology and the New World," *Representations* 33: 212–221.

Giovannini, Adalberto and Helmut Müller. 1971. "Die Beziehungen zwischen Rom und den Juden im 2. Jh. v. Chr.," *Museum Helveticum* 28: 156–171.

Glassner, Jean-Jacques. 2004. *Mesopotamian Chronicles* (ed. Benjamin Foster). Atlanta.

Godelier, Maurice. 1999. *The Enigma of the Gift* (trans. Nora Scott). Chicago.

Goldin, Judah. 1963. "On Honi the Circle-Maker: A Demanding Prayer," *Harvard Theological Review* 56: 233–237.

Goldschmidt, Henry. 2000. " 'Crown Heights Is the Center of the World': Reterritorializing a Jewish Diaspora," *Diaspora* 9: 83–106.

Goodblatt, David. 1987. "Josephus on Parthian Babylonia," *JAOS* 107: 605–622.

Goukowsky, Paul. 1978. *Essai sur les origines du mythe d'Alexandre.* Nancy.

Graf, David. 1993. "Early Hellenistic Travel Tales and Arabian Utopias," *Graeco-Arabica* 5: 111–117.

———. 2003. "Arabs in Syria: Demography and Epigraphy," in Maurice Sartre (ed.), *La Syrie hellénistique* (*Topoi* Suppl. 4): 319–340.

Graham, Mark and Shahram Khosravi. 1997. "Home Is Where You Make It: Repatriation and Diaspora Culture among Iranians in Sweden," *Journal of Refugee Studies* 10: 115–133.

Grainger, John. 1990. *The Cities of Seleukid Syria.* Oxford.

———. 1996. "Antiochos III in Thrace," *Historia* 45: 329–343.

———. 1997. *A Seleukid Prosopography and Gazetteer.* Leiden.

———. 2002. *The Roman War of Antiochos the Great.* Leiden.

———. 2010. *The Syrian Wars.* Leiden.

Grayson, Albert. 1975. *Babylonian Historical-Literary Texts.* Toronto.

Greenblatt, Stephen. 1991. *Marvelous Possessions: The Wonder of the New World.* Chicago.

Gregory, Derek. 1994. *Geographical Imaginations.* Oxford.

Grenet, Frantz. 2004/5. "Maracanda/Samarkand, une métropole pré-mongole. Sources écrites et archéologie," *Annales. Histoire, sciences sociales* 59: 1043–1067.

Grenet, Frantz and Claude Rapin. 1983. "Inscriptions économiques de la trésorerie hellénistique d'Aï Khanoum. L'onomastique iranienne à Aï Khanoum," *BCH* 107: 315–381.

Groningen, B. van. 1933. *Aristote: Le second livre de l'Economique.* Leiden.

———. 1934. "Petite note sur Pap. Tebt. 698," *Aegyptus* 14: 120.

Grosso, Fluvio. 1958. "Gli Eretriesi deportati in Persia," *Rivista di filologia e istruzione classica* 86: 350–375.

Gruen, Erich. 1985. "The Coronation of the Diadochi," in John Eadie and Josiah Ober (eds.), *The Craft of the Ancient Historian:* 253–271. London.

———. 2000. "Culture as Policy: The Attalids of Pergamon," in Nancy de Grummond and Brunilde Ridgway (eds.), *From Pergamon to Sperlonga: Sculpture and Context:* 17–31. Berkeley.

Grzybek, Erhard. 1990. *Du calendrier macédonien au calendrier ptolémaïque. Problèmes de chronologie hellénistique.* Basel.

Guillaume, Olivier. 1983. *Fouilles d'Aï Khanoum II. Les propylées de la rue principale.* Paris.

Gullini, G. 1967. "Un contributo alla storia dell'urbanistica: Seleucia sul Tigri," *Mesopotamia* 2: 135–163.

———. 1968–1969. "Trial Trench on the Canal," *Mesopotamia* 3/4: 39–41.

Gupta, Akhil and James Ferguson. 1992. "Beyond 'Culture': Space, Identity, and the Politics of Difference," *Cultural Anthropology* 7: 6–23.

Guy, Max. 1995. "Cadastres en bandes de Métaponte à Agde. Questions et méthodes," *Études Massaliotes* 4: 427–444.

Habermas, Jürgen. 1962. *Strukturwandel der Öffentlichkeit: Untersuchungen zu einer Kategorie der bürgerlichen Gesellschaft.* Darmstadt.

Habib, Irfan and Vivekanand Jha. 2004. *Mauryan India.* New Delhi.

Habicht, Christian. 1956. *Gottmenschentum und griechische Städte.* Munich.

———. 1957. "Samische Volksbeschlüsse der hellenistischen Zeit," *MDAI* (A) 72: 152–274.

———. 1989. "Athen und die Seleukiden," *Chiron* 19: 7–26.

———. 2006. *The Hellenistic Monarchies: Selected Papers.* Ann Arbor.

Hadley, Robert. 1978. "The Foundation Date of Seleucia-on-the-Tigris," *Historia* 27: 228–230.

Haerinck, Ernie and Bruno Overlaet. 2008. "Altar Shrines and Fire Altars? Architectural Representations on *Frataraka* Coinage," *Iranica Antiqua* 43: 207–233.

Hallo, William. 1984–1985. "The Concept of Eras from Nabonassar to Seleucus," *JANES* 16/17: 143–151.

———. 1988. "The Nabonassar Era and Other Epochs in Mesopotamian Chronology and Chronography," in Erle Leichty, Maria de J. Ellis, and Pamela Gerardi (eds.), *A Scientific Humanist: Studies in Memory of Abraham Sachs:* 175–190. Philadelphia.

Hamilton, J. 1971. "Alexander and the Aral," *CQ* 21: 106–111.

Hammond, Nicholas. 1980. "The Extent of Persian Occupation in Thrace," *Chiron* 10: 53–61.

————. 1998. "The Branchidae at Didyma and in Sogdiana," *CQ* 48: 339–344.

Hammond, Nicholas and G. Griffith. 1979. *A History of Macedonia* II. Oxford.

Hampl, Franz. 1936. Review of Walter Otto, *Zur Geschichte der Zeit des 6. Ptolemäers. Ein Beitrag zur Politik und zum Staatsrecht des Hellenismus. Gnomon* 12: 30–43.

Hannestad, Lise and Daniel Potts. 1990. "Temple Architecture in the Seleucid Kingdom," in Per Bilde, Troels Engberg-Pedersen, Lise Hannestad, and Jan Zahle (eds.), *Religion and Religious Practice in the Seleucid Kingdom:* 91–124. Esbjerg.

Hansman, John. 1990. "Coins and Mints of Ancient Elymais," *Iran* 28: 1–11.

Hartog, François. 1988. *The Mirror of Herodotus: The Representation of the Other in the Writing of History* (trans. Janet Lloyd). Berkeley.

Harvey, David. 2001. *Spaces of Capital: Towards a Critical Geography*. Edinburgh.

————. 2009. *Cosmopolitanism and the Geographies of Freedom*. New York.

Hasluck, F. 1910. *Cyzicus*. Cambridge.

Hatzopoulos, Miltiade. 2001. "Macedonian Palaces: Where King and City Meet," in Inge Nielsen (ed.), *The Royal Palace Institution in the First Millennium BC: Regional Development and Cultural Interchange between East and West:* 189–200. Aarhus.

————. 2006. *La Macédoine: Géographie historique—Langue, cultes et croyances— Institutions*. Paris.

————. 2011. "The Cities," in Robin Lane Fox (ed.), *Brill's Companion to Ancient Macdeon: Studies in the Archaeology and History of Macedon, 650 BC–300* AD: 235–241. Leiden.

Hauben, Hans. 1974. "A Royal Toast in 302 B.C.," *Ancient Society* 5: 105–117.

Haussoullier, Bernard. 1902. *Études sur l'histoire de Milet et du Didymeion*. Paris.

Heckel, Waldemar. 2006. *Who's Who in the Age of Alexander the Great: Prosopography of Alexander's Empire*. Oxford.

Heinemann, I. 1931. "Antisemitismus," *RE* Suppl. 5: 3–43.

Hekster, Olivier and Richard Fowler. 2005. "Imagining Kings: From Persia to Rome," in Olivier Hekster and Richard Fowler (eds.), *Imaginary Kings: Royal Images in the Ancient Near East, Greece and Rome:* 9–38. Munich.

Held, Winfried. 2002. "Die Residenzstädte der Seleukiden," *JDAI* 117: 217–249.

Heller, Anna. 2006. "'Αρχαιότης et εὐγένεια. Le thème des origines dans les cités d'Asie Mineure à l'époque impériale," *Ktema* 31: 97–108.

Helms, Mary. 1988. *Ulysses' Sail: An Ethnographic Odyssey of Power, Knowledge, and Geographical Distance*. Princeton.

Henkelman, Wouter. 2010. "'Consumed before the King': The Table of Darius, That of Irdabama and Irtaštuna, and That of His Satrap, Karkiš," in Bruno Jacobs and Robert Rollinger (eds.), *Der Achämenidenhof:* 667–775. Wiesbaden.

————. 2011a. "Of Tapyroi and Tablets, States and Tribes: The Historical Geography of Pastoralism in the Achaemenid Heartland in Greek and Elamite Sources," *BICS* 54: 1–16.

————. 2011b. "Parnakka's Feast: Šip in Pārsa and Elam," in Javier Álvarez-Mon and Mark Garrison (eds.), *Elam and Persia:* 89–166. Winona Lake.

Hennig, Dieter. 2000. "Straßen und Stadtviertel in der griechischen Polis," *Chiron* 30: 585–615.

Henrichs, Albert. 1999. "Demythologizing the Past, Mythicizing the Present: Myth, History and the Supernatural at the Dawn of the Hellenistic Period," in Richard Buxton (ed.), *From Myth to Reason? Studies in the Development of Greek Thought:* 223–248. Oxford.

Herbert, Sharon and Andrea Berlin. 2003. "A New Administrative Center for Persian and Hellenistic Galilee: Preliminary Report of the University of Michigan/University of Minnesota Excavations at Kedesh," *BASOR* 329: 13–59.

Hercher, Rudolf. 1858. *Aeliani de Natura Animalium, Varia Historia, Epistolae et Fragmenta. Porphyrii Philosophi de Abstinentia et de Antro Nympharum. Philonis Byzantii de Septem Orbis Spectaculis.* Paris.

Herling, Anja. 2003. *Tyloszeitliche Bestattungspraktiken auf der Insel Bahrain.* Göttingen.

Herrenschmidt, Clarisse. 1976. "Désignation de l'empire et concepts politiques de Darius Ier d'après ses inscriptions en vieux-perse," *Studia Iranica* 5: 33–65.

Herrmann, Georgina, K. Kurbansakhatov, and St. John Simpson. 2001. "The International Merv Project Preliminary Report on the Ninth Year (2000)," *Iran* 39: 9–52.

Herrmann, Peter. 1959. *Neue Inschriften zur historischen Landeskunde von Lydien und angrenzenden Gebieten.* Vienna.

———. 1965a. "Antiochos der grosse und Teos," *Anadolu* 9: 29–159.

———. 1965b. "Neue Urkunden zur Geschichte von Milet im 2. Jahrhundert v. Chr.," *MDAI* (I) 15: 71–117.

———. 1987. "Milesier am Seleukidenhof. Prosopographische Beiträge zur Geschichte Milets im 2. Jhdt. v. Chr.," *Chiron* 17: 171–192.

Hoepfner, Wolfram. 2004. "Antiochia die Große. Geschichte einer antiken Stadt," *Antike Welt* 35: 3–9.

Hölbl, Günther. 2001. *A History of the Ptolemaic Empire* (trans. Tina Saavedra). London.

Holleaux, Maurice. 1900. "Un prétendu decret d'Antioche sur l'Oronte," *REG* 13: 258–280.

———. 1942. *Études d'épigraphie et d'histoire grecques* III. *Lagides et Séleucides.* Paris.

Hollis, A. 1994. "[Oppian], *Cyn.* 2,100–158 and the Mythical Past of Apamea-on-the-Orontes," *ZPE* 102: 153–166.

Hölscher, Gustav. 1903. *Palästina in der persischen und hellenistischen Zeit.* Berlin.

Holt, Frank. 1988. *Alexander the Great and Bactria.* Leiden.

———. 1999. *Thundering Zeus: The Making of Hellenistic Bactria.* Berkeley.

———. 2003. *Alexander the Great and the Mystery of the Elephant Medallions.* Berkeley.

Honigmann, Ernst. 1921. "Seleukeia," *RE* Series 2 2.3: 1184–1203.

Honigmann, Ernst and Johanna Schmidt. 1939. "Orontes," *RE* 35: 1160–1164.

Hoover, Oliver. 2004. "*Ceci n'est pas l'autonomie:* The Coinage of Seleucid Phoenicia as Royal and Civic Power Discourse," in Véronique Chankowski and Frédérique Duyrat (eds.), *Le roi et l'économie* (*Topoi* Suppl. 6): 485–507.

————. 2007. "A Revised Chronology for the Late Seleucids at Antioch (121/0–64BC)," *Historia* 56: 280–301.

Hopkins, Clark (ed.). 1972. *Topography and Architecture of Seleucia on the Tigris*. Ann Arbor.

Horden, Peregrine and Nicholas Purcell. 2000. *The Corrupting Sea: A Study of Mediterranean History*. Oxford.

Hornblower, Jane. 1981. *Hieronymus of Cardia*. Oxford.

Horowitz, Wayne. 1988. "The Babylonian Map of the World," *Iraq* 50: 147–165.

————. 1998. *Mesopotamian Cosmic Geography*. Winona Lake.

Houghton, Arthur. 1992. "The Revolt of Tryphon and the Accession of Antiochus VI at Apamea," *SNR* 71: 119–141.

————. 1993. "The Reigns of Antiochus VIII and Antiochus IX at Antioch and Tarsus," *SNR* 72: 87–106.

Houghton, Arthur and Catherine Lorber. 2002. *Seleucid Coins: A Comprehensive Catalogue. Part 1: Seleucus I through Antiochus III*. London.

Houghton, Arthur, Catherine Lorber, and Oliver Hoover. 2008. *Seleucid Coins: A Comprehensive Catalogue. Part 2: Seleucus IV through Antiochus XIII*. London.

Humphreys, Sally. 1997. "Fragments, Fetishes, and Philosophies: Towards a History of Greek Historiography after Thucydides," in Glenn Most (ed.), *Collecting Fragments—Fragmente sammeln*: 207–224. Göttingen.

Hunter, Richard. 2004. "Notes on the *Lithika* of Posidippus," in Benjamin Acosta-Hughes, Elizabeth Kosmetatou, and Manuel Baumbach (eds.), *Labored in Papyrus Leaves: Perspectives on an Epigram Collection Attributed to Posidippus*: 94–104. Washington, D.C.

Huß, Werner. 2001. *Ägypten in hellenistischer Zeit 332–30 v. Chr.* Munich.

Invernizzi, Antonio. 1966. "The Excavations at Tell 'Umayr," *Mesopotamia* 1: 39–62.

————. 1991. "Séleucie du Tigre, métropole grecque d'Asie," *Revue archéologique*: 180–185.

————. 1993. "Seleucia on the Tigris: Centre and Periphery in Seleucid Asia," in Per Bilde, Troels Engberg-Pedersen, Lise Hannestad, Jan Zahle, and Klavs Randsborg (eds.), *Centre and Periphery in the Hellenistic World*: 230–250. Aarhus.

————. 1994. "Fra novità e tradizione: La fondazione di Seleucia sul Tigri," in Stefania Mazzoni (ed.), *Nuove fondazioni nel vicino Oriente antico: Realtà e ideologia*: 115–129. Pisa.

————. 1998. "Elymaeans, Seleucids, and the Hung-e Azhdar relief," *Mesopotamia* 33: 219–259.

————. 2007. "The Culture of Parthian Nisa between Steppe and Empire," in Joe Cribb and Georgina Herrmann (eds.), *After Alexander. Central Asia before Islam*: 163–177. Oxford.

Invernizzi, Antonio (ed.). 1995. *In the Land of the Gryphons: Papers on Central Asian Archaeology in Antiquity*. Florence.

————. 2004. *Seleucia al Tigri: Le impronte di sigillo dagli Archivi*. Alessandria.

Iossif, Panagiotis and Catherine Lorber. 2009. "Seleucid Campaign Beards," *L'Antiquité classique* 78: 87–115.

386 **References**

——. 2010. "The Elephantarches Bronze of Seleucos I Nicator," *Syria* 87: 147–164.

Isager, Signe. 1998. "The Pride of Halikarnassos: *Editio Princeps* of an Inscription from Salmakis," *ZPE* 123: 1–23.

Ivantchik, Askold, Andrei Belinskiy, and Alexei Dovgalev. 2011. "Prospections sur le territoire d'Apamée et élaboration du SIG *Kélainai–Apamée Kibôtos* (2008–2010)," in Lâtife Summerer, Askold Ivantchik, and Alexander von Kienlin (eds.), 2011. *Kelainai–Apameia Kibotos: Stadtentwicklung im anatolischen Kontext / Kelainai–Apameai Kibotos: Développement urbain dans le contexte anatolien:* 137–177. Bordeaux.

Jacobson, Howard. 1975. "The Oath of the Delian League," *Philologus* 119: 256–258.

Jeppesen, Kristian. 1989. *Ikaros. The Hellenistic Settlements III. The Sacred Enclosure in the Early Hellenistic Period.* Aarhus.

Jewsiewicki, Bogumil. 1989. "The Formation of the Political Culture of Ethnicity in the Belgian Congo, 1920–1959," in Leroy Vail (ed.), *The Creation of Tribalism in Southern Africa:* 324–349. Berkeley.

Jones, A. 1931. "The Urbanization of the Ituraean Principality," *JRS* 21: 265–275.

Jones, Christopher. 1993. "The Decree of Ilion in Honor of a King Antiochus," *GRBS* 34: 73–92.

——. 2009. "The Inscription from Tel Maresha for Olympiodoros," *ZPE* 171: 100–104.

Jones, Christopher and Christian Habicht. 1989. "A Hellenistic Inscription from Arsinoe in Cilicia," *Phoenix* 43: 317–346.

Jones, Christopher and J. Russell. 1993. "Two New Inscriptions from Nagidos in Cilicia," *Phoenix* 47: 293–304.

Jones, William. 1877. *Finger-Ring Lore: Historical, Legendary, Anecdotal.* London.

Jonnes, Lloyd and Marijana Ricl. 1997. "A New Royal Inscription from Phrygia Paroreios: Eumenes II Grants Tyriaion the Status of a *Polis*," *Epigraphica Anatolica* 29: 1–28.

Jordan, B. 2000. "The Sicilian Expedition Was a Potemkin Fleet," *CQ* 50: 63–79.

Kahrstedt, Ulrich. 1926. *Syrische Territorien in hellenistischer Zeit.* Berlin.

Kantorowicz, Ernst. 1944. "The 'King's Advent' and the Enigmatic Panels in the Doors of Santa Sabina," *Art Bulletin* 26: 207–231.

Karahashi, Fumi. 2004. "Fighting the Mountain: Some Observations on the Sumerian Myths of Inanna and Ninurta," *JNES* 63: 111–118.

Karttunen, Klaus. 1997. *India and the Hellenistic World.* Helsinki.

Katz, Dina. 2005. "Death They Dispensed to Mankind: The Funerary World of Ancient Mesopotamia," *Historiae* 2: 55–90.

Kelsen, Hans. 1937. "The Philosophy of Aristotle and the Hellenic-Macedonian Policy," *Ethics* 48: 1–64.

Kennell, Nigel. 2005. "New Light on *2 Maccabees* 4:7–15," *JJS* 56: 10–24.

Kern, Otto. 1901. "Magnetische Studien," *Hermes* 36: 491–515.

Keyser, Paul. 2001. "The Geographical Work of Dikaiarchos," in William Fortenbaugh and Eckart Schütrumpf (eds.), *Dicaearchus of Messana. Text, Translation, and Discussion:* 353–372. London.

Khatchadourian, Lori. 2007. "Unforgettable Landscapes: Attachments to the Past in Hellenistic Armenia," in Norman Yoffee (ed.), *Negotiating the Past in the Past: Identity, Memory, and Landscape in Archaeological Research:* 43–75. Tucson.

Kirchberg, Jutta. 1965. *Die Funktion der Orakel im Werke Herodots.* Göttingen.

Koldewey, Robert and Friedrich Wetzel. 1931–1932. *Die Königsburgen von Babylon.* Leipzig.

Košelenko, Gennadij, Andrej Bader, and Vassif Gaibov. 1995. "Walls of Margiana," in Antonio Invernizzi (ed.), *In the Land of the Gryphons: Papers on Central Asian Archaeology in Antiquity:* 39–50. Florence.

———. 1997. "Die Margiana in hellenistischer Zeit," in B. Funk (ed.), *Hellenismus: Beiträge zur Erforschung von Akkulturation und politischer Ordnung in den Staaten des hellenistischen Zeitalters:* 121–145. Tübingen.

Kosmin, Paul. 2009. Review of Andrea Primo, *La Storiografia sui Seleucidi da Megastene a Eusebio di Cesarea. Storia della Storiografia* 56: 131–135.

———. 2011. "The Foundation and Early Life of Dura-Europos," in Gail Hoffman and Lisa Brody (eds.), *Dura-Europos: Crossroads of Antiquity:* 95–109. Boston.

———. 2013a. "Alexander the Great and the Seleucids in Iran," in Daniel Potts (ed.), *The Oxford Handbook of Iranian Archaeology:* 671–689. Oxford.

———. 2013b. "Apologetic Ethnography: Megasthenes' *Indica* and the Seleucid Elephant," in Eran Almagor and Joseph Skinner (eds.), *Ancient Ethnography: New Approaches*: 97–115. London.

———. 2013c. "Rethinking the Hellenistic Gulf: The New Greek Inscription from Bahrain," *JHS* 133: 61–79.

———. 2013d. "Seleucid Ethnography and Indigenous Kingship: The Babylonian Education of Antiochus I," in Johannes Haubold (ed.), *The World of Berossus*: 199–212. London.

———. 2014a. "No Island Is a Man: Antiochus III's Marriage to 'Euboea,'" in Roland Oetjen and Francis Ryan (eds.), *Seleukeia: Studies in Seleucid History, Archaeology and Numismatics in Honor of Getzel M. Cohen.* Berlin.

———. 2014b. "Seeing Double in Seleucid Babylonia: Rereading the Borsippa Cylinder of Antiochus I," in Al Moreno and Rosalind Thomas (eds.), *Patterns of the Past.*

———. Forthcoming. "Indigenous Revolt in *2 Maccabees*: The Persian Version."

Kottaridi, Angeliki. 2011. "The Palace of Aegae," in Robin Lane Fox (ed.), *Brill's Companion to Ancient Macedon: Studies in the Archaeology and History of Macedon, 650 BC–300 AD:* 297–333. Leiden.

Kühne, Hartmut. 1994. "The Urbanization of the Assyrian Provinces," in Stefania Mazzoni (ed.), *Nuove fondazioni nel Vicino Oriente antico: Realtà e ideologia:* 55–84. Pisa.

Kuhrt, Amélie. 1987. "Berossus' *Babyloniaca* and Seleucid Rule in Babylonia," in Amélie Kuhrt and Susan Sherwin-White (eds.), *Hellenism in the East: The Interaction of Greek and Non-Greek Civilizations from Syria to Central Asia after Alexander:* 32–56. London.

———. 2002. *"Greeks" and "Greece" in Mesopotamian and Persian Perspectives: Twenty-First J. L. Myres Memorial Lecture.* Oxford.

Kuhrt, Amélie and Susan Sherwin-White. 1991. "Aspects of Seleucid Royal Ideology: The Cylinder of Antiochus I from Borsippa," *JHS* 111: 71–86.

———. 1993. *From Samarkhand to Sardis: A New Approach to the Seleucid Empire.* Berkeley.

Kupper, Jean-Robert. 1957. *Les nomades en Mésopotamie au temps des rois de Mari.* Paris.

Kuttner, Ann. 2005. "Cabinet Fit for a Queen: The Λιθικά as Posidippus' Gem Museum," in Kathryn Gutzwiller (ed.), *The New Posidippus: A Hellenistic Poetry Book:* 141–163. Oxford.

Kuz'mina, E. 1976. "The 'Bactrian Mirage' and the Archaeological Reality: On the Problem of the Formation of North Bactrian Culture," *East and West* 26: 111–131.

Labat, René. 1988. *Manuel d'épigraphie akkadienne: Signes, syllabaire, idéogrammes.* Paris.

Lackenbacher, Sylvie. 1982. *Le roi bâtisseur: Les récits de construction assyriens des origines à Teglatphalasar III.* Paris.

Lacroix, Léon. 1974. "Héraclès, héros voyageur et civilisateur," *Bulletin de la Classe des lettres et des sciences morales et politiques* 60: 34–59.

Lampl, Paul. 1968. *Cities and Planning in the Ancient Near East.* New York.

Landau, Y. 1961. "A Greek Inscription from Acre," *IEJ* 11: 118–126.

Lane Fox, Robin. 2008. *Travelling Heroes: Greeks and Their Myths in the Epic Age of Homer.* London.

Lassen, C. 1827. *Commentatio geographica atque historica de pentapotamia Indica.* Bonn.

Lauffer, Siegfried. 1956. *Abriß der antiken Geschichte.* Munich.

Lauter, Hans. 1986. *Die Architektur des Hellenismus.* Darmstadt.

Lawrence, A. 1957. *Greek Architecture.* Yale.

Lawton, Carol. 1995. *Attic Document Reliefs: Art and Politics in Ancient Athens.* Oxford.

Le Rider, Georges. 1959. "Monnaies de Characène," *Syria* 36: 229–253.

———. 1965. *Suse sous les Séleucides et les Parthes.* Paris.

Le Roy, Christian. 1986. "Un règlement religieux au Létôon de Xanthos," *RA*: 279–300.

Leblanc, Jacques and Grégoire Poccardi. 1999. "Étude de la permanence de tracés urbains et ruraux antiques à Antioche-sur-l'Oronte," *Syria* 76: 91–126.

Lebreton, Stéphane. 2005. "Le Taurus en Asie Mineure: Contenus et conséquences de représentations stéréotypées," *REA* 107: 655–674.

Lefebvre, Henri. 1991. *The Production of Space* (trans. Donald Nicholson-Smith). Oxford.

Legg, Stephen. 2007. *Spaces of Colonialism: Delhi's Urban Governmentalities.* Oxford.

Lehnen, Joachim. 2001. "Profectio Augusti. Zum kaiserlichen Zeremoniell des Abmarsches," *Gymnasium* 108: 15–33.

Lenfant, Dominique. 2004. *Ctésias de Cnide: La Perse, l'Inde, autres fragments.* Paris.

Leonard, Karen. 2001. "Finding One's Own Place: Asian Landscapes Re-Visioned in Rural California," in Akhil Gupta and James Ferguson (eds.), *Culture, Power, Place: Explorations in Critical Anthropology:* 118–136. Durham, N.C.

Leriche, Pierre. 1985. "Structures politiques et sociales dans la Bactriane et la Sogdiane hellénistiques," in Heinz Kreißig and Friedmar Kühnert (eds.), *Antike*

Abhängigkeitsformen in den griechischen Gebieten ohne Polisstruktur und den römischen Provinzen: 65–79. Berlin.

——. 2003a. "Europos-Doura hellénistique," in Maurice Sartre (ed.), *La Syrie hellénistique* (*Topoi* Suppl. 4): 171–191. Paris.

——. 2003b. "Peut-on étudier la Syrie séleucide?," in Francis Prost (ed.), *L'Orient méditerranéen de la mort d'Alexandre aux campagnes de Pompée. Cités et royaumes à l'époque hellénistique:* 117–146. Rennes.

Leriche, Pierre and Shakir Pidaev. 2007. "Termez in Antiquity," in Joe Cribb and Georgina Herrmann (eds.), *After Alexander. Central Asia before Islam:* 179–211. Oxford.

Lerner, Jeffrey. 2003–2004. "Correcting the Early History of Āy Ḵānom," *Archäologische Mitteilungen aus Iran und Turan* 35–36: 373–410.

Leschhorn, Wolfgang. 1984. *Gründer der Stadt: Studien zu einem politisch-religiösen Phänomen der griechischen Geschichte.* Stuttgart.

Leslie, Donald and K. Gardiner. 1982. "Chinese Knowledge of Western Asia during the Han," *T'oung Pao* 68: 254–308.

Lewis, Naphtali. 1949. "Dio Chrysostom's 'Tyrant of Syria,'" *CP* 44: 32–33.

Liebeschuetz, J. 2004. "Malalas on Antioch," in Bernadette Cabouret, Pierre-Louis Gatier, and Catherine Saliou (eds.), *Antioche de Syrie: Histoire, images et traces de la ville antique* (*Topoi* Suppl. 5): 143–153.

Lilley, Keith. 2009. *City and Cosmos: The Medieval World in Urban Form.* London.

Lincoln, Bruce. 2008. "The Role of Religion in Achaemenian Imperialism," in Nicole Brisch (ed.), *Religion and Power: Divine Kingship in the Ancient World and Beyond:* 221–242. Chicago.

Litvinskiy, Boris. 2010a. *Khram Oksa v Baktrii* III: *Iskusstvo, khudozhestvennoe remeslo, myzykal'nye instrumenty.* Moscow.

——. 2010b. "Problems of the History and Culture of Baktria in Light of Archaeological Excavations in Central Asia," *Anabasis* 1: 23–48.

Litvinskiy, Boris and Igor Pičikjan. 1995. "River-Deities of Greece Salute the God of the River Oxus-Vakhsh: Achelous and the Hippocampess," in Antonio Invernizzi (ed.), *In the Land of the Gryphons: Papers on Central Asian Archaeology in Antiquity:* 129–149. Florence.

Litvinskiy, Boris, Y. Vinogradov, and Igor Pičikjan. 1985. "The Votive Offering of Atrosokes from the Temple of Oxus in Northern Bactria," *VDI:* 84–110.

Liverani, Mario. 2001. *International Relations in the Ancient Near East, 1600–1100 BC.* Houndmills.

——. 2004. *Myth and Politics in Ancient Near Eastern Historiography.* London.

Lloyd-Jones, Hugh. 2005. *Supplementum Supplementi Hellenistici.* Berlin.

Lloyd-Jones, Hugh and Peter Parsons. 1983. *Supplementum Hellenisticum.* Berlin.

Lund, J. 1993. "The Archaeological Evidence for the Transition from the Persian Period to the Hellenistic Age in Northwestern Syria," *Transeuphratène* 6: 27–45.

——. 2003. "Hamā in the Early Hellenistic Period: A Review of the Archaeological Evidence," in Maurice Sartre (ed.), *La Syrie hellénistique* (*Topoi* Suppl. 4): 253–268. Paris.

Ma, John. 2002. *Antiochos III and the Cities of Western Asia Minor.* Oxford.

———. 2003. "Kings," in Andrew Erskine (ed.), *A Companion to the Hellenistic World:* 177–196. Oxford.

MacCormack, Sabine. 1981. *Art and Ceremony in Late Antiquity.* Berkeley.

Macdonald, M. 2003. "'Les Arabes en Syrie' or 'La pénétration des Arabes en Syrie': A Question of Perceptions?," in Maurice Sartre (ed.), *La Syrie hellénistique* (*Topoi* Suppl. 4): 303–318.

Magie, David. 1950. *Roman Rule in Asia Minor.* Princeton.

Maila Afeiche, Anne-Marie (ed.). 2009. *Le site de Nahr el-Kalb.* Lebanon.

Mairs, Rachel. 2011. *The Archaeology of the Hellenistic Far East: A Survey. BAR* 2196. Oxford.

———. 2013. *The Archaeology of the Hellenistic Far East: A Survey.* Supplement 1. www.bactria.org.

Malay, Hasan. 1983. "A Royal Document from Aigai in Aiolis," *GRBS* 24: 349–353.

Malkin, Irad. 1987. *Religion and Colonization in Ancient Greece.* Leiden.

———. 1998. *The Returns of Odysseus: Colonization and Ethnicity.* Berkeley.

———. 2011. *A Small Greek World: Networks in the Ancient Mediterranean.* Oxford.

Manning, Joe. 2010. *The Last Pharaohs: Egypt under the Ptolemies 350–30 BC.* Princeton.

Marcellesi, Marie-Christine. 2004. *Milet des Hécatomnides à la domination romaine: Pratiques monétaires et histoire de la cité du IVe au IIe siécle av. J.-C.* Mainz.

Marek, Christian. 2006. *Die Inschriften von Kaunos.* Munich.

Marfoe, Leon. 1978. *Between Qadesh and Kumidi: A History of Frontier Settlement and Land Use in the Beqa', Lebanon.* Chicago.

Marinoni, Elio. 1972. "La capitale del regno di Seleuco I," *Rendiconti Istituto Lombardo* 106: 579–631.

Marzolff, Peter. 1996. "Der Palast von Demetrias," in Wolfram Hoepfner and Gunnar Brands (eds.), *Basileia: Die Paläste der hellenistischen Könige:* 148–163. Mainz.

Masson, C. 1850. "Illustration of the Route from Seleucia to Apobatana, as Given by Isidorus of Charax," *JRAS* 12: 97–124.

Mastrocinque, Attilio. 1983. *Manipolazione della storia in età ellenistica: I Seleucidi e Roma.* Rome.

———. 1987–1988. "La guerra di successione siriaca: Realtà storica o invenzione moderna?," *AIIS* 10: 65–92.

———. 1993. "'Guerra di successione' e prima guerra di Celesiria. Un falso moderno e una questione storica," *Ancient Society* 24: 27–39.

Matheson, Susan. 1994. "The Goddess Tyche," *Yale University Art Gallery Bulletin* 18–33.

Mauss, Marcel. 1954. *The Gift* (trans. Ian Cunnison). New York.

Mazzarella, William. 2010. "The Myth of the Multitude, or, Who's Afraid of the Crowd?," *Critical Enquiry* 36: 697–727.

Mazzoni, Stefania. 1991. "The Persian and Hellenistic Settlement at Tell Mardikh/Ebla," in Evangelos Arabatzes (ed.), *Ο Ελληνισμος στην Ανατολη:* 81–98. Athens.

McCrindle, John. 1876. *Ancient India as Described by Megasthenês and Arrian.* Calcutta.

McDonald, A. 1967. "The Treaty of Apamea (188 B.C.)," *JRS* 57: 1–8.

McDowell, Robert. 1935. *Coins from Seleucia on the Tigris.* Ann Arbor.

Meadows, Andrew. 2008. "Fouilles d'Amyzon 6 Reconsidered: The Ptolemies at Amyzon," *ZPE* 166: 115–120.

———. 2012. "*Deditio in Fidem:* The Ptolemaic Conquest of Asia Minor," in Christopher Smith and Liv Yarrow (eds.), *Imperialism, Cultural Politics, and Polybius:* 113–133. Oxford.

Meadows, Andrew and Peter Thonemann. 2013. "The Ptolemaic Administration of Pamphylia," *ZPE* 186: 223–226.

Mehl, Andreas. 1980–1981. "ΔΟΡΙΚΤΗΤΟΣ ΧΩΡΑ. Kritische Bemerkungen zum 'Speererwerb' in Politik und Völkerrecht der hellenistische Epoche," *Ancient Society* 11–12: 173–212.

———. 1986. *Seleukos Nikator und sein Reich.* Leuven.

———. 1991. "The Seleucid Cities in Syria: Development, Population, Constitution," in Evangelos Arabatzes (ed.), *Ο Ελληνισμος στην Ανατολη·* 99–111. Athens.

Mendels, Doron. 1987. *The Land of Israel as a Political Concept in Hasmonean Literature: Recourse to History in Second Century B.C. Claims to the Holy Land.* Tübingen.

Mendelsohn, Daniel. 2009. *C. P. Cavafy: The Unfinished Poems.* New York.

Meshorer, Ya'akov. 1982. *Ancient Jewish Coinage I. Persian Period through Hasmonaeans.* New York.

Messerschmidt, Wolfgang. 2000. "Die Ahnengalerie des Antiochos I. von Kommagene," in Jörg Wagner (ed.), *Gottkönige am Euphrat: Neue Ausgrabungen und Forschungen in Kommagene:* 37–43. Mainz am Rhein.

Meyer, Eduard. 1931. "Untersuchungen zur phönikischen Religion. Die Inschriften von Ma'ṣûb und Umm el 'awâmîd und die Inschrift des Bodostor von Sidon," *ZATW* 49: 1–15.

Meyer, Marion. 2006. *Die Personifikation der Stadt Antiocheia: Ein neues Bild für eine neue Gottheit.* Berlin.

Mihailov, Georgi. 1961. "La Thrace aux IVᵉ et IIIᵉ siècles avant notre ère," *Athenaeum* 39: 33–44.

Millar, Fergus. 1977. *The Emperor in the Roman World.* Ithaca.

———. 1993. *The Roman Near East 31BC–AD337.* Cambridge, MA.

———. 1997. "Hellenistic History in a Near Eastern Perspective: The Book of Daniel," in Paul Cartledge, Peter Garnsey, and Erich Gruen (eds.), *Hellenistic Constructs: Essays in Culture, History, and Historiography:* 89–104. Berkeley.

Minkowski, Christopher. 2010. "Where the Black Antelope Roam: Dharma and Human Geography in India," in Kurt Raaflaub and Richard Talbert (eds.), *Geography and Ethnography: Perceptions of the World in Pre-Modern Societies:* 9–31. Oxford.

Minns, Ellis. 1915. "Parchments of the Parthian Period from Avroman in Kurdistan," *JHS* 35: 22–65.

Mitchell, Stephen. 1993. *Anatolia: Land, Men, and Gods in Asia Minor.* Oxford.

Mitchell, Timothy. 1990. "Everyday Metaphors of Power," *Theory and Society* 19: 545–577.

Mittag, Peter. 2000. "Die Rolle der haupstädtischen Bevölkerung bei den Ptolemäern und Seleukiden im 3. Jahrhundert," *Klio* 82: 409–425.

———. 2002. "Beim Barte des Demetrios: Überlegungen zur parthischen Gefangenschaft Demetrios' II," *Klio* 84: 373–399.

———. 2006. *Antiochus IV. Epiphanes: Eine politische Biographie*. Berlin.

Moesinger, Georgio. 1878. *Monumenta syriaca ex romanis codicibus collecta*. Innsbruck.

Montgomery, Hugo. 1965. *Gedanke und Tat. Zur Erzählungstechnik bei Herodot, Thukydides, Xenophon und Arrian*. Lund.

Montgomery, James. 1927. *A Critical and Exegetical Commentary on the Book of Daniel*. Edinburgh.

Mookerji, Radhakumud. 1928. *Asoka*. London.

Moore, Wayne. 1992. "Berytos-Laodicea Revisited," *Schweizer Münzblätter* 42: 117–125.

Morgan, M. 1990. "The Perils of Schematism: Polybius, Antiochus Epiphanes and the 'Day of Eleusis,'" *Historia* 39: 37–76.

Mørkholm, Otto. 1965. "The Municipal Coinages with Portrait of Antiochus IV of Syria," *Congresso Internazionale di Numismatica* II: 63–67. Rome.

———. 1966. *Antiochus IV of Syria*. Copenhagen.

Moyer, Ian. 2011. *Egypt and the Limits of Hellenism*. Cambridge.

Muccioli, Fredericomaria. 2004. "'Il re dell' Asia': Ideologia e propaganda da Alessandro Magno a Mitridate VI," *Simblos* 4: 105–158.

———. 2006a. "Antioco IV 'salvatore dell'Asia' (*OGIS* 253) e la campagna orientale del 165–164 a.C.," in Antonio Panaino and Andrea Piras (eds.), *Proceedings of the 5th Conference of the Societas Iranologica Europaea Held in Ravenna, 6–11 October 2003. I. Ancient and Middle Iranian Studies*: 619–634. Milan.

———. 2006b. "Philopatris e il concetto di patria in età ellenistica," *Studi ellenistici* 19: 365–398.

Mueller, Katja. 2006. *Settlements of the Ptolemies: City Foundations and New Settlement in the Hellenistic World*. Studia Hellenistica 43. Leuven.

Müller, Carl. 1839. *Antiquitates Antiochenae: Commentationes Duae*. Göttingen.

Muntz, Charles. 2012. "Diodorus Siculus and Megasthenes: A Reappraisal," *CP* 107: 21–37.

Murray, Oswyn. 1970. "Hecataeus of Abdera and Pharaonic Kingship," *JEA* 56: 141–171.

———. 1972. "Herodotus and Hellenistic Culture," *CQ* 22: 200–213.

Musti, Domenico. 1966. "Lo stato dei Seleucidi. Dinastia popoli città da Seleuco I ad Antioco III," *Studi classici e orientali* 15: 61–197.

Nagle, D. Brendan. 1996. "The Cultural Context of Alexander's Speech at Opis," *TAPA* 126: 151–172.

Nankov, Emil. 2008. "The Fortifications of the Early Hellenistic Thracian City of *Seuthopolis*: Breaking the Mould," *Archaeologica Bulgarica* 12: 15–56.

Napoli, Joëlle. 2000. "Les remparts de la forteresse de Djazla sur le Moyen-Euphrate," *Syria* 77: 117–136.

Negmatov, Numan, 1986. "Archaic Khojent—Alexandria Eschata (To the Problem of Syr-Darya Basin Urbanization)," *Journal of Central Asia* 9: 41–54.

Neumann, Karl. 1884. "Die Fahrt des Patrokles auf dem kaspischen Meere und der alte Lauf des Oxos," *Hermes* 19: 165–185.

Newell, Edward. 1918. *The Seleucid Mint of Antioch.* New York.

———. 1941. *The Coinage of the Western Seleucid Mints from Seleucus I to Antiochus III.* New York.

Nicolet, Claude. 1988. *L'inventaire du monde: Géographie et politique aux origines de l'Empire romain.* Paris.

Nielsen, Inge. 1994. *Hellenistic Palaces: Tradition and Renewal.* Aarhus.

———. 1997. "Royal Palaces and Type of Monarchy: Do the Hellenistic Palaces Reflect the Status of the King?," *Hephaistos* 15: 137–161.

Niese, Benedictus. 1900. "Kritik der Beiden Makkabäerbücher nebst Beitragen zur Geschichte der makkabäischen Erhebung," *Hermes* 35: 453–527.

Nock, Arthur. 1928. "Notes on Ruler-Cult, I–IV," *JHS* 48: 21–43.

———. 1972. *Essays on Religion in the Ancient World.* Oxford.

Nodelman, Sheldon. 1960. "A Preliminary History of Characene," *Berytus* 13: 83–121.

Nokandeh, Jebrael, Eberhard Sauer, Hamid Rekavandi, Tony Wilkinson, Ghorban Abbasi, Jean-Luc Schwenninger, Majid Mahmoudi, David Parker, Morteza Fattahi, Lucian Usher-Wilson, Mohammad Ershadi, James Ratcliffe, and Rowena Gale. 2006. "Linear Barriers of Northern Iran: The Great Wall of Gorgan and the Wall of Tammishe," *Iran* 44: 121–173.

Nuffelen, Peter van. 2001. "Un culte royal municipale de Séleucie du Tigre à l'époque séleucide," *Epigrahica Anatolica* 33: 85–87.

Oates, David. 1968. *Studies in the Ancient History of Northern Iraq.* Oxford.

O'Donnell, James. 1982. "The Aims of Jordanes," *Historia* 31: 223–240.

Ogden, Daniel. 1999. *Polygamy, Prostitutes, and Death: The Hellenistic Dynasties.* London.

O'Hanlon, Michael and Linda Frankland. 2003. "Co-Present Landscapes: Routes and Rootedness as Sources of Identity in Highlands New Guinea," in Pamela Stewart and Andrew Strathern (eds.), *Landscape, Memory, and History: Anthropological Perspectives:* 166–188. London.

Oikonomides, A. 1988. "The Real End of Alexander's Conquest of India," *Ancient World* 18: 31–34.

Olmstead, A. 1937. "Cuneiform Texts and Hellenistic Chronology," *CP* 32: 1–14.

Oppenheim, A. 1955. "'Siege-Documents' from Nippur," *Iraq* 17: 69–89.

Orth, Wolfgang. 1977. *Königlicher Machtanspruch und städtische Freiheit.* Munich.

Otto, Walter. 1931. "Zu den syrischen Kriegen der Ptolemäer," *Philologus* 86: 400–418.

———. 1934. *Zur Geschichte der Zeit des 6. Ptolemäers. Ein Beitrag zur Politik und zum Staatsrecht des Hellenismus.* Munich.

Panaino, Antonio. 2003. "The *baγān* of the Fratarakas: Gods or 'Divine' Kings?," in Carlo Cereti, Mauro Maggi, and Elio Provasi (eds.), *Religious Themes and Texts of Pre-Islamic Iran and Central Asia:* 265–288. Wiesbaden.

Pandermalis, Dimitris. 1981. "Inscriptions from Dion. Addenda et Corrigenda," in Harry Dell (ed.), *Ancient Macedonian Studies in Honor of Charles F. Edson:* 283–294. Thessaloniki.

Paranavitana, Senarat. 1971. *The Greeks and the Mauryas.* Colombo.

Parke, H. 1985. "The Massacre of the Branchidae," *JHS* 105: 59–68.

Parker, Richard and Waldo Dubberstein. 1942. *Babylonian Chronology 626 BC–AD 75.* Chicago.

Parker, Robert. 2004. "New 'Panhellenic' Festivals in Hellenistic Greece," in Renate Schlesier and Ulrike Zellmann (eds.), *Mobility and Travel in the Mediterranean from Antiquity to the Middle Ages:* 9–22. Münster.

Parkinson, William and Michael Galaty. 2007. "Secondary States in Perspective: An Integrated Approach to State Formation in the Prehistoric Aegean," *American Anthropologist* 109: 113–129.

Parmentier, Richard. 1987. *The Sacred Remains: Myth, History, and Polity in Belau.* Chicago.

Passerini, Alfredo. 1934. "La ΤΡΥΦΗ nella storiografia ellenistica," *Studi italiani di filologia classica* 11: 35–56.

Paton, W. 1890. "An Inscription from Paphos," *CR* 4: 283–284.

Patterson, Lee. 2010. *Kinship Myth in Ancient Greece.* Austin.

Pearce, Laurie. 2011. " 'Judean': A Special Status in Neo-Babylonian and Achemenid Babylonia?," in Oded Lipschits, Gary Knoppers, and Manfred Oeming (eds.), *Judah and the Judeans in the Achaemenid Period: Negotiating Identity in an International Context:* 267–277. Winona Lake.

Pearson, Lionel. 1960. *The Lost Histories of Alexander the Great.* New York.

Pédech, Paul. 1976. *La géographie des Grecs.* Paris.

Pelletier, André. 1955. "Le 'voile' du temple de Jérusalem est-il devenu la 'portière' du Temple d'Olympie?," *Syria* 32: 289–307.

Perring, Dominic. 2001–2002. "Beirut in Antiquity: Some Research Directions Suggested by the Recent Excavations in the Souks," *Aram* 13–14: 129–140.

Peschlow-Bindokat, Anneliese. 1996. "Die Tetrapyrgia von Latmos," in Wolfram Hoepfner and Gunnar Brands (eds.), *Basileia: Die Paläste der hellenistischen Könige:* 170–175. Mainz.

Peters, Frank. 1983. "City Planning in Greco-Roman Syria: Some New Considerations," *Damaszener Mitteilungen* 1: 269–277.

Pfister, F. 1927. "Epiphanie," *RE* Suppl. 4: 277–323.

Philip, Graham, Maamoun Abdulkarim, Paul Newson, Anthony Beck, David Bridgland, Maryam Bshesh, Andrew Shaw, Rob Westaway, and Keith Wilkinson. 2005. "Settlement and Landscape Development in the Homs Region, Syria. Report on Work Undertaken during 2001–2003," *Levant* 37: 21–42.

Philip, Graham, Farid Jabour, Anthony Beck, Maryam Bshesh, James Grove, Alastair Kirk, and Andrew Millard. 2002. "Settlement and Landscape Development in the Homs Region, Syria. Research Questions, Preliminary Results 1999–2000 and Future Potential," *Levant* 34: 1–23.

Picard, Olivier. 1979. *Chalcis et la confédération eubéenne. Étude de numismatique et d'histoire (IVᵉ–Iᵉʳ siècle).* Paris.

Pičikjan, Igor. 1991. "The City of the Branchids," *VDI:* 168–80.

Piejko, Francis. 1988a. "The Inscriptions of Icarus-Failaka," *CM* 39: 89–116.

————. 1988b. "The Treaty between Antiochus III and Lysimachia: Ca. 196 B.C. (with a Discussion of the Earlier Treaty with Philip V)," *Historia* 37: 151–165.

————. 1991. "Antiochus III and Ilium," *ArchPF* 37: 9–50.

Pigulevskaja, N. 1963. *Les villes de l'état Iranien: Aux époques parthe et sassanide.* Paris.

Plantzos, Dimitris. 1999. *Hellenistic Engraved Gems.* Oxford.

Platt, Verity. 2011. *Facing the Gods: Epiphany and Representation in Graeco-Roman Art, Literature and Religion.* Cambridge.

Pomeroy, Sarah. 1984. "The Persian King and the Queen Bee," *AJAH* 9: 98–108.

Portier-Young, Anthea. 2011. *Apocalypse against Empire: Theologies of Resistance in Early Judaism.* Grand Rapids.

Potts, Daniel. 1978. "Towards an Integrated History of Culture Change in the Arabian Gulf Area: Notes on Dilmun, Makkan, and the Economy of Ancient Sumer," *Journal of Oman Studies* 4: 29–51.

————. 1982. "The Road to Meluhha," *JNES* 41: 279–288.

————. 1989. "Seleucid Karmania," in Leon de Meyer and Ernie Haerinck (eds.), *Archaeologica Iranica et Orientalis: Miscellanea in Honorem Louis Vandem Berghe:* 581–603. Leuven.

————. 1990. *The Arabian Gulf in Antiquity.* Oxford.

————. 1999. *The Archaeology of Elam: Formation and Transformation of an Ancient Iranian State.* Cambridge.

————. 2007. "Foundation Houses, Fire Altars, and *Frataraka:* Interpreting the Iconography of Some Post-Achaemenid Persian Coins," *Iranica Antiqua* 42: 271–300.

Potts, Daniel, A. Asgari Chaverdi, C. Petrie, A. Dusting, F. Farhadi, I. McRae, S. Shikhi, E. Wong, A. Lashjari, and A. Javanmard Zadeh. 2007. "The Mamasani Archaeological Project, Stage Two: Excavations at Qaleh Kali," *Iran* 45: 287–300.

Pourshariati, Parvaneh. 2007. "Ḥamza al-Iṣfahānī and Sāsānid Historical Geography of *Sinī Mulūk al-'arḍ w' al-anbīyā,*" in Rika Gyselen (ed.), *Des Indo-Grecs aux Sassanides: Données pour l'histoire et la géographie historique:* 111–140. Bures-sur-Yvette.

Praschniker, Camillo and Max Theuer. 1979. *Forschungen in Ephesos VI: Das Mausoleum von Belevi.* Vienna.

Primo, Andrea. 2009. *La storiografia sui Seleucidi da Megastene a Eusebio di Cesarea.* Pisa.

Proosdij, B. van. 1934. "De morte Achaei," *Hermes* 69: 347–350.

Psoma, Selene, Chryssa Karadima, and Domna Terzopoulou. 2008. *The Coins from Maroneia and the Classical City at Molyvoti: A Contribution to the History of Aegean Thrace.* Athens.

Pugliese Carratelli, Giovanna. 1953. "Asoka e i re ellenistici," *PP* 33: 449–454.

Pulleyblank, Edwin. 1999. "The Roman Empire as Known to Han China," *JAOS* 119: 71–79.

Purcell, Nicholas. 1990. "Maps, Lists, Money, Order and Power," *JRS* 80: 178–182.

————. 2005. "Statics and Dynamics: Ancient Mediterranean Urbanism," in Robin Osborne and Barry Cunliffe (eds.), *Mediterranean Urbanization 800–600 BC:* 249–272. Oxford.

Puskás, I. 1983. "Herodotus and India," *Oikumene* 4: 201–207.

Radt, Timm. 2011. "Die Ruinen auf dem Karasis. Eine befestigte hellenistische Residenz im Taurus," in Adolf Hoffmann, Richard Posamentir, and Mustafar Sayar (eds.), *Hellenismus in der Kilikia Pedias (Byzas* 14): 37–62. Istanbul.

Rajak, Tessa. 1996. "Hasmonean Kingship and the Invention of Tradition," in Per Bilde, Troels Engberg-Pedersen, Lise Hannestad, and Jan Zahle (eds.), *Aspects of Hellenistic Kingship:* 99–115. Aarhus.

Ramsay, William. 1890. *The Historical Geography of Asia Minor.* London.

Rante, R. 2008. "The Iranian City of Rayy: Urban Model and Military Architecture," *Iran* 46: 189–211.

Rapin, Claude. 1992. *Fouilles d'Aï Khanoum VIII. La trésorerie du palais hellénistique d'Aï Khanoum. L'apogée et la chute du royaume grec de Bactriane.* Paris.

Rapin, Claude and M. Isamiddinov. 1994. "Fortifications hellénistiques de Samarcande (Samarkand-Afrasiab)," *Topoi* 4: 547–565.

Ratté, Christopher. 2008. "Reflections on the Urban Development of Hellenistic Sardis," in Nicholas Cahill (ed.), *Love for Lydia:* 125–133. Cambridge, MA.

Ray, J. 1976. *The Archive of Ḥor.* London.

Reinach, Salomon. 1906. *Cultes, mythes et religions.* Paris.

Rey-Coquais, Jean-Paul. 1978. "Inscription grecque découverte à Ras Ibn Hani. Stèle des mercenaires lagides sur la côte syrienne," *Syria* 55: 313–325.

Rice, Ellen. 1983. *The Grand Procession of Ptolemy Philadelphus.* Oxford.

———. 1993. "The Glorious Dead: Commemoration of the Fallen and Portrayal of Victory in the Late Classical and Hellenistic World," in John Rich and Graham Shipley (eds.), *War and Society in the Greek World:* 224–257. London.

Rigsby, Kent. 1996. *Asylia: Territorial Inviolability in the Hellenistic World.* Berkeley.

Ritter, Hans-Werner. 1965. *Diadem und Königsherrschaft.* Berlin.

Robert, Louis. 1937. *Études anatoliennes: Recherches sur les inscriptions grecques de l'Asie Mineure.* Paris.

———. 1949. "Inscriptions séleucides de Phrygie et d'Iran," *Hellenica* 7: 5–29.

———. 1958a. "Observations sur l'inscription grecque," *Journal Asiatique:* 7–18.

———. 1958b. "Sur des types de monnaies imperiales d'Asie Mineure," *Centennial Publication of the American Numismatic Society:* 577–584.

———. 1965. "Aphrodisias," *Hellenica* 13: 109–238.

———. 1966a. *Documents de l'Asie mineure méridionale. Inscriptions, monnaies et géographie* (Hautes études du monde gréco-romain 2). Geneva.

———. 1966b. "Sur un decret d'Ilion et sur un papyrus concernant des cultes royaux," in *Essays in Honor of C. Bradford Welles:* 175–211. New Haven.

———. 1968. "De Delphes à l'Oxus. Inscriptions grecques nouvelles de la Bactriane," *CRAI* 112: 416–457.

———. 1973. "Les inscriptions," in Paul Bernard (ed.), *Fouilles d'Aï Khanoum I:* 207–237. Paris.

———. 1984a. "Documents pergaméniens: 1. Un décret de Pergame," *BCH* 108: 472–489.

———. 1984b. "Pline VI 49, Démodamas de Milet et la reine Apamè," *BCH* 108: 467–472.

————. 1985. "Retour à Pergame: 1. Le décret de Pergame pour Attale III," *BCH* 109: 468–481.

Roisman, Joseph. 2012. *Alexander's Veterans and the Early Wars of the Successors.* Austin.

Rollinger, Robert. 1993. *Herodots babylonischer Logos. Eine kritische Untersuchung der Glaubwürdigkeitsdiskussion an Hand ausgewählter Beispiele.* Innsbruck.

Romm, James. 1992. *The Edges of the Earth in Ancient Thought: Geography, Exploration, and Fiction.* Princeton.

————. 2010. "Continents, Climates, and Cultures: Greek Theories of Global Structure," in Kurt Raaflaub and Richard Talbert (eds.), *Geography and Ethnography: Perceptions of the World in Pre-Modern Societies:* 215–235. Oxford.

Root, Margaret. 1979. *The King and Kingship in Achaemenid Art: Essays on the Creation of an Iconography of Empire.* Leiden.

Rosen, Ralph. 1997. "The Gendered Polis in Eupolis' *Cities*," in Gregory Dobrov (ed.), *The City as Comedy: Society and Representation in Athenian Drama:* 149–176. Chapel Hill.

Rosenberger, Veit. 1995. "Der Ring des Polykrates im Lichte der Zauberpapyri," *ZPE* 108: 69–71.

Rostovtzeff, Michael. 1932. *Seleucid Babylonia: Bullae and Seals of Clay with Greek Inscriptions.* New Haven.

————. 1938. "The Foundation of Dura-Europos on the Euphrates," *Annales de l'Institut Kondakov* 10: 99–107.

————. 1939. "Le Gad de Doura et Seleucus Nicator," in *Mélanges syriens offerts à M. René Dussaud:* 281–295. Paris.

————. 1941. *The Social and Economic History of the Hellenistic World.* Oxford.

Roueché, Charlotte and Susan Sherwin-White. 1985. "Some Aspects of the Seleucid Empire: The Greek Inscriptions from Failaka, in the Arabian Gulf," *Chiron* 15: 1–39.

Roussel, Pierre. 1911. "Laodicée du Phénicie," *BCH* 35: 433–440.

————. 1942–1943. "Décret des Péliganes de Laodicée-sur-Mer," *Syria* 23: 21–32.

Rudé, George. 1964. *The Crowd in History: A Study of Popular Disturbances in France and England 1730–1848.* London.

Sachs, A. and J. Wiseman. 1954. "A Babylonian King List of the Hellenistic Period," *Iraq* 16: 202–212.

Sacks, Kenneth. 1990. *Diodorus Siculus and the First Century.* Princeton.

Şahin, M. 1976. *The Political and Religious Structure in the Territory of Stratonikeia in Caria.* Ankara.

————. 2008. "Recent Excavations at Stratonikeia and New Inscriptions from Stratonikeia and Its Territory," *Epigraphica Anatolica* 41: 53–81.

Sahlins, Marshall. 2004. *Apologies to Thucydides: Understanding History as Culture and Vice Versa.* Chicago.

Said, Edward. 2000. "Invention, Memory, and Place," *Critical Inquiry* 26: 175–192.

Salamé-Sarkis, Ḥassān. 1986. "Inscription au nom de Ptolémée IV Philopator trouvée dans le nord de la Beqa'," *Berytus* 34: 207–209.

Saliou, Catherine. 1999–2000. "Les fondations d'Antioce dans l'*Antiochikos* (*Oratio* XI) de Libanios," *Aram* 11–12: 357–388.

Salles, Jean-François. 1987. "The Arab-Persian Gulf under the Seleucids," in Amélie Kuhrt and Susan Sherwin-White (eds.), *Hellenism in the East: The Interaction of Greek and Non-Greek Civilizations from Syria to Central Asia after Alexander:* 75–109. Berkeley.

Samuel, Alan. 1962. *Ptolemaic Chronology.* Munich.

Sartori, Marco. 1984. "Storia, 'utopia,' e mito nei primi libri della *Bibliotheca historica* di Diodoro Siculo," *Athenaeum* 62: 492–536.

Sartre, Maurice. 2001. *D'Alexandre à Zénobie. Histoire du Levant antique IVe siècle av. J.-C.—IIIe ap. J.-C.* Paris.

Saunders, Trevor. 2001. "Dicaearchus' Historical Anthropology," in William Fortenbaugh and Eckart Schütrumpf (eds.), *Dicaearchus of Messana. Text, Translation, and Discussion:* 237–254. London.

Sauvaget, Jean. 1934. "Le plan de Laodicée-sur-Mer," *Bulletin d'Études Orientales* 4: 81–114.

———. 1941. *Alep: Essai sur le développement d'une grande ville syrienne, des origines au milieu du XIXᵉ siècle.* Paris.

———. 1949. "Le plan antique de Damas," *Syria* 26: 314–358.

Savalli-Lestrade, Ivana. 2003. "L'élaboration de la décision royale dans l'Orient hellénistique," in Francis Prost (ed.), *L'Orient méditerranéen de la mort d'Alexandre aux campagnes de Pompée. Cités et royaumes à l'époque hellénistique:* 17–39. Rennes.

———. 2005a. "Devenir une cité: *Poleis* nouvelles et aspirations civiques en Asie Mineure à la basse époque hellénistique," in Pierre Fröhlich and Christel Müller (eds.), *Citoyenneté et participation à la basse époque hellénistique:* 9–37. Paris.

———. 2005b. "Le mogli di Seleuco IV e di Antioco IV," *Studi ellenistici* 16: 193–200.

———. 2010. "Les rois hellénistiques, maîtres du temps," in Ivana Savalli-Lestrade and Isabelle Cogitore (eds.), *Des rois au prince: Pratiques du pouvoir monarchique dans l'Orient hellénistique et romain:* 55–83. Grenoble.

Sawaya, Ziad. 2004. "Le monnayage municipal séleucide de Bérytos (169/8–114/3? av. J.-C.)," *NC* 164: 109–146.

Scheer, Tanja. 1993. *Mythische Vorväter. Zur Bedeutung griechischer Heroenmythen im Selbstverständnis kleinasiatischer Städte.* Munich.

———. 2005. "The Past in a Hellenistic Present: Myth and Local Tradition," in Andrew Erskine (ed.), *A Companion to the Hellenistic World:* 216–231. Oxford.

Schepens, Guido. 1997. "Jacoby's *FGrHist:* Problems, Methods, Prospects," in Glenn Most (ed.), *Collecting Fragments—Fragmente sammeln:* 144–172. Göttingen.

Schlumberger, Daniel. 1958. "Une bilinguale gréco-araméenne d'Asoka," *Journal asiatique* 246: 1–48.

Schmidt, W. 1910. "Γενέθλιος ἡμέρα," *RE* 13: 1135–1149.

Schmitt, Hatto. 1964. *Geschichte Antiochos' des Grossen und seiner Zeit.* Wiesbaden.

Schmitt, Rüdiger. 2000. "Gabae," *Encyclopaedia Iranica.*

Schober, Ludwig. 1981. *Untersuchungen zur Geschichte Babyloniens und der Oberen Satrapien von 323–303 v. Chr.* Frankfurt.

Schubert, Rudolf. 1914. *Die Quellen zur Geschichte der Diadochenzeit.* Leipzig.

Schuol, Monika. 2000. *Die Charakene. Ein mesopotamisches Königreich in hellenistisch-parthischer Zeit.* Stuttgart.

Schur, David. 2004. "A Garland of Stones: Hellenistic *Lithika* as Reflections on Poetic Transformation," in Benjamin Acosta-Hughes, Elizabeth Kosmetatou, and Manuel Baumbach (eds.), *Labored in Papyrus Leaves: Perspectives on an Epigram Collection Attributed to Posidippus:* 118–122. Washington, D.C.

Schwanbeck, E. 1846. *Megasthenis* Indica. Bonn.

Schwartz, J. 1982. "Numismatique et renouveaux nationalistes dans l'empire séleucide au IIe s. a.C.," in Tony Hackens and Raymond Weiller (eds.), *Actes du 9ème congrès international de numismatique, Berne, Septembre 1979:* I. 243–249. Louvain-la-Neuve.

Schwarz, Franz. 1969. "Daimachos von Plataia," in *Beiträge zur alten Geschichte und deren Nachleben: Festschrift für Franz Altheim:* 293–304. Berlin.

———. 1972. "Candragupta-Sandrakottos: Eine historische Legende in Ost und West," *Das Altertum* 18: 85–102.

Scott, James. 1985. *Weapons of the Weak: Everyday Forms of Peasant Resistance.* New Haven.

———. 1998. *Seeing like a State: How Certain Schemes to Improve the Human Condition Have Failed.* New Haven.

Segre, M. 1928. "Iscrizioni di Licia," *Clara Rhodos* 9: 182–209.

Seibert, Jakob. 1967. *Historische Beiträge zu den dynastischen Verbindungen in hellenistischer Zeit.* Wiesbaden.

Selden, Daniel. 1998. "Alibis," *CA* 17: 289–412.

Sellwood, David. 1980. *An Introduction to the Coinage of Parthia.* London.

Selms, Adiraan van. 1974. "The Name Nebuchadnezzar," in M. van Voss, P. Cate, and N. van Uchelen (eds.), *Travels in the World of the Old Testament:* 223–229. Assen.

Sève-Martinez, Laurianne. 2003. "Quoi de neuf sur le royaume séleucide?," in Francis Prost (ed.), *L'Orient méditerranéen de la mort d'Alexandre aux campagnes de Pompée. Cités et royaumes à l'époque hellénistique:* 221–242. Rennes.

———. 2004. "Peuple d'Antioche et dynastie séleucide," in Bernadette Cabouret, Pierre-Louis Gatier, and Catherine Saliou (eds.), *Antioche de Syrie: Histoire, images et traces de la ville antique* (*Topoi* Suppl. 5): 21–41.

Seyrig, Henri. 1939. "Antiquités syriennes," *Syria* 20: 296–323.

———. 1950. "Notes on Syrian Coins," *NNM* 119: 1–35.

———. 1955. "Trésor monétaire de Nisibe," *RN* 17: 85–128.

———. 1958. "Parion au 3e siècle avant notre ère," in Harald Ingholt (ed.), *Centennial Publication of the American Numismatic Society:* 603–626. New York.

———. 1962. "Le monnayage de Ptolémaïs en Phénicie," *RN* 4: 25–50.

———. 1968. "Seleucus I and the Foundation of Hellenistic Syria," in William Ward (ed.), *The Role of the Phoenicians in the Interaction of Mediterranean Civilizations:* 53–63. Beirut.

Shayegan, M. 2003. "On Demetrius II Nicator's Arsacid Captivity and Second Rule," *Bulletin of the Asia Institute* 17: 83–103.

————. 2011. *Arsacids and Sasanians: Political Ideology in Post-Hellenistic and Late Antique Persia.* Cambridge.

Sherwin-White, Susan. 1982. "A Greek Ostrakon from Babylon of the Early Third Century B.C.," *ZPE* 47: 51–70.

Shipley, Graham. 2000. *The Greek World after Alexander 323–30 BC.* London.

Sick, David. 2002. "An Indian Perspective on the Graeco-Roman Elephant," *Ancient World* 33: 126–146.

Skeat, T. 1961. "Notes on Ptolemaic Chronology II. 'The Twelfth Year Which Is Also the First': The Invasion of Egypt by Antiochus Epiphanes," *JEA* 47: 107–112.

Skurzak, Ludwik.1964. "Le traité syro-indien de paix en 305, selon Strabon et Appien d'Alexandrie," *Eos* 54: 225–229.

Slater, William and Daniela Summa. 2006. "Crowns at Magnesia," *GRBS* 46: 275–299.

Smith, Adam. 2003. *The Political Landscape: Constellations of Authority in Early Complex Polities.* Berkeley.

Smith, R. 1987. "The Imperial Reliefs from the Sebasteion at Aphrodisias," *JRS* 77: 88–138.

————. 1994. "Spear-Won Land at Boscoreale: On the Royal Paintings of a Roman Villa," *JRA* 7: 100–128.

Smith, Martyn. 2004. "Elusive Stones: Reading Posidippus' *Lithika* through Technical Writing on Stones," in Benjamin Acosta-Hughes, Elizabeth Kosmetatou, and Manuel Baumbach (eds.), *Labored in Papyrus Leaves: Perspectives on an Epigram Collection Attributed to Posidippus:* 105–117. Washington, D.C.

Snead, James, Clark Erickson, and J. Andrew Darling (eds.). 2009. *Landscapes of Movement: Trails, Paths, and Roads in Anthropological Perspective.* Philadelphia.

Soja, Edward. 1989. *Postmodern Geographies: The Reassertion of Space in Critical Social Theory.* London.

————. 2009. "Taking Space Personally," in Barney Warf and Santa Arias (eds.), *The Spatial Turn: Interdisciplinary Perspectives:* 11–35. London.

Spek, Robert van der. 1986. *Grondbezit in het Seleucidische Rijk.* Amsterdam.

————. 1995. Review of Rollinger 1993. *Orientalia* 64: 474–477.

————. 2008. "Berossus as a Babylonian Chronicler and Greek Historian," in Spek (ed.), *Studies in Ancient Near Eastern World View and Society:* 277–318. Bethseda.

————. 2009. "Multi-Ethnicity and Ethnic Segregation in Hellenistic Babylon," in Ton Derks and Nico Roymans (eds.), *Ethnic Constructs in Antiquity: The Role of Power and Tradition:* 101–115. Amsterdam.

Stefanidou-Tiveriou, Theodosia. 2000. "Das makedonische Dion und die rechteckige Stadt," *Hefte des archäologischen Seminars der Universität Bern* 17: 49–76.

Stolper, Matthew. 2006. "Iranica in Post-Achaemenid Babylonian Texts," in Pierre Briant and Francis Joannès (eds.), *La transition entre l'empire achéménide et les royaumes hellénistiques* (Persika 9): 223–260. Paris.

Streicker, Joel. 1997. "Spatial Reconfigurations, Imagined Geographies, and Spatial Conflicts in Cartagena, Columbia," *Cultural Anthropology* 12: 109–128.

Strobel, Karl. 1996. *Die Galater: Geschichte und Eigenart der keltischen Staatenbildung auf dem Boden des hellenistischen Kleinasien.* Berlin.

Stronach, David. 1978. *Pasargadae. A Report on the Excavations Conducted by the British Institute of Persian Studies from 1961 to 1963.* Oxford.

Strubbe, J. 1984–1986. "Gründer kleinasiatischer Städte: Fiktion und Realität," *Ancient Society* 15–17: 253–304.

Sumi, Geoffrey. 2004. "Civic Self-Representation in the Hellenistic World: The Festival of Artemis Leukophryene in Magnesia-on-the-Maeander," in Sinclair Bell and Glenys Davies (eds.), *Games and Festivals in Classical Antiquity. Proceedings of the Conference Held in Edinburgh 10–12 July 2000:* 79–92. Oxford.

Summerer, Lâtife, Askold Ivantchik, and Alexander von Kienlin (eds.). 2011. *Kelainai—Apameia Kibotos: Stadtentwicklung im anatolischen Kontext/Kelainai—Apameai Kibotos: Développement urbain dans le contexte anatolien.* Bordeaux.

Sverchkov, Leonid. 2008. "The Kurganzol Fortress (on the History of Central Asia in the Hellenistic Era)," *Ancient Civilizations from Scythia to Siberia* 14: 123–191.

———. 2009. "Die Grabungen im Fort Kurgansol im Süden Usbekistans: Neue Daten zur Geschichte Zentralasiens am Ende des 4. Jhs. v. Chr.," in Svend Hanson, Alfried Wieczorek, and Michael Tellenbach (eds.), *Alexander der Grosse und die Öffnung der Welt:* 145–153. Berlin.

Swain, Joseph. 1944. "Antiochus Epiphanes and Egypt," *CP* 39: 73–94.

Świderek, Anna. 1980. "Le rôle politique d'Alexandrie au temps des Ptolémées," *Prace Historyczne* 63: 105–115.

Syme, Ronald. 1995. *Anatolica: Studies in Strabo* (ed. Anthony Birley). Oxford.

Tadmor, Hayim. 1999. "World Dominion: The Expanding Horizon of the Assyrian Empire," in Lucio Milano, Stefano de Martino, Frederick Fales, and Giovanni Lanfranchi (eds.), *Landscapes, Territories, Frontiers, and Horizons in the Ancient Near East:* 55–62. Padua.

Talmon, Shemaryahu. 1966. "The 'Desert Motif' in the Bible and in Qumran Literature," in Alexander Altmann (ed.), *Biblical Motifs: Origins and Transformations:* 31–63. Cambridge, MA.

Tarn, William. 1901. "Patrocles and the Oxo-Caspian Trade Route," *JHS* 21: 10–29.

———. 1913. *Antigonos Gonatas.* Oxford.

———. 1926. "The First Syrian War," *JHS* 46: 155–162.

———. 1940. "Two Notes on Seleucid History: 1. Seleucus' 500 Elephants, 2. Tarmita," *JHS* 60: 84–94.

———. 1966. *The Greeks in Bactria and India.* 2nd edition. Cambridge.

Taylor, E. 1932. "The Northern Passages," in Arthur Newton (ed.), *The Great Age of Discovery:* 199–224. New York.

Thalmann, William. 2011. *Apollonius of Rhodes and the Spaces of Hellenism.* New York.

Thapar, Romila. 1961. *Asoka and the Decline of the Mauryas.* Oxford.

———. 1987. *The Mauryas Revisited.* Calcutta.

———. 2002a. *The Penguin History of Early India: From the Origins to AD 1300.* New Delhi.

———. 2002b. *Reading History from Inscriptions.* Calcutta.

Thompson, Dorothy. 2000. "Philadelphus' Procession: Dynastic Power in a Mediterranean Context," in Leon Mooren (ed.), *Politics, Administration and Society in the Hellenistic and Roman World:* 365–388. Leuven.

Thompson, E. P. 1971. "The Moral Economy of the English Crowd in the Eighteenth Century," *Past and Present* 50: 76–136.

Thompson, Stith. 1958. *Motif-Index of Folk-Literature.* Copenhagen.

Thomson, James. 1948. *History of Ancient Geography.* Cambridge.

Thonemann, Peter. 2003. "Hellenistic Inscriptions from Lydia," *Epigraphica Anatolica* 36: 95–108.

———. 2005. "The Tragic King: Demetrios Poliorketes and the City of Athens," in Olivier Hekster and Richard Fowler (eds.), *Imaginary Kings: Royal Images in the Ancient Near East, Greece and Rome:* 63–86. Munich.

———. 2006. "Neilomandros: A Contribution to the History of Greek Personal Names," *Chiron* 36: 11–43.

———. 2007. "Magnesia and the Greeks of Asia (*I.Magnesia* 16.16)," *GRBS* 47: 151–160.

———. 2009. "Estates and the Land in Early Hellenistic Asia Minor: The Estate of Krateuas," *Chiron* 39: 363–393.

———. 2012. *The Maeander Valley. A Historical Geography from Antiquity to Byzantium.* Cambridge.

Tigay, Jeffrey. 1983. "An Early Technique of Aggadic Exegesis," in Hayim Tadmor and Moshe Weinfeld (eds.), *History, Historiography, and Interpretation: Studies in Biblical and Cuneiform Literatures:* 169–189. Jerusalem.

Tilia, Ann. 1972. *Studies and Restorations at Persepolis and Other Sites of Fārs.* Rome.

Timmer, Barbara. 1930. *Megasthenes en de Indische Maatschappij.* Amsterdam.

Tomaschek, Wilhelm. 1883. "Zur historischen Topographie von Persien," *Sitzungsberichte der philosophisch-historischen Classe der kaiserlichen Akademie der Wissenschaften* 102: 145–231.

Trautmann, Thomas. 1982. "Elephants and the Mauryas," in S. Mukherjee (ed.), *India: History and Thought. Essays in Honor of A. L. Basham:* 254–281. Calcutta.

Tscherikower, V. 1927. *Die hellenistischen Städtegründungen von Alexander dem grossen bis auf die Römerzeit.* Leipzig.

Tuan, Yi-Fu. 1974. *Topophilia: A Study of Environmental Perception, Attitudes, and Values.* Englewood Cliffs, NJ.

———. 1977. *Space and Place. The Perspective of Experience.* Minneapolis.

Tuplin, Christopher. 1991. "Darius' Suez Canal and Persian Imperialism," in Heleen Sancisi-Weerdenburg and Amélie Kuhrt (eds.), *Achaemenid History VI. Asia Minor and Egypt: Old Cultures in a New Empire:* 237–281. Leiden.

———. 1998. "The Seasonal Migration of Achaemenid Kings: A Report on Old and New Evidence," in Maria Brosius and Amélie Kuhrt (eds.) *Studies in Persian History: Essays in Memory of David M. Lewis* (Achaemenid History 11): 63–114. Leiden.

———. 2008. "The Seleucids and Their Achaemenid Predecessors: A Persian Inheritance?," in Seyed Darbandi and Antigoni Zournatzi (eds.), *Ancient Greece and Ancient Iran: Cross-Cultural Encounters:* 109–136. Athens.

Turner, Victor. 1969. *The Ritual Process: Structure and Anti-Structure*. Chicago.

Vallet, Georges. 1976. "Avenues, quartiers et tribus à Thourioi, ou comment compter les cases d'un damier (à propos de Diod. XII, 10 et 11)," in *L'Italie préromaine et la Rome républicaine. Mélanges offerts à Jacques Heurgon. CÉFR* 27 vol. 2: 1021–1032.

Van't Dack, E., W. Clarysse, G. Cohen, J. Quaegebeur, and J. Winnicki. *The Judean-Syrian-Egyptian Conflict of 103–101 B.C.* Brussels.

Versnel, Hendrik. 1977. "Polycrates and His Ring: Two Neglected Aspects," *Studi storico-religiosi* 1: 17–46.

Veuve, Serge. 1982. "Cadrans solaires gréco-bactriens à Aï Khanoum (Afghanistan)," *BCH* 106: 23–51.

Vilatte, Sylvie. 1990. "Idéologie et action tyranniques à Samos: Le territoire, les hommes," *REA* 92: 3–15.

Völcker-Janssen, Wilhelm. 1993. *Kunst und Gesellschaft an den Höfen Alexanders d. Gr. und seiner Nachfolger*. Munich.

Volkmann, Hans. 1925. "Demetrios I. und Alexander I. von Syrien," *Klio* 19: 373–412.

———. 1959. "Ptolemaios VI. Philometor," *RE* 23.2: 1702–1719.

Waddell, L. 1903. *Report on the Excavations at Pātaliputra (Patna), the Palibothra of the Greeks*. Calcutta.

Walbank, Frank. 1957–1979. *A Historical Commentary on Polybius*. Oxford.

———. 1992. *The Hellenistic World*. London.

———. 1996. "Two Hellenistic Processions: A Matter of Self-Definition," *Scripta Classica Israelica* 15: 119–130.

Wallace, William. 1956. *The Euboian League and Its Coinage*. New York.

Walsh, Elizabeth. 1975. "The King in Disguise," *Folklore* 86: 3–24.

Walsh, Joseph. 1996. "Flamininus and the Propaganda of Liberation," *Historia* 45: 344–363.

Ward-Perkins, John. 1974. *Cities of Ancient Greece and Italy: Planning in Classical Antiquity*. New York.

Warf, Barney and Santa Arias (eds.). 2009. *The Spatial Turn: Interdisciplinary Perspectives*. London.

Weiß, Peter. 1984. "Lebendiger Mythos. Gründerheroen und städtische Gründungstraditionen im griechisch-römischen Osten," *Würzburger Jahrbücher für die Altertumswissenschaft* 10: 179–207.

Welles, Charles. 1970. "Gallic Mercenaries in the Chremonidean War," *Klio* 52: 477–490.

Wenke, Robert. 1975–1976. "Imperial Investments and Agricultural Developments in Parthian and Sasanian Khuzestan: 150 BC to AD 640," *Mesopotamia* 10–11: 31–221.

Westenholz, Aage. 2007. "The Graeco-Babyloniaca Once Again," *Zeitschrift für Assyriologie und vorderasiatische Archäologie* 97: 262–313.

Whitmarsh, Tim. 2011. *Narrative and Identity in the Ancient Greek Novel*. Cambridge.

Wiegand, Theodor. 1904. "Reisen in Mysien," *AM* 29: 254–339.

Wiesehöfer, Josef. 1991. "*PRTRK, RB ḤYLʾ, SGN* und *MRʾ*: Zur Verwaltung Südägyptens in achaimenidischer Zeit," in Heleen Sancisi-Weerdenberg and Amélie

Kuhrt (eds.), *Achaemenid History VI. Asia Minor and Egypt: Old Cultures in a New Empire:* 305–309. Leiden.

———. 1994. *Die "dunklen Jahrhunderte" der Persis. Untersuchungen zu Geschichte und Kultur von Fārs in frühhellenistischer Zeit* (330–140 v. Chr.). Munich.

———. 1998. "Geschenke, Gewürze und Gedanken: Überlegungen zu den Beziehungen zwischen Seleukiden und Mauryas," in Edward Dąbrowa (ed.), *Ancient Iran and the Mediterranean World:* 225–236. Krakow.

———. 2011. "Frataraka Rule in Early Seleucid Persis: A New Appraisal," in Andrew Erskine and Lloyd Llewellyn-Jones (eds.), *Creating a Hellenistic World:* 107–121. Swansea.

———. 2013. "*Fratarakā* and Seleucids," in Daniel Potts (ed.), *The Oxford Handbook of Iranian Archaeology:* 718–727. Oxford.

Wilberforce Clarke, Henry. 1881. *The* Sikandar Nama e bara, *or* Book of Alexander the Great, *written AD 1200 by Abū Muhammad bin Yusuf bin Mu-ayyid-i-Niẓāmu-'d-Dīn, translated for the first time out of the Persian into prose, with critical and explanatory remarks, with an introductory preface, and with a life of the author, collected from various Persian sources.* London.

Wilcken, Ulrich. 1894. "Ein Beitrag zur Seleukidengeschichte," *Hermes* 29: 436–450.

Wilhelm, Adolf. 1898. Review of Charles Michel, *Receuil d'inscriptions grecques I et II. Göttingische gelehrte Anzeigen* 213: 201–235.

———. 1909. *Beiträge zur griechischen Inschriftenkunde.* Darmstadt.

Will, Édouard. 1966. *Histoire politique du monde hellénistique.* Nancy.

Williams, David. 1999. *The Structure of* 1 Maccabees. Washington, D.C.

Winnicki, Jan. 1991. "Der zweite syrische Krieg im Lichte des demotischen Karnak-Ostrakons und der griechischen Papyri des Zenon-Archivs," *Journal of Juristic Papyrology* 21: 87–104.

Winston, David. 1976. "Iambulus' *Islands of the Sun* and Hellenistic Literary Utopias," *Science Fiction Studies* 3: 219–227.

Wolski, Józef. 1947. "L'effondrement de la domination des Séleucides en Iran au IIIᵉ siècle av. J.-C.," *Bulletin International de l'Académie Polonaise* 5: 13–70.

———. 1960. "Les Iraniens et le royaume gréco-bactrien," *Klio* 38: 110–121.

———. 1966. "Les Achéménides et les Arsacides: Contribution à l'histoire de la formation des traditions iraniennes," *Syria* 43: 65–89.

———. 1984. "Les Séleucides et l'héritage d'Alexandre le Grand en Iran," *Studi ellenistici* 1: 9–20.

Woolf, Greg. 1998. *Becoming Roman: The Origins of Provincial Civilization in Gaul.* Cambridge.

Wörrle, Michael. 1979. "Epigraphische Forschungen zur Geschichte Lykiens III: Ein hellenistischer Königsbrief aus Telmessos," *Chiron* 9: 83–111.

Wycherley, Richard. 1967. *How the Greeks Built Cities.* London.

Yardley, J., Pat Wheatley, and Waldemar Heckel. 2011. *Justin, Epitome of the Philippic History of Pompeius Trogus.* Volume II, *Books 13–15: The Successors to Alexander the Great.* Oxford.

Youroukova, Jordanka. 1982. "La presence des monnaies de bronze des premiers Séleucides en Thrace: Leur importance historique," in Simone Scheers (ed.), *Studia Paulo Naster Oblata:* 115–126. Leuven.

Zadok, Ran. 1985. *Répertoire géographique des textes cunéiformes* VIII. *Geographical Names According to New- and Late-Babylonian Texts.* Wiesbaden.

Zambelli, Marcello. 1960. "L'ascesa al trono di Antioco IV Epifane di Syria," *Rivista di filologia e di istruzione Classica* 88: 363–389.

Zambrini, Andrea. 1982. "Gli *Indika* di Megastene I," *ASNP* 12: 71–149.

———. 1985. "Gli *Indika* di Megastene II," *ASNP* 15: 781–853.

Zavyalov, V. 2007. "The Fortifications of the City of Gyaur Kala, Merv," in Joe Cribb and Georgina Herrmann (eds.), *After Alexander. Central Asia before Islam:* 313–329. Oxford.

Zournatzi, Antigoni. 2000. "Inscribed Silver Vessels of the Odrysian Kings: Gifts, Tribute, and the Diffusion of the Forms of 'Achaemenid' Metalware in Thrace," *AJA* 104: 683–706.

Acknowledgments

The enormous enjoyment of writing this book has been due, above all, to those with whom I've discussed, explored, and learned and on whom I've been able to depend. *Aparchai* go to Nino Luraghi, without whose guidance and constant encouragement this project would never have been undertaken or completed; from my very first days as a graduate student he has been a true teacher, friend, and inspiration. Emma Dench has been a brilliant role model and an outstandingly generous mentor; Christopher Jones and Paul-Alain Beaulieu have tirelessly advised and assisted.

Back at Balliol, Oswyn Murray, Lyndal Roper, and Rosalind Thomas showed me what history could be. The seminars, workshops, and café chats at Harvard have taught me much, and I am indebted to colleagues and students alike. Parts of this project have been presented at Berkeley, Berlin, Durham, Madison, Oxford, and Toronto, and I have benefited enormously from the audiences' responses. The comments of Aneurin Ellis-Evans, Duncan MacRae, and the anonymous readers have greatly improved the work.

For their various combinations of assistance, advice, questions, caution, image permissions, travel companionship, and friendship, I am grateful to Carmen Arnold-Biucchi, Tim Barnes, Andrea Berlin, Lisa Brody, Gianluca Casa, Graeme Clarke, Getzel Cohen, Kathleen Coleman, Aldo Corcella, Lauren Curtis, Tiziana D'Angelo, Stephanie Dalley, Susanne Ebbinghaus, Kyle Erickson, Richard Foster, Janling Fu, Jonathan Griffin, Johannes Haubold, Albert Henrichs, Katherine Hill, Gail Hoffman, Oliver Hoover, Benjamin Isaac, Andrew Johnston, Noah Kaye, Christopher Krebs, Martin Kroher, Bekhrouz Kurbanov, Leslie Kurke, Nayanjot Lahiri, Pierre Leriche, Peter Machinist, Joseph Manning, Margaret Miles, Ian Moyer, Dan Potts, Timm Radt, Sarah Insley Say, Ozan Say, Katherine van Schaik, Francesca Schironi, Daniel Schwartz, Andrea Seri, Michael Shenkar, Joe Skinner, Oktor Skjaervo, Kathryn Steevens, Gérard Thébault, Richard Thomas, Daniel Tober, John Tully, and Jason Ur. Crawford

Greenwalt Jr., Isaac Meyers, and Bernard Schwartz are deeply missed. Robert Cioffi, Coleman Connelly, Rebecca Katz, and Elliot Wilson have saved me from several mistakes; any remaining are my fault alone. Maps and figures have been crafted by Isabelle Lewis and C. Scott Walker. The patient support of Sharmila Sen and Heather Hughes at Harvard University Press has eased me through the publishing process. Ivy Livingston, Alyson Lynch, and Teresa Wu have helped with a smile on the many occasions I've found myself at sea.

The generosity of the Loeb Classical Library Foundation, the Scott R. Jacobs Fund, and the Frank Knox, Thomas Day Seymour, and Charles Elliot Norton Fellowships has made research, travel, and publication possible. The American School of Classical Studies at Athens, the British School at Athens, the American Research Center in Sofia, and the Sardis excavation have warmly welcomed me, and I am grateful to the faculty, staff, and members of these institutions.

It gives me untold joy to have at my side Sudeep Agarwala, who has given so much and whose love means the world. My brothers, Michael and Stephen, have always been there, to share and challenge, with good sense and loud laughter. This work is dedicated to my parents, Ruth and Leslie, who teach by example the wonder of travel, the dignity of scholarship, and the importance of place.

Index